THE APOSTLE PAUL IN THE JEWISH IMAGINATION

The Apostle Paul in the Jewish Imagination is a pioneering multidisciplinary examination of Jewish perspectives on Paul of Tarsus. Here, the views of individual Jewish theologians, religious leaders, and biblical scholars of the past 150 years, together with artistic, literary, philosophical, and psychoanalytical approaches, are set alongside popular cultural attitudes. Few Jews, historically speaking, have engaged with the first-century Apostle to the Gentiles. The modern period has witnessed a burgeoning interest in this topic, however, with treatments reflecting profound concerns about the nature of Jewish authenticity and the developing intercourse between Jews and Christians. In exploring these issues, Jewish commentators have presented Paul in a number of apparently contradictory ways. Among other things, he is both a bridge and a barrier to interfaith harmony; both the founder of Christianity and a convert to it; both an anti-Jewish apostate and a fellow traveller on the path to Jewish self-understanding; and both the chief architect of the religious foundations of Western thought and their destroyer. *The Apostle Paul in the Jewish Imagination* represents an important contribution to Jewish cultural studies and to the study of Jewish–Christian relations.

Daniel R. Langton is Senior Lecturer in Modern Jewish–Christian Relations at the University of Manchester. He is the author of *Claude Montefiore: His Life and Thought* (2002), a biography of the founder of Anglo-Liberal Judaism.

The Apostle Paul in the Jewish Imagination

A Study in Modern Jewish–Christian Relations

DANIEL R. LANGTON

University of Manchester

CAMBRIDGE
UNIVERSITY PRESS

CAMBRIDGE
UNIVERSITY PRESS

32 Avenue of the Americas, New York NY 10013-2473, USA

Cambridge University Press is part of the University of Cambridge.

It furthers the University's mission by disseminating knowledge in the pursuit of education, learning and research at the highest international levels of excellence.

www.cambridge.org
Information on this title: www.cambridge.org/9781107425187

First published 2010
First paperback edition 2014

A catalogue record for this publication is available from the British Library

Library of Congress Cataloguing in Publication data
Langton, Daniel R.
The Apostle Paul in the Jewish imagination : a study in modern Jewish-Christian relations / Daniel R. Langton.
p.   cm.
Includes bibliographical references and index.
Summary: "Daniel R. Langton explores a wide variety of Jewish attitudes toward the Apostle Paul in the context of modern Jewish thought, paying particular attention to the role of Jewish identity and ideology" – Provided by publisher.
ISBN 978-0-521-51740-9 (hardback)
1. Paul, the Apostle, Saint – Jewish interpretations.   2. Bible. N.T. – Criticism, interpretation, etc., Jewish.   3. Bible. N.T. Epistles of Paul – Criticism, interpretation, etc.   4. Paul, the Apostle, Saint – Relations with Jews.   5. Paul, the Apostle, Saint – Influence.   6. Jews – Identity. 7. Jews – Civilization.   8. Christianity and other religions – Judaism. 9. Judaism – Relations – Christianity.   I. Title.
BS2506.3.L37   2010
225.9′2–dc22   2009042400

ISBN 978-0-521-51740-9 Hardback
ISBN 978-1-107-42518-7 Paperback

Contents

Acknowledgments   *page* vii

   Introduction   1

PART I.   THE APOSTLE PAUL AND POPULAR JEWISH
                      CULTURAL IDENTITY

1   Paul in the Popular Jewish Imagination   23

PART II.   THE APOSTLE PAUL AND JEWISH IDENTITY: NEW TESTAMENT
                 STUDIES AND THEOLOGICAL APPROACHES

2   Constructions of Paul and Interfaith Relations: Building Barriers or
    Bridges between Judaism and Christianity   57

3   Constructions of Paul in Intra-Jewish Debate: Establishing Jewish
    Authenticity   97

4   Constructions of Paul as a Dialogical Partner: Transformative
    Approaches to Jewish Self-Understanding   154

PART III.   THE APOSTLE PAUL AND JEWISH INTEREST
      IN THE JUDEO-CHRISTIAN TRADITION: ARTISTIC
                  AND LITERARY APPROACHES   175

5   An Oratorio by Felix Mendelssohn, a Painting by Ludwig Meidner,
    and a Play by Franz Werfel   178

6   The Novels of Shalom Asch and Samuel Sandmel   210

PART IV.   THE APOSTLE PAUL AND JEWISH CRITIQUES
   OF THE PLACE OF RELIGION IN SOCIETY: PHILOSOPHICAL
              AND PSYCHOANALYTICAL APPROACHES   231

7   The Philosophical Writings of Baruch Spinoza, Lev Shestov, and Jacob
    Taubes   234

8   The Psychoanalytical Writings of Sigmund Freud and Hanns Sachs   263

     Conclusion   279

Appendix: The Story of Abbu Gulish in The Book of Tales   287

Bibliography   289

Scripture and Other Ancient Writings Index   303

General Index   305

Acknowledgments

This work springs naturally enough from my earlier research on Claude Montefiore, the biblical scholar and founder of Anglo-Liberal Judaism. Prominent among his lifelong interests had been the life and thought of the Apostle to the Gentiles and, in seeking to contextualize this particular interest, I was led to discover a surprising variety of colourful and imaginative readings of Paul by other Jewish thinkers. I thank my friend and doctoral supervisor Tony Kushner for having originally suggested Montefiore as a subject for study, and thus for having started me off along this path. Just as important has been the research culture I have enjoyed at the Centre for Jewish Studies and in the department of Religions and Theology at the University of Manchester, and I am delighted to have the opportunity to thank my colleagues for their support, encouragement, and friendship over the last few years, particularly Philip Alexander, Bernard Jackson, and Bill Williams.

One of the pleasures of writing a book is stumbling across individuals who actually appear interested in what one is doing. In this regard I would particularly like to mention Alan Segal and Mark Nanos, whose stimulating correspondence has been of enormous benefit to me. I would like to thank the following most warmly for their suggestions or help in one way or another: Glenda Abramson, Rocco Bernasconi, Marc Caplan, John Davies, Dave Franks, Michael Hoelzl, Brian Horowitz, Daniel Lasker, David Law, Hyam Maccoby, Ziva Maisels, Stefan Meissner, Peter Oakes, Alex Samely, Reuven Silverman, Renate Smithius, and Tim Stanley. Special thanks go to my brother Michael for proofreading, and to Mirjam Belz and Noam Livne for their help with translation. I have been greatly assisted by the generosity of Kevin Proffitt and the staff of the American Jewish Archives, Cincinnati; Gregory Morris and the staff of St Deiniol's Library, Harwarden; the staff of the Parkes Library at the University of Southampton; and the staff at the Robert Gore Rifkind Center for German Expressionist Studies, Los Angeles.

I gratefully acknowledge the Arts and Humanities Research Council (AHRC) research leave scheme, which made possible a sabbatical in which I was able to write up most of this work. Much of the material was published previously in slightly different forms and has benefitted greatly from the comments offered by the anonymous peer reviewers for *Journal of Jewish Identities*, *Journal for Modern Jewish Studies*, *Journal of Religion and Society*, *Journal for the Study of the New Testament*, *Melilah*, *Mishkan*, *Modern Judaism*, and *Studies in Christian–Jewish*

Relations. The anonymous readers for Cambridge University Press also made a good many useful suggestions for which I am also very grateful.

Finally, I would like to acknowledge the kind permission of Hauswedell & Nolte, Hamburg, to reproduce a rare example of a representation of the Apostle Paul by a Jewish artist, and one which is a focus for discussion in Chapter 5: 'Paulus-predigt' [Paul's Sermon] (1919) by Ludwig Meidner, watercolour, 68 × 49 cm, Buller Collection, Duisberg.

I dedicate this study to the most important women in my life: my mother, my wife, and my daughter.

Introduction

Few Jews, historically speaking, have engaged with the first-century Apostle to the Gentiles. The modern period has witnessed a burgeoning interest, however, with treatments reflecting profound concerns about the nature of Jewish authenticity and the developing intercourse between Jews and Christians. In exploring these issues, Jewish commentators have presented Paul in a number of apparently contradictory ways. He is both a bridge and a barrier to interfaith harmony; both the founder of Christianity and a convert to it; both an anti-Jewish apostate and a fellow traveller on the path to Jewish self-understanding; and both the chief architect of the Judeo-Christian foundations of Western thought and their destroyer. The goal of the present volume is to outline and explain these aspects of the Jewish debate about Paul, as represented in the works of individual Jewish theologians, religious leaders, biblical scholars, artists, musicians, playwrights, novelists, philosophers, and psychoanalysts of the last 150 years.

We will begin with an account of the popular Jewish view of Paul, which is often understood to be derived from a premodern tradition of hostility towards the apostle and which regards him as the damnable inventor of Christianity and the ultimate cause of centuries of Jewish suffering.[1] Here it will be argued that claims for an ancient origin of this hostility have been exaggerated and that the real roots of modern popular Jewish antipathy lie in the apostle's association with much more recent sociocultural developments (Chapter one). At the heart of the study is an examination of the way in which Jewish religious leaders, theologians, and New Testament scholars have treated Paul, and in particular their focus on his background, his attitude towards the Law, the question of his originality, and his relationship to the Jewish Jesus. This will involve consideration of the apostle's place in the context of interfaith dialogue, where he is used both to encourage and to set the limits of understanding between Jews and Christians (Chapter two).[2] It will

---

[1] The brief survey of premodern contributors in Chapter one includes al-Mukammis, Kirkisani, Hadassi, Ibn Kammuna, Profiat Duran, and Isaac Troki, along with the notorious *Toledot Yeshu* (Story of Jesus).

[2] Chapter two includes Heinrich Graetz, Elijah Benamozegh, Kaufmann Kohler, Martin Buber, Leo Baeck, Abba Hillel Silver, Hyam Maccoby, Isaac Mayer Wise, Joseph Krauskopf, Claude Montefiore, Pinchas Lapide, and Mark Nanos.

entail investigation of the disagreements between different Jewish constituencies in the post-Enlightenment world, and the way in which the Apostle to the Gentiles has been caught up in ideological battles concerning authority within Judaism (Chapter three).[3] And it will draw attention to those radical thinkers who have seen parallels in Paul's theological struggles to their own search for Jewish meaning and who have come to regard him as a dialogical partner with whom they can meet the challenges facing the Judaism of their own day (Chapter four).[4] Other kinds of Jewish intellectuals have also wrestled with the apostle. In the widely differing treatments of artists and literary figures, for example, can be found a common fascination with what has been described as the Judeo-Christian heritage and Paul's relation to it (Chapters five and six).[5] Consideration will also be given to the humanistic discourses of philosophy and psychoanalysis, within which one can identify a Jewish interest in Paul manifested in a series of critiques of the place of religion in Western society (Chapters seven and eight).[6]

It is perhaps best to think of the book as a whistle stop tour of a select group of some of the most striking Jewish Pauline commentaries available, mainly, but by no means exclusively, from the nineteenth and twentieth centuries. Each of the thirty-nine thinkers was selected for having produced a dedicated, focused treatment of the apostle's life and legacy, rather than a tangential foray into some aspect of his teachings.[7] Because it is impossible to introduce and contextualise all of them at this point (they encompass the ideological spectrum, from religious traditionalists to the antireligious), the *sitz im leben* or 'life setting' of each will be brought to bear at the appropriate moment. In contrast to earlier treatments of the subject, this study has little to say in terms of understanding Paul better, nor does it propose a blueprint for improving Jewish–Christian interfaith dialogue, nor can it offer a theological contribution to religious understanding.[8] Instead, its aim is the more modest one of simply documenting the fitful emergence and uneven development of Jewish awareness of Paul in a variety of historical contexts. In

---

[3] Chapter three includes Emil Hirsch, Claude Montefiore (again), Joseph Klausner, Micah Berdichevsky, Hans Joachim Schoeps, Samuel Sandmel, Alan Segal, Pamela Eisenbaum, Tal Ilan, Amy-Jill Levine, Paul Levertoff, Sanford Mills, and Joseph Shulam.

[4] Chapter four includes Hugh Schonfield, Richard Rubenstein, Nancy Fuchs-Kreimer, and Daniel Boyarin.

[5] Chapter five includes Felix Mendelssohn, Ludwig Meidner, and Franz Werfel. Chapter six includes Sholem Asch and Samuel Sandmel (again).

[6] Chapter seven includes Baruch Spinoza, Lev Shestov, and Jacob Taubes. Chapter eight includes Sigmund Freud and Hanns Sachs.

[7] There are some important exceptions, such as Spinoza and Freud, who are included for the somewhat arbitrary reason that they are exceptionally influential thinkers for Western civilisation whose original views on Paul have gone largely unnoticed. The figure of thirty-nine is by no means exhaustive of Jewish commentators on Paul but provides a useful sample. At the same time, one must take with a pinch of salt the 'balance' of a survey that gives almost equal space to Zionist, anti-Zionist, Orthodox, Reform, Messianic, feminist, and historically and theologically oriented Jewish views.

[8] For an overview of previous surveys of Jewish Pauline scholarship, see the conclusion to Chapter two.

particular, it investigates the roles that ideology has played in generating the many different Jewish interpretations. As a result, the reader will learn a good deal more about the complex and shifting nature of Jewish identity in the modern world than about the first-century founding figure of Christianity.

The remainder of this Introduction will be mainly concerned with theoretical and methodological issues such as the impact of ideology and identity upon scholarship and the problem of defining 'Jewishness'. It will also provide a brief overview of the complicated relationship between Christian and Jewish Pauline studies. The impatient reader is advised to skip ahead to Chapter 1, where the Jewish commentary begins and where an historical outline of the phenomenon is offered.

PAUL AND THE LANDSCAPE OF JEWISH THOUGHT

What kind of insights into the world of Jewish thought might the reader hope to obtain from a study of Jewish attitudes towards Paul? At one level, the macro level, it will be argued that the very existence of a body of Jewish interpretations of Paul is best explained by reference to the Jewish historical confrontation with modernity. In particular, following the political and legal emancipation of the eighteenth and nineteenth centuries, great pressure was brought to bear on Jews to justify themselves to a hostile Christian world which regarded their emergence from the ghettos with suspicion. At the same time, their increased exposure to alien modes of thought provoked a wide variety of internal debates and responses, ranging from a rejection of modernity and all it stood for to a passionate embrace of all that was unfamiliar and an abandonment of tradition. More urgently than ever before, Western Jews found themselves forced to take a stand on many complex issues as part of a process of defining themselves in relation to the surrounding Gentile social and intellectual environments. These issues included, amongst others, how to relate to Christianity, whether or not to maintain religious practices that ensured social segregation, whether to stress universalist or particularist tendencies within Judaism, and how to counter the vastly increased threats of conversion and assimilation. In this situation it should come as no surprise that, for some Jews at least, the attempt to relate themselves to Christian history and culture brought them face to face with the iconic Apostle to the Gentiles who so powerfully embodied these very same issues. To study Jewish approaches to Paul, then, is to study some of the most profound forces acting upon and shaping the modern Jewish ideological landscape.

On another level, the micro level, it will be argued that when it comes to understanding *individual* Jewish interpretations of Paul, the *individual's* historical and social contexts, and especially his or her ideological perspective, will often provide the key explanatory factors. The reason is simple enough, having to do with the paucity and notorious complexity of the evidence upon which scholarly conclusions about events and ideas dating back two thousand years must be based, and the natural inclination to fill in the gaps according to one's particular biases. Jews who dedicated themselves to the examination of the life and teachings of the apostle believed that they offered fair and objective accounts, whatever conclusions they reached. But along with the Christian scholars whose historical researches ante-dated them, they have frequently deceived themselves on this account. The number of conflicting interpretations and theories that have accrued over the centuries is impressive, and it would be a brave soul who sought to explain the discrepancies and variations within Pauline studies without reference to the profound impact of ideological bias and scholarly fashions.[9] It is not only the dearth of evidence that allows so much room for intellectual manoeuvring. The fact that Paul himself is a towering figure whose indisputable millennia-old influence upon Western civilisa-tion is, in modern times at least, as likely to be reviled as it is honoured, also means that passions run high and that scholarly objectivity is that much more elusive. In the context of the study of Jewish interpretations of Paul, the reader should expect to encounter, again and again, echoes of Jewish ideological developments in a vari-ety of historical backgrounds. Thus this study reflects many of the intra-Jewish conflicts which arose within the community concerning, among other things, whether or not to attempt to modernise religious traditions and to try to reconcile traditional authorities with the findings of biblical criticism, whether or not to champion a shared Judeo-Christian heritage or to challenge Christian political authority, and whether to abandon or augment Judaism in the light of a plethora of -isms including Zionist nationalism, existentialism, pluralism, and feminism.

THE RELATIONSHIP BETWEEN IDENTITY, IDEOLOGY, AND SCHOLARSHIP

Much has been written on the relationship between identity, ideology, and scho-larship.[10] Here, 'ideology' is defined somewhat loosely as a body of ideas that

---

9 For a study of reception history which highlights developments in the nineteenth- and twentieth-century approaches to New Testament studies brought about by changes in the wider sociocultural and international spheres, see John K. Riches, *A Century of New Testament Study* (Cambridge: The Lutterworth Press, 1993). For a survey specifically focusing on the ideological interplay among commentators on Paul, and one which includes the classic formulations of Augustine, Luther, Calvin, and Wesley in addition to twentieth-century scholars, see Stephen Westerholm, *Perspectives Old and New on Paul: The 'Lutheran' Paul and His Critics* (Grand Rapids, MI: William B. Eerdmans, 2004). For a brief introduction to the variety of contemporary scholarly approaches to Paul, which include Jewish, feminist, and liberationist perspectives alongside a renewed interest in the Pauline letters as Holy Writ or as studies in rhetoric, all of which produce quite different ways of thinking about the apostle to the Gentiles, see Ben Witherington, 'Contemporary Perspectives on Paul', in James D. G. Dunn, ed., *The Cambridge Companion to St Paul* (Cambridge: Cambridge University Press, 2003).

10 Ideological scholarship that seeks to redress power differentials between social groups (defined in terms of race, ethnicity, religion, gender, or sexuality) falls under the rubric of 'identity politics'. In the context of the study of religion, for example, see the collection of essays in Jose Ignacio Cabezón and Sheila Greeve Davaney, eds., *Identity and the Politics of Scholarship in the Study of Religion* (London: Routledge, 2004).

reflect the political or social needs and aspirations of individuals, groups, and cultures. Very often an ideology can be characterised in terms of a conscious programme for change, although not always. It might even be thought of as the institutionalisation of a worldview. Examples of different types of ideologies might include Zionist nationalism (political), Orthodox Judaism (religious), and Jewish feminism (gender), though one should bear in mind that these subcategories are not absolute or exclusive. 'Identity' is another amorphous, imprecise concept. In practice, an individual's identity is usually described in terms of race, nationality, ethnicity, culture, religion, gender, and/or sex. It is not always easy to differentiate between an ideology and an individual's identity. Which category should be applied to describe an Orthodox Jewish Zionist feminist, for example? For our purposes, it does not make much difference. Insofar as a scholar is firmly located in a specific time, place, and social setting, and insofar as such systems of belief and constraints encourage certain interpretations of evidence and preclude others, it follows that ideology and identity will almost certainly have some impact upon the scholar's writings, whether consciously acknowledged or not. There is nothing remarkable about this observation. Historians have been trained for generations to allow for different kinds of biases in their sources, and today no academic domain has been left untouched by the winds of postmodernism and religious pluralism, which emphasise the subjectivity of knowledge itself. The rise of Cultural Studies, with its interest in the relation between sociopolitical power and cultural practices such as scholarship, and its privileging of the local and relative over the universal and absolute, is testimony to the widespread recognition of such issues. Few today would admit to being indifferent to the dangers of failing to recognise multiple ideological perspectives or 'truths' concerning any object of study.

In this book, considerable emphasis has been placed on the ways in which individuals' self-identity, ideology, and cultural context have shaped their worldview in general, and their ideas about Paul, Judaism, and Christianity in particular. For those interested in Jewish history and thought, Jewish commentaries on the Apostle to the Gentiles represent a rich source of information about the kinds of anxieties implicit in nineteenth- and twentieth-century discussions concerning the nature of the Jew and Judaism. Paul becomes a familiar figure in debates about how far one should extend the hand of interfaith friendship to Christianity, what distinguishes Judaism from other faiths, and where the borderline between spiritual exploration and apostasy lies. Such debates about Paul and Jewishness provide useful insight into the world of Jewish ideology and identity, and for historians, theologians, and cultural critics this kind of study is to be regarded as an end in itself. For Pauline scholars, however, it might be regarded more usefully as an extended work of historiography, a survey of the intellectual currents that have shaped the modern Jewish study of early Christian origins and Paul's place within it. For them, ideology is less the object of study and more a potential threat to the furtherance of knowledge. As they would see it, Paul himself is of greater interest than the biases bedevilling the scholars who study him. In this context, one particular question about the relationship between scholarship, identity, and ideology has been raised by several Jewish Pauline scholars, and merits further consideration here.[11]

It has been argued that although religious identity and ideology are significant factors in terms of explaining nineteenth- and early twentieth-century Jewish views on Paul, this is less true of later commentators. One suggestion is that scholars have become increasingly aware of their own prejudices and intellectual constraints, and, as professionals, have sought to take these into account.[12] Another is that the religious identity of modern Pauline scholars has been largely irrelevant since the 1950s, since when the wide variety of Jewish ideological perspectives among New Testament scholars has meant that there is little or no predictive value in knowing whether or not a scholar is Jewish.[13] Either way, support is found in the historical observation that circumstances have improved since the days when the prevailing conditions provoked ideological apologetics or polemics:

Where . . . scholars within a particular religious tradition have not enjoyed the benefit of commonly agreed-upon scholarly standards among people of diverse perspectives, or where a religious perspective has been either threatened or persecuted, or, conversely, has gone unchallenged by other views, religious identity is more likely to be predictable, and apologetics rather than scholarship are more likely to prevail.[14]

Such circumstances, the proponents of this view suggest, were more characteristic of the nineteenth and early twentieth centuries than of the second half of the twentieth century onwards. Although in the past many Jews were precluded from

---

[11] Two scholars in particular are relevant to this debate. See Alan Segal, 'Paul's Religious Experience in the Eyes of Jewish Scholars', in David Capes, April D. DeConick, Helen K. Bond, and Troy A. Miller, eds., *Israel's God and Rebecca's Children: Essays in Honor of Larry W. Hurtado and Alan F. Segal* (Waco, TX: Baylor University Press, 2007), 321–44; the French version includes an expanded conclusion: Alan Segal, 'Paul et ses exégètes juifs contemporains', *Recherche de science religieuse* 94:3 (2006), 413–41; and Pamela Eisenbaum, 'Following in the Footnotes of the Apostle Paul', in Jose Ignacio Cabezón and Shelia Greeve Davaney, eds., *Identity and the Politics of Scholarship in the Study of Religion* (London: Routledge, 2004), 77–97.

[12] Segal observes, 'Reading the earlier [Jewish] treatments of Paul, one is struck by how much they tell us about the predicament of modern Jewish life and how little they tell us about Paul. Of the most recent discussants, one is struck about how professional they are.' Segal, 'Paul's Religious Experience in the Eyes of Jewish Scholars', 322. He also writes, 'Jewish scholars writing on Paul have progressed from expressing more general intellectual issues and problems in modern Jewish identity to more professionally disciplined NT agenda.' Segal, 'Paul et ses exégètes juifs contemporains', 437.

[13] Eisenbaum's argument is that because one can no longer speak of a single Jewish perspective, but rather must speak of multiple perspectives among Jewish scholars, the Jewishness of a scholar is effectively meaningless in terms of predicting how it will affect his scholarly judgement. '[T]here is no essential Jewish perspective on Paul if by Jewish we mean a dominant perspective on Paul, developed, articulated, and widely shared by Jewish scholars. . . . [T]he recognition that there can be multiple perspectives among Jewish scholars only bolsters my argument that there is no single Jewish perspective and therefore that religious identity does not determine one's scholarly judgement in any predictable way.' Eisenbaum, 'Following in the Footnotes of the Apostle Paul', 91–2, 93.

[14] Eisenbaum, 'Following in the Footnotes of the Apostle Paul', 78.

university education and suffered social deprivation and persecution, and although Christians were once untrained in rabbinic thought and their religious prejudices went unchallenged, this is no longer true to the same extent today. Nowadays, the professionalisation of the academic study of Christian origins means that standards are largely agreed upon, few groups are threatened, and no one ideological perspective is believed to hold a monopoly on truth. One's identity as an outsider need no longer preclude one's expertise in the study of any particular religious tradition. In principle at least, a Christian who has access to the necessary tools, resources, and training can be as good a specialist in Jewish studies as any Jew (and *vice versa*), and one's religious perspective by no means automatically determines one's conclusions. From this point of view, of course, any attempt to try to present an overview of the history of Jewish commentary on Paul primarily in terms of Jewish identity or ideology will appear too deterministic or simplistic.[15]

At first sight it seems reasonable to agree that Jewish religious identity and ideology play a less obvious role in modern New Testament scholarship than they did in the past. But the claim that Jewish students of the New Testament have de-Judaised themselves (at least to the extent of refusing to allow their Jewishness to interfere with their professional judgement) is problematic on several counts. After all, one can make a distinction between approaches which express an explicit ideological, polemical agenda, and approaches which eschew such hostile activities but which are nonetheless shaped by those particular worldviews. This difference between stronger and weaker manifestations of an individual's identity means that it is logically possible to speak of a Jewish perspective without implying, for example, an overtly anti-Christian one. In addition, historical scholarship can be too easily caricatured as the practice of uncovering a universally true understanding of the past that will be acknowledged by all neutral observers who are given the time and resources to examine properly the evidence. Although our collective knowledge of the past grows all the time, serious differences in the interpretation of the facts remain. No doubt this is partly due to the inherent complexity of the task of trying to reconstruct a comprehensive understanding of the past from fragmentary remains, but it also suggests that knowledge is not neutral and that

---

[15] On balance, Eisenbaum is critical of what she describes as 'the deterministic view of the relationship between identity and scholarship'. She points out that although on one level she is an outsider in the sense that she is a Jewish scholar of Christian texts, nevertheless on other levels she is an insider: first, the New Testament period was a period when the boundaries between Jews and Christians had not yet been established and therefore the identity of the authors is actually ambiguous; and second, within scholarly circles, she regards herself as an equal to her Christian colleagues, because the quality of the argument is based on scholarly criteria and not religious affiliation. Eisenbaum, 'Following in the Footnotes of the Apostle Paul', 80–81. Segal agrees with Eisenbaum, noting, 'It is certainly correct to see ideological considerations in the earlier and self-acclaimed spokespersons for the Jewish community . . . [who] have explicit agendas which speak to Jewish life, Jewish authenticity, Jewish law in modernity, marginality, and support for the state of Israel, among others. But are all Jewish interpreters of Paul involved in the same apologetic?' Segal, 'Paul et ses exégètes juifs contemporains', 438–9.

identity and ideology can play a crucial role in the process. (For some scholars who have internalised the idea of the subjectivity of knowledge, one viable response is to write from their own specific perspective, offering no pretence of neutrality.)[16] In any case, it is by no means self-evident that professional Pauline scholars share an agreed-upon consensus concerning the kinds of questions to be asked and the nature and limits of academic enquiry.[17] The second claim – that it is in fact the diversity of Jewish perspectives that make Jewish identity irrelevant in terms of predicting an individual's scholarly conclusions – should also be treated with caution. For although the undoubted phenomenon of Jewish ideological fragmentation implies that any talk of *a* Jewish perspective is largely redundant, it is by no means self-evident why the variety or kinds of Jewish identity or ideology should therefore be disregarded, as if they cannot determine an individual's research agenda and its paradigms and framework assumptions, to a significant extent.[18] In which case, Jewish identity *does* matter.

It is hoped that the following chapters will convince the reader that, as explanatory factors, ideology and identity remain as useful for making sense of the Jewish engagement with Paul today as they did for the nineteenth and early twentieth centuries, the period covered by the bulk of this work. In the end, the proof of the

---

[16] Segal distinguishes between a work of 'disinterested scholarship' and 'a memoir and an exercise in ideology', which is how he regards Daniel Boyarin's *A Radical Jew*, for example. Although he accepts that 'either path is possible, although they may demand different skills and be directed at different audiences and towards entirely different purposes', it is clear that Segal's sympathies lie with the scholarly pursuit of historical truth, or the 'technical study of the NT', rather than in seeking 'to interest a sympathetic audience with ideology' or offering 'social criticism [from with]in the Jewish community'. Segal, 'Paul's Religious Experience in the Eyes of Jewish Scholars', 342–3. Another way of putting this is to say that Segal stresses the difference between scholars who study Paul for his own sake and 'scholars who turn to Paul to illustrate their theories on other, more properly Jewish subjects.' Segal, 'Paul et ses exégètes juifs contemporains', 439.

[17] Eisenbaum holds up modern Pauline scholarship in order to illustrate that 'inside a broad scholarly arena, one with commonly agreed-upon scholarly standards but that also encompasses a diversity of perspectives, personal religious identity is not determinative of scholarly opinion.' Eisenbaum, 'Following in the Footnotes of the Apostle Paul', 78. But Eisenbaum's 'diversity of perspectives' is composed mainly of liberals and secularists. Segal is more interested in the 'professionalisation' of New Testament scholarship, by which he appears to mean the refusal to offer a value judgement; he maintains that none 'of the more professionally trained scholars attribute any error to Paul or to the Jewish community.' Segal, 'Paul et ses exégètes juifs contemporains', 439. Arguably, Segal's examples have simply offered analyses of what Paul or his contemporaries believed rather than value-laden judgements on the religious veracity or utility or historical legacy of such views, and there is nothing wrong with this. But nor is there any obvious reason that scholarship should be defined exclusively in this way or that a study that included or was even motivated by a strongly held appreciation or condemnation of Pauline thought need be regarded as necessarily unprofessional.

[18] Eisenbaum admits as much. 'Some might argue that the diversity of perspective seen among [modern Jewish Pauline scholars] . . . is due to the different brands of Judaism they represent. . . . I think their individual orientations towards Judaism probably [do] influence them in some way or other. . . .' Although she believes that the shackles of religious (specifically, Jewish) identity and ideology have been largely cast off, nevertheless she does not doubt for a moment the 'perspectival nature of all knowledge.' Eisenbaum, 'Following in the Footnotes of the Apostle Paul', 77, 93–4.

pudding will be in the eating. We will certainly meet contemporaries whose Jewish self-identity and personal ideological programmes appear to have influenced the choice of Paul as a subject of study, the questions asked of his theology, and the assumptions brought to bear in establishing his place in history. Not infrequently, their influence will also be apparent in a strongly held appreciation or condemnation of the apostle in general. We will also see the relevance of Jewish identity and ideology for understanding the reception and perception of the individual's work by others. One has little difficulty in imagining any number of research topics for which a thinker's identity, whether Jew or Greek, bond or free, male or female, would be regarded as irrelevant. But in the light of the history of Jewish–Christian relations, it is a little naïve to think that an individual's Jewish identity could be dismissed as inconsequential when the focus of debate is Paul. The subject is too highly charged for too many Jews and Christians, both within the scholarly community and outside in the wider world.

All this having been said, it is important to stress that a focus on the identity and ideological biases of Jewish Pauline commentators should not be interpreted as an attack on the standard of scholarship discussed. It is logically consistent to speak of bias without doing violence to a researcher's reputation. Good scholarship is characterised by competence in interpreting the evidence as fully as possible in the light of historical knowledge, willingness to follow wherever the evidence leads, coherence and plausibility of argument, independence of mind, and critical awareness of the constraints imposed by the scholarly standards of the day and one's own cultural setting. But one should never forget that the passage of time, the paucity of evidence, and the influence of identity and ideology do mean that whatever scholarly image we have now of Paul is one 'we see through a glass, darkly'. More than that: as we shall discover, the figure who stares back through the glass is very often a reflection in a mirror, however much we might like to think otherwise.

THE PROBLEM OF DEFINING 'JEWISHNESS'

This book is an exploration of the place of the apostle Paul in the Jewish imagination, that is, a study of Jewish interest in Paul. How, precisely, should one understand the term 'Jewish'? When it comes to defining Jewish identity or 'Jewishness' in a systematic way, one's assumptions play a major role. One tendency, not uncommon among theologians, is to essentialise by classifying people and phenomena as Jewish only in so far as they conform to an assumed essence of a normative Jewishness. This essence may or may not be related to theologically derived criteria such as matrilineal decent, conversion to a particular tradition or set of beliefs, adherence to a certain body of law, or a role in salvation history, or to nontheological criteria such as racial, national, or cultural characteristics. From this perspective, responsibility for determining Jewish authenticity rests entirely with the observer, irrespective of whether his views originate from within the community or from outside. For the essentialist, anything or anyone who does not correspond to the given definition is to be excluded as marginal at best and deviant at worst. One might imagine a core of authenticity surrounded by concentric circles of ever decreasing legitimacy. The problem, of course, is that observers do not agree on what exactly constitutes the core of authenticity. Which definition is to be regarded as authoritative depends upon one's existing biases. Furthermore, proponents of essentialism do not tend to recognise the historically conditioned nature of such definitions and often assume that the characteristics of Jewish authenticity have remained fundamentally unchanged down through the ages.[19]

An alternative method of categorisation is that of 'self-definition', the approved method for many social scientists and historians. This nonessentialist approach does not predetermine the outer limits of Jewishness and so 'deviancy' and 'marginality' are terms free of negative connotations. The inclusion of those who define themselves Jewishly can lead to political controversies, such as the acceptance of Messianic Jews despite their dismissal as Christians-by-another-name by a broad spectrum of the Jewish community. But the advantage of a self-definitional approach is that it largely frees the observer from the responsibility for selection and minimises the projection onto the subject of his own ideological biases. For some, 'self-definition' implies that the individual defines himself *primarily* in Jewish terms, but this need not be the case. Arguably, an individual can possess a self-image that includes a Jewish *component*, however he defines it. This is an important point, especially in the context of intercultural studies which take for granted overlapping or hierarchical identities. Nor should one forget that an individual's self-image evolves and transforms in real time and changes according to social context. The self-definitional approach is commonly used because it attempts to accommodate the complex, shifting reality of Jewish identity.[20]

Unfortunately, 'self-definition' excludes many who do not appear to see themselves in Jewish terms and yet who live lives and produce works that strike the sensitive observer as inexplicable without reference to a Jewish dimension of some sort. Celebrated examples include the seventeenth-century philosopher Baruch Spinoza and the nineteenth-century composer Felix Mendelssohn. A work of monumental Jewish scholarship such as the *Encyclopaedia Judaica* will include such problematic individuals because of its working principle that 'anyone born a Jew' is qualified for inclusion, even if he later converted or disassociated himself

---

[19] For a powerful critique of the essentialising tendency, see Laurence J. Silberstein, *Mapping Jewish Identities* (New York: New York University Press, 2000).

[20] For a survey of the changing understandings of Jewishness, especially in the ancient world, see Shaye J. D. Cohen, *The Beginnings of Jewishness: Boundaries, Varieties, Uncertainties* (Berkeley: University of California Press, 1999).

from Jewish life, as are individuals born of only one Jewish parent who are 'sufficiently distinguished'.[21] But no theoretical justification is offered for this approach and it appears to be premised upon unacknowledged essentialist assumptions of a theological and/or racial kind. Is it possible to qualify the self-definitional method, so that a more nuanced treatment of such individuals can be offered that avoids the common essentialist definitions?

The key question, surely, is whether a significant part of an individual's worldview is best explained in terms of his self-identification at some level as a Jew, and whether the failure to take this dimension seriously would result in an impoverished understanding of his life and work. (For our purposes, it does not matter whether the individual's perception of Jewishness or Judaism is real or imagined – or even whether or not it is consciously acknowledged.) For those Jews who later convert to Christianity or who try to disassociate from Jewish life in general, breaking the psychological ties of association is very difficult, if not impossible. This is especially true for those living in the modern period, when the authority of the Church and its belief in the transformative power of baptism were losing ground to the natural sciences and the assumption of eternal and fixed species. Thus a Spinoza or a Mendelssohn would have been well aware that their contemporaries continued to see in them an indelible trace of Jewishness and, at some level at least, they must have internalised this social reality. One should be wary of underestimating the impact of this kind of 'intersubjective' assessment of Jewishness.[22] To put it another way, it might be possible to expand the self-definitional approach to include those born Jews who, after leaving the community, continue to self-identify as Jews on some level. The problem, of course, is how an observer can know whether the individual so identifies if this association is not articulated explicitly. But if one takes seriously such a Jewish dimension to the individual's inner world, then one should admit the possibility of it having a tangible impact on the individual's creative work. Such works then become evidence of the author's state of mind at the time of production. Arguably, Spinoza and Mendelssohn should be included under the self-definitional approach if a case can be made that an awareness of their identification as Jews (in some sense) contributes to a better

---

[21] In their Introduction the editors write, 'In certain biographical entries a problem was to determine who was a Jew. The first principle adopted was that anyone born a Jew qualified for inclusion, even if he or she had subsequently converted or otherwise dissociated himself from Jewish life (where these facts are known, they are stated). The second principle was that a person with one Jewish parent would qualify for inclusion (with the relevant information stated) if he or she were sufficiently distinguished. A person whose Jewish origins were more remote would only be the subject of an entry in very unusual cases. However, a more generous attitude was taken in the case of Marranos, in view of the special circumstances surrounding their history.' Geoffrey Wigoder and Fern Seckbach, 'Editor's Introduction', *Encyclopaedia Judaica*, 7.

[22] In this vein Krausz has argued that 'Jewishness is understood as *a set of characteristic positions in which certain people are cast or ascribed – by themselves and by others.*' Michael Krausz, 'On Being Jewish', in David Theo Goldberg and Michael Krausz, eds., *Jewish Identity* (Philadelphia: Temple University Press, 1993), 266.

understanding of their philosophical and musical compositions. Consequently, both the subject and the observer must share the responsibility for establishing 'self-definition' because however much depends upon the subject's assumptions, attitudes, value judgements, and ideas, just as much hangs on the observer's ability to uncover and interpret them in their historical context. One can make a useful distinction in this regard between essentialist, ahistorical characteristics of Jewishness and historically and culturally determined characteristics of what constitutes Jewishness.[23] Thus the observer will need to mine the 'Semitic discourse', that is, the dominant ways a society understands and represents Jews at a given time and place, in order to reconstruct the meaning of Jewishness in the subject's own cultural environment.[24] In so doing, one should be wary of any overly simplistic categorisation of ideas as either Jewish or non-Jewish; the historian must take great care in grappling with the almost imponderable complexity of the development, transmission, and interpenetration of ideas and attitudes.

It should be clear that inclusion based on the criterion of Jewish self-definition allows one to take into account more fully the rich variety of Jewish experience. Arguably, the self-definitional approach can be expanded to include individuals such as Spinoza and Mendelssohn whose Jewish self-identification on some level also had consequences for their life and work. Thus the approach adopted in this book is not to ask 'Is this commentator on Paul authentically Jewish?' but rather 'What kind of Jewish commentator is this?' and 'How does his or her Jewishness exhibit itself and affect his or her understanding of Paul?' This focus upon Jewish diversity, 'marginality', and Jewish–Christian cultural interrelations means that it will inevitably include the work of individuals who might be regarded somewhat suspiciously in some circles.[25]

THE RELATIONSHIP BETWEEN JEWISH AND CHRISTIAN PAULINE STUDIES

Finally, a few words about the relevance of Christian Pauline Studies to the Jewish treatments included in this book. Among the intellectual influences acting upon Jewish commentators, especially those whose professional lives brought them into

[23] Krausz maintains that one can 'distinguish between essentialism – the doctrine that there are ahistorically fixed conditions for a thing to be that thing – from what, at particular moments in historical evolution, are taken to be necessary conditions for a thing to be a thing.' Krausz, 'On Being Jewish', 267.

[24] The seminal study by Bryan Cheyette, Constructions of 'the Jew' in English Literature and Society: Racial Representations, 1875–1945 (Cambridge: Cambridge University Press, 1993) showed that an analysis of 'Semitic discourse' generates a range of definitions of 'Jewishness' that offer real insight into a culture's particular ideological landscape. Undoubtedly, the 'Semitic discourse' has implications for the self-image of Jews living within that culture, too.

[25] At this point it is probably appropriate to acknowledge my own perspective, which I would describe as nonreligious or agnostic. My working life is dictated by my location in a Centre for Jewish Studies and a nondenominational Department of Religions and Theology at the University of Manchester in the United Kingdom.

regular contact with the New Testament, were scholarly works on Paul written by Christians. The relationship between the two bodies of work is complicated. Many Jewish studies were written as critiques of Christian accounts of history and of Pauline theology in general, but their engagement with the specific findings of contemporary Christian scholarship could be patchy and superficial.[26] And, until recently, Christian interest in Jewish studies of Paul has been rare and patronising in the main as a result of widespread prejudice.[27] Furthermore, if one looks back over the last century and a half, bearing in mind the broad trends of mainstream Pauline studies, then the mutual indifference that characterises much of what was written in the twentieth century hints at the very different paths taken by Paul's Jewish and Christian interlocutors.

The next chapter will describe how the emergence of a scholarly Jewish concern for Paul coincided with the rise of German Liberal Protestant biblical scholarship in the nineteenth century. The new historical-critical research soon concluded that the apostle had been largely responsible for the creation of the Gentile Church; he was presented as the chief agitator in a political conflict that had resulted in the incorporation of non-Jews (the Tübingen school),[28] and as one heavily dependent upon Hellenism, rather than Judaism, for his teachings (the History of Religions school).[29] About this, Jews and Christians could readily agree, even if their value judgements as to whether or not it had been a good thing differed markedly. The

[26] Amongst those who made few or no references to Christian Pauline scholarship were Elijah Benamozegh (1867), Isaac Mayer Wise (1883), Paul Levertoff (1907, 1928), Joseph Krauskopf (1908), Micah Berdichevsky (c.1921), Lev Shestov (1929), Sigmund Freud (1939), and Hanns Sachs (1948).

[27] Christian scholarly disregard for Jewish views on Judaism, in general, has been explained in terms of anti-Semitism or anti-Judaism for some time now. See, for example, Charlotte Klein, *Anti-Judaism in Christian Theology* (London: SPCK, 1978), and Rosemary Radford-Ruether, *Faith and Fratricide; The Theological Roots of Anti-Semitism* (London: Search Press, 1975). Very few Christian scholars before the Second World War acknowledged the Christian tendency to caricature Judaism, but among those who added their voices to the Jewish ones protesting the widespread misunderstandings of Judaism and the Law, ultimately derived from Paul, were George Foot-Moore and James Parkes. See George Foot-Moore, 'Christian Writers on Judaism', *Harvard Theological Review* 14:5 (July 1921), and James Parkes, *The Conflict of the Church and Synagogue: A Study in the Origins of Anti-Semitism* (London: Soncino Press, 1934) and *Jesus, Paul and the Jews* (London: SCM, 1936).

[28] F. C. Baur's Tübingen school of thought, which offered a radical reconstruction of the history of the early Church (and the New Testament itself) as a clash between Jewish Christian and Gentile Christian factions, dominated biblical-critical studies for much of the nineteenth century. As he put it, '[T]he harmonious relation which is commonly assumed to have existed between the Apostle Paul and the Jewish Christians with the older Apostles at their head, is unhistorical, and that the conflict of the two parties, whom we have to recognise upon this field, entered more deeply into the life of the early Church than has been hitherto supposed.' F. C. Baur, *Paul the Apostle of Jesus Christ*, trans. Eduard Zeller, second edition (London: Williams and Norgate, 1876), vi. German original: *Paulus, der Apostel Jesu Christi* (Stuttgart, 1845).

[29] The History of Religions school (*Religionsgeschichtliche Schule*) was established around 1890 and would dominate biblical-critical studies into the 1920s and beyond. Its characteristic focus was on the rituals and practices of Christianity, such as baptism and the Eucharist, and the common methodology was to find parallels in the surrounding Hellenistic and Oriental worlds to explain them. Key figures included Bousset, Cumont, Dieterich, Eichhorn, Gunkel, Reitzenstein, Pfleiderer, and Wrede.

centuries-old sway of the great Christian interpreters of Paul, such as Luther (who had venerated Paul's experience of liberation from bondage under the Law and his contrast of 'justification by faith alone' against 'works-righteousness'), continued to foster a disparaging attitude towards Judaism among Christian scholars into the twentieth century.[30] Nevertheless, some Jewish commentators caught the attention of their Christian counterparts,[31] and, similarly, as long as Christian scholars retained a historical-critical bent and persisted in their emphasis on a sharp disjuncture between the theology of Paul and the teachings of Judaism, Jewish scholars were happy to bolster their own credibility by making reference to them.[32] And yet real engagement, in terms of shared scholarly agenda or technical debates over common questions or methodologies, was noticeable by its absence for considerable periods of the twentieth century. For many Christian Pauline scholars at the turn of the century, the debate had moved back to a focus on Paul's Jewish context, although now this meant the importance for his theology of a Jewish belief in the imminent end of the world,[33] an issue which succeeded in partially reconciling the apostle with the eschatologically minded Jesus (Schweitzer).[34] This had been followed by a more radical development still: the re-prioritisation of theological, rather than historical, interpretations of the apostle.[35] For some this theological

---

[30] The Lutheran reading of Paul privileges 'justification by faith alone', that is, faith in God's grace in granting salvation (for which read Pauline or Protestant faith) over 'works-righteousness', that is, any kind of human effort to achieve salvation (for which read Jewish or Catholic legalism).

[31] Examples of those who were well known to the wider contemporary scholarly community included Claude Montefiore (1894, 1901, 1914), Kaufmann Kohler (1901, 1929), Joseph Klausner (1939), Hugh Schonfield (1946), and Samuel Sandmel (1958).

[32] Examples of those who cited Christian scholars approvingly in this regard included Emil Hirsch (1885), Kaufmann Kohler (1901, 1929), Claude Montefiore (1894, 1901, 1914), Leo Baeck (1901, 1922, 1952), Hugh Schonfield (1946, 1997), Sanford Mills (1969), and Joseph Shulam (1997). Of course, these works often contained criticisms of Christian assumptions concerning Jewish legalism.

[33] Only two Jewish scholars made this idea central to their interpretations, namely Leo Baeck (1952) and Hans Joachim Schoeps (1961).

[34] Schweitzer had given lectures to this effect as early as 1906. As he would put it, later: 'Paul shares with Jesus the eschatological world-view and the eschatological expectation, with all that these imply. The only difference is the hour in the world-clock in the two cases. To use another figure, both are looking towards the same mountain range, but whereas Jesus sees it as lying before Him, Paul already stands upon it and its first slopes are already behind him.' Albert Schweitzer, *The Mysticism of Paul the Apostle*, trans. W. Montgomery (London: ARC Black, 1931), 113. German original: *Die Mystik des Apostels Paulus* (Tübingen: Mohr, 1930). Strictly speaking, Schweitzer was interested in Jewish apocalypticism (that is, the belief and hope that a sudden intervention of God would bring an end to history and to the world) rather than eschatology (that is, last things relating to death, resurrection, judgement, and eternal life). In any case, his emphasis was on a Jewish context for Paul's thought and he was critical of the focus on Hellenism characteristic of the History of Religions school, although he accepted that *after* Paul and Christ's failure to return, Hellenistic thought became more important. 'The Hellenization of Christianity does not come in with Paul, but only after him. . . . Paul was not the Hellenizer of Christianity. But in his eschatological mysticism of being in Christ he gave it a form in which it could be Hellenized.' Ibid., viii–ix.

[35] The treatment by Martin Buber (1950), written in a kind of existentialist theological style, comes closest to this phenomenon. It is no coincidence that Buber writes in the Foreword, 'I am obliged to Rudolf Bultmann for fundamental instruction in the field of New Testament exegesis.' He also

turn required the faithful Christian to engage with the apostle's concerns as revealed in the Word of God in order to discover its actual meaning (Barth),[36] whereas for others it meant translating the apostle's mythical language into modern existential language about the human condition (Bultmann).[37] Overtly historical treatments continued to appear, of course, although often these led to blind alleys, such as overconfidence in the use of rabbinic literature to reconstruct first-century Jewish thought,[38] or overly simplistic models of Hellenistic and Palestinian Judaism.[39] But the paths followed by Barth and Bultmann, whose theological agendas dictated

specially acknowledges Schweitzer. Martin Buber, *Two Types of Faith*, trans. Norman P. Goldhawk (Routledge & Kegan Paul: London, 1951), 13–14. German original: *Zwei Glaubenweisen* (Zurich: Manesse Verlag, 1950).

[36] Barth's approach is described as 'dialectical theology'. In the preface to the second edition to his commentary on Romans (1921), he wrote: 'My complaint is that recent commentators confine themselves to an interpretation of the text which seems to me to be no commentary at all, but merely the first step towards a commentary. . . . Now, [a real commentary] involves more than mere repetition in Greek or in German of what Paul says; it involves the reconsideration of what is set out in the Epistle, until the actual meaning of it is disclosed. . . . By genuine understanding and interpretation I mean that creative energy which Luther exercised with intuitive certainty in his exegesis; which underlies the systematic interpretation of Calvin . . . [who] having first established what stands in the text, sets himself to re-think the whole material and to wrestle with it, till the walls which separate the sixteenth century from the first become transparent! Paul speaks, and the man of the sixteenth century hears. The conversation between the original record and the reader moves around the subject matter, until a distinction between today and yesterday becomes impossible.' Karl Barth, *The Epistle to the Romans*, trans. Edwyn C. Hoskyns, 6th ed. (London: Oxford University Press, 1933), 6–7. German original: *Der Römerbrief* (Bern: Bächlin, 1919).

[37] Bultmann was particularly interested in our ability to observe the effect of forces, acting from within or from without to create a sense of self-alienation or of internal harmony. He is not always easy to understand, but an indication of his approach can be seen in his treatment of Paul's statements 'I am carnal, sold under sin' and 'For I know that nothing good dwells within me, that is, in my flesh' (Rom. 7:14 and 18), together with related texts: '[T]his language stamps *flesh and sin as powers to which man has fallen victim* and against which he is powerless. The personification of these powers expresses the fact that man has lost to them the capacity to be the subject of his own actions. . . . That self which in Rom. 7:17,20 distinguishes itself from the "sin which dwells within me," is flatly labelled in v.14 as "carnal" and "sold under sin". . . . Therefore the "I" and "I", self and self, are at war with each other; i.e. to be innerly divided, or not to be at one with one's self, is the essence of human existence under sin. This inner dividedness means that man himself destroys his true self. In his self-reliant will to be himself, a will that comes to light in "desire" at the encounter with the "commandment", he loses his self, and "sin" becomes the active subject within him (Rom. 7:9). Thereby the self – the "I" – dies. . . . Man, called to selfhood, tries to live out of his own strength and thus loses his self – his "life" and rushes into death. This is the domination of sin. All man's doing is directed against his true intention.' Rudolf Bultmann, *The Theology of the New Testament*, trans. Kendrick Grobel (Waco, TX: Baylor University Press, 2007), 245. German original: *Theologie des Neuen Testaments* (Tübingen: Mohr, 1948–53).

[38] Jewish writers who were, at times, too confident in the relevance of rabbinic literature included Elijah Benamozegh (1867), Isaac Mayer Wise (1883), Claude Montefiore (1914), Micah Berdichevsky (c. 1921), and Harris Hirschberg (1943). Modern scholars are much more cautious and tend not to accept alleged references to Paul in the Talmud or to interpret apparent parallels in the Christian and Jewish literatures as evidence of direct influence.

[39] Claude Montefiore (1914), Samuel Sandmel (1958), and Hans Joachim Schoeps (1961) all overestimated the importance of distinguishing between the categories of Hellenistic and Palestinian Judaism. Modern scholarship tends to stress the significant cultural and intellectual intercourse.

the direction of Pauline scholarship for a good portion of the century, were of little or no interest to the majority of Jewish commentators, whose basic concerns remained closely allied to those raised by the Tübingen and the History of Religions schools, namely, Paul's grand role in an historical understanding of 'the parting of the ways', and specifically the nature of his apparent disagreement with Judaism and the Torah.

The most recent turning point within mainstream Pauline Studies came with the realisation that the tradition of interpretation that privileged inward reflection, a tradition running from Augustine and Luther to Barth and Bultmann, owed more to *their* anguished self-doubts than to Paul's (Stendahl).[40] Eventually, this would lead to the so-called New Perspective on Paul, characterised by an acknowledgement of the distorted view of first-century Judaism that had shaped much Christian discussion of the apostle's attitude towards Israel and the Torah, and a tendency to locate firmly the apostle in a first-century Jewish environment (Sanders).[41] Some Jewish scholars have actively partaken in this revolution and have emphasised Paul's Jewishness in their work.[42] Others, who have welcomed the more positive view of Judaism, and who have contributed to the scholarly debates, have attacked this claim or have been more interested in working out its implications in other contexts.[43] Regardless, the debates and scholarly pursuits of

[40] 'Especially in Protestant Christianity . . . the Pauline awareness of sin has been interpreted in the light of Luther's struggle with his conscience. But it is exactly at that point that we can discern the most drastic difference between Luther and Paul, between the 16th and the 1st century. . . . A fresh look at the Pauline writings themselves shows that Paul was equipped with what in our eyes must be called a rather "robust" conscience. . . . It is most helpful to compare . . . Paul with the great hero of what has been called "Pauline Christianity," i.e., with Martin Luther. In him we find the problem of late medieval piety and theology. Luther's inner struggles presuppose the developed system of Penance and Indulgence. . . . We should venture to suggest that the West for centuries has wrongly surmised that the biblical writers were grappling with problems which no doubt are ours, but which never entered their consciousness.' Krister Stendahl, 'The Apostle Paul and the Introspective Conscience of the West', *Harvard Theological Review* 56:3 (July 1963), 200, 202, 214.

[41] The 'New Perspective' rejects the Lutheran understanding of Paul's theology (and in particular, the doctrine of justification) as primarily a critique of Jewish legalism. Among those most closely associated with its rise are W. D. Davies, *Paul and Rabbinic Judaism: Some Rabbinic Elements in Pauline Theology* (London: SPCK, 1948); Krister Stendahl, *Paul among Jews and Gentiles and Other Essays* (Philadelphia: Fortress Press,1976), E. P. Sanders, *Paul and Palestinian Judaism* (London: SCM Press, 1977); John G. Gager, *The Origins of Anti-Semitism* (Oxford: Oxford University Press, 1983); Francis Watson, *Paul, Judaism and the Gentiles: A Sociological Approach* (Cambridge: Cambridge University Press, 1986); Lloyd Gaston, *Paul and the Torah* (Vancouver: University of British Columbia Press, 1987); James D. G. Dunn, *Jesus, Paul and the Law* (Louisville, KY: Westminster/John Knox Press, 1990); and Nicholas T. Wright, *What St Paul Really Said* (Oxford: Lion, 1997). The 'New Perspective' has been challenged by many conservative Protestants; perhaps the most eloquent critique has been offered by Stephen Westerholm in his *Perspectives Old and New on Paul.* It is worth noting that both Davies and Sanders take Claude Montefiore's approach to Paul as a starting point for their own studies. Davies, *Paul and Rabbinic Judaism*, 1–5. Sanders, *Paul and Palestinian Judaism*, 4–10.

[42] For example, Alan Segal (1990), Nancy Fuchs-Kreimer (1990), Daniel Boyarin (1994), Mark Nanos (1996, 2002), Pamela Eisenbaum (2000), Tal Ilan (2001), and Amy-Jill Levine (2004).

[43] For example, Hyam Maccoby (1986, 1991) was keen to distance Paul from Judaism entirely. Others recognised Paul's Jewishness, of one sort or another, but were less interested in reconstructing Paul's

many Jewish and Christian Pauline scholars are now closer than they had been for a long time.

At the centre of the scholarly debates, polemics, and apologetics lie the enigmatic letters of Paul, probably the most minutely examined collection of correspondence in the history of Western civilisation.[44] For Jews reading the pastoral, nonsystematic theological writings of this first-century itinerant preacher, it is his views of the people of Israel and the Torah which constitute the abiding concerns. And it is precisely here where he is most perplexing. Not only is he difficult to understand, but also he often appears to be contradicting himself. For example, one can point to verses that appear to drip hostility and condemnation.

[B]y the works of the Law no flesh will be justified in His sight; for through the Law comes the knowledge of sin. (Rom. 3:20).

The sting of death is sin, and the power of sin is the law. (1 Cor. 15:56).

[We] are not like Moses, who used to put a veil over his face so that the sons of Israel would not look intently at the end of what was fading away. But their minds were hardened; for until this very day at the reading of the old covenant the same veil remains unlifted, because it is removed in Christ. But to this day whenever Moses is read, a veil lies over their heart; but whenever a person turns to the Lord, the veil is taken away. (2 Cor. 3:13–16).

For as many as are of the works of the Law are under a curse; for it is written, 'Cursed is everyone who does not abide by all things written in the book of the Law, to perform them.' Now that no one is justified by the Law before God is evident; for 'The righteous man shall live by faith' (Gal. 3:10–11).

For neither is circumcision anything, nor uncircumcision, but a new creation. (Gal. 6:15).

For you, brethren, became imitators of the churches of God in Christ Jesus that are in Judea, for you also endured the same sufferings at the hands of your own countrymen, even as they did from the Jews, who both killed the Lord Jesus and the prophets, and drove us out. They are not pleasing to God, but hostile to all men, hindering us from speaking to the Gentiles so that they may be saved; with the result that they always fill

---

historical relation to his first-century Jewish context than they were concerned to engage his thought in the context of contemporary discussions about the search for Jewish meaning (Richard Rubenstein, 1972), or messianism and political philosophy (Jacob Taubes, 1987), or interfaith relations (Pinchas Lapide, 1984).

[44] Of the thirteen letters traditionally attributed to Paul, a number have been rejected as inauthentic since nineteenth-century biblical scholars first cast their sceptical eyes over the texts. Generally speaking, few have disputed Romans, 1 and 2 Corinthians, and Galatians, from which have been derived Paul's core theology and teachings. The tendency has been to include in addition 1 Thessalonians, Philippians, and Philemon, but to dismiss as non-Pauline Ephesians, 2 Thessalonians, Colossians, and the pastoral epistles 1 and 2 Timothy and Titus. The historicity of the Acts of the Apostles, which narrates Paul's transformation from a zealous Pharisee to a leading light of the early church and successful missionary to the pagans, has also been regarded with great suspicion.

up the measure of their sins. But wrath has come upon them to the utmost. (1 Thess. 2:14–16).

Texts such as these are closely associated with teachings that have blighted Jewish-Christian relations for a long time, including the blindness of the Jews,[45] the hypocrisy of the Pharisees,[46] and the disastrous association of Judaism with a negative conception of legalism.[47] Yet other verses that seem to exhibit quite a different attitude can also be readily found, and not infrequently in the very same letters:

Then what advantage has the Jew? Or what is the benefit of circumcision? Great in every respect. First of all, that they were entrusted with the oracles of God. (Rom. 3:1–2).

Do we then nullify the Law through faith? May it never be! On the contrary, we establish the Law. (Rom. 3:31).

What shall we say then? Is the Law sin? May it never be!...So then, the Law is holy, and the commandment is holy and righteous and good. (Rom. 7:7 and 12).

I could wish that I myself were accursed, separated from Christ for the sake of my brethren, my kinsmen according to the flesh, who are Israelites, to whom belongs the

---

[45] The Good Friday Prayer of the Roman Catholic liturgy (1570) draws heavily upon 2 Cor. 3:13–16 in its traditional form: 'Let us pray also for the faithless Jews: that Almighty God may remove the veil from their hearts; so that they too may acknowledge Jesus Christ our Lord.... Almighty and eternal God, who dost not exclude from thy mercy even Jewish faithlessness: hear our prayers, which we offer for the blindness of that people; that acknowledging the light of thy Truth, which is Christ, they may be delivered from their darkness. Through the same Lord Jesus Christ, who liveth and reigneth with thee in the unity of the Holy Spirit, God, for ever and ever. Amen.' *Roman Missal* (1920), 221–2. It was only after the Second Vatican Council, in the revised prayer of the 1970 edition of the Roman Missal, that the reference to the blindness of the Jews and the veil on their hearts was removed.

[46] Throughout Christian history, the label 'Pharisee' has been synonymous with hypocrisy and self-righteousness, partly because of their representation in the Gospels as Jesus' foes (despite the fact that they are also represented in neutral and even friendly terms in relation to early Christians) and partly due to their association with the classic Pauline critique of the Law (despite the fact that Paul only once refers explicitly to the Pharisees in his letters, and actually does so in order to demonstrate his Jewish credentials: 'If anyone else has a mind to put confidence in the flesh, I far more: circumcised the eighth day, of the nation of Israel, of the tribe of Benjamin, a Hebrew of Hebrews; as to the Law, a Pharisee; as to zeal, a persecutor of the church; as to the righteousness which is in the Law, found blameless.' Phil. 3:4–6. In contrast, Jewish tradition accords the Pharisees a more venerated position, because the first postbiblical classic text of Judaism, the Mishnah, is understood to rest upon Pharisaic traditions dating back to before the destruction of the Temple in 70 CE. For a study of the portrayal of the Pharisees in a variety of ancient sources, including in relation to Paul, see Jacob Neusner and Bruce Chilton, eds., *In Quest of the Historical Pharisees* (Waco, TX: Baylor University Press, 2007).

[47] In Christian theology, 'legalism' has a pejorative sense. It is often contrasted with 'justification by faith' (after Luther) and associated with hypocrisy and obsessive casuistry. To speak of 'legalism' is to claim that the letter of the law is valued over the spirit of the law, or the ceremonial over the moral. In particular, the term has often been used of Jewish scholasticism. Useful discussions of 'legalism' in a historical context can be found in Bernard S. Jackson, 'Legalism', *Journal of Jewish Studies* 30:1 (1979) and E. P. Sanders, 'Reflection on Anti-Judaism in the New Testament and in Christianity' in William Farmer, ed., *Anti-Judaism and the Gospels* (Harrisburg, PA: Trinity Press International, 1999).

adoption as sons, and the glory and the covenants and the giving of the Law and the temple service and the promises, whose are the fathers, and from whom is the Christ according to the flesh. (Rom. 9:3–5).

I say then, God has not rejected His people, has He? May it never be! . . . and so all Israel will be saved. (Rom. 11:1 and 26).

Is the Law then contrary to the promises of God? May it never be!. (Gal. 3:21).

One does not have to be a professional biblical scholar to become intrigued by such an apparent display of theological ambivalence. For the historically-sensitive Jew, however, the issues of Paul's teaching and influence, as derived from his letters and from the book of Acts, have become central to the quest for an understanding of the roots of Christian enmity towards the Jew. Upon such verses could be said to hang the history of the Jewish people in the Christian world. But we are getting ahead of ourselves. As hinted at earlier, the Jewish recognition of Paul's significance for Judaism and Jews is a relatively recent phenomenon. Let us begin, then, by investigating how this historical awareness of the Apostle to the Gentiles first developed and, in particular, his place in the popular Jewish imagination.

PART I

∞

THE APOSTLE PAUL AND POPULAR JEWISH
CULTURAL IDENTITY

Paul in the Popular Jewish Imagination

In the post-Holocaust, post–Vatican II world of ecumenicalism and interfaith relations much has been written about Jewish views of Jesus, including works that approach the subject from a cultural perspective, drawing upon literature and artwork.[1] Relatively little has been written about Jewish views of the apostle Paul, and what has been written tends to address the interests and concerns of theologians and New Testament scholars.[2] In what follows, the role of the Apostle to the Gentiles in the popular Jewish imagination will be approached from a sociocultural perspective. The idea of a Jewish tradition of hostility towards Paul will be queried before the argument is made that popular awareness of the apostle had its origins in the nineteenth century. Drawing upon the weekly *Jewish Chronicle* as a useful indicator of public opinion, in Britain at least, some tentative suggestions for the different roles Paul has played in modern popular discourse will also be offered.

THE MYTH OF A JEWISH TRADITION OF HOSTILITY TOWARDS PAUL

The Reconstructionist rabbi Nancy Fuchs-Kreimer once observed in an imaginary letter to Paul, as one rabbi to another, that

Most of my co-religionists, from your era right up till mine, see you as the archetype of the Jewish heretic, the prototypical Jew who abandons the faith and then unjustly criticizes it in a way our enemies can use against us, to put it bluntly – a traitor.[3]

Elsewhere, the historical Jewish attitude to Paul has been presented as portraying him as the 'ultimate enemy of Judaism . . . [and] supreme apostate,'[4] 'its greatest

---

[1] See, for example, Matthew Hoffman, *From Rebel to Rabbi: Reclaiming Jesus and the Making of Modern Jewish Culture* (Stanford, CA: Stanford University Press, 2007). The most comprehensive treatment of Jewish views of Jesus remains Donald Hagner, *The Jewish Reclamation of Jesus: An Analysis and Critique of the Modern Jewish Study of Jesus* (Grand Rapids, MI: Zondervan, 1984).

[2] See the conclusion of Chapter 2 for some examples.

[3] Nancy Fuchs-Kreimer, 'Seven Extant Letters of Rabbi Nancy Fuchs-Kreimer of Philadelphia to Rabbi Paul of Tarsus: Letter 1', The Institute for Christian-Jewish Studies, http://www.icjs.org/scholars/letters.html.

[4] Richard L. Rubenstein, *My Brother Paul* (New York: Harper & Row, 1972), 4, 5.

heretic,'[5] 'the quintessential convert . . . [and] a villain',[6] 'the arch self-hating Jew',[7] and the one 'single-handedly responsible for two thousand years of anti-Semitism and Christian brutality towards Jews.'[8] It is not unusual for commentators to allude to a traditional Jewish view when considering the question of the origins of the modern cultural conception of Paul, a view that might easily be understood to imply centuries of Jewish polemic that reflected and shaped the views of the Jewish people.[9] What evidence is there of such a tradition?

A number of scholars have suggested that references to Paul can be found in ancient Jewish literature.[10] Isaac Mayer Wise argued that, in reality, the apostate

---

[5]   Paul Levertoff, *St. Paul in Jewish Thought: Three Lectures* (London: Diocesan House, 1928), 7.

[6]   Pamela Eisenbaum, 'Following in the Footnotes of the Apostle Paul', 84.

[7]   Nancy Fuchs-Kreimer, 'The Essential Heresy: Paul's View of the Law According to Jewish Writers, 1886–1986' (Ph.D. thesis, Temple University, May 1990), 79–80.

[8]   Pamela Eisenbaum, 'Is Paul the Father of Misogyny and Antisemitism?' *Cross Currents* 50:4 (Winter 2000–2001), 506.

[9]   For example, the Hebrew Christian Paul Levertoff noted that 'for almost nineteen centuries [Paul] had been either ignored by the representatives of Jewish thought or hated and despised by those Jews who happened to hear or read something about his conversion and his attitude towards the Law, Israel and the Gentiles'. Paul Levertoff, *St. Paul in Jewish Thought*, 14.

[10] In addition to the rabbinic sources that follow, one might also consider references to Paul by early Jewish believers in Jesus, but the difficulty in establishing the origins and dates of relevant traditions makes this particularly problematic. One possibility might be the Pseudo-Clementine writings, which were given great prominence by the nineteenth-century Tübingen School for demonstrating conflict between the Judaising and Gentilising followers of Peter and of Paul, respectively. In the *Homilies*, for example, Peter attacks the figure of Simon Magus (who is widely regarded by modern scholars as representing Paul) by arguing that a true understanding of Jesus' teaching comes via eyes and ears rather than via visions or apparitions (17:13.1), alluding to Paul's reference to his vision of Christ in 1 Cor. 15:8. Peter goes on to undermine further Simon/Paul's authority: 'If then, our Jesus appeared to you in a vision . . . and spoke to you, it was as one who is enraged with an adversary; and this is the reason why it was through visions and dreams, or through revelations that were from without that he spoke to you [rather than face to face as with a friend].' (17:19.1). Although Stanton tentatively accepts a date around 200, next to nothing can be said about the Jewish-Christian community which generated *Homilies* 17, and he cautions against associating such traditions with the Ebionites. In another Pseudo-Clementine account, *Recognitions* 1.70ff, a 'certain hostile person' who is clearly intended to be identified as Saul debates and then attacks James before receiving a commission from Caiaphas to arrest Peter in Damascus. Stanton suggests a mid-second-century dating for this particular Jewish-Christian tradition. Graham Stanton, 'Jewish-Christian Elements in the Pseudo-Clementine Writings' in Oskar Skarsaune and Reidar Hvalvik, eds., *Jewish Believers in Jesus: The Early Centuries* (Peabody, MA: Hendrickson Publishers, 2007), 315–17, 322, 324. In *Panarion* 30.16.9 (also known as *Against Heresies*), Epiphanius of Salamis (d.403) cites the (lost) anti-Pauline *Anabathmoi Iakobou*, which is attributed to the Jewish-Christian Ebionites: 'They assert that Paul was from the Greeks . . . the child of both a Greek mother and a Greek father, that he desired to marry a priest's daughter, that for this reason he became a proselyte and was circumcised, that when he still did not receive the girl he became angry and wrote against the Sabbath and the law.' The name 'Ebionites' ('the poor ones') was probably a self-designation current among Palestinian Jewish believers in Jesus in general, which became associated with a specific group for whom there is no certain firsthand evidence after the third century. Irenaeus claimed in *Against Heresies* (c. 180) that they believed that Jesus was a son of Joseph and of the Davidic line who was eligible to be messiah because of his flawless Torah observance, and whose example in this regard should be followed by believers. He also observed that they only used the Gospel of Matthew and that '[t]hey repudiate the apostle Paul saying that he was an apostate from the Law' (*Against Heresies* 1:26.2), a charge which

of Talmudic tradition, Elisha ben Abujah (also known as Acher), had been Paul (Berakhot 57b).[11] Travers-Herford drew a parallel between the rabbinic story of the wayward Gehazi whose master visited him in Damascus to bring him back to the right way (Sotah 47a; Sanhedrin 107b) and the account of Paul's conversion to Christianity in Damascus.[12] Gerhard Kittel and Paul Levertoff suggested that it was Paul who was described in the Mishnah as one who 'profanes the Hallowed Things and despises the set feasts and puts his fellow to shame publicly and makes void the covenant of Abraham our father, and discloses meanings in the Law which are not according to the Halakhah' (Pirke Abot 3.11).[13] Later, Joseph Klausner argued that it was Paul who was referred to in the Talmud as a pupil of Gamaliel who 'went wrong' and who 'interpreted the Torah in a perverse manner' (Shabbat 30b).[14] Harris Hirschberg, drawing upon a raft of Talmudic texts, adduced that Paul and Simon Magus, a figure found in the Acts of the Apostles and the Patristic literature, were one and the same person and that the rabbis' opposition towards the *minim* (heretics) had actually been directed against the apostle's followers.[15] Leo Baeck accepted the alleged reference to Paul in a later rabbinic commentary on Prov. 21:8 which reads 'This man . . . made himself strange to the circumcision and the commandments' (Ruth Rabba 3).[16] And, by claiming an ancient pedigree for a medieval legend, Micah Berdichevsky suggested that the story of Abba Gulish, a pagan priest who was accused of embezzlement and afflicted with blindness as a result of his sins but whose eyesight was miraculously restored to him in Damascus, causing him to convert (to Judaism), was too close to the New Testament account of Paul to be a coincidence.[17] Few modern scholars, however,

Skarsaune regards as entirely plausible, historically speaking. Oskar Skarsaune, 'The Ebionites', in Oskar Skarsaune and Reidar Hvalvick, eds., *Jewish Believers in Jesus: The Early Centuries* (Peabody, MA: Hendrickson Publishers, 2007), 437, 442, 462.

[11] Isaac Mayer Wise, 'Paul and the Mystics', in *Three Lectures on the Origin of Christianity* (Cincinnati: Bloch & Co., 1883), 55–6.

[12] Robert Travers Herford, *Christianity in Talmud and Midrash* (London: Williams & Norgate, 1903), 71, 99f.

[13] Paul Levertoff, *St. Paul in Jewish Thought*, 8. Gerhard Kittel, 'Paulus im Talmud', *Rabbinica, Arbeiten zur Religionsgeschichte des Urchristentums* 1.3 (1920), cited in Donald A. Hagner, 'Paul in Modern Jewish Thought' in Donald A. Hagner and Murray J. Harris, eds., *Pauline Studies: Essays Presented to F. F. Bruce* (Exeter: Paternoster Press, 1980), 160.

[14] Joseph Klausner, *From Jesus to Paul* (trans. William F. Stinespring; London: Allen & Unwin, 1943), 310–11.

[15] Harris Hirschberg, 'Allusions to the Apostle Paul in the Talmud', *Journal of Biblical Literature* 62:2 (June 1943), 73–87. Hirschberg was concerned with rabbinic texts and with Paul's followers as much as with Paul himself. With regard to Paul as represented in the New Testament, he referred to the ethical issues raised in 1 Cor. 5:1 ('It is actually reported that there is immorality among you, and immorality of such a kind as does not exist even among the Gentiles, that someone has his father's wife') and 10:25 ('Eat anything that is sold in the meat market without asking questions for conscience' sake'). Among Christian Pauline scholars, he cited Sanday, Headlam, and Travers-Herford.

[16] Leo Baeck, 'The Faith of Paul', *Journal of Jewish Studies* 3 (1952), 93–110 (109).

[17] Micah Berdichevsky, *Shaul ve-Paul*, ed. Immanuel Bin-Gorion (Tel Aviv: Moreshet Micha Yosef, 1971), 13–17. Berdichevsky discovered the story, which he describes as being 'written in the Hebrew

would be confident in associating such texts with the apostle Paul for, although there is no doubt that the rabbinic material contains oral traditions from earlier periods, controversies continue to rage about their dating and provenance. The trend today is to avoid such sensational claims and to interpret these kinds of texts as references to contemporary Jewish heresies or to competing Christian or other non-Jewish teachings more generally.[18]

Nor have the medieval and early modern periods much to offer, considering how many hundreds of years passed. Paul and his teachings were rarely referred to explicitly.[19] Of course there are exceptions. The ninth-century Iraqi philosopher, al-Mukammis, who converted to Christianity and then returned to Judaism, maintained in the Judeo-Arabic *Book of Urging-on to Attack* that Paul (along with Peter) had given Christianity many of its laws and regulations, which they claimed had been divulged to them by Jesus but which cannot be found in either the Gospels or the Torah.[20] Around the same time, the anonymously authored Judeo-Arabic *Account of the Disputation of the Priest*, which was translated in the twelfth century into a widely distributed Hebrew tract known as *The Book of Nestor the Priest*,

---

of the Mishnaic and Talmudic period' and which he believed had been originally composed in that period, in a collection of aggadot called *Sefer hama'asiyot* or *The Book of Tales* which Moses Gaster, who had published some of this material in 1896, had dated variously from the ninth to the thirteenth centuries. We will return to Berdichevsky and Gaster's *Book of Tales* in Chapter 3.

[18] In the broader context of Talmudic references to Christianity and Christian figures more generally, Sacha Stern maintains that most are later literary creations rather than the legacy of some historical tradition. The surprising scarcity of material might be the result of self-censorship but more likely reflects a lack of interest in others' religions within early Rabbinic Judaism. He suggests that Christianity may well have been assimilated into the single halakhic category of avodah zara (idolatry). Sacha Stern, 'Talmud', *Dictionary of Jewish-Christian Relations*, 416–17.

[19] As the medieval historian Daniel Lasker has observed, '[t]he name Paul rarely occurs in medieval Jewish literature and it can be safely said that only the most knowledgeable Jews had heard of the Christian apostle, his life and his teachings.' In terms of direct references to Paul, Lasker cites al-Mukammis, the anonymous author of *The Account of the Disputation of the Priest*, Profiat Duran, and Isaac Troki. He suggests that, despite the fact that no explicit mention was made of Paul, all medieval Judaism was anti-Pauline in its adherence to observing the commandments of Torah and its acceptance of the commandments' continued salvific value; in this context, Lasker points to Saadia Gaon's *Beliefs and Opinions* and Maimonides' *Commentary on the Mishnah*. He also notes that a number of Jewish commentators regarded Christianity as a distortion of Jesus' teaching by his followers, again without referring to Paul, including Abraham bar Hiyya (fl. 1120), Judah Halevi (d. 1141), Abraham ibn Daud (fl. 1160), Maimonides, and Levi ben Abraham of Villefranche (early fourteenth century). Nevertheless, Lasker concludes by stressing that 'despite the centrality of Paul in Christian thought, and despite the vigorous Jewish refutation of Christianity, Paul remained a marginal figure in the medieval Jewish-Christian debate.' Daniel J. Lasker, 'Anti-Paulinism, Judaism' in *Encyclopedia of the Bible and Its Reception* (Berlin, New York: de Gruyter, 2009), col. 284–6.

[20] The relevant sections of this lost Judeo-Arabic polemic by al-Mukammis (or David ha-Bavli), entitled Kitab al-dara'a (also translated as *Book of Fierce Attack*), are ostensibly cited verbatim in *The Book of Lights* by Jacob Kirkisani (see below). For a translation, see Bruno Chiesa and Wilfrid Lockwood, *Ya'cub al-Qirqisani on Jewish Sects and Christianity: A Translation of Kitab al-Anwar, Book I, with Two Introductory Essays* (Frankfurt am Main, New York: Verlag Peter Lang, 1984), 137–9. For a biographical introduction see Sarah Stroumsa, *Dawud Ibn Marwan Al-Muqammis's Twenty Chapters (Ishrun Maqala)* (Leiden: E. J. Brill, 1989). See Chapters VIIIa and VIIIb of *The Book of Lights* for the references to Paul and Christian laws.

acknowledged Paul as an influential figure within Christianity without demonstrating any real familiarity with his teachings.[21] In his polemic treatment of Jewish
sects known as *Book of Lights*, the tenth-century Iraqi Karaite Jacob Kirkisani firmly
asserted that Paul had introduced and established Christianity.[22] He was quick to
distinguish between Jesus and contemporary Christians, whose heretical belief in
the trinity, conception of God, and divinity of Christ he attributed to Paul, along
with the claims that the commandments need no longer be observed and that religion was to be based on humility.[23] A brief, somewhat confused reference can be
found in the anonymously written *Toledot Yeshu* or *Story of Jesus*, a notorious, popular polemic composed sometime in late antiquity on the basis of earlier traditions,
some of which may go back to the second century CE. Worked and reworked over
the following centuries it spread through Christian Europe and the Islamic Middle
East. Some versions, which are unattested before the thirteenth century, claimed
that Paul had introduced new festivals and rejected circumcision and the dietary
laws; this he had done, it was said, as an agent of the Jewish sages who had sought to
end the conflict between the followers of Jesus and the people of Israel by creating
permanent religious divisions.[24] In *Cluster of Henna* the twelfth-century Karaite

---

[21] I am grateful to Daniel Lasker for pointing me toward these documents. For introductions to and
    translations of *Qissat Mujadalat al-Usquf* and *Sefer Nestor Ha-Komer*, see Daniel J. Lasker and Sarah
    Stroumsa, *The Polemic of Nestor the Priest: Qissat Mujadalat al-Usquf and Sefer Nestor Ha-Komer*,
    2 vols. (Jerusalem: Ben Zvi Institute, 1996). In the *Account of the Disputation of the Priest*, in the
    context of discussing Christ's nature, Paul is said to have distinguished between God and Christ in
    a work apparently entitled *The Book of Paul*. 'Paul said, at the beginning of the seventh chapter:
    "Christ is the son of God, and our scriptures elucidate this." And he said: "I have worked with you
    and [given you] peace from God, the benefactor," after which he said "and Christ is with Him."' The
    first quotation probably relates to Rom. 1:2, 4 ('He promised beforehand through His prophets in
    the holy Scriptures, concerning His Son . . . Jesus Christ our Lord'), whereas the second is obscure.
    In any case, the author concludes that Paul had therefore taught two Gods: 'If you say that He [God]
    is one, then you deny the Gospels, the Psalms and the Book of Paul [sic].' Qissa 47, 48, 50, in Lasker
    and Stroumsa, *The Polemic of Nestor the Priest*, 60–61. In *The Book of Nestor the Priest*, there is an
    additional, confused reference to Paul: 'And Jesus said to Paul, "I will go and see my Father, for
    my Father and I are equal and one."' This anachronistic conversation appears to be taken from a
    conversation (between Jesus and Philip) in John 14:1, 8, and 11 ('I go to prepare a place for you [in
    my Father's house] . . . He who has seen Me has seen the Father . . . I am in the Father and the Father
    is in Me'). *Sefer Nestor* 68, in Lasker and Stroumsa, *The Polemic of Nestor the Priest*, 112.
[22] For a well-contextualised analysis of Kirkisani (or Abu Yusaf Yaqub al-Quiquisani) and his *Kitab al-
    Anwar*, see Daniel J. Lasker, *Jewish Philosophical Polemics against Christianity in the Middle Ages* (New
    York: KTAV, 1977). For a translations of *Kitab al-Anwar*, see Bruno Chiesa and Wilfrid Lockwood,
    *Ya'cub al-Qirqisani on Jewish Sects and Christianity: A Translation of Kitab al-Anwar, Book I, with
    Two Introductory Essays* and Leon Nemoy, *Al-Quirqisani's Account of the Jewish Sects and Christianity*
    (Cincinnati: Hebrew Union College, 1930). It is worth noting that in his *Book of Lights* Kirkisani
    cites extensively from al-Mukammis.
[23] *Kitab al-Anwar*, Chapter 8, translated in Chiesa and Lockwood, *Ya'cub al-Qirqisani*, 135–9. It is worth
    noting that although the reference to freedom from the laws ('He introduced no duties and imposed
    nothing at all. He asserted that religion is nothing but humility . . . ') is understood by Lasker, Chiesa,
    and Lockwood to refer to Paul, Nemoy thought that it possibly referred to Jesus.
[24] Well over a hundred manuscript versions of the *Sefer Toledot Yeshu* exist in Aramaic, Hebrew, Judeo-
    Arabic, Jewish-Persian, Yiddish, Spanish, Landino, and German. There are several distinguishable

Judah Ben Elijah Hadassi of Constantinople argued that Paul had corrupted the teachings of the wise and righteous man Jesus.[25] In his *Examination of the Three Faiths*, Ibn Kammuna, a member of the thirteenth-century Jewish community of Baghdad, cited Acts in noting that Paul, as a Pharisee, had believed in resurrection and angels (in contrast to the Sadducean heretics of the time); he also blamed Paul for the Christian contradiction of Jesus in breaking the laws of the Torah and for the argument that the Law had been obligatory only until the advent of Christ.[26] The anonymous European author of the thirteenth-century *Old Book of Polemic* used Paul's letters as proof texts against Christian customs such as celibacy, and cited his description of the Law as holy.[27] In the fourteenth century, the Spanish philosopher and forced convert Profiat Duran's covert critique of Christian theology, *Disgrace of the Gentiles*, presented Paul as having emphasised Jesus' atoning sacrifice as the means by which believers defeated bodily death and attained eternal life and angelic status; Paul (and Jerome) were among the 'deceivers' who had so distorted Jesus' words and invented a new religion.[28] The sixteenth-century Lithuanian Karaite Isaac Troki, who sought to defend Judaism against Christian

traditions of the *Toledot Yeshu*, but the thirteenth-century 'Helena' group of manuscripts (which are represented in the Wagenseil edition of 1681) includes a section on Jesus' disciples and Paul. They record that the Jewish sages desired to separate from Israel those who continued to claim Yeshu as the Messiah and that they called upon a learned man, Simeon Kepha, for help. This Kepha was able to heal a lame man (as was Simon Peter or Simon Cephas in the Book of Acts) and to convince the followers of Yeshu that he was one of them. Claiming to speak on behalf of Yeshu, he then introduced new festivals and rejected circumcision and the dietary laws. The text of the *Toledot Yeshu* makes it clear that Simon Peter and Paul had been confused within this tradition: 'All these new ordinances which Simeon Kepha (or Paul, as he was known to the Nazarenes) taught them were really meant to separate these Nazarenes from the people of Israel and to bring the internal strife to an end.' Other versions of this account of a secret mole confuse Paul with another figure called Eliyahu, rather than with Simon Peter. For a short critical analysis of this polemical work, which portrayed Yeshu or Jesus as a sorcerer of illegitimate birth who led Israel astray, see Robert E. Van Voorst, *Jesus outside the New Testament: Introduction to the Ancient Evidence* (Grand Rapids, MI: William B. Eerdmans, 2000). For a brief bibliographic discussion of the material that relates to Jesus' disciples and Paul, see Hillel I. Newman, 'The Death of Jesus in the Toledot Yeshu', in *Journal of Theological Studies* 50:1 (April 1999), 60. For a translation of the *Toledot Yeshu* (as quoted above), see Morris Goldstein, *Jesus in the Jewish Tradition* (New York: Macmillan, 1950), 147–54. A new scholarly edition of the *Toledot Yeshu* is being prepared by Peter Schäffer and a team at Princeton.

[25] For a brief introduction to Hadassi, whose work was entitled *Eshkol ha-Kofer*, see Haim Hillel Ben-Sasson, 'Hadassi, Judah', *Encyclopaedia Judaica*, vol. VII, 1046–7.

[26] For a translation of this text, *Tanqih al-Abhath lil-Milal al-Talath*, and short bibliographical introduction to Sa'd Ibn Mansur Ibn Kammuna, see Moshe Perlmann, *Ibn Kammuna's Examination of the Three Faiths* (Los Angeles: University of California, 1971).

[27] For a translation and comprehensive analysis of this text, *Nizzahon Vetus*, see David Berger, *The Jewish–Christian Debate in the High Middle Ages: A Critical Edition of the Nizzahon Vetus* (Philadelphia: Jewish Publication Society of America, 1979).

[28] For a short but well-contextualised analysis of the work of Duran (also known as Efodi), *Kelimmat ha-Goyim* (1397), see Joel E. Rembaum, 'Medieval Jewish Criticism of the Christian Doctrine of Original Sin', *AJS Review* 7 (1982), 353–82. See also Frank Talmage, 'The Polemical Writings of Profiat Duran', *Immanuel* 13 (1981), 69–85.

claims in *Faith Strengthened*, attacked Paul for misreading scripture, for being inconsistent about circumcision and other laws, and for differing with Jesus in his teachings.[29] A more respectful tone was to be found in the early modern period, for example, in the *Theological-Political Treatise* (1670) by the philosopher Benedict Spinoza (1632–77) of Amsterdam, who stressed that the apostle spoke from reason rather than revelation, that he was the most philosophical of the apostles, and that he (Spinoza) found nothing repugnant about Paul's universalism.[30] And, likewise, the German Talmud scholar and anti-Sabbatean Jacob Emden (1697–1776) also wrote appreciatively about Paul in a tract known as *Order of the World, Great and Small*, arguing that he had not sought to denigrate Judaism and that Paul himself had 'never dreamed of destroying the Torah' and was 'well-versed in the laws of the Torah'.[31]

One might be tempted to generate a rough composite image from such surviving references. Setting aside the less hostile estimations of Spinoza and Emden, the premodern Jewish conception of Paul could be said to portray him as the innovator of non-Jewish teachings such as the Trinitarian conception of God, the atoning death of Christ, and celibacy, who had introduced new festivals, and whose antinomian misreading of scripture had led him to reject circumcision and the dietary laws. It would be a mistake to assume that such views were widespread, however. Although the character of premodern Jewish thought in general might be described as 'anti-Pauline' in the sense that it was Torah-observant, in contradiction to the Christian critique of the Law (and often self-consciously so), this had little to do with common knowledge of Paul or his teachings. In terms of actual influence upon the Jewish community, and with no evidence of another

---

[29] For an introduction and translation to *Hizzuk Emunah*, see Isaac Troki, *Faith Strengthened*, trans. Moses Mocatta (New York: Hermon Press, 1970), reprinted from 1850 edition. Writing in response to real or imagined Christian disputants, Troki often began a section with, 'I was once asked by a Christian scholar . . .', 'A member of the Greek Church once addressed me in the following words . . .', or 'An eminent disciple of Martin Luther one day, thus argued with me . . .'. Otherwise he wrote in general terms of Christian divines, or interpreters, or writers and, at least on one occasion, he wrote of 'our Christian brethren'. Troki demonstrated a close familiarity with Paul's writings, citing from Romans, Corinthians, Galatians, Ephesians, and 1 Thessalonians, as well as Timothy and Hebrews. Although he acknowledged that Hebrews is anonymous, he was inclined to see Paul as the author. Acts was also regarded as a legitimate source for Paul; after the Gospels, it is the New Testament text cited most frequently. For a study of Troki's approach to Paul, see Hans-Georg von Mutius, 'Eine jüdische Pauluskritik aus dem 16. Jahrhundert', in *Judaica* 35 (1979), 113–19.

[30] *Tractatus Theologico-Politicus* (Hamburg: Heinrich Kuhnraht, 1670), was actually published anonymously by Jan Rieuwertsz in Amsterdam in 1669. We will return to Spinoza in Chapter 7.

[31] For an introduction and translation of this text, *Seder olam rabbah vezuta*, see Harvey Falk, 'Rabbi Jacob Emden's Views on Christianity', *Journal of Ecumenical Studies* 19:1 (Winter 1982). The title alludes to the two post-exilic Hebrew chronicles on which Emden wrote a commentary in 1757, *Seder Olam Rabbah* and *Seder Olam Zutta*. 'Sabbateanism' is the name of a Jewish messianic movement that emerged in the seventeenth century around the figure of Sabbatai Zvi; it was of particular interest to the Jewish philosopher Jacob Taubes, to whom we will return in Chapter 7.

oral tradition,[32] only the ambiguous asides to Paul in some accounts of the *Toledot Yeshu*, which portray him as an agent of the rabbinic sages, could have had any impact upon the Jewish masses. Furthermore, in their few tangential and infrequent references to the apostle, these unconventional thinkers tended to cite Paul as part of their more general theological engagements with Christianity. In no wise should one think that the fragmentary remarks regarding the Apostle to the Gentiles of these mostly unauthoritative figures influenced Jewish scholars or entered popular Jewish consciousness to any significant extent.

The suggestion, then, that there has been a time-hallowed tradition of enmity towards Paul is difficult to substantiate. The truth is that until relatively recent times Jewish treatments of Christianity have very rarely mentioned Paul, the focus of attention and hostility having been Jesus until the time of the Enlightenment and Emancipation. Even allowing for some of the tenuous examples cited above, the paucity of ancient, medieval, and early modern writings on this subject – upon which a traditional view might have been founded – is striking. There are two possible reasons for this silence: ignorance and repression. One should not discount the possibility that Jews had simply never heard of the apostle because his sphere of influence had been too limited[33] or because they were unfamiliar with the New Testament more generally.[34] Religiocultural interactions between Jews and Christians in the ancient and medieval worlds were a good deal more restricted than was the case in Europe after the Enlightenment, when political and social emancipation of Jews was achieved. Consequently, opportunities for premodern Jews to engage with Christian theology and to familiarise themselves with the historical contributions of specific Christian thinkers were relatively few and far between. On the other hand, assuming that Paul's missionary successes *had* gained him notoriety and that the rabbis *had* viewed him as a serious opponent

---

[32] For example, in his authoritative and sizable anthology of Jewish preaching over the period 1200–1800, Marc Saperstein offers little in the way of reference to Christianity, and none relating to Paul; he observes that extant Jewish sermons tended to be concerned with 'exegesis of traditional [Jewish] texts and on exploration of abstract intellectual problems'. Marc Saperstein, *Jewish Preaching, 1200–1800: An Anthology* (New Haven and London: Yale University Press, 1989), 80.

[33] Assuming a cultural isolation between the ancient Palestinian and Hellenistic Jewish worlds that modern scholarship has increasingly come to challenge, Levertoff suggests that Paul's activities in the countries outside Palestine were irrelevant to the rabbis, whose writings are concerned with problems relating to Palestine and Babylon. Levertoff, *St. Paul in Jewish Thought*, 7. Likewise, Wiefel suggested that Paul's influence had been limited to the Jewish Hellenistic Diaspora, with the result that he had made no impression on the Palestinian Pharisaic establishment. Wolfgang Wiefel, 'Paulus in Jüdischer Sicht' in Marcus Barth, Josef Blank, Jochann Bloch, Frank Mussner, and R. J. Zwi Werblovski, eds., *Paulus – Apostat oder Apostel? Jüdische und Christliche Antworten* (Regensburg: Verlag Friedrich Pustet, 1977), 109.

[34] Rembaum has noted in a survey of medieval Jewish polemical treatises that only relatively late works included references to Pauline sources, a phenomenon he attributes to a very gradual development of knowledge of the New Testament. Joel E. Rembaum, 'Medieval Jewish Criticism of the Christian Doctrine of Original Sin', 353–82.

with a dangerous theology, then they and their successors might well have felt that the best way to deal with his threat was to ignore him and give him as little publicity as possible within their own writings. Nor need one limit such repressive self-censorship to the rabbinical elites. Jews had lived within Christendom from the fourth century until the nineteenth-century Emancipation under oppression, and one could easily interpret their silence as a general reflection of their awareness of the political danger of engaging with Jesus, Paul, or Christianity. [35] This hypothesis is supported by the fact that the few premodern examples to the contrary often emerged from Muslim lands or from countries in which the power of the Church was limited. Whatever the explanation, to the extent that he was thought of at all, Paul appears to have been generally associated with other Christian authorities. Strictly speaking, then, it is difficult to justify talk of a Jewish view of Paul until the nineteenth century, when the history of Jewish awareness of Paul took a decisive turn. From that time onwards, a small number of mainly European and North American Jews, many of whom we will meet in later chapters, began to write about the apostle's background and engage passionately with his specific teachings. However modest this body of Jewish interpretations of Paul, it dwarfed the production of ancient and medieval treatments and distinguished itself by its more focused interest on the man himself. What accounts for this increased interest? Ultimately, it is to be explained by reference to the Jewish community's confrontation with modernity.

THE EMERGENCE OF A JEWISH AWARENESS OF PAUL
IN MODERN TIMES

The historian Michael Meyer has noted the different meanings of 'modernity' for different academic disciplines. For sociologists it can refer to shifts in the web of relations among the members of a society; for social psychologists it means trans-formation of individual dispositions and behavioural patterns; for philosophers and social theorists the key element is the appearance of rationalisation or sub-jectivity. From the perspective of the Jewish historian, Meyer suggests, 'modernity or modernization' is particularly difficult to pin down. He admits that he is not even certain it exists, for some would prefer to speak of a process whereby Jews increasingly participate in the modernisation of their *host* societies. Nevertheless, he offers a range of alternative definitions of 'Jewish modernization', drawing upon contemporary reflections, which include the process by which individual Jews leave the Jewish community; a shift in the nature of the community from one having an organic membership to one having a more voluntary one; the discovery of individual and social progress by means of embracing secular knowledge and learning;

[35] Donald A. Hagner, 'Paul in Modern Jewish Thought', 144–5. See also Stefan Meissner, *Die Heimholung des Ketzers: Studien zurjüdischen Auseinandersetzung mit Paulus* (Mohr: Tübingen, 1996), 10.

the attainment of religious autonomy of the individual.[36] No single definition is entirely adequate, but, taken together, the result was that modern Jews found themselves intensely concerned with redefinition and reinvention on a number of levels.

After the bulwarks against political, social, and intellectual intercourse between Jew and Gentile began to fall with the arrival of the eighteenth-century Enlightenment, it became increasingly difficult to know where to draw the line of distinction between what was Jewish and what was not. In the rupture brought about by modernity, the government-dictated Jewish ghetto identity disappeared, along with the authority of the rabbinate to determine who held Jewish status. For many, this meant the end of the traditional life of the *kehillah* or Jewish community, and in its place appeared a multitude of choices for the wondering and wandering Jewish inhabitants of revolution-weary eighteenth- and nineteenth-century Europe. The Christian world which awaited those who emerged from the ghettos was intimidating and unfriendly, and no one could be sure what strategy was best adopted. Some drifted towards assimilation in an attempt to discard Jewish difference altogether, whether ethnically, culturally, or religiously defined.[37] From the early nineteenth century onwards, Reform Jews trumpeted their Englishness, Frenchness, or Germanness, distinguishing themselves only by their religion. They and their ideological opponents, the neo-Orthodox, also attempted (to varying degrees) to modify their beliefs and practices in conformity to Christian expectations and in response to the Christian critique of Judaism.[38] Late nineteenth-century political Zionists adopted the nationalist outlook of the colonial powers of their day and sought a solution to the threat of anti-Semitism, seeking for a scattered people the normality and dignity of a permanent homeland.[39] But whichever of these (and other) strategies were adopted, Jews everywhere hotly debated where the boundaries between Jew and Gentile should be drawn. To what extent should one maintain social and cultural barriers? How much of the non-Jewish world should be embraced and how much guarded against? Which of Judaism's traditions were tenable in this brave new world? What, if anything, did Christianity and Judaism have

---

[36] Michael A. Meyer, 'Reflections on Jewish Modernization' in Elisheva Carlebach, John Efron, and David Myers, eds., *Jewish History and Jewish Memory* (Hanover, NH: Brandeis University Press, 1998), 369–77.

[37] Two useful introductions to the subject are the collection of essays in Todd Endelman, ed., *Jewish Apostasy in the Modern World* (New York: Holmes & Meier, 1987) and Jonathan Frankel and Steven J. Zipperstein, eds., *Assimilation and Community: The Jews in Nineteenth-Century Europe* (Cambridge: Cambridge University Press, 1992).

[38] A useful overview of the theological and cultural influences on Judaism can be found in Michael Hilton, *The Christian Effect on Jewish Life* (London: SCM Press, 1994). For a full discussion of the influence of Christian thought and practice upon progressive forms of Judaism in an English context, see Daniel R. Langton, 'A Question of Backbone: Comparing Christian Influences upon the Origins of Reform and Liberal Judaism in England', *Melilah* 3 (2004), 1–47.

[39] A comprehensive collection of essays and primary sources exploring the complex nature of Zionism is Jehuda Reinharz and Anita Shapira, eds., *Essential Papers on Zionism* (London: Cassell, 1996).

in common? It was in this time of confusion and compromise that the quintessentially modern question, 'Who is a Jew?' was first articulated. For these reasons the study of Jewish identity in the modern period can, arguably, be equated with the study of the interaction of Jewish and Christian cultures and the process by which they defined themselves in terms of the other.[40] And in this context, the growth of Jewish interest in the Apostle to the Gentiles, whose life and legacy resonated with these very concerns, makes sense as part of a grander project to reinvent Jewishness in the modern world.

Intrinsic to this story was the development of a Jewish historical consciousness at the expense of the Jewish religious collective memory. Before the Enlightenment, Jewish continuity had been assured by the community's faithful adherence to ritual, liturgy, and Torah study. As Yerushalmi has argued, the Hebrew Bible provided ancient and medieval Jews with 'all the history they required'.[41] The rabbis immersed themselves in elaborate interpretations of sacred history, in which they lived and moved and had their being. Later history was of little merit or interest, and could only confirm what tradition had already taught; nor did it shape their sense of who they were. With very few exceptions this understanding of history held sway throughout the medieval Jewish world and on into the modern period,[42] and it therefore comes as no surprise that it is characteristic of the very few references to Paul that are to be found in the Jewish literature from the ninth to the sixteenth century. Polemicists such as al-Mukammis, Kirkisani, Hadassi, Ibn Kammuna, Profiat Duran, and Isaac Troki showed no interest in the historical Paul and his teachings, except insofar as they could use him as a representative figure to contrast better the errors of Christianity and their conceptions of unchanging religious truth. Likewise, the unhistorical flight of fancy found in some versions

---

[40] This idea is increasingly espoused in studies of intellectual and cultural interaction in Jewish–non-Jewish relations. See, for example, Marc Krell on the Jewish theologies of Franz Rosenzweig, Hans Joachim Schoeps, Richard Rubenstein and Irving Greenberg. Marc A. Krell, *Intersecting Pathways: Modern Jewish Theologians in Conversation with Christianity* (Oxford: Oxford University Press, 2003). For the converse, that is, the way in which non-Jewish society has defined itself against the Jew, see Bryan Cheyette's *Constructions of 'the Jew' in English Literature and Society*.

[41] Yosef Yerushalmi, *Zakhor: Jewish History and Jewish Memory*, third ed. (Seattle: University of Washington Press, 1999), 25.

[42] In his anthology of Jewish historical writings, Meyer notes a small number of exceptions to the rule that Jews were uninterested in nonbiblical history until the modern period: There was the second-century *Seder Olam* [Order of the World], a chronicle that included the Bar Kokhba war, and the undated *Seder Olam Zuta* [Small Order of the World], which extended its chronology into sixth-century Jewish Babylonia. Sephardi Jewry produced several relevant works including the anonymously authored *Josippon* (c. 950). The first and second crusades (1096 and 1146) generated Ashkenazi chronicles of Jewish suffering and, likewise, the Spanish Expulsion of 1492 Sephardi lachrymose histories such as *The Vale of Tears* (1558) by Joseph Ha-Kohen. Sixteenth-century Italian Renaissance Jews such as Solomon ibn Verga and Azariah del Rossi incorporated into their writings naturalistic explanations of events alongside divinely providential ones and tried to distinguish between fact and legend. But Meyer maintains, 'Only in the nineteenth century did Jews [in Western Europe] begin to produce integrated and comprehensive histories, not merely fragments or chains of tradition.' Meyer, *Ideas of Jewish History*, 13–21.

of the medieval *Toledot Yeshu* (Story of Jesus), wherein the rabbis send Paul as their undercover emissary to sabotage the early Christian movement and bring about the parting of the ways in conformity with God's will, is paradigmatic in this regard. It illustrates nicely the premodern use of the past, real or imagined, to strengthen the authority of the religious establishment and in particular to reinforce the assumption of divine providence as the ultimate arbiter of events, an assumption that has been described as 'the traditional theological scheme of causality'.[43]

By the time of the Enlightenment, a more secular, philosophical worldview had begun to challenge the theological, with important implications for understanding the past. The earliest stages of this phenomenon can been seen in the writings of Spinoza, who has been credited with a purely naturalistic explanation of Jewish continuity, an explanation that rejected the role of divine providence in favour of the combined historical impact of Jewish separatism and Gentile hostility.[44] Similarly, he perceived the Law as a creation of the Jewish people. Furthermore, his *Theological-Political Treatise* was an early example of rationalist historicism in its criticism of historically suspect stories from the Old Testament and in its demythologising of the priestly traditions that surrounded the Christian authorities Jesus and Paul, with whom he had apparently made his peace. Of course, Spinoza was not writing history but philosophy. Nevertheless, his appreciative views of the Apostle to the Gentiles could be said to be amongst the earliest contributions made towards the development of an historically sensitive Jewish self-awareness that had freed itself from traditional religious authority.[45]

Spinoza would be joined shortly by others for whom revelation and the dictates of authority no longer represented an adequate foundation for knowledge and self-understanding. For the *maskilim*, those who embraced the eighteenth-century Jewish Enlightenment or *Haskalah* and who sought to negotiate an equal place for themselves in European Gentile society, alternative ways of relating to the surrounding world, alternatives to the pietistic rationales of Jewish faith and

---

[43] Ibid., 11.

[44] 'As for their being dispersed and stateless for so many years, it is not at all surprising that, after separating themselves from all the nations in this way, they brought the resentment of all men upon themselves, not only because of their external rites which are contrary to the rites of other nations, but also by the sign of circumcision which they zealously maintain. But experience has shown that it is the resentment of the gentiles to a large extent that preserves them.' Spinoza follows this with a discussion of the Jewish experience in Spain and Portugal. Spinoza, *Theological-Political Treatise*, trans. Michael Silverthorne and Jonathan Israel (Cambridge: Cambridge University Press, 2007) 55 (3:12). According to Yerushalmi, Spinoza's historical observation that Jewish identity was sustained by anti-Semitism rather than Divine Providence was 'an important station on the path to the secularisation of Jewish history, as well as to the historicisation of Judaism.' Y. Yerushalmi 'Divre Spinoza al-kiyum ha-am ha-yehudi' *Proceedings of the Israel Academy of Sciences* (Jerusalem, 1983), 6:186, cited in D. N. Myers, 'Of Marranos and Memory', in Elisheva Carlebach, John Efron, and David Myers, eds., *Jewish History and Jewish Memory* (Hanover, NH: Brandeis University Press, 1998), 8.

[45] Spinoza appreciated Paul as one oriented towards rationality and universalism, who encouraged a discerning approach to the reading of scripture. We will return to Spinoza in Chapter 7.

tradition, had to be found. The chief strategy of these disciples of Moses Mendels-sohn (1729–86) was the inclusion of secular knowledge within Jewish education, and one might well have predicted this to include history. However, any interest in Jewish history as such was tempered by an uneasy notion that drawing attention to centuries of Christian persecution, largely the result of the charge of deicide against Jews, would only hinder them in seeking to convince the Gentile world of their legitimate share in the newfound society of common humanity. Some biographies were written, including those of Maimonides and Mendelssohn himself, but these were produced to provide models of enlightened behaviour,[46] and no *maskil* was prepared go quite as far as Spinoza in holding up Paul as such a model (after all, even Spinoza had written anonymously), although appreciative noises were made in this regard to Jesus.[47] But the philosophical and literary endeavours of the *Haskalah* did prepare the ground for the early nineteenth-century *Wissenschaft des Judenthums*, the German–Jewish movement for the scientific or historical study of Judaism, and with it the first truly historical engagements with Paul by Jews.

Inspired by the Romantic movement of the late eighteenth and early nineteenth centuries, that widespread demonstration of the loss of confidence in both the unadulterated revelation of tradition and the abstracted rationality of the Enlight-enment and *Haskalah*, the scholarly proponents of *Wissenschaft* sought to elevate Jewish historical awareness to an unprecedented degree.[48] Self-consciously react-ing to the philosophically oriented writings of the *maskilim*, its founding fathers, such as Leopold Zunz (1794–1886), were undoubtedly committed to historical scholarship for its own sake, but it soon became apparent to others that by clari-fying the past one was also laying firmer foundations for social strategies for the future.[49] There developed an interest in historicism, that is, the recognition that one's understanding of the past is profoundly shaped by one's location in a specific historical, social, and intellectual setting. Naturalistic, rational interpretations of

[46] David Myers draws attention to the Enlightenment Jews' increasing appreciation for the study of history and, in particular, biography, in *Re-inventing the Jewish Past* (New York: Oxford University Press, 1995), 17. In particular, he cites Shmuel Feiner, 'Ha-Haskalah be-yahasah le-historyah (1782–1881)', Ph.D. thesis (Hebrew University, 1990). But most, like Meyer, are less convinced, seeing biography as a poor substitute for the real thing. Meyer, *Ideas of Jewish History*, 22.

[47] Famously, Mendelssohn wrote, 'I know many a Jew who, like me, . . . acknowledge the innocence and moral goodness of the founder's character [Jesus], yet do so on the clear condition (1) that he never meant to regard himself as equal with the Father; (2) that he never proclaimed himself as a person of divinity; (3) that he never presumptuously claimed the honour of worship; (4) that he did not intend to subvert the religion of his fathers. . . . ' Moses Mendelssohn, public letter to Johann Kaspar Lavater (12 December 1769) in Alexander Altmann, ed., *Moses Mendelssohn Gesammelte Schriften: Jubilaeumsaugabe* (Stuttgart: Friedrich Frommann Verlag, 1971), 7:362.

[48] As Meyer expresses it, 'a reflective conception of Jewish history became central to the consciousness of the Jew.' Meyer, *Ideas of Jewish History*, 22.

[49] Several believed that only Wissenschaft could save Judaism itself, describing it as 'the mighty lever without which there is no Judaism' and 'the only means of the regeneration of Judaism.' Zacharias Frankel, 'Einleitendes' and Wolf Landau, 'Die Wissenschaft, das einzige Regenerationsmittel des Judenthums' in Monatsschrift fürGeschichte und Wissenschaft des Judenthums 1 (1852), cited in Myers, *Re-inventing the Jewish Past*, 20.

history began to be privileged over supernatural, providential ones, because they appeared to offer a more persuasive kind of explanation for who the Jew was and how he had come to find himself in his particular social circumstances. Jewish identity gradually came to be regarded as the sum of Jewish history, so that Jewish religion no longer dictated what would be remembered, but became a part of the complex story. As Yerushalmi put it in his account of the way in which Jewish history became decoupled from Jewish religious collective memory, the modern Jewish perspective assumed that 'it is not history that must prove its utility to Judaism but Judaism that must prove its validity to history.'[50] History became the currency of argument and debate.[51]

It is the ascendancy of historicism in the nineteenth century that makes sense of the apparent oddity that, just as Judaism was being subsumed into a broader account of Jewish history, Christianity began to take on a whole new significance for Jewish intellectuals. The belief that the study of historical challenges to the Jewish people was a worthwhile exercise for ensuring Jewish continuity demanded a reassessment of the community's interactions with Christian thought and culture. In fact, much of what was written from this time can be interpreted in large part as an expression of a desire to work out the relationship and to distinguish between, on the one hand, Jews and Judaism, and, on the other, Gentiles and Christianity.[52] In this crucial period in the development of modern Jewish historiography, then, Christian civilisation loomed large. In the beginning, of course, only a few Jewish individuals took an interest in the apostle Paul himself, such as the renowned German historian and prominent proponent of *Wissenschaft* values, Heinrich Graetz.[53] But before very long others followed suit and, although the first stirrings were undoubtedly due to these early individuals' endeavours, a popular view soon appeared and took on a life of its own. What is perhaps most interesting about this phenomenon was the speed with which a niche was found for the controversial figure of Paul in Jewish communal memory: in effect a false memory

---

50 Yerushalmi, *Zakhor*, 84.

51 For example, at a time of religious reform and ideological conflict, Western Jews of all kinds drew upon historical research to support their conceptions of authentic Judaism, whether this was a Judaism stripped of centuries of detrimental accretions (Reform), or an evolving yet historically continuous Judaism (the 'positive-historical' Breslau school of thought), or a Judaism that remained in its essential truths unchanged although finding new forms to express these truths in each new epoch (neo-Orthodox).

52 Prominent and familiar examples included the multivolume history of the Jewish people by Heinrich Graetz and the historical research on Second Temple Judaism by Abraham Geiger, but earlier members of the movement included Leopold Zunz and Eduard Gans, who also assumed that Jewish history required the reappropriation of its sources from the hands of Christian scholars (along with traditional Jewish scholars), and worked self-consciously to offer material that laid the base for counterhistories.

53 Graetz's *History of the Jews*, published in German between 1853 and 1876, profoundly shaped Western Jewry's understandstanding of Christianity as a flawed religion hostile to Jews and Judaism. He regarded Paul as the inventor of Christianity, a poorly educated antinomian theologian who was to be distinguished from the Jewish Jesus. We will return to Graetz in Chapter 2.

of his central role within a tradition of Christian hostility. In attempting to tell the story of the development of the popular image of the apostle it is necessary to start with a brief consideration of the Jewish historical approach to *Jesus*, which one might have assumed would provide a model for the Jewish scholarly approach to *Paul*, but which in fact is more telling for the differences it highlights.

The majority of modern Jewish writers and scholars drawn to the study of Jesus have been Reform or Liberal, and there are several reasons for this. The tendency among nineteenth-century reform-minded Jews to move away from the idea of Judaism as a nation, and to view it rather as a religious fellowship, was very much related to the new emphasis on ethics as central to their religious message. In this context, Jesus and his ethical teaching appeared interesting and relevant. Also, for those who were critical of Orthodox Jewish ritual, Jesus represented the struggle of free spirituality against the external ritualism of an earlier time, thus mirroring the then contemporary debate between the Orthodox and the Reform. Yet Jewish reclamations of Jesus were driven by more than simply the concern to recover the champion of an earlier Jewish ethical tradition.[54] Since the Enlightenment, Jewish writers had become increasingly engaged in dispute with Christian writers over Christian misunderstandings of rabbinic religion, especially with regard to the Law, which caricatured Judaism as a kind of fossilised legalism. From the nineteenth century onwards, a stock argument among Jewish writers had been that Jesus' ethical teaching had been essentially Jewish, of one sort or another, and had included nothing new or original.[55] Such treatments provided a platform from which to launch attacks on Christianity, in that they stressed the Jewishness and therefore the humanity of Jesus in contradiction to the traditional high Christological view of Jesus as divine. They were also a reminder that the Christian morality championed by Western civilisation could arguably be regarded as imitative and derivative of Jewish religious thought. The German Reform rabbi and *Wissenschaft* scholar, Abraham Geiger, to take one example, spent considerable

---

[54] 'Reclamation' is admittedly a problematic term. In his critique of Hagner's *The Jewish Reclamation of Jesus*, Schwartz concludes, 'If Jews do not find uniqueness in Jesus, I suggest it is ... precisely because such a claim may denote a reclamation in which Jews do not wish to engage'; G. David Schwartz, 'Explorations and Responses: Is There a Jewish Reclamation of Jesus?' *The Journal of Ecumenical Studies* 24 (1987), 104–9 (107). Nevertheless, commenting on a renewed Jewish interest in Jesus' religious teachings in his own day, Sandmel recognised that 'in some Jewish circles not only is there no questioning of the propriety of reclamation, but it is even an axiom in the form that Jesus was a Jew and therefore "ours"'; Samuel Sandmel, *We Jews and Jesus* (New York: Oxford University Press, 1965), 103. For present purposes, 'reclamation' should be understood to mean (1) various attempts at historical reconstruction, taken together with (2) varying degrees of identification with, and acceptance of, aspects of Jesus and his teachings. Although the phenomenon could be labelled as a 'reclamation' in the sense that it describes an attitude that contrasts sharply with the previous centuries of hostility and rejection, it would be more accurate to speak of 'reclamations'.

[55] Celebrated examples include Joseph Salvador, *Jésus-Christ et sa doctrine* (Paris: Guyot et Scribe, 1838), Heinrich Graetz, *Geschichte der Juden von den ältesten Zeiten bis auf die Gegenwart* (Leipzig: Leiner, 1853–75), and Abraham Geiger, *Das Judenthum und seine Geschichte* (Breslau: Schletter, 1865–71).

time and effort to this end.[56] For Geiger the traditional Christian view of the Church as the fulfilment of a failed Judaism was a myth he was determined to overthrow. Instead, he suggested that Christianity should be regarded as a tangential offshoot from Judaism, and that the current search for the faith *of* Jesus by Protestant scholars would only confirm that this ideal faith was essentially Jewish in nature.[57] This way of confronting Christian claims (regarding Jesus and Judaism) by describing Jesus as essentially Jewish, rather than essentially alien and heretical, was new. It can at least be partially explained by the reaction to Christian critique and the underlying psychological need to justify Judaism in the eyes of the Western Christian world. If Jesus had added nothing new to the teachings of the Jewish prophets and sages, then what justification had Christians for condemning Jewish teaching as inferior to Jesus' teaching?[58] One way of justifying Judaism to Christians, then, was to argue for Jesus' Jewishness, to reclaim him as a Jew, albeit with a number of reservations.[59]

Bearing in mind this change in attitude and approach to Jesus, one might have expected a similar reassessment or even reclamation of the apostle Paul. After all, religiously progressive Jews interested in reestablishing Judaism's theological and ideological boundaries would, one might have thought, have been interested in this first-century Jew's attempts to do the same. But for those who were coming to regard Jesus as faithful to Judaism, Paul drew increasing attention as the man responsible for the movement of early Christianity away from its Jewish roots. Such a view seemed to be confirmed by Christian Pauline studies as developed in the Tübingen and later the History of Religions school of thought. Beginning with Tübingen's F. C. Baur in the first half of the nineteenth century, who set himself the task of explaining 'how Christianity, instead of remaining a mere form of Judaism . . . asserted itself as a separate, independent principle [and] broke loose from it',[60] the idea was born that Paul's universalist concern for Gentiles had represented one side of a bitter dispute that had pitted him against the Jewish Christians following Peter, who had refused to abandon Jewish particularism.[61]

---

[56] For an excellent treatment of this paradigmatic case, see Susannah Heschel, *Abraham Geiger and the Jewish Jesus* (Chicago: University of Chicago Press, 1998).

[57] Heschel, *Abraham Geiger*, 14.

[58] This is precisely the way it is phrased, for example, by the British Sephardi authority Paul Goodman in *The Synagogue and the Church* (New York: Routledge, 1908), 233.

[59] These reservations, which differed from one writer to another, were nevertheless unanimously described in terms of a failure of Jesus to remain true to the spirit of Judaism. The sole exception to this rule was Claude Montefiore, who highlighted those elements of Jesus and his teachings that he regarded as un-Jewish and gave them a positive value judgment. See Daniel R. Langton, *Claude Montefiore: His Life and Thought* (London: Valentine Mitchell, 2002), 249–73.

[60] F. C. Baur, *Paul: The Apostle of Jesus Christ* (London: Williams & Norgate, 1871), I:3. German original 1845.

[61] Baur undoubtedly viewed the past through both Protestant and Hegelian lenses. The synthesis of Gentile Christianity, he thought, had been the result of a factional conflict between Pauline Christianity and Jewish Christianity led by Peter. This conflict between Paul's conception of Christianity,

Over the second half of the nineteenth century, the scholarly emphasis shifted away from the issue of the inclusion of Gentiles into Judaism, and towards the centrality of Hellenism for explaining the origins of Christianity. The German History-of-Religions school (*Religionsgeschichtliche Schule*) retained Paul as the central figure, but sought to cut him off entirely from Judaism and the Law. He was presented as very much the proactive radical, having produced the new religion of Christianity out of the flotsam and jetsam of a variety of Hellenistic philosophies.[62] In addition to attributing Christianity's distinctive sacraments of baptism and communion to the gory rituals of the cults of Attis and Dionysus, this approach also accounted for the Christocentricism of the apostle's writings. Unlike Jesus, whose teachings could, in the main, be reconciled easily with Judaism, Paul's fixation upon a cosmic, divine Christ (which resembled the Gnostic Redeemer) and mysticism[63] could not easily be overlooked in favour of his more 'Jewish' teachings.[64] This academic world of syncretistic religions, Gnostic myths, and

characterised by spirituality and internal piety, and Petrine Christianity, concerned with ritualism and outward observance, seemed to foreshadow the later Reformation and the issues underlying the conflict between Protestantism and Roman Catholicism. F. C. Baur, 'Die Christuspartei in der korinthischen Gemeinde, der Gegensatz des paulinischen und petrinischen Christentums in der ältesten Kirche, der Apostel Petrus in Rom,' *Tübinger Zeitschrift für Theologie* 4 (1831), 61–206.

[62] By the early twentieth century, this approach was de rigueur. In Paul (1904, ET 1907), Wrede argued that Paul's central idea of the Christ was formed by his experience at his conversion and the demands of his mission to the Gentiles; no concrete connection to Judaism was made. Bousset's Kyrios Christos (1913, ET 1970) was a corrective to this and argued that Paul had shaken himself free from sacramental and cultic piety of the early Hellenistic Christian communities; nevertheless, Bousset is responsible for sharply contrasting a Palestinian Jewish world and an outside Hellenistic world, the latter of which was more important for its parallels to Pauline thought. Cumont, Reitzenstein, and Dietrich wrote about and edited works on the mystery religions that had entered the Greco-Roman world from the east. Many scholars were interested in the influence of Gnosticism in particular.

[63] Generally speaking, mysticism has been an important theme for many Jewish commentators on Paul although, as we shall see, there has been considerable disagreement as to what, precisely, is meant by the term and whether it is best understood in Gentile or Jewish terms. The kind of texts that are cited as relevant to the subject include, for example, Gal. 2:20 (concerning a profound sense of union with the divine: 'I have been crucified with Christ; and it is no longer I who live, but Christ lives in me; and the life which I now live in the flesh I live by faith in the Son of God'); 2 Cor. 3:18 (concerning a metamorphosis into the divine likeness: 'But we all, with unveiled face, beholding as in a mirror the glory of the Lord, are being transformed into the same image from glory to glory, just as from the Lord, the Spirit'); and 2 Cor. 12:1–6 (concerning mystical visions: 'a man in Christ who . . . whether in the body I do not know, or out of the body I do not know . . . was caught up to the third heaven'). Discussions of the influence of the Greco-Roman mystery religions are frequently brought to bear in the context of discussing Paul's mysticism, too. For example, Rom. 12:4–8 and 1 Cor. 12 and 14 (concerning spiritual gifts such as knowledge, prophecy, speaking in tongues, and distinguishing between spirits, which are bestowed upon believers, who 'though they are many, are one body'); and Rom. 6:1–10 and 1 Cor. 11:23–34 (concerning baptism and the Eucharist, perceived by many commentators as mystical rites of transformation for the believer, freeing him from sin and uniting him with Christ).

[64] Leo Baeck, writing much later, expressed Paul's Christocentricism well: 'The first thing we see is that there is a centre about which everything turns. The point on which everything depends, round which everything revolved in Paul's life, and the point at which his faith became his life was the vision which overpowered him when one day he saw the Messiah and heard his voice. This vision

Hellenistic mystery cults provoked a resonance in the minds of Jewish scholars interested in New Testament studies: for both Christian and Jewish scholars it had become possible to categorise Jesus as a reformer within the Jewish fold and Paul as an innovator outside the Jewish pale. Another important factor was the practical impossibility of reading Paul's writings in isolation from the all-pervasive Lutheran interpretation of Paul as a sustained, polemical attack on the Jewish Law, which contrasted Jewish 'works' with Christian 'faith'; an alternative reading would have to wait until the final decades of the twentieth century.[65] From this perspective, there was little or no incentive for Jews to study Paul other than as a means by which to refute Christian views of Judaism derived from his misrepresentation of the Jewish Law. To summarise, the nineteenth-century origins of the 'traditional' or 'classic' negative Jewish view of Paul can be found in, first, the need to find a replacement for Jesus as Jewish public enemy number one; second, the timely confirmation of contemporary Christian New Testament scholarship that Paul was responsible for the inclusion of Gentiles and the injection of pagan elements into Judaism; and third, the fact that, in the context of defending Judaism against Christian critique, Paul's relevance lay in his misrepresentation of Judaism and the Jewish Law so that, consequently, the most immediate reason to approach him was to attack him head-on as an apostate, an enemy of the Jewish people, and the antithesis of Jesus the Jew. In contrast to Jesus, Paul could not readily be reclaimed or utilised as a means by which to discredit the Christian caricature of Judaism as a fossilised, legalistic religion. In the chapters that follow, it is worth bearing in mind that the assumption of many Jewish commentators that they are writing against the backdrop of a tradition of hostility boasting an ancient pedigree is an assumption based not upon historical reality, but upon a recent cultural construct.

PAUL IN POPULAR JEWISH CULTURE: *THE JEWISH CHRONICLE* AS A CASE STUDY

In the popular Jewish imagination, however, the myth became a reality and for a long time now Paul has commonly been held responsible for Christianity, with all the implications that this entails. How might one hope to demonstrate such a claim? A comprehensive survey of popular sources in Europe and the United States is beyond the scope of this chapter and continues to await the scholarly attention it deserves. In the meantime, as the premier communal newspaper for the Anglo-Jewry since 1841 and as the oldest continuously published Jewish weekly in the world, *The Jewish Chronicle* can be regarded as a useful case study, indicative of Jewish thought and discourse in the public domain over a sustained period, at

---

immediately became, and remained, the central fact of Paul's life . . . One must start from it in order to understand Paul, his personality and his confession.' Leo Baeck, 'The Faith of Paul', 93–110 (94). We will return to Baeck in Chapter 2.

[65] For a brief overview of the phenomenon of the so-called 'New Perspective' on Paul which challenged the traditional Lutheran reading, see the Introduction.

least in one corner of the English-speaking world. It was both reflective of popular opinion and influential in terms of shaping it. As the author of its official history observed, 'By interpreting the world to the Jews in Britain and representing them to the majority society, *The Jewish Chronicle* played a fundamental role in shaping Anglo-Jewish identity. It defined the parameters of debate for communal and other issues. . . [and] it functioned as a forum for the discussion of Judaism.'[66] Debates initiated by learned articles and book reviews gathered momentum within its letters pages, editors pontificated on the great concerns of the day, columnists explained what's what to a lay readership anxious to make sense of the often-confusing Christian culture that surrounds them, and, through a mysterious, interactive process, popular opinion was formed.

In the case of St. Paul, popular opinion occasionally needed to be reminded of why the apostle was an appropriate topic for debate. As one columnist noted in 1922, the conversion of Paul

has had such a tremendous influence upon Jewish history, it opens up so many questions in which Jews are vitally interested, that some account of it may fitly form the subject of comment in a Jewish newspaper. . . . [67]

Nevertheless, the shape of the debate was, and remains, a familiar one. Paul frequently appears in the *Chronicle* when the origins of Christianity are discussed, when an attempt is made to account for its characteristic doctrines, or when someone seeks to define Judaism against the essence of Christianity. A few examples will suffice. As an editorial from 1857 makes clear, it is no longer Jesus who should be held accountable for the transformation of a small Jewish following to a world-shaping religion.

It is the fiery rabbi of Tarsus who is the real founder of Gentile Christianity as developed in process of time. It is Paul who gave the impetus to the small particle detached from Judaism which sent it down to remote ages, and which, as it rolled on, avalanche-like gathered and gathered until it overwhelmed the existing forms of religion.[68]

And in reaction to a public lecture by a Christian religious leader in 1861, the editor made the case more explicitly still.

[W]e cannot admit that it was the teacher of Nazareth [Jesus] that produced the greatest change ever wrought on the face of the earth. This honour is due to rabbi Saul of Tarsus, commonly called St. Paul, and not rabbi Joshua of Nazareth. Had the fiery spirit of the rabbi of Tarsus not boldly broken down the barrier, that separated the Gentile from the Jewish world, and which Jesus left intact, the latter might have passed as the founder

---

[66] The Jewish Chronicle has held a monopoly over the Anglo-Jewish press for much of the last century and a half and has succeeded in maintaining a consensual position and thus a commanding authority. David Cesarani, *The Jewish Chronicle and Anglo-Jewry, 1841–1991* (New York: Cambridge University, 1994), ix.

[67] Theologicus, 'Paul and Paulinism' in *The Jewish Chronicle* (27 January 1922), iii.

[68] Editorial (Abraham Benisch), *The Jewish Chronicle* (17 July 1857), 1076. This is a response to a recent Christian enquiry as to why a Hebrew should not embrace Christianity.

of some obscure Jewish sect. . . . The true founder of Christianity, such as it necessarily must have shaped itself the moment the flood-gates of the Gentile world was opened, and the original Jewish nucleus swept away, is St. Paul, the man who was everything to everybody; among the Jews a Jew, and a Gentile among the Gentiles; who united the simplicity of the dove with the cunning of the serpent, and who, by his cunning, effected between Judaism and paganism that compromise which in process of time was enlarged and developed into historical Christianity such as prevails now in the civilised world. The pope of Rome ought to style himself the successor of St. Paul, the real founder of the Gentile Church, which absorbed the primitive Jewish churches, just as the rod of Aaron swallowed up the rods of the rival magicians.[69]

Although references to Paul are by no means numerous, this way of making sense of him is characteristic of the coverage of *The Jewish Chronicle*. General remarks to the effect that 'Christianity is to a far greater extent the religion of Paul than that of Jesus'[70] represent the most frequent type of discourse in which the apostle appears. Key characteristics of Christian thought, and certainly those which can be regarded as hostile to Judaism, are also often understood to be derived from Paul, rather than from the Jewish Jesus. The report of a public lecture by a Reform minister in 1908 is typical in this respect.

As impartial readers of the New Testament, we [Reform Jews] are able to see clearly to what a great extent that part of Christianity which is opposed to Judaism, which abrogates it, and places it aside, is distinctly apart from the teachings of Jesus and is as distinctly traceable to the effect of the teaching of the Apostle Paul.[71]

A reader who regularly perused the pages of the *Chronicle* would be exposed to numerous book reviews of Protestant New Testament scholarship in which he would be reminded that many of the Christian teachings regarded as 'absolutely repugnant to the Jewish mind . . . [such] as those of the supernatural character of Jesus, the Trinity, the Incarnation, and the Atonement, were the product of Paul's imagination.'[72] Paul's theological creativity was to be held responsible for the parting of the ways, or, as another book reviewer put it,

A Jew [that is, Paul] who speaks of the 'curse of the Law' and believes in a pre-existent Christ, who is the only Son of God, who needs an incarnation and resurrection to effect

---

[69] Editorial (Abraham Benisch) on a lecture given by the Archbishop of Dublin in *The Jewish Chronicle* (5 April 1861), 7.

[70] Mentor, 'Jews and Jesus' in *The Jewish Chronicle* (2 April 1923), 9.

[71] Rev. A. A. Green, lecture to the Cambridge University Nonconformist Union (26 January 1908) in *The Jewish Chronicle* (31 January 1908), 7.

[72] A book review of the Hibbert Lectures by Prof. Pfleiderer of Berlin 1885 on 'The Origin of Paulinism and its Influence on Christianity'. The claim is also made that 'It was Paul who widened the breach beyond the possibility of repair', *The Jewish Chronicle* (17 April 1885), 5. Elsewhere, in a report on a lecture by M. Frank at the Societé des Etudes Juives, Paul was also blamed for the doctrine of 'original sin', *The Jewish Chronicle* (1 January 1886), 9–10.

the salvation of the elect, such a believer has denied his ancestral religion and stands outside the camp of Israel.[73]

It would be difficult to find an alternative to the ubiquitous presentation in the popular press of Paul's invention of Christianity as a pagan-influenced theological system against which the superiority of Judaism could be defined. As such, it represented a useful foil against which to contrast the Jewish religion. As one contributor explained in 1978,

St. Paul it was, and not Jesus, who originated Christianity in the name of Jesus, a Jesus long dead and in no position to protest. Pauline Christianity – there is no other variety extant – is a continuation of Greek saviour cults plus some confusion with and accommodation to Judaism.... It presents little difficulty to show on theological and religious grounds, that Paul was profoundly mistaken, that Judaism and Christianity have divergent world views, that the Hebrew Bible and Greek New Testament are antithetical in just about every consideration....[74]

But in attempting to do justice to the popular Jewish view of Paul, one cannot leave the reader with the impression that it begins and ends with his reputation as the founder of Christianity who synthesised Jewish and non-Jewish elements to create a new faith and who attacked the Law. To anyone even remotely familiar with his place within the Jewish cultural imagination, it is apparent that the general attitude towards the Apostle to the Gentiles is overwhelmingly hostile, even pathologically so. In scholarly and popular sources alike, one will often find references to the apostle couched in vitriolic and hyperbolic language. Abandoning the pages of *The Jewish Chronicle* for a moment, one can readily locate descriptions of Paul as 'Pharisaism's greatest enemy'[75] and 'a bitter and violent enemy of the Law'[76] who called for the 'dissolution of Judaism'.[77] He was someone who exhibited 'Jew-hatred'[78] and whose 'turn-coat theology' created a movement that 'would become the primary source of anti-Semitism in history'.[79] As one polemicist saw it, Paul was

the first enemy of the Jews among the Christians, the first Jewish informer among the gentiles, the first falsifier of Judaism to the gentile world, the foe of Israel, and the

---

[73] A book review by 'G.F.' of Schweizer's *Paul and His Interpreters* in *The Jewish Chronicle* (15 November 1912), 24.

[74] S. Levin, 'Children and the Greek Malady' in *The Jewish Chronicle* (22 December 1978), vii.

[75] Salo Baron, *A Social and Religious History of the Jews*, second ed. (New York: Columbia University Press, 1966), I, 221.

[76] Abba Hillel Silver, *Where Judaism Differed; An Inquiry into the Distinctiveness of Judaism* (New York: Macmillan, 1956), 113.

[77] Paul Goodman, *History of the Jews*, revised by Israel Cohen (London: J. M. Dent & Sons, 1951), 38.

[78] Kaufmann Kohler, 'Saul of Tarsus', *Jewish Encyclopedia*, XI, 85. 'Antisemitism within Christianity Originated with Paul.' Ralf Biermann, 'The False Apostle Paul' in *The Jewish Times*, 27 April 2004.

[79] Tibor Krausz, review of Bruce Chilton, *Rabbi Saul* (2004) in *The Jerusalem Report* (7 March 2005), 41.

foe of the Torah. When among Christians everywhere in the world one hears or reads that Jews are a materialistic people devoid of spirit, a practical people devoid of soul, the source is Paul. When in evil times Christians drag forth our Scrolls of the Law, dishonour them, rend them and burn them, it is owing to Paul, who taught them that the Torah is the quintessence of sin, its apotheosis.[80]

Such sentiments are by no means marginal. Chief Rabbi Jonathan Sacks, writing in 1993, even appeared to identify a genocidal ring to the apostle's teachings, observing that he was

the architect of a Christian theology which deemed that the covenant between God and his people was now broken.... Pauline theology demonstrates to the full how remote from and catastrophic to Judaism is the doctrine of a second choice, a new election.... *No doctrine has cost more Jewish lives.*[81] [Italics added]

These charges, it should be obvious, go further than simply acknowledging Paul as the individual who marked the dividing line between Judaism and Christianity, or the one with whom the Christian Church began. It has been suggested that the animus of the popular view can be explained as resentment for the way in which later Christians used Paul to justify ideas such as Jewish culpability for Jesus' death,[82] or for the denigration of Judaism explicit in the traditional Western Christian reading of Paul.[83] But such explanations assume a more informed, rational basis for Jewish popular feeling than is perhaps warranted. Listening carefully to such emotive allegations, it seems that the raw power of the negative view of Paul is better explained by reference to the wider cultural landscape and, in particular,

---

[80] Chaim Lieberman, *The Christianity of Sholem Asch: An Appraisal from the Jewish Viewpoint* (New York: Philosophical Library, 1953), 87–8.

[81] Jonathan Sacks, *One People? Tradition, Modernity, and Jewish Unity* (London: Littman Library, 1993), 206–7.

[82] Having observed that 'generally Paul has been something of a lightening rod for Jewish anger and criticism of Christianity', the Conservative Jewish professor of Religious Studies at Manhattan College, Claudia Setzer, goes on, 'Where did all this animus come from? In part, it comes from the way Paul has been used against the Jews. For example, his first Epistle to the Thessalonians contains the earliest example of the charge that the Jews killed Jesus (2:14–16).' Claudia Setzer, 'Understanding Paul', unpublished paper given at the twelfth Nostra Aetate Dialogue, Fordham University (October 2004), 2. 1 Thess. 2:14–16 reads 'For you, brethren, became imitators of the churches of God in Christ Jesus that are in Judea, for you also endured the same sufferings at the hands of your own countrymen, even as they did from the Jews, who both killed the Lord Jesus and the prophets, and drove us out. They are not pleasing to God, but hostile to all men, hindering us from speaking to the Gentiles so that they may be saved; with the result that they always fill up the measure of their sins But wrath has come upon them to the utmost.'

[83] In discussing 'the standard view [of Paul] held by Jews up to at least 1950' Eisenbaum asks the question: 'Why was Paul the bad guy? The reason lies with the traditional reading of Paul which has prevailed through most of Western Christian history, one that was given unparalleled, paradigmatic credibility by Luther, Reformation theology, and the rise of modern biblical scholarship... Paul is understood to have rejected his Judaism, which was a legalistic religion in which one achieved salvation through the accumulation of meritorious acts... Judaism is seen to be exclusivist and elitist, ethnically peculiar, and requiring of its members a plethora of arcane rituals.' Eisenbaum, 'Following in the Footnotes of the Apostle Paul', 83–4.

a complex array of ideas and attitudes that possess profoundly negative historical, sociological, and psychological connotations for many Jews, and which populate modern Jewish literature and public discourse. These include attitudes towards apostasy, towards conversion and Christian missionary work, towards those who abandon or subordinate Torah, and towards those who would blur the boundaries of Jew and Christian, to say nothing of the threat of Jewish self-hatred. It is the conscious or unconscious association of these categories with Paul, a kind of conceptual projection or displacement, that accounts for the strong emotion, the widespread acceptance, and the longevity of the negative Jewish view of Paul in modern times. Although it is by no means easy to demonstrate the veracity of such a claim, it will prove useful to return to *The Jewish Chronicle* for establishing the kinds of popular discourse in which Paul appears.

In addition to presenting Paul as the creator of Christianity, then, the columns of the *Chronicle* also portray the apostle as an apostate and frequently associate him with conversion. He is described as a renegade, where 'the meaning of renegade is be understood as an apostate, one who has abandoned his religious faith.'[84] Moreover, he had been a disloyal opportunist who 'cannot escape the reproach of tergiversation and of a turncoat, who, when it suited him, was a Pharisee of the Pharisees'.[85] In the context of more general discussions on conversion, or in the condemnation of particular examples in modern times, Paul's name frequently appears. The typical convert is described as having 'quitted the law of Moses for the precepts of St. Paul,'[86] or having chosen 'to obey the dictates of St. Paul,'[87] or being, 'according to Paul, an apostate from Moses.'[88] The account of one Jew who converted to Christianity, an allegedly gluttonous Jew who apostatised to avoid the dietary laws, ends with a condemnation of his claims to have been persecuted by Jews and that, 'like another St. Paul', he had been converted by a miracle.[89] There is often disgust expressed at the high estimation in which converts were held in the eyes of Christians, one commentator noting bitterly that, in the mould of Paul, 'a Jew when converted becomes a blessing chiefly to the gentiles'.[90] In this context, one may also note the resentment felt by the Jewish community at Christian efforts to convert its members. Unsurprisingly, Paul is seen as the archetypal missionary, whose methods were strongly suspect. His work among the pagans revealed him

---

[84] Letter from 'I.R.P' to the editor in *The Jewish Chronicle* (20 February 1852), 158–9.

[85] Editorial (Abraham Benisch), 'An Analysis of Religious Belief', in *The Jewish Chronicle* (23 June 1876), 187.

[86] James Picciotto, 'Sketches in Anglo-Jewish History: Hebrew Capitalists', in *The Jewish Chronicle* (3 October 1873), 447.

[87] James Picciotto, 'Sketches in Anglo-Jewish History: Isaac D'Israeli', in *The Jewish Chronicle* (14 August 1874), 314. This appears in the context of a discussion of Portuguese converts to Christianity.

[88] Editorial (Marcus Bresslau), 'Clerical Defamation of Jewish Character', in *The Voice of Jacob/The Jewish Chronicle* (14 March 1845), 121.

[89] An Old Traveller, 'Christian Prejudice Fostered by Jewish Converts', in *The Jewish Chronicle* (2 August 1850), 340.

[90] Editorial (Leopold Greenberg), *The Jewish Chronicle* (2 May 1930), viii.

to be 'an adept opportunist . . . [who] saw that to be "accepted" he must mould into the doctrines of Jesus some of the pagan beliefs which the Heathens held.'[91] Nevertheless, his approach, which preferred expediency to principle,[92] had had little effect on Jews of his own day. And this point was worth emphasising in denunciations of modern evangelical missionary efforts.

Can these deluded persons [that is, those who support a Christian mission to the Jews] . . . really believe that the unhallowed words of some salaried missionary will produce a deeper impression on the mind of the modern Jew than the potent preaching of St. Paul to his Hebrew contemporaries?[93]

To label Paul an apostate and to associate him with conversion and missionary activities was to invoke the history and communal memory of painful treatment of the Jewish people at the hands of its most bitter enemies. From a social perspective, the apostate had traditionally been treated as an outcast, totally ostracised from the community. Despised for moral weakness, for succumbing to threats or persecution, for switching sides, the apostate had become a figure of hate. Baptism into Christianity was especially reviled because many of its doctrines (for example, the Trinity and the Incarnation), not to speak of its practices (for example, sacramentalism and veneration of the saints), were regarded as idolatrous. In the medieval and ancient periods, attempts to convert Jews to Christianity were generally unsuccessful (with the exception of Spain and Portugal, where there were forced conversions). Nevertheless, a number of high-profile apostates went on to become notorious persecutors of Jews, such as the thirteenth-century disputants Nicholas Donin (Paris 1240) and Paul Christian (Barcelona 1263). Furthermore, baptism of Jews in the modern period most commonly occurred as a means by which socially ambitious Jews believed they could partake of a wider non-Jewish society which attracted them but which refused to accept them as Jews.[94] Such assimilates were roundly condemned by those within the Jewish community for selling their Jewish identity so cheaply, exchanging their nominal Jewish beliefs for nominal Christian beliefs. A number of these also turned their back on their origins and expressed their own contempt of the primitive tribe from which they had found relief in the superior, cultured world of Christian society. A well-known example was Karl Marx, whose parents had had him baptised as an infant, and who was capable of regarding Judaism as the chief representative of Mammon. Others, for complex reasons we shall shortly explore, were obsessively antagonistic towards Jews and became known as self-haters. The implications for modern perceptions of Paul are obvious. In so far as he is regarded as a convert, he has been construed

[91] Editorial (Leopold Greenberg), *The Jewish Chronicle* (20 December 1929), 10.
[92] Letter to Editor by G. Friedlander in *The Jewish Chronicle* (24 June 1910), 24.
[93] Editorial (Abraham Benisch), *The Jewish Chronicle* (8 May 1863), 4.
[94] For a comprehensive and varied treatment of the subject of cultural assimilation, see the edited collection of essays by Todd M. Endelman, ed., *Jewish Apostasy in the Modern World*.

as a traitor to his people and as someone who not only sold his Judaism cheap, but went on to sell it on cheap to the Gentiles. The Apostle to the Gentiles can also be thought of as the Great Apostate, the prototype of all Jewish converts to Christianity to come, whose theological writings would provide the foundations for fractious debate for millennia to come and who could be held responsible for the Christian mission, that perennial thorn in the flesh of the Jewish community.

Whether Paul was regarded primarily as the inventor of Christianity, an apostate, a convert, or a missionary, all who contributed to *The Jewish Chronicle* agreed that his attitude to the Law was lamentable. Writers often complained about charges of legalism and 'St. Paul's indictment of Judaism as a religion of the dead, a bondage to an obsolete law'.[95] Liberating his followers from the Law was regarded as being integral to his programme of gentilisation.[96] As a result of his innovations, Gentile Christianity discarded many requirements of the Law, such as the keeping of the Sabbath,[97] while spiritualising others – for example, converting dietary impurities into moral ones.[98] In contrast to the Jewish Law, the apostle even undermined the position of women.[99] 'No wonder', observed one regular columnist, 'that Paul was regarded in his day as "an apostate from the Law"'. For, he goes on,

Paul was not only opposed to Jewish Law and its ceremonial observances, but to all law, whether moral or legal. His attitude is thoroughly antinomian . . . Emancipation from Law is one of the foundation principles of the Pauline system . . . Paul's teachings, with their opposition to the Law and their pessimistic view of the world, were in direct antagonism to nine-tenths of the teaching of the [Judaism of the] Old Testament.[100]

This view of Paul as the iconic abrogator of the Law means that he frequently appears in the context of inter-Jewish ideological debate, where his name is employed as a term of abuse to fling at one's opponents. In particular, the Orthodox authorities are often reported as condemning progressive Jews with unflattering

---

[95] Rev. Dr. Abelson, 'A Medieval Theologian', in *The Jewish Chronicle* (24 June 1921), vii. Abelson's focus is on the eleventh-century philosopher Bahya ben Joseph.

[96] Regarding 'Paul's contest about the Law (Torah) . . . He succeeded in gaining the greatest object that lay closest to his heart – the freedom of his Gentile Christians from the Torah.' Letter from 'Yehudi' to editor in *The Jewish Chronicle* (4 May 1923), 13.

[97] 'The gentile Christians – and it is they who have formed Orthodox Christianity as it now is – did not keep the Sabbath since the days of St Paul. In conformity with his teaching, who classified it among the beggarly elements from which Christ had freed his followers, they scorned and even opposed the Sabbath.' Editorial (Abraham Benisch), 'The Sunday Opening of Museums', in *The Jewish Chronicle* (24 March 1876), 828.

[98] Editorial (Abraham Benisch), *The Jewish Chronicle and Hebrew Observer* (18 October 1861), 8.

[99] In a passionate piece about the place of women in religion, it is asserted, '[T]here is no doubt that the Apostle's writings do betray the utmost contempt for the gentler sex . . . These reactionary teachings of the Christian Apostle certainly had the effect of causing women to occupy a lower and more restricted position, during the early centuries of the Christian Church than she had held among the Israelites.' Editorial (Asher Myers?), *The Jewish Chronicle* (6 October 1893), 6.

[100] Theologicus, 'Paul and Paulinism', in *The Jewish Chronicle* (27 January 1922), iii. The article is complementary to the work of Claude Montefiore, but is more critical of Paul.

references to Paul. Thus in the years following the establishment of Reform Judaism in England in the mid-nineteenth century, one could find such pointed criticisms as

God Almighty did not require either the correction of St. Paul or any other mortal. The assertion that a commandment may be broken in word and yet observed in spirit is one of the most dangerous doctrines that was ever brought forward.[101]

And after the establishment of the Liberal Jewish Synagogue a few generations later, Chief Rabbi J. H. Hertz reportedly warned his flock that Anglo-Liberal Jewish attitudes to the Bible and to 'the bondage to the Law' are nothing 'but an echo of Paul, the Christian apostle to the Gentiles'.[102] The significance of this link between Paul and liberal attitudes towards the Torah cannot be overstated. For nineteenth- and twentieth-century progressive Jews, the Law was viewed as the source of Judaism's ethical teaching, but was also regarded as having evolved over time and in accordance with the development of mankind. Biblical criticism, which assumed the human authorship of the scriptures and emphasised a rational, analytical approach to understanding the word of God, alarmed the traditionalists, who believed that it devalued the Law and contributed to the continued decline of Torah observance that had begun with the Enlightenment. Such progressive forms of Judaism exhibited a relaxed attitude towards *halakhic* observance. Although some Reform leaders adopted an openly hostile stance towards rabbinic authority and interpretation of the Law, others came to see the ethical teachings of the Hebrew Bible and the developments of the rabbis as part of the wider revelation that included non-Jewish religious thought. The suspicion of many within the Orthodox camp that the reformers had been unduly influenced by Christian thought and practice made the association with Paul all the more appropriate. The schism regarding the status of the Law and its binding nature for the Jew became a gaping chasm, an unchanging post-Enlightenment landmark around which intra-Jewish religious debates continue to rage. The same holds true for the highly fraught context of the secular–religious divide within the modern state of Israel, where the practice of likening Paul to one's enemies remains alive and well. When, for example, the Israeli political party Shas gained in 1999 a concession that obligated senior cabinet members to avoid public desecration of the Sabbath, the *Chronicle* suggested 'they have probably done more damage to the purity of Judaism than any misguided believer since Saul of Tarsus.'[103] In controversies over the meaning of the Law in modern Jewish life, the Apostle to the Gentiles has

---

[101] Editorial (Abraham Benisch), 'The Seven Words against the Lord Jesus', in *The Jewish Chronicle and Hebrew Observer* (20 September 1863), 3.

[102] Chief Rabbi Joseph Hertz, 'The New Paths: Whither Do They Lead?' in *The Jewish Chronicle* (25 December 1925), 14.

[103] The reason given was that the law actually undermined the sanctity of the Sabbath. 'For when, in return for recognising the government, a group, with rabbinical authority, outlaws public Sabbath breaches by senior ministers, it is, by implication, allowing junior ministers to do what they like on

come to be so closely implicated that it is by no means obvious where antagonism towards one's ideological opponent ends and hostility towards Paul begins.

In more recent times, it is possible to find allusions to Paul in the context of criticism of the Messianic Jewish movement within the pages of the *Chronicle*. The controversial claimants of this hybrid religious identity, whose Jewish authenticity is uniformly denied by the Jewish community as a whole, have been likened to the apostle for, amongst other things, their missionary activities.[104] The biting dismissal of one well-known subgroup, the evangelical 'Jews for Jesus', is representative: 'Ever since the days of Paul, there has been a technical name for Jews for Jesus: Christians.'[105] The association is by no means a coincidence. The Messianic Jew or Hebrew Christian represents for the vast majority of Jews a deceptive and misleading confusion of the Jewish and Christian traditions. Such messianic groups are resented for the misappropriation of religious language, symbols, institutions, and objects. Similarly, it is easy to see how Paul can be viewed as someone who confuses the categories of Jewish and Christian, who in fact deliberately set out to blend ideas and teaching from Jewish and non-Jewish sources, not least with his emphasis on the Messiah as the Son of God and his allegorical reading of the Bible. Paul was also, of course, a seasoned missionary to both Jew and Gentile, whose attitudes and activities towards the dissemination of the gospel have provided the inspiration and model for centuries of Christian – and by association Messianic Jewish – missionary practice to follow. The fact that Messianic Judaism, in the forms with which we are familiar, emerged largely in the nineteenth and twentieth centuries[106] does not in any way negate the displacement of the intense Jewish resentment of such groups onto the Messianic Jew from Tarsus.

If one were to attempt to generate an artificial, composite image of Paul from the pages of *The Jewish Chronicle*, the figure produced would have few redeeming features. To speak of the ways in which the Apostle to the Gentiles appears in popular discourse is to speak of a patchwork quilt of suspicion and hostility that regards him both as the creator of Christianity and as a convert to it, as an embittered apostate from Judaism and as the translator of Jewish teachings for the

---

the seventh day (and senior ones to break Sabbath in private).' Norman Lebrecht, 'When Ministers Get Their Hands on the Ministries', in *The Jewish Chronicle* (9 July 1999), 25.

[104] A critique of Messianic Judaism by Arye Forta begins by referring to Paul. 'In the first century . . . Paul roamed the Graeco-Roman world trying to convince Jews that their religion was a temporary thing, to be abolished as soon as Jesus came along.' Rabbi Arye Forta, 'Misguided Missions', in *The Jewish Chronicle* (9 June 1989), 31.

[105] John Diamond, 'Right Envelope but with the Wrong Message', in *The Jewish Chronicle* (12 November 1999), 31. It is worth noting that Paul never used the term 'Christian'.

[106] For a useful overview of the modern history of Messianic Judaism, see Dan Cohn-Sherbok, *Messianic Judaism* (London: Continuum, 2001). The most sophisticated analysis of modern messianic Jewish theology is Richard Harvey, *Mapping Messianic Jewish Identities* (Milton Keynes: Paternoster Publishing, 2009). Although dated, the most comprehensive study of the historical phenomenon remains Hugh Schonfield, *The History of Jewish Christianity from the First to the Twentieth Century* (London: Duckworth, 1936).

Gentiles. In the mind of the modern Jew, the unfamiliar yet threatening figure of Paul was to be associated with progressive theological trends which undermined the authority of the Law, resented as the exemplar for opportunistic Christian missionary activities, and despised as a forerunner of the Messianic Jews who blurred the boundaries between Jew and Christian. He was the very personification of all the pain and destruction that the Christian Church had wrought upon the Jew in nineteen hundred years.

Finally, in the context of exploring the ways in which the popular Jewish view of Paul maps onto existing social categories with negative connotations, one might also point to the shadow cast by the phenomenon of Jewish self-hatred. After all, Paul's story appears to echo the familiar story of the modern Jewish self-hater, as some have pointed out. Kaufmann Kohler is perhaps the most influential scholar to have so described the apostle, but others commentators who have addressed the question of Pauline self-hatred or Jew-hatred include Lapide, Fuchs-Kreimer, and Brumberg-Kraus.[107] Unfortunately, here it is necessary to abandon the firm ground of The Jewish Chronicle and enter the realm of speculation, for evidence is not easy to come by, not least because 'Jewish self-hatred' lies in the eye of the beholder. Theodore Lessing first coined the term in his book Jewish Selfhatred (1930),[108] in which he utilised clinical reports on Jews who regarded the Jewish people with utter disgust, as vermin and as a stain upon mankind, who urged Aryans to exterminate them, and who themselves deliberately remained childless or committed suicide. Such self-haters believed that ultimate responsibility for his ill treatment lay with the Jew himself. In its extreme form Lessing regarded the phenomenon as an acute pathology of psychosis. In Jewish Self-Hatred (1986), Sander Gilman articulated the phenomenon as an internalisation of non-Jewish constructions of Jewish identity and expanded Jewish self-hatred to include Jewish anti-Judaism and Jewish anti-Semitism.[109] Todd Endelmann, in an essay entitled 'Jewish Self-hatred in Britain and Germany', (1999) criticised the tendency among some in the Jewish community to use the term as a means by which to undermine

---

[107] Kohler's scholarship emphasises 'Pauline Jew-hatred' and the apostle's 'hatred of Judaism and the Jew'. Kaufmann Kohler, 'Saul of Tarsus', Jewish Encyclopedia, XI, 85, and The Origins of the Synagogue and the Church (New York: Macmillan, 1929), 266. Lapide suggests that his own view is unlike that of other Jews who, having read Christian accounts of Paul, have asked, 'Is he the father of that enmity towards Jews which claims to be Christian? Or might he not even have contracted the malady of Jewish self-hatred?' Pinchas Lapide and Peter Stuhlmacher, Paul: Rabbi and Apostle, trans. Lawrence W. Denef (Minneapolis: Augsburg Publishing House, 1984 [1981]), 32–3. Fuchs-Kreimer admits that 'in the symbolic world of modern Judaism, Paul became the arch self-hating Jew who left his people for convenience.' Fuchs-Kreimer, 'The Essential Heresy', 79–80. Brumberg-Kraus also accepts that Jewish scholars have labelled Paul as an 'alienated or as a self-hating Jew'. Jonathan D. Brumberg-Kraus, 'A Jewish Ideological Perspective on the Study of Christian Scripture', Jewish Social Studies 4/1 (1997), 124.

[108] Theodore Lessing, Der Jüdische Selbsthass (Berlin: Jüdischer Verlag, 1930).

[109] Sander Gilman, Jewish Self-hatred: Anti-Semitism and the Hidden Language of the Jews (Baltimore: Johns Hopkins, 1986).

and express contempt of another's view, citing the debates around declining religious observance, intermarriage, and the Arab–Israeli conflict. Nevertheless, he argued that the term was useful in a historical context, if one focused upon actions and motivations. His preferred definition distinguished self-haters from converts, assimilationists, and other Jews who had severed their ties to Jews and Judaism for a wide variety of reasons and drew attention to the inability of the self-haters to move on and their obsession with articulating anti-Jewish views, disparaging, belittling, and cursing their origins and fate.[110] He maintained that self-hatred should not be confused with either Jewish self-criticism, which he viewed as a hallmark of the modern Jewish world, or some kind of disease or mental-illness, because Jewish internalisation of non-Jewish values and perspectives was widespread throughout the modern Western world, and because the strength of feeling did not always lead to self-hating behaviour.

So what has the concept of Jewish self-hatred to do with Paul? Conceivably, Paul could be categorised as a self-hater in so far as he is perceived to be a Jewish opponent of Jews and Judaism, or because his views are regarded as antagonistic to Judaism. But there is more to it than that. The very concept of a self-hating Jew, which is strictly speaking a modern phenomenon, provides yet another means, another social category, by which to make sense of this first-century Jew. Arguably, Paul can be viewed as a Diaspora Jew who ceased to regard the Jewish way of life as superior to that of the Gentiles. Crucially, he appears obsessed with a common Christian criticism relating to the burden of the Law, and with defining Jewish observance in terms of this burden. The all-consuming nature of Paul's apparent critique of Judaism suggests the ultimate self-hater, one who could not simply move on and leave Jews alone. Here, the point is not whether the wider Jewish community has been conscious of their displacement of the concept of the 'self-hating Jew' onto Paul – they are not, or, at least, there is no hint of this in a source such as *The Jewish Chronicle*. Rather, it is simply to suggest that such a displacement, such a conceptual spillage, might have played *some* part in the development of the modern appreciation of the Jewish Saul of Tarsus who became Paul, Apostle to the Gentiles.

CONCLUSION

An attempt having been made to outline the place of Paul in the popular Jewish imagination, a number of observations can be offered. Although some assume a tradition of Jewish hostility towards the apostle, the reality is that he was largely ignored until modern times. The growing awareness of Paul came about as the result of a crisis of confidence among post-Enlightenment Jews, and in particular

---

[110] Todd Endelmann, 'Jewish Self-Hatred in Britain and Germany' in M. Brenner, ed., *Two Nations: British and German Jews in Comparative Perspective* (Tübingen: Mohr Siebeck, 1999), 335.

the demise of the authority of Jewish religious communal memory, which led many to reassess their relationship with Christian history and culture. In particular, the nineteenth-century Jewish reclamation of Jesus and trends within contemporary Christian scholarship meant that some Jewish scholars began to regard Paul as the inventor of Christianity. However, the intensity of negative feeling towards the apostle within the popular Jewish imagination – insofar as it is reflected in a communal newspaper such as *The Jewish Chronicle* and thus insofar as Anglo-Jewry offers a useful case study[111] – is best explained in terms of an association, conscious and unconscious, of the Apostle to the Gentiles with wider cultural attitudes towards apostates and converts, those who would abrogate the Torah, those who would confuse the distinction between Jew and Christian, missionary activities, and, arguably, the phenomenon of Jewish self-hatred.[112] But the popular Jewish

---

[111] *The Occident*, a Jewish monthly national newspaper that ran from 1843 until 1869, reveals similar emphases among North American Jewry on the rare occasions it mentions Paul. Once, after the editor of *The Jewish Chronicle* had rather uncharacteristically criticised *The Occident* for its cynicism in regarding all converts as insincere and had gone so far as to defend the sincerity of the conversion of the great apostate himself, a biting response had been offered by Isaac Leeser, the renowned Sephardic rabbi, preacher, and founder of the Jewish press of America: 'We do not esteem Paul greatly . . . Of course Saul or Paul was a Jew; but he taught in opposition to Judaism . . . The apostles themselves had surely no great sympathy with Paul; he went to the gentiles, while they adhered the Jews, and kept the law . . . Indeed, we hold him to have been a man of consummate skill; he wanted to spread Judaism among the gentiles; but of ceremonial Judaism this was impossible, so he divested it of ceremony, and added the plurality in the Deity, as a doctrine better suited to the heathen world than the pure unity of the Jews. We would respectfully ask the editor of the Chronicle, whether he discovers not many inconsistencies in the character of Saul of Tarsus? At times with the Jews, then with the gentiles; at times entering the Synagogues, and then saying, he quits his brethren; at times living as a Jew, and then neglecting the ceremonies totally. We cannot reconcile all this; hence we do not esteem his character, even assuming all that is said about him in the Acts as literally true.' Isaac Leeser, 'The Jewish Chronicle and the Occident', *The Occident* III:1 (April 1845), 44. Another commentator, responding to Christian missionary efforts, asserted forcefully that 'the Jew wars against the very ideas Paul puts forth, and to enforce which oceans of blood have been shed; and that . . . we will resist them as we have done hitherto.' Editorial (Isaac Leeser), 'The Presbyterian Synod of New York and the Jews', *The Occident* VII:10 (January 1850), 483.

[112] A brief survey of twentieth-century Anglo-American encyclopaedia entries also supports these findings, albeit once again from an English-speaking perspective. The *Jewish Encyclopedia* (1901) suggested that Paul, 'the actual founder of the Christian Church', had created a 'new faith, half pagan and half Jewish.' His 'antinomian theology' had been the product of his 'fierce hatred of the Jew', also described as 'Pauline Jew-hatred'. His teachings had contained 'an irrational or pathological element'. Nevertheless, as a missionary, the 'many mythological and Gnostic elements in his theology which appealed more to the non-Jew than the Jew, [meant that] he won the heathen world to his belief'. (79–87). We will return to this entry by Kaufmann Kohler in Chapter two. *The Encyclopedia of Jewish Knowledge* (1934) described Paul as the 'actual founder of Christianity' and 'an opponent of Judaism', whose theology differed from that of the Talmudic rabbis as a result of his idea of 'a denationalised Judaism' and his concept of original sin 'and all the ideas of necessary redemption that flow out of it' (493–4). *Vallentine's Jewish Encyclopaedia* (1938) presented him as 'the real founder of Christianity', explaining that 'without his work the followers of Jesus would have remained a small Jewish sect destined to disappear'. He had been 'as zealous a believer as he had been a persecutor' and his missionary activities had led him to travel extensively. Although not anti-Jewish, he had engendered opposition as a result of his 'violations of Jewish law and custom' (505–6). *The Universal Jewish Encyclopedia* (1942) emphasised Paul's 'highly successful' missionary role, which had been made

conception of Paul and the antagonism that the wider Jewish community has felt towards this shadowy yet threatening figure are by no means the whole story. As we shall see, there has been a broad spectrum of reactions among Jewish thinkers, and a significant proportion have empathised with the apostle and appreciated his achievements. Why some of those who chose to engage with the apostle found in him something to admire, whereas others did not, will be the focus of enquiry in the following chapters.

possible by his recognition 'that by complete denial of law he could outdo Jewish missionary work and even draw to himself proselytes' (and although he never sought to destroy the law, it was 'not difficult for him spiritually to free himself from it'). He himself had believed that 'Christianity was a Judaism adapted for the times' but, as 'the first Christian theologian', he had 'extended Christianity beyond the teachings of Jesus, and constituted Christianity as a religion independent of and separate from Judaism' and even 'opposed to Judaism'; this was achieved largely as a result of his teaching on original sin and the mystical sacraments of baptism and the Eucharist (415–17). The *Standard Jewish Encyclopedia* (1959) emphasised Saul's conversion to Christianity, although suggesting that he 'contributed greatly to development of a distinctive Christian theology'. He generated 'thousands of new converts who did not adopt Jewish loyalty or Jewish observance, as converts of the other disciples had done', and taught that 'those who believe in Jesus are "the true Israel"' and that 'Divine election of "Israel after the flesh" was invalidated when the Jews rejected Jesus.' He believed that with the atonement of Christ, 'the law had been abrogated' (1484). The *Encyclopaedia Judaica* (1972) was perhaps the least negative of these articles, although it commented that 'neither his Jewish nor his Greek learning were extensive or deep'. Although Paul had not been the first to preach Christianity to gentiles, 'he was the most important of these missionaries'. His importance, however, lies in the fact that 'not only did Paul refuse to restrict his activities to gentiles; he also strongly opposed the observance of all Jewish practices in his gentile Christian communities.' Crucially, '[a]lthough he was not the only Christian who, by abrogation of the Jewish halakhah [law], paved the way for the separation of Christianity from Judaism, his arguments against the Jewish way of life had a very strong impact upon the development of gentile Christianity' (190–91). We will return to this entry by David Flusser in Chapter 3.

PART II

❧

THE APOSTLE PAUL AND JEWISH RELIGIOUS IDENTITY: NEW TESTAMENT STUDIES AND THEOLOGICAL APPROACHES

Constructions of Paul and Interfaith Relations: Building Barriers or Bridges between Judaism and Christianity

As we have seen, for Jewish thinkers in the nineteenth and twentieth centuries who wished to define themselves against Christianity, Paul had come to be seen as a replacement for Jesus as a symbol of Christianity *per se*. Concerned to defend themselves against Christian critiques of Judaism, they had preferred to champion the newly discovered Jewish Jesus as an ally rather than as a figure representative of the antithesis of Judaism; and so Paul emerged as his unfortunate successor. In this chapter we will consider how, for Jews who saw themselves as ideological opponents of Christianity, Paul's alien origins and absorption of foreign influences could be effectively contrasted with Jesus' Jewish authenticity. In this context, the apostle's influence and significance were more easily undermined than those of Jesus, his motives could be questioned, and the common view of his understanding of Judaism and the Law could be attacked as a betrayal of the faith of his master Jesus. We will also explore the options open to Jewish thinkers who wished to encourage better relations between Jews and Christians and who, with Paul as the new figurehead for Christianity, now had to address his place in the Jewish–Christian discourse as well as Jesus'. Although difficulties remained with many aspects of the apostle's theology, a small number of writers were ideologically predisposed to overlook his apparent weaknesses and, remarkably, to attempt to use him as a bridge to dialogue, that is, to view him as a means by which to better become familiar with and strengthen ties to the surrounding Christian world. This involved confronting the now self-evident classic Jewish view and arguing for the importance of a debate on Paul as a means to developing a close Judeo-Christian alliance in the face of a hostile, increasingly secular world. It meant emphasising the apostle's role in bringing the Jewish God to the non-Jewish world by means of his ethical and universalist teachings. In their desire to improve interfaith relations, a few even suggested that, in stark contrast to the hateful figure of popular imagination, Paul had actually been a good Jew.

BUILDING BARRIERS WITH PAUL

For some writers, including several traditionalists of one sort or another, the study of Paul provided an opportunity to express hostile attitudes towards Christianity itself. Heinrich Graetz, Elijah Benamozegh, Leo Baeck, Kaufmann Kohler, and

Martin Buber not only should be regarded as writing in a time-honoured tradition of anti-Christian polemic (joined in recent times by Abba Hillel Silver and Hyam Maccoby), but also arguably should be credited with the formation and establishment of the classic Jewish view of the apostle Paul itself.

Heinrich Graetz (1817–91) was a German Jewish historian and Bible scholar whose popular *History of the Jews*, published in German between 1853 and 1876, has endured as one of the most influential pieces of modern Jewish scholarship.[1] Influenced by the neo-Orthodox thought of S. R. Hirsch, he was more committed still to historical criticism and was a key figure of the Breslau School.[2] He has been credited with instilling the average Western Jew with a working hypothesis of Christianity, that is, as a flawed religion hostile to Jews and Judaism.[3] Throughout his work, Christian offences against the wandering Jews are treated in considerable detail, but his criticism also included other groups, such as Jewish converts to Christianity, Jewish mystics, and Hasidic and Reform Jews. Graetz marks an early stage in the so-called Jewish reclamation of Jesus, however, and Jesus himself is presented as an ideal of Jewish piety whose 'high-mindedness, earnestness and spotless moral purity were . . . undeniable', and as a figure of pride within Jewish history (the few criticisms Graetz had were put down to the unorthodox influences of the Essenes).[4]

Paul, on the other hand, represented for Graetz the arrival of Christianity proper, and was ultimately responsible for its success. As he saw it,

Without Jesus, Saul would not have made his vast spiritual conquests, but without Saul, Christianity would have had no stability. . . . Saul combined a weak and an iron nature; he seemed created to establish what was new, and to give form and reality to that which seemed impossible and unreal.[5]

Admitting a Pharisaic background, Graetz preferred to emphasise Paul's limited familiarity with Jewish writings and the Hebrew Bible.[6] His conversion to Christianity had been influenced by the female citizens of Damascus having 'gone over to Judaism', which had persuaded him that 'the time foreseen by the prophets

---

[1] Heinrich Graetz, *Geschichte der Juden*, 13 volumes (Berlin: 1853–76). The key volume for Paul is volume III, *Von dem Tode Juda Makkabi's bis zum Untergang des jüdischen Staates* (1854). The translation used here is Heinrich Graetz, *History of the Jews from the Earliest Times to the Present Day*, ed. and trans. Bella Loewry (London: Jewish Chronicle, 1901), II. The German edition includes scholarly apparatus, in contrast to the more popular English edition, although in neither case does he make reference to New Testament scholarship. For his treatment of Paul, Graetz was heavily dependent upon Romans, 1 Corinthians, and Galatians; he was also prepared to accept the historicity of Acts.

[2] Graetz was a professor at Zacharias Frankel's Jewish Theological Seminary in Breslau from 1853. In his writings he sought to trace the essence of Judaism down through the ages, as Hirsch had done, the key difference being the stamp of his historical positivist assumptions.

[3] Herbert Danby, *The Jew and Christianity* (London: Sheldon Press, 1927), 73.

[4] Graetz, *History of the Jews*, 149.

[5] Graetz, *History of the Jews*, 225.

[6] Graetz, *History of the Jews*, 225.

[had] now arrived, when every nation should recognize the God of Israel'.[7] His famous vision had convinced him that Jesus had risen from the grave ('not very lucid evidence as to a fact which was actually supposed to have happened') and that the messiah had indeed arrived.[8] For Graetz, as for many Jewish commentators to come, Paul's consequent abrogation of the Torah was not difficult to explain: he had been an opportunistic missionary for whom the Law had got in the way, it being 'a hindrance to the reception of heathen proselytes'.[9] His justification for waiving the Law, that is, his claim that belief in Jesus as the messiah had made the Law unnecessary, was an argument that Graetz regarded as 'resting on ... sophistry'.[10] Furthermore, Paul's considerable missionary successes should actually be credited to Judaism, for in winning over the heathens 'he had to unfold to them the glorious past of the Judaean nation ... [and] to contrast the pure belief in God with the wild practice of heathendom'.[11] And it was *Jewish* ethics that attracted converts tired of the 'widespread disease of immorality which was rife throughout the Roman Empire'.[12] In spite of Paul's dependence upon Judaism, Graetz felt that the apostle had consciously sought to distinguish his Christianity from Judaism. It was competition with Jews that led him to attempt to disconnect the teachings of Christ from those of Judaism, with the result that he 'conceived Christianity to be the very opposite of Judaism', that is, one system founded on Law and compulsion, the other on freedom and grace.[13] Racial feelings that had helped set Greek Christians against Judaic Christians had been fanned by the apostle, who 'sent out violent epistles against the adherents of the Law, and laid a curse on those who preached salvation in a manner differing from his own'.[14]

Without citing non-Jewish or pagan influences, Graetz argued that the Apostle to the Gentiles and his followers had betrayed Judaism because their superficial Jewish learning had allowed them to value success at conversion over loyalty to the Torah.[15] The balance of the influential *History of the Jews* would demonstrate the

[7] Graetz, *History of the Jews*, 226.

[8] Graetz, *History of the Jews*, 227.

[9] Graetz, *History of the Jews*, 231. It is worth noting that Graetz does not attribute Paul's teaching in terms of guilt for failing to fulfil the law.

[10] Graetz, *History of the Jews*, 228. 'A saying of his teachers may then have occurred to Saul that the Law was only binding until the time of the Messiah, and that as soon as the Redeemer came its importance and significance would cease.' Graetz, *History of the Jews*, 226.

[11] Graetz, *History of the Jews*, 229.

[12] Graetz, *History of the Jews*, 230.

[13] Graetz, *History of the Jews*, 231.

[14] Graetz, *History of the Jews*, 233.

[15] This emphasis on superficial Jewish learning among early Christians in general and Paul in particular might be described as a standard, even as an instinctive, Jewish response. An articulate recent expression of this position is offered by David Klinghoffer, who writes, 'The insistence on his [Paul's] own Jewish authenticity is so, well, insistent that you start to wonder. What does this Pharisee of Pharisees, this Hebrew of Hebrews, feel he needs to prove, and why? Jews, that critical people, to this day are quick to notice subtle suggestions of inauthenticity – hints that individuals who claim to be Jewish or to represent Jewish values are nothing and do nothing of the sort. There

terrible consequences that this mistake, and the subsequent rise of Christianity, would bring. For Graetz, it was no exaggeration to describe him as 'the destroyer of Judaism'.[16]

Graetz's historical, positivist understanding of Judaism reflected his commitment to secular learning and his determination to distance himself as much from the superstitious traditions of Eastern European Jewry as from Reforming modernists of Western Europe. Writing around the same time was another Jewish thinker who could also draw upon a vast reservoir of western literature and ideas, the Italian rabbi and philosopher Elijah Benamozegh. Epitomising the open and well-integrated Italian Jewish scholarly tradition, Benamozegh (1823–1900) lived his life in Livorno (Leghorn), a flourishing cosmopolitan centre of Jewish culture that was entirely free from hostility towards Jews. Although he was almost as familiar with Greek philosophy and Christian theology as with the Talmud, his first love was nevertheless Jewish mysticism or *kabbalah*. Acutely aware of how modern Jews (such as Graetz) dismissed *kabbalah* as superstition, Benamozegh spent a lifetime trying to demonstrate its worth and centrality to Judaism, most importantly in his *magnum opus* entitled *Israel and Humanity*, which was published posthumously in 1914.[17] The subject also featured heavily in *Jewish and Christian Ethics* (1867),[18] most interestingly in the context of explaining elements of Pauline thought.[19] Despite a respectful tone (he asserts at one point, 'we should be sorely grieved, could it be thought for an instant that we wished to calumniate the Christian ethics'),[20] this work was clearly polemical in its aims, contrasting as it did the ethical foundations of the two religions to the detriment of Christianity.[21]

---

is a certain quivering sensitivity in the Jewish soul, almost a sixth sense. With Paul, the hints that he was not what he claimed to be were right on the surface. A perusal of his letters immediately raises troubling questions about the veracity of his self-description.' David Klinghoffer, *Why the Jews Rejected Jesus* (New York: Doubleday, 2005), 95.

[16] Graetz, *History of the Jews*, 228.

[17] Emanuel Benamozegh, *Israël et l'humanité: étude sur le problème de la religion universelle et sa solution* (Paris: E. Leroux, 1914), trans. Maxwell Luria as *Israel and Humanity* (New Jersey: Paulist Press, 1995).

[18] *Morale juive et morale chrétienne: examen comparatif suivi de quelques réflexions sur les principes de l'islamisme* (Paris: Michel Lévy frères, 1867), translated as *Jewish and Christian Ethics with a Criticism on Mahomedism*, trans. anonymous (San Francesco: Emanuel Blochman, 1873).

[19] Benamozegh did not often cite his sources for Paul, the exceptions being Acts 15 (the Jerusalem Council) and 17 (Paul's missionary efforts in pagan cities) and Rom. 8:22–23 ('For we know that the whole creation groans and suffers the pains of childbirth together until now. And not only this, but also we ourselves, having the first fruits of the Spirit, even we ourselves groan within ourselves, waiting eagerly for our adoption as sons, the redemption of our body') as evidence of the influence of Gnostic–kabbalistic doctrines of the Palestinian School, but he certainly alluded to Acts 22:3, Rom. 3:20, 5:12–21, 6:15, 7:1–6, and 11:25–6, and Gal. 4:1–6. Although prepared to cite Christian writers such as Ernst Renan in other connections, he did not do so with regard to Paul. Nor did he tend to refer to Jewish writers.

[20] Benamozegh, *Jewish and Christian Ethics*, 15.

[21] This attack on Christianity was by no means vitriolic. Elsewhere, he stated, 'Unlike Paul, we do not say of this Providence [God] that it knows neither Jews nor Greeks, for that implies an inadmissible levelling of differences, a suppression of all nationality. We affirm, rather, that Providence recognises equally Jews, Greeks, and Barbarians – in a word, all races and peoples, who ought to be perceived as one though without losing their individual identities.' Benamozegh, *Israel and Humanity*, 133.

The crucial issue for Benamozegh was the abrogation of the Law, which he attributed in part to Jesus' belief that the messianic era was about to begin and to his confusing it with the final day of resurrection.[22] That it became a central tenet within early Christianity was, however, primarily the responsibility of the apostle Paul,[23] who had been a disciple of the sage Gamaliel.[24] Ironically, Benamozegh suggested, this cornerstone of Pauline thought had been ultimately derived from the Pharisaic tradition. For the Pharisees had believed that the reign of the Law would end with the resurrection, when a new earth would call for a new Law.[25] If one identified the resurrection (or day of judgement) with the messianic era, as the early Jewish-Christians did, then consequences for the Law after Jesus were clear. Paul also picked up on another Jewish tradition.

Already had the Bible and the Hebrew prophets, highly prizing life, said in a thousand places that the law, virtue, commands of God cease at the door of the tomb; that the dead no longer praise the Lord; that the sepulchre gives forth no song of thanks. . . . Pharisaism formulizes [these passages] into one general saying. . . . The Pharisees say: 'With the dead is liberty (from the Psalms), when one is dead he is freed from precepts.' [Shabbat 151b] It is almost incredible, but this is the sole pivot upon which the words and thoughts of Paul incessantly turn, in the thousand places where he speaks of the liberty of the dead. Here is the origin, the cause of one of the boldest fictions that ever emanated from the human mind – a fiction, the consequences of which were incalculable. Paul wants the faithful to identify themselves with Christ, to believe that they are his very embodiment, and that their flesh is condemned, crucified and dead with him. By this death which they share with him they acquire the most precious freedom, viz., the freedom from the law. [Rom. 7:1–6][26]

Thus Paul had taken a psalm which spoke of the freedom that attends death, together with a rabbinic commentary that interpreted this to mean freedom from the Law, and had added to this his conviction that any believer who identified with Christ had died with him (in some spiritual sense). He had concluded that any believer who had died with Christ had thereby been liberated from the Law. As a result of Paul's teaching that the Law was the source of death and sin and nothing better than wretched slavery, and the idea that faith in Jesus was now the highest virtue,[27] Benamozegh claimed that Christianity had lost its moral compass.[28] He bemoaned 'the fatal precedent that Christianity established against morality by

[22] Benamozegh, *Jewish and Christian Ethics*, 12.
[23] In discussing those who took the most active part in the abolition of the Law, he commented, 'the chief place certainly belongs to Paul.' Benamozegh, *Jewish and Christian Ethics*, 14.
[24] An allusion to Acts 22:3. Benamozegh, *Israel and Humanity*, 112.
[25] Benamozegh, *Jewish and Christian Ethics*, 22–3.
[26] Benamozegh, *Jewish and Christian Ethics*, 20–21. Shabbat 151b: 'Once man dies he is free from [all] obligations, and thus R. Johanan interpreted: Among the dead I am free: once a man is dead he is free from religious duties.'
[27] An allusion to Rom. 6.
[28] 'Paul, who wants faith without works, is the greatest enemy of the ceremonial law'. Benamozegh, *Jewish and Christian Ethics*, 17.

this abrogation of the Law',[29] and argued that Protestantism, in particular, had followed Paul when it 'proclaimed moral works *useless* and *pernicious*, faith alone being sufficient for salvation.'[30] The danger, of course, was that 'morality itself be annihilated' and that the believer would 'free himself from virtue, from moral obligations, as well as from ceremonial injunctions'.[31]

The abrogation of the Law was not the only aspect of Paul's thought that could best be explained by reference to Jewish sources. Thus Paul's conviction that the Jews had become hard-hearted in order to allow the salvation of the Gentiles recalled a Talmudic passage about a horse and an ox.[32] And, anachronistically, Benamozegh believed that knowledge of *kabbalah* was evident, too. For example, there were some remarkable parallels to Pauline categories.

The spirituality to which Christians are invited is naturally linked to the Cabalistic model of the Holy Spirit, the Bina; both [Christians and Cabalists] make the same use of the study and dissemination of the Cabalistic mysteries. . . . By the same [Cabalistic] system, for raising themselves to the Bina, they acquired the name *children*, which, as opposed to that of *slaves*, the Cabala used long before Christianity. They acquired at the same time the '*liberty*' proper to this degree . . . which the Cabala never used in its practical sense, but which the Christians first, and then the Gnostics, so strangely used.[33]

And *kabbalah* also taught, like Paul, that original sin had come about through Adam's sin, which had necessitated the Law to make reparation.[34] But these characteristic teachings of original sin, of the 'liberty' of 'slaves' and transformation

---

[29] Benamozegh, *Jewish and Christian Ethics*, 13.

[30] Benamozegh, *Jewish and Christian Ethics*, 15. Interestingly, Benamozegh contrasts Protestantism with Catholicism, which, at the Council of Trent, admitted the necessity of good works. 'It was a return to the old Hebrew ethics, it was a total rejection of the Apostle to the Gentiles, it was a great diminution of the importance, the efficacy of the redemption.' Ibid.

[31] Benamozegh, *Jewish and Christian Ethics*, 22.

[32] Benamozegh linked Rom. 11:25–6 ('a partial hardening has happened to Israel until the fullness of the Gentiles has come in; and so all Israel will be saved') with Sanhedrin 98b ('The Holy One, blessed be His name, says: "These on one side are My creatures, those on the other are also the work of My hands. How, therefore, can I sacrifice one group for the other?" R. Papa said: "Thus men say, When the ox runs and falls, the horse is put into his stall."') and Rashi's commentary on it ('This is what the Master would never have considered doing before the downfall of the ox, for He very much loved His ox. And when the ox eventually succeeded in recovering from his fall, the Master felt sorrow when he expelled His horse in turn from the stable. Likewise, when the Holy One, blessed be He, saw the fall of Israel, He conferred greatness on the Gentile peoples of the earth; and when Israel returns to God and receives God's mercy, God will suffer from having to dispose the nations on account of Israel'). Benamozegh, *Israel and Humanity*, 127.

[33] Benamozegh, *Jewish and Christian Ethics*, 20.

[34] Benamozegh asked, 'what is the Cabalistic doctrine regarding original sin, spiritual new-birth? Is it not the *law* or *death* which it names as the sole means of making the ticcoun [tikkun] or reparation for the first sin [that is, the sin of Adam]? Well, of these two means, says Paul, we [Christians] have chosen the last [that is, death].' Here he alluded to Rom. 5:12–14, 20 ('Therefore, just as through one man sin entered into the world, and death through sin, and so death spread to all men, because all sinned – for until the Law sin was in the world, but sin is not imputed when there is no law. Nevertheless death reigned from Adam until Moses. . . . The Law came in so that the transgression would increase.') Benamozegh, *Jewish and Christian Ethics*, 21.

to 'children',[35] and of the abrogation of the Law through the death of the believer with Christ, all stemmed from Paul's tragic misinterpretation of Jewish traditions, a tragic misunderstanding that would lead to tragic human consequences.

All relations about to cease, all ties to be broken, society to disappear, and this ephemeral life to have, perhaps, no morrow; all affections, wants, tears, rights, duties, the living, throbbing reality of life sacrificed to an abstraction, to a chimera, to a rabbinical subtlety of Saul's [sic] . . . Paul has a theory which Georgias, Hobbes, or the deceased Proudhon, the inventor of anarchy, would not have disowned, and which, once admitted, would be the *coup de grace* to all justice, all law, all morality, all society – namely, that not only is the Law a result of the first sin [of Adam], but that it *constitutes and is the cause of our sins* – that without the Law there is no sin, and that consequently you have but to suppress the Law to make sin disappear. Nothing can be more exact than the statement: *It is through the Law that we know sin.* [Rom. 3:20][36]

Benamozegh readily admitted that, historically, Christianity had not fully accepted the logic of Paul's teaching 'and the enticement to the licentiousness which these doctrines authorized', but he was firm in his insistence that the influence of such teachings had shaped a number of Christian sects down through the centuries.[37] Furthermore, he suggested that even Paul had been dismayed by the inevitable consequences of his own theology, which, famously, had resulted in his famous inconsistency: '"What, then" he cries, "shall we sin because we are not under the Law, but under Grace?" [Rom. 6:15]'.[38] Like Graetz, Benamozegh concludes with an unfavourable assessment of the legacy of Pauline thought, Christianity having a foundation that was 'fraught with dangers',[39] although he accounted for the bulk of Paul's ideas in terms of a misinterpretation of traditional Jewish and kabbalistic sources.

Early constructors of the classic view were not restricted to the traditionalist camp. Another systematic philosophical comparison between Judaism and Christianity was made by the Liberal rabbi Leo Baeck (1873–1956), a leader of German Jewry during the Nazi period, and a survivor of the concentration camp Terezín.

---

[35] An allusion to Gal. 4:1–6. 'Now I say, as long as the heir is a child, he does not differ at all from a slave although he is owner of everything, but he is under guardians and managers until the date set by the father. So also we, while we were children, were held in bondage under the elemental things of the world. But when the fullness of the time came, God sent forth His Son, born of a woman, born under the Law, so that He might redeem those who were under the Law, that we might receive the adoption as sons. Because you are sons, God has sent forth the Spirit of His Son into our hearts, crying, "Abba! Father!"'

[36] Benamozegh, *Jewish and Christian Ethics*, 24, 25–6.

[37] He cites the Adamites of the first and twelfth centuries, the Turlupines in the fourteenth century, and the Picards in the fifteenth century. Benamozegh, *Jewish and Christian Ethics*, 25.

[38] Benamozegh, *Jewish and Christian Ethics*, 27.

[39] 'The foundation, then, as we see, upon which Christianity rests, far from having that solidity which the beauty of the structure seems to promise, are, on the contrary, fraught with dangers, that a rigid logic could not fail to show.' Benamozegh, *Jewish and Christian Ethics*, 28.

In his response to the Protestant Adolf Harnack's *Essence of Christianity* (1901),[40] Baeck argued that Harnack was mistaken to suppose that Jesus had removed the Jewish husk from the pure biblical faith of the prophets of Israel or that Jesus had rejected Jewish legalism for the Christian 'rule of love'. Baeck, whose work represented a powerful reclamation of Jesus as a Jew, asserted that what Harnack regarded as the husk was in fact the kernel of Jesus' faith: a Jewish commitment to internalising the divine commandment.[41] Baeck suggested that because Christian scholars had been unable to identify something new in Jesus' teaching which would have justified the creation of new religion, they had taken to representing Jesus as the one who had recovered true faith from the postprophetic developments of Judaism. But if Jesus' teachings were better regarded as Jewish rather than Christian, 'a disciple of the rabbis' as he put it,[42] then how should Christianity proper be explained? For Baeck, the essence of Christianity was to be found in its overemphasis upon 'romanticism', the mystical dream of the spirit longing for redemption, which could readily be contrasted with 'classical' Judaism, which balanced law and mystery.[43] Ultimately, this essence of Christianity could be traced back to Paul.

Later in life, Baeck's polemical stance waned, and with it his anti-Paulinism. But until after the war, Baeck's presentation of the Apostle to the Gentiles was an authoritative champion of the classic view. Paul had been the instigator of a new religion that had mixed Jewish and pagan religious elements. The history of this new religion was actually a history of two antagonistic tendencies, Jewish and Pauline, fighting over the heart of Christianity. In 'Mystery and Commandment' (1921/1922),[44] Baeck contrasted the equal mix of 'mystery' and 'commandment' in Judaism with the lopsided emphasis on 'mystery' in Christianity. Paul had reacted against the endlessness of the Law, which could not be fulfilled once and for all.[45] 'Paul left Judaism', Baeck argued,

when he preached *sola fide* (by faith alone) and thereby wound up with sacrament and dogma. Mystery became everything for him, not only that which is concealed, but also that which is manifest. Hence mystery finally had to become for him something

---

[40] Adolf Harnack, *Wesen das Christentums* (Leipzig: J.C. Hinrichs, 1901). Leo Baeck, 'Harnack's Vorlesungen über das Wesen das Christentums' in *Monatsschrift für Geschichte und Wissenschaft des Judenthums* 45 (1901), 97–8, 117–20.

[41] Baeck, 'Harnack's Vorlesungen über das Wesen das Christentums', 118.

[42] Ibid., 110.

[43] 'Romanticism...lacks any strong ethical impulse, any will to conquer life ethically. It has an antipathy against any practical idea which might dominate life, demanding free, creative obedience for its commandments and showing a clearly determined way to the goal of action....All...law is repugnant to it.' Leo Baeck, 'Romantic Religion' (1922), in Leo Baeck, *Judaism and Christianity*, trans. Walter Kaufmann (New York, Leo Baeck Institute 1958), 192.

[44] Originally published in 1921/1922, Baeck's 'Mystery and Commandment' is reproduced in Baeck, *Judaism and Christianity*, 169–85. In the essay, Baeck cites no specific texts from the New Testament, nor does he refer to Christian or Jewish commentators on Paul.

[45] Baeck, 'Mystery and Commandment', 179.

tangible, namely, sacraments, and something molded, namely dogma. . . . The boundary of Judaism was crossed only by Paul at the point where mystery wanted to prevail without commandment, and faith without the law.[46]

In 'Romantic Religion' (1922),[47] Baeck argued that Paul was less a creator of ideas than a connector. As an heir to their romanticism, he had merged the Hellenistic mysteries with living Jewish ideas.[48] In contrast with Judaism, which was 'classical' in that it taught that freedom came from obedience to commandment, Pauline religion was 'romantic', teaching that freedom came as a gift.[49] Salvation was not something worked for but something granted, with the result that morality and responsibility for the future were less important than mysteries and sacraments. Paul was not Jewish in any meaningful sense: 'What is called the victory of Christianity was in reality this victory of romanticism'[50] and 'what had been most essential in the ancient mysteries is preserved in this Pauline religion.'[51] As far as Jewish influences were concerned, Baeck even believed that Paul had undermined the Jewish ethical foundations to his own teachings.[52] In the end Baeck identified Paul's chief mistake as identifying too closely with the romantic, mythical tales of saviour-gods who descended to earth.

This myth was the bridge on which Paul went over to romanticism. To be sure, this man had lived within Judaism deep down in his soul; and psychically he never quite got away from it. Even after his conversion to mystery and sacrament, he only too often found himself again on the old Jewish ways of thought, as though unconsciously and involuntarily; and the manifold contradictions between his sentences derive from this above all. The Jew that he remained in spite of everything, at the bottom of his soul, again and again fought with the romantic in him, whose moods and ideas were ever present to him. But in spite of this, if we are to label him as he stands before us, the apostle of a new outlook, then we can only call him a romantic.[53]

Others we were even less prepared to acknowledge a Jewish dimension. Kaufmann Kohler (1843–1926) was a German-born North American radical Reform rabbi. He famously convened the Pittsburgh Conference of Reform Rabbis, which

---

[46] Baeck, 'Mystery and Commandment', 177.

[47] Originally published in 1922, Baeck's 'Romantic Religion' is reproduced in Baeck, *Judaism and Christianity*, 189–292. In the essay, Baeck's few citations of texts from the epistles include Rom. 10:4 ('Christ is the end of the Law'), Gal. 3:28 ('here is neither Jew nor Greek, here is neither bond nor free'), and Rom. 14:23 ('Whatsoever does not issue from faith is sin'); he does not cite Christian or Jewish commentators on Paul, except for Luther.

[48] Baeck understood romanticism in terms of '[t]he exuberance of emotion, the enthusiastic flight from reality, the longing for an experience . . . the sentimental attitude which seeks escape from life into living experience and turns the attention towards a phantastic and marvellous beyond.' Baeck, 'Romantic Religion', 196, 197.

[49] Baeck, 'Romantic Religion', 211.

[50] Baeck, 'Romantic Religion', 198.

[51] Baeck, 'Romantic Religion', 202.

[52] Baeck, 'Romantic Religion', 248.

[53] Baeck, 'Romantic Religion', 202–3.

claimed, *inter alia*, that Mosaic and rabbinical dietary restrictions should be rejected; that Israel should be regarded as a religious community rather than as a nation; that Judaism was a progressive religion, striving to accord with reason; and that Christianity and Islam should be regarded as partners in establishing a reign of truth and righteousness among men. Partly as a result of the stinging criticism Reform Jews received from their Orthodox opponents, who claimed that the Reform movement was profoundly influenced by Christianity, and partly because of an enhanced sensitivity towards the Christian critique of Judaism (all the more frustrating in the light of the tolerant attitude that Reform presented towards Christianity), Kohler was keen to distance Reform Judaism from Christianity. As we have seen, this was made possible by a reclamation of Jesus as a Jew and a new interest in Paul as the proper (negative) representative of Christianity. For Kohler, once Jesus was extracted from the highly unreliable and biased Gospels,[54] the Christian messiah appeared as Torah observant,[55] his thought closely related to 'essenism',[56] and his ethical teachings reflecting an imminent expectation of the end of the world.[57] The picture uncovered was of a Jew, if not a particularly remarkable one.[58] Someone else, then, must have been responsible for creating Christianity. Kohler's analysis of Paul, which involved an influential article, 'Saul of Tarsus', in the *Jewish Encyclopaedia* (1901–16) and a chapter in *The Origins of the Synagogue and the Church* (1929),[59] not only demonstrated whom he held to blame for Christianity, but provided a splendid opportunity to demonstrate the clear blue water that lay between the two faith systems.

---

[54] Kohler, *The Origins of the Synagogue and the Church*, 211. In his works on Paul, Kohler mentioned Montefiore and Lowy among Jewish writers, and Cheyne, Deiterich, Jowett, Krenkel, and Reitzenstein among Christians. His Encyclopedia entry in particular was peppered with references to Acts and to the Epistles, which he regarded as 'partly spurious and partly interpolated'.

[55] Kohler, *The Origins of the Synagogue and the Church*, 218.

[56] Kaufmann Kohler, 'Jesus of Nazareth', *Jewish Encyclopedia*, VII, 169.

[57] Kaufmann Kohler, 'Christianity in Its Relation to Judaism', *Jewish Encyclopedia*, IV, 51.

[58] Kohler once compared Jesus and Paul in a polemical tract: 'Who of the two was the more typical Jew? Jesus, the mild, silver-tongued preacher of Galilee, who probably never stepped beyond the boundaries of Judea, nor spoke in other language but that of his countrymen, nor preached to any but Jewish hearers, whose every word is an echo of rabbinical sayings, and who emphatically declared that he had not come to destroy but to fulfil the old covenant? Or Paul, the irritable, ghost-seeing fanatic from the Greek isle of Tarsos, who acted like an infuriated zealot when in Judea, and poured forth all the wrath of his hot temper against the Jews when a preacher of Christ among the Gentiles, whose writings are a quaint mixture of Hellenistic philosophy, of semi-pagan mysticism (or gnosticism) and oriental superstition, and who took a special pride in being a Roman among Romans, a Greek with Greeks, and a Hebrew with Hebrews? There is nothing genuinely Jewish about Paul except the name of Saul, which he in time dropped, whereas every feature of Jesus betrays the influence of rabbinical lore, and particularly the school of Hillel, the meek, the original exponent of the Golden Rule.' Kaufmann Kohler, *Christianity vs. Judaism: A Rejoinder to the Rev. Dr. R. Heber Newton* (New York: Stettiner, Lambert and Co., 1890), 3.

[59] Kaufmann Kohler, 'Saul of Tarsus', *Jewish Encyclopedia*, XI, 79–87; *idem*, 'Paul the Apostle to the Heathen', in *The Origins of the Synagogue and the Church*, 260–70.

For Kohler, Paul's conception of life was not Jewish, as a consequence of his non-Jewish background.[60] In contrast to Graetz, Kohler argued that Paul was entirely Hellenistic in thought and sentiment, was quite unfamiliar with the Hebrew version of the Bible, and, despite the claims of some Christian scholars, had not received rabbinic training.[61] He instead emphasised Gnostic influences to account for Paul's teachings on Christology and ritual, and the Hellenistic mystery religions for his teachings relating to the Son of God, baptism, communion, and mysticism.[62] As for Paul's view of the Law, Kohler believed that his original position had been to claim transcendence rather than opposition, but as a result of his conflict with Jews he had come to regard the Law (both ceremonial and moral) as 'an intrinsic evil'.[63] Worse still, despite his success in bringing Jewish ethics to the pagans,[64] Kohler believed that there was evidence that Paul hated Jews and Judaism.[65] Paul's new faith, 'half pagan and half Jewish', was ultimately foreign to Jewish life and thought.[66] In the surrender of reason implicit in accepting the 'mystery of the cross',[67] Paul's Christianity was 'radically in conflict with the spirit of Judaism',[68] which was concerned with the practical goal of the moral perfection of the human race.[69] Likewise, there was a profound difference between Jewish faith and 'Paulinism', which 'substituted for the natural childlike faith of man in God . . . a blind artificial faith prescribed and imposed from without'.[70] In an attempt to contrast the essence of Paul's Christianity with that of Judaism, Kohler adopted the same strategy that Orthodox opponents adopted towards Reform Judaism, namely, to condemn it as inauthentic by emphasising alien, non-Jewish origins.

Martin Buber (1878–1965) was also interested in comparing and contrasting Judaism and Christianity, and was more explicit still in using Jesus and Paul to accomplish this. An influential neoconservative theologian, philosopher, and Zionist, the Viennese-born Buber was forced out of Germany by the Nazis and emigrated to Palestine in 1938, where he lectured at the Hebrew University. After the war he travelled extensively, developing and propagating themes he believed he had derived from Hasidism to wider Jewish and non-Jewish audiences. These themes included the hallowing of everyday life and the discovery of God in the context of interpersonal relationships. Buber published *I and Thou* in 1923,[71] which outlined

---

[60] Kohler, 'Saul of Tarsus', 80.
[61] Kohler, 'Saul of Tarsus', 79.
[62] Kohler, 'Saul of Tarsus', 82–4.
[63] Kohler, 'Saul of Tarsus', 84–5.
[64] Kohler, 'Saul of Tarsus', 86.
[65] Kohler, 'Saul of Tarsus', 85. Kohler, *The Origins of the Synagogue and the Church*, 266.
[66] Kohler, 'Saul of Tarsus', 79.
[67] Kohler, *The Origins of the Synagogue and the Church*, 265.
[68] Kohler, 'Saul of Tarsus', 87.
[69] Kohler, 'Saul of Tarsus', 83.
[70] Kohler, 'Saul of Tarsus', 83, 86.
[71] Martin Buber, *Ich und Du* (Berlin: Schocken Verlag, 1923).

his philosophy of dialogue and identified two types of interpersonal categories, namely I–Thou and I–It. The first he described as a dialogue of two respectful partners, characterised by mutuality, openness, presentness, and directness. The second was something less, a monologue, a necessary and common form of relationship, but one without the potential for generating the radical development offered by the first. Theologically, Buber came to see the individual's relationship with God in these terms. On one hand, the *halakhah* or Law could be regarded as an expression of an impersonal, collective interaction with a group, and therefore as an expression of a generalised I–It relationship. On the other hand, a *mitzvah* or commandment was a direct call from the Divine-Thou to the Human-I. This call could be internalised by the individual, whose response became an act of partnership with the One who commanded. *Mitzvah* therefore expressed a dialogical relationship between the individual and God. Buber suggested that Judaism compared favourably with other religions for its emphasis on this dialogical partnership between God and man, which stressed man's role in seeking to bring about redemption and the hallowing of the world.

In *Two Types of Faith* (1950),[72] Buber brought his dialogical philosophy to bear directly on the two central figures of Christianity, Jesus and Paul. Going even further than those before him, Buber reclaimed his 'great brother' Jesus as the embodiment of authentic Judaism.[73] Paul, on the other hand, was a 'gigantic figure . . . whom we must regard as the real originator of the Christian conception of faith'[74] and who therefore represented a quite distinct set of values. Strictly speaking, Buber's treatment was focused more on the faith-systems of these two figures than on any historical reconstruction of the men themselves.[75] He did not specifically attempt to define Paul's background or to assess the degree of non-Jewish influence upon Paul. But the prominence in his analysis of the Gnostic features of Paul's theology (for example, the powers that rule the world, the enslavement of the cosmos, the setting free of men)[76] and his emphasis on the mystery religions (for example, the

---

[72]   Martin Buber, *Zwei Glaubenweisen* (Zurich: Manesse Verlag, 1950). The English translation is Martin Buber, *Two Types of Faith*. Buber acknowledges the special influence of Bultmann, who is referred to throughout, and Schweitzer; amongst the other authorities cited are Bousset, Burkitt, Dalman, Delitzsch, Dibelius, Hatch, Lohmeyer, Loisy, Weiss, and Wellhausen. Among Jewish scholars, he mentions Schechter and Schoeps. He cites texts from most of the Epistles, but is most dependent for his reading of Paul on Galatians and especially Romans.

[73]   'From my youth onwards I have found in Jesus my great brother. That Christianity has regarded or does regard him as God and saviour has always appeared to me a fact of the highest importance which, for his sake and my own, I must endeavour to understand. . . . I am more than certain that a great place belongs to him in Israel's history of faith and that this place cannot be described by any of the usual categories'. Buber, *Two Types of Faith*, 12–13.

[74]   Buber, *Two Types of Faith*, 44.

[75]   Buber did not directly address the question of the reliability of the historical sources. But because he assumed throughout a good familiarity with Romans (and Galatians), and because there was almost no reference made to Acts, it comes as no surprise that Buber's Paul was presented as highly Hellenistic in character.

[76]   Buber, *Two Types of Faith*, 83.

doctrine of a dying and rising god)[77] leave one in no doubt as to his belief that Paul originated in an essentially non-Jewish environment.

Developing Kohler's views, Buber contrasted the Hellenistic or Greek *pistis* (faith or belief in the truth of a proposition), which he argued was embodied in Paul, with the Jewish *emunah* (faith as trust), which was embodied in Jesus.[78] Jesus' Jewish *emunah* reflected an intimate, trusting relationship with God, and was paradigmatic of the I–Thou relationship. As had others before him, Buber 'reversed the theological gaze' by turning on its head the traditional Christian interpretation of the antagonistic relationship between Jesus and the Pharisees, and emphasising instead their similarities. In contrast to their spontaneous spirituality, though, Paul's Hellenistic *pistis* was predicated on the I–It relationship. Admittedly, Paul's theology had been a reaction against a particular view of the Law, a kind of legalism still found in rabbinic Judaism. Paul, he suggested, had been influenced by an inauthentic, Hellenistic understanding of the Law, which was characterised by

the judicial computation of items of guilt and innocence against each other, and in connexion with this . . . the rightness of conduct which justifies the individual before God. . . . [This was] a deflation of that original fullness of life, a limitation common to Alexandrian [Hellenistic] and contemporary rabbinical Judaism. . . .[79]

According to Buber, Paul's solution had been the doctrine of justification, the teaching that faith in Christ made one righteous and the denial that 'works' (the fulfilment of the Law) could bring about this transformation. But dispensing with Law or *halakhah* had not been much of an improvement, in that 'The simple face-to-face relationship between God and man in the Genesis story is replaced by [Paul with] an interpenetration which comes about by faith and faith alone, the dialogical by the mystical situation'.[80] Paul's mystical solution of faith in Christ, the intermediary between man and God, thus typified the I–It relationship no less than did rabbinic *halakhah*. Paul could therefore be contrasted with Jesus (and the Pharisees) as turning away from the biblical conception of the kingdom of God, which emphasised the immediacy between God and man. Furthermore, Paul's introduction of a dualism between faith and action, based on the impossibility of the fulfilment of the Law, demonstrated his profoundly mistaken understanding of the true nature (à la Buber) of commandment or *mitzvah*, once again in contrast to Jesus. And finally, Paul's pessimistic world-view, described as 'Paulinism',

---

[77] Buber, *Two Types of Faith*, 100.
[78] Paul's bias towards *pistis* reinforced Buber's belief that the apostle's background had been one of 'a peripheral Judaism, which was actually "Hellenistic"'. He referred to Schweitzer, who had suggested that Paul 'has his roots in the Jewish world of thought, not in the Greek', as a foil for his argument. Buber, *Two Types of Faith*, 14.
[79] Buber, *Two Types of Faith*, 46–7.
[80] Buber, *Two Types of Faith*, 47.

also indicated his movement away from the authentically Jewish, intimate, direct encounter with the Eternal Thou. As Buber saw it,

The Gnostic nature of the essential features of [Paul's] conception is obvious – the derivative powers, which, ruling the world, work against the primal divine power and waylay the human soul, the enslavement of the cosmos, the problematic character of the law, the overcoming of the 'rulers' and the setting free of man.... None of this concerns the God-head, but the intermediate being set up or permitted by Him.[81]

Thus Buber concluded, 'I no longer recognize the God of Jesus, nor his world, in this world of Paul's.'[82]

Buber explicitly stated that Paulinism, this pessimistic worldview that combined a belief in an unredeemed cosmos controlled by inevitable forces with a powerful sense of personal alienation, could be found in both Christian and Jewish thought (and in secular culture, too).[83] But despite his protestations that he was free of apologetic motivation,[84] Buber undoubtedly believed that the tendency was more pronounced in Christianity than in Judaism.[85] He argued that it dominated the writings of Christian theologians such as Emil Brunner, author of *The Mediator* (1934), maintaining that the Christian stress on fate was evident in Christianity's need for a mediating redeemer.[86] Ultimately, the explanation for this difference between Judaism and Christianity could be found in the very different beginnings of the two faith communities. As he explained, 'The origin of Jewish Emunah is in the history of a nation, that of Christian Pistis in that of individuals'.[87] Although the trust of the people of Israel had been fostered by their Father's guidance through wilderness and dangers, the belief of Christians had come about as a challenge to accept a man crucified in Jerusalem as their saviour.[88] This challenge, of course,

---

[81] Buber, *Two Types of Faith*, 83.

[82] Buber, *Two Types of Faith*, 89.

[83] Buber used not only the Christian theologian Brunner but also the Jewish writer Franz Kafka to make this point: 'In the human life of our day, compared with earlier epochs, Christianity is receding, but the Pauline view and attitude is gaining the mastery in many circles outside that of Christianity'. Buber, *Two Types of Faith*, 162.

[84] 'There is scarcely any need to say that every apologetic tendency is far from my purpose. For nearly fifty years the New Testament has been a main concern in my Studies, and I think I am a good reader who listens impartially to what it said'. Buber, *Two Types of Faith*, 12.

[85] 'The periods of Christian history can be classified according to the degree in which they are dominated by Paulinism, by which we mean of course not just a system of thought but a mode of seeing and being which dwells in the life itself . . . Those periods are Pauline in which the constrictions of human life, especially of man's social life, so mount up that they increasingly assume in man's consciousness of existence the character of a fate. The light of God appears to be darkened, and the redeemed Christian soul becomes aware, as the unredeemed soul of the Jew has continually done, of the still unredeemed concreteness of the world of men in all its horror'. Buber, *Two Types of Faith*, 162, 166–7.

[86] Buber, *Two Types of Faith*, 150, 163–5.

[87] Buber, *Two Types of Faith*, 170.

[88] Buber, *Two Types of Faith*, 170–72.

had been Paul's, and therefore responsibility for the consequent parting of the ways, and for the enormous influence of Paulinism, was his. The classic view of the apostle was thus reinforced and strengthened.

Buber had articulated his 'two types of faith' thesis with great care, explicitly denying a polemical agenda. With a much more strident tone, the North American Reform rabbi and Zionist leader Abba Hillel Silver (1893–1963) wrote a study in 1956 entitled *Where Judaism Differed: An Inquiry into the Distinctiveness of Judaism* in which he also contrasted Judaism with Christianity. It was, of course, produced in a very different context under very different circumstances, as reflected by some of his other writings that included works on democracy, messianism, Zionism, and modernity.[89] In *Where Judaism Differed*, Silver's underlying concern had been to challenge the conception of a shared Judeo-Christian heritage that appeared ubiquitous in postwar North American society, and, crucially, to justify the place of Judaism in its own right. As he put it, 'The one universal God does not require one universal church in which to be worshipped.'[90] Jesus and the apostle Paul were important characters in this discussion, although it was Pauline theology that is identified as the key to understanding what separates the two faith communities. As Silver saw it, Jews had certainly rejected Jesus' messianism, but it was Paul's onslaught on the Law, his gospel of redemption through the atoning death and resurrection of Jesus, and the doctrine of God incarnate in man that had made the breach permanent.[91] By the second century, he said, the Christian Church was energetically pressing its attack on the Law under Pauline inspiration.[92]

When it came to explaining Paul's view of the Law, Silver was suspicious about the apostle's claims to have been zealous for the traditions of his fathers before his conversion. Paul must have been impatient with the Law even before he was converted, he reasoned, or he could not have spoken of it later as 'a curse'.[93] Silver observed that there must have been other Jews, even before then, especially in the Hellenistic diaspora, who fretted under the constraints of the Mosaic ceremonial code and who dreamt of a universal monotheistic faith, which all the nations

---

[89] Abba Hillel Silver, *History of Messianic Speculation in Israel from the First Through the Seventeenth Centuries* (New York: Macmillan, 1927); Abba Hillel Silver, *The Democratic Impulse in Jewish History* (New York: Bloch, 1928); Abba Hillel Silver, *Religion in a Changing World* (New York: Richard R. Smith, 1931).

[90] 'There is much which all religions have in common and much which differentiates them. Their common purpose in the world will not be advanced by merger or amalgamation. . . . To ignore these differences is to overlook the deep cleavages which existed in the past and to assume a similarity of doctrine and outlook which does not exist in the present.' Silver, *Where Judaism Differed*, 338–9. Of course, when the 'common purpose' had to do with the support of Israel, Silver, an influential Zionist leader, was keen to emphasise a shared tradition with Christian Zionists.

[91] Silver, *Where Judaism Differed*, 96.

[92] Silver, *Where Judaism Differed*, 101.

[93] Silver, *Where Judaism Differed*, 112–13.

of the world could share.[94] The difference, Silver maintained, was that Paul had eventually found the excuse he need in Jesus the Messiah, an authority who had ushered in a new age and a new dispensation. As a result, Paul had been able to set aside the Law as a regrettable interlude, a custodian until the true faith was revealed.[95] That explained his loss of interest in the Torah, but what had made the apostle so 'bitterly intolerant' of it?[96] How was it that Paul could have spoken of the Law as sin?[97] It surely could not have been the Damascus Road vision of the resurrected Jesus that had made the apostle so hostile, he noted pointedly, because Jesus had not been an enemy of the Law.[98] The answer for Silver was the apostle's 'proselytizing zeal', for it was the Law that Paul regarded as *the* stumbling block to the conversion of the Gentile world, and this goal, ultimately, was what energised him.[99] Could Paul's attitude to the Law, or this justification for his attitude to the Law, ever be justified? For Silver the issue was admittedly complex. As he put it,

There has always been a debate among Jews as to the extent to which one is free to interpret the Written Law and by what technique, and whether the Oral Law is binding and to what extent. Orthodox, Conservative, and Reform Jews have continued the debate to this day. But no organised Jewish religious group ever maintained that the Law could be dispensed with altogether, that the Law was a curse or that faith alone was sufficient.[100]

Nor was Paul's un-Jewish teaching about the Law the only dangerous teaching of Paul's that had come to dominate Christianity. The core of his theology was, according to Silver, the messiah's role in the forgiveness of sins, for which biblical proofs, such as the Suffering Servant in Isa. 53, were later found.[101] This doctrine

---

94 Silver suggests that, whatever his original hopes, the apostle was ambivalent about this universal monotheistic faith and what it meant for the election of Israel. 'The universalism of Paul was not free of local patriotism. Israel "after the flesh" was still the chosen people. At times there appears to be no contradiction in his mind between a national faith and its universal mission. At other times there decidedly is.' Silver, *Where Judaism Differed*, 115–16.

95 'Now that faith has come, we are no longer under a custodian' (Gal. 3:25). Silver, *Where Judaism Differed*, 114. Ironically, the apostle soon discovered that he could not reject the Torah in its totality, for he had became too dependent upon it to substantiate and bear witness to Jesus and his role in history. This had not prevented him, however, from teaching that the Law given to Moses at Sinai was a punishment for the sins of the people of Israel. Ibid., 113.

96 '"Christ is the end of the Law" (Rom. 10:4). The covenant of Sinai is Hagar, bearing children for slavery. The covenant of Abraham is Sarah. "Cast out the slave and her son!" (Gal. 4:30).' Silver, *Where Judaism Differed*, 115.

97 Silver, *Where Judaism Differed*, 115.

98 Silver, *Where Judaism Differed*, 112–13.

99 Silver, *Where Judaism Differed*, 115.

100 Silver, *Where Judaism Differed*, 118.

101 This ideas had influenced later writers such as Mark, who had incorporated into his Gospel an episode where Jesus declares all food clean. Silver could not countenance that such a teaching, which had no basis in Jewish Law, could be reconciled with Jesus' 'consistent and positive attitude towards the Law.' Rather, here was an example of Paul's teaching (concerning a messiah who offers

of vicarious expiation had led to another, that of Original Sin, for which proofs were found in Genesis. The doctrine described the belief that the guilt of Adam's disobedience had been transmitted to all his descendents, who now languished in condemnation.[102] For Silver, however, biblical proofs did nothing to change the fact that this redemptive role of Christ was a new focus, one that could be contrasted with the Torah's centrality for Judaism, or even that of the Kingdom of God for Jesus.[103] Moreover, Paul's conception of Original Sin had had serious consequences, which had further distanced Pauline Christianity from the Synagogue. Silver argued that, in order to exalt God's unconditioned grace and the gift of the redemptive sacrifice of Jesus, Paul had been forced to deny man free choice. The apostle's denial of the efficacy of good works was likewise made in order to exalt the role of faith in the risen Christ and his redeeming sacrifice.[104] Silver saw this as dangerously naïve, noting, 'Paul did not fully confront all the ethical implications of these teachings... [which] if logically followed through, would utterly paralyze man's moral will.'[105] This was, of course, a teaching which was entirely at odds with that of Judaism. The consequences for early Christianity, where there was no attempt to reform or to reconstruct society in any practical sense, were as inevitable as they were lamentable.[106]

Silver's treatment of the apostle was very much the work of a popular theologian.[107] His writings reflect a wider attitude, namely, that as far as most members of the Jewish community were concerned, Paul's real legacy had been the error-strewn Church that functioned as an instrument of Jewish suffering, and which no commitment to an ideal of a shared Judeo-Christian heritage could afford to overlook. For Silver, who, as a militant communal leader, had been largely responsible for the rise in prominence of the voice of Zionism within North American politics in the 1940s and who believed passionately that the Jewish

---

forgiveness of sin by his death and, though the authority of the holy spirit, even during his life) being written back into Jesus' life-story. Silver, *Where Judaism Differed*, 107–8.

[102] Rom. 5:12, 18–19. 'Therefore, just as through one man sin entered into the world, and death through sin, and so death spread to all men, because all sinned.... So then as through one transgression there resulted condemnation to all men, even so through one act of righteousness there resulted justification of life to all men. For as through the one man's disobedience the many were made sinners, even so through the obedience of the One the many will be made righteous.' Silver, *Where Judaism Differed*, 111.

[103] Silver, *Where Judaism Differed*, 111.

[104] Rom. 8:29–30. 'For those whom He foreknew, He also predestined to become conformed to the image of His Son, so that He would be the firstborn among many brethren; and these whom He predestined, He also called; and these whom He called, He also justified; and these whom He justified, He also glorified.'

[105] Silver, *Where Judaism Differed*, 288.

[106] 'The Christian renounced the world at baptism. "Slaves, obey in everything those who are your earthly masters," advised Paul (Col. 3:22).' Silver, *Where Judaism Differed*, 178.

[107] Silver mentioned only two Pauline scholars, Dean Inge and Prof. Murray. He was mainly dependent on Paul's letters to the Romans, Corinthians, and Galatians.

people had to be accepted on their own terms, too much was at stake to tolerate any nonsense about a shared religious brotherhood. Respect for Christianity, yes. Sentimental idealisation of it, no. He concluded,

There is much which all religions have in common and much which differentiates them. Their common purpose in the world will not be advanced by merger or amalgamation. . . . To ignore these differences is to overlook the deep cleavages which existed in the past and to assume a similarity of doctrine and outlook which does not exist in the present.[108]

More recently, the Anglo-Orthodox Jewish scholar Hyam Maccoby (1924–2004) reinforced the classic view of Paul with his study *The Mythmaker: Paul and the Invention of Christianity* (1986).[109] Maccoby's writings include works on Jesus, on medieval disputations, and on the phenomenon of anti-Semitism, and are concerned to draw attention to past injustices and myths in the history of Jewish–Christian relations. Regarding the myths that had grown up around Jesus, Maccoby emphasised politics as the key to understanding this very Jewish figure. A typical Pharisee whose teachings were reminiscent of Hillel's,[110] Jesus had had no intention of subverting the Law, whether in the sense of scriptural laws or Pharisaic reforms.[111] But Jesus had also been something of a prophet, a man of action, whose teachings concerning the kingdom of Heaven and messianic claims put him in a 'head-on collision with Rome'.[112] In contrast to Jesus, the key to understanding Paul was, according to Maccoby, his non-Jewish background (echoing Kohler and Buber). Paul had been born a Gentile,[113] his background largely pagan, primarily Gnosticism and the mystery religions (particularly that of Attis).[114] Heavily dependent upon reconstructed traditions of the anti-Pauline Jewish-Christian Ebionites (as found in, for example, *Against Heresies* by the fourth-century bishop Epiphanius), Maccoby maintained that Paul had converted to Judaism and had worked for the

---

[108] Silver, *Where Judaism Differed*, 338–9.

[109] Maccoby cited both Christian and Jewish commentators on Paul, including Baur, Bultmann, Davies, Gager, Gaston, Käsemann, Pagels, Parkes, Reitzenstein, Sanders, Schweitzer, Stendahl, Kohler, Montefiore, Sandmel, Schoeps, and Schonfield. He used Acts more extensively than many other scholars and, among the Pauline epistles, he drew heavily from 1 Corinthians, Galatians, and Romans. Maccoby offered a more academic treatment of the subject in *Paul and Hellenism* (London: SCM, 1991), in which he again emphasised that the roots of Pauline anti-Semitism lay in Gnosticism and that Paul's worldview was one dependent upon Gnostic, Hellenistic, and Greco-Roman mystery religions. In general, there is little in the way of revision; it simply continues and reinforces his de-Judaising programme for Paul.

[110] Hyam Maccoby, *Revolution in Judaea: Jesus and the Jewish Resistance* (London: Ocean Books, 1973), 232.

[111] Maccoby, *Revolution in Judaea*, 141.

[112] Maccoby, *Revolution in Judaea*, 143, 129, 133.

[113] Hyam Maccoby, *The Mythmaker: Paul and the Invention of Christianity* (London: Weidenfeld and Nicolson, 1986), 15.

[114] Maccoby, *The Mythmaker*, 16.

Sanhedrin until disappointed in his lack of advancement, whereupon he founded a new religion as part of his quest for fame.[115] Paul's inauthentic origins were confirmed by the observations that his Greek writing and references to Greek poets was unique among Pharisees, and by his poor Hebrew.[116] Maccoby suggested that the apostle's writings would have been shocking to Jews but familiar to non-Jews; his use of 'Christ' as a divine title did not correlate to the concept of the Jewish messiah; and the concept of 'being in Christ' was alien,[117] as was the opposition between flesh and spirit.[118] Tarsus had been a city with few if any Pharisees, and Paul's exposure to Pharisaism must have been very limited.[119]

For Maccoby it was Paul's abrogation of the Law that most clearly distinguished him from both Pharisaism and 'the Nazarene variety of Judaism'.[120] Fundamentally, Paul's view stemmed from his inability to observe Judaism and his obliteration of the distinction between Jew and Gentile – and therefore the obligation of either to observe the Law.[121] Maccoby argued that Paul's view of the Law as having limited authority was justified in Gal. 3:19–20 mainly in Gnostic terms, whereby Paul presented angels as the authors of the Torah.[122] The argumentation that was understood by many Pauline scholars as rabbinic argumentation (such as Rom. 7:1–6) was, according to Maccoby, merely a poor attempt to emulate that genre.[123]

Maccoby's polemical agenda was undisguised; he was open about the conclusions that he wished the reader to draw from his investigation as to the Jewish authenticity of Paul's background.

[W]as Paul a Pharisee? It will be seen that this is not merely a matter of biography or idle curiosity. It is bound up with the whole question of the origins of Christianity. A tremendous amount depends on this question, for, if Paul was not a Pharisee rooted in Jewish learning and tradition, but instead a Hellenistic adventurer whose acquaintance

---

[115] 'A source of information about Paul that has never been taken seriously enough is a group called the Ebionites. Their writings were suppressed by the Church, but some of their views and traditions were preserved in the writings of their opponents, particularly in the huge treatise on *Heresies* [or *Panarion*] by Epiphanius. From this it appears that the Ebionites had a very different account to give of Paul's background and early life from that found in the New Testament and fostered by Paul himself. The Ebionites testified that Paul had *no* Pharisaic background or training; he was the son of Gentiles, converted to Judaism, in Tarsus, came to Jerusalem when an adult, and attached himself to the High Priest as a henchman. Disappointed in his hopes of advancement, he broke with the High Priest and sought fame by founding a new religion. This account, although not reliable in all its details, is substantially correct. It makes far more sense of all the puzzling and contradictory features of the story of Paul than the account of the official documents of the Church.' Maccoby, *The Mythmaker*, 17.

[116] Maccoby, *The Mythmaker*, 70.

[117] Maccoby, *The Mythmaker*, 62–3.

[118] Maccoby, *The Mythmaker*, 93.

[119] Maccoby, *The Mythmaker*, 93.

[120] Maccoby, *The Mythmaker*, 15–16.

[121] Maccoby, *The Mythmaker*, 95.

[122] Maccoby, *The Mythmaker*, 188–9.

[123] Maccoby, *The Mythmaker*, 68–71.

with Judaism was recent and shallow, the construction of myth and theology which he elaborated in his letters becomes a very different thing. Instead of searching through his system for signs of continuity with Judaism, we shall be able to recognize it for what it is – a brilliant concoction of Hellenism, superficially connecting itself with the Jewish scriptures and tradition, by which it seeks to give itself a history and an air of authority.[124]

For Maccoby, Paul was to be regarded as the inventor of Christianity and its symbol.[125] In his concern to draw upon the authority of his alleged Jewish learning, even as he sought to undermine it, Paul came to represent a religion that down through the centuries would attack Judaism (he had been responsible for Christian anti-Semitism),[126] but at the same time treat it as its storehouse of history, a source of authority and blessing, and the very framework by which it would define itself (for example, the new Israel, the true Judaism). This paradox partly explains Maccoby's fascination. As he put it,

To be Jewish and yet not to be Jewish, this is the essential dilemma of Christianity, and the figure of Paul, abjuring his alleged Pharisaism as a hindrance to salvation and yet somehow clinging to it as a guarantee of authority, is symbolic.[127]

The authors considered here demonstrate a tendency to compare and contrast the Jewish Jesus with the non-Jewish Paul for purposes that can only be described as anti-Christian. Arguably, Graetz, Benamozegh, Baeck, Kohler, and Buber were instrumental in establishing the common or classic view of Paul in the modern Jewish mind, and the tradition lives on in the more popular works of Silver and Maccoby. According to such writers, Paul combined superficiality of Jewish learning, missionary opportunism, and Christian anti-Semitism. He was understood to have corrupted Jesus' Judaism with non-Jewish thought, possibly as a consequence of his pagan background. Furthermore, the resultant impersonal, pessimistic system Paulinism (characteristic of Christianity) could be diametrically opposed to the intimate, optimistic system of Judaism. The message was clear: Maccoby's 'inventor of Christianity' represented, in Graetz's words, a mortal threat to Judaism itself.

BUILDING BRIDGES WITH PAUL

For those writers, mainly but not exclusively progressives, who were swept along by the promises of Emancipation, committed to Enlightenment concepts of progress,

---

[124] Maccoby, *The Mythmaker*, 18.
[125] In a discussion on the Eucharist, Maccoby seeks to demonstrate that the Gospel tradition of the last supper can be traced back to Paul and thus to Hellenistic mystery meals. Maccoby, *Paul and Hellenism*, 90ff.
[126] Maccoby, *The Mythmaker*, 180–84.
[127] Maccoby, *The Mythmaker*, 18.

and dedicated to improving relations between Jew and Christian, an alternative presentation was required to counter the potent anti-Christian implications of the increasingly dominant view of Paul. Although adherents of the alternative view, such as Isaac Mayer Wise, Joseph Krauskaupf, and Claude Montefiore, often agreed with details of the classic critique of Paul, they tended to begin their analyses by distancing themselves from it. Paul functioned as a means by which they could reinforce their more general message that Jews need not fear Christianity or Christian culture. For others such as Leo Baeck who returned to Paul in his later years, and, more recently, Pinchas Lapide and Mark Nanos, a reappraisal of the apostle was necessary for the postwar interfaith environment. For such reasons the disjuncture between Paul and Jesus was set to one side in favour of what could be admired in the apostle's teachings, and attempts were made to downplay his alleged critique of Judaism and the Law.

The North American Reform rabbi Isaac Mayer Wise (1819–1900) gave a series of public lectures on the roots of the Christian religion, published in 1883 as *Three Lectures on the Origin of Christianity*. A moderate reformer, this immigrant from Bohemia introduced synagogue modifications regarding mixed pews, choral singing, and confirmation and established the short-lived Zion College (which combined Hebrew and secular studies), but at the same time he was responsible for ensuring that the agreements reached at the national Reform conference known as the Cleveland Platform (1855) confirmed that the Bible was divine and that 'it must be expounded and practiced according to the comments of the Talmud'. Wise was concerned to encourage the integration of his congregants with the non-Jewish world around them, to reassure them that in the New World there was no need to perpetuate the Old World fears of Christianity. The Apostle to the Gentiles was a case in point, and deserved his own lecture.[128] Paul could easily be contrasted negatively with Jesus in terms of the Law (and Wise made the comparison), but this was not as important to Wise as was the presentation of Paul as a 'master machinist, one of those brilliant stars in the horizon of history' whose contribution to world history could be attributed to his Jewishness.[129]

Wise's main source of information on Paul was not the New Testament or early Christian writings, but rather the rabbinic literature. Identifying Paul with a heretic referred to in the Talmud, Wise explained,

The rabbis called him Acher, 'another', i.e. one who passes under another or assumed name. They [the rabbis] maintain that his name was Elisha ben Abujah. But this name must be fictitious, because it is a direct and express reference to Paul's theology. It signifies 'the saving deity, son of the father god', and Paul was the author of the 'son of God' doctrine. The fact is, he was known to the world under his assumed name only.[130]

[128] Wise, 'Paul and the Mystics', 53–75.
[129] Wise, 'Paul and the Mystics', 67.
[130] Wise, 'Paul and the Mystics', 55–6.

Wise's hypothesis and almost exclusive dependence upon the Talmud[131] are unique among the Jewish writers on Paul. They enabled him to argue (anachronistically) for a Pharisaic–kabbalistic background for Paul. For Wise, Paul's vision of Paradise in 2 Cor. 12 ('I know a man in Christ who 14 years ago was caught up to the third heaven . . .') correlated with Acher's experience of Paradise as mentioned in the Talmud, and he argued that at the time of Paul–Acher there had been a 'growth of superstition among the Hebrews, among whom a class of mystics had sprung up'.[132] It therefore seemed only sensible to conclude that Paul's background had been one of Jewish mysticism.[133] Not only was this central figure of Christianity recognisably Jewish, but also Paul's motivations were entirely comprehensible to North American Reform Jews. According to Wise, 'All Jews of all ages hoped and expected that the kingdom of heaven should be extended to all nations and tongues; but Paul went forth to do it; this is his particular greatness'.[134] In addition to his universalism, his rejection of Jewish nationalism[135] and preparedness to compromise regarding the Law for progress were also admirable.

Paul cared not for an hundred and one laws, as long as the essence and substance could be saved and preserved . . . he held that the laws are local, the spirit is universal, that laws are limitations, the spirit is free and the property of all men of all ages and climes . . . he was determined to drop everything which could retard his progress.[136]

Although Wise echoed others in attributing originality to Paul for paganising the Gospels – the apostle was responsible for the Christian idea of the Son of God, for a theological kingdom of Heaven, for vicarious atonement, for abrogation of the Law, and for beginning a new covenant[137] – he did not do this in order to attack Christianity. Wise anticipated later Jewish commentators in claiming that Paul

---

[131] Generally, Wise rejected the New Testament evidence regarding Paul in favour of the stories of Acher found in the Talmud (except for the 'we' passages in Acts). For example, he declared that Paul's 'principal activity', commencing after the dubious record of Acts ended, was 'in opposition to Rabbi Akiba and his colleagues'. And again, 'We know from the Talmud that he married and left a daughter. We know also numerous stories of Acher or Paul and his disciple, Rabbi Meir.' None of this is even hinted at in either the Epistles or Acts. Wise, 'Paul and the Mystics', 72–3. He spoke of the 'genuine epistles' without defining them, but he cited directly Rom. 9:3 ('For I could wish that I myself were accursed, separated from Christ for the sake of my brethren, my kinsmen according to the flesh'), Rom. 11:11 ('I say then, they did not stumble so as to fall, did they? May it never be! But by their transgression salvation has come to the Gentiles, to make them jealous'), 2 Cor. 12:4 ('[a man] was caught up into Paradise and heard inexpressible words, which a man is not permitted to speak'), and he alluded to Acts 21:24 regarding Paul's adherence to the law, 1 Cor. 15 concerning Christ's resurrection, and 2 Cor. 11:32–33 and Gal. 1:17 regarding opposition and his forced escape from Damascus. Wise makes no mention of Christian or Jewish scholars.

[132] Wise, 'Paul and the Mystics', 57–9. For example, Hagigah 14b, where four individuals are described as entering paradise, including Acher.

[133] This explained, for example, the similarity of Paul's conception of Christ to the kabbalistic semidivine figure of the *Saar Haolam*. Wise, 'Paul and the Mystics', 58–9.

[134] Wise, 'Paul and the Mystics', 53–4.

[135] Wise, 'Paul and the Mystics', 63.

[136] Wise, 'Paul and the Mystics', 67–8.

[137] Wise, 'Paul and the Mystics', 62–4.

was the author of Gentile Christianity,[138] but this did not prevent him from partly reclaiming Paul as a Jewish hero, explaining (if not justifying) Paul's teachings as a result of a Jewish mystic's attempt to offer the Gentiles something of the gift God had granted Israel. Wise's interest was to encourage a magnanimous, sympathetic value judgement of Christianity; thus he did not attempt to contrast Paul negatively with Jesus, but rather highlighted what he saw as a profound similarity. As he put it, 'In him [Paul], the spirit of Jesus was resurrected as eminently and vigorously as John had resurrected Jesus'.[139]

The Prussian-born North American Reform rabbi Joseph Krauskopf (1858–1923) also fits this pattern of approaching Paul as part of a wider project to acclimatise Jews to the Christian world, to familiarise them with Christian figures in an unthreatening way, to emphasise similarities, and to look forward to a common destiny. A graduate of the first class of the Hebrew Union College at Cincinnati, he was a radical reformer who was closely involved with Kohler in the Pittsburgh Platform of 1885 and who introduced Sunday services at his Philadelphia congregation in 1887. He published many lectures in the areas of religion, ethics, and social science and was a founding member of the Jewish Publication Society of America, a powerful instrument for expanding the literary and intellectual horizons of North American Jewry.

Hidden away in a book called *A Rabbi's Impressions of the Oberammergau Passion Play* (1908), Krauskopf included a lecture entitled 'Paul: The Founder and Spreader of Christianity'. In form and tone it is reminiscent of Wise's treatment, although its explanation of Paul's theology rested on his integration of Grecian Philonic Gnosticism and 'the controversial and casuistical method of reasoning [of the Jewish school]', rather than on pseudo-kabbalistic mysticism.[140] Like Wise, Krauskopf enthused about the historical impact and character of Paul.[141] The apostle had both reflected and foreshadowed the distinguished characteristics of some of the greatest religious leaders in history, including the enterprising spirit of Moses, the fire of Isaiah, the patience of Hillel, the temper of Shammai, the zeal of Savonarola, and the daring of Luther.[142] Again, like Wise, Krauskopf recognised Paul's involvement in the creation of Gentile Christianity but did not use this as an opportunity to attack or discredit Christianity. Rather, in line with his Reformist tendencies, he chose to focus on what he regarded as the positive, universalist aspects of Paul's teachings. 'As members of a civilised society', he suggested, 'we owe him [Paul] unstinted praise for coming to the rescue of Gentile peoples'.[143] For Paul had been a Jewish hero whose theology, although not without serious

[138] Wise, 'Paul and the Mystics', 53–4, 62.

[139] Wise, 'Paul and the Mystics', 53.

[140] Joseph Krauskopf, *A Rabbi's Impressions of the Oberammergau Passion Play* (Philadelphia: Edward Stern & Co., 1908), 205.

[141] Krauskopf cited no Pauline scholars and offered no references. He was suspicious of the historicity of Acts.

[142] Krauskopf, *A Rabbi's Impressions*, 198.

[143] Krauskopf, *A Rabbi's Impressions*, 215.

flaws,[144] had brought the unenlightened Gentiles closer to God by teaching them Jewish ethics.[145] The key teaching in this context had been the Prophets' dream of a universalist Judaism.

What the prophets of Israel had long dreamed and hoped took form in that moment [when Paul resolved to be the 'Apostle to the Gentiles']. What millions of Jews had professed for centuries, this one man proposed to execute single-handed. He would open the way for the realization of the prophets' dream of a federation of all people into a brotherhood, under the sway of universal peace and goodwill. He would spread his new theology to the ends of the vast Roman empire, and preach it, till it received the homage of every tongue and knee.[146]

With Paul, argued Krauskopf, Judaism's existence as a tribal religion had ended. As a result of his missionary efforts 'the ethical teachings of Judaism crossed the border of their birthplace'.[147] Paul had gone on to sweep aside every barrier between Jew and Gentile, including Jewish ritual. In comparison with his new theology, 'the authority, with which centuries of observance had vested these rites and ceremonies [of Judaism], could have no weight'.[148] Like the prophets before him, Paul emphasised deed rather than form, and from this perspective Paul's abrogation of the Law appeared commendable.[149] But despite these achievements, ultimate success had eluded the apostle – for he had failed to unite Jews and Gentiles. The reason Krauskopf gave for this failure, the regret he expressed at this lost opportunity, and the remedy he proposed dramatically demonstrated his lack of interest in negative Jewish–Christian polemics.

According to Krauskopf, Paul's mistake had been to fail to compromise with the Jewish Christians. 'Had they but compromised their differences', he opined, 'they might have laboured together, and in unison, and converted, not only Gentiles, but also the Jews'.[150] His disappointment that the Nazarenes had not surrendered their fondness for ceremonialism and exclusiveness, and that Paul had not abandoned his mysticism, was palpable.[151] Had things gone differently, the parting of ways

---

[144] Paul had been too influenced by mysticism and pagan teachings, and his education had been shallow; Krauskopf accepted that Paul had enjoyed both Greek and Jewish studies, but deduced from the reasoning displayed in his epistles that he had 'acquired more of what was faulty in both systems of education, than of what constituted their chief merits'. Krauskopf, *A Rabbi's Impressions*, 204–5.

[145] 'Christianity was established in the name of a Jew and by a Jew'. Krauskopf, *A Rabbi's Impressions*, 212.

[146] Krauskopf, *A Rabbi's Impressions*, 207–8.

[147] Krauskopf, *A Rabbi's Impressions*, 207.

[148] Krauskopf, *A Rabbi's Impressions*, 208.

[149] In fact, nowhere does Krauskopf criticise Paul's view of the Law. Remarkably, the Torah itself is not explicitly mentioned in the piece, and Paul's attitude towards ritual and ceremony is presented in a positive light.

[150] Krauskopf, *A Rabbi's Impressions*, 212.

[151] Krauskopf, *A Rabbi's Impressions*, 212.

might have been avoided and a Jewish religion that united Jew and Gentile might have emerged.

They [the early Christians] would, in time, have given up hoping for the Second Advent of their Master. They would have concentrated their attention upon the pure, ethical precepts which he had taught, would have recognised in them the pure Judaism of old, and their pure life, aided by Paul's zeal, would have cemented the different Jewish sects into a close brotherhood, and prevented the breach which Paul's Christianity introduced. Such a compromise would not have interfered with Paul's success among the Gentiles. It was not as much his mystical and mythical Grecian Christ that conquered the Gentiles, as it was the preaching of the pure-hearted and noble-minded Judaic Jesus. It was not so much the Gnostic theosophy, as it was the ethics of Judaism, that found a ready echo in Gentile hearts, especially in those days of corruption, of tyrannous rule. . . . Such a compromise might have brought the prophets' dream of One God over all, One Brotherhood of all, peace and goodwill among all, nearer realization than it is to-day, and Paul might have ranked as one of the great men of Israel.[152]

Despite this disappointment, Paul remained an inspiration for those who, early in the twentieth century, were more interested in a reunification of Jew and Gentile than in highlighting the differences and demarcating the boundaries between the two communities.

Each of us may draw from the results of his [Paul's] labour the hope that the compromise, that could not be effected eighteen centuries ago, may yet be brought about. The spirit of our age greatly favours such a compromise. . . . Obsolete forms and meaningless rites are crumbling away. Offensive doctrines are disappearing. The Judaic Jesus is slowly regaining his lost ground. The Ethics of Judaism are gradually supplanting the Gnosticism of Paul. When the Jew shall have completely cast away his obstructive exclusiveness and ceremonialism, and the Christian his Christology, Jew and Gentile will be one.[153]

For all his faults and with all the injuries his Christology had led to, Krauskopf felt that there was more reason to be grateful to the Apostle to the Gentiles than to find cause for censure. In particular, Paul's universalist tendency made him a potential partner of Reform Judaism and an example of how to win over the non-Jewish world. Not only had he taught Jewish ethics to the Gentile world, which no Jew had achieved before, but also he had demonstrated that Judaism could be stripped of 'obsolete, meaningless and repellent ceremonies, rites, and observances' and, in its pure and simple form, might become a world-conquering religion.[154]

Another progressive religious leader with a similar agenda was the Anglo-Jewish biblical scholar and philanthropist Claude Montefiore (1858–1938), who also came to Paul as part of a wider project to integrate the best of the non-Jewish world

---

[152] Krauskopf, *A Rabbi's Impressions*, 212–13.
[153] Krauskopf, *A Rabbi's Impressions*, 215–16.
[154] Krauskopf, *A Rabbi's Impressions*, 215.

with the best of Jewish thought. Montefiore had been educated at Oxford under the Anglican minister Benjamin Jowett. Together with Lily Montagu, he founded Liberal Judaism in Britain, which was in part an attempt to model a progressive form of Judaism on certain aspects of Christian thought.[155] In terms of scholarship he was unusual for his obsessive interest in Christianity and the New Testament.[156] A fervent anti-Zionist, he argued that familiarity with Christian thought and culture was useful for Jewish integration into Western society. It was in this context that he sought to neutralise the apostle's negative image for Jews, and he went about this in two ways.

First, Montefiore sought to demonstrate that Paul was not as anti-Jewish as he might seem. Certainly, Paul's description of Judaism was quite unrecognisable to him. As he put it in 1901,

St Paul beats the air with words, which, magnificent as they are, seem out of relation to the actual Jewish religion . . . [Paul's arguments] leave the impression: either this man was never a Rabbinic Jew at all, or he has quite forgotten what Rabbinic Judaism was and is.[157]

Montefiore did not, however, attempt a defence of Judaism against Pauline criticism. Instead, he suggested that (1) Paul's criticisms actually represented the Judaism with which he, Paul, had been familiar, and (2) this Judaism had not been rabbinic Judaism. In *Judaism and St Paul* (1914), Montefiore went on to describe Paul's experience of a poorer, inferior diaspora Hellenistic Judaism. In his opinion, the religion Paul had suffered under and criticised had been

more systematic, and perhaps a little more philosophic and less child-like, but possibly for those very reasons it was less intimate, warm, joyous and comforting. Its God was more distant and less loving. . . . The early religion of Paul was more sombre and gloomy than Rabbinic Judaism; the world was a more miserable and God-forsaken place; there were fewer simple joys and happinesses. . . . The outlook was darker: man could be, and was, less good. . . . God was not constantly helping and forgiving.[158]

Regardless of the validity of Montefiore's idea of Hellenistic Judaism as a kind of second-rate Judaism, the point made here is that he sought to present Paul as one who need not be viewed as an enemy of Judaism *per se*.

---

[155] See Langton, *Claude Montefiore*.

[156] Montefiore made extensive reference to the works of Christian Pauline scholars; examples include Pfleiderer, Weizaecker, Cone, Clemen, Jowett, Drummond, Everett, Kabisch, Wellhausen, Sanday, Holtzmann, Delitzsche, Loisy, Reitzenstein, Lake, Hereford, Bartlet, andBousset. He was particularly concerned to correct common Christian misconceptions of Rabbinic Judaism such as those offered by Weber. His references to Jewish scholars were less frequent but included M. Friedlaender, Schechter, Abelson, Abrahams, and Buechler.

[157] Claude G. Montefiore, 'Rabbinic Judaism and the Epistles of St. Paul', *Jewish Quarterly Review* 13 (1901), 205–6.

[158] Montefiore, 'Rabbinic Judaism and the Epistles of St. Paul', 81–2.

Second, Montefiore sought to draw the sting from Paul by reexamining the idea that the apostle had made a god of Jesus. He based his assessment upon a limited number of letters that he regarded as authentic.[159] One effect of this was to reject as Pauline the more developed Christology of other epistles. He fully recognised the central importance of Christ in Paul's message; for the apostle, 'Christianity is not the Law plus Christ. It is Jesus Christ alone'.[160] But he imagined Paul's authentic view to have been that Christ, although preexistent before his human birth, had originally been created by God, and suggested that the apostle had not sought to 'imply the co-eternity or co-equality of Christ with God'.[161] Obviously, because he was seeking to introduce the apostle to a Jewish audience in as positive a light as possible, it was in Montefiore's interest to play down Paul's conception of the divinity of Christ where he could. Nevertheless, this was a remarkable statement and set Montefiore, as a Jewish commentator, apart. He had attempted to rescue Paul, to reinterpret the common reading of him, when the vast majority of his Jewish readers had been content to reject him *in toto*. Both as a Jew and as a Liberal, Montefiore had opposed any claim of divinity for Jesus. Although the superimposition of one's beliefs onto Jesus has by no means been an uncommon occurrence among either Christians or Jews who wished to enrol Jesus as a supporter of their ideas, it was surely remarkable that Montefiore, as a Jew, should have chosen to treat the Great Apostate in such a way.

With his hope for a future religion that would encompass the best of both Judaism and Christianity, Montefiore was keen to credit Paul with his contributions to religious evolution. In particular, he was interested in Paul's ethical writings, which he found deeply inspirational. He suggested that the apostle's religious and moral enthusiasm was the secret to his 'perennial power over the hearts of men' and he found in his hatred of sin a continual challenge.[162] He recognised and admired Paul's attempt to base his religion upon the love of God, that is, on the love of God for man and on the love of man towards God, and was keen to commend this to his Jewish audience, implying that this could be learned from Christianity. He wrote admiringly of the wealth of ethical language.[163] The apostle's exhortations did not exceed the best moral teachings of the Old Testament and rabbinic literature because, as he reminded his Jewish readers, it had originated from these sources. Yet he could not help but admire their 'spirit and sureness of touch, a vigour and connectedness essentially their own'.[164] There was a unity

---

[159] These were 1 Thessalonians, Galatians, 1 and 2 Corinthians, Romans, and Philippians. Claude G. Montefiore, 'First Impressions of St. Paul', *Jewish Quarterly Review* 6 (1894), 428.

[160] Claude G. Montefiore, *Judaism and St. Paul: Two Essays* (London: Macmillan, 1914), 129.

[161] Montefiore, 'First Impressions of St. Paul', 430.

[162] Montefiore, 'First Impressions of St. Paul', 428.

[163] Montefiore, 'First Impressions of St. Paul', 468.

[164] Montefiore, 'First Impressions of St. Paul', 466.

in Paul's ethics; in contrast to the rabbis' writings Paul's beliefs were 'deducible from certain principles, so that they become something more than isolated and heterogeneous maxims. They may fairly be said to flow from the one central principle of Love'.[165]

Ever concerned with what practical use he could make of religious teachings, Montefiore pointed out several other advantages that he felt Paul's ethical writings possessed over the rabbis': they were easily available, were conveniently contained within a single volume, and were 'nobly expressed and redolent of enthusiasm and genius'.[166] It would be quite wrong to give the impression that Montefiore had only positive things to say about Paul. Quite the reverse: the vast mass of Paul's theology had to be rejected. Nevertheless, the fact that he found most of Paul unacceptable only makes his effort to undermine the classic view even more striking. Ironically, although his positive presentation of Paul, almost exclusively focused upon his ethics, is incongruous with Christian tradition, it is so precisely because his primary concern was to interpret Paul to Jews for whom the classic, negative image was repulsive; thus, in sharp contrast to previous Jewish practice, he openly praised what he felt the epistles had to offer Judaism and quietly rejected all that he believed was unserviceable.

We have already referred to Leo Baeck in the context of a negative assessment of Paul. But after the war, when Baeck found himself living away from old Europe and its ingrained anti-Semitism, he was prepared to more fully acknowledge Paul's Jewishness, as can be seen in his essay 'The Faith of Paul' (1952).[167] It is a particularly interesting shift in attitude, bearing in mind that Baeck continued to base his analysis upon Romans, 1 and 2 Corinthians, and Galatians; this, one might have thought, would have led him to emphasise non-Jewish influences upon Paul.[168] Yet his experiences of Christians in Britain and North America and his conviction of the necessity of building bridges with Christian allies meant that Baeck became keen to stress the Jewishness of Paul. One way of achieving this was to emphasise the great extent to which Hellenistic or Greek ideas were accepted and adopted within the Jewish Diaspora. For example, he argued that very many aspects of Hellenistic thought were reminiscent of the teachings of the 'schools of Jewish "wisdom"'. Likewise, the utilisation of Stoic philosophic terminology remained

---

[165] Montefiore, 'First Impressions of St. Paul', 466–7.

[166] Montefiore, *Judaism and St. Paul*, 208–9.

[167] Baeck, 'The Faith of Paul'.

[168] Acts was a 'source that is in every regard secondary', although he admitted that it was of some use in confirming information given in the letters. He also rejected 2 Cor. 6:14–7:1, an apparent interpolation concerning the dangers of associating with unbelievers, as post-Pauline. Baeck, 'The Faith of Paul', 93–4. Here, as elsewhere, the influence of German Lutheran scholarship (Tübingen) upon modern Jews is apparent; he made reference to the Pauline scholars Barth, Bousset, Bultmann, and Deissmann.

'within the Jewish compass'.[169] Thus the Hellenistic elements of Paul's thought as expressed in his letters did not, in Baeck's opinion, make the apostle a 'Hellenist' as was commonly claimed. Indeed, Paul's approach to the Hellenistic world was the same as that of some Palestinian teachers.[170] Tarsus, in which Paul had grown up, was a place of 'Hellenism, with all its philosophies, beliefs, annunciations, and cults' and yet 'Paul was a Jew of Tarsus, not a Syrian or Persian or Egyptian of Tarsus. . . . His background was that of the Jewish people.'[171] The fact that Paul's background was one of Judaism expressed through a Hellenistic medium did not, for Baeck, make it any less Jewish.

Of particular note in Baeck's construction of a Jewish Paul was his interpretation of the apostle's view of the Messiah, which he described as 'Jewish Messianism such as it was determined by the [apocalyptic] Book of Daniel'.[172] But he also emphasised the power of Paul's vision of Christ over his theology. Thus the apostle's starting point was 'the vision allotted to him which gave him the assuredness that Jesus was the Christ' and his background 'of the Jewish people'. Baeck put it most eloquently when he wrote,

Nor did Paul, by stressing his apostolate to the Gentiles, deviate from the genuine Jewish creed. It is not only history that tells us of the Jewish mission. . . . Jewish philosophy, or theology, of history, includes always the Gentiles. The terms 'Jewish people' and 'Gentiles' are interrelated in their meaning. . . . The 'coming' of the Messiah and the 'coming' of the Gentiles are interconnected. This is Jewish faith, and such was Paul's faith.[173]

He maintained that there was nothing un-Jewish about the apostle's position, and thus it was more accurate to say that, for Paul, the Law had been transcended rather than abrogated. Referring to the rabbinic literature for support, he argued that Jews of that time had believed that history was divided into three epochs: 2000 years of chaos (*tohu wabhohu*); 2000 years of Law or Torah beginning with the revelation on Mt. Sinai; and 2000 years of 'the Messianic age', which would be finally followed by 'that world which is wholly Shabbath, the rest in the life of eternity'.[174] He argued that Paul's vision of Christ had convinced him that the age of the Messiah had arrived. In Baeck's opinion, then, it was by no means outside the pale of Jewish thought for Paul to have assumed that the Law had now been transcended. Nor was it un-Jewish for him to have exclaimed, 'All things are lawful

---

[169] Baeck, 'The Faith of Paul', 101.
[170] Baeck, 'The Faith of Paul', 101.
[171] Baeck, 'The Faith of Paul', 102–3.
[172] Baeck distinguished between the Prophetic view and the Apocalyptic view of the Messiah, yet both streams of thought remained within the Jewish tradition as far as he was concerned. Baeck, 'The Faith of Paul', 98, 103.
[173] Baeck, 'The Faith of Paul', 108.
[174] Baeck refers to Sanhedrin 97a, Pesiq Rabbati 4a, and Tamid vii 4. Baeck, 'The Faith of Paul', 106.

unto me' (1 Cor. 6:12) because this closely paralleled the rabbinic teaching that in the 'Days of the Messiah . . . there will be no merit or guilt'.[175] Baeck concluded,

We are, therefore, not entitled to say Paul rejected or condemned the Law – if he had done so he would have broken asunder the structure of his belief . . . That a new epoch was to begin one day was not contended by anybody; it was the common belief of the Jewish people. . . . What separated Paul from the Jewish people was the question of fact – the problem of whether the Messiah had, finally, been manifested, whether his kingdom had come in truth.[176]

The tendency to see in Paul an opportunity to develop Jewish–Christian partnership, to listen sympathetically to the voice of a potential ally, has recently reappeared in postwar interfaith dialogue. In this context the contribution of Pinchas Lapide (1922-) is significant, particularly with regard to his book *Paul: Rabbi and Apostle*, originally published in German in 1981.[177] A Canadian-born Orthodox Jew, he moved to Israel in 1938, where he later lectured on the New Testament at the American College in Jerusalem. During the Second World War Lapide was an officer in the Jewish Brigade of the British army. He went on to serve Israel as a diplomat and a journalist (as head of the Jerusalem press bureau). He lived in Germany and lectured throughout Europe, a frequent participant in Jewish–Christian dialogue concerned with reconciliation between Jews and Christians and between Jews and Germans.

Paul: Rabbi and Apostle was the record of a public discussion between Lapide and a Christian Pauline scholar in the context of interfaith relations.[178] A study in interfaith diplomacy, it is an attempt to reassess a figure whom Lapide regarded as replacing Jesus as the key figure of dialogue.[179] As he put it,

In this third decade of Christian–Jewish dialogue Jesus is no longer the central figure in the discussion between Church and synagogue. Thanks to the current surge of

---

[175] Baeck drew on Shabbat 151a, where Rabbi Simeon ben Eleazar interpreted Eccles. 12:1 ('The years that draw nigh, in which I say, I need no will, no choice') as referring to the Messianic age. Baeck, 'The Faith of Paul', 106.

[176] Baeck, 'The Faith of Paul', 107.

[177] Pinchas Lapide and Peter Stuhlmacher, *Paul: Rabbi and Apostle*, trans. Lawrence W. Denef (Minneapolis: Augsburg Publishing House, 1984). German original: *Paulus: Rabbi und Apostel*.

[178] Lapide pointed out that the issue of establishing Paul's authentic letters is unresolved; this did not stop him from citing extensively from Romans, Galatians, Ephesians, 1 and 2 Corinthians, Philippians, 1 and 2 Thessalonians, and 1 Timothy. He referred to a number of Christian Pauline scholars, including G. Bornkamm, G. Klein, Käsemann, Barth, Wilckens, and Stuhlmacher. He specifically mentioned Buber as a Jewish commentator.

[179] Elsewhere Lapide explained that 'Jesus – who enlarged upon Torah, who built fences around the Law and radicalised the fulfilment of the commandments – would nowadays be someone like a Hassidic rabbi with many disciples and their pronounced messianic expectation. Paul, on the other hand, would be a Reform rabbi in the Diaspora, in New York for instance, whose main concern was the ethos of the prophets of Israel – entirely as it is lived and taught by the Reform rabbis today.' Lapide, *Paulus zwischen Damaskus und Qumran* (Mohn: Gütersloh, 1993), 25.

interest in Jesus within the State of Israel, the Nazarene, long shrouded in silence, is beginning to be acknowledged among his own people and in his own land. With this new recognition the vanguard of Christian theology has gradually, though hesitantly, also begun to take Jesus' Jewishness into account and to draw the conclusions this hardly coincidental reality requires. Such is not yet the case with Paul.[180]

On the one hand Lapide's suggestion that Paul was very much an individual, something of a 'mystic, a fanatic, lone wolf',[181] succeeded in distancing Paul from Judaism. The apostle's sense of feeling forsaken by God, which led to a heightened sense of sin/evil, was described by Lapide as characteristic of 'marginal Jewish circles'.[182] His teachings were also alien. Paul was responsible for the 'absurd caricature' of the Torah/divine instruction as Nomos/Law, and for the 'doctrine of Original Sin', which did not reflect an authentic Jewish experience.[183] On the other hand, Lapide was prepared to confirm the traditional Christian understanding of the apostle as a Pharisee. The apostle's style was described as reflecting rabbinic thought forms and emphasis was placed upon his dependence on the Law.[184]

Crucially, the book was intended as a refutation of the classic Jewish critique of Paul. Lapide made it clear that his view was unlike those of other Jews who, having read Christian accounts of Paul, asked, 'Is he the father of that enmity towards Jews which claims to be Christian? Or might he not even have contracted the malady of Jewish self-hatred?'[185] Throughout, Lapide expressed a concern to accommodate his Christian partners in dialogue whenever possible. This is clear, for example, in his acknowledgment of a messianic role for Jesus and in his remarkable assessment of the Jewish reception of Paul's presentation of Jesus.

[W]e can conclude that despite Paul and all of his well-intentioned statements, Jesus was not the Messiah of Israel. He did, however, become the Saviour of the Gentile Church, the redeemer of idolatry and faithlessness, the one who made it possible for those 'having no hope and without God in the world' to become 'fellow citizens with the saints' and 'partakers of the promise', as Paul puts it in Ephesians 2 and 3. No Jew living today doubts that Jesus has, as the Christ so convincingly proclaimed by Paul, become the Saviour of the Gentile church; nor do we question the messianic mission of Christendom in this as yet unredeemed world.[186]

Lapide's occasionally incoherent, self-contradictory presentation might be best understood as an attempt to create an Apostle to the Gentiles suitable for strengthening interfaith relations. One key factor in this politically correct construct was the suggestion (echoing the Gaston–Gager hypothesis, which was partially motivated

---

180 Lapide and Stuhlmacher, *Paul*, 31.
181 Lapide and Stuhlmacher, *Paul*, 53.
182 Lapide and Stuhlmacher, *Paul*, 44–5.
183 Lapide and Stuhlmacher, *Paul*, 39, 44–5.
184 Lapide and Stuhlmacher, *Paul*, 34–5, 40.
185 Lapide and Stuhlmacher, *Paul*, 32–3.
186 Lapide and Stuhlmacher, *Paul*, 50.

by the ecumenical implications of Auschwitz)[187] that the end of the Law (Rom. 10:4) was relevant only for Christian believers, for whom it no longer functioned as a way to justification.[188] For Jews and Jewish proselytes, however, the Mosaic Law was understood to retain its full validity. Again, Lapide's optimistic and conciliatory tone is striking.

Of course all of this [that is, Paul's refusal to impose the law] applies only to Gentile Christians. For Jews and for Jewish proselytes the Mosaic law, as Paul sees it, retains it full and unaltered validity. He emphatically underscores this in his letter to the Galatians, 'I testify again to every man who receives circumcision that he is bound to keep the whole law' (Gal. 5.3). And for surety in his letter to the Romans he amplifies what he has said, 'It is not the hearers of the law who are righteous before God, but the doers of the law who will be justified' (Rom. 2.13). And shortly thereafter he confesses, 'For I delight in the law of God, in my inmost self' (Rom. 7.22). Mark well, Paul is here speaking of the Torah of God and *not* the 'law of Christ', whatever he might have meant by that concept. That sounds just as orthodox as the word in 1 Tim 1.8, 'We know that the law is good, if any one uses it lawfully'. I am certain that no contemporary rabbi, even in Jerusalem, would have the slightest cause for disagreement with these words of Paul.[189]

Lapide argued that Paul was actually very dependent upon the Law, appealing to it as an authority and retaining it as the foundation of his worldview, his Christology, his theory of salvation, and that he had many positive things to say about it. It would be wrong, Lapide suggested, to regard Paul as antinomian.[190] In this way he explicitly distanced himself from Jewish writers who regarded Paul as the founder of Christianity or as one who had repudiated Judaism.[191] Paul's teaching represented not a break but an evolution with the coming of the messianic age; he had simply disagreed with the Pharisees as to when the Gentiles would be reconciled with God.[192] Lapide argued that Paul had not hated Israel and had regarded God's promises to Israel as valid.[193] And yet he recognised that Paul certainly posed a series of problems to the modern Jew: Why reject the Law? Why invent an un-Jewish doctrine (original sin) and solve it with an un-Jewish remedy (human sacrifice)? Why sacrifice valid principles for propagandist purposes? Why twist the religion of Jesus into a religion about Jesus? Why transform a positive (Jewish) view of human nature into a negative (Hellenistic) one?[194] Lapide's solution was to explain

---

[187] Gager has commented, 'I believe that our history, or rather what we think and know of it, does matter in the present. I would not claim that Paul, or even Christianity as a whole, is responsible for modern anti-Semitism. But Paul in the traditional reading has been an important part of that story. If that version should turn out to be wrong, the story will need to be revised.' John G. Gager, *Reinventing Paul* (New York: Oxford University Press, 2001), 18.

[188] Lapide and Stuhlmacher, *Paul,* 37.

[189] Lapide and Stuhlmacher, *Paul,* 42.

[190] Lapide and Stuhlmacher, *Paul,* 40, 43.

[191] Lapide and Stuhlmacher, *Paul,* 48.

[192] Lapide and Stuhlmacher, *Paul,* 48, 49.

[193] Lapide and Stuhlmacher, *Paul,* 37, 42.

[194] Lapide and Stuhlmacher, *Paul,* 53–4.

the apostle in terms of salvation history. If Israel's role had been to bring the world to the one true God, then Paul's Christianity could be regarded as a significant interim station. After all, it had been Paul and not the Pharisees who had brought the Gentiles to faith in God.[195] This solution, which paints a picture of a Paul who is essentially irrelevant to the Jewish people, can perhaps best be explained in terms of a calculated appeal to his Christian partners in dialogue, a gesture of interfaith generosity entirely in keeping with his sympathetic treatment of Jesus.[196]

Such interest and concern for harmonious interfaith relations reached their ultimate expression in Pauline studies in the work of Mark Nanos (1954–), a Reform Jewish scholar of early Judaism and Christianity, and winner of the 1996 National Jewish Book Award for Jewish–Christian relations. In *The Mystery of Romans* (1996) and *The Irony of Galatians* (2002),[197] Nanos came to Paul from a self-consciously Jewish perspective, concerned about the role of previous interpretations of Paul in shaping Christian views of Jews and things Jewish.[198] In particular, he acknowledged 'the victims of certain interpretations of Paul's voice, especially those who have suffered the Shoah. Their suffering cannot be separated from prejudices resulting from those interpretations any more than it can be wholly attributed to them'.[199] Rather than condemn Paul's apparent misconceptions of Judaism and/or the Law, or work diplomatically around them, he presented a radical new understanding of the apostle as a Torah-observant Jew who played no intentional role in the parting of the ways or in the creation of a separate Gentile form of Christianity.[200]

Nanos's approach was possible largely due to the postwar shift in mainstream scholarly attitudes towards the complexity of Jewish existence in the first century. Taking seriously the fragmented nature of ancient Judaism(s), 'marginal' forms of Jewish identity and the Jewish origins of Christianity itself, he approached the New Testament as a Jewish book.[201] Paul, he claimed, should not be regarded as an apostate or as a bad Jew, but as a thoroughly Jewish, Torah-observant Pharisee.[202] Paul was a 'practicing Jew – 'a good Jew' – albeit a Jew shaped by his conviction in

---

[195] Lapide and Stuhlmacher, *Paul*, 53.

[196] Lapide's concern resulted in the recognition of the Christian claim that Jesus rose from the dead. Pinchas Lapide, *The Resurrection of Jesus: A Jewish Perspective* (London: SPCK, 1983) from the German original 1977.

[197] Mark Nanos, *The Mystery of Romans: The Jewish Context of Paul's Letter* (Minneapolis: Fortress Press, 1996). Mark Nanos, *The Irony of Galatians: Paul's Letter in First-Century Context* (Minneapolis: Fortress Press, 2002). Nanos's commentaries include extensive cross references to the rest of the New Testament. He also refers extensively to both Jewish and Christian Pauline scholars.

[198] Nanos, *Galatians*, 2, 4; Nanos, *Romans*, 16.

[199] Nanos, *Galatians*, ix.

[200] Nanos, *Galatians*, 252–3.

[201] Nanos, *Romans*, 4.

[202] Paul was not anti-Judaic, or an apostate, nor did he abrogate Torah. Nanos, *Romans*, 4–6, 7. He was thoroughly Jewish, even in his concern for the Gentiles. Nanos, *Romans*, 3, 9–10. He was a Torah-observant Pharisee, as reflected in his interest to transform Priestly purity concerns into daily lifestyle and a matter of self-definition. Nanos, *Galatians*, 3, 7–9; *Romans*, 193–5.

Jesus as Israel's Christ, who did not break with the essential truths of the Judaism(s) of his day.[203]

According to Nanos, Paul believed that with the life and death of the messiah a new eschatological age had begun, which enabled Gentiles to come to God as equals to Jews.[204] Paul's original insight was that now, in the messianic era, the Shema's claim that God is One applied to both Jew and Gentile, as *Jews and Gentiles*.[205] Crucially, Gentiles need no longer convert to Judaism and observe the Torah as Jews (involving, *inter alia*, circumcision and dietary laws), or even begin the ritual process to become Jewish proselytes; their faith in Christ now automatically gave them the spiritual status of proselytes.

Paul is not arguing... that the boundary has collapsed so that there is no longer Jew or Gentile, circumcised or uncircumcised, any more than he is arguing that the social boundary of difference between male and female or slave and free has been eliminated; both kinds still exist, and they are different with respect to one another. These Gentiles have not become Jewish proselytes but fellow heirs of Abraham while remaining members of the nations. For Paul, the differences of identity remain, but the discrimination that accompanies such roles in the present 'evil' age does and must not remain, for those in Christ, those of the age to come (cf. Gal. 3.26–4.7). They have become the equivalents of proselytes – righteous ones of God though not of Israel, of a new community creation consisting of Israel and the nations worshipping together – by the act of God in Christ.[206]

And what of the Torah? In Paul's eyes, the only legal requirements for Gentile Christians were those that the Jewish Law required of righteous Gentiles, namely, those specified in the apostolic decree in the Acts of the Apostles, which approximated to the Noachide laws.[207] Observance of anything less would suggest Gentile arrogance towards their Jewish brothers and the Jewish Law, whereas observance of anything more would suggest disbelief in the grace God had shown them as Gentiles.[208] Paul's negative comments about the Law did not reflect a problem with the Law *per se* but with the ethnocentric exclusivism of non-Christian Jews

---

[203] Nanos, *Romans*, 9.

[204] Nanos, *Romans*, 36–7, 177–9.

[205] Nanos, *Romans*, 9–10, 37.

[206] Nanos, *Galatians*, 99–100.

[207] Nanos, *Romans*, 34–5, 177–9. The Apostolic decree (Acts 15.19–32; 16.15; 21.25) drew upon the ancient Mosaic model for laws incumbent on the stranger (Lev. 12, 17, 18, 20) and upon the Noachide laws later outlined in the rabbinic literature in the second or third centuries (t. Avodah Zarah 8.4). They included the prohibitions relating to things sacrificed to idols, blood, things strangled, and fornication. Nanos, *Romans*, 50–56.

[208] For Nanos, this perspective explains Romans, where Paul had attempted to restrain Gentile-Christian superiority, and Galatians, where he had attempted to restrain Jewish-Christian superiority. Romans was not written to discourage association with Judaism but to remind the Gentile addressees that they needed to observe the *halakhot* for righteous Gentiles, in order to offend the Roman Jews whom Paul hoped soon to be preaching to. It is worth noting that Nanos differs from the New Perspective, in which Paul in Romans is understood to *defend* Gentile-Christian freedom against Jewish ethnocentricism, in that he sees Paul *restraining* Gentile-Christian freedom halakhically.

who disagreed that the new age had dawned and who rejected the claim that the conventional ritual admittance for Gentiles into Israel was no longer necessary.[209] Both groups could come before God in their own way, although Paul regarded the Noachide laws as a (Jewish) legal necessity for Gentile believers in Christ[210] and the obvious *modus vivendi* for them to coexist with non-Christian Jews, with whom they closely associated in synagogue and Jewish communal life.[211] Nanos concluded that

Paul has, mistakenly, been made a creator of gentile Christianity that rejected Judaism and the Law as operative, rather than the champion of the restoration of Israel who fought for the inclusion of 'righteous gentiles' in this new community of equals, in fulfilment of the eschatological hope of Israel.... [212]

Nanos differed from previous Jewish writers in that he did not attempt to focus primarily upon Paul himself, but instead concentrated upon the historical contexts of individual epistles, specifically, Romans and Galatians. Nevertheless, the picture of the author that emerges has potentially enormous implications for Jewish–Christian relations. Firstly, Paul's writings should be regarded as a contribution to an intra-Jewish rather than Jewish–Christian debate concerning how Gentiles are to be included in Israel in the messianic age. As such, he should no longer be viewed as the inventor of Gentile Christianity, but rather as an instrument of Jewish and Gentile rapprochement. Second, Paul's own Torah observance, and his expectation that Jewish believers in Jesus would continue to observe the *halakhah*, demands of Gentile Christians a very different view of the Law than has traditionally been held.[213] It also raises the question of how Gentile Christians in the twenty-first century should respond to Paul in terms of observing the apostolic decree themselves and recognising the legitimacy and even necessity of Torah observance for Jewish followers of Christ. Third, Nanos's appreciative tone and readiness to recognise the theological dilemmas facing the Jewish Apostle to the Gentiles – and his solutions – heralds a new chapter in the Jewish interest in the apostle as a key historical figure of Jewish history and thought.

It seems fair to conclude from the Pauline studies offered by Wise, Montefiore, Kraupskopf, Lapide, and Nanos that a tradition of conciliation and empathy has existed alongside the hostile, antagonistic one. Although Paul is here, too, portrayed

---

[209] Nanos, *Romans*, 9–10, 177–9. According to Nanos, the Galatians were not troubled by Jewish-Christians or Christian Judaisers, but rather by well-meaning representatives in Galatian synagogues 'entrusted with the responsibility of conducting Gentiles wishing more than guest status within the communities through the ritual process of proselyte conversion by which this is accomplished. They may be proselytes – former Gentiles – as well'. Nanos, *Galatians*, 6–7, 228–9.

[210] Nanos, *Romans*, 34–5, 177–9.

[211] Gentile God-fearers would have shared in synagogue life, participated in the lifestyle of the Jewish community, and eaten together. Nanos, Romans, 55–7. Nanos, *Galatians*, 258, 264.

[212] Nanos, *Romans*, 173, 174–5.

[213] In this context, Nanos suggests that Romans is more relevant than Galatians, because Paul in Romans is calling for Gentile respect for the Jewish law, whereas in Galatians he is emphasising the limits of the law for Gentiles. Nanos, *Romans*, 15–16.

as a key representative of Christianity, the negative value-judgement is dramatically reversed. This is a tradition that seeks to explain Paul for the purpose of mutual understanding between Jew and Christian and, whether he is regarded as a mystic, a prophetic purveyor of Jewish universalism, or a Pharisee, his historical stature is acknowledged and applauded.

CONCLUSION

Although we have only just begun to look at individual Jewish scholars' views of Paul, the question naturally arises: Is it legitimate to speak of a Jewish reclamation of the apostle Paul? In several surveys of Jewish Pauline scholarship the claim is made that there has been a radical change in attitude in the post-War period.[214] Earlier nineteenth-century antagonistic treatments that had been generated in the face of Christian anti-Jewish hostility are said to have given way to nonpolemical works of more objective scholarship in the context of improved social conditions for twentieth-century Jews. A new tendency for Jewish commentators to locate Paul within the context of the Judaic thought of his own day is understood to have been encouraged by a lessening of the anti-Judaic assumptions of Christian scholarship after the holocaust. Hagner (1980),[215] for example, suggests that the modern Jewish study of Paul has taken a new direction with an increasingly open-minded approach to Paul; a conscious effort to bring Paul within the sphere of Judaism; a recognition that Paul's concerns for Gentiles and universal religion are ultimately derived from his Jewishness; an admiration for Paul as a great and influential theologian; and a proclivity to praise and highlight those aspects of Paul which can be characterised as 'Jewish'.[216] For Hagner, who is an Evangelical Christian, these developments only made the continued Jewish rejection of the gospel message all the more frustrating. As he complains,

Despite all the energy expended by Jewish scholars to uncover Paul's authentic Jewishness and to approach him positively and appreciatively, it is all the more remarkable that his theology is rejected *in toto*.[217]

---

[214] In addition to the surveys discussed below, it is also worth making reference to Paul Levertoff's short contribution, *St. Paul in Jewish Thought: Three Lectures*, because he comments, 'It is very remarkable indeed that St Paul, who for almost nineteen centuries had been either ignored by the representatives of Jewish thought or hated and despised by those Jews who happened to hear or read something about his conversion and his attitude towards the Law, Israel and the Gentiles, should, in our days, be considered by some Jews as one of the greatest religious geniuses and heroes of humanity' (14). However, Levertoff's survey, once it has highlighted a few texts from the rabbinic literature, only offers a selective overview of the treatments of Schiller-Szinessy, Claude Montefiore, and Franz Werfel. We will return to Levertoff in Chapter three.

[215] Hagner, 'Paul in Modern Jewish Thought', 143–65. Hagner's survey includes Claude Montefiore, Kaufmann Kohler, Joseph Klausner, Marin Buber, Leo Baeck, Samuel Sandmel, Hans Joachim Schoeps, Schalom Ben-Chorin, and Richard Rubenstien.

[216] Hagner, 'Paul in Modern Jewish Thought', 157–8.

[217] Hagner, 'Paul in Modern Jewish Thought', 158.

Meissner (1996)[218] also divides his larger survey into two groups, citing a 'paradigm shift' between earlier writers who regarded Paul as 'an apostate and founder of Christianity' who had debased pure Jewish theism with pagan-Hellenistic interpolations, and twentieth-century writers who had come to 'positively appreciate' the apostle as 'an important figure of Jewish religious history'.[219] For him, 'the homecoming of the heretic' was made possible by a combination of post-Holocaust commitment to dialogue, exposure of the anti-Judaic tendencies of earlier Christian views of Judaism, and the improved social position of postwar Jewish communities.[220]

Eisenbaum (2004)[221] likewise distinguishes between two periods of Jewish Pauline studies, that is, before and after 1950, but although she agrees that Jewish scholars of the earlier period saw Paul as 'the bad guy', she suggests that a more complicated picture emerges after 1950, when they became 'gradually more varied in their understanding of Paul.'[222] She does, however, contrast the earlier writers, who are described as 'apologists for Judaism', with the later ones, who are said to have adopted 'a scholarly stance, not a confessional one'.[223] The new diversity of perspectives on Paul continues to proliferate, she claims, 'precisely because there now exists more freedom from the constraints of personal identity', meaning, presumably, that the context for such work is less prejudiced and encourages greater academic freedom.[224]

Segal (2007) is just as keen to emphasise the difference between earlier writers who tended to 'use Paul as a symbol for their own particular theoretical understanding of Judaism and Christianity' and more recent Jewish commentators who are 'better understood as proponents of one or another school of New Testament criticism rather than representing a distinctive Jewish school of historiography.'[225] He differs from Eisenbaum slightly by attributing the change to an increased professionalism within New Testament scholarship so that 'Jews today are being educated in NT [New Testament] programs as NT scholars.'[226] As a result, although Segal accepts that some ideological concerns can affect Jewish scholars, he suggests

---

[218] Meissner, *Die Heimholung des Ketzers*. Old paradigm: Joseph Salvador, Samuel Hirsch, Heinrich Graetz, Elia Benamozegh, Isaac Mayer Wise, Kaufmann Kohler, Moritz Friedlaender, Claude Montefiore, Gottlieb Klein, Joseph Klausner, Martin Buber, and early Leo Baeck. New paradigm: late Leo Baeck, Hans Joachim Schoeps, Samuel Sandmel, Schalom Ben-Chorin, David Flusser, Richard Rubenstein, Michael Wyschogrod, Hyam Maccoby, Lester Dean, Alan Segal, Pinchas Lapide, and Daniel Boyarin.

[219] Meissner, *Die Heimholung des Ketzers*, 136–7.

[220] Meissner, *Die Heimholung des Ketzers*, 138–43.

[221] Eisenbaum, 'Following in the Footnotes of the Apostle Paul', 77–97. Pre-1950: Martin Buber and Leo Baeck. Post-1950: Richard Rubenstein, Alan Segal, Daniel Boyarin, and Marc Nanos.

[222] Eisenbaum, 'Following in the Footnotes of the Apostle Paul', 84, 89, 93.

[223] Eisenbaum, 'Following in the Footnotes of the Apostle Paul', 92.

[224] Eisenbaum, 'Following in the Footnotes of the Apostle Paul', 97n38.

[225] Alan Segal, 'Paul et ses exégètes juifs contemporains', 414. See also Segal, 'Paul's Religious Experience in the Eyes of Jewish Scholars', 321–43.

[226] Segal, 'Paul et ses exégètes juifs contemporains', 437.

'that they have been surpassed by ordinary scholarly exchange in the field [of New Testament scholarship].'[227]

Arguably, one can overstate the case for a paradigm shift.[228] We will have reason to question such a claim in the chapters to come, yet already, at this stage, it is possible to note that even the most generous of the modern approaches remain cautious about reclaiming Paul and his theology without qualification, and by no means have all of the key concerns and protestations of hostile commentators actually been addressed by those who wish to welcome the heretic home. Bearing in mind the emotional power of the popular view discussed in the previous chapter, it is not terribly surprising to learn that any new scholarly appreciation for the apostle has completely failed to impress wider Jewish opinion, which remains uninterested. Nor can one point to the kind of general Jewish scholarly consensus regarding Paul's Jewishness that one finds on the subject of Jesus' Jewishness, for example.[229]

Furthermore, any suggestion that the positive appreciation of Paul's Jewishness should be put down to a greater objectivity in scholarship should be regarded with suspicion. Eisenbaum's claim that the necessary conditions for this improvement were brought about by growing mutual respect between Jews and Christians in the postwar period overlooks the fact that positive Jewish portrayals of Paul long antedated the arrival of the interfaith era. Segal's claim that many Jewish scholars

---

[227] Segal, 'Paul et ses exégètes juifs contemporains', 440.

[228] Two earlier studies make no such claim. Halvor Ronning, 'Some Jewish Views of Paul as Basis of a Consideration of Jewish–Christian Relations', *Judaica* 24 (1968), 82–97, and Wiefel, 'Paulus in Jüdischer Sicht', 109–44, 151–67. Ronning's survey is short and only draws upon the Pauline studies of Claude Montefiore, Heinrich Graetz, Martin Buber, and Kaufmann Kohler. Rather than point to a nonexistent shift in attitudes among his thinkers as an indication of improved Jewish–Christian relations, he suggests that what is required is an honest appraisal of Jewish criticism of Christianity in general and Paul in particular. Nevertheless, for Ronning as a Christian scholar this does not imply that either side should stop trying to win the argument. 'The task', he explained, 'is to try in all *honesty* to change each other.' Ronning, 'Some Jewish Views of Paul', 95. Wiefel's survey is also limited in size. He analyses the negative appraisals of the historians Heinrich Graetz and Joseph Klausner and the philosophers Hermann Cohen and Martin Buber, and the more ambiguous religious-phenomenological approaches of Leo Baeck and Hans Joachim Schoeps, for what benefit he believes they offer Pauline studies more generally. The modern Jewish reception of Paul is of more than simple historical interest, he writes, for it 'helps to comprehend better Paul's personality and thinking'. In particular, modern Jewish Pauline scholarship represents a critical view of 'the character of the Pauline way of thinking as theology, at his Christ centrism, and at his insistence on the presence of salvation.' Wiefel, 'Paulus in Jüdischer Sicht', 165.

[229] It is noteworthy that the extensive survey by Fuchs-Kreimer (1990), which did not restrict itself entirely to New Testament scholarship, did not identify such a trend. Rather, drawing heavily upon the work of Christian scholars, she called for the very Jewish reassessment of Paul that Hagner, Meissner, and Eisenbaum see developing in the post-war period. Fuchs-Kreimer, 'The Essential Heresy'. Meissner reports that in a phone conversation three years later, however, Fuchs-Kreimer agreed that 'the positions which in 1986 . . . still appeared exceptional, represent with hindsight a shift in trend that one could absolutely describe as a paradigm shift.' Meissner, *Die Heimholung des Ketzers*, 6n30.

have become less biased because they have been trained to be professional New Testament experts only raises the question of which came first: the professional training or the disinclination for anti-Christian polemics? The key factor, surely, is the increased readiness of post-Enlightenment Jews to relax the boundaries of 'Jewishness' and an attraction to historical figures and beliefs that, traditionally, existed outside the mainstream. From this point of view, the Jewish study of Paul can be seen as a window onto the debate regarding the reformulation of Jewish religious self-definition. This would explain why the majority of positive appreciations of Paul were authored by progressives, who tend to be less exclusivist in defining Jewishness and more likely to embrace the pluralist assumptions of the modern academy.

Equally important is an awareness of the variety of ideological strategies adopted by modern Jews for relating to the Christian 'other'. Generally speaking, there have been two options. One can define oneself in terms of what is shared or one can define oneself in terms of what differentiates. Depending upon one's worldview and ideology, one can build bridges or one can build barriers. This way of looking at things is supported by the observations that, as we have seen, Jewish Pauline scholarship, from the beginning of the modern period until the present day, has included both those who recognise *and* those who deny the Jewishness of Paul. Thus one should be cautious about attributing the positive view, which has certainly gathered speed in the last couple of decades, to some kind of value-free scholarship made possible by the post-Holocaust respect for Judaism and Jewish learning.

The selective overview of Jewish thinkers offered above does not trace a chronological narrative that moved from anti-Christian polemic to a warmer appreciation of Paul resulting from more objective scholarship. Rather, it explores the ways in which Jewish scholars have used Paul to undermine or to reinforce relations between Jewish and Christian communities. It should be clear that the so-called Jewish reclamation of Paul is but one of several strategies available to modern Jews who are driven to define Judaism in terms of Christianity.[230] Whether positive appreciations of the apostle or vehement condemnations of him, Jewish commentaries on Paul should first and foremost be regarded as an opportunity for the ideological articulation of this complex relationship. Of course, when Jewish Pauline scholarship is approached for what it has to tell us about modern Jewish

---

[230] Likewise, Fuchs-Kreimer's survey of Jewish Pauline scholarship identifies four major functions of Jewish writings on the New Testament in the modern period, three of which clearly describe ways in which Jews relate to non-Jews: (1) to defend the integrity of first-century Judaism and by extension modern Judaism against the perceived attack in New Testament writings; (2) to define a boundary between Judaism and its 'other' in the West (that is, Christianity) in order to justify the continued separate existence of the Jewish people; (3) to link Jews with the majority culture by establishing a bond between Judaism and treasured aspects of Christian civilisation; and (4) to enable Jews to learn from and be challenged by a rediscovered Jewish, albeit sectarian, source for Jewish thought within the New Testament. Fuchs-Kreimer, 'The Essential Heresy', 8–9.

identity, the overtly polemical, religious agenda of the authors considered here represents only a part of the story. Other Jewish Pauline scholars have arguably abandoned the well-trodden paths of interfaith bridge- or barrier-building, and some have used their studies as a means by which to explore issues that reflect rather an in-house debate about the nature of Judaism and Jewish identity. To this we now turn.

3

Constructions of Paul in Intra-Jewish Debate: Establishing Jewish Authenticity

As we have seen, Jewish views of the apostle Paul are often discussed in the context of Jewish–Christian relations. This is because for many Jewish writers Paul represents an opportunity to contrast Jewish and Christian worldviews, or, for a select few, Paul potentially offers a chance to build relations and emphasise commonalities with Christians. Either way, Paul is used as a means by which to define Jewish religious views in relation to Christianity. For some writers, however, often those who are keen to distance themselves from anti-Christian polemics, alternative or additional agenda are apparent. A number of mainly progressive thinkers have used their studies as platforms from which to engage in a quite different kind of apologetic: an intra-Jewish one. As a result, Jewish Pauline studies can be regarded as a kind of ideological battlefield in which some of the most contentious issues for modern religious Jews feature prominently.

PAULINE STUDIES AS A FOREIGN THEATRE OF INTRA-JEWISH WARFARE

In 'A Jewish Ideological Perspective on the Study of Christian Scripture' (1997), the North American Reconstructionist rabbi and scholar Jonathan Brumberg-Kraus set out to identify and account for themes and areas that generate ideological conflict within Jewish New Testament scholarship in general.[1] He observed that a common feature of such studies was that the writers often emphasised their lack of interest in Jewish–Christian polemics and stressed their own scholarly objectivity in contrast to Jewish studies before them. This happened, he suggested, because of the importance of demonstrating commitment and loyalty to the Academy, which is coloured through and through with Christian thought and value judgements.[2] At the same time, Brumberg-Kraus suggested that the study of the New Testament had become a platform for ideological apologetics, a kind of foreign theatre of war in which *intra-Jewish* conflicts are commonly played out. Certain trouble zones or subject areas within New Testament studies appear to push the scholar beyond the

---

[1] Brumberg-Kraus, 'A Jewish Ideological Perspective', 121–52. Brumberg-Kraus's doctorate was in New Testament studies. Jonathan D. Brumberg-Kraus, 'Conventions of Literary Symposia in Luke's Gospel with Special Attention to the Last Supper', Ph.D. dissertation, Vanderbilt University (1991).

[2] Brumberg-Kraus, 'A Jewish Ideological Perspective', 135–9.

strict academic objectivity for which he or she strives, revealing ideological agendas
of one sort or another. The arguments often run along Progressive–Traditionalist
lines on issues such as how to establish Jewish authenticity, how to regard the Law
in the modern world, how to respond to non-Jewish culture and ideas, how to
regard marginal figures, how to relate Judaism and nationalism, and how to relate
Judaism and Christianity.

In the context of Jewish approaches to Paul specifically, Brumberg-Kraus's short
article only had space to focus on Jewish hostility towards the apostle. He emphasised the scholarly trend that contrasts Paul with Jesus and argues that the apostle
'was more inclined to Gentile forms of piety – Gnosticism or the mystery religions, or Greek-speaking Hellenistic Judaism (as opposed to "normative" rabbinic
or Palestinian Judaism)'.[3] It is typical of many Jewish scholars, Brumberg-Kraus
suggested, to label Paul as alienated or self-hating and to emphasise his *goyishkayt*.[4]
This highlighting of the negative view of Paul (a view which is common among traditionalists in particular) is unfortunate in that it neglects a number of writers on
Paul who have clearly sought to consider the apostle outside the familiar context of
Jewish–Christian polemics, that is, to go beyond the traditional, hostile view. And
in fact these individuals provide further illustrations of Brumberg-Kraus's observations about intra-Jewish apologetics. Participants in this ideological mêlée might
include Emil Hirsch, Claude Montefiore, Joseph Klausner, Micah Berdichevsky,
Hans Joachim Schoeps, David Flusser, Samuel Sandmel, Alan Segal, Pamela Eisenbaum, Tal Ilan, Amy-Jill Levine, Paul Levertoff, Sanford Mills, and Joseph Shulam.

OLDER BRITISH AND NORTH AMERICAN PROGRESSIVE PERSPECTIVES

Emil Gustav Hirsch (1851–1923), the Luxembourg-born son of the well-known
Reform rabbi Samuel Hirsch, strikingly demonstrated his position within the
contemporary intra-Jewish debate by the use he made of Paul. One of the most
radical Reform rabbis in the United States, he was the editor of the journals *The
Jewish Reformer* and *The Reform Advocate*, which he used to champion an evolutionary understanding of Judaism whereby ethical monotheism and the social
justice of the prophets took precedence over *halakhah* or Jewish religious law.
Although open to new influences and ideas, supporting the idea of Sunday as
the Jewish Sabbath, for example, he was suspicious of the growing Jewish secular nationalist or Zionist movement and was as scathing about Jewish ideological
alternatives to Reform as he was concerned to retain those who would assimilate
into the wider Christian society. His attitude towards the successful missionary
apostate, Paul, then, was always going to be highly charged.

---

[3] Brumberg-Kraus, 'A Jewish Ideological Perspective', 124.
[4] Brumberg-Kraus, 'A Jewish Ideological Perspective', 125. Brumberg-Kraus himself concludes by
noting that it is twentieth-century rather than first-century Jewish sensibilities that find Paul's
Christianity alien, the result of centuries of hostility.

In a characteristically eloquent sermon to his Chicago congregation, entitled 'Paul, the Apostle of Heathen Judaism, or Christianity' (1894),[5] Hirsch provocatively set out his position with regard to the traditional founding figure of Christianity, emphasising that Jesus had actually founded no new religion or creed. 'The religion of Jesus', he stated unambiguously, 'is our religion: Judaism, universal'.[6] Furthermore, Jesus' Jewish teachings, as expressed in the Sermon on the Mount, were to be highly prized not least because they contrasted so obviously with the later teachings and attitudes of the hostile Gentile Church.[7] After all, the Church was an amalgamation of Jewish and Greek thought and rather than this fusion occurring in the person of the Jewish Jesus, the focus in which 'sunlight from Palestine's hills and waves from Athens' acropolis met' was actually the mind of Paul.[8] By no means did this result in a wholesale condemnation of the Apostle to the Gentiles. Above heroes of the battlefield, or of thought, or the giants of industry, Hirsch maintained,

None of these has so materially, so deeply, so lastingly stamped his own thought upon the human race as has, and does to the present day, the poor misshappen [sic] Jew, Roman citizen though he was, whose cradle stood at Tarsus and whose school years were spent at the feet of Jerusalem's patriarchs. Should ever, by some hap or other, the greatest lights be extinguished in the galaxy spanning the centuries, longer than any other star would scintillate above in power his name. Yea, none has so deeply, I repeat, affected the destiny of the human family as has Paul the Apostle to the Gentiles. On his account wars were waged; by his doctrine humanity was cleft into hostile camps; his words have been the burden of many a human soul and again have been the stay

---

[5] The format of a sermon meant that Hirsch did not provide references to the New Testament, although he did refer on one occasion to a Christian authority, Edwin Hatch, whose 1888 Hibbert Lectures had been entitled 'The Influence of Greek Ideas and Usages upon the Christian Church'.

[6] Emil Hirsch, 'Paul, the Apostle of Heathen Judaism, or Christianity' reprinted in G. W. Foote and J. M. Wheeler, eds., *The Jewish Life of Jesus, Being the Sepher Toledoth Jeshu or Book of the Generation of Jesus*, trans. from the Hebrew (London: Progressive Publishing Company, 1885), 3. The introduction notes that this was a discourse 'delivered before Sinai Congregation, Chicago, 1894' and was bound with other discourses given in 1894 by Hirsch including 'The Jews and Jesus', 'Jesus, His Life and Times', and 'The Doctrines of Jesus', 26.

[7] 'The Sermon on the Mount is undoubtedly the most abundant casket of jewels drawn from the treasure house of high moral inspiration. There is no other necklace so valuable as this; the world has prized it; and as long as suns will rise and moons will wax and wane in the nightly sky, as long as man has not lost that appreciation for purity which is the best heirloom given to him, these words of Jesus will come to the soul as the whispered proclamation of the highest. A greater contrast cannot well be conceived, than that of the church three hundred, and two hundred years after Jesus' time, to his own – if his own they were – words and appeals.' Hirsch, 'Paul, the Apostle of Heathen Judaism, or Christianity', 3.

[8] Hirsch describes him admiringly: 'The apostle was a man of little prepossessing appearance; a man racked by disease; a man whose eyes were weak; a man who had to win his livelihood in the sweat of his brow; a man of whom no-one would have dreamt that under the misshapen body burned a fire-consumed soul. In such ungainly frame God's spirit loves to dwell occasionally. This tent-maker, bleary-eyed, disease-racked, lifted the Roman world out of its hinges.' Hirsch, 'Paul, the Apostle of Heathen Judaism, or Christianity', 26.

of as many other human hearts. He has cited the demons of terror to gather around the bed where agonized poor human mortal clay in terror and anxiety of what would come after the final struggle of life; and he has winged with confidence of peaceful hope and assurance other souls impatient to shuffle off this mortal coil and to enter the truer kingdom of light, of love and of life. Whatever our own religious opinions may be, this fact alone should assure for his words and his doctrines a careful and a close attention.[9]

This central figure in the history of Western civilisation is recognised by Hirsch as a learned Jew who studied at the Jerusalem Pharisaic academy of Gamaliel, and who 'grew up a strict observer of the law and well versed in the dialectics which anchored the legal enactments upon the rock bed of the Pentateuchal text.'[10] The conversion experience, when 'Saul the persecutor was changed into Paul the Apostle',[11] is treated by Hirsch as the key to understanding the apostle's thought. He sets aside the efforts of 'bungling rationalism' to present the account on the road to Damascus as a fabricated story or the result of a lightning-induced daze, nor can he accept orthodox Christianity's interpretation of it as the risen Christ. 'How do *we* account for the phenomenon?' he asks of his fellow Reform Jews. The answer lay in a combination of modern psychology's insight into autohypnotism or self-suggestion. 'Have you not had similar experiences', Hirsch asked his audience, 'have you not in the busy streets of Chicago turned to see whether face was behind you or form had followed you?'[12] Paul had been so bound up in a certain problem, so haunted by a specific issue, that he had almost lost touch with reality. The problematic issue had been, of course, that of the proper observation of the Law. Again, Hirsch asked his audience to stand in the shoes of the apostle and to understand him in his shared humanity.

[Paul asks himself] Why is it that the law does not satisfy me; why is it that I, the strict adherent of legal Judaism, am in constant danger of violating the law? Some of you who have been brought up under Jewish orthodox influence know what is implied in being a loyal Jew of the old school: not a motion of the hand but is tied to an article of the code; not a twitching of the finger but will brush against some other paragraph of the law. The conclusion is not far off – although it is not altogether true – that one is not free, but bound under the law, a slave under the law. That mechanical legalism cannot still the inborn yearning, is an unavoidable experience. It adds a new thorn to the flesh. This experience must have been Paul's. He must have fretted and chafed under the 'yoke of the law,' for he committed the error of overlooking the spirituality of the 'Law'.[13]

---

9   Hirsch, 'Paul, the Apostle of Heathen Judaism, or Christianity', 4–6.
10 Hirsch, 'Paul, the Apostle of Heathen Judaism, or Christianity', 11–12.
11 Hirsch, 'Paul, the Apostle of Heathen Judaism, or Christianity', 17.
12 Hirsch, 'Paul, the Apostle of Heathen Judaism, or Christianity', 12–13.
13 Hirsch, 'Paul, the Apostle of Heathen Judaism, or Christianity', 14–15.

While not fully accepting the Pauline criticism of the Law, Hirsch had no difficulty using the occasion as an opportunity to attack what he regarded as Orthodoxy's unhealthy obsession with the *halakhah*. As he went on to argue, 'From his premises, Paul is right in saying that the law, instead of decreasing sin, increases it. There is none that is perfect, that is the experience of the law.'[14]

Although Paul's ideas were often at odds with true Jewish sensibilities,[15] Hirsch maintained, nevertheless the apostle's decision to set aside the Law was 'the bold step' that made possible the fantastic success of Christianity. For Judaism before Paul's time had failed to win over the Gentiles; the barrier of the Law had kept out a waiting world. Admiringly, Hirsch observed, 'Paul, with one bold sweep of the pen opened up the gates for the conquest and conversion of the world.'[16] Were there lessons for the modern Jew, Hirsch wondered?

Had the Jews of that time been able to read the inscription on the wall, had they looked at the hand on the dial, they might have reclaimed the world with ethics, lived and taught by Jesus of Nazareth; they might have gone forth and brought to the thirsty the water, to the hungry the bread of life. But they would not, as today they will not. The times were ripe; Judaism neglected the opportunity. Paul embraced it. He preached in words comprehensible to the pagan world the doctrine which he had discovered in his own God-touched heart.[17]

And so Hirsch concludes that, despite the exception he might take to the Pauline system of thought in its totality, God had undoubtedly used Paul to carry Jewish thought into the world.[18] Certainly, Paul had underrated ethical action in contrast to a mystical faith.[19] Yet his exaggerated reaction against the legalism of the synagogue (which, with the advent of Reform Judaism, was now a moot point) was nevertheless echoed in a modern world rife with apostasy. In particular, the Orthodox Jewish fixation on the *halakhah*, he argued, drove many into irreligious assimilation, or Christianity, or modernist movements such as Felix Adler's Society for Ethical Culture, which advocated a socioethical worldview without the burden of a religion.[20]

Why is it that so many brought up among our orthodox will have nothing of Judaism after they escape from their tutors? Why is it that ethical culture finds nowhere so eager recruits as from the ranks of the orthodox Jews? [Moses] Mendelssohn's fate illustrates

---

[14] Hirsch, 'Paul, the Apostle of Heathen Judaism, or Christianity', 22.
[15] Hirsch identifies Paul's identification of Judaism with the Law, his dismissal of ethical action, and his mystical faith leading to salvation. Hirsch, 'Paul, the Apostle of Heathen Judaism, or Christianity', 24.
[16] Hirsch, 'Paul, the Apostle of Heathen Judaism, or Christianity', 23.
[17] Hirsch, 'Paul, the Apostle of Heathen Judaism, or Christianity', 23–4.
[18] Hirsch, 'Paul, the Apostle of Heathen Judaism, or Christianity', 25.
[19] Hirsch, 'Paul, the Apostle of Heathen Judaism, or Christianity', 24.
[20] This Society, often simply referred to 'ethical culture', was established 1876 by Hirsch's colleague, rationalist Reform rabbi Felix Adler (1851–1933). Hirsch maintained an impassioned opposition to this movement in his writings and sermons.

the reason. His own children went forth from Judaism and separated from it. The Mendelssohns are no longer Jews, they are officially Christians; it was the legalism of Mendelssohn that superinduced their apostasy.[21]

Just as Paul had sought freedom from the burden of guilt that he had carried only to replace 'the slavery of the Law' with 'the shackles of creed and dogma', so many modern Jews rallied to the cry 'Separate from Judaism!' without realising that their newfound 'freedom will soon yield to a new slavery.'[22] Reform Judaism, Hirsch assured his audience, understood that the highest human and liberal tendencies were best preserved in an historical framework, an already existent, naturally evolved system of ethico-religious thought. Thus, unlike Paul or those in the ethical culture movement, there was no need for Jews to leave Judaism in order to win the world.[23]

The first president of the World Union of Progressive Judaism, Claude Montefiore (1858–1938), also used Paul to critique his ideological enemies. A clear indication of this English scholar's position could be seen in his warning about directly comparing Paul's writings with those of the rabbis. His rationale for viewing such a contrast as 'unfair' was, for a Jewish writer, unusual, to say the least:

St Paul was a religious genius of the first order, who writes in the flush of fresh enthusiasm. The Midrash is a confused jumble of sermons, parables, sayings, and anecdotes without system or plan. There are indeed occasional flashes of genius, but most of it is of a very second and third-rate order of literary merit.[24]

Although recognising the 'contradictions and antinomies' in Paul's theology, he felt that there was still an overall coherence which made Paul far more systematic (that is, superior) than the rabbis.[25] In the context of the theological debates raging between progressive and traditionalist apologists, the jibe that Paul was superior to the rabbis would not have gone unnoticed.

As a liberal, Montefiore maintained that 'all the light has not shone through Jewish windows' and that inspiration and wisdom could be drawn from sources outside the corpus of traditional Jewish religious writings.[26] He argued, for example, that the teachings and attitudes of Jesus as portrayed in the New Testament represented, in some sense, those of an ideal liberal Jew.[27] Developing this progressive principle further, he suggested that even Paul could be approached for religious inspiration.

[21] Hirsch, 'Paul, the Apostle of Heathen Judaism, or Christianity', 24–5.
[22] Hirsch, 'Paul, the Apostle of Heathen Judaism, or Christianity', 25.
[23] Hirsch, 'Paul, the Apostle of Heathen Judaism, or Christianity', 26.
[24] Montefiore, 'Rabbinic Judaism and the Epistles of St. Paul', 170.
[25] Montefiore, 'Rabbinic Judaism and the Epistles of St. Paul', 170.
[26] Claude G. Montefiore, cited in Norman Bentwich, 'Claude Montefiore and His Tutor in Rabbinics: Founders of Liberal and Conservative Judaism', 6th Montefiore Memorial Lecture (Southampton: University of Southampton, 1966), 15.
[27] Langton, *Claude Montefiore*, 256–61.

In seeking to introduce Paul to a Jewish audience, Montefiore had been well aware of the obstacles in his path, not least the challenge of impartiality. He wrote,

It may be that the Jew is both too near Paul and too far from him to do him justice or even adequately to understand him. The ashes of old controversies still glow within the Jew's mind and heart. Just as it is very hard for the modern Christian . . . to understand and appreciate the Rabbinic religion, so it may also be very hard for the modern . . . Jew to appreciate and understand Paul.[28]

Nevertheless, his characteristic optimism led him to argue that if there were spiritual benefits to be gained from reading Paul – and he was convinced there were – then it would be in the interests of modern Jews to approach the epistles with a more open mind.

Ultimately, Montefiore regarded most of Paul's theology as fatally flawed. Paul's pessimism, his Christology, much in his conception of sin and of the Law, his demonology, and his view of human destiny had 'all gone by the board'.[29] Nor could Paul be of much use with regard to the Holy Spirit, or the character of God. This was because Paul's doctrine concerning these had to be pruned and curtailed before any use could be made of it, and even what remained did not significantly go beyond what had been taught in the Old Testament, the Apocrypha, and the rabbinical literature.[30]

Even so, there were fragments of the apostle that it suited Montefiore's purposes to concentrate upon, aspects which he regarded as having considerable relevance to Liberal Jews. At the top of this list was, of course, Paul's introduction of a practical (although imperfect) universalism. A stress on the universal aspects of Jewish religion was an integral part of the teaching of Montefiore's own Liberal Judaism. It does not come as a surprise, then, to find him praising those aspects of Paul's teaching that were concerned with 'breaking down the wall of distinction between Jew and Gentile'.[31] He himself had come to the same conclusion as Paul, namely that 'Judaism could not become a universal religion together with its inviolate Law'.[32] He believed that Paul's knowledge of the Hellenistic mystery cults had influenced his pre-Christian thinking and made him ready and eager to discover a universal method of salvation, suited and predestined for all humankind. But although he commended Paul for preaching universalism and solving the 'puzzle of the universal God and the national cult',[33] he could not accept the new form of religious particularism that Paul had forged. Neither could he credit Paul with

[28] Montefiore, *Judaism and St Paul*, 133–4.
[29] Montefiore, *Judaism and St Paul*, 141.
[30] Claude G. Montefiore, *The Old Testament and after* (London: Macmillan, 1923), 208.
[31] Letter from Benjamin Jowett to C. G. Montefiore, 14 September 1884. Lucy Cohen, *Some Recollections of Claude Goldsmid-Montefiore 1858–1938* (London: Faber & Faber, 1940), 35.
[32] Montefiore, *Judaism and St Paul*, 145.
[33] Claude G. Montefiore, *Liberal Judaism and Hellenism and Other Essays* (London: Macmillan, 1918), 119.

originating the idea. He felt that, keeping in mind Old Testament universalist passages such as those found in Jonah, Isaiah 51, and several Psalms, 'one has to acknowledge that Paul has only smoothed more completely, more definitely, what these others had begun to smooth before him'.[34] Liberal Judaism and its teachings of ethical monotheism, of course, polished off the job, and presented the clearest expression of this important Jewish tradition.

Again, Montefiore admired the apostle's teaching in not giving needless offence for the benefit of those who were 'weaker' in faith. This was a policy that he had attempted to practice in the context of the Anglo-Jewish response to his own Liberal teachings, especially with regard to the lax Liberal observation of the dietary laws.[35] Similarly, Montefiore felt that the controversial use of the vernacular in synagogue services could be justified along the lines of argument that Paul had offered so many centuries before.[36] There was even one element of Paul's objection to justification by works that was worth salvaging. According to Montefiore, the apostle had taught that one failed to win righteousness by fulfilling the Law because one could never fulfil it; worse still, one failed to win righteousness even if one did fulfil the Law. In spite of his recognition that 'no Jew ever looked at the Law from this point of view', Montefiore admitted that he felt there was, indeed, a danger that 'works righteousness' could lead to self-righteousness and self-delusion.[37] Interestingly, he also admired Paul's mysticism, 'its solemnity, its power and its beauty' even as a 'double outsider... that is, a Jew who is not a mystic'.[38] He especially appreciated Paul's teaching regarding the reproduction of the death and the risen life of the messiah in the experience of each individual believer, seeing in it a parallel to the rabbinic teaching that a proselyte, brought to the knowledge of the One God, was made new and recreated.[39] Paul's attitude towards suffering could also be learned from. He observed:

Paul not only rises superior to his sufferings, but he rejoices in them. And perhaps in this exultation and rejoicing lies the most peculiar and instructive feature of his career, the feature, moreover, in which he was, though perhaps unconsciously, in fullest accordance with the teaching of his Master and Lord.[40]

Thus Montefiore approached Paul as a source of inspiration and religious insight. More significantly, Pauline studies provided him with an opportunity to articulate

---

[34] Montefiore, *The Old Testament and after*, 287.

[35] Montefiore, *Judaism and St Paul*, 183.

[36] He quoted Paul's comments, 'If I know not the meaning of the language, the speaker is unintelligible to me' and 'How shall the unlearned say Amen to your thanksgiving, if he does not understand what you say?' Montefiore, *Judaism and St Paul*, 192–4.

[37] Montefiore, 'First Impressions of St. Paul', 443–44.

[38] Montefiore, *Judaism and St Paul*, 194. In a letter to Lucy Cohen, he remarked, 'I am no good at mysticism, only respectful'. Cohen, *Some Recollections*, 113.

[39] Montefiore, *Judaism and St Paul*, 193–4, 200.

[40] Montefiore, *Judaism and St Paul*, 201.

progressive, Liberal Jewish ideas; what more effective way to demonstrate the extent of his commitment to liberal principles and tolerant worldview than by a generous reassessment of the apostle to the Gentiles for the Jewish people?

ZIONIST PERSPECTIVES

A quite different reassessment was made by Joseph Klausner (1874–1956), a Jewish historian and prominent Zionist, whose approach to Paul was profoundly shaped by his nationalist ideology. Born near Vilna, Lithuania, Klausner studied in Germany and became a committed Zionist, attending the first Zionist Congress in Basle in 1897. Following the Bolshevik Revolution (October 1917), he emigrated from Odessa, Russia, to Palestine. From 1925 he taught modern Hebrew literature and the history of the Second Temple Period at Hebrew University. He became increasingly nationalist in his views and was regarded as the ideologue of the Revisionist Party, which from the 1920s and 1930s was the principal opposition to Weizmann's leadership. Not Orthodox, Klausner would probably have identified with the Conservative movement if it had existed in Eretz Yisrael at that time.[41] His historical writings on Jesus and Christian beginnings were the first such comprehensive treatments in Hebrew; in addition to *Jesus of Nazareth* (1922), he wrote *From Jesus to Paul* (1939).[42]

Klausner's interest in both Jesus and Paul stemmed from a concern to reclaim influential Jews for Jewish history or, more precisely, to utilise them in the Zionist project to construct a strong nationalist identity. This involved contrasting Jewish and Christian worldviews, as Klausner made clear in his conclusion.

My deepest conviction is this: Judaism will never become reconciled with Christianity (in the sense of spiritual [religious and intellectual] compromise), nor will it be assimilated by Christianity; for Judaism and Christianity are not only two different religions, but they were also *two different world-views*. Judaism will never allow itself to reach even in theory the ethical extremeness characteristic of Christianity; this extremeness has no place in the world of reality, and therefore is likely in actual fact to be converted into its direct opposite – into brutality such as has been seen in the Middle Ages and in our own time in any number of 'Christian' countries.[43]

---

[41] Kling argued that, although observant of tradition in matters of religion, Klausner was not Orthodox and many of his friends were secular Zionists. Simcha Kling, *Joseph Klausner* (Cranbury, NJ: Thomas Yoseloff, 1970).

[42] Klausner, *Jesus of Nazareth*. Hebrew original *Yeshu ha-Notsri* (Jerusalem: Shtibel, 1922). Klausner, *From Jesus to Paul*. Hebrew original *Mi-Yeshu ad Paulus* (Tel Aviv: Mada, 1939). Klausner cited Christian scholars such as Baur, Bauer, Bousset, Bultmann, Clemen, Deissmann, Delitzsche, Herford, Loisy, Reitzenstein, and Schweitzer and Jewish scholars such as M. Friedlaender, Graetz, and Kohler. He advised caution in using Acts of the Apostles, but believed that it contained much useful information. He regarded as authentic Romans, Galatians, Ephesians, and 1 and 2 Corinthians, 'and they corroborate much of what we know of Paul from Acts'.

[43] Klausner, *From Jesus to Paul*, 609.

The Zionist concern with the differences between Jewish and non-Jewish world-views provides the key to Klausner's understanding of Paul. The apostle's background had been one of Hellenistic Judaism and paganism. Far from *Eretz Yisrael*, Paul had been 'detached from authentic, living Judaism, which was rooted in its own soil'.[44] This accounted for his message, 'a whole new doctrine which was not Judaism, [but] which was in fact anti-Judaism, the complete antithesis of Judaism'.[45] Specifically, it accounted for his teachings regarding dying and rising gods.[46] But Klausner was drawn to Paul for more than simply the opportunity to hold him up as a representative of a hostile Christian religion or non-Jewish worldview. At the same time, there was a desire to reclaim Paul the Jew as a significant player in world history, to recognise even in the apostle to the Gentiles the genius and power of authentic Judaism. Klausner was appreciative of certain of Paul's 'lofty and beautiful' teachings,[47] and he acknowledged that the influential Christian thinker's dependence upon Torah (and even the oral law) had helped protect Judaism down through the centuries.[48] In attempting to have his cake and eat it, Klausner explained,

Intensive research over many years has brought the writer of the present book to a deep conviction that there is nothing in the teaching of Paul – not even the most mystical elements in it – that did not come to him from authentic Judaism. For all theories and hypotheses that Paul drew his opinions *directly* from the Greek philosophical literature or the mystery religions of his time have no sufficient foundation. But it is a fact that most of the elements in his teaching which came from Judaism received unconsciously at his hands *a non-Jewish coloring* from influence of the Hellenistic-Jewish and pagan atmosphere with which Paul of Tarsus was surrounded during nearly all of his life, except for the few years which he spent in Jerusalem. . . . [49]

Klausner was prepared to accept that Paul had probably studied for a while under Gamaliel in Jerusalem, his Pharisaic training evidenced by his use of scripture.[50] While there, he had possibly met Jesus and had come to vigorously oppose him.[51] A combination of Jesus' crucifixion and Stephen's martyrdom had provoked an epileptic fit or vision that had put Paul on a very different path, his guilt at opposing Jesus only being relieved by his devotion to the risen Christ.[52] Thereafter, Paul had

---

[44] Klausner, *From Jesus to Paul*, 465.

[45] Klausner, *From Jesus to Paul*, 443.

[46] Klausner, *From Jesus to Paul*, 344–5.

[47] Klausner, *From Jesus to Paul*, 603.

[48] Klausner, *From Jesus to Paul*, 606–9. The early Church Father Augustine portrayed the Jews as guardians of scripture, and argued that they should be protected so that their Law, which they did not accept testified to the truth of Christianity, should not be forgotten. Ironically, Klausner sees Paul in a similar role on behalf of the Jews, unwittingly acting as their protector as a result of his dependence upon the Law.

[49] Klausner, *From Jesus to Paul*, 466.

[50] Klausner, *From Jesus to Paul*, 309–12, 606–9.

[51] Klausner, *From Jesus to Paul*, 314–15.

[52] Klausner, *From Jesus to Paul*, 325–30.

devoted himself to the Gentiles, adopting a *Realpolitik* approach which Klausner recognised as making possible the success of Christianity, the contradictions he had introduced being both inevitable and necessary for that success.[53] The apostle's talent for adaptability ('a thorough-going opportunist . . . a clever politician') had allowed Paul to appeal to the Gentiles by teaching of the Jewish messiah without reference to Jewish nationality.[54] In that he believed that Jesus' teaching would not have won over the non-Jewish world, Klausner regarded Christianity as the creation of Paul, 'who was much more denationalized and divided in soul than was Jesus – the latter being a Jew of Palestine only, and hence not affected by foreign or conflicting influences'.[55] At the same time, he accepted that, as far as Paul was concerned, his negation of the importance of Israel's Torah that he had taught and preached had not cut him off from the people of Israel.[56]

Klausner's use of Paul as an object lesson, illustrating the opposing worldviews of Judaism and Christianity, was fundamentally a Zionist critique. Paul's inauthenticity was, he claimed, rooted in his lack of intimacy with the Land. His creation of a world religion was made possible only by denationalising Judaism, something that neither the prophets nor Jesus had sought to do. All the same, one is left in no doubt that that any positive assessment of his significance should be understood in terms of the influence of authentic Judaism. After all was said and done, Paul was a Jew and a significant figure in the national history of the Jewish people.[57] The unresolved tension accounts in part for Klausner's somewhat confusing claim that Paul's new religion was 'Judaism and non-Judaism at the same time'.[58]

Micah Joseph Berdichevsky (1865–1921), also known as Mikha Yosef Bin-Gorion, was another well-known Hebrew writer and thinker who offered a Zionist treatment of Paul. Born into a Hasidic rabbinic family in Ukrainian Medzibezh, Berdichevsky underwent a traditional *yeshiva* education that was undermined by his surreptitious reading of *Haskalah* works. These writings of the Jewish Enlightenment eventually resulted in rebellion and a lifelong literary obsession with the inner turmoil of individuals torn between modern ideas and traditional ways of life

---

[53] Klausner, *From Jesus to Paul*, 429–30.

[54] Klausner, *From Jesus to Paul*, 312, 431, 446.

[55] Klausner, *From Jesus to Paul*, 309–12, 590.

[56] Klausner, *From Jesus to Paul*, 415–16.

[57] An eloquent example of this national pride in Paul was offered much earlier by the first reader in rabbinics at Cambridge University, Solomon Schiller-Szinessy, writing in an altogether more conciliatory tone with regard to Christianity. 'How the feeble, almost blind and epileptic little Jew [Paul] dethroned the mighty gods of Olympus, is it not duly set forth in the history of the world in general and in that of the Christian Church in particular? And can this narrative be read by a Jew without deep emotion? Next to the pride which a religious Jew naturally feels in being a child of the race and religion of Israel, he surely must feel proud of that man and his race and religion who had the power over nations and kingdoms, not merely to root out and to pull down, to destroy and to throw down heathenism, but also to build and to plant Christianity – the Judaism of the Gentiles.' S. M. Schiller-Szinessy, 'St Paul from a Jewish Point of View', *The Expositor*, ed. W. Robertson Nicoll (London: Hodder and Stoughton, 1886), IV:329–30.

[58] Klausner, *From Jesus to Paul*, 465.

and thought. After leaving Russia he studied in both Switzerland and Germany, where he settled; his compositions in Yiddish, German, and Hebrew included articles and stories, collections of Hebrew myths, and analyses of the origins of Judaism, with particular emphasis on the Samaritans. He has been described as one of the founding fathers of secular Jewish nationalism, not least because his compilations of Jewish legends championed a nationalistic, worldly alternative to the religiously normative view of Jewish history.[59] But it is for his scholarly writings on Christianity that this giant of modern Hebrew literature is of interest here. In addition to the posthumous *Jesus Son of Hanan* (1959)[60] – which controversially identified Jesus of Nazareth with the Jesus ben Hanan mentioned in Josephus *and* with the New Testament martyr Stephen – Berdichevsky also wrote the equally incendiary *Saul and Paul* (1971). Both were probably originally written in Berlin, shortly before the author's death.[61]

Shaul ve-Paul represents one of the most striking interpretations of the apostle to the Gentiles offered by any Jewish author, and one which ran entirely contrary to the traditional Christian account of the Jewish Saul who converted to become the Christian Paul and apostle to the Gentiles. The main idea appears to have been that Saul and Paul were two different individuals whose distinct traditions had been amalgamated by the early Christians into the familiar New Testament narrative. In developing his theory, Berdichevsky identified the earliest version of Paul's blinding and conversion as the mysterious Hebrew legend of Abba Gulish, a non-Jewish pagan priest who converted to Judaism and spread his teaching among the Gentiles of the Hellenistic world. (This legend, to which we shall turn shortly, can be read in translation in the Appendix). Later, Berdichevsky suggested, the Gentile followers of Paul and the Jewish followers of Jesus merged this figure with another, a Jew called Saul, to create the composite, fictitious figure of Saul-Paul, who functioned as a unifying figure between the two groups and as a bridge between the Hellenistic and the Jewish elements of Christian thought.

As the work of an uprooted, marginal thinker, capable of embracing logically contradictory positions and emotions, Berdichevsky's manuscript does not make for easy analysis.[62] To make matters worse, he failed to complete his study of Paul,

59   Berdichevsky, *Miriam and Other Stories*, trans. Avner Holtzman (New Milford: The Toby Press, 2004), 9.
60   Micah Yosef Berdichevsky [Bin Gorion], *Yeshu ben Hanan*, edited by Immanuel Bin Gorion (Jerusalem: Mosad Ha-Rav Kuk, 1959).
61   Micah Yosef Bin Gorion [Berdichevsky], *Shaul ve-Paul*, edited by Immanuel Bin Gorion (Tel Aviv: Moreshet Micha Yosef, 1971). The fragmentary nature of the work makes dating difficult, with some parts self-evidently written long before the other parts.
62   For example, Berdichevsky's primary interest in the parallels between Paul and Abba Gulish are undermined by his speculative identification of Paul with several other individuals including Apollos in the New Testament and possibly even Rabbi Akiva in the Talmud. Bin Gorion, *Shaul ve-Paul*, 36, 127, 129–30. More difficult still is the confusing interchangeability of the names Saul, Saulus, Paul, Paulus, Saul-Paul, and Abba Gulish. It appears that Berdichevsky had not entirely decided upon the strict distinction between the Jewish figure of Saul and the Gentile figure of Paul or Abba Gulish. Within the first part of the book, he could write, for example, 'Another detail which may give proof

and it was left to his literary executors to collate the material and publish it in fragmented form.[63] In terms of sources for the life of Paul, Berdichevsky's interest in the New Testament was limited. His use of Acts was focused primarily upon passages where the apostle was involved in a mission to the Gentiles and where he confronted Hellenistic worship and ritual. He was also suspicious of the Epistles, which he regarded merely as literary forms expressing the views of a fictional character.[64] Nevertheless, he accepted that the New Testament did offer evidence of a Jew called Saul, about whom little is actually known, who was also mentioned in Jewish sources. According to Berdichevsky, the first authentic reference to this Saul is Acts 13:2–3, where he is said to have been chosen by the Holy Spirit;[65] just as

of Abba Gulish and Abba Saul being identical. Paul the Apostle was also slandered against in that he had embezzled funds meant for the poor'. Bin Gorion, *Shaul ve-Paul*, 18. Within the Notes section, he explicitly identifies Abba Gulish with both Abba Saul and Paul (for example, ibid., 126, 127) and explicitly distinguishes between Saul and Paul (for example, ibid., 127, 128, 129). Nevertheless, Berdichevsky's son and editor, Immanuel Bin Gorion, understood the two-person theory to be his father's main thesis, explaining, 'The book was to be given the title *Saul and Paul* in order to demonstrate from the start that, in the author's opinion, these are two traditions; not necessarily a case of Saul the Jew turning into Paul the apostle to the Gentiles, but a case of the original figure being one of a non-Jew.... [Only later] was created that intermediate figure, Saul of Tarsus.' Comments by Immanuel Bin Gorion in Bin Gorion, *Shaul ve-Paul*, 7, 145. The two-person theory is also the reading adopted in, for example, Yotam Hotam, 'Berdichevsky's *Saul and Paul*: A Jewish Political Theology', *Journal of Modern Jewish Studies* 6/1 (March 2007), 51–68, and Brumberg-Kraus, 'A Jewish Ideological Perspective on the Study of Christian Scripture', 124.

[63] Comments by Immanuel Bin Gorion in Bin Gorion, *Shaul ve-Paul*, 7. Berdichevsky's wife, Rachel Bin Gorion, translated some of the book from the original German into Hebrew and his son, Immanel Bin Gorion, finished the translation, arranged it, and added editorial comments together with a short introduction, a summary chapter, and an endnote. Of Micah's material, the first part, which was entitled Consecutive Chapters and which was almost completed, includes the story of Abba Gulish and analyses the different versions of the accounts of Paul's conversion, offers a commentary on a number of episodes in the Acts of the Apostles such as Paul's visits to Athens and Ephesus, and considers such themes as the distinction in Christian tradition between the killed hero (Jesus) and the escaped hero (Paul). The second part, which was entitled Diverse Chapters, includes standalone studies of various Pauline topics such as the purpose of Paul's visit to Jerusalem, speeches in Paul's defence, and his views on baptism. It begins with a short introductory piece in which Berdichevsky offers a critical reading of Acts of the Apostles. The third part, which is entitled Notes, is a set of jottings from his work journal which includes possible alternative versions. Berdichevsky had planned to write another section that identified traces of Paul (and Peter) in the writings of Josephus and also include an appendix devoted to the epistles attributed to Paul and demonstrating that 'Pauline' polemic had been directed again the Samaritans (this being a favourite subject in Berdichevsky's researches).

[64] 'More than once (in the books of the New Testament) we have before us a fictional apostle's letter'. Bin Gorion, *Shaul ve-Paul*, 102. According to Immanuel Bin Gorion, his father also searched for traces of Paul and his teachings in Flavius Josephus, although with what success we do not know because he never wrote the chapter. He had been particularly interested in the case of the unknown man on whose account the Jews were expelled from Rome (*Antiquities* 13.3.5). Comments by Immanuel Bin Gorion in Bin Gorion, *Shaul ve-Paul*, 7.

[65] Bin Gorion, *Shaul ve-Paul*, 126. Acts 13:2–3: 'While they were ministering to the Lord and fasting, the Holy Spirit said, "Set apart for Me Barnabas and Saul for the work to which I have called them." Then, when they had fasted and prayed and laid their hands on them, they sent them away.' In fact, according to Berdichevsky, the Saul of the New Testament is himself a composite character. He regards the young man at whose feet Stephen's executors laid their cloaks (Acts 7) as a distinct figure from the Saul who persecuted the early Christians. Although 'later legend combined them

significantly, Christian tradition held that he had received his divine calling from the risen Jesus.[66] The same character could also be found in Jewish literature. No doubt referring to a sage from the mishnaic period called Abba Shaul, Berdichevsky stated, 'Abba Saul is a figure of importance among the tannaim [sages]'.[67] He also makes the unsubstantiated assertion that '[i]n modern Hebrew literature, Paul the apostle is sometimes called Abba Saul.'[68] In summary, the only thing known for sure about this Saul (from Berdichevsky's point of view) was that he was Jewish.[69]

Berdichevsky's conceit is that one need not identify this Jewish Saul with the figure of Paul. To learn more about Paul, one should rather turn to the tale of Abba Gulish. This apocryphal story was valued very highly by Berdichevsky because he believed it to be derived from a Hebrew tradition that was ancient enough to be taken seriously as an alternative to the New Testament account(s) of Paul. Although the legend was discovered in a medieval manuscript, he emphasised that it was 'written in the Hebrew of the Mishnaic and Talmudic period'; that is, it possessed an ancient pedigree.[70] Because it was not to be found in the Talmudic literature, he was also hopeful that it was relatively free from religious bias.[71]

into a single figure', Berdichevsky was not convinced that 'the same young man who looked after the garments became the zealous persecutor of Stephen's followers and the destroyer of the community'. Ibid., 32.

[66] '[Saul] had the privilege to be called, according to legend, by Jesus . . . Jesus appeared to him ['Saul-Paul'] after his [Jesus'] death'. Bin Gorion, *Shaul ve-Paul*, 127–8.

[67] 'Tannaim' refers to the sages living in the first to second centuries who were involved in the compilation of the Mishnah. For brief references to Abba Saul, see Niddah 24b and Avot 2:8. Bin Gorion, *Shaul ve-Paul*, 18, 21–2. Later, he asserts that the story of Paul (Abba Gulish), who had opposed pagan idols with the knowledge of the one true god, had influenced Talmudic and Midrashic tales of Abraham attacking statues of idols. Such influence was suggestive to him of an early date for the story of Abba Gulish. Ibid., 129.

[68] Bin Gorion, *Shaul ve-Paul*, 17.

[69] As Immanuel Bin Gorion notes, '[W]e can only say with certainty about . . . the one called Saul, that he was Jewish, which is obviously not the case with Paul'. Comments by Immanuel Bin Gorion in Bin Gorion, *Shaul ve-Paul*, 145.

[70] The story was included in a collection of *aggadot* called *Sefer hama'asiyot* or *The Book of Tales* which Moses Gaster (1856-1939) had found and dated variously from the ninth to the thirteenth centuries, and which he had published as an appendix to Moses Gaster, *Judith Montefiore College Ramsgate: Report for the Year 1894-5 and Report for the Year 1895–6 . . . Together with the Ancient Collections of Agadoth, the Sefer ha-Maasiyoth* (Ramsgate: Judith Montefiore College, 1896), and later republished in *The Exempla of the Rabbis: Being a Collection of Exempla, Apologues and Tales culled from Hebrew Manuscripts and Rare Books* (London/Leipzig: Asia Publishing Company, 1924). For a discussion of Gaster's interest in *Sefer hama'asiyot*, see Philip S. Alexander, 'Gaster's *Exempla of the Rabbis*: A Reappraisal' in G. Sed-Rajna, ed., *Rashi 1040-1990: Hommage à Ephraim E. Urbach* (Paris: CERF, 1993), 793–805. Berdichevsky was delighted to discover that the story was also to be found in the *Midrash ha-Gadol* (published as David Zvi Hoffman, *Great Midrash: Exodus*, 2 vols. [Berlin: Verein MeKize Nirdamin, 1913–21]), a compilation of commentaries on the Torah dating from perhaps the fifteenth-century which apparently drew upon a lost source that included the tale of Abba Gulish and whose text is identical to that of the *Sefer hama'asiyot* (except for its attribution). Bin Gorion, *Shaul ve-Paul*, 11, 13, 15–16.

[71] Berdichevsky explains his rationale: 'It will not be surprising to say that Rabbinical texts, written in the Talmudic and Midrashic period, are capable of reflecting a much earlier period. Ancient themes, excluded from the Holy Scriptures due to dogmatic or historical tendencies, have come up again and

In the story of Abba Gulish we have a Hebrew text about Saul-Paul and his path to the faith.... But it is no secondary [or derivative] text of Paul's conversion as presented in Acts of the Apostles. The story of Abba Gulish needs to be seen as a relic from an earlier time.... [A] picture emerges which is nearer the historical background than that presented in Acts.[72]

This story tells of a pagan called Abba Gulish who served as a priest in 'an idolatrous temple' in Damascus and who used to pilfer the donations. Habitually calling upon his idol for healing and receiving none, he one day called upon 'the Sovereign of the Universe', who promptly cured him. Moving to Tiberias, where he converted to Judaism, 'he ran after the *mitzvot* [commandments]' and began a new life as an administrator for the poor. Eventually he was overcome by temptation and began embezzling money again – with the consequence that he went blind. Returning to Damascus, he stood before the Gentiles (who believed that he had lost his sight because he had scorned the idol) and delivered a public speech. Pointing out that in all the time he had stolen from the temple donations the idol had never punished him, he went on to confess that he had resumed his criminal activities in Tiberias until struck down. He therefore attributed his condition not to the idol but to the One 'whose eyes roam the whole world and no misdeed is beyond Him to see [and punish]', whereupon, after his having witnessed to God's power and judgement, his sight was miraculously restored. The account concludes, 'from the nations thousands and tens of thousands... [found] shelter under the wings of the shekhinah', that is, converted to Judaism.[73]

According to Christian tradition, Paul had been a Jewish convert to Christianity, whereas Abba Gulish had been a pagan who converted to Judaism. What, then, made Berdichevsky think that Abba Gulish and Paul were one and the same person? His evidence was a string of intriguing parallels in the stories. He highlighted the importance placed in both accounts upon Damascus,[74] and noted that both Paul and Abba Gulish had been treasurers[75] associated with accusations of

become preserved in Talmudic literature, some in disguised and some in open fashion. In the body of religious tractates whose main aim is to strengthen and exalt monotheistic faith, you occasionally come across idolatrous residues form the earlier days, and these residues completely contradict the book's intentions and morality'. Bin Gorion, *Shaul ve-Paul*, 18.

[72] Bin Gorion, *Shaul ve-Paul*, 17. Rather confusingly, Berdichevsky says in this paragraph: 'Abba Gulish is to be read as Abba Saul.' Because his main thesis is to *distinguish* between the Jewish Saul and the Gentile Abba Gulish or Paul, this must be put down to a copying error or confusion or evidence of Berdichevsky's experimentation with an alternative theory.

[73] See the appendix 'The Story of Abbu Gulish in *The Book of Tales*' for the full English translation.

[74] Bin Gorion, *Shaul ve-Paul*, 126. Famously, Paul's conversion was on the road to Damascus, and Chapters 9, 22 and 26 of Acts of the Apostles tell how he remained in the city after his conversion. Other references to his time in the city include 2 Cor. 11:32 ('In Damascus the ethnarch under Aretas the king was guarding the city of the Damascenes in order to seize me') and Gal. 1:17 ('nor did I go up to Jerusalem to those who were apostles before me; but I went away to Arabia, and returned once more to Damascus.')

[75] Bin Gorion, *Shaul ve-Paul*, 126. For example, Acts 11:29–30 recounts how Paul delivered famine relief to Jerusalem: 'And in the proportion that any of the disciples had means, each of them determined

embezzlement of funds meant for the poor.[76] Both men were described as zealous against idolatry,[77] both became fully convinced of the new faith's power and truth having had their blindness miraculously healed,[78] and both were responsible for the conversion of many Gentiles.[79] Pointing out that, as a convert, Abba Gulish would not have been appointed administrator of poor money entrusted to the temple priest, Berdichevsky came to the conclusion that the text as it stood did not make sense, and that it must have been referring to 'a *new* community whose members, who had just come to the faith, appointed him their treasurer'.[80] The conversion of Abba Gulish, he argued, had been from idolatry to an early form of Christianity rather than to Judaism. Thus the story was in fact a *Christian* one, albeit preserved in modified form by a Jewish source. In Berdichevsky's mind, the legend of Abba Gulish represented an alternative but more authoritative version of the conversion of Paul. He argued that the recognition of Paul's pagan background also explained his success among them, for real influence over the Gentiles could only have been exerted by one who had emerged from among them, and all the more so by a former priest.[81] When properly reconstructed, the story ran as follows:

[Paul] was an idolatrous priest in a temple in Damascus; and there appears to have been there a small Christian community, which was persecuted by the idolatrous priests, and especially by [Paul]. At a time of severe illness and inner distress, [Paul] appealed to the god of the Christians and was healed; at that moment he became a Christian. On behalf of the Christian community he was appointed as treasurer, became blind, went back to Damascus and could see again. Thanks to the miracle, he succeeded in converting Damascenes to Christianity.[82]

---

to send a contribution for the relief of the brethren living in Judea. And this they did, sending it in charge of Barnabas and Saul to the elders.' Other references to Paul's fiscal responsibilities include Acts 24:17 ('Now after several years I came to bring alms to my nation and to present offerings') and Gal. 2:10 ('They [i.e., the Christian leaders in Jerusalem] only asked us to remember the poor – the very thing I also was eager to do.')

[76] Berdichevsky infers this from 2 Cor. 8:20–21, where Paul wrote of 'taking precaution so that no one will discredit us in our administration of this generous gift'. Bin Gorion, *Shaul ve-Paul*, 18.

[77] Citing the accounts of Paul's speeches to the pagans (Acts 17:16–34) and in Ephesus (Acts 19:23–41), Berdichevsky points out that Paul's theology simply focuses on idolatry and is therefore a lot less refined than in other speeches, implying greater authenticity. Bin Gorion, *Shaul ve-Paul*, 126.

[78] Saul's three days of blindness ('And he was three days without sight, and neither ate nor drank', Acts 9:9) are also compared to the biblical accounts of how Joseph held his brothers under arrest for three days (Gen. 42:17) and Jonah's three-day sojourn in the bowels of the fish (Jon. 1:17). Bin Gorion, *Shaul ve-Paul*, 34.

[79] Comments by Immanuel Bin Gorion in Bin Gorion, *Shaul ve-Paul*, 149. The book of Acts outlines Paul's missionary success among the gentiles and relative failure among the Jews on three great missionary journeys (Acts 13:4–15:35, 15:36–18:22, 18:23–20:38).

[80] Bin Gorion, *Shaul ve-Paul*, 18.

[81] Bin Gorion, *Shaul ve-Paul*, 126.

[82] Bin Gorion, *Shaul ve-Paul*, 126. This is one of several occasions when, rather confusingly, Berdichevsky writes 'Saul' despite the fact that the logic of the two-person theory requires 'Paul'. It may be a copying error or reflect some confusion in his thought. Possibly this is a draft in which Berdichevsky was experimenting with an alternative theory in which Saul, Paul, and Abba Gulish

The Hebrew version of the story might have been adapted by its editors so that the name 'Jesus' had been replaced by 'Sovereign of the Universe', but the essence of the story remained the same: the hero was a pagan who became an emissary to the pagans on behalf of a community of the faithful.[83] Without explaining how there came to be an embryonic Christian community in Damascus for Paul or Abba Gulish to join in the first place, Berdichevsky was nonetheless convinced that the former pagan priest had soon found himself leading this Gentile Christian group and, ultimately, should be held responsible for its spectacular success.

Over time, Berdichevsky suggested, this new anti-idolatrous Gentile movement sought to attach itself to the existing monotheistic tradition of Judaism.[84] With the destruction of the Temple, Judaism itself had become fragmented, and it so happened that the form of Judaism that the Gentile Paulinists found most conducive was the Jewish-Christian movement, that is, the followers of Jesus.[85] The Gentile known as Abba Gulish or Paul and the Jew Saul were two different people, but, as a means by which to give Gentile Christianity greater credibility, they were merged within Christian tradition. Berdichevsky argued that 'only after the characters of Saul and Paul were joined together was a story of conversion attributed to Saul, also.'[86] As he explained,

A religious movement became attached to Abba Gulish the convert. The circle of the followers of Jesus . . . which converged after his death, was initially independent and developed separately. Later on the two movements merged. . . . Paul, the gentile, became connected with the figure of Saul since the latter had the privilege to be called by Jesus, according to legend.[87]

The predominance of the miraculous conversion story within Christian tradition could be accounted for psychologically in terms of the desire of many early Christians to sever their oppressive ties to their past, 'and Paul's example served as a source of encouragement for them.'[88]

Berdichevsky was keen to stress several key findings. First, Christianity's roots had been pagan, not Jewish. Second, Gentile Christianity's ancient strategy to

---

are one person. According to the two-person theory, he cannot actually mean 'Saul', because he argues elsewhere that Saul was a distinct person, a Jew who is referred to in the early part of Acts and (as Abba Shaul) in a few tractates in the Talmud. He cannot mean 'Saul-Paul' because he is explicit elsewhere that this character of Christian tradition is a fictional construct that amalgamates the Jewish Saul with the Gentile Paul. In this quotation, then, 'Saul' has been replaced with 'Paul.'

[83] Bin Gorion, *Shaul ve-Paul*, 126.

[84] 'Paulinism and Islam are two religions which arose by themselves and only later sought to become tied to Judaism'. Bin Gorion, *Shaul ve-Paul*, 129.

[85] Bin Gorion, *Shaul ve-Paul*, 128.

[86] Bin Gorion, *Shaul ve-Paul*, 126–7. References to Paul's conversion can be found in Acts 9:1–39, 22:1–22, 26:9–24, 1 Cor. 9:1 and 15:3–8, and Gal. 1:11–12, 15–16. In Acts, the name Saul is used until 13:9, after which Paul becomes the preferred name ('Then Saul, who was also called Paul, filled with the Holy Spirit, looked straight at Elymas . . . ').

[87] Bin Gorion, *Shaul ve-Paul*, 127, 128.

[88] Bin Gorion, *Shaul ve-Paul*, 37.

invest itself with authority by associating with Judaism had now been revealed and discredited. Third, the universalist tendency of its founder, Paul, had been trumped by the Jewish nationalist spirit for, according to Berdichevsky, the historical development had been from the notion of a cosmic Christ to that of a Jewish messiah, and not *vice versa*, as many scholars would have it. According to his own researches,

Gentile Christianity won 'ordination' from Judaism after the fact . . . Christianity did not reach the Gentiles via Jewish Christianity. It stands more to reason that Christianity, which was Gentile from its beginning, succeeded in gaining followers among the Jews. Accepted opinion indicates, of course, a reverse process: Jewish Christianity existed first, and then a Gentile Christianity was added to it; the two competed and finally the Gentile Christianity won. But it is near certain that things occurred in a different order. It appears that Christianity was born within Diaspora Jewry; through the conversion of many Gentiles, new ideas and redemptive hopes arose. These *general* ideas slowly took on a *national* form; thus it turned out that the saviour of humankind gradually became the saviour of Israel. . . . [T]he Jewish-national Christianity rose up against the international ambitions which had preceded it.[89]

Both Klausner and Berdichevsky had sought to criticise Paul from a Zionist perspective. But whereas Klausner had ultimately found fault with the Diaspora Pharisee in his lack of nationalist feeling yet, at the same time, had been uncomfortable about disowning him entirely, Berdichevsky's critique was quite unambivalent. Attributing historicity to a Hebrew Jewish legend rather than a Greek Christian one, Berdichevsky saw Paulinism as an essentially pagan philosophical system. But whereas many before and after him would find the seeds of Christianity in the Jewish Paul's adoption of non-Jewish, Hellenistic ideas, Berdichevsky went one step further and denied Paul even a Jewish birth. In this way he refuted the idea that Christianity was simply Judaism polluted by pagan thought; rather, by attributing its emergence to a pagan priest, the Zionist scholar sought to demonstrate the fundamentally non-Jewish, alien nature of Christianity.[90]

---

[89] Bin Gorion, *Shaul ve-Paul*, 128. This was reflected in the Christian literature. 'In the Acts of the Apostles, the figure of Paul became secondary in importance compared to the figure of Saul; in other words, Saul overcame Paul'. Ibid., 129.

[90] Fundamentally, the logic of Berdichevsky's anti-Christian polemic fails at an internal level. He assumed three concentric rings of Jewish authenticity in the ancient world (that is, Palestinian Jewry, Diaspora Jewry, and converts to Judaism) and stressed that the first two had already diverged considerably in the first century. It was the third circle, that of the pagan converts to Diaspora Judaism, he says, that had been the source of early Christianity (Bin Gorion, *Shaul ve-Paul*, 128). It is therefore difficult to see how, if Berdichevsky had finished his book, he would have reconciled the claims that Paul converted to Christianity *and* that he was responsible for its pagan origins. If the 'small Christian community' in Damascus which Abbu Gulish/Paul joined was 'Christian' in any meaningful sense, then where did they get their ideas from if not from a Jewish-Christian source? Why call them 'Christians' (*notzrim*) if they are understood to have no connections to the Christ, Jesus of Nazareth? If, on the other hand, these 'Christians' whom Abba Gulish/Paul joined as a convert had been composed of pagan converts to Judaism who had veered away to create a new

A 'PROTESTANT JEWISH' PERSPECTIVE

The anti-Zionist scholar of religious history, Hans Joachim Schoeps (1909–1980), wrote about Paul in such a way as to extol a quite different understanding of Judaism. Born in Berlin of Jewish parents who died in the Holocaust, Schoeps emigrated to Sweden in 1938 and returned to Germany after the Second World War, where he taught religious/intellectual history at the University of Erlangen, specialising in early Christianity. A proponent of German nationalism from his youth, he was mistaken by many as supporting Nazi ideology; in 1933 he argued that it was possible to distinguish German Jews from Eastern European Jews and Zionists (a view he later retracted). His particular understanding of German nationalism required a theological component, and for Schoeps this component could easily be Judaism; he regarded himself as converted to Judaism by a Jewish friend. His theology was influenced by the Swiss Protestant theologian Karl Barth and emphasised the basic sinfulness and poverty of humanity and a lack of access to God. In addition, he excluded all legal as well as national cultural elements, emphasising a brotherhood 'whose spirit was poured into the world by Christ'. His theological Judaism viewed Jewish identity in terms of belonging to the Sinaitic covenant, rather than to a Jewish race.

Seeking to draw a line under the question of whether Paul's background had been Hellenism, Hellenistic Judaism, or Palestinian Judaism, Schoeps argued in *Paul: The Theology of the Apostle in the Light of Jewish Religious History* (1961) that, methodologically, it was useful to recognise the influences of all three in understanding Paul.[91] Paul demonstrated a characteristic rabbinic style, suggesting rabbinism as a starting point.[92] Much of his Jewish teaching had been eschatological, including a personal messiah and a day of punishment.[93] Such areas of interest were unfamiliar to the Hellenistic world and so Hellenism should be regarded as only nuancing Paul's teachings.[94] Paul could be thought of as a Diaspora Pharisee who became a disciple of Gamaliel in Jerusalem.[95] As for the influence of pagan Hellenism, this

universalist religion (a kind of proto-Christianity), why not say so, and why not explicitly define which of their beliefs should be regarded as foundational for Christianity? The unresolved tensions that proliferate throughout the work reveal the Zionist author's primary concern, namely, to preserve the Jewish land, religion, and people from the charge that they had given birth to Christianity; he could not tolerate the idea of Israel tainted by the link to the Diaspora religion *par excellence*.

[91] Hans Joachim Schoeps, *Paul*, 47, originally published as *Paulus: Die Theologie des Apostels im Lichte der Jüdischen Religionsgeschichte* (Tübingen: Mohr, 1959). Schoeps cited literally hundreds of Christian Pauline scholars and a number of Jewish commentators, including Benamozegh, Ben Horin (sic), Klausner, and Montefiore. With regard to Paul himself, he treated comprehensively the 'genuine letters' of Romans, 1 and 2 Corinthians, Galatians, Philippians, 1 Thessalonians, and Philemon, although he also made extensive use of Acts, Ephesians, Colossians, 2 Thessalonians, and 1 and 2 Timothy.

[92] Schoeps, *Paul*, 37–40.

[93] Schoeps, *Paul*, 43, 97–9.

[94] Schoeps, *Paul*, 40, 47.

[95] Schoeps, *Paul*, 37.

had not been direct but had been filtered through the medium of Hellenistic Judaism, which had distorted it.[96] Schoeps was cautious in terms of defining Hellenistic
Judaism too precisely, but although its exact nature remained unclear, he felt that
it had not been in irreconcilable opposition to Palestinian Judaism.[97]

When it came to the question of the Law, Schoeps accepted that the legacy of
Paul had been a distortion of the Law for the Christian Church.[98] The apostle
had undoubtedly been influenced by Hellenistic Judaism, which had viewed the
Law in terms of 'ethical self-justification and ritual performance'.[99] At the same
time, Schoeps suggested that the key to understanding the apostle was to set him
in his proper context, that of 'aeon theology'.[100] The apostle had not been against
the Law in principle but had come to reject its validity in the new messianic era
(inaugurated in this case by Jesus), as later messianic movements would do.[101] (He
was not the first to suggest that Paul's attitude towards the Law could be explained
in terms of Jewish beliefs concerning the messianic age.[102]) Schoeps claimed to
approach Paul as 'an impartial historian of religion, and as one who also wishes
to do justice to the Judaism whence Paul sprang . . . not hindered by confessional
alliances. . . . '[103] He made frequent references to mainstream, history-of-religions
Pauline scholarship in order to emphasise his 'purely' academic approach. But in
his presentation of Paul's view of the Law, Schoeps exceeds his scholarly remit and
uses his analysis to criticise intrinsic elements of traditional Judaism, in so far as
it had failed to comprehend the true meaning of Torah.[104] Defending his line of
inquiry as a legitimate one for a historian of religion, Schoeps put Paul's original
question about the Law (in its pre-Christian form) to the Jewish religion:

If we understand the matter rightly, 1900 years ago he [Saul] posed a question which
tradition did not adequately answer as a Pharasaic theologian. We know the problem
only in its Pauline setting, and so must translate it back into Judaic terms. It would then
run somewhat as follows: If here and now the law as a whole does not seem 'fulfillable',
does not the fact perhaps suggest that the law is not an exhaustive expression of the

---

[96] Schoeps, *Paul*, 23, 213.
[97] Schoeps, *Paul*, 25–6.
[98] Schoeps, *Paul*, 261–2.
[99] Schoeps, *Paul*, 262.
[100] Schoeps, *Paul*, 97–9.
[101] Schoeps, *Paul*, 172–3.
[102] Leo Baeck, like Schoeps, argued that beliefs about different 'epochs' explained Paul's theology. Leo
Baeck, 'The Faith of Paul', 106–8. The Orthodox Jewish scholar Herbert Loewe was not convinced,
however. In 1938 he wrote, 'It was held in Messianic times, mankind would gradually improve
and that certain prescriptions would become obsolete. . . . In a sense this idea is similar to that of
Paul's conception of the Torah as paidagogos. But it is not Antinomian. It implies a spontaneous
evolution, as a result of the outpouring of the Holy Spirit, which shall regenerate mankind, not
a violent or abrupt abolition. Even in the days of the Messiah, certain obligations must remain,
ingrained though they may be in human nature.' Herbert Loewe, *Rabbinic Anthology* (New York:
Schocken Books, 1974), 669.
[103] Schoeps, *Paul*, xi.
[104] The title of the relevant chapter is 'Paul's Criticism of the Law as a Problem Intrinsic to Judaism'.

will of God? [Should] the fulfilling of the law of Moses be understood literally and completely as a fulfilling of the will of God? . . . [105]

In classic liberal terms, Schoeps criticised the failure among Jews down through the centuries to distinguish adequately between the nonessential and essential, the literal and the deeper understanding of Judaism.[106] Crucially, Jews had lost the ability to recognise the symbolic value of the Law as a representation of God's will, rather than the will of God itself. In modern times, however, the situation had begun to improve with the arrival of thinkers such as Martin Buber and Hermann Cohen, whom Schoeps commended for distinguishing 'the law within the law' or 'the idea of the law' from the multiplicity of the particular commands. His criticism of traditional Judaism was clear:

Not until the epoch of the liberal Judaism of the last hundred years have the presuppositions arisen which enable us to understand this duality and to make an end of the straightforward identification of the law and the divine will which was so typical of Talmudic Judaism.[107]

Schoeps went on to suggest that modern Judaism could appreciate, 'like Christianity', Paul's concern and the tension that he had felt between the works of the Law and faith. In fact, modern Judaism better appreciated the paradoxical duality than did Christianity because it maintained that tension and refused to join Paul in dissolving the tension prematurely (by abandoning works of the Law). Schoeps's resolution of the problem thrown up by Paul and his understanding of the role of Paul in the context of developments within Judaism are worth citing at length:

The Jewish solution of it [the dichotomy between faith and works] flows not from Christ but from the focusing of the two poles in God. The Jewish answer is [on the one hand] the faith of Israel in God as Creator of the world, Revealer of the Torah, and Redeemer of Israel – and [on the other] of humanity as a whole. This faith is the fundament for the doing of works of the law. It precedes the doing of the law, which is intended only to express self-commitment to this faith and to prove obedience in the breadth and variety of life. For revelation precedes the law. It is not the law itself. Only when revelation is believed, or, in Jewish terms, when man adopts the attitude of the fear of God, can the law be done in faith. Then the question of the 'fulfillability' of the law loses its sting. Quantitatively it becomes a task laid on man and an appeal to him to do as much as possible. Qualitatively it is a challenge to man's constantly renewed self-examination to see that he does the law with the right faith and disposition – which is the Jewish counterpart to Paul's insistence on faith. Finally, the significance of Paul for the Jews consists also in the fact that he addressed not only Jews and Greeks, but

[105] Schoeps, *Paul*, 280.
[106] Schoeps, *Paul*, 283.
[107] Schoeps, *Paul*, 283.

man in general. His affirmations about man who is a sinner and who is yet capable of the right faith, concern the Jews also.

The right faith is in fact synonymous with the fear of God; and just because the latter was distorted in Paul's perspective we wish in conclusion to assess its importance as the basis of the law for Jewish thinking as a whole. Perhaps the true mission of the Rabbi Saul within Judaism itself – a mission not up to the present discharged – will be found to consist in the fact that with his criticism of the law he is able to arouse the Jews' attention to the importance of the fear of God, which they are all too liable to forget.[108]

For Schoeps it was 'right faith' that legitimates Torah observance, which should be valued only as an expression of commitment to this faith. The Law, in and of itself, was of no substance; without 'right faith' it was meaningless. Modern Judaism had lost sight of this truth, Schoeps asserted; elsewhere he made this more explicit still, stating categorically, 'Talmudic Judaism erred in making a straightforward identification of the law and the divine will'.[109] Paul's attitude to the Law (although not his Christocentric justification for his attitude) therefore offered a necessary and welcome reminder of its place in the great scheme of things. It is difficult to see this addendum to his scholarly study of Paul as anything other than a confessional challenge and contribution to the intra-Jewish debate between progressive and traditional Judaism. What is remarkable is that, like Montefiore's, Schoeps's platform for reform was framed by reference to Paul, that is, in terms of 'the true mission of the Rabbi Saul within Judaism itself – a mission not up until the present discharged'.[110]

AN ORTHODOX JEWISH CRITIQUE OF PROGRESSIVE JUDAISM?

Arguably, one of the most widely read accounts of Paul in modern times has been David Flusser's entry 'Paul of Tarsus' in the *Encyclopaedia Judaica* (1971),[111] which contrasts sharply with Kohler's overtly anti-Christian polemical article in the *Jewish Encyclopaedia*. Austrian-born of assimilated Jewish parents, Flusser (1917–2000) was educated at Catholic schools and his interest in Judaism was, in part, a reaction against his parents' disinterest. He escaped the Holocaust, emigrating in the late 1930s to Palestine, where he became an observant Jew and studied the Talmudic literature. His university studies in Prague had brought about a meeting with one pastor, a member of the Bohemian Brethren, who positively influenced

---

[108] Schoeps, *Paul*, 284–5.
[109] Schoeps, *Paul*, 283.
[110] Schoeps, *Paul*, 285.
[111] David Flusser, 'Paul of Tarsus', *Encyclopaedia Judaica*, 190–92. As a New Testament specialist, Flusser was familiar with Christian Pauline scholarship and cited frequently Paul's epistles; his interpretation relied in the main upon his reading of Romans, 1 Corinthians, and Galatians.

his view of Jesus and Christianity.[112] He went on to Hebrew University, where he spent the next 50 years as professor of early Christianity and comparative religion.

In no way did Flusser attempt to attack Christianity through Paul, or present him as an enemy of the Jewish people. He pointed out that Paul's attitude towards Jews had been positive, teaching that the election of Israel had not been abrogated and that they would eventually be saved (Rom. 9–11).[113] He recognised the apostle's background in Pharisaic Judaism, which he felt had probably been the result of his family coming from Galilee.[114] With regards to the Law, Flusser approached Paul's view of Torah on two levels. He suggested that when Paul had written, 'No human being will be justified by the works of the law' (Rom. 3:20), he had originally referred to Jewish law, but he also accepted that 'justification by the works of the Law' had come to be understood in a broad theological sense (as a legalistic religious system), and was by no means condemnatory about this classic Protestant understanding.[115]

In fact, Flusser's attitude to Christianity was remarkably relaxed, going so far as to suggest that Jews could learn from Christians that 'some concepts of the second Temple are not sufficiently stressed in Modern Judaism.'[116] He pointed to a growing discontent and uneasiness, in this period, concerning divine justice as manifested in the world, and a tendency towards a belief that 'Man is sunk in sin; only by the gift of the spirit of God can he emerge.'[117] Paul's teachings regarding grace and the inadequacy of the Law to merit God's favour are obvious expressions of this

---

[112] Flusser discussed his childhood in Catholic Bohemia, where he said he did not experience 'any sort of Christian aversion to my Jewish background', and the profound impact of his friendship with pastor Josef Perl in Prague in David Flusser, *The Sage from Galilee: Rediscovering Jesus' Genius* (Grand Rapids: Eerdmans, 2007), xviii–xxix. For a useful overview of his scholarly interest in early Christianity, see John G. Gager, 'Scholarship as Moral Vision: David Flusser on Jesus, Paul, and the Birth of Christianity', *The Jewish Quarterly Review* 95:1 (Winter 2005), 60–73.

[113] Flusser, 'Paul of Tarsus', 192.

[114] Flusser, 'Paul of Tarsus', 190.

[115] Flusser, 'Paul of Tarsus', 191. Flusser later offered a more nuanced reading of Paul's view of the Law, for example, drawing attention to Paul's assertion in Gal. 2:15–16 ('We being Jews by nature... [know that] no one is justified by the works of the law'), and suggesting that Paul's was a typically Jewish position, commenting 'any Jew would find it most curious if a rabbi were to say, 'You are redeemed by doing the Law.' He also emphasised that Paul's apparently negative attitude towards the Law had not necessarily applied to Jewish observance but only to non-Jewish believers, observing, 'Paul never says in so many words that there is anything that can release a Jew from his observation that the Law and its works... Paul accepted and delivered to the Churches the rule that Christians from Jewish stock should practice what they did before their call.' David Flusser, 'Paul's Jewish-Christian Opponents in the Didache', in S. Shaked, D. Shulman, and G. Stroumsa, eds., *Gilgul: Essays on Transformation, Revolution and Permanence in the History of Religions* (Leiden: 1987), 33, 80–81.

[116] J. Oesterreicher, 'Review of *Jesus*' in *The Bridge; Brothers in Hope* 5 (1970), 329, cited in Fuchs-Kreimer, 'The Essential Heresy', 222.

[117] David Flusser, *Ha Natzrut be Aynay ha Yehudi (Christianity from the Jewish Perspective)* (Jerusalem: Siphrut Poalin, 1979), 362, cited in Fuchs-Kreimer, 'The Essential Heresy', 228. Freud similarly suggested that 'a growing feeling of guiltiness has seized the Jewish people – and perhaps the whole of civilization at that time'. *Moses and Monotheism* (New York: Knopf, 1939), 136.

concern. But Flusser was convinced that such concepts of grace had not been unique to the early Church; he felt that they had developed in the intertestamental period, eventually being taken on board by the Essene community.[118] He maintained that this wider Jewish interest in God's grace was the proper context in which to locate both the Essenes' belief that they (a small, elect group of Jews) had been preordained to become the righteous, and the conviction of Paul and the early Church that God's chosen ones now comprised their group (of Jewish and Gentile Christians). Without feeling the need to posit a direct connection, Flusser was convinced that Paul, just as much as the Essenes and their forerunners, had come to pessimistic conclusions about human inadequacy in a common intellectual climate. Whatever difficulties one might have with his attempt to parallel Paul's concept of grace (God's offer of salvation without the need of the Law) with that of the Essenes (God predestines, without ending observance of the Law), the result of Flusser's presentation was to place Paul's concept of grace well and truly within the context of competing, developing, expanding Jewish theologies and interpretations of Judaism in the first century.[119] The idea was essentially a Jewish phenomenon, then, and need not be denounced as alien or Christian.

Although on one hand Flusser can be said to have risen above Jewish–Christian polemics, on the other hand there is an interesting moment when, in his encyclopaedia entry, this religiously observant scholar subtly associates the Christian apostle Paul with progressive Judaism. Flusser casually observed that 'Paul comes close to a rationalistic, liberal approach . . . as a result of his new Christological worldview.'[120] This, he said, was demonstrated by the apostle's relaxed attitude to the Law in general and to food in particular (1 Corinthians 10:23–26).[121] Although Paul had not claimed that the Torah had ceased to be valid for Christian Jews, this was only because, *inter alia*, he had not wished to shame those weaker in faith, because 'everyone should remain in the state in which they are called' (1 Cor. 7:20), and because he had not wanted to provoke the Jerusalem church.[122] In reality Paul had developed from 'a purely liberal attitude' to a point where the new covenant represented freedom from the yoke of the Jewish Law.[123] The link made between the abrogating Apostle to the Gentiles and liberal Jews can hardly have been intended as a supportive gesture for the latter, and could easily be interpreted as a hint at the

---

[118] David Flusser, 'A New Sensitivity to Judaism and the Christian Message', in *Harvard Theological Review* 61 (1968), 109.

[119] E. P. Sanders criticises Flusser's methodology in *Paul and Palestinian Judaism*, 15–16.

[120] Flusser, 'Paul of Tarsus,' 191.

[121] Flusser, 'Paul of Tarsus', 191. 1 Cor. 10:23–6: '"Everything is permissible" – but not everything is beneficial. "Everything is permissible" – but not everything is constructive. Nobody should seek his own good, but the good of others. Eat anything sold in the meat market without raising questions of conscience, for, "The earth is the Lord's, and everything in it."'

[122] Flusser, 'Paul of Tarsus', 191.

[123] Flusser, 'Paul of Tarsus', 191.

dangers of liberalism and its relatedness to Christian theology. In this context it is noteworthy that Flusser felt the need to distance Paul from rabbinic Judaism, by emphasising that Paul's Jewish learning had not been extensive or deep and that his abrogation of the Law could not be linked to rabbinic teachings, as suggested by Schoeps and others.[124]

MODERN NORTH AMERICAN PROGRESSIVE PERSPECTIVES

With the implicit critique offered by Flusser, one can readily see that it has not only been those who promote a progressive Jewish worldview who have made the link between a Pauline and a liberal attitude towards the Law. Perhaps for that reason, some progressive Jewish writers have struggled with this promotional use of Paul more than others. Montefiore and Schoeps exhibited fewer qualms than, for example, did Samuel Sandmel. Sandmel (1911–79) was an Ohio-born biblical scholar whose parents had fled Eastern Europe to escape pogroms. Following a mainstream North American education, he trained as a Reform rabbi at Hebrew Union College, where he was ordained in 1937. After serving as a navy chaplain based in California and the Pacific (1942–6), he took his doctorate at Yale in New Testament Studies. Sandmel's duties as a rabbi for the Hillel Foundation (1939–49) meant he had special responsibilities for Jewish youth and was very conscious of the threat of assimilation. His academic career as professor of Bible and Hellenistic literature at HUC made him an internationally recognised authority on the relationship between Judaism and the New Testament. He wrote in the tradition of liberal Judaism, approaching Jesus as a source of inspiration, yet concerned to prevent conversion. His writings, which took into account non-Jewish scholarship, include *A Jewish Understanding of the New Testament* (1956), *We Jews and Jesus* (1965), and *Anti-Semitism in the New Testament* (1978).[125]

Sandmel well illustrates what Brumberg-Kraus views as the predicament of the modern Jewish New Testament scholar who must simultaneously address both the Jewish and the wider academic communities.[126] On one hand, as a Jew, Sandmel was concerned to demonstrate his familiarity with, and ability to contribute to, mainstream (Christian) scholarship, and also to criticise the use of Paul as 'the whip with which ... scholars beat Judaism'.[127] On the other hand, his assumptions of Paul's Jewishness and sympathetic engagement with the apostle's view of the

[124] Flusser, 'Paul of Tarsus', 190, 191.
[125] Samuel Sandmel, *A Jewish Understanding of the New Testament* (New York: Ktav Publishing House, 1956), *We Jews and Jesus* (New York: Oxford University Press, 1965), and *Anti-Semitism in the New Testament* (Philadelphia: Fortress Press, 1978).
[126] Brumberg-Kraus, 'A Jewish Ideological Perspective', 135.
[127] Samuel Sandmel, 'Leo Baeck on Christianity', Leo Baeck Memorial Lecture 19 (New York: Leo Baeck Institute, 1975), 16.

Law clearly reflected a rejection of the Orthodox prerogative to determine what actually constituted authenticity, and thus his Pauline studies could be regarded as a platform from which was issued a liberal Jewish apologetic.

As with Montefiore, the key to understanding Sandmel's Paul as presented in *The Genius of Paul: A Study in History* (1958) is the distinction made between Palestinian Judaism and Hellenistic Judaism, and the location of Paul within the latter category. As he explained,

> To call Paul a Hellenistic Jew is not to put a value judgment on the nature of his Jewish fidelity, but is only to state a fact. The Hellenistic world into which Paul was born, we know now, was one of many religious expressions and of earnest philosophical disputations.... There is no reason to be sceptical of his statement that in his study of Judaism he had surpassed his fellow students of his own age. Nor should we doubt that he had achieved a skilful knowledge of Judaism. His statement that he had learned the traditions of his fathers is to be accepted – but the content of those Graeco-Jewish 'traditions' is not to be confused with that which later centuries recorded as the product of the Jewish schools in Palestine and Babylonia.[128]

For Sandmel, Palestinian Judaism could be distinguished from Hellenistic Judaism in terms of universal/cosmic and individual/local worldviews. For example, the Palestinian Jews viewed the messiah as a divine agent who would help them out of their national predicament, whereas Paul saw in him the means to save individuals from the human predicament.[129] Similarly, Paul's background, which was to be gleaned from the Epistles and not the Acts of the Apostles,[130] explained a lot about his understanding of the Law. Like another well-known first-century Hellenistic Jew, Philo of Alexandria, Paul did not regard the Mosaic Law as primary. But whereas Philo's concerns had been theoretical (he had had no difficulty in observing the Law himself), Paul's problems were of a more personal nature. Rather than a difficulty with the Law itself, Paul's problem lay in his own failure to observe it. 'Had Paul not found this personal difficulty', Sandmel maintained, 'he would not have been led to a virtual abrogation of the Law'.[131] Furthermore, it was as a Hellenistic Jew that Paul interpreted his discovery of freedom from the Law as

---

[128] Samuel Sandmel, *The Genius of Paul*, 16–17.

[129] Sandmel, *The Genius of Paul*, 18–19.

[130] 'I have no hesitation in choosing Paul's evidence as preferable, more reliable, and more authentic than that of Acts. I conclude that Paul, a Hellenistic Jew, had never been in Palestine until after he had joined the new movement.' Sandmel, *The Genius of Paul*, 13. He accepts as authentic the Epistles of Romans, 1 and 2 Corinthians, Galatians, Philippians, 1 Thessalonians, and Philemon and doubts the rest. Ibid., 4. Sandmel, a professional New Testament scholar, cited many Pauline scholars, but among these who he claimed had most influenced him were Baur, Bultmann, Davies, Hawkins, Loymeyer, and Schmidt. He also gave special mention to Baeck, Schoeps, and Montefiore; Graetz's interpretation had been 'brilliant (but wrong)' and he denounced 'Klausner's incredibly bad *From Jesus to Paul*.' Ibid., 221–8.

[131] Sandmel, *The Genius of Paul*, 32.

applicable universally to each and every individual.[132] Interestingly, Sandmel was concerned to defend Paul's view of the Law against the charge of opportunism. He denied the assumed scenario in which Paul's failure to win over Jews had led to his abandonment of the Law in order to attract Gentile converts. Rather, Paul's view of the Law had cost him the support of Jews.[133] Whatever he might have thought of Paul's apparent abrogation of the Law, then, Sandmel did not doubt his integrity.

Despite this emphasis on Hellenistic Judaism, Sandmel went on to place Paul in the Jewish prophetic tradition, which he identified closely with the mystical tradition.

Paul was a mystic who encountered God – in the form of Christ. Paul's 'conversion' is the change wrought in him because of that experience. As a result of it, Paul sees what to him are new and heightened insights within his inherited and precious Judaism.

Now we must be more specific about the character of this heightened insight. In my judgement, no term better serves initially to classify the convert Paul than the word 'prophet'. Paul had the sense of a call from God, of communion with him, and a commission from God. . . . [134]

In so doing, Sandmel offered a very different perspective on Paul's view of the Law. In order to understand a prophet, Sandmel felt that one needed to take into account the historical situation, for this determined his message. Amos had dealt with the accrued social injustice of the settled agricultural north, prophesying that God disapproved of the conduct rampant in Israel, especially of the extravagances of cult; and Isaiah, fervently convinced that Israel should trust in God and not in political alliances, prophesied that God would punish Israel for its infidelity by bringing in a destructive foe. It seemed reasonable to Sandmel to apply this way of thinking to Paul. Thus,

Paul confronts a situation different from that of Amos, Isaiah, and Jeremiah. These pre-exilic prophets denied the validity of ritual ceremony or of a written code at a time previous to the existence of the Pentateuch, for the latter, in spite of its traditional ascription to Moses, is a post-exilic compilation, coming no less than a century after Jeremiah's time, and almost five centuries before Paul's. But by Paul's time the Pentateuch had become the very center of his religious heritage. Amos could ignore it, for it did not exist; Paul (and Philo) must deal with it and account for it.

Paul's denial of the validity of the Pentateuchal legislation is akin to Amos' denial of ritual sacrifice (5.21–22) and to Jeremiah's denial of the existence of any valid written code (7.21–22). The impetus in all the cases was identical; the end result was the same:

---

[132] Sandmel, *The Genius of Paul*, 32.
[133] Sandmel, *The Genius of Paul*, 28–9, 32.
[134] Sandmel, *The Genius of Paul*, 75.

Communion is the only essential, and ritual is useless. What is different is only the environment and the particulars confronted.[135]

As a result, the common charge that Paul had abrogated the Law was, in Sandmel's opinion, a misunderstanding. Any negative remarks Paul had made about the Law had been provoked by the negative reception of his message and possibly as a result of psychological trauma.[136] It was a kind of critique of institutionalised religion.[137] In reality, Paul had simply sought to emphasise internal over external worship, as had the prophets before him, and had done so in terms of the Law, living as he had in an age of Law.[138] Despite any reservations he harboured concerning the apostle to the Gentiles, the liberal Jewish scholar looked kindly upon this way of approaching the Law, and was prepared to give Paul the benefit of the doubt.

In a number of Jewish studies of Paul, the apostle's creative abilities are regarded as evidence of religious genius. Sandmel's emphasis on this aspect of Pauline theology can be gauged from the title of his book, The Genius of Paul, and from his assertion that Paul was the second founder of Christianity.[139] There can be no doubt that Sandmel disagreed with much of Paul's teaching and was concerned about the allure of Christianity more generally. He recorded his instinctive, personal 'antagonism to [Paul's] aspersions of the Torah'.[140] He argued that rabbinic Judaism and Christianity shared little more than the Bible as a starting point and viewed the Law in opposing ways.[141] And in an introduction to We Jews and Jesus (1965) he made clear his concern to inform Jewish students about Christianity in order to prevent assimilation or conversion, no doubt reflecting his experiences with

---

[135] Sandmel, The Genius of Paul, 75–8.
[136] Sandmel, The Genius of Paul, 56. Sandmel's positive evaluation of Hellenistic Judaism meant that an alternative cause of Paul's animosity towards the law was necessary. We will return to Sandmel in Chapter six to discuss his unpublished novel The Apostle Paul, in which he suggests that Paul's mother had been abandoned by his father and had been unable to remarry without the religious certificate of divorce. As a result, she had killed herself, and anti-halakhic seeds had been sown in the young Paul's heart. It is worth noting that the 1950s and 1960s saw the gradual emergence of psychobiography as a popular genre. Such biographies tended to highlight prototypical scenes in the subjects' formative years as models for understanding their personality traits, with the aim of establishing a logically coherent narrative of the subject's life-story and development. The focus on historically significant figures meant that the genre included studies of a number of religious individuals, such as Erik Erikson's Young Man Luther: A Study in Psychoanalysis and History (New York: W. W. Norton, 1958) and Gandhi's Truth: On the Origins of Militant Nonviolence (New York: W. W. Norton, 1969).
[137] Sandmel, The Genius of Paul, 218.
[138] In this, Sandmel's Paul is similar to Montefiore's Jesus, also 'a prophet in the age of Law'.
[139] Sandmel, The Genius of Paul, 114. 'That in him [Paul] Christianity becomes Hellenized, transformed in terms of the environment of the religious genius who was the transformer, Paul did not create Christianity, he re-created it.' Ibid., 116.
[140] Samuel Sandmel, Two Living Traditions: Essays on Religion and the Bible (Detroit: Wayne State University, 1972), 14.
[141] Sandmel, The Genius of Paul, 59–60.

the Hillel Foundation.[142] Nevertheless, as a Progressive Jewish scholar he was concerned to include marginals, and, despite the views of some commentators,[143] he was reluctant to condemn Paul as an inauthentic kind of Jew or as an enemy of the Jewish people. Furthermore, he was prepared to recognise and accept Paul's own Jewish self-identity, and even to criticise the use of the term 'Christian' in connection with him.[144] He felt so strongly committed to a progressive view of the historical nature of Jewish identity that he was not prepared to abandon his principles, even in the context of discussing one of the most notorious marginal Jews of all time.

This tendency to approach Paul as a marginal-but-legitimate Jew has become *de rigueur* among a number of the more recent studies,[145] and appears to confirm Brumberg-Kraus's suggestion that the research of progressive Jewish New Testament scholars naturally tends to confront traditional or orthodox Jewish assumptions about Jewish history (for example, challenging the centrality of authoritative rabbis and a normative, *halakhic* Judaism). They do this, he claims, by generating histories of Jewish diversity (that is, by emphasising marginal experiences and the profound interactions between Jewish and non-Jewish cultures).[146] One example that reflects this increasingly widespread assumption about complex or hybrid religious identities is *Paul the Convert* (1992) by the North American Jewish scholar Alan Segal (1945).[147] Brought up in a Reform congregation and later joining the Conservative synagogue, Segal has a background corresponding to Liberal Judaism in Britain. He is a professor of religion at Columbia with interests in early rabbinic Judaism and Christianity, Gnosticism, mysticism, and magic.

In Segal's view, Paul's essentially Jewish background was best expressed in terms of Pharisaism *and* Jewish mysticism. Although maintaining that 'one must recognise that Paul was a Pharisaic Jew who converted to a new apocalyptic Jewish sect and then lived in a Hellenistic, gentile Christian community as a Jew among gentiles',[148] Segal argued that Paul must also have been profoundly influenced by

---

[142] 'I have tried to provide a small book that Jewish parents, after they themselves have read it, might put into the hands of college-age students. It has been my observation that a Jewish youngster, away from home and sharing in the great adventure of higher education with fellow students who are Christians, could benefit from such an endeavour.' Sandmel, *We Jews and Jesus*, ix.

[143] Stendahl mistakenly suggests that Sandmel's aim in emphasising Paul's Hellenistic characteristics was to locate him 'outside the Jewish fold'. Krister Stendahl, 'Review of *A Jewish Understanding of the New Testament*', *Ecumenical Review* (July 1975), 295–6.

[144] Sandmel, *We Jews and Jesus*, 21.

[145] In addition to Alan Segal, below, examples include Daniel Boyarin, *A Radical Jew: Paul and the Politics of Identity* (Berkley: University of California Press, 1994) and Nanos, *Romans* and *Galatians*.

[146] Brumberg-Kraus 'A Jewish Ideological Perspective', 135–9.

[147] Segal, *Paul the Convert*. The study draws largely on Romans, 1 and 2 Corinthians, and Galatians, but its particular focus also requires heavy use of Acts of the Apostles, along with Jewish mystical and rabbinic writings. Segal engages extensively with contemporary Pauline scholarship, particularly representatives of the New Perspective including Sanders, Krister, Gager, and Dunn, and adds to this sociological scholarship concerning the phenomenon of conversion.

[148] Segal, *Paul the Convert*, 6–7.

Jewish apocalyptic and mystical thought.[149] Specifically, he noted the stress Paul placed upon 'conversion' and 'transformation' in the nonpastoral epistles (and the dramatic effect of his encounter with Christ on the road to Damascus, as recorded in Acts).[150] This aspect of Pauline theology, he felt, had its roots in what was later described as *Merkabah* mysticism (after the mishnaic term for the 'chariot' that Ezekiel saw in his vision of Ezek. 1.26), which spoke of 'angelic transformation' attained by having gazed upon the glory of God in human form.[151] Paul's subsequent Christian interpretation of his 'conversion' and its religious significance – for example, his identification of Christ as the human figure of God enthroned in heaven (envisioned by Ezekiel)[152] – could then be viewed as a reexpression of *Merkabah* terminology. According to Segal, recent research into conversion experiences demonstrated that converts naturally found the meaning of their conversion and their visions in the community that valued them, and so 'any convert and especially a converted Pharisee who knew of mystical and apocalyptic traditions would give these experiences Christian interpretations if that person had chosen to join a Christian community'.[153] Thus Paul's Jewish (mystical) background provided the framework for a self-understanding of his conversion experience, which he later reexpressed in specifically Christian terms. And this was also the key to making sense of Paul's view of the Law:

Those who stress that Paul was merely a Jew whose messiah has come have missed Paul's point. Paul was a Jew who did not have to convert to become a Christian. Theoretically, he could have just slid over as an adherent by claiming Judaism was fulfilled by the messiah's arrival. In that case, he would have insisted that the rules of Jewish life be imposed on all Christians, as did the Jewish Christians. Or he would have insisted that the gentiles remain God-fearers and not become part of the community. But Paul, though Jewish, and because he had been a believing Pharisee, had to go through a radical reorientation to enter Christianity. Paul then said that everyone needs radically to reorient his or her way of thinking in order to become a Christian. . . . No one should think that Paul's writing is a dispassionate or impartial theology of Torah. Paul's description of Torah is a consequence of his conversion experience, not the other way around; for conversions do not follow the pattern of philosophical questioning.[154]

---

[149] Segal, *Paul the Convert*, 42–8. Segal, who closely associates Paul's apocalypticism with his mysticism, compares, for example, the apostle's discussion of the future glorification of the mortal body (2 Cor. 5:1–10) with the transformations described in apocalyptic text of 2 Enoch.

[150] For Segal, Acts of the Apostles was most useful for what it confirmed in Paul's letters. At the same time, although he admitted that many of the details of Paul's 'dramatic conversion' (an event central to his thesis) were missing from Paul's letters, he disapproved of the fact that 'many readers of Paul deny that he was a convert, because the reports of his conversion come only from Luke'. Segal, *Paul the Convert*, 5.

[151] Segal, *Paul the Convert*, 47, 48. An important consequence of this theory for the study of first-century Judaism(s) is the realisation that Paul was the only Jewish mystic of this period to relate his experience confessionally.

[152] Segal, *Paul the Convert*, 58.

[153] Segal, *Paul the Convert*, 37, 38.

[154] Segal, *Paul the Convert*, 147.

Regarding the discussion about Abraham, faith, and the Law in Galatians 3:6–14, Segal doubted whether Paul had meant to imply that the Torah itself was wrong, but rather that the oral Torah, as understood by the Pharisees, was an all-or-nothing proposition.[155] Paul's own position, which he promoted as a radical alternative, was closer to that of a Diaspora Jewish accommodation than to a strict Pharisaic view.[156] Although the Law might serve a useful purpose as a standard for moral behaviour generally, the special laws of Judaism did not actually figure in his redefinition of the community.[157] To understand Paul was to understand that

[f]aith means more to Paul than remaining faithful and steadfast to the covenant. It is not something that Judaism or Jewish Christianity exhibits, but it *is* inherent in gentile Christianity. The paradigm for this type of religion is Paul's own conversion from the surety of his Pharisaic observances to the freedom and uncertainties of his gentile Christianity. By faith, Paul essentially means a radical reorientation and commitment, as social science describes a radical new commitment in contemporary conversions. This also means a radical change in the community to which Paul gives allegiance. Those who are faithful are those who believe in Christ without the works of the law, the gentile Christian community.[158]

It was the intensity of Paul's mystical conversion experience that had forged in the apostle's mind a new unity based on faith in the promises of God, as opposed to the distinction between Jew and Gentile.[159] And although this was a remarkable new theology, it made perfect sense in the context of the Jewish historical context. Segal's particular take on Paul thus reflected an interest in unravelling the variegated nature of first-century forms of Judaism – and the value of the apostle for this task. As he himself commented,

Most scholars assume that once Paul had converted, his writings became irrelevant to Judaism. This is simply not so: Paul wrote to a brand-new Christian community that was still largely Jewish, giving us the only witness to a world of everyday Hellenistic Judaism now vanished. . . . Techniques of theurgy [magic, divine intervention] and heavenly ascent were secret lore in rabbinic literature . . . which dates from the third

---

[155] Gal. 3:6–14: 'Even so Abraham believed in God, and it was reckoned to him as righteousness. Therefore, be sure that it is those who are of faith who are sons of Abraham. The Scripture, foreseeing that God would justify the Gentiles by faith, preached the gospel beforehand to Abraham, saying, "All the nations will be blessed in you." So then those who are of faith are blessed with Abraham, the believer. For as many as are of the works of the Law are under a curse; for it is written, "Cursed is everyone who does not abide by all things written in the book of the Law, to perform them." Now that no one is justified by the Law before God is evident; for, "The righteous man shall live by faith." However, the Law is not of faith; on the contrary, "He who practices them shall live by them." Christ redeemed us from the curse of the Law, having become a curse for us – for it is written, "Cursed is everyone who hangs on a tree" – in order that in Christ Jesus the blessing of Abraham might come to the Gentiles, so that we would receive the promise of the Spirit through faith.'

[156] Segal, *Paul the Convert*, 118–19.

[157] Segal, *Paul the Convert*, 125.

[158] Segal, *Paul the Convert*, 121.

[159] Segal, *Paul the Convert*, 146.

century. Paul alone demonstrates that such traditions existed as early as the first century.... Paul is a first-century Jewish apocalypticist, and as such, he was also a mystic. In fact he is the only early Jewish mystic and apocalypticist whose personal, confessional writing has come down to us....[160]

Ostensibly, Segal and other progressive Jewish scholars have showed little direct interest in the implications of their studies for Jewish-Christian or for modern intra-Jewish relations. Paul is for them, as for many non-Jewish New Testament scholars, a purely academic, historical problem. At the same time, any study that locates Paul firmly within the Jewish spectrum, and which is founded upon their particular assumptions concerning diversity and cultural interrelations, is, in a very real sense, a contribution to the wider intra-Jewish debate on Jewish identity – at least in so far as it reinforces a nontraditional way of understanding Jewish history.

PERSPECTIVES CONCERNED WITH GENDER

Of course, with regard to ideological agenda and nontraditional ways of understanding Jewish history, feminism has proven to be a particularly potent approach for Pauline scholarship in recent decades. In terms of sketching out an ideological landscape, it seems sensible to consider Jewish feminists together, although it should be borne in mind that a feminist approach – or, more accurately, a concern for gender – also characterises other Jewish commentators on Paul (such as Daniel Boyarin) and that each of those considered here could just as easily have found themselves located elsewhere in this book, for their agenda are by no means exclusively feminist (whatever that might mean); for two, at least, a commitment to multiculturalism is just as relevant. But for obvious reasons, the ideological struggle in which those concerned with gender are currently engaged within the Jewish community and the place that the apostle plays in that context warrants special acknowledgement.

Pamela Eisenbaum (1961–), a specialist in Christian origins and Hellenistic Judaism, belongs to a new wave of feminist Pauline scholars. Brought up in Conservative and Orthodox synagogues, she now regards herself as Reform in terms of Torah observance ('which is to say that I am not an observant Jew').[161] As a New Testament specialist who works in a Christian theological college, she has repeatedly felt the need to defend her Jewish identity, which she describes as founded upon her identification with Jewish history and tradition. She notes that her interest in Paul is 'no coincidence' in that she 'care[s] deeply about modern Jewish–Christian relations in the wake of the Holocaust' and argues that the way Christians think

---

[160] Segal, *Paul the Convert*, xiii, 34–6.
[161] Eisenbaum, 'Following in the Footnotes of the Apostle Paul', 78.

about Paul affects the way they think about Judaism.[162] In her article 'Is Paul the Father of Misogyny and Antisemitism?' (2000–2001),[163] she sought to articulate a decidedly liberal, multicultural reading of the apostle.

Eisenbaum makes it clear that her scholarship is especially influenced by trends that include feminism and the new perspective on Paul which 'makes it impossible to see Paul as completely alienated from his Judaism'.[164] The apostle clearly regarded himself as Jewish throughout his life, she argues, which makes perfect sense since Christianity *per se* did not yet exist in the mid-first century; no followers of Jesus would have regarded themselves as members of a new religion at that time.[165] Taking as her key text Galatians 3:28 ('There is no longer Jew or Greek, there is no longer slave or free, there is no longer male and female, for all of you are one in Christ Jesus'), Eisenbaum suggests that the common feminist interpretation that sees Paul preaching here a radical egalitarianism, however much it might act as a corrective to conservative views of women as inferior to men, is still unsatisfactory. In her view, Paul's message has less to do with the destruction of human categories of existence in order that people might come to see that they share the *same* human essence, and more to do with his construction of a new social relations, such that people who are *different* can regard themselves as meaningfully related to each other and part of a shared world.[166]

In constructing this argument Eisenbaum is aware that ideological bias plays an important role in determining the emphases given to various texts from Paul's epistles. She suggests that the range of possible interpretations is partly the fault of apostle himself, who appears at times 'to speak out of both sides of his mouth; he has good as well as bad things to say about women and Jews.'[167] She sympathises

---

[162] Eisenbaum, 'Following in the Footnotes of the Apostle Paul', 93.

[163] Eisenbaum, 'Is Paul the Father of Misogyny and Antisemitism?' Among Pauline scholars, Eisenbaum refers to Davies, Dunn, Gager, Gaston, Meeks, Raisanen, Schüssler Fiorenza, Stendahl, Theilman, and Westerholm. Jewish commentators mentioned include Boyarin and Maccoby. Gal. 3:28 is central to her thesis, but she also draws heavily upon Romans. Eisenbaum's eagerly anticipated *Paul Was Not a Christian: The Original Message of a Misunderstood Apostle* (New York: HarperOne, 2009) was not published at time of writing.

[164] Eisenbaum, 'Is Paul the Father of Misogyny and Antisemitism?' 508.

[165] Eisenbaum, 'Is Paul the Father of Misogyny and Antisemitism?' 508. Eisenbaum does feel obliged to note that 'Critics of the new perspective claim that it is motivated more by contemporary Jewish–Christian relations in light of the holocaust than by an accurate reading of Paul.' Ibid.

[166] Eisenbaum, 'Is Paul the Father of Misogyny and Antisemitism?' 518–19.

[167] Eisenbaum, 'Is Paul the Father of Misogyny and Antisemitism?' 509. Texts cited in support include Rom. 3:1–2 ('Then what advantage has the Jew? Or what is the benefit of circumcision? Great in every respect. First of all, that they were entrusted with the oracles of God.') and Gal. 3:10 ('For as many as are of the works of the Law are under a curse; for it is written, "Cursed is everyone who does not abide by all things written in the book of the Law, to perform them"'); Rom. 9:4–5 ('who are Israelites, to whom belongs the adoption as sons, and the glory and the covenants and the giving of the Law and the temple service and the promises, whose are the fathers, and from whom is the Christ according to the flesh, who is over all, God blessed forever') and Gal. 2:12 ('For prior to the coming of certain men from James, he used to eat with the Gentiles; but when they came, he began to withdraw and hold himself aloof, fearing the party of the circumcision'); 1 Cor. 7:3–4

with those of a liberal bent who see in Paul's words an inclusive vision in which all distinguishing marks are erased.[168] But although in the twenty-first century there is no difficulty acknowledging the abolition of the categories 'slave and free', Eisenbaum asserts that the dissolution of the category-pairs of 'Jew or Greek' and 'male and female' is 'neither attainable nor desirable'.[169] Thus the common liberal interpretation is regarded as undermining the goal of liberation – insofar as this goal is understood to appreciate cultural and sexual difference,[170] that is, insofar as it is predicated upon the beliefs of modern multicultural North America.[171]

In justifying her position, Eisenbaum is dependent upon texts such as Romans 3:1–2 ('What advantage has the Jew? Or what is the value of circumcision? Much in every way'), and concludes 'Paul did not relegate Jewishness to an lower order of being; it is his interpreters who do that.'[172] 1 Corinthians 7:17–20 is particularly important in this regard:

Let each of you lead the life that the Lord has assigned, to which God called you. This is my rule in all the churches. Was anyone at the time of his call already circumcised? Let him not seek to remove the marks of circumcision. Was anyone at the time of his call uncircumcised? Let him not seek circumcision. Circumcision is nothing, and uncircumcision is nothing; but obeying the commandments of God is everything. Let each of you remain in the condition in which you were called.

This text, she argues, mitigates against the reading of Galatians 3:28 that sees Paul as propounding a programme to eradicate difference.[173] As she interprets the apostle, 'Human difference is an essential part of Paul's worldview. As a Jew, Paul assumes some differences exist because that is the way God made the world.'[174] The key thing is that he did not regard the differences as consequential to God

---

('The husband must fulfill his duty to his wife, and likewise also the wife to her husband. The wife does not have authority over her own body, but the husband does; and likewise also the husband does not have authority over his own body, but the wife does') and 11:7 ('For a man ought not to have his head covered, since he is the image and glory of God; but the woman is the glory of man').

[168] Eisenbaum, 'Is Paul the Father of Misogyny and Antisemitism?' 511–12.

[169] Eisenbaum, 'Is Paul the Father of Misogyny and Antisemitism?' 512.

[170] 'Some liberal intellectuals, many who identify themselves as feminist, believe there are essential differences between men and women, differences which may or may not be complementary, but which in any case cannot be transcended.' Eisenbaum, 'Is Paul the Father of Misogyny and Antisemitism?' 512.

[171] Eisenbaum, 'Is Paul the Father of Misogyny and Antisemitism?' 512. Here Eisenbaum makes it clear that she realises that the liberal interpretation does not see Paul calling for the obliteration of cultural difference, but rather calls for a claim to 'common humanness' – but she points out that this does imply a 'human sameness' as a profound level.

[172] Eisenbaum, 'Is Paul the Father of Misogyny and Antisemitism?' 514.

[173] Eisenbaum, 'Is Paul the Father of Misogyny and Antisemitism?' 515.

[174] Eisenbaum, 'Is Paul the Father of Misogyny and Antisemitism?' 515.

or relevant for salvation. Furthermore, Eisenbaum finds it implausible that Paul had a problem with the Law but believes that, rather, he was fiercely concerned for those to whom it had not been revealed, that is, the Gentiles.[175] Thus when a text appears to denigrate circumcision (for example, Gal. 5:6), Paul's first-century Jewish male identity should be kept firmly in mind.[176] This worldview held circumcision to be a characteristic of the natural state of the Jew; although he believed passionately that the Gentiles should not try to become Jews by taking on the Law and circumcision, this did not mean that he had abandoned his belief in two (legitimate) species of people, whom he described simply as the circumcised and uncircumcised.[177]

In offering a new reading of Gal. 3:28, Eisenbaum suggests that it is the metaphor of the family that lies behind Paul's utopian vision. Perfectly in line with progressive Jewish feminist sensibilities, she sees him attempting to show how different kinds of people can be brought together into a unity.

It is not two identical creatures who come together to create a family, but two different ones. 'Male and female' means difference is required at a fundamental level for the construction of family.... [And] Paul, who is already a member of Abraham's family, is attempting to make his Gentile followers members of Abraham's family [but] ... similarly, Jew and Gentile coming together in harmony while remaining distinct is the goal of Paul's mission.... [178]

A more overtly feminist agenda can be found in work of Tal Ilan (1956–), an Israeli-born professor of Jewish Studies at the Freie Universtät in Berlin. Ilan describes herself as a 'positivist historian' whose ideology 'partly consists of reconstructing the past as an end in itself'[179] and partly lies in recovering the place of Jewish women in antiquity, as reflected in the title of her *Integrating Women into Second Temple History* (2001).[180] She explains that her historical reconstructions, although dependent on a careful analysis of reliable evidence, draw heavily upon feminist theoretical observations and methodologies. They are 'based on the premise that women were always present in history but only became invisible in the historiography' and are concerned to place women at the centre in order to unbalance the old androcentric theoretical-historical paradigm.[181] In an essay

---

[175] Eisenbaum, 'Is Paul the Father of Misogyny and Antisemitism?' 515.

[176] Gal. 5:6: 'For in Christ Jesus neither circumcision nor uncircumcision means anything, but faith working through love.'

[177] Eisenbaum, 'Is Paul the Father of Misogyny and Antisemitism?' 517.

[178] Eisenbaum, 'Is Paul the Father of Misogyny and Antisemitism?' 520, 521.

[179] Tal Ilan, 'Paul and Pharisee Women' in Jane Schaberg, Alice Bach, Ester Fuchs, eds., *On the Cutting Edge: The Study of Women in Biblical Worlds* (London: Continuum, 2003), 83.

[180] Tal Ilan, *Integrating Women into Second Temple History* (Peabody, MA: Hendrickson, 2001).

[181] Ilan, 'Paul and Pharisee Women', 83.

entitled 'Paul and Pharisee Women' (2003),[182] Ilan argues that her feminist reading of the sources for Pharisaic Judaism throws new light on Paul's discussion of intermarriage in 1 Corinthians and confirms his Pharisaic background.[183]

Ilan begins her enquiries with a rereading of sources relating to first-century Pharisaism or *perushim*. Certain rabbinic texts speak of two constituents of Jewish society, *haverim* (companions) and *amei-aratzot* (people of the land), the former being distinguished from the latter in terms of their emphasis on purity and stricter interpretation of the food laws.[184] Although previous commentators have refrained from identifying the *haverim* with the Pharisees, Ilan makes a sustained argument that this was a name that they used for themselves[185] and then goes on to demonstrate that women were included in the 'pharisaic havura'.[186] In particular, she focuses upon the discussions in Tosefta Demai, Chapter 2, which deal with the problem of marriages between a *haver* and an *am-haaretz*. Here a key question was whether a woman required an initiation into the sectarian lifestyle so that she would not be an impediment to her Pharisee-*haver* husband, or whether she was already 'trustworthy', having been brought up or already initiated into this lifestyle. When the situation was reversed and a wife or daughter of a Pharisee-*haver* later married someone who did not belong to the sect, they are understood to 'remain trustworthy, unless they become suspect' (v. 17), implying that such women held independent (equal) sectarian status until proven otherwise. Ilan's point is that marriage between sectarian and nonsectarian members was regarded as viable, and that such a marriage did not automatically violate the integrity of the sect member. (The same chapter also considered the place of slaves and asserts the independence of their sectarian status, too.) It is not entirely surprising, then, that she seeks to apply her new insight to 1 Corinthians, an epistle in which the apostle Paul recommends that married Christians should attempt to preserve their marriages to non-Christians (and should not dismiss their slaves). Ilan suggests that the Corinthians had assumed that Jesus' opposition to divorce only referred to fellow Christians. Paul's advice in 7:12–14, with its egalitarian similarities to Tosefta Demai 2:16–17, asserts that intermarriage does not disqualify the believer's Christian status, whether male or female.[187] In arguing that 'If a Christian has a

---

[182] Tal Ilan, 'Paul and Pharisee Women'.

[183] For her reading of 1 Cor. 7, Ilan draws upon the Christian feminists Elisabeth Schüssler Fiorenza, Antoinette Clark Wine, Lone Fatum, and Elizabeth Castelli. She makes no references to Jewish commentators on Paul.

[184] Ilan, 'Paul and Pharisee Women', 87. The text cited is from the Tosefta (a legal compilation similar to the Mishna) T. Demai 2.

[185] For this Ilan draws primarily upon T. Shabbat 1:15, T. Hagigah 3.

[186] Again, Ilan concentrates on T. Demai 2. Ilan sets aside the observation that nowhere in the early rabbinic literature is the female equivalent of *haver* (that is, *havera*).

[187] 1 Cor. 7:12–14: 'But to the rest I say, not the Lord, that if any brother has a wife who is an unbeliever, and she consents to live with him, he must not divorce her. And a woman who has an unbelieving husband, and he consents to live with her, she must not send her husband away. For the unbelieving husband is sanctified through his wife, and the unbelieving wife is sanctified through her believing

heathen wife and she is willing to live with him, he must not divorce her' and *vice versa*, and in his assumption that Christians can own Christian and non-Christian slaves,[188] he 'imagines a situation very similar to that of Pharisee men and women married to members of the *am-haaretz*.'[189]

Ilan's essay takes seriously Paul's claim that he was a Pharisee and asks what aspects of the Pharisaic worldview he brought with him into his role as apostle to the Gentiles, especially regarding attitudes towards women.[190] A short analysis of the attempts of 'Christian and Diaspora Jewish feminists' to answer this question leads her to suspect that ideological biases were responsible for the common conclusion that the positive Jewish influence upon Paul had been Diaspora or Hellenistic Judaism, and not Pharisaic Judaism, which was regarded as pregnant with chauvinist failings.[191] As neither a Christian nor a Diaspora Jew, then, she claims to offer an alternative feminist perspective.

If the table fellowship of the Pharisee (Palestinian!) *havura* loomed large in Paul's vision, some of his rhetoric, and particularly... his 'rhetoric of equality', is actually carried over from that environment. When in his First Letter to the Corinthians Paul discusses the situation of mixed couples – Christian men and non-Christian women, Christian women and non-Christian men – he envisions the *haverim* (and *haverot*) and their *am-haaretz* partners. His belief that they can stay together without compromising their allegiance to Christianity may be based on his previous experience as a Pharisee, where he had seen such mixed couples work out their disagreements and go on living together.[192]

For Ilan, the apostle Paul offered two opportunities to further her ideological agenda. First, in her attempt to identify the Pharisees with the *haverim*, she sought to demonstrate the active participation of women within the pharisaic sect, thereby incorporating women into the male-dominated history of ancient Judaism. Paul's claim to be a Pharisee and his sensibilities with regard to intermarriage similar to those of the *haverim* appear to offer support in this regard. Second, Ilan is happy to challenge both the Christian and Diaspora feminist critique of Pharisaic Judaism by suggesting that the apparently egalitarian ethos of 1 Corinthians 7 can be put

husband; for otherwise your children are unclean, but now they are holy.' Tosefta Demai 2:16–17: 'A daughter of an *am-haaretz* married to a *haver*, the wife of an *am-haaretz* married to a *haver*, the slave of an *am-haaretz* sold to a *haver*, should undergo initiation (in order to become trustworthy). A daughter of a *haver* married to an *am-haaretz*, the wife of a *haver* married to an *am-haaretz* . . . they remain trustworthy.'

[188] Ilan here draws on 'Were you not a slave when you were called? Do not let that trouble you' (1 Cor. 7:21) and the epistle to Philemon in which Paul assumes that the Christian Philemon can own the Christian slave Onesimus. Ilan, 'Paul and Pharisee Women', 95.
[189] Ilan, 'Paul and Pharisee Women', 94–5.
[190] Ilan, 'Paul and Pharisee Women', 97.
[191] Ilan, 'Paul and Pharisee Women', 97–8.
[192] Ilan, 'Paul and Pharisee Women', 98.

down to Paul's close familiarity with the Palestinian *haver*-Pharisaic, rather than to a Hellenistic or Diaspora Jewish background.

Another feminist scholar with a penchant for criticising the anti-Jewish bias of some Christian feminist studies is Amy-Jill Levine (1956–), professor of New Testament Studies at the Protestant Vanderbilt Divinity School in Nashville, Tennessee, a location that has been described as 'the buckle of the bible-belt'. The southern Jewish scholar, who attends an Orthodox synagogue, credits her commitment to interfaith dialogue at least partly to having been brought up in a Roman Catholic neighbourhood.[193] She is the general editor of a series of feminist commentaries on the New Testament. In one, *A Feminist Companion to Paul* (2004), she hints at the importance she places upon the pragmatic, pastoral dimension of scholarship, observing, 'most feminists . . . find it insufficient to restrict analysis to first-century history. To respond to Paul is also to respond to all those who have been and continue to be influenced by him.'[194]

In *The Misunderstood Jew* (2006), a popular work that focuses primarily on the implications of modern scholarship,[195] Levine has a chapter entitled 'From a Jewish Sect to a Gentile Church' in which Paul, described as 'the church's first great evangelist',[196] plays the prominent role. After his encounter with the risen Christ, 'the Pharisee from Tarsus'[197] went to Arabia and to Damascus where, along with other followers of Jesus, he 'started the process of articulating a theology that would translate the Jewish Jesus into a gentile saviour.'[198] Any idea that he invented Christianity in the sense of repackaging Judaism for the non-Jews, however, is wrong, according to Levine. It ignores, for example, the prophet Zechariah's vision of the Gentiles streaming to Zion *as Gentiles*.[199] She makes little or no reference to Hellenistic influences. Instead, Paul, 'good Jew that he was', is shown to be in agreement with the later Talmud when he taught that the God of Israel was also the God of the Gentiles and that there was therefore no need for them to convert in order to receive his love and beneficence.[200]

There is a definite sense in which Levine appears to have conservative evangelical Christians in mind when she makes some of her observations regarding Paul. She wonders at the long-term legacy of the apostle's 'statement directed to a small,

---

[193] Amy-Jill Levine, *The Misunderstood Jew: The Church and the Scandal of the Jewish Jesus* (New York: Harper Collins, 2006), 1. Brought up in North Dartmouth, Massachusetts, Levine's introduction to the church was, she recalls, through 'ethnic Catholicism, and it was marvellous'.

[194] Amy-Jill Levine, *A Feminist Companion to Paul* (London: Continuum, 2004), 2.

[195] With regard to Paul's letters, Levine cites primarily from Romans, 1 Corinthians, and Galatians. She also mentions several Christian commentators, including S. Wesley Ariarajah, Nirmla Vasanthakumar, Elisabeth Schüssler Fiorenza, and Bärbel von Wartenberg-Potter.

[196] Levine, *The Misunderstood Jew*, 59.

[197] Levine, *The Misunderstood Jew*, 65.

[198] Levine, *The Misunderstood Jew*, 66.

[199] Levine, *The Misunderstood Jew*, 85.

[200] Levine, *The Misunderstood Jew*, 69. Levine cites Sanhedrin 105a, 'Righteous people of all nations have a share in the world to come.'

first century Greek congregation' that Christ would soon return (Thessalonians) and the North American right's fixation on the rapture and end times.[201] She contrasts 'the [Christian] proclamation heard so often today that "I am saved"' with Paul, who 'tends to put the idea of salvation into the future. Jesus justifies and sanctifies (in the present), but one is saved in the future [in Paul's view].'[202] And, in contextualising Saul's actions in persecuting the church, she points out how he resembled Protestants of all types who attacked members of the Church of Latter Day Saints for teaching something contrary to the basic tenets of their theology.[203]

At the same time, the modern context of interfaith dialogue provides an important backdrop to the study. For example, Levine's Paul had hoped that the Jewish representatives of the church would have prioritised the good of the institution as a whole over their particular practices. In discussing the controversy of Paul's attitude to food laws, Levine suggests that the fact that Peter and the other Jewish followers of Jesus in Antioch were determined to follow Jewish dietary practice might be seen as their recognition of the importance of their own cultural and religious identity. The lesson to be drawn is that

Multiculturalism, then and now, cannot function if there is a homogenous default that causes one group to give up what is of enormous value to them, especially if what is to be forsaken is divinely mandated Torah.[204]

In making the traditional Jewish case clearly and unambiguously, Levine emphasises a number of times the idea that, as far as Jews were concerned, Paul's Christ was redundant because they already believed in the resurrection of the dead and in a just God who forgave sin: 'there was nothing broken or missing in their system that his death or resurrection could fix or fill.'[205] And in a chapter dedicated to interfaith dialogue, she emphasised that Paul's explanation in Romans 11 for the 'failure' of the Jewish people to recognise Jesus (by stating that a 'hardening' had come upon the Jews until the Gentile mission was accomplished) was 'not altogether a model of good Jewish–Christian relations . . . since Paul does identify those hardened Jews as "enemies of God" and as lopped off the root of Israel (Romans 11).'[206]

Other Jewish commentators have written about Paul as a means to challenge Christian assumptions and/or to inculcate Jewish–Christian dialogue, of course. It is perhaps in her sensitivity to feminist approaches to New Testament studies that Levine is more distinctive. In addition to challenging Christian feminist

---

[201] Levine, *The Misunderstood Jew*, 60.
[202] Levine, *The Misunderstood Jew*, 67.
[203] Levine, *The Misunderstood Jew*, 65.
[204] Levine, *The Misunderstood Jew*, 76.
[205] Levine, *The Misunderstood Jew*, 67.
[206] Levine, *The Misunderstood Jew*, 218. Levine treats the passage in greater depth, 82–4.

presentations of *Jesus* freeing women from an oppressive, misogynistic Judaism, Levine also wishes to correct similar ideas about *Paul*. Against those who see the apostle as sexist and placing restrictions on women,[207] as a result of his rabbinic training, she points out the anachronism of the charge: that he belonged to no rabbinic school, and that the rabbinic literature is dated to after Paul.[208] Against those who would see him as advocating a positive role for women to play against the background of Judaism, where women's role was passive, she diplomatically draws upon Christian feminist writers whose familiarity with the sources give the lie to such 'noxious stereotypes'.[209] She also insists that the Jewish community has always regarded women as full members and demonstrates from a variety of texts from intertestamental literature, Josephus, and the Talmud the positive, active role of women within Judaism, all the while acknowledging that 'both church and synagogue are patriarchal institutions; neither was egalitarian in the first century.'[210] A particular case in point, which Levine critiques twice in the book, is the claim that Paul's abolition of circumcision and introduction of baptism as an initiation rite opened up the new faith to Gentiles, men *and* women, and abolished a rite that venerated male fertility. Such commentators, Levine suggests, overlook the alternative interpretation of baptism, a symbol of rebirth, as a substitution of birth into the church for the biological mother's role. 'That is, baptism can be just as much a problem symbolically as circumcision when it comes to questions of gender.'[211] In any case, she argues, Paul promoted the idea of baptism not because of some feminist impulse or concern that women should not bear the mark of circumcision, but because circumcision indicated conversion to Judaism, which he regarded as unnecessary.[212] That Paul is cast as neither a hero nor a villain in this context must be put down to Levine's remarkable balance of ideological self-awareness and well-honed sensitivity to historicity.

Levine is an important commentator on Paul whose Jewish feminist perspective means that she will battle with Christians, and Christian feminists, who seek to elevate Christianity at the expense of denigrating and misrepresenting Judaism. Her practical, programmatic approach to Jewish–Christian relations, and her use of Paul in this context, is premised upon the need to correct the erroneous views that Jews and Christians have of each other for the purposes of more harmonious interfaith relations. Bearing in mind that, as Levine herself points out, being biased is not the same things as being wrong, she explains,

---

[207] Levine cites 1 Cor. 14: 34–5. 'The women are to keep silent in the churches; for they are not permitted to speak, but are to subject themselves, just as the Law also says. If they desire to learn anything, let them ask their own husbands at home; for it is improper for a woman to speak in church.'

[208] Levine, *The Misunderstood Jew*, 178.

[209] Levine, *The Misunderstood Jew*, 178–9. Levine cites Elisabeth Schüssler Fiorenza and Wanda Deifelt.

[210] Levine, *The Misunderstood Jew*, 73.

[211] Levine, *The Misunderstood Jew*, 179.

[212] Levine, *The Misunderstood Jew*, 73.

I am convinced that interfaith conversation is essential if we are to break down the prejudices that have kept synagogue and church in enmity, or at best tolerance, for the past two millennia. In other words, I am placing my scholarship in service to personal, pastoral, and even political ends.[213]

The Jewish feminist perspective, as reflected in the work of Eisenbaum, Ilan, Levine, and others, has become a permanent feature – and an increasingly influential voice – within the modern Jewish ideological landscape. Whatever the difficulties, the fact that feminism has gained so many victories in the wider, non-Jewish world means that this relatively recent phenomenon will continue to impact on the whole Jewish community. That Paul, who has always attracted the attention of Christian feminist New Testament scholars, also acts as a research focus for Jewish feminists is, perhaps, not remarkable. In the case of Hebrew Christians or Messianic Jews, the struggle for acknowledgment and recognition has met with much stiffer opposition. Marginalised as they are, their use of Paul is perhaps just as predictable, however.

HEBREW CHRISTIAN AND MESSIANIC JEWISH PERSPECTIVES

Although the boundaries are fuzzy, one can legitimately differentiate between *Hebrew* or *Jewish Christians*, who, despite a Jewish self-definition, tend to belong to Christian denominations and to adhere to a mainstream Gentile lifestyle in terms of religious observance, and *Messianic Jews*, whose Jewish ethnicity is their primary identity and who religious rituals are modelled upon conventional Jewish practices. For our purposes, however, they can be treated together. Both groups regard Jesus as the messiah and believe that any form of Judaism that does not recognise him has lost its way; they are as concerned to correct Gentile misconceptions about the Jewish roots of their faith as to draw Jews into their fellowship; and they have achieved the remarkable feat of uniting the vast majority of other Jews in opposition to them, because they are perceived as promoting Christianity under another name. In response, these Jewish followers of Jesus are passionate in defending their claim to Jewish authenticity. In this context, a study of the apostle Paul represents a useful arena in which to propagate a controversial position in the face of both Jewish and Christian antagonism. Since it is somewhat rare to have such writers included in a survey of Jewish views of Paul, extra space will be accorded here to three examples that together span the twentieth century.[214]

---

[213] Levine, *The Misunderstood Jew*, 5.

[214] Leon Levison's *Life of St. Paul* (Edinburgh: Marshall Brothers, 1916), which adopts a relatively orthodox Hebrew Christian position, is an obvious omission. One might also have included more popular works, such as Michael Brown's *What Do Jewish People Think about Jesus? And Other Questions Christians Ask about Jewish Beliefs, Practices, and History* (Grand Rapids, Mich: Chosen Books, 2007), which addresses Paul's significance from a messianic Jewish perspective and with a Jewish audience very much in mind, asking, 'Was Paul really an educated Jew who knew the Hebrew

Paul Levertoff (1878–1954) was born Feivel Levertoff in Belarus to a Hasidic family, where he received a traditional Jewish education.[215] Following Talmudic studies at the Volozhin *yeshiva*, he went on to the University of Königsberg in Prussia, where he converted to Christianity in 1895. He became a missionary, working for various societies throughout Europe,[216] and demonstrated a flair for translation and scholarship. After a stint as a lecturer in rabbinics in Leipzig,[217] he moved to Wales, where he was ordained as an Anglican minister, and then on to East London, where he established an independent Messianic Jewish congregation, although for a time he was closely associated with the International Hebrew Christian Alliance. A particular interest in his theology was the attempt to reconcile the teachings of the New Testament with Hasidic thought, and he is best remembered for his partial translation of the Zohar for Soncino Press.[218] His *Ben ha-Adam* (1904)[219] was the first treatment of Jesus in modern Hebrew.

Levertoff's interest in Paul came to the fore early with his study entitled *St Paul: His Life, Works and Travels* (1907),[220] when he was working for the London Society for Promoting Christianity amongst the Jews.[221] There is little in this short work that would have raised an eyebrow among Christian readers, but Levertoff intended it for a Jewish audience and wrote his treatment of Paul in modern Hebrew, as the first author to do so.[222] In his introduction, he laments the fact that every time he

language well?' 'Did Paul abolish the law?' 'What did Paul mean when he said that "all Israel will be saved"?').

[215] For a useful overview of Levertoff's life and writings, see Jorge Quiñónez, 'Paul Phillip Levertoff: Pioneering Hebrew-Christian Scholar and Leader', *Mishkan* 37 (2002), 21–34.

[216] He worked for the London Society for Promoting Christianity amongst the Jews from 1896 to 1910, and the United Free Church of Scotland Jewish Committee as their evangelist in Constantinople (1910–11). He was director of the East London Fund for the Jews (also known as London Diocesan Council for Work among the Jews) 1923–54.

[217] He taught at the Institutum Judaicum Delitzschianum 1912–18, although he was held under house arrest as a Russian citizen 1914–16. In addition to rabbinics he also taught Yiddish and a variety of courses in Jewish Studies and the New Testament.

[218] Harry Sperling, Maurice Simon, and Paul Phillip Levertoff, trans., *Zohar* vol.3 (London: Soncino Press, 1933) and Maurice Simon and Paul Phillip Levertoff, trans., *Zohar* vol.4 (London: Soncino Press, 1933).

[219] *Ben ha-Adam: Chayey Yeshua ha-Mashiach upealeav* (London: 1904), the English title given as *Son of Man: A Survey of the Life and Deeds of Jesus Christ*. The author of the second Hebrew attempt, Joseph Klausner, is dismissive of Levertoff's study, complaining that 'the plain purpose of the writer in spite of what he says to the contrary in his Preface is to win adherents to Christianity from among Russian Jews who read Hebrew.' Klausner, *Jesus of Nazareth*, 124.

[220] Paul Levertov, *Polus ha-Shaliach o Sha'ul ish Tarsus: Chayav, po'alav u-nesi'otav* (London: 1907), the English title given as *St Paul: His Life, Works, and Travels*.

[221] Also of interest are his series of three lectures Paul P. Levertoff, 'St Paul in Jewish Thought: Three Lectures' (London: Diocesan House, 1928), where he offered a select survey of Jewish commentators, including Schiller-Szinessy, Montefiore, and Werfel; he also mentioned the Christian scholar Kittel. In discussing Paul, he cited Acts, Romans, 1 and 2 Corinthians, Galatians, Philippians, Colossians, and Timothy. No references or scholarly citations are offered in the 1907 book. In addition, Levertoff translated Franz Werfel, *Paulus unter den Juden* (Berlin: Zsolnay, 1926) as Franz Werfel, *Paul among the Jews: A Tragedy*, trans. Paul Levertoff (London: A.R. Mowbray & Co., 1928).

[222] Levertov, *Polus ha-Shaliach*, iv.

writes about 'messianism' (as he calls Christianity), it is necessary for him justify his reasons. He argued that there should be no more need to explain a book on Paul than there was a book on Maimonides, because the essential character of Messianism 'is so *Hebrew* and . . . ought to be common to the lips of every child of Israel'.[223] In offering a full picture of the life of Paul the Apostle in a concise and popular manner,[224] Levertoff was clear that his aim is a missionary one.[225] Nevertheless, he regarded himself as Jewish[226] and his vision was of a profoundly Hebraic interpretation of what it meant to be a follower of the Messiah, Jesus of Nazareth. For example, he sprinkled the text with Hebrew and Aramaic phrases that are laden with Jewish religious meaning.[227]

According to Levertoff, Paul's work was a continuation of the life and mission of Jesus of Nazareth.[228] Although Jesus had not been able to reveal the full significance of his appearance in the world ('The generation was not yet worthy of it') and his disciples had failed to comprehend it, Paul was able to articulate the essence of Jesus' messianic title 'Son of Man' and to develop his ideas. In contrast to the other disciples, who were simple and unlearned men, Paul was a scholar whose writings represent 'the most complete interpretation of Messianism there is in the world.'[229] In particular, because Jesus could not explain the meaning of his own death, Paul had done so, and his (thirteen) letters reveal a progressive realisation

---

[223] Levertov, *Polus ha-Shaliach*, ii.

[224] Levertov, *Polus ha-Shaliach*, iii.

[225] He hopes to 'awaken such a desire in the hearts of those who stand apart from Messianism, and to strengthen the impression in those who have already been bestowed with a little of Messianism – that is our aim in our literary work in general and in writing this book in particular.' Levertov, *Polus ha-Shaliach*, iii. He also writes of his hope that it will 'produce beneficial fruit for our people, the People of Israel, and will show a way and an opening to salvation, this being our prayer rising from the depths of the heart which is hurting and concerned for its people.' Levertov, *Polus ha-Shaliach*, iv.

[226] Levertoff's daughter recalls his mantra: 'Christianity is Judaism with its hopes fulfilled.' Olga Levertoff, 'Paul Levertoff and the Jewish-Christian Problem' in Lev Gillet, ed., *Judaism and Christianity: Essays Presented to the Rev. Paul P. Levertoff* (London: JB Shears and Sons, 1939), 97. As Levertoff saw it, 'The "New Testament" was founded and built upon the foundation of the "Old Testament"; the latter signifies the age of prophecies and aspirations, the former – the age of realisation and fulfilment'. Levertov, *Polus ha-Shaliach*, 18.

[227] He describes Paul as one of 'the great men' (*eshlae ravrevei*), or attributes the root of Messianism in terms of 'a secret and hidden force' (where *tamir v'nelam* refers to God). He is also careful to explain the Christian religion (*ha-dat ha-Nozrit*), a label with very negative connotations, in terms of the exalted founder-figure of Jesus of Nazareth (*Nazrat*), and generally prefers to write of the Messianic religion (*ha-dat ha-mashichit*). The stoning of Stephen is described in the traditional language of martyrdom as 'sanctifying the Name' (*kiddush ha-shem*). Levertov, *Polus ha-Shaliach*, 2, 20–21, 23.

[228] Levertov, *Polus ha-Shaliach*, ii, 5.

[229] Levertov, *Polus ha-Shaliach*, 5. He went on, 'The most sound way to understand Paul's writings is to look at them as the continuation of the teachings of Jesus himself. They contain many of those ideas that Jesus took with him and never uttered in words. . . . Of course, if Jesus had expressed them himself, then the explanation would have been different. But although Paul's ideas always bear the stamp of his rational personality, yet their essence is without doubt the essence of the ideas of Jesus himself.' Ibid., 5–6.

of the sacrificial significance of the messiah's death[230] and God's plan 'to demolish
the iron wall that had been put between Jew and Gentile', a task which could not
have been given to Jesus, who had been 'plucked away while in the prime of his
youth'.[231] Thus Paul could take his place alongside Moses, David, Isaiah, and other
great Jewish personalities and heroes who, during the weightier periods of world
history, had been drawn to the stage by the invisible hand of providence and who
had 'forced the current of history to direct itself to a particular goal.'[232]

   Although mainly adhering to the traditional Christian account, Levertoff occasionally fills in gaps in the apostle's biographical record, such as the family decision
to send the precocious Saul to *yeshiva* to prepare to be a rabbi (rather than to be a
merchant), to wonder whether he attended university in Tarsus, where he would
have become familiar with Greek thought and methods of debate,[233] and to suggest
that his mentor, Gamaliel the Great, was tolerant of Greek wisdom.[234] Although
Levertoff spends considerable time praising the benefits of a rabbinic education
for a missionary who would always gravitate towards the local synagogue in his
travels,[235] he also notes that Saul would have been taught that peace of mind and
God's reward could only be obtained by observance of the commandments.[236]
He believes that Saul went through severe spiritual sufferings in that the more he
tried to observe the Law, the more powerful grew 'the evil inclination'.[237] Saul's
increasingly desperate, guilt-ridden zeal for the Law led him to persecute early
messianism, and Levertoff writes sympathetically of Saul's shock at its account
of a crucified messiah, 'a terrible desecration of the Name and a betrayal of all
that makes Israel holy'.[238] Only during the tranquillity and quietness of his journey on the road to Damascus did Saul's personal sense of guilt and the powerful
impression made by messianics such as Stephen and their teachings of a suffering
messiah bring about the famous vision and blindness, and 'the total shattering of
the previous system of his life'.[239] In the period that followed, Levertoff suggested

---

[230] '[T]o Paul it was given to discover and reveal the full height and depth of the work of "the Son of
God" as a saviour for humankind. He very seldom speaks of the Messiah's life on earth, though we
know from several hints in his writings that he knew it well. For him, the messiah was always – that
sublime, glorious creature whose head was crowned with the splendour of the heavenly rays, who
appeared to him on the road to Damascus, who held his hand and brought him to the foundations
of heavenly peace and the joy of the new life.' Levertov, *Polus ha-Shaliach*, 41.

[231] Levertov, *Polus ha-Shaliach*, 6–7.

[232] Levertov, *Polus ha-Shaliach*, 1, 2.

[233] Levertov, *Polus ha-Shaliach*, 15–16. 'Did he draw water from the springs of science descending from
Mount Helicon before going to sit by the water flowing down from Mount Zion? . . . The speech
he made in Athens [in Acts] shows us how he could, if he only wished, employ a style superior in
splendour to that of his letters'. Ibid.

[234] Levertov, *Polus ha-Shaliach*, 17.

[235] Levertov, *Polus ha-Shaliach*, 18.

[236] Levertov, *Polus ha-Shaliach*, 19.

[237] Levertov, *Polus ha-Shaliach*, 20–21.

[238] Levertov, *Polus ha-Shaliach*, 23.

[239] Levertov, *Polus ha-Shaliach*, 26–9.

that Paul, 'an ardent nationalist', came to realise that his hope for a Jewish messiah who would save the world was realised in Jesus. About his self-imposed exile in the Arabian desert, near Mount Sinai, Levertoff once again emphasises Paul's place in authentic Jewish tradition.

Exalted memories hovered over that place and the shadows of great men went about it. There Moses saw the burning bush and listened to the voice of Jehovah from the top of the mountain; there Elijah secluded himself in his wanderings, full of zeal for Jehovah and there he drank from the fountains of salvation. What place was better suited than this place for the thoughts of the man following them?[240]

In his solitude, Paul's meditations led him to conclude that neither Gentiles, who were immersed in idolatry, nor Jews, who knew the Torah but did not do it,[241] could achieve righteousness. In the case of Jews,

their knowledge made the weight of their guilt all the greater, because they sinned while facing the light. While the Gentiles went in darkness and to a certain extent only sinned without evil intent, the Children of Israel sinned wilfully and intentionally. Their being chosen was their disgrace! They aroused Jehovah's wrath more than the Gentiles whom they hated and despised, and Jehovah's judgement was harsher upon them.[242]

This was all part of God's plan: like 'an expert doctor who sometimes strives to bring about a headache by artificial means prior to a cure', God allowed the Gentiles to follow their desires and the Jews Torah, 'so that man's nature, evil from his youth, would be fully revealed in all its distressing character'.[243] Levertoff's Paul is an abrogator of the Law, and even a Lutheran in that he believed that faith alone was necessary for salvation,[244] although this is presented as an idea foreshadowed in the Old Testament.[245] Echoing Christian Church fathers,[246] Levertoff's Paul believed that Adam's descendents were burdened both by a state of sin which

---

[240] Levertov, *Polus ha-Shaliach*, 33.

[241] Levertoff cites Abot 1:17, 'It is the deeds that count and not the study'. Levertov, *Polus ha-Shaliach*, 35.

[242] Levertov, *Polus ha-Shaliach*, 35–6.

[243] Levertov, *Polus ha-Shaliach*, 36.

[244] 'The Torah had never been the definite way to salvation.... It only served as a negative means by which to demonstrate the necessity of salvation.' Levertov, *Polus ha-Shaliach*, 36. 'The one human condition for receiving God's righteousness is – faith; and this is as possible for a gentile as for a Jew.' Ibid., 38.

[245] 'In truth, the secret had already been known in the past, too. It was heralded by the Prophets and also hinted at in the Torah. The Torah gave testimony for it only negatively; the Prophets grasped it more positively. Abraham, too, had already glanced into that secret: he became righteous through God not by action but by faith.... But the patriarchs and the prophets saw only the first rays of sunrise; daylight in its full force burst through only in Paul's day.' Levertov, *Polus ha-Shaliach*, 38–9.

[246] Interestingly, Levertoff translated some of Augustine into Hebrew. Paul Levertoff, *The Confessions of St Augustine* (London: Luzac & Co., 1908).

they were unable to free themselves from and by a physical nature incapable of righteousness.[247]

In a chapter entitled 'His Great Dispute', Levertoff discusses the key question of the relationship between messianism and Judaism. He argues that although many of the Children of Israel had regarded the Law as a heavy burden that was necessary if God was to create a unique people (for this required 'a furnace and a trial for the spirit of the Israelite People'),[248] others, who were proud and arrogant, saw it as evidence that they were a superior nation and even added new laws to separate themselves further from the surrounding peoples.[249] This 'national arrogance' led them to an expectation that the kingdom of the messiah would in fact be the kingdom of Israel.[250] 'National arrogance and ancient traditions' also meant that even after Peter's dream, which had demonstrated that both the circumcised and the uncircumcised were acceptable to God, the question of whether Gentiles should be included without conversion to Judaism remained contentious.[251] Paul had come to a similar conclusion independent of Peter. Partly this was because 'he was a man of the world and understood better than his fellows and compatriots in Jerusalem how dangerous were the conditions which they imposed, for the spreading of Messianism outside Palestine', bearing in mind that neither the 'haughty Romans' nor 'the high-minded Greeks' would have agreed to undergo circumcision and 'generally to imprison their lives within the narrow confines of the national traditions of the People of Israel.'[252] In other words, Paul was an opportunist of sorts, for 'a religion entailing such heavy burdens could not possibly become a world religion.'[253] Partly, the opposition which Paul faced was due to the self-interest of the messianic Jews, who did not want to be ostracised from their fellow Jews and who were therefore determined to avoid the complications of socialising with Gentiles with their different modes of behaviour and customs. There would also have been religious jealousy, too, regarding Gentile inclusion.[254] Paul's success in defeating these Judaisers was highly significant: 'If the outcome had been reversed, Messianism would now be a forgotten Jewish sect, not the faith of most enlightened peoples.'[255]

Perhaps Levertoff's most interesting comments lie in his speculations regarding the attitude of pro-Pauline Jewish messianics towards the Law. Admitting that it was possible that they believed themselves to be free from the burden of the Law along with their Gentile brothers in Christ, Levertoff points out that Paul never

[247] Levertov, *Polus ha-Shaliach*, 39.
[248] Levertov, *Polus ha-Shaliach*, 80.
[249] Levertov, *Polus ha-Shaliach*, 80.
[250] Levertov, *Polus ha-Shaliach*, 81.
[251] Levertov, *Polus ha-Shaliach*, 82.
[252] Levertov, *Polus ha-Shaliach*, 83.
[253] Levertov, *Polus ha-Shaliach*, 83.
[254] Levertov, *Polus ha-Shaliach*, 84.
[255] Levertov, *Polus ha-Shaliach*, 86.

explicitly argued against circumcision in particular nor observance of the Law in general for Jews by birth. Thus,

we see clearly that he did not see it as part of his work to interfere with the Jews holding on to their national customs. . . . [I]f any man of Israel held on to Israelite customs as a mark of his nationality, Paul was very far from reproachful; on the contrary, he himself had a certain fondness for those customs.[256]

Effusive in his admiration for Paul, Levertoff regarded him as a Jewish hero who took Jesus' true Judaism or 'messianism' to the Gentile world. The apostle's letters, especially Romans, Galatians, and 2 Corinthians, were 'one of the most sublime resources of human thought and whose influence is still spreading to this very day.'[257] They revealed Paul's originality which 'gave the human race a new world of thoughts and ideas . . . [and] all progress and renewal that has ever taken place within Messianism took its cue from these writings.'[258] Paul's innovations, although strictly limited to working out the teachings implicit in Jesus' ministry, lay in his genius for understanding the non-Jewish world and articulating to them the nature of true Judaism. Although Levertoff spoke about Paul in general historical terms, his fellow Hebrew Christian missionary, Sanford Mills, and the Israeli messianic Jew, Joseph Shulam, would reach similar conclusions in their commentaries on the apostle's epistle to the Romans, specifically.

Sanford C. Mills was born in Poland to an Orthodox Jewish family and given a traditional Jewish education before he moved with his parents to the United States in 1921. He converted to Christianity as a young man and dedicated his career to the mission field, mostly among Gentiles, although he was also associated with the American Board of Missions to the Jews.[259] He regarded himself as 'a Hebrew Christian' and 'Jewish',[260] although he was also happy to be described as 'a Christian gentleman' and a Baptist who firmly believed in the pre-millennial, pretribulation rapture.[261] His commentary, *A Hebrew Christian Looks at Romans* (1968),[262] is written primarily with a Gentile audience in mind, although it was

---

[256] Levertov, *Polus ha-Shaliach*, 88.

[257] Levertov, *Polus ha-Shaliach*, 69–70.

[258] Levertov, *Polus ha-Shaliach*, 70. Admittedly, the letters were often written hurriedly, and were certainly unsystematic in nature. Ibid., 71.

[259] Daniel Fuchs, 'Introduction', in Sanford C. Mills, *A Hebrew Christian Looks at Romans*, second edition (Grand Rapids, MI: Dunham Publishing, 1969), 10. Fuchs was Secretary of the Board. Mills writes of himself as one 'who has spent decades of time as a field evangelist in the active work of Jewish missions.' Mills, *A Hebrew Christian Looks at Romans*, 290.

[260] Mills, *A Hebrew Christian Looks at Romans*, 167, 173.

[261] Rev. Noel P. Irwin, 'Foreword' in Mills, *A Hebrew Christian Looks at Romans*, 8–9. Irwin was pastor of Calvary Baptist Church, South Bend, Indiana.

[262] Sanford C. Mills, *A Hebrew Christian Looks at Romans* (Grand Rapids, MI: Dunham Publishing, 1968). The second edition (1969) will be used here. Mills offered numerous proof-texts from throughout the New Testament and accepted Acts as entirely historical. He drew upon many Christian commentators on Romans and on biblical Greek, including Barclay, Haldane, Kittel, Luther, and Sanday, and a few Jewish writers on Jewish subjects, such as Montefiore and Hertz.

also regarded by supporters as 'a valuable contribution to Jewish evangelism.'[263] For the former, Mills offered correctives to Christian doctrine arrived at from his knowledge of Talmud, Targum, and Tanakh;[264] for the latter, he offered a strange mix of empathy and Baptist fire-and-brimstone invective in response to their stubbornness of heart.

Mills was concerned from the outset to demonstrate that Paul was not, 'as the Jews say,' the one who changed Jesus' message and spread Christianity throughout the world. The gospel preached by Paul was not foreign to the preaching of Christ but was one with it; crucially, it was a *Jewish* gospel through and through.[265] Thus 'there is no such thing as a Gentile church... [for] such an idea is a monstrosity in theology'.[266] It followed that a Hebrew Christian was not abandoning his faith. Rather, 'a Jew who becomes a Christian, a believer in the Lord Jesus Christ, is a *completed Jew.*'[267] Despite a general rejection of the gospel among the populace, there had always been a remnant of true Jews who were prepared to accept Christ.[268] Paul himself is described as a 'Hebrew Christian warrior of the cross'[269] who was a highly trained and educated Pharisaic Jew.[270] Many of his teachings that were often regarded as Gentile inventions were no such thing. For example, in a discussion about Christ's redemptive sacrifice he argued that, despite what was often claimed, 'substitutionary atonement is not foreign to Judaism' and was an integral component to the Day of Atonement.[271] He was prepared to acknowledge, however, that Paul did deliver 'body blows to Judaism',[272] especially in terms of the apostle's view of the Law, which was 'to bring Jew and Gentile to the realisation that both are sinners. For by the Law is knowledge of sin.'[273] But Mills was wary of exaggerating Paul's attitude towards the Law, cautioning his readers, 'we must guard ourselves against antinomianism, a sect which holds that faith alone, not obedience to the moral law, is necessary for salvation.'[274]

---

[263] Rev. Noel P. Irwin, 'Foreword' in Mills, *A Hebrew Christian Looks at Romans*, 9.

[264] For example, Mills was concerned to correct Catholic conceptions of Mary mothering God and the proper protocol for 'Believer's Baptism'. Mills, *A Hebrew Christian Looks at Romans*, 24, 173ff.

[265] 'The Gospel is not new. Basically and fundamentally the Gospel is Jewish, Jewish in origin, Jewish in its message, "for salvation is from the Jews" (John 4:22). It is not from the Gentiles.' Mills, *A Hebrew Christian Looks at Romans*, 20–21.

[266] Mills, *A Hebrew Christian Looks at Romans*, 103. 'The term "Israelites" [Romans 9:4] applies only to the nation of Israel.... It does not and cannot mean the Church of the New Testament, in any sense of the word. To apply the term Israelites to the Church does violence to the Word of God.' Ibid., 291.

[267] Mills, *A Hebrew Christian Looks at Romans*, 75.

[268] For Mills it was 'not true to say that the Jews, *as a people*, rejected Jesus as their messiah. The *Jewish leaders and their politicians* rejected Him, but the multitudes, the common people, as recorded in the Gospels and the Book of Acts, followed Him.' Mills, *A Hebrew Christian Looks at Romans*, 297.

[269] Mills, *A Hebrew Christian Looks at Romans*, 492.

[270] Mills, *A Hebrew Christian Looks at Romans*, 29, 76.

[271] Mills, *A Hebrew Christian Looks at Romans*, 102.

[272] Mills, *A Hebrew Christian Looks at Romans*, 77.

[273] Mills, *A Hebrew Christian Looks at Romans*, 90.

[274] Mills, *A Hebrew Christian Looks at Romans*, 104.

A constant theme in the book is Mills' call for renewed mission to Jews. He points to the efforts made to take the gospel to China and Africa, and bewails the lack of interest in Jews in this context.

We all believe that the Jews are lost, but what are we doing for them today? We talk of the Jews in prophecy. We speak of the Tribulation Period as a time of Jacob's trouble. We elaborate upon the atrocities that the Jews will suffer, and of the handful, the remnant, that will be saved. This is good. But how terrible it is when we realize that we have done and are doing so little for the Jews in the missionary program of many of our churches.[275]

Although Mills did not underestimate the problem facing missionaries to the Jewish people in the light of centuries of their maltreatment by Christians,[276] he was frustrated by lack of Christian commitment to this end. He wrote disparagingly of those Christians who did not take Paul seriously at his word that the Gospel was for 'the Jew first'[277] and expressed disappointment in having attended 'hundreds of Christian meetings where mission of all kinds, domestic and foreign, have been presented', yet having rarely ever heard 'any mention made of the plight of the Jews, and their need of the Gospel.' The Jew, he said, is 'joked about, and in many cases, slandered when he isn't maligned, and often pointed to as an example of disobedience, but scarcely ever prayed for, and almost never represented as a people needing the Gospel.'[278] His passionate plea was to refuse to give up on Jews.

By what stretch of the imagination can anyone claim that the Jews have had their chance and lost it, and that now they have been set aside in order that the Gentiles may have *their* chance during the present age? How can it be claimed by anyone familiar with the history of Christianity that the Jews have had their chance and lost it, when the

---

[275] Mills, *A Hebrew Christian Looks at Romans*, 106.

[276] 'The Gentiles, from the beginning of Jewish history until the present time, have far exceeded the sum total of Israel's transgressions and guilt. The guilt of one Gentile nation, Germany, in just ten years has been a million times greater than the guilt of all the Jews throughout their entire existence. The history of the Roman Empire, the Roman Catholic Church, Spain, Italy, France, England, and Russia, teems with Jewish persecution, murder and exile.' Mills, *A Hebrew Christian Looks at Romans*, 365–6. Mills himself writes of having experienced anti-Semitism in his youth. 'The writer is a Jewish Christian and he cannot be blind to the Jew-hate of today and the experiences of his people Israel through past an present ages. He knows from childhood what it means to be called "a dirty Jew". The memory of this and other painful experiences can never be forgotten. Opprobrious epithets such as "Christ-killer!" and the haunting words of the Polish people, "Why can't you go home to your own country?" still ring in his ears. Who can blame the Jews in Israel if they do not want the Gospel preached to them? The terrors of past persecutions, ostracisms and banishments by those who called themselves Christians but never knew the meaning of the word, make it extremely difficult for Jewish in Israel, and elsewhere, to tolerate the Gospel.' Ibid., 431–2.

[277] 'Usually, the person who will not accept the fact "to the Jew first" will not take it [the Gospel] to the Jew at all. This has been the experience of this writer for over twenty-five years.' Mills, *A Hebrew Christian Looks at Romans*, 106.

[278] Mills, *A Hebrew Christian Looks at Romans*, 290. Partly, Mills explained this in terms of 'the unscriptural philosophy of the "Gentile Church", claiming that we are now in the "Gentile Church age". Ibid., 350.

Jews, at best, have only heard the Gospel in its entirety for about forty years, from 30 to 70 AD?[279]

Espousing a Baptist ideology, Mills' pronouncements were Bible-based,[280] anti-Catholic,[281] and suspicious of evolution.[282] It is his antirabbinic statements that are of most interest here, however. Thus he attacks the rabbis' rite of circumcising the dead,[283] the laws of *kashrut*,[284] their Talmudic learning,[285] their prayers,[286] and their refusal to accept traditions that supported Christian teachings.[287] In general, Jews are condemned for their pride, because they know the truth but do not follow it,[288] and two thousand years of suffering are interpreted as God's punishment for their sins.[289] Even when defending their probity, he cannot help but condemn them for their 'works-righteousness'.[290] Despite all this, Mills was quick to draw upon stories and sayings from traditional Jewish literature that he believed strengthened his reading of Paul's epistle to the Romans.[291] Most important in this context

---

[279] Mills, *A Hebrew Christian Looks at Romans*, 389.

[280] 'The Word of God must always be the final authority. We cannot, we must not, question it.' Mills, *A Hebrew Christian Looks at Romans*, 22. It was also progressive revelation, in that it led towards the Gospel. Mills, *A Hebrew Christian Looks at Romans*, 92. 'This writer is not only Jewish, but he is also biblical.' Mills, *A Hebrew Christian Looks at Romans*, 173.

[281] Mills, *A Hebrew Christian Looks at Romans*, 24, 31, 62.

[282] Mills, *A Hebrew Christian Looks at Romans*, 50.

[283] Mills, *A Hebrew Christian Looks at Romans*, 60–62.

[284] Mills, *A Hebrew Christian Looks at Romans*, 66.

[285] Mills, *A Hebrew Christian Looks at Romans*, 68.

[286] Mills, *A Hebrew Christian Looks at Romans*, 157, 222.

[287] 'Modern Judaism does not accept this [idea of Adam's sin bringing death to all, Zohar in Num. fol. 52]. The Jews, like all religionists, change "with every wind of doctrine". Like all the unregenerate theologians, the Jewish rabbis teach that their own works will save them. . . . The Bible teaches contrary.' Mills, *A Hebrew Christian Looks at Romans*, 164. 'Modern Judaism has changed this idea that God created the evil in man [citing, *inter alia*, Sanhedrin 91b and Tanhumah-Beshalla 3].' Ibid., 222.

[288] Mills, *A Hebrew Christian Looks at Romans*, 65, 76.

[289] Mills, *A Hebrew Christian Looks at Romans*, 67, 70. 'Israel as a nation may be wallowing in sin. She may be scattered among the nations and seemingly lost in the maelstrom of iniquity.' Ibid., 366.

[290] 'The problem with Israel is, and has always been, a lack of faith. The Jewish people do not lack morals, or standards, or laws. They boast of having all of these. The divorce rate among Jews is low; dope addiction among Jewish teen-agers is surprisingly low; the number of Jews in penal institutions is insignificant; and alcoholism is rare among Jews. They are a moral people. Works of righteousness supercede faith in the Jewish mind. To a Jew, no matter what a man believes, so long as he is morally upright he is a righteous individual. "Prayer, charity and fasting overcometh all evil deeds." This brief prayer summarizes the Jewish concept of righteousness – *works!*' Mills, *A Hebrew Christian Looks at Romans*, 329–30.

[291] Parallels offered include 'all things work together for the good' (Rom. 8:28) with 'Whatsoever heaven does is for the best' (Berahhot 60b) (274); 'for there is no respect of persons with God' (Rom. 2:11) with the story of Yochannan Ben Van Zakki [sic] who exclaimed, 'If I am to come into the presence of this kind of King, should I not weep?' (61); Paul's call to live 'in diligence not slothful' (Rom. 12:11) with 'The day is short, the work is much, and the workmen are indolent (slothful), and reward much; and the Master of the house is insistent' (Mishnah 2:15) (417); Paul's call to 'put ye on of Christ' (Rom. 13:14) with the rabbinic 'putting on of the cloak of the Shekinah' (442); Paul's claim that 'not the hearers of the law are just before God, but the doers of law shall be justified' with

was the link he frequently made between original sin and the evil inclination (or 'evil imagination', as he called the *yetzer ha-ra*).[292] As with Levertoff before him, the overall impression made by Mills is that of pride in his Jewish heritage and a burning desire to evangelise Jews. To recover the Jewish roots of the Christian gospel as enunciated by Paul is therefore a means to a very specific end. At the same time, Mills, even more than Levertoff, uses his treatment of Paul to express his indignation at the indifference of Gentile Christians to the precious Jewish resources and understanding available to them. They share an awareness that both Jewish and Christian audiences were frustratingly ill-disposed towards their message.

The final example of a Pauline study by a Jewish believer in Jesus is different from the previous examples in that it is by an individual who, as a Messianic Jew, belongs to no Christian congregation. Nevertheless, it follows a similar approach in arguing for Jewish legitimacy and in fact takes the idea of locating Paul and his ideas within a Jewish context to its logical extreme by attempting a systematic review of relevant Jewish literature from the Biblical and post-Biblical periods. Joseph Baruch Shulam (1946–) is a Bulgarian-born Jew whose family immigrated to Israel in 1948. In 1962 he came to believe that Jesus (or Yeshua) was the Messiah and joined the Messianic Jewish community in Jerusalem; he is now an Elder of the Messianic *Congregation Roeh Israel*.[293] He has taught at Abilene Christian University in Jerusalem and has written *A Commentary on the Jewish Roots of Romans* with Hilary Le Cornu (1997),[294] which draws upon parallels in biblical, Qumranic, and rabbinic literature to establish Paul as a profoundly Jewish writer whose authentic Jewish theology is best interpreted in a Jewish literary context.[295]

Gamaliel's son, 'a classmate of Paul's', in Pirque Aboth 1:18 (61). The Davidic ancestry of the messiah (Rom. 15:12) is also reinforced by reference to Rabbi David Kimchi, Rabbi Aben Ezra, the Targums of Jonathan, and the Prayer Book (471).

[292] Mills, *A Hebrew Christian Looks at Romans*, 94, 178, 222, 230, 265–6. He cites in support *inter alia* Midrash Haneelam in Zohar Gen. fol. 68:1, Midrash Kobeleth fol. 70:2, Sanhedrin 91b, Tanhumah-Beshalla 3, Caphtor fol. 14:2, and Bereshita Rabba 12.

[293] After attaining an M.A. in the history of Jewish thought in the Second Temple Period from Hebrew University and 3 years study of rabbinics and Jewish thought at Diaspora Yeshiva in Jerusalem, Shulam established the Netivyah Bible Instruction Ministry, which aims 'to study and teach the Jewish background of the New Testament, providing a bridge between Jews and Christians and Judaism and Christianity, and nurturing the Messianic Jewish community in Israel.' Shulam, *A Commentary*, 529.

[294] Joseph Shulam and Hilary Le Cornu, *A Commentary on the Jewish Roots of Romans* (Baltimore, MA: Lederer Books, 1997). Shulam's research assistant, Le Cornu (1959–), studied at Edinburgh and at Hebrew University. A staff member of Netivyah Bible Instruction Ministry, she is also committed to Messianic Judaism, having worked at the Messianic Midrasha in Israel.

[295] Shulam and Le Cornu are not interested in Pauline scholarship, but Christian authorities cited include Dodd, Headlam, Käsemann, Kittel, Murphy-O'Connor, Sanday, Sanders, Stendahl, Tomson, and Weiss; Jewish writers include Boyarin, Klausner, Flusser, Safrai, and Scholem. The commentary shares the traditional scholarly acceptance of Romans, 1 and 2 Corinthians, Galatians, Philippians, 1 Thessalonians, and Philemon as authentic, and also includes Colossians and 2 Thessalonians.

In the Introduction to the commentary, Paul is acknowledged as a Roman citizen, either because his parents had been Roman citizens or because, as a citizen of Tarsus, he was automatically entitled to such status.[296] It is his Jewish credentials which Shulam emphasises, however. Thus the future apostle was probably educated under the supervision of 'Rabban Gamaliel' or Gamaliel the Elder of the school of Shammai, after his Pharisaic parents had 'encouraged him to seek a good rabbinic education in Jerusalem'. As a result of his choice of education, Paul's main identity lay with rabbinic Judaism, and he became 'a master in rabbinic thought and forms'.[297] No mention is made of any conversion. He was known by his name Sha'ul as well as by the Roman name Paul,[298] and spoke Hebrew as well as Greek.[299] Although the letters of this Diaspora Jew were written in Greek, they nevertheless reflect his training in a rabbinic tradition and Hebrew linguistic and thought patterns.[300] Shulam has no doubts whatsoever in this regard. As he puts it,

Paul himself, of course, was Jewish, and his language, terminology, methodology, and style all reflect the Jewish education which he received and the Jewish traditions in which he was brought up.[301]

Texts (mainly from the Acts of the Apostles) are cited to show how the apostle referred to himself as a Pharisee,[302] lived his life as a Pharisee, and was 'Torah-observant, obedient to rabbinic regulations, and proud of his Jewish heritage.'[303]

---

[296] Shulam, A Commentary, 12.

[297] Shulam, A Commentary, 5, 12.

[298] Shulam cites Acts 7:58 ('When they had driven him out of the city, they began stoning him; and the witnesses laid aside their robes at the feet of a young man named Saul'); 8:1 ('Saul was in hearty agreement with putting him to death. And on that day a great persecution began against the church in Jerusalem, and they were all scattered throughout the regions of Judea and Samaria, except the apostles'); 9:1 ('Now Saul, still breathing threats and murder against the disciples of the Lord, went to the high priest'); 9:11 ('And the Lord said to him, "Get up and go to the street called Straight, and inquire at the house of Judas for a man from Tarsus named Saul, for he is praying"'); and 9:17 ('So Ananias departed and entered the house, and after laying his hands on him said, "Brother Saul, the Lord Jesus, who appeared to you on the road by which you were coming, has sent me so that you may regain your sight and be filled with the Holy Spirit"'). Shulam, A Commentary, 23.

[299] Shulam cites Acts 21:40 ('When he had given him permission, Paul, standing on the stairs, motioned to the people with his hand; and when there was a great hush, he spoke to them in the Hebrew dialect, saying . . .'), 21:37 ('As Paul was about to be brought into the barracks, he said to the commander, "May I say something to you?" And he said, "Do you know Greek?"'). Shulam, A Commentary, 23.

[300] Shulam, A Commentary, 1.

[301] Shulam, A Commentary, 3.

[302] Shulam cites Acts 23:6 ('But perceiving that one group were Sadducees and the other Pharisees, Paul began crying out in the Council, "Brethren, I am a Pharisee, a son of Pharisees; I am on trial for the hope and resurrection of the dead!"') and 26:5 ('since they have known about me for a long time, if they are willing to testify, that I lived as a Pharisee according to the strictest sect of our religion') and Phil. 3:5 ('circumcised the eighth day, of the nation of Israel, of the tribe of Benjamin, a Hebrew of Hebrews; as to the Law, a Pharisee').

[303] Shulam, A Commentary, 12. Shulam cites Acts 22:3 ('I am a Jew, born in Tarsus of Cilicia, but brought up in this city, educated under Gamaliel, strictly according to the law of our fathers, being

At the same time, he is said to have had a close relationship with the Sanhedrin, as indicated by their letters of recommendation permitting him to bring followers of Yeshua to Jerusalem to trial. What little doubt Shulam shows concerning the accuracy of the New Testament evidence about Paul's life tends to be expressed as criticism of occasional lapses of knowledge of Jewish custom or Law. For example, the account in the Acts of the Apostles of the execution of Stephen is censured for having missed the *halakhic* significance of Paul's role as cloak-holder, which reflected his official capacity as a representative of the priestly authorities.[304]

Shulam is keen to convince the reader that the apostle's key arguments and goals are derived from the prophets, and that his teachings about Israel, the end times, the nature of the messiah, and God's interest in the Gentiles are well integrated in the theological landscape of Second Temple Judaism. The idea that there is anything new about Paul's conclusions is, he argues, the result of overemphasis upon the Hellenistic background of the New Testament and ignorance among Christian scholars regarding its Jewish and rabbinic character.[305] Jewish scholars, too, have been misled by the overwhelming power of the Reformation view of Paul as the champion of a 'theology of grace', and later as the main exponent of the Gentilisation of Jewish scriptures and the resultant new Christian faith.[306] It is therefore incumbent upon this messianic Jew to correct the erroneous view of mainstream Jewish and Christian scholars of the place of Paul in salvation history.

It has become obvious through time that this neglect or contempt for the Jewish character of the New Testament has played a large part in the formation of the claim that Paul was in fact the author of a new religion (Christianity). We are endeavouring

---

zealous for God just as you all are today'), 23:6 ('But perceiving that one group were Sadducees and the other Pharisees, Paul began crying out in the Council, "Brethren, I am a Pharisee, a son of Pharisees; I am on trial for the hope and resurrection of the dead!"'), 26:4–7 ('So then, all Jews know my manner of life from my youth up, which from the beginning was spent among my own nation and at Jerusalem; because they have known about me for a long time, if they are willing to testify, that I lived as a Pharisee according to the strictest sect of our religion. And now I am standing trial for the hope of the promise made by God to our fathers; the promise to which our twelve tribes hope to attain, as they earnestly serve God night and day. And for this hope, O King, I am being accused by Jews'), and 28:17 ('After three days Paul called together those who were the leading men of the Jews, and when they came together, he began saying to them, "Brethren, though I had done nothing against our people or the customs of our fathers, yet I was delivered as a prisoner from Jerusalem into the hands of the Romans"'), Rom. 9:3 ('For I could wish that I myself were accursed, separated from Christ for the sake of my brethren, my kinsmen according to the flesh'), 2 Cor. 11:22 ('Are they Hebrews? So am I. Are they Israelites? So am I. Are they descendants of Abraham? So am I'), and Phil. 3:5–6 ('circumcised the eighth day, of the nation of Israel, of the tribe of Benjamin, a Hebrew of Hebrews; as to the Law, a Pharisee; as to zeal, a persecutor of the church; as to the righteousness which is in the Law, found blameless').

[304] Shulam cites Sanhedrin 42b as evidence of the halakhic requirement for an official to stand at the door of the court with a cloak, in order to signal for the accused to be brought back if new witnesses appeared, even four or five times. Shulam, *A Commentary*, 12.

[305] Shulam, *A Commentary*, 3.

[306] Shulam, *A Commentary*, 4.

as far as possible to redress this 'historical aberration' and to demonstrate that the New Testament is a Jewish book *and that Jews who believe in Yeshua remain Jews.*[307] [Italics mine]

Once one has rescued Paul from the charge of inventing Christianity, Shulam suggests, the Jewish authenticity of the first-century apostle's thought can be extrapolated to those whose have come to acknowledge his messiah in the modern era.

The methodology adopted in the book resembles in many respects the methodology of postmodern literary theory and the concept of intertextuality. Although little or no attempt is made to historically situate Paul's letter or to conduct any kind of source criticism,[308] the text is to be interpreted subjectively by the reader in the light of parallel readings from other texts; the commentary simply assists in this process by facilitating the reader's access to a range of potentially relevant texts.[309] The uncritical inclusion of materials found in rabbinic works compiled centuries after Paul wrote Romans, which Shulam acknowledges that some will regard as anachronistic, is justified by the observation that such rabbinic literature contained oral traditions of an ancient pedigree.[310] Shulam's treatments of Romans 5 and 12 are illustrative of these issues. In the first case, Shulam purports to demonstrate the apostle's use of rabbinic exegetical principles:

Romans 5 is a masterful illustration of an analogy [*binyan av*] built upon a string of variations of a *fortiori* [*kal ve-chomer*] inferences: 'if while we were enemies, we were reconciled to God . . . how much more we shall be saved by his life;' [v.10] 'if by the transgression of the one, death reigned through the one, how much more those who receive the abundance of grace . . . will reign in life through the one, Yeshua the Messiah.' [v.17][311]

In the second case, Shulam defends Romans 12:9–21[312] against those commentators who are uncomfortable with the apparently politically quietist attitude Paul

---

[307] Shulam, *A Commentary*, 4.

[308] The one gesture in this direction is made when Shulam argues that Paul's letters are written for the public forum and therefore 'the genre of rabbinic thought takes precedence over that of private communication'. Having said that, he makes it clear that 'since Paul is not engaged in talmudic debate with other Rabbis, his letter is not as tightly bound by the constraints of dialectic argument in the Talmud itself.' As a source, 'Romans could be added to the list of contemporary midrashic compilations of the period', for it (i) is an exposition of scripture and (ii) employs midrashic principles such as verbal analogy (*gezerah shavah*), analogy (*binyan av*), and a fortiori (*kal ve-chomer*). Shulam, *A Commentary*, 6, 7.

[309] Shulam, *A Commentary*, 9.

[310] Shulam cites the Israeli Second Temple specialist, David Flusser: 'The entire corpus of rabbinic literature is an expression of a constant stream of oral transmission. . . . Thus the specific character of rabbinic literature not only permits us, but even obligates us to include post-Christian rabbinic sources as an inseparable part of the investigation of the Jewish roots of Christianity.' David Flusser, *Judaism and the Origins of Christianity* (Jerusalem: Magnes Press, 1988), iii–xv, cited in Shulam, *A Commentary*, 9.

[311] Shulam, *A Commentary*, 17, 191, 199.

[312] Rom. 12:9–21: 'Rejoice with those who rejoice, and weep with those who weep . . . If possible, so far as it depends on you, be at peace with all men. Never take your own revenge, beloved, but leave room for the wrath of God, for it is written, "Vengeance is mine, I will repay" says the Lord.'

espouses by pointing to two principles derived respectively from the Talmud (relating to conversion) and from the Qumran community (relating to the Day of Judgement). Hillel reportedly said that in order to win converts, 'a man should not rejoice when among people who weep or weep when among those who rejoice.... This is the general rule: A man should not deviate from the custom of his companions or from society.'[313] Likewise, certain Qumran documents suggest that it is correct to submit to evil rulers so that God will punish them in the Day of Judgement.[314] By juxtaposing such parallels, Paul's apparently *laissez-faire* attitude becomes embedded within a Jewish worldview that many within the Messianic community today would recognise as a pragmatic strategy rather than an expression of quietism. And, in fact, much of the *Commentary on the Jewish Roots of Romans* is profoundly shaped by such ideological aims and objectives. As Shulam himself puts it,

We offer this commentary on the book of Romans as a Jewish text in the hope that it will bring to the reader a broader and deeper appreciation of the Jewish nature of the New Testament writings as a whole.... [W]e also hope that this volume will go some way in redressing the historical mistake committed by the Church of cutting itself off from its own roots. Our most fervent desire is perhaps that this commentary will also serve to return Yeshua himself to his own people, in demonstrating that the New Testament is not a Christian book representing a different faith but a Jewish text embodying an authentic Jewish interpretation of the Tanakh [Old Testament].[315]

Thus Paul not only embodied Messianic Jewish theology for Shulam, but his writings also remain a key resource for modern Messianic Jews who wish to correct Gentile errors of understanding, to reclaim Paul as a Jew, and, it is clearly implied, to convince the People of Israel of the good news of their messiah's coming.

Historically, the Hebrew Christian community has been notoriously fragmented, something that is perhaps inevitable insofar as it is composed of strong-willed, Jewish individuals who have taken the momentous, socially disastrous decision to recognise Jesus as the messiah. Nevertheless, a few generalisations can be made about the use of the apostle Paul as a platform from which to articulate their views. Jewish believers in Jesus such as Levertoff, Mills, and Shulam are uncompromising in their insistence that their perspective not only is legitimately Jewish but in fact is the most authentic form of Jewishness extant. Although they are not slow to criticise the misunderstandings of Gentile Christians, which perhaps explains the medium of commentary, they are quicker still to strike out preemptively against the views of other Jews who are opposed to their very *raison d'être*. This is unsurprising and simply reflects the fact that the issue of Messianic Judaism is one of the rawest, most bitter ideological disputes within modern Jewry. From the popular Jewish perspective, Paul's place in this dispute has already been touched upon in a previous chapter. For the thinkers discussed above, the image of Paul that emerges is of a

---

[313] Derekh Erez Rabbah 7:7. Shulam, *A Commentary*, 417.
[314] Shulam cites (Community) Rule 1QS 9:21–3, 10:17–25. Shulam, *A Commentary*, 411.
[315] Shulam, *A Commentary* (1997), 17.

messianic hero who, following the path opened up by his Nazarene master, realised the Jewish dream of bringing all mankind to God, who was profoundly attached to (and not hostile towards) Jewish tradition and custom, and whose ostensibly unfamiliar emphases, such as original sin, are presented as entirely unproblematic from a Jewish perspective. In contrast to other Jewish approaches, such Jewish believers in Jesus offer a caveat-free reclamation of a Jewish Paul.

CONCLUSION

Most of the writers in this chapter are progressives who belong to an interpretative tradition or ideological worldview that had been profoundly influenced by ideas in the surrounding Christian environment and by broader processes relating to modernity in general. With their having committed themselves to an understanding of Judaism that emphasised among other things Jewish diversity, universalism, and a critical attitude towards the Law, their value-judgements on a range of issues were markedly different to those of Jewish traditionalists. And, in principle, the apostle to the Gentiles was no exception. A consistent application of progressive theory meant that Paul could not but appear to them in a very different light than he appeared in to those who did not share their presuppositions. Thus it did not seem entirely unreasonable to regard him as a Jew, it was not difficult to acknowledge his universalistic outlook as a worthy enterprise, and it was even possible to liken his criticism of the Law to their own. And yet these writers went much further than simply recognising theological parallels between themselves and the apostle. In bringing with them their own questions, assumptions, and interests, they went on to use him as a platform from which to promote their own individual ideological positions, almost always with a view to undermining traditionalist conceptions of Jewish authenticity. A common tendency, taken to its extreme by Schoeps, was to emphasise internal spirituality and principles over external observance of the Law and ritual (although, of course, the same argument could be criticised by an Orthodox scholar such as Flusser). In addition, Hirsch contrasted Paul's missionary successes and his providential role in propagating Jewish thought to the failings of traditional Judaism, which only encouraged assimilation. Montefiore used Paul as a foil to emphasise universalist conceptions of Judaism over particularist ones and to demonstrate an eclectic approach to religious truth. Sandmel's treatment emphasised the prophetic (as against the legal) tradition within Judaism and at the same time promoted a more inclusive conception of Jewish identity, and Segal's presentation tested the limits of an ever-widening definition of Jewishness. In arguing for a surprisingly nonmisogynistic interpretation of a Jewish Paul, scholars such as Eisenbaum, Ilan, and Levine unhesitatingly express their concern for gender in studying Judaism, past and present. And although not progressives, Hebrew Christians like Paul Levertoff and Sanford Mills, together with Messianic Jews such as Joseph Shulam, argued that Gentile Christianity and Jewish tradition alike had misunderstood the teachings of Rabbi Shaul of Tarsus, and promoted a controversial vision of 'fulfilled' Judaism. In all these cases, one does not simply trace the ideological biases of the authors 'in between the lines', so to speak; nor does one have to strain very hard to identify their opponents or the objects of their antagonism. Their treatments of Paul dovetail with a range of issues that feature prominently within modern intra-Jewish ideological discourse and, whatever else their studies accomplished, they also functioned as contributions to a wider cultural debate concerning the nature of Judaism and Jewish identity.

How is it that *Paul*, of all people, can be found at the centre of this intra-Jewish ideological mêlée? The answer may lie in Paul's traditional symbolism as a personification of the break with the Law. For those with a taste for scandal or for those determined to demonstrate their independence of mind, he provides an ideal opportunity to discuss this profoundly divisive issue without necessarily having to identify with his particular reasoning. More significantly, Paul also allows progressive writers to express two apparently paradoxical tendencies. On the one hand, they seek to demonstrate an interest in ostensibly non-Jewish religious thought, a willingness to include literature outside the received canon of Jewish religious literature. On the other hand, they want to push the limits of Jewish pluralism and to demonstrate a relaxed view of what it means to be part of the Jewish community – and once the Epistles of Paul the Jew are added to the multiplicity of authentic Jewish voices down through the ages, the antiquity and legitimacy of the intra-Jewish debate regarding the significance (or insignificance) of the Law is reinforced. The writings of nonliberal thinkers such as Klausner and Berdichevsky also help explain Paul's appeal. Setting aside their particular contributions to intra-Jewish debates (in which Zionist criteria were used to establish Jewish authenticity), they were clearly attracted by Paul's stature in world history. For Jews concerned with how to make Judaism relevant to the modern world, Saul of Tarsus' provocative example of how to relate to the non-Jewish world demanded a response. The apostle's success, his undeniable relevance, called for careful consideration.

4

Constructions of Paul as a Dialogical Partner: Transformative Approaches to Jewish Self-Understanding

Although it has become something of a cliché to talk of a Jewish obsession with defining what makes one Jewish, with what distinguishes the Jew from the non-Jew, and with where to draw the boundaries, it is no less true for all that. In addition to the dilemma posed by the cacophony of voices claiming to represent authentic Judaism, there is the question of how to navigate a safe path through the vast surrounding Gentile environment that has been so profoundly influenced by Christian thought and culture. Understandably, the characteristic attitude towards the non-Jewish world is often one of ambivalence. A particularly disconcerting discovery for many has been the extent to which non-Jewish worldviews have been internalised, the recognition that many of their attitudes and value-judgements are in fact indistinguishable from those of the unwashed world around them. For some, this discovery has been enough to send them hurrying off to self-imposed ghettos of strict religious observance. For others, it has led to the real-isation that the non-Jew is not as alien, not as 'other', as they had been taught to believe.

Historically, it could be argued that the ambivalence with which Paul is regarded by Jewish commentators as a group reflects this ambivalence towards non-Jewish culture more generally. As we have seen in the two previous chapters, there is as much uncertainty and suspicion as there is interest in and appreciation of the theological achievements and historical significance of the apostle to the Gentiles. Even the same author is capable of being both complimentary and condemnatory, both fascinated and repelled, by the life and teachings of this curious first-century figure. Paul has become symbolic of the desire to be accepted within the Gentile world, the readiness to make compromises, and the fear of the risk of losing something of one's Jewishness in the process. The study of the apostle allows one to explore where the limits lie from a safe distance, to give oneself the freedom to think dangerous thoughts without necessarily committing oneself to them. A small number of Jewish scholars have gone further, however. They have approached the study of the apostle as an opportunity to reexamine their own assumptions about a variety of religious issues and to develop new ways of expressing their own, often idiosyncratic, theologies. Essentially, they find in Paul a man whose concerns and dilemmas so closely parallel their own that they come to value him as a kind of existential *agent provocateur*, someone whose experiences and reflections powerfully assist them in their own search for Jewish self-understanding. Examples of writers whose grappling with the apostle as a fellow Jewish seeker of truth results in a reassessment and development of their own understanding of Jewish identity includes Hugh Schonfield, Richard Rubenstein, Nancy Fuchs-Kreimer, and Daniel Boyarin.

HUGH SCHONFIELD

Hugh Schonfield (1901–88) was an eccentric Anglo-Jewish Bible scholar and broad-caster with an Orthodox Jewish upbringing. At sixteen he came to believe that Jesus had been the messiah and came to distinguish between two kinds of Christian-ity: an inside and an outside Christianity, one concerned with Jesus' messiah-ship, and the other with Gentile doctrines, which he could not accept. Schonfield became fascinated with the origins of Christianity and, largely self-taught, he attempted to revive the Ebionites or Nazarenes in *A History of Jewish-Christianity* (1936) and other works.[1] Despite his involvement with the International Hebrew Christian Alliance, he appears to have kept himself largely apart from Christian and Hebrew–Christian congregations and regarded himself as 'a Jew and one who has become a Nazarene'.[2] At 37 he had a vision that convinced him that he was to establish a servant nation and in 1950 the Commonwealth of World Citizens was announced with 40 members.[3] He retreated somewhat from his advocacy of Judeo-Christianity in some of his later works,[4] where he stressed his

---

[1] Schonfield, *A History of Jewish-Christianity*.

[2] For a critical introduction to Schonfield, see Richard Harvey, 'Passing over the Plot? The Life and Work of Hugh Schonfield (1901–1988)', *Mishkan* 37 (2002), 35–48. Harvey stresses Schonfield's independence of mind, describing him as the 'the enfant terrible of the Hebrew Christian movement of the twentieth century' in reference to his unorthodox beliefs (for example, rejection of the doctrine of the trinity) and political conflicts (for example, Schonfield was expelled from the Executive Committee of IHCA, of which he was a member from 1925 to 1937).

[3] The origins of this organisation, later renamed the Mondcivitan Republic, are described in Hugh Schonfield, *The Politics of God* (London: Hutchinson, 1970), xi–xviii.

[4] In his most famous work, *The Passover Plot* (London: Hutchinson, 1965), Schonfield argued that a very human Jesus had planned his own arrest and had attempted to feign his death as part of a carefully orchestrated messianic coup that had sought to fulfil the promises of the Hebrew Bible. There was nothing Jewishly inauthentic about Jesus' messianic self-belief, Schonfield argued, nor had this Galilean Jew sought to establish a new religion; rather, non-Jewish followers in the centuries that followed had transformed this Jewish messiah into the divine Christ of the Gentile Church. Schonfield completely rejected the idea of Jesus' deity: 'The God-man of Christianity is increasingly incredible ... Such a man could have his godlike moments, but could never be consistently a reflection of the Divine' (10, 12). But he did recognise Jesus' messiahship: 'The Messianic Hope which Jesus espoused and in a unique manner personified has not yet exhibited its full potentialities, and so he is still the leader, worthy to be followed, not of a lost cause, but of one ever demanding fuller realisation' (185). As Schonfield saw it, to be a messiah or 'anointed one' was an honourable calling to which anyone might aspire, and we should 'be strengthened and encouraged because he is bone of our bone and flesh of our flesh and not God incarnate. The mind that was in the Messiah can therefore be in us, stimulating us to accomplish what those of a more careful and nicely balanced disposition declare to be impossible. Thus the victory for which Jesus relentlessly schemed and

Jewish identity, as a result of which he has been described as a pioneer of the messianic Jewish movement.

Schonfield assumed a Jewish background for Paul in his key work *The Jew of Tarsus* (1946) and the posthumous publication *Proclaiming the Messiah* (1997).[5] Having ignored Hellenistic influences, he highlighted instead Jewish influences such as that upon the liturgy in Romans,[6] and the passionate motivation to win over Gentiles to monotheism.[7] In contrast to the writers considered so far, however, Schonfield exhibited a psychological empathy with Paul of a quite different order, especially in *The Jew of Tarsus*.[8] His primary concern was to understand and explain Paul's sense of destiny, and this was often achieved by drawing upon his own spiritual experiences. Similarities between his own world and predicament and those of Paul are hinted at from early in the work. Shortly after the Second World War, contemplating the ancient world of first-century Palestine, he said,

I was transported into an age not so unlike our own, where a small country was occupied by a Great Power, where Resistance Movements courageously defied the destruction of the soul of their people, an age in which many had lost their faith and confidence in the future, and where superstition and anti-Semitism flourished: but an age also in which a little Jew had a splendid vision of a new world order.

For such a Jew, always practical as well as mystical, to have the vision was to act upon it. With Roman citizenship, Greek contacts, and Jewish culture, the love of God in his

---

strove will be won at last. There will be peace throughout the earth' (187). Jewish readers warmed to the idea of a de-deified Jesus who sought to realise the prophets' dreams, and the conception of a messiah as a kind of ethical model, and to an author who described himself as a 'Jewish boy' who was 'not connected with any section of the Church' and who sought to persuade 'my Christian friends' that their religion was still too influenced by paganism to be able to recognise God as pure spirit (9, 10, 12).

[5] Hugh Schonfield, *The Jew of Tarsus: An Unorthodox Portrait of Paul* (London: MacDonald, 1946), 30, 31. He considered but rejected the hostile evidence of the Ebionites that Hyam Maccoby had focused upon in *The Mythmaker: Paul and the Invention of Christianity*. E. P. Sanders's *Paul and Palestinian Judaism*, which emphasises Paul's Jewishness, was set aside because, like Maccoby, Sanders was 'mainly concerned with theological matters, or influenced by them, whereas what is required is an objective historical approach, which I have pursued for the greater part of a long life.' Hugh Schonfield, *Proclaiming the Messiah: The Life and Letters of Paul of Tarsus, Envoy to the Nations* (London: Open Gate Press, 1997), 7. Though it was published posthumously, Schonfield actually completed *Proclaiming the Messiah* in 1988. In his works he referred to the entire New Testament corpus, and also the Church Fathers and rabbinic writings, although *The Jew of Tarsus* tended to prioritise Romans, 1 Corinthians, Galatians, and Acts. A proudly independent scholar, he was not much interested in the scholarly literature. Christian scholars he referenced in one or another work included Burkitt, Oesterley, Ramsey, Sanders, and the convert Edersheim, whereas Jewish scholars included Eisler, Gaster, Klausner, Maccoby, and Vermes; he referred to the *Jewish Encyclopedia* repeatedly.

[6] Schonfield, *The Jew of Tarsus*, 224–5.

[7] Schonfield, *The Jew of Tarsus*, 144–5.

[8] Schonfield, *The Jew of Tarsus*, 94–5.

heart, and the Brotherhood of Man in his soul, he set out to unite the world under the beneficent rule of a Messiah.[9]

Paul had inhabited a complex Jewish milieu of the first century. Schonfield felt that too much attention had been paid to Hellenistic parallels to his religious worldview (for example, belief in angels and demons, magic, preexistence, transmigration of souls, predestination, resurrection), which he maintained was actually, like the Apostles' Creed, 'pure Pharisaic doctrine in most of its terms'.[10]

Regarding the Law, Schonfield drew upon his own experiences to understand Paul's attitude, which was one of guilt at failing to observe the commandments, especially those of the oral law, since his angst-ridden youth in Tarsus. With a somewhat free hand, Schonfield drew a picture of Paul's psychology.

Not many Jews would be as introspective as the youthful Saul of Tarsus, and his later reminiscences already tell us a good deal about his character. The Law and its commandments were holy and just; but he was carnal, sold like a slave into sin's foul bondage. Somehow the thing he did was the thing he knew he ought not to do, and he hated what he did. The realisation dawned upon his rather morbidly sensitive mind that in him nothing good had its abode; for though the desire to do the right thing was there, how to perform it always and at all times presented an insoluble problem. In his inner life he delighted in the Law of the Lord: he loved and worshipped God with all his soul. But another law seemed ever to rule his actions conflicting with the Divine Law, and bringing him into the captivity of sin. So with his will he served the Law of God, and with his flesh the law of sin. How to escape the chains that grappled with him iron bands to the rotten carcase of evil? [sic]

Heightened and overdrawn as this language may be when employed in the service of an ardent debate, it still seems to echo the struggles and anxious fears of adolescence. Saul, evidently, was not a normal boy, even while he strove obstinately, uncomfortably, and, as he felt, vainly to keep himself right in a heathen world and environment. He had become early obsessed with a secret guilt-complex, which he was unable to shake off, and one would imagine, therefore, in the absence of knowledge that his mother had died during his childhood. His father, who we do know was a Pharisee, may have

---

9 Schonfield, *The Jew of Tarsus*, x.
10 Schonfield, *The Jew of Tarsus*, 46. The Apostles' Creed is an early statement of Christian belief, widely used for liturgical purposes, which has nothing explicit to say about the divinity of Christ or the Holy Spirit: 'I believe in God the Father Almighty, Maker of heaven and earth: And in Jesus Christ his only Son our Lord, Who was conceived by the Holy Ghost, Born of the Virgin Mary, Suffered under Pontius Pilate, Was crucified, dead, and buried: He descended into hell; The third day he rose again from the dead; He ascended into heaven, And sitteth on the right hand of God the Father Almighty; From thence he shall come to judge the quick and the dead. I believe in the Holy Ghost; The holy Catholick Church; The Communion of Saints; The Forgiveness of sins; The Resurrection of the body, And the Life everlasting. Amen.' 'The Apostles' Creed', *Book of Common Prayer* (New York: The Church Hymnal Corporation, 1979), 54–5.

been particularly puritanical, and though he had at least one sister, she failed to give him the love he needed.[11]

Paul's Pharisaic education had been unfulfilling,[12] and Schonfield's own childhood experience echoed this experience.[13] For Schonfield, as for Schoeps, Paul's abrogation of the Law stemmed from a Jewish belief that in the messianic age attitudes towards the Law would be transformed – and Paul believed that this new age was imminent or had even begun.[14] In this context it made sense for Paul to believe that those Gentiles who were true believers were to be regarded as true Israelites without the need to observe the Law, and at the same time to expect Jewish believers to continue to do so (just as he himself did).[15]

In neither of his studies did Schonfield doubt the Jewish authenticity of the 'Envoy to the Gentiles'. On the contrary, he claimed that 'Paul was a Jew and remained one at heart all his life', arguing that Paul had never intended to create Christianity: his religion had been that of Moses, the prophets, and the messiah and he had believed there was only one God and one people of Israel.[16] Old Testament references were abundant in the Epistles, employed in the rabbinical manner, and so were doxologies and liturgical formulae. To demonstrate this, he took the letter of Romans and related it to the oldest parts of the Jewish liturgy, the *Shema* and its attendant prayers *Yotser*, *Ahabah* and *Geullah*, and the *Shemoneh 'Esreh*.[17] Later, in *Proclaiming the Messiah*, Schonfield stressed the Jewish authenticity of Paul's mysticism, arguing that Rabbinic Judaism devoted itself to mystical and psychic matters, in addition to ethics and the Law of Moses.[18]

---

[11] Schonfield, *The Jew of Tarsus*, 29–30. The reference to Paul's sister is derived from Acts 23:16 when Paul was plotted against by 'the Jews' in Jerusalem ('But the son of Paul's sister heard of their ambush and he came and entered the barracks and told Paul').

[12] Schonfield, *The Jew of Tarsus*, 94–5.

[13] Reminiscing on his own 'Jewishly fairly orthodox home', Schonfield offered 'confirmatory experiences of his own' as to the negative psychological results upon Paul of failing to fulfil the Law: 'What twinges of conscience there were over the sharpening of a pencil or plucking a leaf from a hedge on the sabbath! What a problem of faith was raised by attending synagogue in one's school cap because the badge was a Maltese cross!' Schonfield, *The Jew of Tarsus*, 30.

[14] Schonfield, *The Jew of Tarsus*, 146.

[15] Schonfield, *The Jew of Tarsus*, 195, 230. 'The conclusion that Paul reached by his Biblical erudition was that by an act of faith, rather than by law, believing Gentiles have been accorded Israelite status.' Schonfield went on, 'Consequently non-Jewish Christians are not in fact Gentiles: they are now Israelites. The Land of Israel is *their* homeland. One wonders what would happen if Christians of today believed Paul.' Schonfield, *Proclaiming the Messiah*, 73.

[16] Schonfield, *Proclaiming the Messiah*, 71.

[17] *Yotser*, Rom. 1:25; *Ahabah*, Rom. 2:17–18; *Shemoneh 'Esreh*, Rom. 4:17; *Chashkivenu*, prayer which follows the evening *Shema*, Rom. 8:35–39; prayer after reading from the Prophets, Rom. 9:4; morning prayer, Rom. 9:5; *Shemoneh 'Esreh*, Rom. 15:33. Schonfield, *The Jew of Tarsus*, 225.

[18] Schonfield asserts that Paul had been devoted to a mystical understanding of the first chapter of Genesis (*Ma'aseh Bereshith*), rather than to the other branch of mysticism that focused upon the Heavenly Chariot in Ezekiel (*Ma'aseh Merkabah*). Schonfield, *Proclaiming the Messiah*, 9, 69. In the second of his studies, Schonfield suggests that Paul's 'physical handicap . . . may have disposed him to psychic experiences, and his [ugly] appearance may also have been compensated for by mystical

Perhaps the most fascinating feature of Schonfield's treatment was his suggestion that Paul had at one time believed that he himself was the promised messiah.[19] This curious interpretation was justified at some length in *The Jew of Tarsus* in terms of how Paul must have interpreted messianic texts from the Hebrew Bible.[20] Thus, for example, Schonfield conjectured,

[In Saul's imagination, m]ore definitely had the Psalms announced him [as Messiah]. It was written in the 2nd *Psalm*: 'Yet have I anointed My king upon My holy hill of Zion. I will declare the decree: the Lord hath said unto me. Thou art My son; this day have I begotten thee. Ask of Me, and I shall give thee the Gentiles for thine inheritance, and the uttermost parts of the earth for thy possession'. Did not that word 'ask' (*Heb. Sheal*) indicate him Shaul? Should not he read: 'Saul (is sent) from Me, and I will give thee the Gentiles for thine inheritance'? Such a word-play was entirely in accordance with rabbinical methods of interpretation.[21]

Schonfield's conception is, however, best explained by the projection of his own sense of destiny and purpose onto Paul. After all, he too was a marginal Jew who never quite fitted in and who had a vision in which he had been called to initiate God's plan for world peace. He easily recognised the worldview of this kindred spirit and fellow Nazarene. He himself had had a vision in which he had been called to initiate God's plan for world peace.[22] Schonfield went on to suggest that it was Paul's crisis of identity and eventual acceptance of Jesus' messiahship that led to his breakdown on the road to Damascus. Paul was not downcast for long, however, in that he became convinced that he was possessed by the spirit of the messiah and thus his sense of grand purpose as 'Acting or Vice-Messiah' was assured.[23] Insight into how Schonfield naturally came to view Paul in this way can be found in the account he gives elsewhere of his own paranormal abilities (including automatic writing and prophecy), reflecting the worldview of one who believes in his own special abilities.[24]

What Schonfield found in Paul was a kindred spirit, a fellow man of destiny who faced similar challenges and self-doubts. It was not so much that Paul had

---

pursuits'. This interest in disability and/or unattractiveness is repeated throughout. Ibid., 9, 25, 29, 70.

[19] Schonfield defines the function of the messiah as 'to bring his people back to their service for God, in order that Israel should lead the nations to God.' Schonfield, *Proclaiming the Messiah*, 17.

[20] Schonfield, *The Jew of Tarsus*, 80, 83–5, 89–90.

[21] Schonfield, *The Jew of Tarsus*, 83.

[22] Schonfield, *The Politics of God*, xvi–xx.

[23] Schonfield, *The Jew of Tarsus*, 100. Elsewhere he suggests 'Paul now had what might be described as a Jesus fixation. He had become in the most direct sense the earthly reflection of the heavenly Christ, thus reconciling his status with his earlier beliefs in his own special destiny.' Schonfield, *Proclaiming the Messiah*, 71.

[24] Schonfield, *The Politics of God*, xi–xiii. Schonfield makes explicit the link between messianic destiny and paranormal abilities when he asserts, '[H]aving psychic experiences played no small part in convincing him [Paul] that he had a special destiny of a Messianic nature well before he was aware of the claims of Jesus'. Schonfield, *Proclaiming the Messiah*, 9.

anything to offer the modern Jew or Christian. Rather, from the perspective of salvation history, Paul had played an important historical role of drawing Gentiles into membership of a 'servant nation', the focus of a Divine Plan laid out in detail in the manifesto *The Politics of God* (1970). Schonfield believed that he was in a better position to interpret Paul than those who had written before, and was attracted to him because Paul reinforced Schonfield's self-understanding as a Jew and his own sense of messianic mission to the nations.

RICHARD RUBENSTEIN

Perhaps the most self-reflective of the Pauline studies was by the New York–born antiestablishment theologian Richard Rubenstein (1924–). Brought up in an assimilated Jewish family, he was from early in life on obsessed with his own Jewish identity. In later years he stressed his training at Hebrew Union College (Reform Judaism) and membership of the Reform Synagogue, but despite his hostility to the Conservative movement he completed his rabbinical studies and was ordained at the Jewish Theological Seminary, a Conservative Jewish training seminary in New York. A widely discussed university lecturer, Rubenstein is something of a freethinking radical, who eventually rejected institutional religion. His study of Paul clearly demonstrates the profound influence of Freudian psychology, and a number of his theological writings came to be closely associated with the 1960s' Christian death-of-God theology.[25]

Rubenstein began his study *My Brother Paul* (1972) with a twofold explanation of its title, which was an attempt to express his positive appreciation for Paul (echoing Buber's recognition of Jesus as 'my great brother') and to distance himself from 'the tradition in Jewish scholarship that regards him [Paul] as the ultimate enemy in early Christianity'.[26] In essence, he felt that the Jewish community should not have set Paul aside so easily, and that it was unfair to hold him responsible for the traumatic parting of the ways.[27] Whatever the complexities of his background

[25] See, for example, Richard L. Rubenstein, *After Auschwitz* (Indianapolis: Bobbs-Merrill, 1966). It is worth noting that, as discussed earlier in relation to Samuel Sandmel, psychobiographical studies of historical figures had become quite popular by the 1960s. Regarding mainstream Pauline scholars, Rubenstein referred to, among others, Barrett, Barth, Bultmann, Davies, Dibelius, Käsemann, Lohmeyer, Schweitzer, and Stendahl. Among Jewish commentators, he referred to Baeck, Buber, Freud, Klausner, Montefiore, and Schoeps. He regarded the authentic Pauline Epistles as having been 1 Thessalonians, Romans, Galatians, 1 and 2 Corinthians, Philippians, Philemon, and Colossians.

[26] He wrote of 'a desire to express my fundamental positive appreciation for Paul as well as my dissent from the tradition in Jewish scholarship that regards him as the ultimate enemy in early Christianity.... As a theologian of Jewish origin, I am painfully aware of the fact that in the history of Judaism Paul is regarded as the supreme apostate. When Jewish theologians contrast their insights about man's relation to God with those of Christianity, the Christian theologian they are most like to oppose is Paul. Seldom, if ever, have Jewish scholars found it possible to express appreciation of Paul.' Rubenstein, *My Brother Paul*, 4, 5.

[27] As Rubenstein explained later, 'In reality it was not Paul but Jesus who instituted the irreparable breach with the established Judaism. The conflict between the claims of charisma and the authority

as a Hellenistic Jew, Rubenstein argued that the apostle had demonstrated many Jewish assumptions (shared by Pharisees, Sadducees, and the community of the Scrolls), including covenant and election, and a reinterpretation of scripture.[28] In explaining his position, Rubenstein hinted at a keen interest in the psychology of marginal Jewish thinkers.

The greatest single failing of Jewish attempts to understand Paul has been a persistent refusal to take Paul seriously as both a loyal Jew and a theologian of extraordinary competence. I do not suggest that Paul was correct in his rejection of the Judaism of his time. Empathy for Paul is not agreement with him. Some men have personality structures that make it impossible for them to find fulfilment in traditional Judaism. They are neither better nor worse than traditional Jews; they are simply different. Paul was such a man. We are more likely to account for the differences between Paul and the rabbis by considering the differences in their experience than by attempting to establish whether Paul's religious position or that of his adversaries was the 'true' one.[29]

Certainly, Rubenstein's own experience of institutional religion was not a happy one. Describing his own earlier attempts to conform religiously, he commented, 'The more obedient I became, the more intensely I felt that I was falling short'.[30] He reflected upon thirty-five years of interaction with the organised Jewish community as a 'largely unpleasant experience'. Following his controversial publication of *After Auschwitz* (1966), in which the Shoah was used to justify disbelief in the God of tradition, a number of Jewish communities opposed his attaining any position of influence.[31] In any case, his wife Betty Rubenstein observed that he was temperamentally ill equipped for life as a congregational rabbi.[32] Although Rubenstein fully accepted 'the viability of Judaism for Jews who are acculturated normally',[33] he was obviously predisposed towards other malcontents.

In terms of methodology, Rubenstein was determined to avoid the self-deception of many well-known Christian Pauline scholars who had recreated Paul in their

---

of tradition that Paul's career elicited were far less intensive than that produced by the career of Jesus.' Rubenstein, *My Brother Paul*, 121–2.

[28] Rubenstein, *My Brother Paul*, 117–18.

[29] Rubenstein, *My Brother Paul*, 4–5.

[30] Rubenstein, *My Brother Paul*, 10.

[31] 'I lost any desire to participate in organised Jewish life several decades ago. Long ago, my writings concerning Jewish life and thought were deemed outside of the Jewish mainstream. As a result a mainstream consensus evolved that I was to be marginalised and, if possible, denied an opportunity to express my views either in print or through an academic employer.' R. Rubenstein, 'Reflections on Identity and Memory', in Charles Selengut, ed., *Jewish Identity in the Post-modern Age: Scholarly and Personal Reflections* (Minnesota: Paragon House, 1999), 182, 195. This piece also touches on his experimentation with various Jewish and non-Jewish religious identities. See also 'The Point of View of the Observer', in *My Brother Paul*.

[32] B. Rubenstein, 'A Brief Biographical Sketch', in Betty Rubenstein and Michael Berenbaum, eds., *What Kind of God? Essays in Honour of Richard L. Rubenstein* (New York: University Press of America, 1995), xiv.

[33] Rubenstein, *My Brother Paul*, 19.

own image.[34] Rubenstein conceded that he himself was not immune to such pitfalls of historical analysis and biography. Nonetheless, he was convinced that engaging with Paul was worthwhile, not least for the stimulus it provided for exploring human nature.

Beyond a certain point, the quest for the 'historical' Paul may very well be a will-o'-the-wisp. This does not mean that there remains no point in studying the Apostle's life or his thought. If it is true that each scholar presents his own Paul, it is also true that Paul's writings have elicited an extraordinary range of informed responses concerning the human condition in practically every generation since his own time. The theologies of Augustine and Luther are but two examples of Paul's perennial influence, for the reading of Paul proved decisive for both these men.[35]

Rubenstein's justification for dedicating his time to such a study was based not only upon his conviction that Paul was a theologian of considerable power whose concerns would be grappled with for generations to come, but more specifically on his discovery that the issues that most concerned 'one of the most influential Christian theologians of all time' closely paralleled his own.[36] What were these issues?

Paul's chief concern, according to Rubenstein, was not about the mechanics of God's forgiveness (that is, the traditional Christian focus), nor how God stands in relation to man (à la Buber). It was rather the question of how to defeat death.[37] Rubenstein maintained that Paul had initially persecuted the Church in order to reduce the tension arising from internal conflict between his hopes that the messiah had come and his worldly realism. His attraction to the new movement was ultimately due to a fixation with his own mortality, a fixation with which, as Rubenstein suggested, one could readily empathise.

Like the rest of us, Paul did not want to die. Until Paul learned of the Resurrection, it is likely that he was convinced that death was inevitable for all men. There may have been a time when he harboured the secret hope that, were he to fulfil the Law perfectly, God might save him from death. Some rabbis maintained that were a person to lead a sinless life of complete obedience to God's will, he might not die. Nevertheless, Paul knew that even the greatest of the Israelites had died, save perhaps for Elijah. Eventually he must have concluded that no matter how scrupulously he kept God's commandments, he too was going to die.

One can safely guess that Paul's first response to the reports of Jesus' Resurrection was intense scepticism if not derisive rejection. Still, some part of Paul must have wanted the report to be true, for *if Jesus had been victorious over death, there was also hope for*

---

[34] And to a great extent, he was successful. For example, although the traditional reading of Rom. 7 is understood to reflect the apostle's personal suffering in his failure to fulfil the Law, Rubenstein was prepared to accept recent scholarship that rejected the idea, even though the older reading must have appeared attractive to Rubenstein, who himself had suffered acute feelings of inadequacy in his own observance of the Law.

[35] Rubenstein, *My Brother Paul*, 1, 2.

[36] Rubenstein, *My Brother Paul*, 5.

[37] Rubenstein, *My Brother Paul*, 41.

Paul. Hence the Christian claim that Jesus had risen must have elicited an awesome hope within him, the hope that his own annihilation might be overcome. After all, death was no less threatening to Paul the Pharisee than to Paul the Apostle.[38]

Rubenstein had come to regard his earlier life of religious observance and later academic striving as a vain attempt to escape his own mortality; only the death of an infant son and the experience of Freudian analysis shook him free of this illusion.[39] It was with considerable empathy, then, that he interpreted Paul's complex attitude to the Law, worldly status, power, and wisdom in terms of the apostle's conviction that his primal fear of death had been defeated in Christ, upon whom he was fixated.[40] Other underlying characteristics of Paul's worldview could also be explained in psychological terms.

One of the most powerful themes dominating the apostle's thought, according to Rubenstein, was Jewish messianism. Citing Freud, who himself had written on Paul,[41] he presented a psychoanalytical account of Judaism, arguing that, unlike other religious systems that allowed periodical infringements of the rules, Judaism did not. The psychological release was instead relegated to the future, that is, to the messianic age when the inhibitions and frustrations of the day-to-day world would finally be annulled. This was why 'Jewish messianists from the time of Paul to Sabbatai Zvi and even some of the early reform rabbis have seen the "end of the Law" as one of the most important consequences of the Messianic Age'.[42] From this perspective the traditional view of Paul and the Law appeared unworthy. As Schonfield, Schoeps, and others had done, Rubenstein argued that it had been a mistake to view Paul as antinomian. Rather, Paul had believed that the messiah had abolished the authority of the Law.[43] Paul, arguing within the world of Rabbinic Judaism, had made his case in Rom. 7:1–6 that Christians were no longer bound by the premessianic Law.[44] Nor, argued Rubenstein, should the apostle's distinction between letter and spirit be regarded as inauthentic; it reflected a strategy similar to that of the Pharisees with their twofold Law (that is, the oral law making sense

---

[38] Rubenstein, *My Brother Paul*, 42–3.
[39] Before the breakthrough, Rubenstein had convinced himself that his failure to observe the Law had somehow caused the death of his newborn son. Rubenstein, *My Brother Paul*, 14–18.
[40] Rubenstein, *My Brother Paul*, 40.
[41] See Freud, *Moses and Monotheism*. We will return to Freud in chapter eight.
[42] Rubenstein, *My Brother Paul*, 36.
[43] Rubenstein, *My Brother Paul*, 39.
[44] Rubenstein, *My Brother Paul*, 40. Rom. 7:1–6: 'Or do you not know, brethren (for I am speaking to those who know the law), that the law has jurisdiction over a person as long as he lives? For the married woman is bound by law to her husband while he is living; but if her husband dies, she is released from the law concerning the husband. So then, if while her husband is living she is joined to another man, she shall be called an adulteress; but if her husband dies, she is free from the law, so that she is not an adulteress though she is joined to another man. Therefore, my brethren, you also were made to die to the Law through the body of Christ, so that you might be joined to another, to Him who was raised from the dead, in order that we might bear fruit for God. For while we were in the flesh, the sinful passions, which were aroused by the Law, were at work in the members of our body to bear fruit for death. But now we have been released from the Law, having died to that by which we were bound, so that we serve in newness of the Spirit and not in oldness of the letter.'

of the written).[45] In Rubenstein's reading, Paul's frustration in failing to observe the Law is empathetically portrayed as a natural and not uncommon reaction to the *halakhah*, and the fault is laid at the door of institutional Judaism, which had failed to provide a religious outlet for such psychological tension.

Bearing in mind the difficulty of making sharp distinctions between Palestinian and Hellenistic Judaism,[46] Rubenstein suggested that Paul's upbringing in Tarsus (and his exposure to different ways of thinking) explained his desire to unify humanity in Christ and potentially offered insight into the plight of minority groups who live on the sufferance of their hosts.[47] A fascination with non-Jewish thought is apparent throughout Rubenstein's own work, and he maintained that it was right and proper that 'the varieties of contemporary Jewish identity overflow the boundaries of all the religious and secular ideologies of Jewish life'.[48] Interest in minority groups also resonated, because he was a committed adherent of the American civil rights movement and felt duty bound to defend unpopular marginal groups such as the Unification Church.[49]

Despite his shared interests, Rubenstein disagreed with the majority of Paul's teachings. But there can be no doubt that in Paul Rubenstein found a kindred spirit, a conflicted, sensitive, and innovative religious thinker who had been grossly mis-understood by Jewish commentators. He was adamant that Paul should not be regarded as the prototype of 'the Jewish turncoat'. In contrast to the medieval period, when apostates had shifted to the dominant Christian community, Ruben-stein argued that Paul's conversion had been to a persecuted sect, the implication being that this had been an act of courage and integrity. Nor should the apostle's anger and impatience with his fellow Jews be compared to later degrading Christian attempts to convert Jews.[50] At the root of Rubenstein's appreciation was his belief that Paul had had the profound insight that our common perception of reality was only a part of the story. As he put it,

If any single idea dominates the way I have come to see Paul, it is this: *Under the impact of the Christian religious revolution, which was at least initially an internal Jewish revolution, Paul came to understand, as did later Jewish mystics, that reality as appre-hended by commonsense offers only hints of the deeper and truer meaning of the human world.* Paul thus prepares the way for and anticipates the work of the twentieth-century's most important secularised Jewish mystic, Sigmund Freud.[51]

---

[45] Rubenstein, *My Brother Paul*, 117–18.
[46] Rubenstein, *My Brother Paul*, 19.
[47] Rubenstein, *My Brother Paul*, 129–30.
[48] Rubenstein, 'Reflections on Identity and Memory', 179.
[49] Rubenstein, having studied the Moonies, associated with them in the face of popular hostility. He was fascinated by their emergence from a nexus of shamanistic, Confucian, and Buddhist roots, and their embracing of Protestant missionism and modernity. Rubenstein, 'A Brief Biographical Sketch', xix–xx.
[50] Rubenstein, *My Brother Paul*, 116–17.
[51] Rubenstein, *My Brother Paul*, 22.

Whatever else his observations might suggest, this vision of a precociously modern Paul indicates that Rubenstein, as part of his programme of Jewish self-discovery, was not entirely successful in avoiding the temptation to recreate the apostle in his own image.

NANCY FUCHS-KREIMER

The Reconstructionist rabbi Nancy Fuchs-Kreimer (1952–) also believes that Paul can be approached as part of an effort to redefine what it meant to be Jewish. A graduate of Yale Divinity School, she was ordained at the Reconstructionist Rabbinical College in Philadelphia in 1982 and received her Ph.D. in Jewish–Christian relations from Temple University in 1990. Involved with interreligious dialogue and having written on modern Jewish identity for many years, it is her earlier studies, as a doctoral student, that are most pertinent here.

Fuchs-Kreimer produced the most comprehensive survey of Jewish writers on Paul to date with her unpublished thesis, 'The Essential Heresy: Paul's View of the Law According to Jewish Writers, 1886–1986' (1990). She argues forcefully that new developments in Pauline studies and a reassessment of Judaism within Christian theology had profoundly changed the landscape and called for a reassessment of what the traditional 'arch-enemy of the Jewish establishment' had to offer Judaism.[52]

Fuchs-Kreimer grounds her approach to Paul upon two postwar developments within Christian New Testament studies. The first is the successful contextualising of Paul in Pharisaic Judaism, rather than Hellenism, which rejects the Law/grace dichotomy as central to Paul's thought (that is, the so-called 'new perspective' on Paul in distinction to the traditional Lutheran understanding). The second is 'a new wave of Christian theology' that calls for a revisionist approach to integrating Paul into a positive view of the Jewish people.[53] Assuming that Judaism had for centuries defined itself in distinction to the traditional Western Augustinian/Lutheran reading of Paul and his problem with the Law (which she calls 'new culture's Paul'),[54] Fuchs-Kreimer is intrigued by the potential ramifications of this 'new perspective' for modifying previous Jewish approaches to Paul – and thus for modifying Judaism's self-understanding itself. As she puts it,

If the understanding of what Paul really thought were to change, if Jews were confronted by a new cultural reality, a new 'culture's Paul', would that change the nature of Jewish understanding of the boundary between Judaism and Christianity? How would this, in turn, effect [sic] the Jewish understanding of Judaism and its distinctive contributions?[55]

---

[52] Fuchs-Kreimer, 'The Essential Heresy', vii.
[53] Fuchs-Kreimer, 'The Essential Heresy', 20. Pauline scholars cited included Stendahl, Sanders, Sloyan, Gaston, and Gager. Theologians included Thoma, van Buren, and Mussner.
[54] Fuchs-Kreimer, 'The Essential Heresy', 292.
[55] Fuchs-Kreimer, 'The Essential Heresy', 20.

What was this 'new culture's Paul'? Fuchs-Kreimer argues that Paul should be seen as a man of integrity and no longer as an unprincipled opportunist of the traditional view, which was the understandable but mistaken result of the need to 'insulate Judaism from criticism by demoting the status of the critic'.[56] The charge that he was giving the Gentiles what they wanted makes no sense in the light of Galatians, an epistle in which he could be seen trying desperately to convince apparently unwilling Gentile believers *not* to place themselves under the Law.[57] Similarly, although she understands the psychological need to view Paul as 'the paradigm of the Jewish convert to Christianity . . . the arch self-hating Jew who left his people for convenience',[58] she criticises previous attempts to undermine Paul's Jewishness, or portray his thought as alien to Judaism, arguing,

As a questing Jew prior to his conversion, Paul can certainly not be 'read out' of Judaism. One can argue that his final conclusions were beyond the boundaries Judaism set at his time or in subsequent eras. This does not mean, however, that he was not a Jew who raised Jewish issues with which a Jew would not want to deal.[59]

Paul had not been 'a malcontent' before his call to be an apostle, nor should his theology be read, à la Luther, as a critique of Judaism; Paul the Pharisee had not suffered from guilt under the Law.[60] On the other hand, he had moved away from the Law for the purpose of justifying a new community. Fuchs-Kreimer suggests that this had been due to a fixation on the role of the Gentiles, and a belief that the actions of a biblical God of history could be unexpected and that creative interpretations of the consequences were called for. Distinguishing herself from the majority of previous writers who regarded Paul's emphasis on Christ as problematic, Fuchs-Kreimer argues that Paul had 'insisted upon God as primary, even above the law God had given. Thus Paul was insistent in his anti-idolatry.'[61] With this fresh perspective on the apostle to the Gentiles in mind, she goes on to consider the implications for Jewish self-understanding. These include the following:[62]

1. The need for Jewish theologians to take Paul seriously as posing theological issues for Judaism, especially in the realm of the universalism/particularism debate. Judaism not only needs a more sophisticated theology to account for non-Jewish religions than was represented by the Noachide laws, but also explicitly requires one for Christianity. Pauline Christianity, deriving from Judaism, offers ideas that ought to be engaged with. 'If Paul was

---

[56] Fuchs-Kreimer, 'The Essential Heresy', 300.
[57] Fuchs-Kreimer, 'The Essential Heresy', 79.
[58] Fuchs-Kreimer, 'The Essential Heresy', 79.
[59] Fuchs-Kreimer, 'The Essential Heresy', 300.
[60] Fuchs-Kreimer, 'The Essential Heresy', 300–301.
[61] Fuchs-Kreimer, 'The Essential Heresy', 301–2.
[62] Fuchs-Kreimer, 'The Essential Heresy', 302.

neither an opportunist nor a foreigner, but rather a serious Jew of his time', Fuchs-Kreimer argues, 'then Judaism must look upon Paul as a Jewish theologian. As such, it is a theological issue for Jews to decide what their attitude ought to be to this Jewish thinker and the unique variation of Judaism which he helped shape and which most Jews rejected.... A religious community [Christianity] with universal claims has grown up using Jewish scripture and basing itself on the Jewish story [due to the influence of Paul]. What Judaism might have to say about that is indeed a question for Jewish theology.'[63]

2. The abandonment of the practice of using Paul for anti-Christian polemical purposes. Fuchs-Kreimer suggests that if Christian scholars such as Paul van Buren and Rosemary Radford-Ruether could attempt radical reassessments of their own polemical traditions, then it was incumbent upon Jewish theologians to repudiate theirs, too, and this should include misrepresentations of the apostle Paul.[64]

3. The abandonment of the use of the Law/grace dichotomy to distinguish between Judaism and Christianity. In light of what little is known about first-century Pharisaism, Fuchs-Kreimer argues that it is no longer tenable to regard Paul as attacking Judaism by means of this contrast. On the other hand, because Judaism had subsequently come to glory in being the 'religion of deed' in contrast to Paul's 'religion of grace' (that is, to define itself against Paul), then 'Ironically, the criticism may fit modern Judaism far better than the Judaism Paul was supposedly writing about'.[65] Modern Jews, whether Orthodox or Progressive, tended to define Judaism in terms of the Law (in a literal or metaphorical sense), and proudly maintained that by their actions they would bring salvation to the world. Fuchs-Kreimer comments that this was unfortunate, in that

many Jews feel more and more the need for a metaphoric way to say, through their religion, what has not been said quite as often in modern Judaism: some things are not in our power ... we need not justify ourselves because we are already loved, not forgiven for this or that wrong, but fundamentally and unalterably accepted.[66]

Created in opposition to Paul, she suggested, some of the themes of modern Judaism were understandably vulnerable to Pauline attack.[67] If, on the other hand, one abandoned the Law/grace debate as a means by which to distinguish Judaism from Christianity, then a more productive consideration of this other way of perceiving the world might be possible. In such a context

---

[63] Fuchs-Kreimer, 'The Essential Heresy', 306.
[64] Fuchs-Kreimer, 'The Essential Heresy', 307.
[65] Fuchs-Kreimer, 'The Essential Heresy', 307.
[66] Fuchs-Kreimer, 'The Essential Heresy', 309.
[67] Fuchs-Kreimer, 'The Essential Heresy', 307.

Paul's views were cogent, and Judaism would be free to treat these issues in ways that might better speak to human needs.[68]

4. The replacement of the Law/grace dichotomy by another, namely, 'peoplehood' and 'universal church'. Fuchs-Kreimer identifies three possible responses to Paul's question: What does the God of Israel have in mind for the Gentiles? The first is to focus on a common humanity and renounce the special metaphysical claims for both faith communities; the second is to accept theologically that God's plan for the Gentile is Christianity; and the third is to reject the idea that Christianity is the solution but to accept that the question demands a response, although it is as yet unclear what this response will look like.[69] Despite accepting that Paul's own creedal solution was inadequate (in that it appeared to negate the need for the continued existence of the Jewish people), Fuchs-Kreimer argues that his attempt should inspire Jewish theologians to address the issue.

The very fact that Jewish peoplehood, at one point in its history, spawned a universal church through the efforts of Paul and others points poignantly to the universalism inherent in Jewish peoplehood and challenges Jews to address that legacy again.[70]

5. The desirability of learning from Paul the importance of placing God at the centre of Jewish thought. Fuchs-Kreimer suggests that Jews, if honest, would admit that they had 'attempted to domesticate God' by asserting control over their own lives. She criticises the 'favourite midrash of modern Jews' (*Baba Mezia* 59b), which depicts a rabbinic dispute in which the decision goes with the majority, even when a voice from heaven represents the minority opinion, and from which is derived the lesson that God was charmed by his children's independence and their defeat of him. As a God-intoxicated Jew, she claims, the apostle offers a necessary counter to this kind of idolatry. In contrast to many Jews today, 'Paul chose to believe that it was God acting in a surprising way, a God who is greater than the law (which Paul did not criticize in and of itself), a God who is entitled to surprise mankind'.[71]

Each of Fuchs-Kreimer's implications regarding the nature of Judaism maps onto familiar areas of contention within the traditionalist–progressive ideological conflict. Since the nineteenth century, a key debate has concerned the proper balance of the universalist and particularist tendencies within Judaism and how

---

[68] Fuchs-Kreimer, 'The Essential Heresy', 311.

[69] Fuchs-Kreimer cited Samuel Sandmel as championing the first, Franz Rosenzweig, Hans J. Schoeps, and Pinchas Lapide the second, and Michael Wyschogrod the third. Fuchs-Kreimer, 'The Essential Heresy', 313–14.

[70] Fuchs-Kreimer, 'The Essential Heresy', 315–16. It is worth noting that Jewish Reconstructionism has tended to focus attention on the Jewish people rather than the Jewish religion *per se* ever since Mordecai Kaplan wrote *Judaism as Civilisation* (New York: Macmillan, 1934).

[71] Fuchs-Kreimer, 'The Essential Heresy', 316–17.

to relate to the Christian religion and its icons. The challenge of defining the role of Judaism in the modern world without reference to Christianity or Christian civilisation (here, by rejecting the grace/Law dichotomy) lies behind much of the discourse. For Fuchs-Kreimer, a change in attitude towards Paul means seeing him as a legitimate contributor to these ongoing debates. In terms of what Paul himself has to offer, Fuchs-Kreimer follows Montefiore in seeing him as a kind of limited spiritual inspiration (specifically with regard to his God-centeredness). But the most significant implication of her analysis is that the unhealthy antagonism to Pauline Christianity is a tragic historical misunderstanding, which has profoundly stunted Judaism's growth, and that a revision of the classical Jewish attitude to Paul will result in freedom from the practice of defining itself against Christianity. This would, in turn, encourage a reorientation of Judaism to address itself to the needs of individuals, unperturbed by apparent similarities with Christianity. However difficult it might be to discuss the specific consequences, the potential was enormous.

DANIEL BOYARIN

Like Schoeps, Rubenstein, and Fuchs-Kreimer, Daniel Boyarin (1946–) regards Paul as profoundly relevant to the modern Jewish world and is interested in issues of pluralism and identity in the context of a personal critique of Jewish tradition. A dual citizen of the United States and Israel, Boyarin is a professor of Talmudic culture at the University of California at Berkeley. He trained at the Jewish Theological Seminary (Conservative Judaism) and has research interests in Talmudic culture, rabbinic literature, sexuality and gender, and Jewish–Christian relations. He describes himself as a postmodern, actively practising rabbinic Jew who has familiarised himself with modern cultural studies. His approach is very much one of treating Paul as a cultural critic, and as someone who set the agenda in terms of ethnicity and gender for Jews and Christians.[72]

In *A Radical Jew: Paul and the Politics of Identity* (1994), Boyarin suggests that Pauline studies should be approached as an integral part of the study of Judaism in late antiquity.[73] In line with other recent writers such as Segal, he views Paul as a precious, unique resource for Jewish studies.

I would like to reclaim Pauline studies as an important, even an integral part of the study of Judaism in the Roman period and late antiquity. Paul has left us an extremely precious document for Jewish studies, the spiritual autobiography of a first-century Jew. There is hardly another document, save parts of Josephus and Philo, which even

---

[72] Boyarin, *A Radical Jew*, 4.
[73] Boyarin, *A Radical Jew*, 1. Boyarin refers to Pauline commentators, including both Christians such as Barclay, Baur, Betz, Bultmann, Davies, Dunn, Fiorenza, Gager, Gaston, Hays, Käsemann, Luther, Sanders, Stendahl, Watson, Westerholm, and Wright, and Jewish commentators such as Sandmel, Segal, and Schoeps. For Paul, he draws most heavily on Romans, 1 Corinthians, and Galatians.

comes close to fitting such a description. Moreover, if we take Paul at his word – and I see no *a priori* reason not to – he was a member of the Pharisaic wing of first century Judaism, with which Josephus may have also been connected but with which Philo certainly was not.[74]

But more than offering a window for the historian to perceive the complexity of first-century Judaism, Boyarin believes that Paul confronted issues that continue to be of vital relevance to modern Jewish identity.[75] In particular, he is fascinated by Paul's intellectual background, which made him a Hellene by linguistic culture and a Hebrew by training.[76] For Boyarin, Hellenistic Judaism represented an ancient attempt to reconcile apparently contradictory tendencies: one of universalism, characterised by the capacity for all people to be saved and by the idea of different deities being manifestations of the one deity; the other an emphasis on the particular privileges of the Jewish people and their one God, a reaction against universalism.[77] Thus any modern Jew struggling with the challenge of universalism for Judaism should be interested in the study of such a culture. But this raises the question: Should Jewish theologians take seriously the views of this particular proponent of Hellenistic Judaism? Boyarin is quite unapologetic in making the case for taking the apostle to the Gentiles seriously. As he puts it,

I would like to reclaim Paul as an important Jewish thinker. On my reading of the Pauline corpus, Paul lived and died convinced that he was a Jew living out Judaism. He represents, then, one option which Judaism could take in the first century. Paul represents a challenge to Jews in the first century, and I will argue that he presents a challenge to Jews now as well. Assuming, as I do, that Paul was motivated not by an abnormal psychological state but by a set of problems and ideas generated by his cultural, religious situation, I read him as a Jewish cultural critic, and I ask what it was in Jewish culture that led him to produce a discourse of radical reform of that culture. I ask also in what ways his critique is important and valid for Jews today, and indeed in what ways the questions that Paul raises about culture are important and valid for everyone today. Further, I want to inquire into the limitations, inadequacies, contradictions, and disastrous effects of some of the Pauline solutions to those problems. Finally, I wish to interrogate our situation and ask whether we have better solutions to the cultural, social problems raised by the Pauline corpus.[78]

It is clear that this reclamation of Paul, this use of the apostle as a means by which to probe the limits of Jewish interaction with the surrounding world, by no means implies approval of Paul's solutions. But it does mean that, for Boyarin at least, the study of his background, his view of the Law, and his approach to Gentiles and women is a profitable exercise.

---

[74] Boyarin, *A Radical Jew*, 1–2.
[75] Boyarin, *A Radical Jew*, 2.
[76] Boyarin, *A Radical Jew*, 59.
[77] Boyarin, *A Radical Jew*, 57–9.
[78] Boyarin, *A Radical Jew*, 2–3.

According to Boyarin, Paul should be regarded as a radical reformer of Jewish culture as a result of the influence of Greek universalistic ideas.[79] His genius was in utilising a dualist ideology (Platonism) to solve the challenge of universalism for Judaism, that is, in attempting to justify the integration of the Gentiles into the People of God by means of an allegorical interpretation of the Law.[80] This allegorical reading was made possible after Christ's life and death, and reveals the spiritual law that lies behind the literal Law; that is, it reveals a law that marks out a Universal People of God and makes no ethnic distinctions. Consequently, the (literal) Law must be regarded as less glorious and, if read apart from Christ, which is what it truly signifies, it brings death.[81] (Paul never explicitly identifies these two kinds of law, but this, according to Boyarin, is because allegory/dualism underlies all of Paul's thought, being implicit in Hellenistic Judaism itself).

Boyarin suggests that this new approach to the Law, derived from his impulse towards unity, freed Paul to construct a new view of humanity that was nondifferentiated and nonhierarchical, a view that is summed up in Gal. 3:28: 'There is neither Jew nor Greek, slave nor free, male nor female, for you are all one in Christ Jesus'. It is this view that Boyarin is fascinated and provoked by, and with which he struggles. He ultimately concludes that, although laudable in intent, Paul's view had negative consequences for ethnicity in that it required cultural specificities (for example, Jewishness) to be subsumed into a dominant culture, a single essence for which cultural specificity is unimportant. It had negative consequences for gender, too, in that Paul's equality depends upon the eradication of sexuality by upholding maleness as the norm to which women were to aspire.[82] But Boyarin is no less critical of rabbinic Judaism, in which ethnic difference, cultural specificity, historical memory, and sexuality were highly valued, but where the negative consequences included the potential for a racist social system and limited social and religious freedom for women.[83] Of course, Paul is useful in constructing such a critique. To take the example of religious Zionism:

When ... an ethnocentric Judaism becomes a temporal, hegemonic political force, it becomes absolutely, vitally necessary to accept Paul's critical challenge – although not his universalizing, disembodying solution – and develop an equally passionate concern for human beings. We, including religious Jews – perhaps especially religious Jews – must take the theological dimension of Paul's challenge seriously. How *could* the God of all the world have such a disproportionate care an concern for only a small part of His world?! ... If, on the one hand, rabbinic Judaism seems to imply that Israel is the

---

[79] Boyarin, *A Radical Jew*, 85, 52.
[80] Boyarin, *A Radical Jew*, 85. Although profoundly influenced by Platonism (that is, a dualistic philosophy where the physical world is a representation of the ideal world), he does not reject the body (that is, he retains the biblical view). Ibid., 7.
[81] Boyarin, *A Radical Jew*, 54–6.
[82] Boyarin, *A Radical Jew*, 8–9.
[83] Boyarin, *A Radical Jew*, 8–9.

true humanity, a potentially vicious doctrine of separation and hierarchy, Paul argues that humanity is the true Israel, an equally vicious doctrine of coerced sameness and exclusion.[84]

In the end, neither system is satisfactory for Boyarin, whose own expertise in secular, nontraditional studies can be viewed both as a counterpoint from which to criticise traditional worldviews and as a modern-day parallel to Paul's internalisation of non-Jewish philosophies.[85]

For Boyarin, a reconstruction of Jewish identity in light of new ways of thinking is integral to Jewish existence, and Paul, a paradoxical figure, provides him with a paradigm of this concept of the Jew. As he puts it,

[Paul] represents the interface between Jew as a self-identical essence and Jew as a construction constantly being remade. The very tension in his discourse, indeed in his life, between powerful self-identification as a Jew . . . and an equally powerful, or even more powerful, identification of self as everyman is emblematic of Jewish selfhood. Paul represents in his person and thematizes in his discourse, paradoxes not only of Jewish identity, but . . . of all identity as such. When the Galatians wish to take on Jewish cultural practice, Paul cries out to them with real pathos: Remain as I am, for I have become as you are. The paradoxes and oxymorons of that sentence are, I submit, those of identity itself, and exploring the Pauline corpus with this kind of quest in mind will lead us to a deeper and richer appreciation of our own cultural quandaries as male or female, Jew or Greek, and human. [86]

Thus the struggle to comprehend and engage with this marginal Jew allows Boyarin to move from the exploration of Jewish identity to the more complex issue concerning the nature of identity itself.

CONCLUSION

Previously we considered the way in which many Jewish thinkers have become polarised in their attempt to understand Judaism in relation to Christianity.

[84] Boyarin's suspicion of religious Zionism is justified in terms of Paul's critique of Jewish ethnocentricism, despite the fact that he cannot accept Paul's own universalist solution. Boyarin, *A Radical Jew*, 257.

[85] 'Rather than seeing Paul as a text and my task that of a philologist, I see us engaged across the centuries in a common enterprise of cultural criticism. When, for instance, I deal with the question of the signification/significance of circumcision in Paul and in the rabbinic response to him, I speak about it in terms drawn from post-structuralist inquiries into the significance of the "phallus", a seemingly appropriate line of inquiry which to my knowledge has yet to be pursued. . . . When I inquire into Paul's pronouncements on the relations between the sexes, I do so with the full agenda of feminist cultural criticism in my personal reading agenda. And I am concerned as well to register the response of an actively practicing (post)modern rabbinic Jew to both Paul and Pauline interpretation, particularly insofar as these (especially the latter) have often been inimical to my religious/ethnic group and practice. My inquiry and response involve, as well, the ways that the Pauline discourse of the Jew as "figure" has heirs today in both marxian and other theoretical discourses.' Boyarin, *A Radical Jew*, 4.

[86] Boyarin, *A Radical Jew*, 3.

Whereas some can only see a chasm between the two faiths and regard Paul as emblematic of that which separates them, others seek to span the gulf and see the apostle as a bridging figure who embodies that which is shared between the two faiths. We also saw how some Jewish thinkers, acutely aware of his unique and powerful standing in the history of Western civilisation, have used the apostle to the Gentiles to justify their own individual ideological positions within a wider intra-Jewish debate; in practice, this was largely a matter of progressives criticising traditionalist conceptions of Jewish authenticity. In this chapter we have looked at Jewish writers who regard Paul as a fellow traveller on a journey of exploration of Jewish religious identity. For Schonfield, Paul is a fellow visionary whose role in salvation history has been disastrously misinterpreted in the past and who is useful for reinforcing belief in the activity of God in the world. For Rubenstein, Paul is a fellow existentialist, a man before his time who was capable of profound psychological insights, and whose anxiety concerning his own mortality reinforces Freudian interpretations of Judaism and the human condition. For Fuchs-Kreimer, Paul is an icon of religious prejudice but also a fellow worker in the task of rejuvenating Judaism; his critique of particularism, his actual understanding of and teachings regarding grace, and his attempt to work out a worthy theology of the non-Jew all demanded adequate Jewish responses (even if she herself could not quite articulate what these responses should be). For Boyarin, Paul is a fellow cultural critic who approached perennial dilemmas (regarding universalist and gender issues in particular) in such a way as to make avoidance of the issues, and acceptance of the status quo, impossible. There is no doubt that, in thinking through the implications of postmodern cultural criticism, Boyarin's approach, like Fuchs-Kreimer's, represents a powerful, politically charged challenge for the wider Jewish community. Nevertheless, the impression given by these authors is that they are primarily concerned with an internally orientated reassessment of Jewish thought and identity. They take delight in having discovered such an unlikely ally, an ally who takes seriously their own concerns, who is to be taken seriously in return, and who represents more to them than merely a means to defend an established ideological position. The dilemma for each is not how to judge Paul's views in the light of Jewish theology (because Jewish theology is, for each, lacking in some way). Nor is it to establish to what extent his views can be regarded as authentically Jewish (because his voice is clearly regarded by each as a legitimate Jewish voice). Rather, the primary concern of these authors is how to draw upon or develop the views of this partner-in-dialogue to help meet the challenge of making sense of Judaism in the modern world. Instinctively they dismiss the small-mindedness of those who disagree with them. The apostle is appreciated as a like-minded spirit who was unafraid to ask questions that cut to the heart of what it meant to be a Jew or to apply himself to working out practical and theological solutions, whatever these may be. The paradoxes that characterised his life and thought are no stumbling block for them but rather evidence that he was straining to articulate that which lies at the root of the Jewish predicament. The very act of grappling with Paul as an equal shows their willingness to go beyond the familiar debating ground and to explore revolutionary possibilities; and each of them is passionate in their belief that Paul has been profoundly misunderstood – and undervalued – by the Jewish community. Their remarkable sense of kinship to this first-century follower of Jesus Christ is a powerful demonstration of the ever-increasing complexity of modern religious identity in general and the nebulousness of modern Jewish identity in particular.

In this and the previous two chapters we have explored the variety and richness of the different visions of Paul generated by Jewish theologians, New Testament scholars, and religious leaders. Such figures certainly represent an important section of the Jewish community, but, interested as we are in the treatment of Paul in Jewish culture more generally, their status as leaders and spokespersons for that community mean that their opinions should be regarded only part of the story. All too often within the study of Jewish–Christian relations (and in interfaith dialogue in particular) one forgets that such elites represent only a limited sample of the many conflicting voices that make up the Jewish community and that more interesting developments are often taking place elsewhere. It is important, then, to consider approaches to Paul undertaken by Jewish thinkers who can in no wise be regarded as speaking in an official or Jewishly authoritative capacity. We will therefore now turn to an examination of the place of Paul in the Jewish artistic imagination.

PART III

THE APOSTLE PAUL AND JEWISH INTEREST
IN THE JUDEO-CHRISTIAN TRADITION:
ARTISTIC AND LITERARY APPROACHES

The origin of the idea of a Judeo-Christian tradition, or heritage, or civilisation, or ethic, lies well before the advent of the modern interfaith movement.[1] It has been suggested that its roots can be traced back to the Enlightenment, when the rationalists and the Deists started disassociating themselves from the adherents of revelational religion, be it Jewish or Christian.[2] Later, in the context of nineteenth-century Christian biblical criticism, (German) Protestant scholars offered a response to Enlightenment criticism, by insisting upon the distinction between Judaism and Christianity, and arguing that profound differences had been evident from the start, in that Pauline Christianity had been the triumph of Gentile, universalising tendencies over the Jewish, particularising tendencies of the Torah-observant Jerusalem Church – in other words, that Christianity may have initially manifested itself as a Judeo-Christian entity, but quickly distinguished itself from Judaism.[3] And during the Nazi period the *Deutsche Christen* or German Christians similarly aimed to purge Christianity of its Jewish roots; that is, they sought to eradicate any residual elements of Judeo-Christianity from within their faith, which for them, ironically, included the writings of Paul. All these are negative conceptions of 'Judeo-Christian', but, according to the Oxford English Dictionary, the term itself first appeared in 1899 in an entirely neutral sense to describe a 'Judeo-Christian "continuity" theory'. This theory postulated the development of Church ritual out of the practices of Second Temple Judaism. The use of the term 'Judeo-Christian' in this context allowed the scholar to focus on those elements of the two communities which overlapped each other, for which a historic continuity could be demonstrated. The label also appealed to North American scholars in the 1930s and 1940s who, reacting against the arguments of the nineteenth-century German scholars, wanted to express their commitment to the prophetic values of

---

[1] For the following overview of the history of the idea of the Judeo-Christian tradition the author has greatly benefited from reading Mark Silk, 'Notes of the Judeo-Christian Tradition in America', *American Quarterly* 36:1 (Spring 1984); Arthur Cohen, *The Myth of the Judeo-Christian Tradition; and Other Dissenting Essays* (New York: Schocken Books, 1971); and Jacob Neusner, *Jews and Christians: The Myth of a Common Tradition*, second edition (London: SCM Press, 1990). These last two represent vehement critiques of the idea of the tradition.

[2] Cohen, *The Myth of the Judeo-Christian Tradition*, 196–7.

[3] For example, the Tübingen School led by Ferdinand Christian Baur, discussed in Chapter one.

social justice and biblical faith, and to demonstrate how rooted Christian values were in the world of the Hebrew Bible.[4] In wider cultural, nontheological circles, too, the term was cropping up in the sense of a shared set of ethics.[5] And during the Second World War, the 'Judeo-Christian tradition' was useful as a way to unite the 'fighting faiths' of Anglo-American democracy against the Fascists and later to include Jews in a united front against the godless Communists.[6]

The classic critique of the tradition was offered by the author and theologian Arthur Cohen, who argued that such beliefs, which he described as 'schematic, loose, general, archetypal', were of little import in light of the philosophic or theological issues that were overlooked in such presentations – for example, the question of whether the Messiah had already come or not.[7] This issue in particular represented an irreparable divide between Jews and Christians, and convinced him that the so-called Judeo-Christian tradition was an artificial construct that had set aside 'the sinew and bone of actuality', the historical reality of profound theological difference.[8] His analysis concluded,

We can learn much from the history of Jewish–Christian relations, but the one thing we cannot make of it is a discourse of community, fellowship, and understanding. How then do we make of it a tradition? . . . It has become in our own day a myth which buries under the fine silt of rhetoric the authentic, meaningful, and irrevocable distinction which exists between Jewish belief and Christian belief.[9]

Nevertheless, whether explicitly articulated or not, the idea of a shared body of Western attitudes, ideals, and values derived from a shared biblical tradition boasts a venerable pedigree and is undoubtedly woven into the very fabric of post-Enlightenment European culture.

In Chapter five we will meet the composer Felix Mendelssohn, the painter Ludwig Meidner, and the playwright Franz Werfel. In Chapter six we will look at the novelists Shalom Asch and Samuel Sandmel. What links these individuals together is that they were drawn to Paul in their explorations of what has come to be called the Judeo-Christian tradition. They used their artistic engagement with

---

[4] For example, the theologians Reinhold Niebuhr, G. Ernest Wright, and Paul Minear.

[5] For example, George Orwell wrote of 'the Judeo-Christian scheme of morals' in 1939. George Orwell, 'Stendhal', *The New English Weekly* 15 (27 July 1939), 237.

[6] Deborah Dash-Moore, 'Jewish GIs and the Creation of the Judeo-Christian Tradition', *Religion and American Culture* 8:1 (1998).

[7] "[F]or where Jews and Christians divide, divide irreparably, divide finally . . . is that for Jews the Messiah is to come and for Christians he has already come." Cohen, *The Myth of the Judeo-Christian Tradition*, xii.

[8] Cohen's attempt to trace the origins and development of the idea has been incorporated into my earlier account. He concluded, "The renewal of the doctrine of the Judeo-Christian tradition . . . is a post-War phenomenon. Christianity has a bad conscience and Jews seem anxious to pique it. Unfortunately, the penance which some Christians seem willing to perform and which some Jews seem anxious to exact, whatever its personal value, does not legitimate the creation of a 'Judeo-Christian tradition'." Cohen, *The Myth of the Judeo-Christian Tradition*, 200.

[9] Cohen, *The Myth of the Judeo-Christian Tradition*, xiii, xvi.

him as an opportunity to work through such theological issues as universalism within Judaism, transnational knowledge of God, and the reality (or otherwise) of a shared religious essence. In the following examination of their largely appreciative portrayals of this founding figure of Christianity and his theological deliberations, considerable emphasis will be placed on their respective social backgrounds and cultural milieus. It will be seen that these rare Jewish artistic renderings of Paul represent five very different attempts to explore interfaith relations, which is hardly surprising, because the historical period covered runs from the early nineteenth to the mid-twentieth century. It is hoped that this focus upon the artistic imagination will pay dividends in broadening our understanding of the diversity of Jewish responses to Paul, especially when one takes seriously the complex nature of Jewish identity in European and North American culture in the modern period.

5

∽

An Oratorio by Felix Mendelssohn, a Painting by Ludwig Meidner, and a Play by Franz Werfel

For some the very idea of 'Jewish art' is nonsensical, the paucity of artistic material of any kind generated down through the centuries being attributed to the second commandment's prohibition of graven images.[1] Amongst others, the debate about what exactly constitutes 'Jewish art' falls into two schools of thought: it is understood either to be art *produced* by Jews, or art whose subject matter is *about* Jewish life or Judaism. Of course, any definition that regards Jewish art as a reflection of the Jewish experience is a very broad definition indeed, bearing in mind the varieties and complexities of the modern Jewish experience.[2] Arguably, one unifying theme of modern Jewish art is the exploration of identity; and in this the interests of Jewish artists dovetail neatly with those of other Jewish intellectually creative efforts. One might well have predicted as much, considering how Jewish artists have struggled to find a place for themselves and their own interests in a Western culture dominated by Christian themes and motifs, or when one thinks of the number who have been refugees of one sort or another.[3] Another common theme which makes perfect sense for a Jewish artist struggling to make sense of his identity in a Christian world, and which is again shared with nonartistic forms of Jewish discourse, is that of biblical interpretation.[4] The French painter of Russian-Jewish origin, Marc Chagall (1887–1985), who painted biblical figures alongside characters from the *shtetl* and who was haunted by Christian motifs such as the Crucifixion, is perhaps the best-known artist illustrating these tendencies.

[1] For an overview of this issue, see Joseph Gutmann, 'The "Second Commandment" and the Image in Judaism' in Joseph Gutmann, ed., *No Graven Images: Studies in Art and the Hebrew Bible* (New York: Ktav, 1971).

[2] 'Jewish art is art which reflects the Jewish experience' was the agreed definition of the seminar participants who set themselves the task of defining Jewish art in 1984. See Vivian B. Mann and Gordon Tucker, *The Seminar on Jewish Art: January–September 1984* (New York: Jewish Theological Seminary of America and the Jewish Museum, 1985), 10.

[3] Examples of painters include Marc Chagall, Jacques Lipchitz, George Grosz, Mordechai Ardon, Abraham Rattner, Oskar Kokoschka, Jankel Adler, and Felix Nussbaum. For an excellent overview of the subject, see Ziva Amishai-Maisels, 'The Artist as Refugee', in Ezra Mendelsohn and Richard I. Cohen, eds., *Art and Its Uses: The Visual Image and Modern Jewish Society*, Studies in Contemporary Jewry, VI (New York: Oxford University Press, 1990), 111–48.

[4] The artist and critic, Menachem Wecker, notes that 'One of the most fascinating trajectories that Jewish artists take – though still an under-treaded path – is painting as a means of biblical interpretation.' Menachem Wecker, 'The Challenge of Defining Jewish Art', *Forward* (18 August 2006).

In this chapter we will look at a piece of music, a painting, and a play.[5] The artists themselves have complicated relationships with the Jewish community into which they were born, and some would question their inclusion here, especially in the case of Mendelssohn. It is true that all three can be regarded as products of the *German* culture of their own day, and one is inclined to agree with the sentiments expressed by the editors of the *Jewish Encyclopedia* entry on 'Attitude of Judaism toward Art', that

Modern Jewish art no longer bears the specific character of the Jewish genius, but must be classified among the various nations to which the Jewish artists belong.[6]

But it is also true that, although very different from each other, the experiences of Mendelssohn, Meidner, and Werfel were shared by other Jews living in their times and took place at important transitional moments in the course of modern European Jewish history. Arguably, it is an awareness of the nature of their disparate cultural experiences as Jews that makes possible a fuller appreciation and understanding of their art. In particular, the unusual choice of Paul as a subject for each of them speaks volumes about their particular life-experiences, even as it brings together the themes of biblical interpretation and the exploration of Jewish identity.

FELIX MENDELSSOHN'S PAUL: 'JUDAISM IN TRANSITION'

Felix Mendelssohn (1809–47) was a grandson of the famous Jewish Enlightenment philosopher Moses Mendelssohn, and a son of the banker Abraham Mendelssohn, who had him baptised as a seven-year-old. A musical child prodigy who has been compared frequently to Mozart, Felix went on to become a renowned conductor and composer whose work mediated between the Classical and Romantic traditions.[7] Among the many symphonies, concertos, oratorios, and piano and chamber music pieces that he wrote in his short lifetime, two of his most famous were the oratorios *Elijah* (1846) and, of greatest interest here, *St. Paul* (1836).[8]

---

[5] There are precious few examples of Jewish artistic treatments of Paul. The Russian-born Israeli sculptor Avraham Melnikoff's plaster sculpture 'St Paul Preaching' is another fascinating example, about which little is known. Melnikoff (1892–1960) exhibited the piece in 1935 at the Bloomsbury Galleries in London as part of a one-man show, to critical acclaim. *The Jewish Chronicle* described his portrayal of Paul as that of 'a flaming Chasid, as a fanatic, resenting sculptural control.' *Jewish Chronicle* (10 May 1935), 22. Before returning to Israel in 1958, Melnikoff destroyed the work 'in protest against the resurgence of racism which he now conceives of as inherent in Christianity.' Ilana Ortar, *Melnikoff: The Awakening Judah* (Haifa: University of Haifa Art Gallery, 1982), 45–6.

[6] Joseph Jacobs, Kaufmann Kohler, Judah David Eisenstein, 'Art, Attitude of Judaism toward', *Jewish Encyclopedia*, I, 142.

[7] For a comprehensive biographical study, see R. Larry Todd, *Mendelssohn: A Life in Music* (Oxford: Oxford University Press, 2003).

[8] The first German edition was Felix Mendelssohn-Bartholdy, *Paulus* (Bonn: N. Simrock, 1836). The first English edition was Felix Mendelssohn, *St. Paul* (Birmingham: 1837).

A passionate debate currently rages amongst scholars as to whether Felix defined himself Jewishly or not. No one disputes that he was a proud German and a sincere Christian. Rather, the focus of the debate is how important, if at all, Felix's Jewish heritage was to his religious worldview and, by extension, to his work. The history of this controversy is long and not a little sordid. An influential anti-Semitic attack by Wagner in 1850, shortly after Felix's death, had sought to marginalise his works by reference to their perceived Jewish characteristics,[9] and the Nazis took up this theme and went on to ban performances of his music starting in 1938. In a classic study by Werner in 1963, the negative value judgement of Felix's Jewishness was reversed and a portrayal of a great musician was offered that stressed Jewish influences and pride in his Jewish heritage.[10] However, recent research by Sposato has discredited much of Werner's presentation, showing that he modified the wording of key correspondence in making his case. Sposato argues instead that Felix saw himself as 'enlightened, rationalist, and, in short, a typical German *Neuchrist*',[11] as Jewish converts to Christianity were called, brought up and baptised as a Protestant and eventually becoming a follower of the highly influential Reformed theologian Friedrich Schleiermacher (1768–1834),[12] with no documented interest in his Jewish ancestry. Certainly, evidence to the contrary is hard to come by and appears to amount to a report that Felix once commented on the irony that he, as a 'Jew-boy', had brought about a revival of the church composer J. S. Bach.[13] Nevertheless, other scholars, including Botstein, Steinberg, and Todd, although accepting Sposato's demolition of Werner's account, continue to regard Felix's Jewish background as important for making sense of the man and his music.

[9] Wagner published 'Das Judenthum in der Musik', *Neue Zeitschrift für Musik* (Leipzig: 1850) under a pseudonym. He describes Mendelssohn's music as 'vague, fantastic shadow-forms', having already explained that '[a]lthough the peculiarities of the Jewish mode of speaking and singing come out the most glaringly in the commoner class of Jew, who has remained faithful to his fathers' stock, and though the cultured son of Jewry takes untold pains to strip them off, nevertheless they shew an impertinent obstinacy in cleaving to him.' Richard Wagner, *Judaism in Music and Other Writings*, trans. W. Ashton Ellis (London: University of Nebraska Press, 1995), 89, 96.

[10] Eric Werner, *Mendelssohn, a New Image of the Composer and His Age*, trans. Dika Newlin (New York: Collier-Macmillan, 1963).

[11] Jeffrey S. Sposato, 'Creative Writing: The [Self-] Identification of Mendelssohn as a Jew', *The Musical Quarterly* 82:1 (Spring 1998), 192.

[12] Felix proclaimed himself 'a follower of Schleiermacher' in 1830 in a letter to his friend Julius Schubring, himself a disciple of the theologian who sought to reconcile Lutheran and Reformed theology; he also cultivated a personal friendship with Schleiermacher. Jeffrey Sposato, *The Price of Assimilation: Felix Mendelssohn and the Nineteenth-Century Anti-Semitic Tradition* (Oxford: Oxford University Press, 2006), 48, 186n39. The differences between the Reformed (Calvinist) and Lutheran churches in Prussia had their origins in the major theological dispute between Zwingli and Luther on the question of the real presence of Christ in the bread and wine of the Eucharist; this profoundly influenced how the two denominations understood Christ to be present and active in the world. There was an attempt by Friedrich Wilhelm III to unite the two denominations in Prussia in 1817, which was followed by some attempts to reconcile the two churches' theological and liturgical differences, but this did not meet with great success.

[13] 'To think that it must be a comic-actor and a Jew-boy [*Judenjunge*] who brings back to the people the greatest Christian musical work!' Eduard Devrient, *Meine Erinnerungen an Felix Mendelssohn* [My Memories of Felix Mendelssohn] (Leipzig: J.J. Weber, 1872), 62.

All agree that in nineteenth-century German society, Felix could not have avoided his Jewishness even if he had so desired.[14] But although Sposato stresses that he chose not to define himself as such, the others remain convinced of the importance of his Jewish heritage to understanding him.[15] In particular, Botstein argues that Felix's lifework was the completion of a 'syncretic' project to 'universalise Judaism', a project that first began with his grandfather Moses Mendelssohn.[16] In fact, there is not as much distance between the two camps as appears at first sight. Sposato's meticulous study is certainly prepared to acknowledge a development in Felix's writing which, by the end of his life, had arrived at what is described as a 'strategy of dual perspective', that is, 'an attempt to reconcile his Christian faith and his Jewish heritage.'[17] It is agreed, then, that Felix's shifting attitude towards Jews and his consciousness of both Jewish and Christian perspectives – and its implications for his self-understanding – can be traced in his works. For those interested in complex Jewish identity, whatever the precise label given, his oratorio about the Apostle to the Gentiles has some particularly useful insights to offer.

Before the musical work itself is considered, a brief discussion of the intellectual influences within Felix's family is in order for the purpose of establishing the foundations of his own religious constitution. One might be tempted to begin with his grandfather, Moses Mendelssohn (1729–86),[18] whose writings can be seen as an attempt to relate eighteenth-century rationality and theism. After all, Felix was

---

[14] Sposato himself observes, 'That Mendelssohn identified in part as Jewish is beyond question. How could he not have, with queens, princes, fellow musicians, and friends all, to a greater or lesser extent, seeing him as such?' but he argues forcefully that this was of little or no real consequence. Sposato, *The Price of Assimilation*, 14.

[15] Steinberg responds directly to Sposato's categorisation of Mendelssohn by asserting that 'Felix Mendelssohn's cultural moment and biographical formation cannot be understood as those of a "typical *Neuchrist*" but rather as a paradigm of a multicultural and uncertain moment in German Jewish history that was available only to the Biedermeier generation, that is, the generation of 1815–1848. The assertion that Mendelssohn should be considered a Protestant rather than Jew simply replaces one conceptually and historically inadequate label with another.' Michael P. Steinberg, 'Mendelssohn's Music and German-Jewish Culture: An Intervention', *The Musical Quarterly* 83:1 (Spring 1999), 32. Todd draws upon both Botstein and Sposato, concluding 'we must begin to realize the significance of the composer's own project of assimilation, of finding ground between his adopted faith and the rationalist Judaism of his grandfather, Moses Mendelssohn.' Todd, *Mendelssohn: A Life in Music*, xxviii.

[16] Writing before Sposato, Botstein's argument was that '[Felix] Mendelssohn was syncretic, not sectarian. His Christian faith focused on the extent to which Christianity was a universalization of Judaism.' Leon Botstein, 'The Aesthetics of Assimilation and Affirmation: Reconstructing the Career of Felix Mendelssohn' in R. Larry Todd, ed., *Mendelssohn and His World* (Princeton: Princeton University Press, 1991), 23.

[17] Sposato suggests that a changing attitude towards Jews is apparent from the time of Felix's revival of the St. Matthew Passion in 1829, through the libretto drafted for A. B. Marx's *Mose* in 1833 and the oratorios of *St. Paul* (1836), *Elijah* (1846), and *Christ* (1847). The new attitude revealed in the last two works was 'one no longer fuelled by a need to demonize the Jews in order to prove the sincerity of his Christian faith.' Sposato, *The Price of Assimilation*, 178–9.

[18] Botstein is among those who would do so. 'Felix Mendelssohn's advocacy of his grandfather's work is certainly positive evidence of his connection to being Jewish. A revival of or an increase in awareness of his grandfather's writings by definition had to invoke a visible affirmation of Felix's Jewish heritage . . . Felix's knowledge of and lifelong admiration for Moses Mendelssohn's work was

instrumental in having Moses's collected works published only four years after the completion of *St. Paul*.[19] The book that made Moses's reputation, *Phaedon* (1767), was a discussion of immortality which drew heavily upon natural theology and assumed the universality of rational thought.[20] Felix read this extended commentary on Plato's treatise in 1831, only a year before he began work on the *St. Paul* oratorio.[21] If Felix had also read Moses's classic study, *Jerusalem or on Religious Power and Judaism* (1783), which also featured a deist-like vision of a God who reveals his purposes and ethical demands through the natural world and by means of a common access to reason,[22] then this would have important implications for his conception of the Jewish religion. However, with the exception of *Phaedon*, there is no direct evidence that Felix actually read Moses's works, and although it is difficult to imagine that his famous grandfather's writings and ideas were of no interest to the cultivated, intellectual household in which Felix was brought up,

---

nontrivial.' Leon Botstein, 'Mendelssohn and the Jews', *The Musical Quarterly* 82:1 (Spring 1998), 212.

[19] It is, however, important not to overestimate Felix's role in this. He was approached to assist with the publication of Moses Mendelssohn's works in 1840, but it was his uncle, Joseph, and Joseph's son Benjamin, who were actually responsible for bringing this product to a successful conclusion. Todd, *Mendelssohn: A Life in Music*, 16–17.

[20] '[T]he endowments he [man] possesses of body and mind, he knows to be the gift of the all-good Father. All beauties, all harmony, goodness, wisdom, providence, ways and means, which he has acknowledged hitherto in the visible and invisible world, he considers as thoughts of the Almighty, which are given him to read in the book of creation, in order to advance him to a higher perfection.... [W]e fulfil the views of the supreme bring on earth by developing our intellectual capacities.... In our eyes the world of moral beings speaks the perfection of its author, as strongly as the world of nature.' Moses Mendelssohn, *Phaedon or the Death of Socrates* (London: J. Cooper, 1789), 174–5, 181, 197. (German original: Moses Mendelssohn, *Phaedon oder über die Unsterblichkeit der Seele in drey Gesprächen* (Berlin: Stettin, 1767).) In an appendix to the third edition, Moses goes so far as to suggest that 'A friend of reason, such as he [Socrates] was, would certainly have gratefully accepted from other philosophers that part of their doctrine which was based on reason, no matter what country or religious party they otherwise belonged to. Where rational truths are concerned, one can agree with anyone, and nevertheless find many things untrustworthy which he accepts on faith.'

[21] Todd, *Mendelssohn: A Life in Music*, 244.

[22] In *Jerusalem* Moses wrote 'It is true that I recognize no eternal truths other than those that are not merely comprehensible to human reason but can also be demonstrated and verified by human powers.... I consider this an essential point of the Jewish religion and believe that this doctrine constitutes a characteristic difference between it and the Christian one.... Eternal truths... insofar as they are useful for men's salvation and felicity, are taught by God in a manner more appropriate to the Deity; not by sounds or written characters, which are comprehensible here and there, to this or that individual, but through creation itself, and its internal relations, which are legible and comprehensible to all men. Nor does He confirm them by miracles... but He awakens the mind, which He has created, and gives it an opportunity to observe the relations of things, to observe itself, and to become convinced of the truths which it is destined to understand here below.' Moses Mendelssohn, *Jerusalem or On Religious Power and Judaism*, trans. Allan Arkush (New England: Brandeis, 1983), 89, 93. (German original: Moses Mendelssohn, *Jerusalem oder über religiöse Macht und Judentum* (Berlin: Maurer, 1783).) Moses also believed that the revealed Law could likewise be explained in terms of a rational purpose, and could be regarded as 'the foundation for the national cohesion.' Mendelssohn, *Jerusalem*, 126–8.

one must be cautious about attributing to them too great an influence.[23] Firmer ground is found in Felix's father, Abraham Mendelssohn-Bartholdy (1776–1835), a profoundly important figure in the composer's life and one whom Felix deeply respected and from whom he sought approval throughout his life. Although Abraham died just before the oratorio was completed, his impact upon its development was considerable, and it is worth spending some time considering the views of the father for what they tell us about the kind of religious environment in which the son was raised. In common with other assimilationist Jews of his day, Abraham was attracted to a rationalist perspective, and his religious worldview was wary of theism of any sort. Although he rejected Judaism, he did not offer a ringing endorsement of Christianity, either, as he made clear in several letters to his children. In 1820, at around the time of the confirmation of Felix's sister, Fanny, Abraham discussed his conception of religion at some length.

Does God exist? What is God? Is He part of ourselves, and does He continue to live after the other part has ceased to be? And where? And how? All this I do not know, and therefore I have never taught you anything about it. But I know that there exists in me and in you and in all human beings an everlasting inclination towards all that is good, true and right, and a conscience which warns and guides us when we go astray. I know it, I believe it, I live in this faith, and this is my religion.... This is all I can tell you about religion, all I know about it; but this will remain true, as long as one man will exist in the creation, as it has been true since the first man was created. The outward form of religion your teacher has given you is historical, and changeable like all human ordinances. Some thousands of years ago the Jewish form was the reigning one, then the heathen form, and now it is the Christian.... We have educated you and your brothers and sister in the Christian faith, because it is the creed of most civilized people, and contains nothing that can lead you away from what is good, and much that guides you to love, obedience, tolerance, and resignation.... By pronouncing your confession of faith you have fulfilled the claims of *society* on you, and obtained the *name* of a Christian. Now be what your duty as a human being demands of you, *true, faithful, good*, obedient and devoted till death to your mother, and I may also say to your father, unremittingly attentive to the voice of your conscience... and you will gain the highest happiness that is to be found on earth, harmony and contentedness with yourself.[24]

---

[23] Sposato notes that in a letter dated February 1842 Felix wrote that he did not possess 'a single page of his [Moses'] writing', which he reads as indicative of a lack of interest. Sposato, *The Price of Assimilation*, 36. On the other hand, Botstein has argued that 'Felix Mendelssohn clearly was familiar with the writings of his grandfather. This is made explicit in the letter he sent to Joseph Mendelssohn on 20 February 1840. Felix complained about the errors in and incompleteness of the existing Vienna edition of his grandfather's work.' Leon Botstein, 'Neo-Classicism, Romantism, and Emancipation: The Origins of Felix Mendelssohn's Aesthetic Outlook', in Douglass Seaton, ed., *The Mendelssohn Companion* (London: Greenwood Press, 2001), 20n15.

[24] Letter from Abraham Mendelssohn to Fanny Mendelssohn (1820) reproduced in Sebastian Hensel, *The Mendelssohn Family*, trans. Carl Klingemann, second edition (New York: Harper, 1882), 1:79–80.

For Abraham, then, the label 'Christian' was a matter of convenience, an appellation adopted for society's sake, and his real concern for his daughter was for her to find happiness in an ethical, dutiful life. Ultimately, the label made little difference for, as he put it elsewhere, 'There are in all religions only one God, one virtue, one truth, one happiness.'[25] In a letter to Felix in 1829, Abraham wrote

I had learned, and until my last breath will never forget, that the truth is one and eternal; its forms, however, are many and transitory; and so I raised you, to the extent that the constitution under which we then lived permitted it, free from any religious form, which I wished to leave you to your own convictions, should they demand it, or to your choice, based on considerations of convenience. That was not to be, however, and I had to choose for you. Given the scant value I place on all [religious] forms, it goes without saying that I felt no inner calling to choose for you the Jewish, the most obsolete, corrupt, and pointless of them [all]. So I raised you in the Christian, the purer [form] accepted by the majority of civilised people, and also confessed the same for myself, because I had to do myself what I recognized as best for you.[26]

Once again, there is the sense of grudging necessity in raising his children as Christians, as dictated by the bigotry of wider society,[27] even if an outmoded Judaism was entirely out of the question. For Abraham, 'religion' was, in essence, a universal ethic towards which humankind is progressing that had once been clothed in the apparel of Judaism and was now wrapped in the garments of Christianity. It was a historical view of religion that simultaneously linked Judaism and Christianity but went beyond them, and, arguably, Abraham did not see his conversion (six years after his son's baptism) or change of name (to Mendelssohn-Bartholdy) as a rejection of Moses Mendelssohn's core values, but rather as a continuation or extension of them, the fulfilment of an ideological trajectory; for him, the Mendelssohn name symbolised 'Judaism in transition'.[28] This schema of

---

[25] Letter from Abraham Mendelssohn to Fanny Mendelssohn (1819) reproduced in S. Hensel, *The Mendelssohn Family*, 1:77.

[26] Letter from Abraham Mendelssohn to Felix Mendelssohn (1829). M. Schneider, *Mendelssohn oder Bartholdy?* (Basel: Internationale Felix-Mendelssohn-Gesellschaft, 1962), 18–19, cited in Sposato, *The Price of Assimilation*, 16.

[27] Abraham discussed the matter with his wife's brother, who had changed his name from Salomon to Bartholdy, and who apparently convinced him to do likewise in correspondence: 'You say you owe it to the memory of your father [to remain a Jew] – do you think you have done anything evil by giving your children the religion which you consider the best one *for them*? Rather it is an act of homage which you and I and all of us owe to Moses Mendelssohn's efforts in the interests of true Enlightenment.... A man can remain loyal to an oppressed, persecuted religion; he can impose it on his children as a candidature for a lifelong martyrdom – *as long as he thinks that it alone will bring salvation*. But as soon as he no longer believes that, it is barbarism to do anything of the kind.' Letter to Abraham Mendelssohn (undated) reproduced in S. Hensel, *The Mendelssohn Family*, 1:75.

[28] Abraham wrote to Felix, 'My father felt that the name Moses den Mendel Dessau would handicap him in gaining the needed access to those who had the better education at their disposal. Without any fear that his own father would take offence, my father assumed the name Mendelssohn. The change, though a small one, was decisive. As Mendelssohn, he became irrevocably detached from an entire class, the best of whom he raised to his own level. By that name he identified himself

a transitional relation between Judaism and Christianity is worth noting because, as will be argued, it was implicit in Felix's composition of *St. Paul*, despite the fact that the connection was minimised by the Lutheran and Reformed theologies with which he publicly associated himself.

The oratorio, which had been commissioned in 1832, was first performed in Germany in 1836; it launched Felix's international career and was his most popular work during his lifetime.[29] Musically, it courted controversy with its use of chorales, which were normally associated with Church or liturgical music, and the innovative decision to have the words of Christ to Saul on the road to Damascus sung by an all-female choir, rather than the bass performance that was conventionally used to represent the voice of Christ. The oratorio is divided into two parts. The first includes Stephen's martyrdom (Nos. 1–11), Saul's persecution of the Christians (Nos. 12–13), and his conversion on the road to Damascus (Nos. 14–22). The second part treats Paul and Barnabas' commission (Nos. 23–6), the Jews' opposition to Paul (Nos. 27–32), the Gentiles' opposition to Paul, after having first thought him a god (Nos. 32–40), and his departure from Ephesus, ready to face martyrdom (Nos. 41–5). Throughout, the choruses and solos are interspersed with narrative, most of which is dependent upon the story given in the Acts of the Apostles, but which also draws heavily on other materials from the New and Old Testaments.[30] Felix spent almost four years writing and redrafting the libretto in consultation with the musician, Adolf Bernhard Marx, the orientalist, Julius Fürst, and the theologian, Julius Schubring,[31] and there can be no doubting the seriousness with which he

---

with another group. Through the influence which, ever growing, persists to this day, the name Mendelssohn acquired great authority and a significance which defies extinction. This, considering that you were reared a Christian, you can hardly understand. A Christian Mendelssohn is an impossibility. A Christian Mendelssohn the world would never recognise. Nor should there be a Christian Mendelssohn; for my father himself did not want to be a Christian. 'Mendelssohn' does and always will stand for a Judaism in transition, when Judaism, just because it is seeking to transmute itself spiritually, clings to its ancient form all the more stubbornly and tenaciously, by way of protest against the novel form that so arrogantly and tyrannically declared itself to be the one and only path to the good.' Letter from Abraham Mendelssohn to Felix Mendelssohn (8 July 1829), reproduced in Michael P. Steinberg, 'Mendelssohn's Music and German-Jewish Culture', 37–8.

[29] Performances followed in England, Switzerland, Denmark, Holland, Poland, Russia, and the United States.

[30] Number of verses cited from biblical books: Leviticus (2), Psalms (15), Isaiah (3), Jeremiah (3), Matthew (3), Acts (77), Romans (4), 1 Corinthians (2), 2 Corinthians (1), Philippians (1), 2 Timothy (6), James (1), 1 John (1), Revelation (4).

[31] Adolf Bernhard Marx (1795–1866) was a music critic and composer whom Mendelssohn initially approached to compose the libretto; he contributed to the soprano recitative preceding Stephen's defence. Julius Fürst (1805–73) was a Hebraist and Orientalist who deserves the credit for most of the opening chorus of the first scene as well as for the aria *Jerusalem*. Julius Schubring (1806–89) was a theologian and close adherent of Schleiermacher who suggested the placement of the chorales as well as the text and melody for the second chorale. Sposato's research has determined that, despite their valuable assistance, 'Mendelssohn remained staunchly independent while composing the actual *Paulus* libretto'. Sposato, *The Price of Assimilation*, 84–5.

involved himself in the editorial work.[32] Although the project obviously meant a lot to his father, Abraham, who took an active interest in his son's treatment of the transformation of the Jewish Saul into the Christian Paul,[33] a story which so powerfully resonated with the spiritual journey of the Mendelssohn family,[34] there is little or no evidence from Felix's own pen as to his actual theological intentions.[35] Although this is frustrating for the historian, authorial intention does not tell us everything about a work of art, especially one concerned with such personally emotive themes as religious belief and conversion. In any case, speculation as to intention in this case (whether conscious or unconscious) must be based primarily on two aspects of the editorial composition, namely: What themes can be derived from the texts selected by Felix? And what should be made of the materials and corresponding themes that he chose *not* to include?

First, there are the materials chosen. Many commentators, both in Felix's day and afterwards, have complained about the amount of space devoted to the martyrdom of Stephen.[36] After all, the dramatic potential for Saul, such as it is, lies in his

[32] As to his methodology, Felix wrote that 'When I am composing, I usually look out [sic] the Scriptural passages myself.' Letter from Felix Mendelssohn to J. Fürst (20 July 1820) reproduced in Paul and Carl Mendelssohn Bartholdy, eds., *Letters of Felix Mendelssohn Bartholdy, from 1833 to 1847*, trans. Lady Wallace (London: Longmans, 1863), 39. He was also determined to be true to the texts. In a letter to one of his theological advisors, he asks to know '[w]hether you are of the opinion that any of the principal features in the history or the acts, and also in the character and teaching of St. Paul, have been either omitted or falsified.' Letter from Felix Mendelssohn to Julius Schubring (1833) reproduced in P. and C. Mendelssohn Bartholdy, eds., *Letters of Felix Mendelssohn Bartholdy*, 5.

[33] After Abraham's death, before he completed the oratorio, Felix wrote 'The only thing that now remains is to do one's duty, and this I strive to accomplish with all my strength, for he [Abraham] would wish it to be so if he were still present, and I shall never cease to endeavour to gain his approval as I formerly did, though I can no longer enjoy it. . . . I shall now work with double zeal at the completion of 'St. Paul' for my father urged me to it in the very last letter he wrote to me, and he looked forward very impatiently to the completion of my work.' Letter from Felix Mendelssohn to Julius Schubring (6 December 1835) reproduced in P. and C. Mendelssohn Bartholdy, eds., *Letters of Felix Mendelssohn Bartholdy*, 88.

[34] Robert Schumann's complaint at the depiction of Paul as a 'convert rather than a converter' is well taken. Robert Schumann, *On Music and Musicians*, ed. Konrad Wolf, trans. Paul Rosenfeld (New York, 1946), 198. The subject of the oratorio was agreed upon with Felix's friend, A. B. Marx, who was to write the libretto while Felix was to write one on Moses in return; in the event, Felix decided not use Marx's text. Interestingly, Marx tried to persuade him that St. Peter would be a more suitable topic than St. Paul, who was perceived as very much the rationalist Protestant. Todd, *Mendelssohn: A Life in Music*, 264, 266.

[35] Although he undoubtedly intended it as a sermon (*Predigt*), as he put it in one letter, confirming his Protestant faith, this does not help a great deal in clarifying the actual nature of that faith. Letter from Felix Mendelssohn to Carl Klingemann (20 December 1831), cited in Todd, *Mendelssohn: A Life in Music*, 338.

[36] In fact even his father, Abraham, complained, but Felix's polite reply (included within a letter to his sister) does not offer any explanation. 'The non-appearance of St. Paul at the stoning of Stephen is certainly a blemish, and I could easily alter the passage in itself; but I could find absolutely no mode of introducing him at the time, and no words from him to utter in accordance with the Scriptural narrative; therefore it seemed to me more expedient to follow the biblical account, and to make Stephen appear alone. I think, however, that your other censure is obviated by the music; for the recitative of Stephen, though the words are long, will not occupy more than two or three

(very marginal) involvement in the murder of a Christian saint and his consequent inauguration as a persecutor of the new sect – and this might easily have been dealt with in less than the eleven sections it actually takes. However, one key theme to emerge is that of the contrast between the ideas of the Jews, whose religion was focused on the Law and Temple, and Stephen's more spiritual conception of the nature of their God as the creator of the natural world.[37] To begin with, Felix reproduces the testimony of the Jewish false witnesses, who shout 'We verily have heard him blaspheme against these holy places, and against the law' (Acts 6:14), and has 'the Jews' sing

Now this man [Stephen] ceaseth not to utter blasphemous words against the law of Moses, and also God. . . . He hath said, and we have heard him, [that] Jesus of Nazareth He shall destroy all these our holy places, and change all the laws and customs which Moses delivered us (Acts 6:11, 14).

Furthermore, in the space of a few sections, Felix has the chorus of Hebrews twice chant Lev. 24:16, in which the Law demands death for blasphemy.[38] In recounting the speech that Stephen made in response, about the rebellious history of the Hebrews, Felix is especially careful to include the passages in Acts which condemn them for idol worship – 'but they refused him [Moses] and would not obey his word, but thrust him from them, and sacrificed to senseless idols' (Acts 7:39–40) – and where he denigrates the importance of the Temple, drawing attention instead to God's sovereignty over nature.

Solomon built Him an house; albeit the Most High God dwelleth not in temples which are made with hands; for heaven is His throne, and earth is but His footstool. Has not His hand made all these things? (Acts 7:47–8)

This central theme is reinforced by the choice of the text for the first chorus of the oratorio, which exclaims, 'LORD, Thou alone art God; and Thine are the heavens, the earth and the mighty waters' (Acts 4:24). Likewise, in a later episode in Lystra in which Paul is mistaken by the Gentiles for a god after having performed a healing, a similar critique is made of the Gentiles, who appear even more confused about the nature of God than had been the Jews. Felix cites at length Paul's reaction to the Gentiles' intention to sacrifice to and adore him as a god:

O wherefore do ye these things? We also are men of like passions with yourselves; who preach unto you, in peace and earnestness, that you should turn away from all these

---

minutes, – or *including* all the choruses – till his death, about quarter of an hour.' Letter from Felix Mendelssohn to Rebecca Dirichlet (23 December 1834), reproduced in P. and C. Mendelssohn Bartholdy, eds., *Letters of Felix Mendelssohn Bartholdy*, 62–63.

[37] Sposato sees this critique of the Jewish obsession with the Law as evidence of anti-Semitism (which he prefers to the term 'anti-Judaic' in this context). Sposato, *The Price of Assimilation*, 10–11.

[38] The first Hebrew chorus is 'Take him away. For now the holy name of God he hath blasphemed; and he who blasphemes Him, he shall perish', whereas the second is 'Stone him to death. He blasphemes God; and who does so shall surely perish. Stone him to death.'

vanities unto the ever living God, who made the outstretched heavens, the earth and the sea. As saith the Prophet: 'All your idols are but falsehood, and there is no breath in them. They are vanity, and the work of errors: in the time of their trouble they shall perish.' God dwelleth not in temples made with human hands. (Acts 14:15; Jeremiah 10:14, 15; Acts 17:24)

Felix immediately follows this with Paul's question, 'For know you not that ye are His temple, and that the spirit of God dwelleth in you? . . . For the temple of God is holy, which temple you are' (1 Cor. 3:16, 17), and with a chorus that confirms, 'But our God abideth in heaven: His will directeth all the world. We bow to only His decree, Who made the skies, the earth and sea' (Ps. 115:3). As if to drive home the significance of the debate regarding the nature of God, Felix has Jews and Gentiles come together to assault Paul in a joint chorus in Section 38:

This is Jehovah's temple. Ye children of Israel, help us. This is the man who teacheth all men, against the people, against this place, and also our holy law. We have heard him speak blasphemies against the law. He blasphemes God. Stone him. (Acts 21:28)

Thus Felix's editorial choices imply that Jew and Gentile alike have misunderstood the nature of God, and have set up idols, temples, and laws as a result of their ignorance of the true Creator of the Universe.[39] In contrast, Felix projects onto Paul (and Stephen) a Deist-like admiration of the divine watchmaker, whose temple is to be found within man and who is properly worshipped through the spiritual appreciation of nature, as suggested by the paean of praise of God as the source of all knowledge that ends the first part of the oratorio.[40] What is of significance here is that Felix's particular understanding of Christianity as the path towards universal, rational enlightenment is by no means an obvious emphasis for a treatment of the life of St. Paul. To explain it, one might look to the foundational influence of his family. For although the kind of belief that characterises the oratorio has been described as 'an aesthetically blank lowest common denominator of the Christian community in the act of worship',[41] its assumptions concerning the rationalist underpinnings of religion and the shortcomings of its Jewish garb might as easily be said to have characterised the letters that Abraham Mendelssohn, the assimilated Jew, wrote to his children.[42] Likewise, in attempting to explain

---

[39] Sposato observes that, in the libretto, Gentiles respond more positively to Paul's missionary endeavours than do the Jews, and he suggests that this reflects a typical tendency of Lutheran and German Protestantism to glorify their Gentile heritage, which he calls 'philo-Heathenism'. Sposato, *The Price of Assimilation*, 92–4. But the reading of the libretto adopted here sees Mendelssohn equally critical of the shortcomings of Jewish legalism and Gentile idolatry.

[40] 'O great is the depth of the riches of wisdom and knowledge of the Father! How deep and unerring is He in His judgements! His ways are past our understanding. Sing to His glory forever more: Amen.' (Rom. 11:33)

[41] Peter Mercer-Taylor, 'Rethinking Mendelssohn's Historicism: A Lesson from St Paul', *The Journal of Musicology* 15:2 (Spring 1997), 227.

[42] Botstein makes a similar observation regarding the source for Felix's rationalism. 'Insofar as Mendelssohn actually succeeded in integrating a Judaic element in the Protestant theology of the text of

the theme of natural religion, one is sorely tempted to consider the parallels to Moses Mendelssohn's famous adherence to a God who reveals his universal will to those who can detect it by observation of his creation, rather than find its source in Lutheran 'philo-Heathenism'.[43] Of course, an interest in natural religion was very much in line with the wider German Enlightenment *Zeitgeist*, and there is nothing remarkable about finding in the work of any composer of this time the rationalist emphasis characteristic of contemporary theology and philosophy of religion. But the point is that, for a Mendelssohn at least, such ideas were not regarded as being in opposition to Judaism. Although the origin of such emphases must remain the subject of speculation, it is at least reasonable to suggest that Felix's conception of religion had been shaped by the Mendelssohn family's well-documented commitment to rational, universalist religion. In particular, his was a vision consistent with Abraham Mendelssohn's belief in a universal ethic that, in Paul's day, had progressed beyond the culturally determined limitations of paganism and ancient Judaism, and that would undoubtedly move on again in time.

In addition to Felix's critique of Judaism's misplaced confidence in the Temple and the Law, and his portrayal of the rebellious character of the Hebrews as described in Stephen's speech, the oratorio provides further evidence of its author's negative attitude towards ancient Jewry.[44] Sposato has demonstrated how, through

---

St. Paul Julius Schubring provided him, it was in the highlighting, through the choral numbers, of the abstract and rational substance of faith. Despite the prominence of the figure of Christ in *St. Paul* and the centrality of the conversion, it is the rational, ethical essence of faith that stands out.... *St. Paul* represented Mendelssohn's musical-dramatic defence of the theological stance of Abraham Mendelssohn, who ultimately converted to Christianity himself. In *St. Paul*, baptism is the route to a rational enlightenment.' (Botstein overestimates the role of Schubring and exaggerates the prominence of Christ in the libretto.) Leon Botstein, 'Songs without Words: Thoughts on Music, Theology, and the Role of the Jewish Question in the Work of Felix Mendelssohn', *The Musical Quarterly* 77:4 (Winter 1993), 574–5.

[43] Sposato attributes the theme of 'natural religion' to a German tradition that denigrated Judaism's significance for the Gentiles. In particular, he observes that both Luther and Schleiermacher had believed that God had revealed his law in nature, and therefore 'most of it . . . was also written into the hearts of the Gentiles before their conversion, thereby inviting Germans to view their ancestors not just as pre-Christian, but as proto-Christian, and therefore a people they could look back on with pride and respect.' *The Price of Assimilation*, 93–4.

[44] According to Sposato, Mendelssohn 'tried to distance himself from his [Jewish] heritage as much as possible.... The editorial practices in his sacred music libretti also support this view of Mendelssohn, containing as they do numerous examples of the composer unnecessarily including anti-Semitic texts, such as that in the chorus "His blood be upon us and our children" in his edition of *St. Matthew Passion* and those that add to his stereotypical depiction of the Jews as a law-obsessed people in *Paulus*.' S. Sposato, 'Creative Writing: The [Self-] Identification of Mendelssohn as a Jew', 204. For Sposato, this anti-Jewish strain is enough to demonstrate Felix's rejection of a Jewish identity, at least at the time of writing his *Paulus*. But this is to dismiss the complex racial understanding of 'Jewishness' in nineteenth-century European Semitic discourse. Sposato himself observes that Felix's attitudes towards the Jews shifted throughout his lifetime, from which some might infer a lifelong struggle with a Jewish self-identification. Thus Felix's negative representation of the Jews in *Paulus* could be plausibly interpreted as an antagonistic posture adopted for complicated psychological and

successive drafts of Section 38, Felix eventually replaced the biblical account of Gentile opposition with that of an essentially Jewish opposition.[45] And early in the second part, Felix focuses on the envy of the Jews at Paul's popularity with the masses, their arguments with him, and eventually their conspiracy to ambush and kill him. Furthermore, several choruses of Jews vigorously assert their rejection of the Saviour and their hostility to Paul and 'all deceivers'.[46] This negative portrayal of Jews has been put down to the influence of Abraham Mendelssohn,[47] but in any case it represents a mechanism by which Felix can explain the apostle's momentous decision to turn from the Jews to the Gentiles, which is the point of Sections 23–31. It concludes with his famous parting shot,

Ye were chosen first to have the word of the Lord set before you; but, seeing that ye put it from you, and judge yourselves unworthy of the life everlasting, behold ye, we turn, even now, unto the Gentiles. (Act 13:46)

For Felix, however, more significant than the failings of the Jews was the universalisation of the knowledge of the one true God – and in his mind, this was only made possible through sacrifice and martyrdom. The theme of sacrifice is very important and helps account for the structure of the oratorio and even for his interest in Paul in the first place. It is implicit in the death of Stephen himself, whose martyrdom was necessary to put Paul on the path to becoming the Apostle to the Gentiles, and whose story, as already noted, seems to have been given disproportionate attention.[48] The divinely ordained enlightenment of the Gentiles is a phenomenon referred to repeatedly throughout the work,[49] and is emphasised

social reasons that reflect the complex reality of the Jewish conversion existence at that time and place, rather than simply as evidence that he did not self-identify as a Jew.

[45] Jeffrey S. Sposato, 'Mendelssohn, "Paulus", and the Jews: A Response to Leon Botstein and Michael Steinberg', *The Musical Quarterly* 83:2 (Summer 1999), 284–8.

[46] One chorus sings 'Thus saith the Lord, "I am the Lord, and beside me there is no Saviour"' (Isaiah 43:11) and another 'Is this he, who, in Jerusalem, destroyed all calling on that name which here he preacheth? May all deceivers ever be confounded! Force him away!' (Acts 9:21).

[47] 'By far the strongest influence on *Paulus*'s treatment of the Jews was [Felix] Mendelssohn's father.... [D]uring Felix's youth, Abraham Mendelssohn continually encouraged his son to separate himself from his Jewish roots, both through instruction and by example.' Sposato, *The Price of Assimilation*, 90.

[48] Felix also chooses to include the references in Stephen's speech relating the persecution and suffering of God's messengers: 'Which of the Prophets have not your fathers persecuted? And they have slain them which showed before the coming of Him, the Just one, with whose murder ye have here been stained' (Acts 7:52) and a similar gospel passage, 'Jerusalem, Jerusalem, thou that killest the Prophets, and stonest them which are sent unto thee' (Matthew 23:37).

[49] Texts that Felix uses to allude to the Gentiles' salvation include: Acts 4:26, 29 ('And the kings of the earth took their stand and the rulers were gathered together against the Lord and against his Christ.... And now, Lord, take note of their threats, and grant that Your bond-servants may speak Your word with all confidence'); Isa. 60:1, 2 ('Arise, shine; for your light has come, And the glory of the LORD has risen upon you. For behold, darkness will cover the earth And deep darkness the peoples; But the LORD will rise upon you And His glory will appear upon you'); Rev. 6:15 ('Then the kings of the earth and the great men and the commanders and the rich and the strong and every slave and free man hid themselves in the caves and among the rocks of the mountains'), 15:4 ('Who

in the opening chorus of the second part, which preempts Paul's rejection of the Jews:

The nations are now the Lord's; they are His Christ's. For all the Gentiles come before Thee and shall worship Thy name. Now are made manifest Thy glorious law and judgements. (Rev. 11:15, 15:4)

Felix's interest in the cost of universalisation also explains the length of the final section, which is devoted to Paul's farewell to the elders of Ephesus. Although not offering much in terms of drama, the four final sections are replete with references to Paul's readiness to suffer death in the cause of taking the gospel message throughout the world, including, 'Bonds and affliction abide me there [in Jerusalem]; and ye shall see my face no more' (Acts 20:23, 25), 'For I am prepared not only to be bound, but also to die at Jerusalem, for the name of the Lord our saviour Jesus Christ' (Act 21:13), and 'And though he be offered upon the sacrifice of our faith, yet he hath fought a good fight.... Henceforth there is laid up for him a crown of righteousness' (2 Tim. 4:7, 8). Some commentators have complained at Felix's tendency towards sentimentalism, and, arguably, the final sections could be regarded as an over-indulgent expression of the pathos of Paul's life. Others have seen here confirmation of his Christological concerns.[50] But they also echo Moses Mendelssohn's emphasis on the universality of religious truth, and Abraham Mendelssohn's painful conviction of the necessity of severing his children's ties to the outmoded religious language of Judaism in favour of Christianity. Thus once again, Felix's internalisation of his two forebears' philosophies, a strange combination of Jewish rationalism and pseudo-Christian rationales, appears implicated in his meditation of the sacrifice necessary to achieve universal knowledge of the one true God.

Second, there is the issue of materials and themes left out by Felix. To anyone familiar with Lutheran understandings of Paul and his life story, as derived from the Acts of the Apostles and his letters, the absence of an explicit reference to the

will not fear, O Lord, and glorify Your name? For You alone are holy; For all the nations will come and worship before you, for your righteous acts have been revealed'); Rom. 10:15, 18 ('How will they preach unless they are sent? Just as it is written, "How beautiful are the feet of those who bring good news of good things".... But I say, surely they have never heard, have they? Indeed they have; "their voice has gone out into all the earth, and their words to the ends of the world"'); Acts 13:47 ('For so the Lord has commanded us, "I have placed you as a light for the gentiles, that you may bring salvation to the end of the earth."'), 2:21 ('And it shall be that everyone who calls on the name of the Lord will be saved'); 2 Tim. 4:17 ('But the Lord stood with me and strengthened me, so that through me the proclamation might be fully accomplished, and that all the Gentiles might hear; and I was rescued out of the lion's mouth'); 1 John 3:1 ('See how great a love the Father has bestowed on us, that we would be called children of God; and such we are For this reason the world does not know us, because it did not know Him').

[50] Sposato recognises the theme of sacrifice but does not make the link to universalism and interprets it as evidence of the influence of contemporary Christological models that see the hero, be it Moses or Paul, as the suffering servant of God whose suffering is brought about by the Jews. Sposato, *The Price of Assimilation*, 92.

Pauline doctrine of faith alone, or to his abrogation of the Law in that context, or to original sin, or to the Jerusalem Council's decision, after heated debate, to accede to Paul's position that the Gentiles were equally acceptable to God, is puzzling, to say the least.[51] Such omissions were undoubtedly deliberate, as we can see from the evidence of a contributor to the libretto in a complaint he made after Mendelssohn's death.

That he [Mendelssohn] would not accept my suggestions for the Pauline doctrine of the justification by faith, but, at the appropriate place, substituted merely the general assertion: 'Wir glauben all an einen Gott' [We all believe in one God] was something that did not satisfy my theological conscience, though, perhaps, any extension of the work in this direction would have made it too long.[52]

Put another way, one might ask: to what does Paul convert? Not, as one might have expected from the pen of a convert to Lutheranism, to an understanding of justification by God's grace, and salvation by faith alone in the divine Christ. In fact, one is struck by the general lack of interest in Jesus.[53] Although it would be an exaggeration to claim that Mendelssohn sought to eliminate him, the impression made is certainly one of neglect. Next to nothing is said of Jesus' messianic role or of his redemptive sacrifice.[54] The gloriously powerful cosmic Christ of the Pauline epistles does not emerge from the text. Rather, Jesus is referred to in the context of bringing an end to the Temple and the Law (Section 5) and is associated as a martyr with Stephen (Section 6). Admittedly, Christ is also seen by Stephen in a vision standing by the side of the Father (Section 6), and the unconventional use of women's voices to represent the words of the ascended Christ on the road to Damascus certainly produces an ethereal, otherworldly effect (Section 14). But this

---

[51] The doctrine of justification by faith alone, that is, the teaching that salvation is brought about through faith in God's grace rather than through works of righteousness, is derived from an interpretation of Eph. 2:8 ('For by grace you have been saved through faith; and that not of yourselves, it is the gift of God'), an interpretation famously championed by Martin Luther. Accounts of the debate of the early church in Jerusalem are given in Acts 15 and in Galatians 2. Its leader, James, ruled 'Therefore it is my judgment that we do not trouble those who are turning to God from among the Gentiles, but that we write to them that they abstain from things contaminated by idols and from fornication and from what is strangled and from blood. For Moses from ancient generations has in every city those who preach him, since he is read in the synagogues every Sabbath' (Acts 15:19–21).

[52] Julius Schubring, 'Reminisences of Felix Mendelssohn-Bartholdy', reproduced in Todd, ed., *Mendelssohn and His World*, 230. The particular formulation 'We all believe in one God' is from a hymn by Martin Luther but Schubring, at least, did not regard it as providing an appropriate emphasis of the doctrine of justification by faith alone.

[53] I am grateful to Canon John Davies, formerly of the University of Southampton, for this observation. Admittedly, this is a somewhat subjective claim because others do identify Christ as a focus to the work. Botstein notes 'the prominence of the figure of Christ in *St. Paul*', referring primarily to the female chorus, and Sposato sees the sacrificial ('suffering servant') motif as Christological in origin. Botstein, 'Songs without Words', 574. Sposato, *The Price of Assimilation*, 92.

[54] Except for three citations of Matthew, the Gospels are completely ignored. Mendelssohn's overwhelming preference is for the Acts of the Apostles (77 citations), in which very little is offered in the way of direct quotations of Jesus.

only reinforces the impression that the heavenly Jesus is met only in the subjective visions of men, supportive of a rationalist perspective.[55] Of course, the audiences for the oratorio could fill in the gaps, and no doubt Mendelssohn was happy for them to do so, but the fact remains that the familiar Lutheran reading of Paul that emphasised God's grace as made manifest in the life, death, and resurrection of Christ, who redeems the inhabitants of a fallen world through faith alone, is conspicuous by its absence. Jesus appears primarily as a liberator from outward religion and thereby as a pioneering exemplar for Stephen and Paul.

Felix's portrayal of Paul is one of an individual's realisation of the God who exists on a plane far beyond the reach of idol or Temple and whose Laws are better observed from the natural world than from the Torah. Furthermore, it champions an understanding of faith that assumes an unchanging ethical core which, from time to time, requires liberation from the religious misunderstandings and theological confusions that human minds (Jewish and Gentile) have accrued over time. The parallels with the views of his father (and grandfather) suggest some obvious sources of influence. But could one not argue that the themes of the libretto could just as likely be explained by more widespread Protestant beliefs? Sposato and Todd both see this particular oratorio as representative of a stage in Felix's life-story when he was concerned to demonstrate his Christian credentials and to achieve his father's goal of assimilation into Prussian society.[56] But contemporary German Lutheran theology, although undoubtedly in intellectual ferment and however varied, can safely be said to have had offered little in

---

[55] Felix appears to have been aware that in his revision of the conventions he was sailing close to the wind, theologically speaking, and was courting the condemnation of those who might be suspicious of his religious motives. Schubring recalled that his own suggestion that the voice of Christ be set for four parts ('he [Felix] could not reconcile himself to the notion of producing the effect of a very powerful bass voice') had a strange effect on Felix: 'After looking at me for a long time, he said: "Yes, and the worthy theologians would cut me up nicely for wishing to deny and supplant Him who arose from the dead."' But he went ahead anyway and had Christ's words set to a four-part female chorus, which did provoke some theological complaints. The composer, 'who was well aware of the circumstance, laughed, but did not say much.' Julius Schubring, 'Reminisences of Felix Mendelssohn-Bartholdy' reproduced in Todd, ed., *Mendelssohn and His World*, 231–2. The otherworldly effect has also been explained as an example of Jewish influence. According to Heinrich Jacob, Felix had applied the commandment 'Thou shalt make thee no graven images' to his music, utilising a device that stressed the great distance between Man and God. Heinrich E. Jacob, *Felix Mendelssohn and His Times*, trans. Richard and Clara Winston (New Jersey: Prentice Hall, 1963), 217.

[56] Todd concludes that 'The completion of the oratorio [*Paulus*] and its successful reception were critical steps towards achieving Abraham's cherished agendum – full assimilation of his family into Prussian society.' Todd, *Mendelssohn: A Life in Music*, 338. Sposato writes that 'Mendelssohn, in this, his first oratorio, tried to assuage real or imagined doubts about his Christian faith by writing a work that conformed to popular expectations, both through its call for the conversion of the nonbelievers and its depiction of the narrow-mindedness of those who refuse to see the light (namely, the Jews). *Paulus* also demonstrates, however, the mental anguish that such a depiction caused Mendelssohn, anguish that led to his eventual reevaluation of this approach. . . . Mendelssohn's tendency to depict the Jews negatively in *Paulus* derived from an overwhelming personal desire to assimilate into German Christian culture.' Sposato, *The Price of Assimilation*, 79, 88.

way of encouragement in these directions. On the contrary, one might point to the emergence of Lutheran Confessionalism in the 1830s and 1840s, that is, a movement away from the idea of the Church as the universal Body of Christ and towards a distinctive identity based on traditional Lutheran doctrine and exclusive church worship. Mendelssohn's apparent inclinations towards universalism and even a kind of rationalist, natural religion, as found in *St Paul*, strained against such intellectual currents. The same might be said in relation to the prominent Reformed theologian Friedrich Schleiermacher, a personal friend of Mendelssohn. On the one hand, Schleiermacher recognised that Christianity could claim no monopoly on revelation, believed it impossible to formulate a theology which was valid for all time, and regarded the articles of Christian belief as edifying expressions rather than fixed proofs – all ideas with which Mendelssohn could sympathise. On the other hand, Schleiermacher also gave absolute prominence to the redemptive work of Christ in his theology, denied any meaningful continuity between Judaism and Christianity (dismissing Judaism as almost entirely without value), and emphasised religious feeling over and against what he saw as the simplistic rationalism of natural theologians and deists – ideas which seem at odds with the reading of the theology underlying the libretto given here.[57]

For those prepared to dismiss as intrinsically implausible the idea that Felix had shrugged off entirely his Jewish self-consciousness, *St. Paul* offers a chance to explore the dilemmas of identity facing this 'Jew-boy' musical genius. Living in a world even more confusing than that of his grandfather, Felix was one of many assimilated Jews who were not allowed to forget their Jewish heritage, who

---

[57] Schleiermacher wrote that 'Christianity... is essentially distinguished from other such faiths by the fact that in it everything is related to the redemption accomplished by Jesus of Nazareth.... Christianity cannot in any wise be regarded as a remodelling or a renewal and continuation of Judaism.... Neither can it be said that purer original Judaism carried within itself the germ of Christianity.... [Except for prophecy] almost everything else in the Old Testament is, for our Christian usage, but the husk or wrapping of its prophecy, and that whatever is most definitely Jewish has least value'. Friedrich Schleiermacher, *The Christian Faith*, trans. H. R. Mackintosh and J. S. Stewart (Edinburgh: T&T Clark, 1999), 52, 61, 62. (German original: *Der christliche Glaube* (Berlin: 1821–2).) For Sposato, Schleiermacher's anti-Judaic sentiments are indicative of Mendelssohn's own position. Sposato, *The Price of Assimilation*, 93–4. Schleiermacher's attitude towards natural religion and the 'empiricism' of Deism was highly critical: 'The essence of natural religion actually consists wholly in the negation of everything positive and characteristic in religion and in the most violent polemic against it.'. Friedrich Schleiermacher, *On Religion*, trans. Richard Crouter (Cambridge: Cambridge University Press, 1988), 192, 207. (German original: *Reden über die Religion* (Berlin: 1799).) This attitude stems from his central project, as described by one commentator: 'The way in which God is apprehended in the immediacy of feeling of utter dependence... leads [Schleiermacher] to a conception of the relation of God and the world which does not fit into the common classifications of deism, theism, pantheism.... He was plainly seeking a view beyond naturalism and supernaturalism. Deism was obviously abhorrent, for it posits an externality of God to the world and the self that is utterly at odds with the feeling of utter dependence, and makes God only "a being."' Claude Welch, *Protestant Thought in the Nineteenth Century: 1799–1870* (New Haven: Yale University Press, 1972), I:79.

were acutely aware that their contemporaries regarded them as, if not religiously Jewish, then at least racially or culturally Jewish. In Felix's world, *Neuchristen* were frequently met with suspicion concerning their spiritual sincerity and their new social proximity. If at times he felt the need to distance himself from Judaism, as his father had demanded and as seems to have been the case in *St. Paul*, this simply reflected the complexities of the reality of his situation as a prominent member of the Mendelssohn family and his struggle with his father's observation that, as far as society was concerned, 'a Christian Mendelssohn is an impossibility'.[58] In fact, Felix seems to have shared fewer of Abraham's social concerns about Jewishness as a marker of marginal status, even softening the libretto's anti-Judaism after his father's death,[59] and he appears to have interpreted his father's ideological problems with Judaism primarily in terms of a rejection of the Temple, the Law, and superstition.[60] Thus Paul represented for Felix the moment when these more primitive religious crutches were done away with. And once gone, Christianity (as redefined by Abraham Mendelssohn) and Judaism (as redefined by Moses Mendelssohn) can be viewed as theological stages on a journey towards a greater religious knowledge, suggesting the possibility that baptism was not to be regarded as betrayal.[61] In this sense Felix's religious identity was rooted in a universal religion of ethics which was imperfectly revealed in both Judaism and Christianity and which lay beyond either, a religion that had been expressed at different times and places in different ways but that was, in its essential trajectory, shared by both his father and grandfather, even if it was now called 'Protestantism'. For Botstein,

---

[58] Letter from Abraham Mendelssohn to Felix Mendelssohn (8 July 1829) reproduced in Michael P. Steinberg, 'Mendelssohn's Music and German-Jewish Culture: An Intervention', 37–8.

[59] Sposato has shown that Felix 'softened the anti-Jewish intensity of certain scenes,' after his father's death. Jeffrey S. Sposato, 'Mendelssohn, "Paulus", and the Jews: A Response to Leon Botstein and Michael Steinberg', 288–9.

[60] For example, a letter from Felix's sister hints at a tension between the composer and his father regarding the need for a less Jewish-sounding surname. 'It's suddenly come to Father's attention that your name was mentioned merely as Felix Mendelssohn in several English newspapers. He thinks he detects an ulterior motive in this fact and wants to write to you today about it. . . . I know and approve of your intention to lay aside someday this name [Bartholdy] that we all dislike, but you can't do it yet because you are still a minor. . . . Suffice it to say that you distress Father by your actions. If questioned, you could easily make it seem like a mistake, and carry out your plan later at a more appropriate time.' Letter from Fanny Mendelssohn to Felix Mendelssohn (8 July 1829) reproduced in Marcia J. Citron, ed., *The Letters of Fanny Hensel to Felix Mendelssohn* (New York: Pendragon, 1987), 66–7. As Sposato notes, Mendelssohn's reply makes it clear that he was not interested in any such plan, and he retained the double-barrelled name throughout his career. Sposato, *The Price of Assimilation*, 26–8.

[61] This is the view of Botstein. '[Baptism] into Protestantism was not necessarily a betrayal of the beliefs of one's forefathers. Rather, as the music of *St. Paul* suggests, for Felix Mendelssohn, baptism marked the synthesis of past and present. It represented human progress in the modern age in which the Jewish tradition was preserved. The ultimate aim of the Jewish religion – the triumph of rational human wisdom in the name of God – understood in the sense of Moses Mendelssohn and realized by modern Protestantism, was therefore embraced psychologically by Felix Mendelssohn and rendered central to his vocation as a musician.' Leon Botstein, 'Songs without Words', 574–5.

the oratorio promoted the idea that this Protestantism 'could become a legitimate synthesis of Western Christianity and Judaism.' As Botstein sees it,

Mendelssohn was a proud, self-consciously Jewish Protestant who believed in a rational God and the progress of Enlightenment.... [H]is utopian Protestant project [was] rooted in the Judaism of his grandfather that was centred on enlightenment, harmony and the transcendence of nationalism and religious difference. Mendelssohn spoke to his fellow humans through music on the assumption that a rational ethics could govern human behaviour.... Music was an instrument of spiritual education and guidance and not an end in itself.[62]

Thus the sensitive observer cannot help but feel that important aspects of Felix's creative work can best be explained by reference to a dimension to his inner world that had been shaped by his Jewish heritage. The short period in which he edited the text and wrote the music of *St. Paul* gives us a tantalising glimpse into a kind of Judeo-Christian religious consciousness that has long since ceased to exist. It would be almost three generations later before one would find another German Jewish artist interested in representing Paul, but he, too, would assume a unity beneath the apparent duality of Judaism and Christianity.

LUDWIG MEIDNER, PAUL, AND REVELATION

The painter and poet Ludwig Meidner (1884–1966) was born in Bernstadt in the Prussian province of Silesia to assimilated Jewish parents whom he described as liberal in religion.[63] Not long after his bar mitzvah, he decided that he was an atheist and socialist and burned his *tefillin*.[64] After a period of infatuation with Nietzsche and Marxism, followed by a brief affair with Christian mysticism, he finally returned to Judaism, eventually to be lauded as one of the foremost representatives of expressionism in Europe.[65] He was a product of German and French art academies,[66] and profoundly influenced by the social depression, political angst,

---

[62] Leon Botstein, 'Mendelssohn, Werner, and the Jews: A Final Word', *The Musical Quarterly* 83:1 (Spring 1999), 48, 49–50.

[63] Ernst Scheyer, 'Ludwig Meidner, Artist-Poet' Manuscript, Los Angeles County Museum of Art, Rifkind Center (undated), 3. Scheyer offers an excellent short biography of Meidner, firmly contextualising the art within his life-story.

[64] Also known as phylacteries, *tefillin* are two boxes containing biblical verses and the leather straps attached to them, which are used in the ritual of traditional Jewish prayer.

[65] Meidner also had the distinction of being exhibited in the notorious Nazi exhibition 'Entartete Kunst' ('Degenerate Art', 1937), where one of 84 confiscated works (a self-portrait) was prominently displayed under the heading 'Revelation of the Jewish Racial Soul'. A short biographical sketch of Meidner and outline of his experiences of the Third Reich can be found in Stephanie Barron, *'Degenerate Art': The Fate of the Avant-Garde in Nazi Europe* (New York: H. N. Abrams, 1991), 298–300.

[66] Meidner studied at the Royal School of Art in Breslau 1903–5 and at the Julien and Cormon Academies in Paris 1906–7.

and nervous energy of the artistic community of pre-War Berlin.[67] His intellectual curiosity and his German-Jewish appreciation for Christian civilisation allowed him to retain an interest in Christianity throughout his life,[68] and his watercolour 'Paul's Sermon' (1919)[69] is a rare rendering of this subject by a Jewish artist.[70]

Meidner is perhaps best known for his series of 'Apocalyptic Landscapes' that anticipated the horrors of the First World War with their burning cities, twisted buildings, dark skies lit by fiery explosions, and anguished suffering of those fleeing the terror of an overturned world.[71] He began painting these disturbing visions of nightmare and apocalypse in 1912 and continued with them until his conscription into the German army in 1916. After the war, sated with death and destruction, he changed direction and focused instead on portraiture and biblical themes.

From his youth, religious motifs of one sort or another had appeared in Meidner's work. An early sketch of the medieval Spanish-Jewish philosopher and poet 'Jehuda ben Halevy' (1901) had been accompanied by lines from a poem by Heinrich Heine, the literary giant and convert to Christianity.[72] Other ink drawings that date from 1902, while he was apprenticed to a builder, frequently contained medieval Christian imagery of praying monks.[73] Yet he would later claim to have remained

[67] Meidner later wrote that, at the time, he had been 'full of anger, wistfulness and brokenness; and whenever fatigue impinged on me, the dark desire pulled me up again, a grim will, an unrest; the ambition, whatever it was, abruptly commanded me to stand and take my place.' L. Meidner, *Septemberschrei – Hymnen-Gebete-Lästerungen*, Berlin, 1918, S. 66, cited in Thomas Grochowiak, *Ludwig Meidner* (Recklinghausen: Bongers, 1966), 119. Grochowiak, an artist himself, offers perhaps the most comprehensive and critical treatment of Meidner's art available.

[68] Meidner's cultural milieu brought him into contact with several other well-known Jewish comment-ators on Paul. Whilst in France he met 'the very young Schalem [sic] Asch.' In 1913–14 he co-edited a journal that included contributions by Franz Werfel, who became a regular visitor to Meidner's attic in the 1920s. Finally, Meidner was married by Rabbi Leo Baeck of the Berlin Synagogue in 1927. E. Scheyer, 'Ludwig Meidner, Artist-Poet', 12, 28, 41a, 47.

[69] L. Meidner, 'Pauluspredigt' [Paul's Sermon] (1919), watercolour, 68 × 49 cm. Buller Collection, Duisberg.

[70] It is known that Meidner produced several other studies of Paul. One was confiscated by the Nazis and destroyed. L. Meidner, 'Die Verzückung Pauli' [The Ecstasy of Paul] (undated), drawing? unknown dimensions, National Gallery Berlin? S. Barron, *'Degenerate Art'*, 300. Another was 'Vision der Apostel Paulus' [Vision of the Apostle Paul] (1919), lithograph print, 25.4 × 17.62 cm, the Robert Gore Rifkind Center for Herman Expressionist Studies.

[71] Despite his expressionist credentials, the influence of Cubism and Futurism is clear in these paintings, in which the forms are sharp and angular, the brushwork is fiercely eruptive, and the themes are overwhelmingly of the destruction of modern urban landscapes. That he is not better known has been put down to the fact that 'Meidner never belonged to any of the major artistic groups of his time'. Carol S. Eliel, *The Apocalyptic Landscapes of Ludwig Meidner* (Munich: Prestel, 1989), 59. Along with the Polish painter Jacob Steinhardt (1887–1968) and the German painter Richard Janthur (1883–1956), he did, however, found the small Pathetiker Group in 1912, which stressed dramatic content over artistic form.

[72] 'Gently flowed the rabbi's blood and / Gently to its end his song he / Sang and his last sigh in dying/ Was the sigh, Jerusalem.' Heinrich Heine, 'Jehuda ben Halevy' (1851). The drawing is reproduced in the Appendix in E. Scheyer, 'Ludwig Meidner, Artist-Poet'.

[73] 'To find salvation from the storms of adolescence under floods of tears, fantastic figures, monks, flagellants, hermits in their humble piety. All that was awkwardly drawn, but oh, so honestly

nonreligious, even antireligious, until almost thirty years old. The story of the winding path back to his ancestral faith is an interesting one. As he explained in personal correspondence in 1934,

I have been an atheist until my 29th year – from this time [1912] surrendering to a religious-mystical but individual experience. Since the last year of the war, I was totally steeped in Christian thinking and feeling. 1919–1923 I was occupied with Christian theology, especially with the Apostle Paul. Then came the turning point after storm years: return to Judaism, acquaintance with Chassidism; reception of Jewish religious practice since 1924; since 1927, the year of my marriage, regulated by the exact observance of [the] Jewish ceremonial [codex] the Schulchar Oruch [*Shulchan Aruch*]. Peace of mind had been achieved, my years of struggle were over.[74]

Thus, during the period from 1912 until 1924 when he found his peace in Judaism, Meidner was engaged in a personal search for spiritual meaning that culminated in several years of immersion in the life and thought of the apostle Paul. The starting point in this journey can be traced back to a strange episode in Berlin in December 1912.

One evening, while I was painting, I realized all of a sudden that I could not do anything. I could not paint. Then, all at once, I . . . could see myself painting. My arm worked by itself, and I was extremely surprised. Then something came over me: the Holy Spirit. The curious thing was, though, that I did not believe in God. I cannot, at this point, describe the presence of the Holy Spirit. This was exceptionally eruptive. In all, it lasted for two to three minutes, but it left a distant echo. I realized that this is what we call ecstasy. Because I did not believe in God, I was incapable of recognizing that this was intimately connected with God. It repeated itself, however, evening after evening, so that I began to yearn for it. It came over me even in the street, so that I had to hang on to something; it was as if a storm was trying to sweep me away. I told my friends about it, but they thought me crazy. [Marc] Chagall said about me: 'He is incredibly gifted, but mad!' I had a New Testament at home. Before, I had only ever used it for anti-religious reasons. I opened a Psalm [sic] and suddenly realized: this is [describing] exactly what I have experienced; and in only a few seconds it hit me: this is the truth![75]

Further appreciation of Meidner's artistic temperament can be gleaned from his description of his ideal working conditions. These comprised a dimly lit, poorly furnished attic studio and lonely nights of exhausting activity, all of which seemed designed to inculcate the mysterious and precious divine winds of inspiration.

experienced, quite independently felt.' Ludwig Meidner, *Im Nacken das Sternenmeer* (Leipzig: Kurt Wolff, 1916), cited in E. Scheyer, 'Ludwig Meidner, Artist-Poet', 29. See also his 'Töte das Fleisch' [Mortify thy Flesh] (1902), ink pen, 20 × 32 cm, which portrays a group of cowled monks in prayer, several of whom are scourging themselves bare-backed before two looming crosses.
74 Meidner to Franz Lansberger (21 Feb 1934). Meidner–Lansberger correspondence, Leo Baeck Institute, New York, cited in E. Scheyer, 'Ludwig Meidner, Artist-Poet', 37.
75 According to 'Meidner's own testimony' (no reference), cited in Grochowiak, *Ludwig Meidner*, 119.

The gas lamp is the true light. It is a source of inspiration. It hums quietly and if one listens at a late hour and for a long time, one perceives a distant but powerful singing. Daylight is too rationalistic and sceptical. Furthermore, during the day one also lacks courage for one's ideas and intuition. Under the lamp, on the other hand, one is incredibly brave, bold and great. One has to keep late hours every night to paint and to draw. The staying up all night releases secret powers. This was well understood by those who lived a mystic-ascetic life in long passed epochs.[76]

Did he believe that he was tapping into his own inner, creative resources or experiencing divine revelation? Either way, his endeavours eventually found expression in the new artistic direction he took in 1917, while still enlisted. Meidner began reading the Old Testament and filling pocket books and, after the War, canvasses with personifications of prophecy and revelation. In the past, he had been interested in Nietzsche and the idea of the poet as a superior being who, once liberated from the repression of his own subjectivity, has the potential to speak revelatory truth.[77] With his biblical drawings and paintings, Meidner appears to be further exploring this idea and the connections between artistic and prophetic experiences of inspiration. His imagination was now fired by figures of prophets, sibyls, apostles, and penitents. As he recounts,

Secretly, I hid myself away in old, mystical books, and one day it hit me that this so-called dead Holy Scripture was an inexhaustible source of joy and profound truths. Having previously leafed through it with misunderstanding and arrogance, I was now powerfully gripped by those soothing verses of the Psalms or the dreadful speeches of Isaiah; like a sleeping man, they aroused me and whirled me up like dust to the heights of heaven.[78]

This cycle of Prophets was a long, quite repetitive series of compositions, and included both unnamed individuals and biblical luminaries such as Moses, Jeremiah, Elijah, and Elisha. The angry characters erupting from the pages of the Bible are contorted, writhing, frustrated, and ecstatic in their search for illumination. From 1919 Meidner found himself drawn to Catholic mysticism, and particularly the works of Thomas à Kempis and the testimonies of Saint Teresa of Avila. He even contemplated conversion.[79]

---

[76] L. Meidner, *Eine autobiographische Plauderei* IV (Leipzig: Klinkhardt & Biermann 1923), 2, cited in Grochowiak, *Ludwig Meidner*, 127.

[77] German Expressionism had been profoundly influenced by Nietzsche's *The Birth of Tragedy* (*Die Geburt der Tragödie*, 1872) and *Thus Spoke Zarathustra* (*Also sprach Zarathustra*, 1883–5) and especially the idea of the abandonment of rationality and the return to the irrational and primitive impulses.

[78] L. Meidner, Septemberschrei, S. 18, cited in Grochowiak, *Ludwig Meidner*, 120.

[79] 'Meidner's relations to the Catholic Church are further intensified through the acquaintance with the Black Monk Jan Verkade, who invited me to visit. Later, Meidner remembers: "Had I not fallen ill at the time when Verkade invited me to come to Beuron, I possibly would have been christened. Providence would not have it, and so I turned back to the faith of my forefathers."' Grochowiak, *Ludwig Meidner*, 125.

Above all, however, it was the apostle Paul's teaching and preaching that obsessed Meidner, for he found in the archetypal Jewish convert a reflection of his own emotional contradictions, spiritual crises, and intellectual concerns. After all, Paul, too, had been struck by ecstatic visions, he had understood what it was to be enflamed by an overwhelming quest for purity of purpose, and he had similarly devoted his life to warning of impending disaster those who refused to listen. Furthermore, the diminutive, awkward Meidner was drawn to the unimpressive figure of Paul, and empathised with the complexities of living as an alien in both the Jewish and the Gentile worlds. Finally, Meidner, who actually lived a relatively ascetic lifestyle, was nevertheless haunted by his abandonment of the faith of his ancestors, and debated long and hard with Paul as to the relation of the spirit to the Law. In the end, of course, the observant life of Orthodox Judaism won out over any attraction to the interior life of Christian mysticism. But before that homecoming, and while still wrestling with an apostle who seemed to hold the secret to a release from spiritual torment and despair, the painting of Saint Paul was produced.

'Paul's Sermon' (1919) is not as easy to interpret as some might suggest. The artist and critic Thomas Grochowiak sees this work (along with the rest of the Prophet series) through the lens of Meidner's earlier 'Apocalyptic Landscapes', describing it as 'loaded with threatening apocalyptical eeriness and tense to the bursting point'. He also takes the title at face value, suggesting a narrative in which one of Paul's sermons is suddenly interrupted by a nightmarish vision of future apocalypse.

Just before his [Paul's] hands were waving full of spirits. But suddenly they are frozen, his arms protectively folded over his head. And his wide-open eyes, which seem to see terrible things happening, are full of fear and foreboding. Both the sceptics and his followers who are sat around him seem either unsuspecting or curious. The apostle advances hesitatingly, ducked before the beams of divine power and bent under the weight of his vision of horror.[80]

But to anyone familiar with the New Testament, the heavenly 'beams of divine power' above Paul will immediately bring to mind the apostle's description of his conversion in the book of Acts: 'But it happened that as I was on my way, approaching Damascus about noontime, a very bright light suddenly flashed from heaven all around me' (Acts 22:6). It seems more probable that the painting is a representation of the famous episode of the apostle's revelation of the risen Christ on the road to Damascus. In any case, the power of the scene relies heavily on the dramatically atmospheric skyscape, the two shards of light splintering the oppressive, overhanging, dark blue firmament.[81] Four figures are seated on the

---

[80] Grochowiak, *Ludwig Meidner*, 125.
[81] The beams of light are certainly reminiscent of the explosive streaks illuminating his earlier apocalyptic cityscapes, for example his 'Apokalyptische Landschaft' [Apocalyptic Landscape] (1912), oil painting, 94 × 109 cm. Küsters Collection, Recklinghausen.

red road, but these do not appear to be 'unsuspecting or curious' members of an audience; rather, these are travelling companions who have been caught up in the light storm.[82] Paul's own account in Acts explains their frightened upturned faces and the cupping of their ears: 'And those who were with me saw the light, to be sure, but did not understand the voice of the One who was speaking to me' (Acts 22:9). How else to represent this text graphically? These shaken individuals, illuminated by the supernatural radiance, strain to hear the heavenly voice that is thundering down on Paul.[83] The apostle himself appears to have stumbled forward, flinching, unbalanced by the violence of the revelation, hiding his face with arms that might have been outstretched in righteous admonition of his fellow travellers seconds before. His wide eyes flick heavenwards, the shock and awe of the moment etched on his flushed cheeks and prominent wrinkled forehead. The stocky build, balding head, and hooked nose of traditional Christian portrayals are apparent,[84] but there can be no doubting that Paul is here perceived in line with the other biblical prophets from this series, the continuity between the Old and New Covenants fully assumed in Meidner's mind.[85]

But if the painting is of the conversion of Paul, why then is it entitled 'Paul's Sermon' (*Pauluspredigt*)? Perhaps this can be explained in terms of Meidner's conviction that the power to communicate – in art as in prophecy – relies upon the ability to recapture and relive the original moment of ecstasy, revelation, and inspiration. From 1915, when he also dedicated himself to portraiture, many of his works were of leading expressionist writers and poets. Such artists concerned themselves with the individual's spiritual awakening and the search for truth through the outward expression of inner, subjective realities.[86] It seems reasonable that his preoccupation with the nature of inspiration, whether artistic or religious, can assist in relating the title to the content of the piece. Perhaps it is best regarded

[82] One of the figures is hooded, and reminds one of the medieval heirs of Saint Paul that Meidner had previously drawn penned such as 'Töte das Fleisch'.

[83] According to Acts of the Apostles, the voice called out 'Saul, Saul, why are you persecuting Me?' (Acts 22:7).

[84] Meidner appears to have done his homework. A second-century account (*The Acts of Paul and Thecla*) famously describes the apostle as 'A man of middling size, and his hair was scanty, and his legs were a little crooked, and his knees were far apart; he had large eyes, and his eyebrows met, and his nose was somewhat long.' Of course, Meidner would also have been familiar with the brief description in 2 Cor. 10:10, 'For they say, "His letters are weighty and strong, but his personal presence is unimpressive and his speech contemptible."'

[85] The apostle's gesture and posture are paralleled in several earlier compositions featuring Old Testament seers, for example, 'Prophet' (1919), feather and brush, 111 × 73 cm. Museum of Art, Düsseldorf. The Prophets series has been interpreted unanimously as an attempt to capture the instant of revelation (whether of apocalypse or not). The similarities to Meidner's Paul further supports the claim made here that the composition must represent something more than simply a sermon.

[86] Politics was also an area infused with religious fervour. The year before, following the November Revolution of 1918, Meidner had published an avant-garde, socialist artist's manifesto in which he had exclaimed, 'Painters, poets – who else is obliged to fight for the just cause but we? The voice of God in us again and again wakes our enraged fists.' Ludwig Meidner, 'An alle Künstler' [To All Artists] (1918), cited in E. Scheyer, 'Ludwig Meidner, Artist-Poet', 38.

as a study of how Paul understood and successfully drew upon his experience of inspiration for his preaching. Hence, in this work, the observer is eavesdropping on a sermon in which the apostle retells the story of his conversion in such a dramatic way that, in reliving it, he succeeds in transporting his listeners back to the eruptive moment itself.[87] Such is the power of prophetic inspiration, suggests Meidner, that the listener becomes, if only for an instant, a pilgrim on the road to Damascus and a participant in a divine revelation. And who better to elucidate this truth than the prophetic artist of apocalypse, who had himself felt the touch of the spirit?

At the time of the painting, Meidner was a spiritually awakened and cultured European intellectual who, in an existential search for an alternative to the Judaism of his youth, had found himself mesmerised by the spirit-filled life and writings of Saint Paul. The exhilaration of divine inspiration had, he believed, been shared by prophets of the Hebrew Bible, New Testament apostles and medieval Christian mystics alike. The essential experience of Jew and Christian had been the same. The watercolour of Paul thus represents an important moment in a rebellious German Jew's spiritual journey back to the faith of his fathers: it was a moment when his indeterminate sense of religious identity allowed him to freely associate with the Apostle to the Gentiles, and to see him as part of an ancient Judeo-Christian tradition of revelational prophecy, a subject of profound importance to him both religiously and artistically.

FRANZ WERFEL AND THE PAULINE TRAGEDY

Franz Werfel (1890–1945) was an Austrian expressionist poet, novelist, and play-wright whose favoured themes included religious faith and heroism and the broth-erhood of mankind. Born into a culturally assimilated Jewish family in Prague, he later freely admitted that his religious inclinations were somewhat unortho-dox. One biographer would go so far as to conclude that, as a result, Werfel was committed to 'a transcendent, almost supra-historical dogma' that allowed him to see his faith as both Jewish and Christian.[88] Although he always maintained his Jewishness, he did not feel comfortable with organised religion of any sort. At the time of the production of his play *The Eternal Road* (1935),[89] a work that expressed the ambiguity of his religious position with its debates between faithful Jews and doubting apostates, he explained,

---

[87] If Meidner spent three or four years steeping himself in Paul's theology, as he claimed, then he could not have failed to notice the number of times that Paul himself referred to the transformational experience in his preaching (Acts 22:1–11 and 26:9–18) and Epistles (1 Cor. 9:1 and 15:3–9; Gal. 1:11–17).

[88] Lionel B. Steiman, *Franz Werfel: The Faith of an Exile* (Ontario: Wilfrid Laurier University Press, 1985), 167.

[89] Franz Werfel, *Der Weg der Verheissung* (Vienna: Paul Zsolnay, 1935). The English translation is *The Eternal Road*, trans. Ludwig Lewisohn (New York: Viking Press, 1936).

I had to discover my Jewishness on my own, from early on in a strange, unconscious way, which has strengthened itself in my soul through knowledge and sorrow so that nothing can take it from me, neither Christians or even Jews.[90]

And yet, although Werfel never converted to Christianity, he described himself as a 'believer in Christ' and filled his writings with eulogies and pastiches of Christian spirituality.[91] Following his escape as an identified Jew after the annexation of Austria in 1938, he found religious solace at Lourdes before fleeing the Nazi invasion of France and eventually settling in the United States. There, in fulfilment of a vow made during his escape, he wrote perhaps his most famous novel, the life of the Catholic visionary of Lourdes, *The Song of Bernadette* (1941).[92] Such works hint at his mystical conception of faith, the disappointment he felt towards historical manifestations of religion, especially Judaism, and his fascination with the moral power of religion as expressed through the lives of pious individuals. As he once explained,

History and religion are in a sense unreconcilable [sic] contrasts. For history rationalises the moment of divine wonder which operates at the beginning of every elemental religious manifestation. The rational dissection of the genesis of a religion offends the sensibility, not only of believing minds, but also of unbelieving ones, in so far as they are sincere. In all of us there is a subtle refinement of feeling, a holy shyness, which shrinks from hearing the numinous explained to us.[93]

Considering Werfel's background, it comes as no surprise to discover that, from relatively early on in his career, he had been drawn to the apostle Paul as a means by which to explore his Judeo-Christian heritage. The play, *Paul among the Jews: A Tragedy*, was written in 1926, and is the only example of a theatrical treatment

[90] A speech given by Werfel to a Jewish group in New York (1935), cited in Steiman, *Franz Werfel* (1985), 222n4.

[91] Steiman discounts rumours that Werfel converted before his death, although, in making his argument, he accepts that such rumours were entirely understandable. Thus Steiman explains away the religious influence of Werfel's bourgeois Catholic wife, Alma, and his funeral service (conducted by a Catholic priest friend); nor does he take at face value Werfel's assertion in 1916 that he was 'christusgläubig' (a believer in Christ) and, in 1941, that the marrow of his poetic, epic, and dramatic work was his 'mystical, even Catholic faith'. The evidence of his writings themselves, which indicate something of an obsession with Christian spirituality, is interpreted alongside Werfel's unshakable Jewish self-definition and parallel obsession with the Jewish character. Steiman, *Franz Werfel*, 165–6.

[92] Franz Werfel, *Das Lied von Bernadette* (Stockholm: Bermann-Fischer, 1941). The English translation is Franz Werfel, *The Song of Bernadette*, trans. Ludwig Lewisohn (New York: Viking Press, 1942).

[93] Franz Werfel, *Paul among the Jews; A Tragedy*, trans. Paul Levertoff (London: A.R. Mowbray & Co., 1928), i. Werfel's mysticism made him wary of relying too heavily upon historical explanations of religion in general and the parting of the ways in particular.

of the subject by a Jewish playwright.[94] It is prefaced with a note that informs the reader that the author is a Jew whose interest is in those who suffer for the sake of religion. In essence, the play is a series of conversations (*inter alia*, between Paul and the disciples, and between Paul and his former teacher, Gamaliel the Elder) from which Paul emerges uncompromised and ready to unleash his gospel upon the world. Werfel makes it clear that, for him, it is the study of 'men possessed by religion', rather than 'ideas, confessions of faith, doctrines, dogmas, degrees of belief', which is required to comprehend 'the great tragic hour of Judaism'. What is this tragic hour of Judaism? It is, for Werfel, the failure of the Jewish people to retain Paul for Israel.[95]

The drama begins some time after Paul's conversion, upon his return to Jerusalem, where the early Christians or Nazarenes wait to meet their former persecutor in some agitation.[96] We are informed by the Christian women in whose house he is staying that the apostle is frequently afflicted by fits, described as the torments of an evil angel.[97] Upon his first meeting with the disciples, we see Paul, the self-confessed murderer of Stephen, reeling under a great burden of guilt, and overawed by the presence of those who knew his messiah in the flesh.[98] It does not take long, however, before he is arguing with them over whether the gospel should be given to the Gentiles, and provoking horror for the suggestion that the Law has been abrogated by the messiah.[99] James, the brother of Jesus and the voice of Jewish Christianity, asserts that

The Messiah Jesus lived within the Law. He preached to the lost sheep of Israel. He did not wish to cast the children's bread to the dogs.... With blood and wisdom have *we*

---

[94] Franz Werfel, *Paulus unter den Juden* (Berlin: Zsolnay, 1926). The English translation is *Paul among the Jews*. Werfel explains in his introduction that his key sources of information are the Acts of the Apostles and certain rabbinic traditions relating to rabbis Shimon and Zadok. Werfel, *Paul Among the Jews*, ii–iv. The play was written following a visit to Palestine and was originally intended to be the first part of a trilogy about the life of Paul. Karlheinz Martin's production was moderately well received in Berlin. For a comparison of *Paul among the Jews* with Werfel's two other historical dramas, *Juarez and Maximilian* (1924) and *The Kingdom of God in Bohemia* (1930), which are both interpreted as meditations on political leadership, on the Christian message of forgiveness, and on the link between religion and revolution, see John Warren, 'Franz Werfel's Historical Drama: Continuity and Change' in Lothar Huber, ed., *Franz Werfel: An Austrian Writer Reassessed* (Oxford: Berg, 1989), 125–73.

[95] Werfel, *Paul among the Jews*, ii.

[96] At one point James, the brother of Jesus, asks, 'Why did not the Lord, my Brother, appear unto [the Pharisaic teacher] Gamaliel, the righteous one of Israel? Why did he not come to enlighten the good teacher, instead of the malicious disciple?' Werfel, *Paul among the Jews*, 49–50.

[97] 'An evil angel torments him. Hast thou seen how crazy are his eyes and how his fists are clenched, his lips all crooked, and his dreadful voice when he cried "Flesh, Oh thou my angel of darkness!"' Werfel, *Paul among the Jews*, 37.

[98] Werfel, *Paul among the Jews*, 53–4. 'Ye [Peter] were elected from the beginning. I am merely one of the saved. From the abyss come I, where souls perish.' Ibid., 55.

[99] Paul maintains that 'The kingdom of God cometh to all men ... [and] Jesus, the Messiah, is above the Law.' Werfel, *Paul among the Jews*, 56.

created the Church of the Messiah. She lives eternally in the Law of Moses. The Lord himself said: 'Till earth and heaven pass away, not one jot or tittle shall pass away from the Law. . . . '[100]

When pressed, Paul, the recent convert, is forced to reveal his justification for holding such different views from his Lord and master. Werfel does this by having Paul ask the rhetorical question, 'Did the Christ Himself perfectly comprehend the mystery of the Christ?' The implication is that such was Paul's inner conviction that even the messiah's teachings had to give way to the apostle's own spiritual insight. Of such men as these, Werfel seems to be saying, are religions born.

On two occasions in the play, Paul confronts his former teacher, Rabbi Gamaliel, portrayed as the wisest Jewish mind of his day. These are the crucial discussions, the points on which the play, and the future of the world, turn. From the first meeting, we learn that Gamaliel had only ever lost one disciple, and that the estrangement of this beloved student has caused him great sorrow; at no point had he ever given up the hope that Saul would return to the fold.[101] And, initially, the only thing that seems to separate the two men, whose respect for each other is undiminished, is the classic distinction between the Jew and Christian: one believes that the messiah has come, the other that he will come.[102] It soon becomes apparent, however, that Paul's views are more dangerous, threatening as they do the validity of the Torah, and he is arrested.[103] Unwilling to countenance the execution of Paul, which is called for by many who witness the disputation, Gamaliel submits to the call for the Exorcist who can rid Paul of the demon which is believed to possess him.[104] In the event, the exorcism fails and Paul is only rescued from a stoning when his former teacher once again intervenes, drawing the criticism of the mob. (Gamaliel's gentleness and fairhandedness is pronounced throughout. Werfel has him abroad at the time of Jesus' crucifixion, and hints that he would not have permitted the execution to have taken place, had he been present, blasphemy or not.)[105] At the

---

[100] Werfel, *Paul among the Jews*, 56–7. Later James complains, 'He [Paul] goes about preaching that sin is the fruit of the Law. How is one to understand this? If so, we, Jews, are lower than the Gentiles! . . . Perchance he is really possessed. . . . ' Werfel, *Paul among the Jews*, 92.

[101] Werfel's Gamaliel believes that he had taught the deeper meanings of the Torah to Saul too early and that this 'awakening' had brought about his disciple's demise. At the same time, in a short exchange with some of his other students, the old sage admits that Saul's 'perception was too advanced' to be good for him. One of his disciples concludes that perception is the origin of all heresy. Werfel, *Paul among the Jews*, 75–6.

[102] Paul exclaims that 'The Law is fulfilled and love hath come', to which Gamaliel responds gently, 'Love *will* come.' Werfel, *Paul among the Jews*, 77–8.

[103] 'The Law *is* fulfilled. The Promised One *has* appeared. . . . The Law has no longer power, for the new world has come into being.' Werfel, *Paul among the Jews*, 78.

[104] Rabbi Zadok is so shocked that he wonders how 'This world is still standing, after such words have been spoken!' Werfel, *Paul among the Jews*, 78. The Exorcist is one of the more colourful characters of the play, and is described as 'The terrible man, who keeps all the six hundred and thirty [sic] commandments, and their children, and their children's children. Since he observes them all, God can't do anything to him.' Werfel, *Paul among the Jews*, 39.

[105] Werfel, *Paul among the Jews*, 82.

second and final debate, Gamaliel puts enormous effort into convincing Paul of
the error of his ways, now conscious of what is at stake.[106] Paul, for his part, regards
this as the deciding battle between Judaism and Christianity, declaring, 'In the
name of Christ must I fight with Moses.'[107] We now learn the original cause of
Paul's dissatisfaction with his former life as Werfel reinforces the traditional image
of the young Pharisaic student of Gamaliel as frustrated and unable to observe the
Law. Paul laments,

Early did they inculcate me with the Torah. Then was the world filled with flaming
angels of the Law, who beset all my paths. And all their swords blazed against me,
thousands and millions of them! I scourged my body in order to keep the Law. But,
alas! What is this body of feverish dream-chasing flesh, stamped with Adam's curse,
about to do? Nothing! Nothing!... The Torah redeemed me not, it cursed me only
with the knowledge of my sin!'[108]

Sympathetic to this torment, which Paul claims was only assuaged by his discovery
of the messiah, the old sage offers support and encouragement before hinting
that he is prepared to call for a rapprochement between the Jewish people and
Jesus, whom he describes as 'a holy man of God.'[109] When Paul insists that the
messiah had brought about the end of the Law, Gamaliel counters by reminding
Paul that Jesus, messiah or not, would have disagreed.[110] Once again, Paul's justifies
his distinctive teaching by setting aside the limited knowledge of the man Jesus,
merely a rabbi from Nazareth, in favour of his own understanding of 'the Messiah,
the incarnate Shekina, God's Son, [existent] before the world came into being.'[111]
In the face of such presumption, Gamaliel retracts his offer and, apparently on
behalf of generations of Jews as yet unborn, bitterly condemns his recalcitrant
student as 'a drunken apostate' and 'Israel's self-hatred.'[112] Perhaps, he agonises,
it would be better to sacrifice one soul for the sake of the purity of God's Torah.
In the end, however, he spares Paul, despite being prophetically aware of the fatal
consequences of his failure for the world. He prays,

---

[106] During the debate, the participants learn that the Romans are stepping up their oppression. Rabbi
Huna suggests that 'The reason is clear: we have permitted heresy and the insulting of the Torah.'
Werfel, *Paul among the Jews*, 114.

[107] Werfel, *Paul among the Jews*, 131.

[108] Werfel, *Paul among the Jews*, 135.

[109] Gamaliel announces that 'I have decided that thou [Paul] shouldst lead back Rabbi Jehoshua of
Nazareth to Israel!...I have found a holy man of God. And I will testify of him. With thee I
will stand up before the Tribunal!' At the same time, he finds some (human) fault with Jesus.
'Even illumination is guilty, when it is too dazzling for weak eyes. Very dangerously hath Jehoshua
illuminated the Law, and beside, it was too premature.' Werfel, *Paul among the Jews*, 136–7.

[110] Paul argues that 'This Tie has become rotten, Rabbanu! Like a discarded wine-skin the Word lies
upon the road!' Gamaliel replies, '*This* this man did not say!' Werfel, *Paul among the Jews*, 139.

[111] Werfel, *Paul among the Jews*, 139.

[112] Werfel, *Paul among the Jews*, 142.

Can I let Thine enemy go, my God? Let him go to a strange land, him, who wishes to destroy thy inexhaustible Torah and our holy responsibility towards men, in order that he may preach his phantom gospel? Oh, they will listen to him, and the phantom will become their Law, for a shadow lies but lightly, but Thy Law lies heavily![113]

Thus Werfel captures the instant of the parting of the ways, 'that decisive hour in which Christianity separated itself from its mother environment.'[114] Is Paul to be condemned for his beliefs or the establishment of a religion that will go on to win the world at the expense of the Jewish people? Apparently not. The apostle's raw passion and spiritual sincerity exonerate him, just as the wisdom and patience of his teacher support the moral claim of the stance adopted by the Pharisees. That these two 'men possessed by religion', these equally admirable representatives of Christianity and Judaism, fail to reconcile is, for Werfel, *the* tragedy of Jewish history.[115] At the same time, there is no doubt that in the playwright's mind, Israel's loss is, ultimately, world religious civilisation's gain.

Soon after the play was published, suspicions of Werfel's Jewish identity began to be voiced publicly. In response to a barrage of inquiries as to his baptismal status, he insisted in one newspaper interview, 'I have never moved away from Judaism, I am in feeling and thinking a conscious Jew.'[116] Among his critics was Sigmund Freud, who was uncomfortable at the appearance of anti-Jewish motifs such as the People's stiff-necked refusal to recognise Christ, and who saw the play as a glorification of Christianity which was, as a religion, only a social construction, after all. Werfel, who was interested in psychoanalysis and who had met Freud, replied,

I wrote this play as a Jew. And no moment in history seemed to me more . . . 'tragic' than that when the antinomian direction (Christ) breaks away from the Torah and the Nation, and in the person of the renegade Paul conquers the world. . . . It is not a question of religions; they are only the conscious manifestation of the two important groups of characters into which the Jewish being was split at that time.[117]

Thus, according to Werfel's self-proclaimed Jewish account, the parting of the ways is to be understood as a kind of neurosis within the Jewish people itself, an internal matter unrelated to Christianity *per se* (despite his identification of Paul's universality and abrogation of the Law as the root causes of the split).

How did such a view fit into the playwright's wider ideological programme? There can be little doubt that Werfel held Catholic spirituality in the highest esteem

---

[113] Werfel, *Paul among the Jews*, 143.
[114] Werfel, *Paul among the Jews*, i.
[115] 'What men, what earnestness, what eternal momentous events are displayed here!' Werfel, *Paul among the Jews*, ii, iv.
[116] Interview with *Israelisches Wochenblatt* (1926), cited in L. B. Steiman, *Franz Werfel* (1985), 222n3.
[117] Letter from Werfel to Freud (1926), reproduced in Michel Reffet, 'Franz Werfel and Psychoanalysis', 122n26. Reffet notes that Freud's side of the correspondence has been lost.

and was not a little awed by its powerful sway over world history; furthermore, complaints from the Jewish community did nothing to prevent his continuing to write empathetically on the theme of Christian religion for years to come. In light of his apparent theological confusion, Werfel is perhaps best understood as 'a marginal man . . . [living] on the line between Judaism and Christianity'.[118] The play *Paul among the Jews* certainly did not call for a religious synthesis, for he did not believe that one could logically reconcile Jewish and Christian theologies – this he made clear in the debates between Paul and Gamaliel. But, convinced that they shared a common ground in the face of political opposition, and committed to a postwar vision of the universal brotherhood of humanity, he sought an understanding or rapprochement between the two faith communities. In an unusual variant of the theme of the Judeo-Christian tradition, Werfel hinted at their complementary roles – Christianity going on to conquer the pagan world in demonstration of its spiritual potency, Judaism going on to suffer centuries of degradation with a dignity that expressed just as powerfully its own spiritual purity. Both witnessed to the reality of the presence of the Spirit of God. Written from his unsystematic, mystical perspective, the tragedy that the story of Paul symbolised for Werfel was the failure of the two 'conscious manifestations' of the split 'Jewish being', that is, Judaism and Christianity, to recognise in each other the mystery of true faith.

CONCLUSION

To anyone even remotely familiar with the place of Paul within the wider Jewish cultural imagination, one would have to say that the views of the artists in this chapter are unrepresentative, to put it mildly, even setting aside the controversial figure of Mendelssohn. In their attempt to render an artistic portrait of the Apostle to the Gentiles, neither Meidner nor Werfel appears to have associated him with the negative stereotypes of the popular Jewish view. No doubt this can be accounted for by their respective personal and sociocultural backgrounds. Certainly, both had seen in Paul a kindred spirit and in interpreting his life and theology they had created a mirror in which were reflected their own problems and experiences. At the same time, their remarkably sympathetic treatments had been facilitated by the artistic medium itself, which offers the advantage of not obliging the author to reconcile ideas or beliefs that, to others, might appear to be in tension; in fact, art communicates very effectively the often paradoxical nature of subjective experience. Despite the fact that all three readily acknowledged Paul's responsibility for the 'parting of the ways', they had believed that it was more important to emphasise the commonalities than the differences. Thus Paul had represented an

---

[118] 'Franz Werfel was a marginal man. He lived on the line between Judaism and Christianity, sensuality and asceticism, left and right, earth and heaven.' L. B. Steiman, *Franz Werfel* (1985), 189.

opportunity to explore their own ideas of the meaning of the Judeo-Christian heritage. What the composer Mendelssohn, the painter Meidner, and the playwright Werfel all shared was a belief that deep down Judaism and Christianity were of the same substance.

Of course, these men possessed highly idiosyncratic views of the two religions. The faith of Mendelssohn had been influenced by his father's idea of a universal ethic lying beneath the historically conditioned religions; it was interwoven with the contemporary Christian regard for natural religion so that it is difficult to know where one began and the other ended. His treatment of the story of Paul had been an eloquent celebration of the rational foundation that was shared between Christianity and his grandfather Moses's conception of Judaism. For Meidner, whose familiarity with Christianity was skewed towards its mystical traditions, the thread that joined it to Judaism was to be found in the supernatural phenomenon of prophetic inspiration, into which context he firmly placed Paul. At the time of his painting, Meidner saw no reason to distinguish between Jewish and Christian prophetic revelation, and the ecstatic figure of Paul was a powerful artistic expression of this sentiment. For Werfel, Paul represented Judaism's sacrifice and contribution to a greater Judeo-Christian ideal, the two faiths being regarded as two parts of a greater whole. Paul had been a sincere, spiritually gifted but tragically misunderstood figure, and an empathetic reading of his story would greatly assist in a rapprochement between Jew and Christian in the modern era. Rather than say that each had attempted to reclaim Paul for Judaism, it might be better to say that each had sought to reclaim him for a vision of a Jewish-Christian heritage. One can uncover a similar concern in other forms of artistic expression, too. Let us move the discussion from the context of German-Jewish fine arts to that of the North American-Jewish historical novel.

6

~

The Novels of Shalom Asch and Samuel Sandmel

North American Jewish novels of the mid-twentieth century were largely concerned with explorations of identity and in particular with tensions between secular society and Jewish tradition. A number of high-profile writers appeared to have set themselves in opposition to their Jewish heritage.[1] In the eyes of many, authors such as Chaim Potok (1929–2002), Saul Bellow (1915–2005), and especially Philip Roth (1933–) appeared to be committed to the demystification of Judaism and the deconstruction of Jewish life, revealing it warts and all and emphasising its disoriented secularism. Although some interpreted this phenomenon as an attempt to normalise the Jewish people, many others believed that they went too far in undermining Jewish values. One literary critic recalled that the 'Jewish book-buying public were shocked and hurt to find [Jewish] writers representing their institutions as shams, their communities suffused with pettiness, spite, lust, hypocrisy, and pretence'.[2] Mordecai Kaplan, founder of Reconstructionist Judaism and himself highly critical of unreflective loyalty towards Jewish tradition, believed that the impact of North American Jewish literature had had a highly detrimental effect on Jewish life in North America in general:

[T]hanks for the most part to the Jewish self-hating attitude of the intellectual elite among our Jewish writers, our Jewish masses are likely to become, at best, only marginal Jews, and at worst, drop outs.[3]

Certainly, many works of literature published in the decades around the mid-century were concerned to formulate North American Jewish cultural identity in

---

[1] In a discussion about the characters that American Jewish novelists have created, the literary critic Aarons observes, 'Jews by birth, these characters are in many ways "marginal" Jews, Judaism in America, for the most part, appears in this literature as rootless, in flux, even antagonistic. One's relation to Judaism, to the history of the Jews, is a preoccupation in the literature of American Jewish writers. What it means to be a Jew in America has been a fundamental issue for American Jewish writers....' Victoria Aarons, *A Measure of Memory: Storytelling and Identity in American Jewish Fiction* (Athens, GA: University of Georgia Press, 1996), 13.

[2] Robert Alter, *After the Tradition: Essays on Modern Jewish Writing* (New York: E. P. Dutton, 1969), 10.

[3] Preface by Mordecai Kaplan in Bernard Cohen, *Sociocultural Changes in American Jewish Life as Reflected in Selected Jewish Literature* (Rutherford, NJ: Fairleigh Dickinson University Press, 1972), 9.

painfully secular terms. From this perspective, the two North American Jewish writers considered in this chapter are atypical. Neither the Yiddish author Shalom Asch nor the New Testament scholar and amateur novelist Samuel Sandmel was particularly interested in the tension between Judaism and secularism; rather they focused upon the fraught relationship between Judaism and an older 'other', namely Christianity. It was in their desire to understand it from the time of its first-century roots that they turned their attention to Paul. On the other hand, neither sought to undermine Jewish values, and Judaism was portrayed as neither intrinsically superior nor inferior to Christianity; in this sense at least, both could be said to have been engaged in a programme of normalisation, even if not as radical as those of other authors of the same period. The key issue, and one on which Asch and Sandmel were diametrically opposed, was how to relate Judaism to Christianity, that is, how to respond to the claim of a Judeo-Christian tradition. Both explicitly set out to examine claims of a common religious vision and both were preoccupied with the so-called Gentile Problem, that is, the relationship of the non-Jewish world to the God of Israel and to the people of Israel. Furthermore, both were committed to improving interfaith relations and believed that their fictional treatments of Paul represented important contributions towards this aim. But in their novels they adopted very different approaches. Whereas Asch eulogised about shared religious foundations and sought to dissolve the distinctions, Sandmel insisted upon maintaining the theological differences, even as he valued them. They represent two very different ways of thinking about the Judeo-Christian tradition in mid–twentieth century North American culture.

SHOLEM ASCH AND THE MISUNDERSTOOD APOSTLE

The Polish-born novelist, essayist, and dramatist Sholem Asch (1880–1957) had enjoyed an Eastern European traditional Jewish upbringing before becoming interested in secular literature and eventually emerging as the first Yiddish writer to boast a truly international reputation. He lived in North America during the First and Second World War, where he published most of his works, but also spent time in Poland, France, and Israel, and in his writings he drew upon the lives of both Jews and Gentiles from these countries. His profound attachment to and wide-ranging interests in the legacy of the Jewish past coloured all his works, ranging from a timeless and romanticised *shtetl*, to seventeenth-century pogroms, to the challenges of modern Jewish life in Russia, Germany, and Poland, to the pioneer experience in Palestine, to the Nazi persecution, to treatments of biblical figures such as Moses and Isaiah. A constant theme was the inner beauty and freedom of Jewish spirituality; another focus was his subjects' moral dilemmas and religious challenges. Concerned to expand his horizons throughout his career, he composed a trilogy about Christianity's founding figures, Jesus, Paul, and Mary,

a universally familiar theme which emphasises a shared Judeo-Christian spiritual heritage;[4] quite possibly, he was angling for a Nobel Prize in literature.[5]
But although the English translations of these sympathetic studies met with critical acclaim, the Jewish press was hostile. The North American Yiddish daily *The
Forward* not only refused to publish them, but also dropped him as a writer and initiated a public campaign, attacking him for encouraging conversion by preaching
Christianity.[6]

Asch's novel, *The Apostle* (1943),[7] is a remarkable reconstruction of the life of
Paul for several reasons. First, it adopts a highly positive approach to the apostle
and treats the early Christians or 'Jewish Messianists' very sympathetically indeed.
Nowhere in this historical novel, which is peppered throughout with New Testament references, is there any sense of Jewish antagonism to, or even criticism
of, Christianity. Second, in attempting to account for the apostle's conversion and
theological teachings, Asch abandons the time-honoured understanding (common
to Jews and Christians alike) that the preconversion Saul had become frustrated
and guilt-ridden by his failure to keep the legal observances and had subsequently
found in Christ a means by which to do away with the Law. He went even further
and maintained that although Paul came to regard the Law as subsumed under
a new Messianic dispensation, and unnecessary for Gentile believers, he did not
demand that Jews or Jewish Christians abandon observance of the Torah and, in
fact, observed it strictly himself.[8] Third, in terms of assessing Paul's career, Asch
is firmly of the opinion that Paul lived and died as an authentic Jew, and that
his eccentric views had not compromised his Jewishness. But before considering

---

[4] Sholem Asch, *The Nazarene*, trans. Maurice Samuel (New York: Putnam, 1939); *The Apostle*, trans.
Maurice Samuel (New York, 1943); *Mary*, trans. Leo Steinberg (New York: G. P. Putnam's Sons,
1949).

[5] Asch had already been nominated in 1933 for his novel *Three Cities*, trans. Willa and Edwin Muir
(London: 1933), and might have thought that Christian themes would give him a wider and more
receptive readership.

[6] For a well-contextualised survey of Asch's writings and their reception, see the collection of essays
Sholem Asch Reconsidered, Nanette Stahl, ed. (New Haven, CT: Beinecke Rare Book and Manuscript
Library, 2004). See also Charles A. Madison, *Yiddish Literature: Its Scope and Major Writers* (New
York: F. Ungar, 1968), 221–61.

[7] Sholem Asch, *The Apostle*, trans. Maurice Samuel (New York: G. P. Putnam's Sons, 1943). The
edition used here is Sholem Asch, *The Apostle*, trans. Maurice Samuel (London: Macdonald, 1949).
For reasons that will become apparent, the Yiddish original was never published.

[8] This reading of Asch's Paul is shared by Anita Norich, who writes of *The Apostle*, 'He [Asch's Paul]
is a strictly observant Jew, observing all the laws that Asch himself had long abandoned, but also
changing certain laws in order to teach new ones [to the Gentiles].' Anita Norich, 'Sholem Asch
and the Christian Question', in Stahl, ed., *Sholem Asch Reconsidered*, 255. The idea that Paul had
believed in the continued observance of the Law for *Jews* and had only rejected it as a means for
Gentile salvation was only seriously posited by New Testament scholars such Gaston and Gager in
the 1980s; they argued that Paul's negative statements about the Law were never meant to be applied
to Torah-observant Jews. See Gager, *The Origins of Anti-Semitism* and Gaston, *Paul and the Torah*.
Only very recently has the thesis that Paul was himself strictly Torah-observant been suggested by
Mark Nanos in *Romans* and *Galatians*.

these aspects more closely, it is worth outlining Asch's observations regarding the apostle's early influences and background.

Asch's Saul is described as 'all motion and restlessness, as if in his veins ran quicksilver instead of blood,' an ascetic firebrand who fasts frequently, has taken a vow of chastity, and provokes both admiration and concern for his uncompromising religious fervour.[9] Throughout his career he sees visions and dreams upon which he bases his actions and beliefs, and it seems fair to say that the poet in Asch is swept away by this first-century free spirit. A student of the great Pharisaic authority, Gamaliel the Elder, Paul has trouble keeping up with the rabbinic curriculum, not because of any innate inability but because of his determination to follow the rabbinic ideal of learning a trade, which for Saul meant tent-making. For Asch, this dedication to an occupation not only gave Saul financial security, reflecting the man's independent streak, but also provided an opportunity to suggest that, in contrast to other Pharisaic students, Saul learned the ways of life not from legal theory but by contact with reality, with the poor and oppressed of first-century Palestinian society. In contrast to the yeshiva students, then, 'The young man Saul knew the meaning of life.'[10]

Paul's early life outside Palestine, about which we know so little, is often regarded with considerable suspicion by his commentators. After all, if the traditional negative image of Paul is correct, one might expect to find the roots of his heresy or spiritual corruption here. Asch, in contrast, appeared to approve of Saul's cosmopolitan upbringing. Born in Tarsus, Asia Minor, Saul was a Diaspora Jew whose exposure to Hellenistic thought and culture meant that 'two souls lived side by side in the heart of the young Saul, and they struggled for mastery, even as Jacob and Esau had struggled in the womb of their mother, Rebecca.'[11] The creative tension of one who has lived and breathed in different worlds appealed to the well-travelled Asch and formed the key to his understanding of the apostle's life. From early on, Saul is shown preoccupied with the Gentile Problem, puzzled as to why God had created both Jews and non-Jews; and from well before his conversion he is convinced that the messiah will restore the Kingdom of God throughout the earth, and not simply restore the Kingdom of Israel.[12] The apostle's interest in the wider world is thus again contrasted with the parochialism of Palestinian Jewry.

Saul's religious devotion soon brings him into conflict with the followers of a new sect, that of the followers of the executed messiah Jesus or Yeshua. Convinced that he had been chosen from before he was born to assist God in bringing about the coming of the messiah,[13] Saul is appalled by their claim that the messiah has been

---

[9] Asch, *The Apostle*, 17. 'Paul had never held – not even in his youth – a too high opinion of womenfolk.' Asch, *The Apostle*, 365.
[10] Asch, *The Apostle*, 84.
[11] Asch, *The Apostle*, 77.
[12] Asch, *The Apostle*, 40, 79.
[13] Asch, *The Apostle*, 80, 182.

and gone. He is instrumental in the death of the first Christian martyr, Stephen, and soon obtains the backing of the Sadducean priesthood to hunt down the heretics. Interestingly, Asch's portrayal of these unfortunate victims of Saul's attentions is one of unanimous saintliness, forgiveness, and love. No doubt this is partly for dramatic effect, highlighting the barbarism of the rabid rabbi. But there is no doubt that among Asch's early Messianists are Jews whose religiosity has become enriched and deepened by their mysterious acceptance of the reign of the dead Jewish messiah, Yeshua.[14] By the time of Saul's celebrated conversion experience on the road to Damascus, Asch has worked Paul into a demented lather, angry and confused by the heresy of so many gentle, pious (Hellenistic and Palestinian) Jews, and unsure whether his actions are truly in keeping with God's will. Ostracised by his Pharisaic teachers and fellow students, who regard the death of Stephen as a murder, an execution without due process,[15] he is haunted by a dream of a fallen angel who transforms into the martyr.[16] The sense of profound guilt that Saul feels for the killing of Stephen, his exhausting persecution of the Jewish Messianists, a propensity to ecstatic visions and fits, and the stormy weather all conspire to bring him to his knees, shaken to the ground by the voice of Yeshua, who introduces himself as the one 'whom thou persecutest.'[17]

For Asch, then, it is ultimately Saul's overwhelming sense of guilt that is the catalyst that changes the direction of his life, but it is noteworthy that this guilt has nothing to do with a failure to observe the Law.[18] In contrast to the traditional Lutheran image of a Pharisaic Jew wracked by guilt at his failure to observe the Law, Saul is portrayed throughout the book as a strict observer of *halakhah* – so much so that he was unable to comprehend the teaching of his master Gamaliel who suggested that the human, not the laws and commandments, was the chief thing.[19] Having rejected the idea that Paul had a problem with the Law to begin with, Asch also ignores the common belief that Paul was obsessed by sin.[20] He focuses instead upon Paul's early interest in the Gentile Problem. It is the apostle's concern for the non-Jew, the result of his Diaspora background, which throws most light upon his conversion and subsequent teachings.

---

[14] Asch, *The Apostle*, 53.

[15] Asch, *The Apostle*, 125.

[16] Asch, *The Apostle*, 156.

[17] Asch, *The Apostle*, 186. Asch is citing Acts 9:5, 'And I said, "Who are You, Lord?" And the Lord said, "I am Jesus whom you are persecuting."'

[18] Asch maintains throughout the book that Paul's sense of guilt for his part in the death of Stephen never left him, and that he even believed that this was the cause for the Jewish rejection of his message. Asch, *The Apostle*, 179, 390. He changes his name to Paul partly to distance himself from his crime. Asch, *The Apostle*, 300.

[19] Asch's Gamaliel observes, 'But not the laws and commandments are the chief thing; we are the chief thing. The laws and commandments were created for us, not we for them.' Asch, *The Apostle*, 96.

[20] There are only two discussions of sin, in the first of which Paul observes, 'Sin is heritage, a part of the blood. Every drop flowing in my vein is heavy with sin, which I inherited with the blood of the first man, who was Adam.' Asch, *The Apostle*, 477–8, 517.

For example, Asch implies that Paul's complex view of the messiah came about as a result of Paul's sensitivity to the needs of the Gentiles. As a result of self-induced starvation, heat exhaustion, and other ascetic and mystical exercises, Paul comes to believe that his long-awaited unknowable, unimaginable messiah, who was in the heavens before the world was created, is one and the same as the man Yeshua. This emanation of God's highest will – higher than Wisdom, the daughter of heaven – can be described as the Son of God, because he alone brings true redemption to the world and offers unification with God. Thus Yeshua, or Jesus, is the Son of God, who links heaven and earth as had the ladder in Jacob's dream. For Paul, 'The ladder was Yeshua the Nazarene . . . [and] upon this ladder we mount to Heaven.'[21] Crucially, then, Paul is the author of the idea that Jesus was more than King Messiah, that he was the Son of God, a universal might, a radiation of the divinity, come to reconcile the entire world to God.[22] As Asch puts it, 'Paul began to weave a new robe for the Messiah',[23] and he suggests that such teachings provoked hostility from the Jewish disciples even as they attracted the Gentiles.[24]

Similarly, Asch spends considerable time describing the idolatry and debauched worship of the ancient Roman empire, and presents the apostle favourably as a champion engaged in a one-man Jewish war against the pagan gods.[25] Paul does not unreservedly condemn the Gentiles, however, but is drawn to what is described as 'the Gentile world at its best', that is, the Greek-thinking world's ceaseless aspiration for truth. Asch's apostle is deeply moved, for example, by the story of Oedipus Rex,[26] which is interpreted as a metaphor for the Gentile search for truth no matter what the cost.[27] It is as though Asch himself is keen to justify Paul's concern and interest in the non-Jewish world.

As the story progresses, Paul's own missionary endeavours soon convince him that the Gentiles can be brought to God through faith in the Messiah and without recourse to the Law. He finds a ready audience in the Gentile god-fearers who attend synagogue and who are relieved to hear that the heavy burden of the Jewish Law is not necessary in order to share in the promise of the messiah of Israel.[28] As a

---

[21] Asch, *The Apostle*, 187–9.

[22] Asch, *The Apostle*, 203, 194.

[23] Asch, *The Apostle*, 606. Later, after the powerful testimony of the execution of James, or Reb Jacob ben Joseph, Paul goes even further, believing that even physical death has been conquered by the messiah, the logic being (1) that the messiah comes to bring unification and reconciliation with God; (2) that this unification is achieved through faith, when the believer becomes one with the messiah, who is himself part of the divinity ('being in Christ'); (3) that those 'in Christ' share in the reality of the messiah Yeshua's own bodily resurrection. Thus, unified with God's messiah, one shares in his dominion over even physical death. Ibid., 636.

[24] Asch, *The Apostle*, 203, 455–60.

[25] Asch, *The Apostle*, 282–7.

[26] According to Greek legend, an oracle foretold that Oedipus would one day kill his father and marry his mother. Neither his knowledge of this prophecy nor his best efforts to prevent its fulfilment allowed him to avoid this fate, and in his despair this mythical king of Thebes blinded himself.

[27] Asch, *The Apostle*, 402, 601.

[28] Asch, *The Apostle*, 364.

means by which to explore and illustrate Gentiles' needs, Asch spends considerable time describing the relationship between Paul and his Gentile disciple Titus. In a very interesting episode, Titus is brought by Paul to Jerusalem as a proof of what the gospel could achieve among the pagans. A reflective Titus visits the Temple, which he finds 'indescribably impressive', although the Jews' profound religious earnestness and their strict observance of all the minutiae of the laws leave him cold. He is aware that he cannot be 'admitted to this Temple or this God' and is immensely grateful to Paul for having taught him of an alternative to both the distant Jewish Law and his old abandoned gods and temples.[29] The happiest day in Paul's life, according to Asch, is the day he convinces the Jerusalem Council of believers that the Gentiles need not obey the Jewish religious laws in their entirety.[30] With this achievement, however, Asch makes it clear that Paul becomes responsible for the schism that would lead to a Gentile Church, for there are many Jewish Messianists inhabiting the pages of the book who are horrified by the apostle's conception of the messiah and who disagree with his abrogation of the Law for the Gentiles.[31] Asch has them attack Paul as 'the traitor of Israel' and 'he who would tear out the Torah by its roots.'[32] And Jews, too, anxious about the controversies he stirred up in the Diaspora communities, condemn him for having 'sold the election of Israel to the Gentiles.'[33] From his presentation it would seem that Asch did not agree with such views, but rather empathised with Paul's universalistic yearnings.

One remarkable feature of Asch's account is that although Paul preaches to Jews that 'the Messiah has abrogated the little law that stands between them and the world,'[34] and presses for a lightening of the Law for the Gentiles, Asch concludes that the apostle had never separated himself from his own people[35] and that 'Paul had remained in his inner structure the complete Jew.'[36] Paul is presented throughout as a strict adherent of the Torah,[37] carrying scrolls of the Prophets wherever he

---

[29] Asch, *The Apostle*, 333.

[30] Paul achieved this victory in part by pointing out how difficult it would be to 'keep watch and ward over all the transgressions and to report in every [Gentile] place all the fences which the Rabbis have drawn about our lives'. Ibid., 340ff.

[31] Asch, *The Apostle*, 455.

[32] Asch, *The Apostle*, 460.

[33] Asch, *The Apostle*, 545.

[34] Asch, *The Apostle*, 389.

[35] Asch, *The Apostle*, 422.

[36] Asch, *The Apostle*, 537.

[37] Asch observes of the postconversion Paul, 'His personal attitude in matters concerning the Jewish ritual was so correct that even the strictest Pharisees of the Jewish community in Antioch could find no fault with him. He preached the lightening of the discipline for the Gentiles, but he himself gave full obedience to the Law. He was scrupulous in the observation of the laws and kosher and non-kosher food; the Sabbath he regarded as sanctity....' And 'Although Paul preached to the Gentiles that there was no need for them to obey the law of Moses, he was in his own life a strictly obedient Jew, submitting to the commandments as though the Torah had been given to him direct at Sinai, for his own use but not for the use of others....' In discussion with a Jewish-Christian

travels[38] and maintaining the laws of kashrut and Sabbath observance.[39] He derives his ethical teachings from the body of Jewish Law that he had studied under Gamaliel in Jerusalem,[40] often demanding even stricter discipline of his followers than that required by the rabbis.[41] And in discussing the meaning of the messiah for the Jewish people, Paul denies that he had ever preached that Jews should cease from circumcision, rather urging them to continue this practice.[42] Ultimately, he reasons that the coming of the messiah does not end the Law so much as fulfil it,[43] for the messiah was the personification of the Torah, being the equivalent expression of God's will.[44] And there is no doubt in the author's mind that the last words of the Apostle to the Gentiles were those of the Shema.[45]

For Asch, Paul was 'granite between the millstones' of the Jewish and Gentile Christian communities.[46] He never fully reconciled himself with the Jewish messianists and yet never abandoned the observance of the Law himself.[47] As a result, he was something of an irritant to both camps. At the same time, the tone of the treatment suggests that Asch greatly admired Paul's independence of mind, his interest in and dedication to the non-Jewish world, and his sincere Jewish faith and dedication to Jewish morality.

The Apostle was never published in its original Yiddish. Written during the war at a time when the Jewish people suffered tremendous persecution, its timing meant that few in the Jewish community were prepared to tolerate Asch's empathetic treatment of the founder of Christianity. Amongst the many and varied criticisms he incurred was a book-length polemic, published in 1953, in which Asch

---

Paul exclaims, 'As to the Torah, the Laws and commandments, am I not an observant Jew, even as you are? Do I not observe the laws and commandments?' and then performs a ritual at the Temple to demonstrate the truth of his claim. Asch, *The Apostle*, 293, 448, 536.

[38] Asch, *The Apostle*, 416.

[39] Asch, *The Apostle*, 293. At certain times, Asch suggests that Paul probably 'relaxed his orthodoxy' in order to sit at the same table as his Gentile followers, but he would not have partaken of unclean food. Ibid., 271.

[40] Asch, *The Apostle*, 609.

[41] Asch, *The Apostle*, 426.

[42] After a controversy with some Jewish disciples, and in response to those who feared that he was building up a barrier between himself and his flesh and blood, the Jews, Paul remarks: 'God forbid!... Have I ever preached, God forbid, that the Jews shall cease from circumcision?... I say, those that are circumcised, let them remain circumcised. But if the external circumcision of the body become the only gate through which there is entry into the Kingdom of Heaven... then I say all our labour is in vain; for if justification is only through the Torah, then the messiah died in vain.' Asch, *The Apostle*, 466. In the context, 'circumcision' appears to refers to the Law as a whole.

[43] Asch, *The Apostle*, 389. On occasion, Paul appears to waver with regard to the Torah's relevance for the Jews; for example, in the writing of Romans he claims that they, along with the Gentiles, should abandon it. Ibid., 517–19.

[44] Asch, *The Apostle*, 346.

[45] Asch, *The Apostle*, 750.

[46] Asch, *The Apostle*, 530.

[47] As Asch put it, 'Deep and bitter was the inner struggle of the apostle. It was as if he were tearing at his own flesh.... Faithfulness to the Gentiles, passion of the Messiah, love of his own people – these were at war in him.' Asch, *The Apostle*, 521.

is described as having 'carried on in the course of years a missionary activity on a scope never before known among Jews' and in which his treatment of Paul is castigated as a betrayal of Judaism.[48] He was horrified by the frequent charge that he was a Christian apologist and denied it adamantly.[49] His interest in Jesus and Paul, who he insisted had been misunderstood as enemies of the Jewish people, had, he said, been entirely honourable.[50] Rather than bringing Jews to conversion, he sought to persuade Christians to see them as *Jewish* heroes. The short epilogue to the book, whose form emulates the traditional prayer of thanks that customarily finished a Jewish work of scholarship, indicates how he felt about it and at what cost he wrote it.

I thank thee and praise thee, Lord of the world, that thou has given me the strength to withstand all temptations and overcome all obstacles, those of my own making and those made by others, and to complete the two works 'The Nazarene' and 'The Apostle', which are one work; *so that I might set forth in them the merit of Israel, whom thou elected to bring the light of the nations of the world*, for thy glory and out of thy love of mankind.[51] [Italics added]

And yet, reading *The Apostle* alongside his autobiographical *My Personal Belief* (1942),[52] one can easily understand how it was that the work received an almost unanimously censorious reception from his Jewish contemporaries. For in this attempt to demonstrate to a non-Jewish audience how a sense of a shared Judeo-Christian heritage could overcome the heritage of 'blood and fire', Asch frequently appeared to deny any significant difference between Christianity and Judaism. He spoke of 'the Jewish–Christian spirit',[53] and he argued that the two faiths 'are founded on the same principle and derive from one source, which is God.'[54] He maintained that he was not interested in writing an apologia for his own Jewish faith,[55] but rather in exploring the possibility that North America offered for the

---

[48] Chaim Lieberman, *The Christianity of Sholem Asch*, 1, 139. Lieberman, a member of the editorial board of the Yiddish daily *The Forward*, whose book was published in Yiddish, English, and Hebrew, devotes a chapter to the analysis of *The Apostle*. To describe this 276-page work as a vitriolic character assassination would be a gross understatement.

[49] 'It is absolutely false that I preach Christianity to the Jews. Some ascribe to me things that are alien to me. I do not preach Christianity.' Sholem Asch, 'The Guilty Ones', in *Atlantic Monthly* (December 1940), cited in C. A. Madison, *Yiddish Literature* (1968), 255. Madison preferred to write of Asch's 'continued belief that the salvation of mankind lies in the recognition of the Judeo-Christian concord.' Ibid., 260.

[50] In fairness to Asch's detractors, Asch's portrayal of Jesus, or Yeshua, is idiosyncratic, even by his standards. His view of Yeshua seems to shift over time from that of a Jewish leader, a rabbi, and a prophet in *The Nazarene* (1939) to become the Son of God – not of Joseph – and a miracle-working preacher of a new religion who rises from the dead in *Mary* (1949).

[51] Asch, *The Apostle*, 752.

[52] Sholem Asch, *My Personal Faith*, trans. Maurice Samuel (London: G. Routledge, 1942).

[53] Asch, *My Personal Faith*, 156.

[54] Asch, *My Personal Faith*, 181.

[55] Asch, *My Personal Faith*, 101.

recognition of equality in the God of Jews and Christians.[56] Consequently, he called for an end to the destructive theological segregation that existed between the two communities.

> There must be a levelling of the barriers which separate faith from faith – for we are all children of one community . . . because the blood that flows in our veins is the flood of faith, everywhere the same, and everywhere fed by the same roots. . . . It is my deepest belief that just as I have a share in the God of Israel through my faith in him, that I stand under his authority and am included in the promise of redemption, so my Christian brother has his equal share in the God of Israel, stands equally in the promise of redemption. For he is a son of Israel equally with me. His faith has made him a son of Abraham, Isaac and Jacob. My rights are his, and I have a share in his religious values as he has a share in mine.[57]

It is reasonable to regard Asch's study of Paul as an integral component of an ambitious programme to promote a shared Judeo-Christian tradition,[58] to the extent that, as one commentator put it, Asch 'may have seen himself as fulfilling Paul's legacy in our own times, as one bridging Judaism and Christianity in his own person'.[59] That works such as *The Apostle* provoked suspicion of his loyalties was a price that Asch deeply resented but one that he was prepared to pay in order to promote his greater vision of religious harmony. An entirely different approach to understanding Paul, but which also aimed at improving Jewish–Christian relations, was articulated in another work of historical fiction, written by a well-known North American Jewish New Testament scholar.

SAMUEL SANDMEL AND THE RELIGIOUS GENIUS OF THE APOSTLE

Samuel Sandmel's novel *The Apostle Paul* (undated)[60] was the more intellectually rigorous of the two literary endeavours and drew heavily upon his professional expertise in the world of first-century Judaism. For this reason it is worth briefly pointing out a few themes that characterise his historical study *The Genius of Paul* (1958) before examining the novel itself. Here, Sandmel emphasised the apostle's

---

[56] Asch, *My Personal Faith*, 196, 201.

[57] Asch, *My Personal Faith*, 192, 196.

[58] Norich argues that, in the case of Asch, the phrase 'Judeo-Christian tradition' has a particularly North American ideological resonance which erases the distinctions between equality and similarity: 'The assertion that we are all equal comes to rely on a prior claim that we are all alike.' Anita Norich, 'Sholem Asch and the Christian Question', 252–3.

[59] Keziah Alon, 'Christians, Jews and Others: A Study in the Literary Heritage of Sholem Ach and Avraham Aharon Kabak', *Theory and Criticism* 26 (Spring 2005), 193. Alon argues that Asch felt a religious obligation to write the novel, justified it in later commentaries, hoped that it would achieve social transformation, and identified with its subject, Paul. As a result, she concluded that *The Apostle* was better described as a theological novel than as an historical novel. Ibid., 198.

[60] Samuel Sandmel, *The Apostle Paul: A Novel* (unpublished, undated), 472pp, in Samuel Sandmel Papers, Manuscript Collection No. 101, Series C/1/17.7 and 18.1 at the American Jewish Archives, Cincinnati, U.S.A.

theological creativity as an individual at the same time as locating him firmly in the world of Hellenistic Judaism, which he was careful to present as different but not inferior to Palestinian Judaism. His study was a Liberal Jewish contribution to the wider intra-Jewish debate about what constitutes authentic Judaism. As was argued earlier, an important subtext was the presentation of a *marginalised* Jew as a *legitimate* Jew, thereby undermining Orthodox claims to determine what actually constituted authenticity. Although he accounted for Paul's abrogation of the Law in terms of Paul's personal guilt at failing to observe the Law (and not as an opportunistic strategy to win over Gentiles), he was also interested in stressing the continuity of Paul's message with those of previous 'prophets' who had similarly criticised those who prioritised external activities (for example, ritual and written codes) over internal ones (for example, communion with God).[61] At the same time, as he wrote elsewhere, Sandmel was also concerned to prevent Jewish assimilation and believed that the best method to prevent it was to offer a modern Jewish critique of Christianity's origins, stressing the differences.[62] The attractions and the fears of the Christian Other could be assuaged by familiarising the Jew with its founding figures, such as Paul. These and other progressive Jewish themes reappear in the novel, which is first and foremost a novel of ideas.

Sandmel attempted to write *The Apostle Paul: A Novel*[63] without constant allusion to the centuries of hostility between Judaism and Christianity that would follow. Rather than concentrate on history-in-the-making, he drew the reader close into Paul's private world, focusing on the minutiae of everyday life in the first century and offering glimpses into the personal events that would profoundly shape Paul's thought. Werfel and Asch had regarded Paul's personality as central to understanding the parting of the ways, but Sandmel's aim was to go even further and to offer a pseudo-Freudian analysis that sought to explain why Paul was the way he was by extensive reference to his childhood, his relationship to his parents, his sexual experiences, and his internal struggle with forces that lay below his conscious life. In this novel we see a historian allowing his imagination to run free in order to solve a series of academic problems relating to understanding Paul the man. The apostle is taken seriously as a person, with specific psychological problems and gifts. He is a passionate thinker, a creative genius, and a paranoid, whose world is one of competing worldviews and confrontation with ideological opponents.

Sandmel begins the story with Paul's childhood in Tarsus, where he and his pious mother live out a fretful, meagre existence within the small Jewish merchant

---

[61] Samuel Sandmel, *The Genius of Paul*, 75–8.
[62] Sandmel, *We Jews and Jesus*, ix.
[63] Although the date of writing cannot be established with any certainty – there is no firm internal evidence one way or the other – it seems likely that the novel was written after *The Genius of Paul* (1958), because it appears to expand on a number of ideas found in the scholarly work and to add many new hypotheses, as will be discussed below.

community, Paul's father having disappeared years before on a trading adventure.[64] The author offers a colourful tapestry of first-century Diaspora life, a vibrant, sexually charged, hunger-ridden world where Jew and Gentile mix freely both socially and intellectually. The first part of the book (entitled 'The Boy') includes several invented episodes in Paul's early life that will have a powerful impact in shaping his outlook on life. First, the sensitive, lonely adolescent is drawn into sexual experimentation with pagan girls and women, experiences which he both enjoys and is troubled by, for he knows that such pleasurable liaisons are prohibited by the Law.[65] Along with this, his hunger – and his tendency to experiment – leads him in a moment of weakness to eat non-kosher meat, for which, again, he suffers guilty pangs of conscience.[66] Second, his independent and inquisitive mind makes him unpopular with the teachers of Torah at the local synagogue, who interpret his precocious questions as challenges to their authority. Happily, the fatherless boy becomes friendly with one of them, an elderly scholar who sees a future rabbi in the young troublemaker and takes him under his wing. This teacher, Menelaus, has a penchant for Gentile thought, however, which he is convinced can be reconciled with Jewish scriptural tradition through allegorical interpretation.[67] Paul's private studies of Plato and other Greek thinkers, which Sandmel explores in considerable depth, are soon interrupted by the death of the old man,[68] but not before he has been introduced to a Gentile philosopher called Proprius whose critique of

---

[64] Sandmel did not subscribe to the idea that Paul was a Roman citizen. Even when he has Paul later demand a trial before his imprisonment, no mention is made of it. Sandmel, *The Apostle Paul: A Novel*, 285.

[65] There is a distinctly Freudian flavour to these episodes. Afterwards, Paul immediately starts to think about death and, on one occasion, becomes confused as to 'whose body had served him', that of a local prostitute or that of his mother. Sandmel, *The Apostle Paul: A Novel*, 73, 105, 113.

[66] 'Then Paul became aware that he needed desperately to eat a piece of the Gentile bread and a piece of the meat, even if it were pork. . . . He was aware of no taste, but only that the forbidden food was in his mouth. He chewed it and managed to swallow it. He walked home slowly, wondering if God or an angel would suddenly block his way. . . . ' Sandmel, *The Apostle Paul: A Novel*, 47–8.

[67] As Menelaus explains by way of example, 'In the simple stories – of Adam and Eve in the garden – there is a hidden profundity which escapes the ordinary Jew. . . . I learned in Alexandria that Adam is Scripture's way of speaking about the mind: what the mind is and how it works. Eve is the senses, through which the mind receives perceptions. And the serpent is pleasure, to which the mind and the senses sometimes succumb, and thereby lose virtue, which is the Garden of Eden.' Sandmel, *The Apostle Paul: A Novel*, 80–81.

[68] Amongst other things, they discuss the application of Greek wisdom to the biblical interpretation of Abraham's call. Having argued that it is wrong to anthropomorphise God, and that God cannot be perceived with the senses because they are prone to error, it is suggested that only the mind, when trained to be free from such error, can apprehend God. Paul demonstrates his understanding by applying this Platonic idea to the Bible: 'Then when God spoke to Abraham, Abraham did not hear a voice like ours which the ears can harken to. Instead, his mind – can you say heard? – his mind heard God'. In answering Paul as to what exactly entered the mind of Abraham, Menelaus suggests that 'Not God himself, but something from him. Perhaps what we call the holy spirit.' Emphasising a symbolic reading, Menelaus explains that Abraham left Ur because the Chaldeans were astronomers, dependent on their fallible senses for their wisdom, and so Abraham moved to Charran where he could cultivate his mind. Sandmel, *The Apostle Paul: A Novel*, 110–11.

Judaism plants in his mind a connection between the Law and evil.[69] Inevitably, such experiences, taken together with his friendships with pagan neighbours, result in Paul's concern for the Gentile Problem, that is, the question of the fate of non-Jews. Third, Paul's mother commits suicide in her despair at the refusal of the rabbinic establishment to issue her a divorce from her missing husband, in order to allow her to remarry a new suitor.[70] Paul's interpretation of the cause of his mother's death, having received the news that no divorce could be granted, was damning: 'Why had she killed herself? It was a judgement of men, not of God. Law was evil. Even the law of Moses. Especially the law of Moses.'[71] In these incidents, Sandmel suggests, we see the origins of Paul's dissatisfaction with the Law, which, in his partial knowledge, appeared to him at odds with common sense and human necessity, and which brought considerable guilt and suffering in its wake.

His education incomplete, but with nothing more to keep him in Tarsus, Paul sets off in the second part of the book (entitled 'The Conversion') to discover the wider world. Over many years of travel, Paul finds himself torn in two directions. On the one hand, he experiences a growing sense of alienation from the Jewish community and increasingly eschews it.[72] On the other, he is drawn to an obsessive study of Torah. Eventually Paul settles in Antioch where, despite the limits of his education, he gains a reputation in the worldly wise Diaspora Jewish community as a solitary holy man and scholar. He finds a patron in the invented figure of Theophrastus, a synagogue leader who is concerned to improve Jewish–Gentile relations for political reasons.[73] Persuaded to use his rhetorical skills with local Gentile leaders

---

[69] As Proprius explains, 'The rulers of the world use laws to sustain their rule. . . . If I spoke [using superstitious language] I would say that laws exist through the sway over this world of demons. Laws surely do not come from the good, or the wise – not laws as they exist. No, laws come from the forces of wickedness. . . . You speak of Moses your law-giver; you delude yourselves that your laws do not come from demons, as I assure you they do.' Sandmel, *The Apostle Paul: A Novel*, 117–19, 130.

[70] The legal case is worked out in some detail. After rejecting the idea of appointing an agent for the missing father who might produce a writ of divorce on his behalf (because this action would be taken after the event and would invariably be regarded as a legal fiction), the petitioners from the Tarsus synagogue instead construct an argument premised on the idea that the intent of Deuteronomy was to protect the wife from a husband's negligence. Sandmel, *The Apostle Paul: A Novel*, 123–4.

[71] Sandmel, *The Apostle Paul: A Novel*, 161–2, 132–6.

[72] During this period of self-exile, Paul avoids Jewish markets and synagogues. 'The Jews seemed to him too willing, too eager to embrace him as one of their own, but he could not in honesty respond to these overtures, for he himself did not feel that he was one of them. He had only implied that he was a Jew; he had not said so explicitly. No, he was not one of them. Not at all.' Partly this was due to his theological beliefs. 'Jews seemed to lack the understanding that was so clear to him that the high point in the ancient past was the age of Abraham, Isaac, and Jacob. The age of Moses was a sharp descent. A descent and an aberration. Why could his fellow Jews not see that? His fellow Jews! Were they indeed his fellow Jews? Had he not severed relations? Had he not said several times that he was once a Jew but no longer one?' Sandmel, *The Apostle Paul: A Novel*, 163b, 213.

[73] As Theophrastus explains, 'We Jews do not explain ourselves to the Greeks, to the people who matter. We need to do this. But we do not have anyone here in Antioch able to do so.' Following the Alexandrian pogrom in 38 C.E., Theophrastus confides to Paul, 'As soon as I heard of this, I felt it urgent to tell you. Now I see all the more clearer how important your work has been.' Sandmel, *The Apostle Paul: A Novel*, 211, 227.

in after-dinner conversations in order to convince them of the beauty of Judaism, he is also asked to propound his knowledge of Torah from the synagogue pulpit to convince Jews of God's universal love for all mankind.[74] Although some among the Jewish community are suspicious of Paul, there are those such as Theophrastus who are prepared to overlook his theological eccentricities (such as his disinterest in *halakhah*) in favour of an effective programme of Gentile proselytisation which will act as a buffer against future pogroms.[75] The few Christians whom Paul does meet at this time offer an initially interesting account of the arrival of a Galilean messiah and the impending Day of Judgement, but he is quickly repelled by their poor Jewish learning in general and by their limited conception of a Christ who is unconcerned for the Gentile world in particular.[76] Less sensitive than others to the potential political danger of their messianic claims, Paul nevertheless publicly condemns their ideas and thereby legitimates their violent treatment at the hands of the synagogue authorities.[77]

In this preconversion period, Sandmel has several interesting hypotheses to offer. He deliberately limits Paul's expertise to allegorical readings of the two scrolls he possesses, namely Genesis and Exodus, and a few of the prophetic writings, maintaining that he had only basic knowledge of other books and no interest whatsoever in the emerging Pharisaic body of *halakhah* or legal teachings. Sandmel also has Paul develop some key ideas that would later characterise Pauline Christian teaching, including the conviction that he was the 'prophet to the Gentiles' spoken of in Jeremiah,[78] that circumcision should not be required for conversion

---

[74] During Paul's sermon at the synagogue in Antioch 'a wondrous fluency came to him' as he spoke on Abraham. 'He spoke of Abraham's righteousness, the result of Abraham's faith' and argued that his promised descendents could not mean only the Jews. 'Perhaps it was God's will that the Gentiles should be converted, and enter into the Jewish people, and thereby the descendents of Abraham would be beyond counting.' He directly addressed the fears of the Diaspora community, asking, 'Should the Jews of Antioch lose their children to the pagans? Or, rather, should the Jews of Antioch bring the pagans into Judaism and raise them to the heights which Jews alone had attained to?' Sandmel, *The Apostle Paul: A Novel*, 199–201.

[75] Theophrastus continues his support for Paul, even when he has become a Christian, claiming 'I want all the Gentiles to become Jews. Even if they become Jews like you....' Sandmel, *The Apostle Paul: A Novel*, 379.

[76] His speculative explanations as to the angelic nature of Jesus, the *mashiah* or 'anointed one' who John Mark and Andreas claim was resurrected, are met with incomprehension. Sandmel, *The Apostle Paul: A Novel*, 233–5.

[77] In the manuscript held at the American Jewish Archives, the pages dealing with the confrontation (236–40) are missing. However, Paul later refers his dealings with John Mark and Andreas, 'I knew them. I quarrelled with them. Neither is a learned man, and neither is bright. They did not persuade, they only antagonised. I was not friendly to them. In fact, I too stirred up our people against them. I came to regret that. But their ways compelled me to oppose them'. Sandmel, *The Apostle Paul: A Novel*, 315.

[78] Paul reads Jer. 1:5 ('Before I formed you in the womb, I knew you, and before you came from the belly, I consecrated you, I made you a prophet to the Gentiles') and ponders, 'What did "a prophet to the Gentiles" mean? Surely only a small portion of Jeremiah was concerned with Gentile nations; overwhelmingly it was about Judeans and their trespasses, and God's punishment of them. Then why was Jeremiah designated a prophet to the Gentiles? Could it possibly be that he, Paul, had

to Judaism,[79] and that the Law had been authored by wicked angels rather than by God himself.[80] Perhaps the most surprising innovation from this period was Paul's belief in the necessity of the idea of God descending to earth as a man. Some days after a discussion with a Gentile who had contrasted the Jewish God's otherworldly transcendence with the frequent visitations of Olympian Zeus,

Paul found himself reverting to the question, why had God not come to earth in the form of a man? Was there not a certain force in the contention . . . that a God who is pure in spirit is above the understanding of most men? Would not Gentiles be the more able to grasp the central belief in Judaism if only on some occasion in the past God had come to earth in the form of a man? Not in a manner as unseemly as Zeus! Not at all! . . . Not that it was impossible for God to come to earth as a man. Nothing, nothing at all was impossible for God. If the angels who came to Abraham could come as men, surely God himself could do so. No, it was not impossible. Yet God was so majestic, so elevated that he would possibly lose his unique goodness were he, even for a brief span, to become man. No, God could not do this. But was there not in heaven, higher than the angels, the spirit of God, the unique mind of God? . . . If it were too much to

been led to wander from the synagogue, from his fellow Jews, in order that he too might become a prophet to the Gentiles? . . . Scripture, he was certain, must mean more than a record of the past. Scripture, ancient though it was, was speaking of the present, of Paul's time.' Sandmel, *The Apostle Paul: A Novel*, 190–91.

[79] In reflecting on how a young God-fearing Gentile called Baalmalka could not join the synagogue without formal conversion, Paul became indignant. 'How unfair for a man like Baalmalka to be faced with the pain of circumcision as a requirement for becoming part of the synagogue. True, God had commanded circumcision, enjoining it on Abraham and his descendents. But God, through Jeremiah, had taught too that it was the impure heart that required circumcision, not the foreskin. Of course, circumcision was a symbol, a symbol of purity. . . . He Paul, would never, were he still in Judaism, demand literal circumcision of a Baalmalka. Or of any grown man. Surely many men would have come into Judaism, as many women did, were the requirement of literal circumcision abolished. Indeed, Father Abraham had first come to righteousness and only thereafter had he come to circumcision; clearly circumcision could not be a requirement for attaining righteousness.' Sandmel, *The Apostle Paul: A Novel*, 194. Sandmel suggests that this was not an unreasonable view: he has the synagogue leader in Antioch, Theophrastus, join with Paul in seeking to release Paul from the burden of circumcision, albeit for political rather than theological reasons. Ibid., 329.

[80] Drawing together rabbinic traditions he remembers from his schooldays, the Hellenistic-Jewish obsession with Spirit, and close readings of Torah scrolls, Paul rationalises the link between the Law and evil. 'Moreover, there was missing from this account about Moses any mention of the Spirit, the breath of God. . . . Surely the Spirit, which God could choose to pour onto whatever mortal He wished, must have hovered about Him, just as it had hovered above the waters at the time of creation. Strange that the passage [of the giving of the Law] made no mention of the Spirit. . . . It was strange . . . to recall the vivid [rabbinic] accounts about the angels who had attended the great moment at Sinai and yet to find no mention of them at all in the biblical passage. . . . It seemed inevitable that the heavenly hosts must have been present. Perhaps it was they, and not God Himself, who had disclosed the Law to Moses. . . . And, as the angels were intermediaries between God and man, so the man Moses was an intermediary between the angels and the Hebrews. But were there not wicked angels as well as good ones? The generation of Noah – had it not been spawned by the wicked angels who had come to earth and been allured by the beauty of human women, and, as a consequence of succumbing to abominable lust, had filled the earth with horrendous corruption? Surely it was the wicked angels who had transmitted the laws to Moses. That must be the case, for the laws were created because men were evil, because sin had entered into man; had man not been sinners, laws would have been unnecessary.' Sandmel, *The Apostle Paul: A Novel*, 184b–186.

expect God himself to come to earth as a man, surely God might some day let his spirit come to earth and take on flesh! If only that could happen![81]

Sandmel delights in long excursions into Paul's theological deliberations, which are portrayed sympathetically as intense bursts of thought that amalgamate brilliantly various strands of tradition and legend that Paul has been exposed to in his wanderings. The idea of God taking on flesh, for example, is not presented simply as the result of exposure to classical myths, but rather as the innovative conclusion of one who is passionate about the need to draw the Gentiles to the God of Abraham, who has been profoundly influenced by Greek conceptions of the mind and spirit, and whose allegorical reading of Torah and past experiences of institutional Judaism have freed him from traditional theological constraints.

It is clear that in his dealings with Jews and Gentiles Paul remains his own man, finding his own idiosyncratic way with his own intellectual resources. It is only at the end of Part Two of the book that he comes to embrace Christianity, and, even then, he does this very much on his own terms. While in Damascus, this highly introspective lapsed Jew becomes haunted by the story he has heard from the Christians about a worthy Galilean who had been crucified by the Romans, a Galilean whom some now regarded as the messiah. Recurrent nightmares of the cruel death of this stranger become intertwined with the death of others, including his own mother and characters from the Torah. One dark and gloomy morning, after another tormented night obsessing about death, Paul finds himself reading the account of the Burning Bush. In the blinding vision of the risen Jesus that suddenly follows, he hears the words, 'I have chosen you, Paul. Chosen you to speak of me to the Gentiles, to prepare them for my return. I choose you above all men.'[82] As Sandmel portrays it, this breakthrough assuages Paul's existential concerns (about his life's purpose and his fear of death) and, at the same moment, resolves for Paul both the Gentile Problem and the ancient paradox of a transcendental God who can commune with mankind – for the vision of Jesus is immediately interpreted by Paul as the spirit of God come down to earth to bring about universal salvation.[83] The section ends with Paul's meditation on the life of Abraham and his dawning sense of realisation that

The laws of Moses were unnecessary. They could not save a man, since they implied that a man could rely on himself. No, only faith in God, unreserved faith, could bring salvation. It was that salvation, that righteousness that Abraham had achieved. Abraham was the ancestor of the Jews; Abraham's was the true Judaism. The true Judaism had now been restored in the call of Paul. As God had bidden Abraham to leave his land and become a blessing to the Gentiles, so Paul would leave the erroneous Judaism of laws and synagogues and self-centred people and he too would become a blessing to the Gentiles.[84]

---

[81] Sandmel, *The Apostle Paul: A Novel*, 224–5.
[82] Sandmel, *The Apostle Paul: A Novel*, 244–5.
[83] Sandmel, *The Apostle Paul: A Novel*, 245.
[84] Sandmel, *The Apostle Paul: A Novel*, 247.

In the third part of the novel (entitled 'The Apostle'), Paul has to work out the profound implications of his conviction that he is God's chosen instrument for bringing about 'a covenant of all the peoples.' This is no easy task, however. Sandmel is keen to stress the apostle's fiery individualism and to show that his theological convictions came to him independent of existing Christian teaching. His antiauthoritarian personality leaves him in a precarious place within the early church and leads to troubled relationships with sympathetic synagogue leaders and powerful Gentile god-fearers alike. Partly to outline his message of 'the true Judaism' against those who would oppose him, and partly to help administer the small churches made up of a growing band of disciples, Paul begins to compose a systematic manual, which he draws upon in writing several of his letters.[85] At the same time, these letters demonstrate his reactive approach to the errors he sees in the pagan, Jewish, and Christian worlds around him. Sandmel works very hard to confound the reader's expectation that there was a straightforward ideological shift between Paul's preconversion and postconversion identities. Instead, the Jewish and Christian dimensions of his identity seem to ebb and flow with the social context and with his particular train of thought. As he weaves a radical new worldview, Paul appears to move effortlessly between the worlds of Torah study, Hellenistic philosophy, and primitive Christian dogma. Sandmel achieves this effect by having Paul constantly, but subtly, modify his ideas. His critique of the Law and Jewish tradition with which he was familiar neatly illustrates this.

Paul's Hellenistic Jewish childhood had taught him a certain respect for the sages' interpretation of the Law, which often considered the intent of the Law as well as the plain meaning.[86] Over time, he developed an ambiguous attitude towards it. On the one hand, he hated the Law for the part it had played in his

---

[85] In reaction to reports of chaos in the small churches he had founded and of dissent between his followers and those of Peter/Cephas, Paul is forced to action. 'Prepare a manual? Never! He would sooner revert to the laws of Moses, and that he would never do. Then, strangely, he remembered that Theophrastus [the synagogue leader in Antioch] had once broached to him the suggestion that he write some tract for the Gentiles, explaining Judaism to them. Why not a tract for the ecclesias, setting forth clearly the unique views that were his, so that his views could be preserved and known? He was sure that in a face-to-face debate he could best [Peter] Cephas, even though he was not as strong as once he was. But a debate could soon be forgotten, whereas a tract could be read, copied, reread, copied – a tract could live forever. Such a tract would be useful especially for the ecclesias that it seemed likely that he would never be able to visit.' In Sandmel's account, the main body of the text was based around the first draft of his letter to the Galatians, 'for it contained much of Paul's main teachings'. Later, in prison in Rome, Paul almost completed this systematic treatise, drawing upon it when writing letters to his churches at Philippi and Corinth. Sandmel, *The Apostle Paul: A Novel*, 420–21, 423, 445–6.

[86] When he was a boy, an uncle in Tarsus had explained that 'even in Judea there are those – they are called Pharisees – who have said that it is the intent in the Law, not the words themselves, which are important.' Sandmel, *The Apostle Paul: A Novel*, 66. His teacher, Menelaus, had argued, 'One must always ask about a passage, how have our sages understood it? Their understanding is better than ours, for it was arrived at in these [Pharisaic] debates, and it has become the holy understanding because holy men of the past have transmitted it to us', and had promptly quashed Paul's sceptical response, 'I have my own mind. I have my own understanding.' Ibid., 89.

mother's death. On the other hand, he was drawn to it and felt at times as though it had been written especially for him.[87] Before he converted, and while in the employ of Theophrastus, the leader of the synagogue in Antioch, he was able to hide the extent of his doubts about the Law from the community.[88] But on a trip to Jerusalem soon after his conversion, he became suspicious that the Pharisaic sages had twisted the plain meaning of the writings.[89] Back in Antioch, and in a discussion with Theophrastus, he argued that Jews *need* not observe circumcision, although they could if they so wished.[90] He was increasingly intolerant of the traditional place of honour given to Moses and became convinced that some of the synagogue readings were inappropriate for the followers of 'true Judaism', especially those which lauded the laws.[91] At first, in discussion with Peter/Cephas, Paul acquiesced with the Christian leader's application of the Noachide laws to Gentile converts, even though 'for Paul, the seven laws of Noah were as obsolete as the six hundred and thirteen laws of Moses.'[92] However, as his self-confidence grew, he preached a sermon that led to a divisive split with Torah-observant Jewish Christians from Jerusalem. He argued,

The laws that had come from Sinai were admirable . . . without equal among the Greeks and barbarians. But it needed to be understood that Sinai had become a symbol of slavery, for Jews had become enslaved to the laws, losing the freedom they should have had, the freedom which had marked Abraham. In their enslavement, Jews had become deluded into relying on the merit of their own works, rather than in freedom putting themselves into the arms of God. . . . It was the Christ alone who set men free, free of sin, free of guilt, free of mortality.[93]

When Peter, under the influence of the Judaisers from Jerusalem, stopped eating with Gentiles, Paul openly expressed his contempt for his 'outer reflection of inner dishonesty'. Paul was keen to differentiate his own attitude, reasoning, 'Hypo-crisy was different from conscious accommodation'. As he explained, 'Should the situation arise in which to win Jews for Christ Paul would need to give the impression of his full fidelity to the laws, that would not be hypocrisy. Indeed, to win

---

[87] 'Some passages he read and re-read, some he read and had to revert to for either he did not understand, or else he thought that he was being repelled; and unless a passage could speak to him in some congenial way, the feeling of repulse did not leave him. The more he read the more the feeling came over him that the sacred books were written primarily for him, primarily to teach him, Paul. The books were his own special possession, much more so than of the people he had been born into.' Sandmel, *The Apostle Paul: A Novel*, 190.

[88] In particular, Paul felt guilty that he had deceived his Jewish audience by saying nothing of his views on the laws, that 'Abraham had first achieved righteousness, and only thereafter had become circumcised.' Sandmel, *The Apostle Paul: A Novel*, 203, 213.

[89] Sandmel, *The Apostle Paul: A Novel*, 313.

[90] Sandmel, *The Apostle Paul: A Novel*, 321.

[91] Sandmel, *The Apostle Paul: A Novel*, 330.

[92] Sandmel, *The Apostle Paul: A Novel*, 342.

[93] Sandmel, *The Apostle Paul: A Novel*, 356.

people to Christ, he was fully prepared to be a Jew to Jews and a pagan to pagans.'[94] In a final discussion with Theophrastus towards the end of his life, he made his personal position clear: 'I do not believe that the Temple is of any consequence. The death of Jesus is greater than all the hundreds of animals sacrificed at the Temple.... Nor do we require the New Year or the Day of Atonement, for the Christ is our atonement ... [or] the food laws and circumcision.'[95] Throughout this theological development, Paul returns repeatedly to the story of Abraham, which had captivated him since his school days. The centrality of the patriarch's faith convinces him of the proper focus of Judaism and leads him to see how little of Jewish tradition is necessary for Gentiles to find their right place before God. As he explained,

Father Abraham lived before the laws arose through Moses. Because the Christ has come, we are in the situation again of Father Abraham. He was a man who achieved righteousness without observing the laws. We can also achieve righteousness without observing the laws.... [I]f you will search the holy writings, you will not find one word about Abraham's observing the laws of Moses.... [Abraham's] circumcision was a symbol of righteousness achieved, not a prior necessity for achieving it.[96]

The novel ends with Paul's reconciliation with Peter in Rome, before his violent death at the hands of robbers – an ending in which the narrator, pointing to the imponderable nature of history, suggests that it was by no means obvious that the apostle's work would live on beyond him.[97]

What was it that Sandmel hoped to achieve with a novel that he had not achieved with his historical study? The answer might have something to do with the freedom that fiction writing gives an author to tease out unsubstantiated hypotheses. It is one thing to suggest in a work of scholarship that, for example, Paul had incorporated Hellenistic philosophy or that he had harboured a bitter resentment of the Law from an early age. It is quite another thing to put flesh on these bones through the emotive power of storytelling, to paint a convincing picture of how an eccentric Torah teacher or a mother's suicide might account for such interests and attitudes.

---

[94] Sandmel, *The Apostle Paul: A Novel*, 358.
[95] Sandmel, *The Apostle Paul: A Novel*, 377.
[96] Sandmel, *The Apostle Paul: A Novel*, 377.
[97] The fourth and final part of the book (entitled 'The Memory') is an enchanting series of letters ostensibly written by Luke, the author of Acts, a work in which the apostle Paul plays a central role. Here Sandmel ties up a number of loose ends, such as the celebrated discrepancies between Paul's epistles and the account found in Acts. In between requests to his patron Theophilus ('beloved of God', addressed in Luke 1:3 and Acts 1:1) for further payments and complaints that his work is unappreciated, Luke freely admits to improving the story to better represent the orderly development of the Church. Thus Luke justifies his exaggerated use of Gamaliel as a means by which to authenticate the claim that Christianity was the true Judaism, his rewriting of the role of Peter as less antagonistic, his glossing over Paul's persecution of the believers, and his distancing of Paul from the doctrine of faith alone in order to portray Paul as a less divisive and more reconciliatory figure. Sandmel, *The Apostle Paul: A Novel*, 465–6, 469.

Also, as noted earlier, a key assertion in Sandmel's scholarly work had been the idea that Paul could be thought of as an authentic Jewish prophetic voice at a particular moment in history, that is, a prophet in the age of Law. This was a problematic assertion for a Jewish thinker to make in the light of the Pauline church's later oppression of Jews. But the novel, written as it is from the day-to-day perspective of the protagonist, allowed Sandmel to illustrate just how complex Paul's identity really had been. By showing how his sense of self developed over time and how different dimensions of his identity came to the fore in different social settings, Sandmel made impossible any simplistic judgement regarding Paul's Jewish, Hellenistic, or Christian credentials. Rather, he warns of the artificiality of defining Judaism too narrowly, especially as it has developed and interacted with non-Jewish culture throughout history. He certainly rejected the idea that Paul was the author of a theology hostile to Jews; rather, he had been obsessed with the task of uncovering the true Judaism that he believed would ultimately reconcile them with their non-Jewish brothers. Thus, without minimising Paul's differences, which Sandmel was keen to see acknowledged in any talk of a Judeo-Christian civilisation, he nevertheless brought him back within the Jewish fold: Sandmel's Apostle to the Gentiles was a link in an unbroken chain of prophets, from Abraham to Isaiah and Jeremiah.

Again, a novel written from the protagonist's perspective allows the author to humanise the subject and to show the messy impact of personality clashes and character development. This was certainly an important factor in Sandmel's presentation; among Christians alone, Sandmel highlights quarrels with James, Peter, Apollos, Barnabas, Timothy, Titus, and a host of other fictional characters. And, arguably, a reader who has seen the human face of the subject, who believes that he or she understands the psychology of the subject, is less inclined to fear or hate that subject. After finishing the novel, it would have been a hard-hearted reader who remained unmoved by the tragically flawed personality of Paul, whose spiritual intensity, personal dynamism, self-reliance, and theological creativity were offset by his rash character, suspicious and pessimistic nature, short temper, antiauthoritarian disposition, and perfectionism. Paul's traditional reputation as some kind of anti-Semitic monster, *the* archetypal enemy of Judaism and ultimate apostate, was problematised by Sandmel's presentation of a very human Jewish prophet.

One final reason for having written the novel might have something to do with providing Sandmel with an opportunity to explore more contemporary issues. And here, perhaps, we see what it was about Paul and his theology that so captivated Sandmel. The reader is struck by the similarities to Paul's pagan surroundings and 1950s and 1960s North America with its challenge to Jewish values: assimilation, a sexually charged popular culture, pluralism and competing philosophies, many of which appear to undermine Jewish tradition, a certain nebulousness of what constitutes Jewish identity, a sense of alienation from institutional religion generally and criticism of an intransient established order (and *halakhah*) in particular, the desire to experiment, religious and theological compromise and innovation, and interests in the link between individual freedom and community, in social justice, and in internationalism. In this context, a certain amount of compromise, and even of confusion, appears reasonable, and the generation of alternative world-views and strategies for how to reconcile oneself to the non-Jewish world are seen as valid enterprises. In *Paul the Apostle* Sandmel effectively argued that one need not agree with Paul's conclusions to see him as a spiritually sincere Jew confronting challenges similar to those faced by progressives in the multicultural United States. Thus, in a way, Sandmel's Paul can be understood as the North American Jewish Everyman.

CONCLUSION

In comparing the literary treatments of Asch and Sandmel, it is clear that both had sought to present Paul as a spiritually gifted but tragically misunderstood figure. Both had attempted in their own way to reclaim him and to reconcile him with Judaism; he was to be viewed as a flawed but unfairly forgotten *Jewish* hero, who should be honoured not least for the sake of improved Jewish–Christian relations. Yet there were important differences between their approaches, which can best be explained by their respective backgrounds. Paul offered Asch a dramatic licence to explore his own sense of Jewish identity. Forever seeking to broaden his horizons and irked by the close confines of the Jewish community, the Yiddish writer had preferred to explore the margins, where he could express his Jewishness in his own terms, even if this had generated some suspicion. In contrast, Sandmel had been a well-known and respected Jewish religious leader and scholar. His greater confidence in himself as a Jew and in his academic expertise had meant that his portrayal of Paul had been even more magnanimous in recognising the apostle's achievements. Nevertheless, in recognising Paul as a Jewish prophet, Sandmel never relaxed for one instant his conviction that the boundary between Judaism and Christianity in the twentieth century was unbreachable.

Asch's emphasis on a common Judeo-Christian heritage was certainly one way of relating two communities; it worked on the assumptions that improved rela-tions would come about by highlighting what is shared in common, rather than what differentiates, and by emphasising Judaism's contribution to Western culture. Another way, of course, was to acknowledge the differences but present them in such a way that they appeared nonthreatening; this way worked on the assump-tions that diversity was to be embraced and that one does not fear or hate what one understands. As we have seen, Sandmel adopted this second strategy. Sadly, we will never know whether this way of engaging with Paul would have met with greater success, for the amateur novelist never found a publisher for his manuscript.

PART IV

THE APOSTLE PAUL AND JEWISH CRITIQUES

OF THE PLACE OF RELIGION IN SOCIETY:

PHILOSOPHICAL AND PSYCHOANALYTICAL

APPROACHES

After the Enlightenment and the attendant phenomena of the dissolution of the ghetto and the widespread establishment of legal emancipation, there was no longer one norm of Jewish existence (if there ever had been). The first wave of Jews who did not abandon Judaism for another faith but who nevertheless found themselves living outside the Jewish community represented a new phenomenon. In earlier times, the existence of a Jew who was at odds with his community, who held ideas that were deemed by the religious authorities as heretical, and who was attracted to non-Jewish ways of thinking was untenable. And yet, over time, as a result of a tremendous variety of pressures and influences that accompanied modernity, the 'secular Jew'[1] emerged to become a permanent feature of the Jewish landscape. From that time to this, a good deal of discussion has taken place as to whether such individuals can meaningfully be described as Jewish. One seminal contribution was a collection of essays entitled *The Non-Jewish Jew* (1968) in which the Polish-Jewish journalist Isaac Deutscher made an impassioned defence of this new species of Jew.[2] Insistent that 'the Jewish heretic who transcends Jewry' was part of a Jewish tradition whose revered membership had begun with Spinoza, he went on to describe some of their characteristics. The non-Jewish Jews, he says, who went beyond the boundaries of the Jewish community and who looked for ideals and fulfilment elsewhere, nevertheless

had in themselves something of the quintessence of Jewish life and of the Jewish intellect.... [T]hey dwelt on the borderlines of various epochs. Their minds matured where

---

[1] Yerushalmi has described Spinoza as 'the first great culture-hero of modern secular Jews.' Yosef Yerushalmi, *Freud's Moses: Judaism Terminable and Indeterminable* (New Haven, CT: Yale University Press, 1991), 10.

[2] Isaac Deutscher, 'The Non-Jewish Jew', in *The Non-Jewish Jew and Other Essays* (Oxford: Oxford University Press, 1968), 25–41. Later, Deutscher observed, 'The definition of a Jew is so elusive precisely because the Diaspora exposed the Jews to such a tremendous variety of pressures and influences, and also to such a diversity of means with which they had to defend themselves from hostility and persecution.... To speak of the "Jewish community" as if it were an all-embracing entity, then, is meaningless.' Deutscher, *The Non-Jewish Jew*, 51–2.

the most diverse cultural influences crossed and fertilised each other. . . . Each of them was in society and yet not in it, of it and yet not of it. It was this that enabled them to rise in thought above their societies, above their nations, above their times and generations, and to strike out mentally into new horizons and far into the future. . . . All of them had this in common, that the very conditions in which they lived and worked did not allow them to reconcile themselves to ideas which were nationally or religiously limited and induced them to strive for a universal *Weltanschauung* [worldview]. . . . Their manner of thinking is dialectical, because, living on borderlines of nations and religions, they see society in a state of flux. They conceive reality as being dynamic, not static. . . . [They] comprehend more clearly the great movement and the great contradictoriness of nature and society . . . [and] agree on the relativity of moral standards. None of them believe in absolute good or absolute evil. They all observed communities adhering to different moral standards and different ethical values . . . [T]he genius of the Jews who have gone beyond Jewry has left us the message of universal human emancipation.[3]

Here, Deutscher reminds us of three important realities of modern Jewish identity. First, that Jewish self-consciousness, however difficult to describe or account for, is no less real for having abandoned the two ideological pillars of religion and nationalism. Second, that those Jews who no longer feel at home within the Jewish community continue to feel a sense of alienation from the wider society. Yet this experience of living at an ideological and cultural crossroads had the benefit of bestowing upon them a more flexible view regarding prevailing assumptions, even ethical assumptions, and of encouraging them to strike out intellectually in contrary directions. Third, having escaped from one intellectual ghetto, such Jews are determined not to be imprisoned in another, and are drawn as moths to the flame to grander, more universalistic visions of human endeavour.

In Chapter seven we will meet the philosophical freethinkers Baruch Spinoza, Lev Shestov, and Jacob Taubes. In Chapter eight we will look at the writings of the psychoanalysts Sigmund Freud and Hanns Sachs. What unites these thinkers is their interest in Paul as part of their analyses of the place of religion in Christian society and of the rational foundations of Western civilisation in general. Although the forms of their critiques do not immediately strike one as Jewish *per se*, Deutscher's observations suggest that it would be a mistake to disavow them too quickly. The attempt of each to generate a philosophical or psychological frame of reference, that is, to appeal to a more universalist system of thought, cannot be fully understood without reference to the historical context in which they, as Jews, found themselves. Deutscher may not have expressed it in such terms, but it is possible to interpret the work of such non-Jewish Jews as a secularisation of the Jewish messianic idea, a call to redemption (of one sort or another) in an unbelieving

---

[3] Deutscher, *The Non-Jewish Jew*, 26–7, 30, 35, 36, 41.

age.[4] In any case, circumstances dictated that, whether they liked it or not, each was regarded as Jewish by his non-Jewish contemporaries, the same contemporaries whom they wished to convict of dangerously erroneous ways of thinking about socio-political authority in Christian society. And as we shall see, the difficulties that a Jewish commentator faced in such a situation might also help explain why, quite unexpectedly, they discovered in Paul's writings support for their own ideological concerns and drew so heavily upon him in their various challenges to the Christian establishment.

---

[4] According to Wolin, Deutscher regarded the greatness of Spinoza, Marx, and others as lying in their 'definitive break with their Jewish past'. Setting aside the question of whether or not this is a fair assessment of Deutscher, Wolin, who embraces the category of the non-Jewish Jew, goes on to make a persuasive argument that such non-Jewish Jews cannot be adequately explained without reference to religious content, influences, and motifs. He offers the idea of secular messianism as an example of how non-Jewish Jews remain at some level Jewish. Richard Wolin, 'Reflections on Jewish Secular Messianism', in Jonathan Frankel, ed., *Jews and Messianism in the Modern Era: Metaphor and Meaning*, Studies in Contemporary Jewry, VII (Oxford: Oxford University Press, 1991), 186–96.

7

The Philosophical Writings of Baruch Spinoza, Lev Shestov, and Jacob Taubes

'Jewish philosophy' has been defined in a number of different ways. Some regard it as the explication of Jewish beliefs and practices by means of philosophical concepts and norms.[1] Others, such as L. E. Goodman, would place less stress on religious belief.

Jewish philosophy is philosophical inquiry informed by the texts, traditions and experiences of the Jewish people. Its concerns range from the farthest reaches of cosmological speculation to the most intimate theatres of ethical choice and the most exigent fora of political debate. What distinguishes it as Jewish is the confidence of its practitioners that the literary catena of Jewish tradition contains insights and articulates values of lasting philosophical import.[2]

In so far as the views expressed by the Jewish-born thinkers in this chapter reflect common experiences among post-Enlightenment Jews, in so far as their Jewish backgrounds helps account for their contributions to the wider political debate and theory, and in so far as their arguments draw heavily upon traditional literary resources, the Bible in particular, one could argue that they belong to the honourable tradition of Jewish philosophy. As Jewish philosophers, however, Baruch Spinoza, Lev Shestov, and Jacob Taubes do have certain serious shortcomings. A philosophical tradition should be understood first and foremost in terms of the key philosophic problem, or set of problems, that gave rise to it in the first place. For these thinkers, the key problem concerns the nature of religious authority within society. All three are damning of the social and legal influence of Christianity in their own time and place but, more than that, their great suspicion of religion in general implicates Judaism, too. Worse still, their philosophical critiques of political authority draw not only upon traditional Jewish sources but also upon the Apostle to the Gentiles; all three make the claim that the Church has seriously misunderstood the apostle and has failed to recognise the threat that he represents to the established social order. Historically speaking, of course, Jewish philosophers from Philo of Alexandria onwards have been willing to examine and integrate into their systems ostensibly non-Jewish modes of thinking. Very few have

---

[1] Warren Zev Harvey, 'Philosophy, Jewish', *Encyclopedia Judaica*, XIII, 421.
[2] L.E. Goodman, 'Jewish Philosophy', *Routledge Encyclopedia of Philosophy*, 85.

demonstrated such a keen curiosity about Paul before, however, and it will be left to the reader to decide how significant are their shortcomings as Jewish philosophers.[3] In the meantime, we will begin with a figure who features in every book of Jewish philosophy but whose interest in Paul is rarely commented upon.

BARUCH SPINOZA AND PAUL THE RATIONALIST

Baruch Spinoza (1632–77) was born of Portuguese Jewish parents in Amsterdam and died in poverty, reviled for his free thought and largely unrecognised for his profound contributions to modern Western philosophy, political theory, and biblical criticism. Because he was expelled from the synagogue and estranged from the Jewish community, many commentators have concluded that his Jewishness was of little relevance to him or to his philosophical work. Certainly, one of his chief aims was to free philosophy from religious authority, and in the *Theological-Political Treatise* (1670)[4] he attempted to place religion on a new basis, one more natural and political than traditional and theological. From this perspective, his view of the Law as a product of the Jewish people (and not vice versa) amounted to its abrogation.[5] On the other hand, more recently, other commentators have noted that his writings represent a continuous dialogue with the Torah, the Prophets, and philosophers such as Maimonides, that he sought the transformation of Jews rather than their conversion, and that he himself never converted to Christianity. From this point of view, Spinoza should be regarded as a forerunner of the modern emancipated secular Jew and credited with the emergence of a critical attitude to tradition within Jewish thought.[6] Although we possess no definitive evidence

---

[3] This may well be a doomed exercise. As the historian of Jewish philosophy, Isaac Husik, famously asserted, 'There are Jews now and there are philosophers, but there are no Jewish philosophers and there is no Jewish philosophy.' Along with many others, he believed that the way in which premodern Jews had merged Judaism and philosophy was impossible to envisage after the Enlightenment. Isaac Husik, *A History of Medieval Jewish Philosophy* (New York: Macmillan, 1930), 432.

[4] *Tractatus Theologico-Politicus* (Hamburg: Heinrich Kuhnraht, 1670) was actually published anonymously by Jan Rieuwertsz in Amsterdam in 1669. The edition used here is Benedict de Spinoza, *Theological-Political Treatise*, trans. Michael Silverthorne and Jonathan Israel.

[5] Such luminaries as Herman Cohen, Emmanuel Levinas, and Leo Strauss have regarded Spinoza as a self-hating Jew, anti-Jewish, and demeaning of Judaism. See Steven B. Smith, *Spinoza, Liberalism, and the Question of Jewish Identity* (New Haven: Yale University Press, 1997), 16–20, 166–96, for an excellent overview of previous Jewish (and non-Jewish) appreciations of Spinoza.

[6] Perhaps the most convincing presentation of such a view is offered in Steven B. Smith, *Spinoza, Liberalism, and the Question of Jewish Identity*. Smith argues, 'Spinoza put Jewish concerns and problems at the forefront of his thought in order to exercise a profound transformation of them. Not conversion but secularisation was the final aim of the *Treatise*. It was an attempt to turn Judaism from an authoritative body of revealed law into what today would be called a modern secular identity.' He also observes, 'The *Treatise* is, to my knowledge, the first modern work to advocate the restitution of Jewish sovereignty and a Jewish State.' Ibid, xiii, 19. See also Yosef Yerushalmi, *Freud's Moses*, 10, where Spinoza is held up as the first example of the modern secular Jew.

of his self-understanding,[7] few nowadays would dismiss entirely the idea that it included a Jewish dimension.

One of Spinoza's purposes in writing his *Theological-Political Treatise* was to make the case for freedom of thought as a stabilising force for society.[8] He maintained that the people were controlled by the clergy, whose authority was built on irrational and superstitious teachings, observing that

It may indeed be the highest secret of monarchical government and utterly essential to it, to keep men deceived, and to disguise the fear that sways them with the specious name of religion. . . . [I]n the religion of the common people, serving the church has been regarded as a worldly career, what should be its unpretentious offices being seen as lucrative positions and its pastors considered great dignitaries. As soon as this abuse began in the church, the worst kind of people came forward to fill sacred offices and the impulse to spread God's religion degenerated into sordid greed and ambition. Churches became theatres where people went to hear ecclesiastical orators rather than to learn from teachers. Pastors no longer sought to teach, but strove to win a reputation . . . by teaching new and controversial doctrines designed to seize the attention of the common people. . . . [F]aith amounts to nothing more than credulity and prejudices. And what prejudices they are! They turn rational men into brutes since they completely prevent each person from using his own free judgement and distinguishing truth from falsehood. They seem purposely designed altogether to extinguish the light of the intellect. Dear God! Piety and religion are reduced to ridiculous mysteries. . . . [9]

He argued that by allowing people to think and philosophise freely the foundations of society would be established more securely. Contrary to his enemies' aspersions, his famously unorthodox identification of God with 'nature' did not lead him to reject religious practice altogether. Rather, he believed that religious observance should be protected by a sovereign who required of his subjects adherence only to that common belief which was acceptable to a wide variety of existing sects,

---

[7] The evidence is notoriously ambiguous. Taking just one letter as an example, Spinoza can be understood to express pantheistic, Jewish, and Christian sentiments: 'I hold an opinion about God and Nature very different from that which modern Christians are wont to defend. For I maintain that God is, as the phrase is, the immanent cause of all things, but not the transcendent cause. Like Paul . . . I assert that all things live and move in God. . . . I would dare to say that I agree also with all the ancient Hebrews as far as it is possible to surmise from their traditions, even if these have become corrupt in many ways. . . . I say that it is not entirely necessary to salvation to know Christ according to the flesh; but we must think far otherwise of the eternal son of God, that is, the eternal wisdom of God, which has manifested itself in all things, more especially in the human mind, and most of all in Christ Jesus.' Letter from Spinoza to Henry Oldenburg (November or December 1675), reproduced in Franz Kobler, ed., *A Treasury of Jewish Letters: Letters from the Famous and the Humble*, II (New York: Jewish Publication Society, 1953), 553.

[8] The subtitle of the Treatise reads, 'Containing several discourses which demonstrate that freedom to philosophize may not only be allowed without danger to piety and the stability of the republic but cannot be refused without destroying the peace of the republic and piety itself.'

[9] Spinoza, *Theological-Political Treatise*, 6, 7–8 (Preface:7, 9)

and who otherwise respected freedom of conscience.[10] In this way, the influence of the clergy would be minimised and philosophers such as himself would be able to concentrate on the advancement of knowledge and the betterment of society without concern for the constraints of traditional authority. In this ambitious project, the apostle Paul was to prove useful to Spinoza in a number of ways.[11]

First, Paul bridges the gap between the religious and the philosophical in that, according to Spinoza, 'none of the Apostles engaged with philosophy more than Paul'.[12] By this he meant that Paul appeared to favour rational argument to a greater extent than did the other disciples, whose claim to authority more often appealed to divine revelation. In this context, Moses, too, was also compared unfavourably to the Apostle to the Gentiles.

This is how all of Moses' arguments in the Pentateuch are to be understood; they are not drawn from the repertory of reason, they are simply turns of phrase by which he expressed God's edicts more effectively and imagined them more vividly.... By contrast, the long deductions and arguments of Paul, such as are found in the Epistle to the Romans, were by no means written on the basis of supernatural revelation.[13]

Although he was prepared to take seriously both the Old and New Testaments (after applying rationalist criteria to their reading), Spinoza was a good deal more sceptical of the authority of contemporary priests. Their authority was founded upon tradition and unverifiable claims to special knowledge of the divine will. Scholastic assertions that 'the natural light of reason' could teach nothing of any value concerning salvation could be dismissed easily for, as decriers of reason, scholastics were not entitled to use it to defend their nonrational views; their insistence on something superior to reason was 'a mere fiction'. For Spinoza, the shortcomings of their worldview would be clear for all to see.

I would add just this, that we can know no one except from his works. Anyone who abounds in the fruits of love, joy, peace, long-suffering, kindness, goodness, faithfulness,

---

[10] The civil right of the citizen is defined as 'the freedom of each person to conserve themselves in their own condition' and is to be protected by the authority of the sovereign power. There are limits to individual religious conscience, of course. The shared doctrine is the 'divine command to love their neighbour as themselves' (discussed previously in 13:3) and he argues that in accepting such a command, individuals surrender their natural liberty to God. He maintains that this adherence to divine law can only occur in a civil state and not in the state of nature, and that ultimately, as a consequence, 'all men are obliged to obey his [the sovereign's] decrees and commands about religion'. Spinoza, *Theological-Political Treatise*, 202, 205, 206–7 (16:13, 19, 21).

[11] In relation to Paul, Spinoza made no mention of Jewish scholars, but he did refer several times (with reference to Romans) to a Jewish convert to Protestantism, John Immanuel Tremellius (1510–80), who was an expert in biblical languages. Along with Romans, he cited from 1 Corinthians, Galatians, 1 and 2 Timothy, and Acts of the Apostles in the *Theological-Political Treatise*.

[12] Spinoza puts this down to Paul's need to find a language appropriate to the Gentiles. He goes on to say that the other apostles 'who preached to the Jews, the despisers of philosophy, likewise adapted themselves to their minds ... and taught a religion devoid of philosophical theory.' Spinoza, *Theological-Political Treatise*, 162 (11:9).

[13] Spinoza, *Theological-Political Treatise*, 157 (11:3, 4).

gentleness and self-control, against whom (as Paul say in his Epistle to the Galatians 5.22) there is no law, he, whether he has been taught by reason alone or by Scripture alone, has truly been taught by God, and is altogether happy.[14]

Thus Paul was not only a model of philosophic integrity whose teaching method was superior to those of both Christian and Jewish founding fathers, but also a potent weapon to wield against the contemporary enemies of reason.

Second, Paul's universalistic teachings are of great interest and are drawn upon early on in the treatise to demonstrate that God cannot be delimited by any creed or claimed as the property of any one people. Once again, it is Moses, together with his parochial descendents, who is contrasted negatively with Paul. Contemporary Jewish teachers, to whom Spinoza refers as Pharisees, claimed that the divine gift of prophecy or revelation had been given only to the Hebrew nation. To prove this, they pointed to the passage in Exodus where God makes a covenant with them as a result of Moses' petition. After a sideswipe at the Jews whose 'obstinate temper and spirit' had provoked Moses' plea for 'the election of the Hebrews', Spinoza offers a plain reading of the story to argue that nothing in the text indicated God's refusal to reveal himself to other nations.[15] Intriguingly, he admits that Paul seemed to disagree with him.

However, I find another text, in the Epistle of Paul to the Romans, which weighs still more with me [than does Exod. 33–4], namely 3.1–2 where Paul appears to teach something different from what we are asserting here. He asks: 'What therefore is the pre-eminence of the Jew? Or what is the advantage of circumcision? Much in every way; for it is of the first importance that the pronouncements of God were entrusted to them.'[16]

It is revealing that such is his predilection for Paul that Spinoza is prepared to gloss over this apparent discrepancy as an anomaly. Instead he places greater emphasis on the universalism in Paul's thought and continues by demonstrating how the apostle made no distinction between different peoples when it came to the human condition of sin, consciousness of which accompanied knowledge of the Law. And because all mankind experienced this sin, the 'law' that accompanied it, and which was also familiar to all, must refer to a universal sense of right and wrong rather than to the Mosaic Law developed by the ancient Hebrews.

But if we consider the principal doctrine Paul is trying to preach here, we shall find that it does not conflict with our view at all; on the contrary, he is saying the same thing. For at verse 29 of this chapter he affirms that God is the God of the Jews and of the gentiles. . . . Again, 3.9 and 4.15 state that all men equally, that is, both Jews and gentiles, were under sin, but that there is no sin without commandment and law. It is entirely

---

[14]　Spinoza, *Theological-Political Treatise*, 80 (5:19–20).
[15]　Spinoza, *Theological-Political Treatise*, 51–2 (3:10).
[16]　Spinoza, *Theological-Political Treatise*, 52 (3:10).

evident from this that the law has been revealed to everyone without exception . . . that all men have lived under it, and that this law is the law which aims at true virtue alone, and is not the law which is shaped by the form and constitution of one particular state and adapted to the character of a single people. Finally, Paul concludes that God is the God of all nations, that is, God is equally well-disposed to all . . . and that is why God sent his Christ to all nations. . . . Hence Paul teaches exactly what we want him to affirm.[17]

Spinoza has no difficulty taking the next step and suggesting that the internal sense of ethical behaviour possessed by all peoples was possible precisely because all men could come to know God's laws through rational thought and observation of nature. This idea was an important one to Spinoza (and to later Enlightenment thinkers and deists) and, once again, he chooses to justify it by reference to Paul.

[W]e must not forget this passage of Paul, found at Romans 1.20, where . . . Paul says, 'for the hidden things of God, from the creation of the world, are seen through the understanding in his creatures, as well as his power and divinity which is for ever, so that they are without a way of escape'. With this he indicates plainly enough that each man fully understands by the natural light of reason the power of God, and His eternal divinity, by which men can know and deduce what they should seek and what they should avoid.[18]

And what were the practical implications of such a natural law? For Spinoza, the just society would base its laws on those common ethics that inculcated good relations between men. In a section headed, 'Where it is shown that the teachings of Scripture are very simple, and aim only to promote obedience', Spinoza drew upon Paul to argue,

Since obedience to God consists solely in love of our neighbour (for he who loves his neighbour, with the intention of obeying God, has fulfilled the Law, as Paul observes in his Epistle to the Romans, 13.8), it follows that the only knowledge commended in Scripture is that which everyone needs to obey God according to this command, that is if, lacking this knowledge, they must necessarily be disobedient or at least deficient in the habit of obedience.[19]

Third, Spinoza argues that a close reading of Paul's writings suggests the proper approach to the sacred scriptures, the interpretation of which was conventionally regarded as a priestly prerogative. The readiness of the apostle to distinguish between teachings revealed through prophecy and his own teachings demonstrates the need to discern between revelation and other forms of knowledge.[20] Paul

---

[17] Spinoza, *Theological-Political Treatise*, 52–3 (3:10).
[18] Spinoza, *Theological-Political Treatise*, 67 (4:12).
[19] Spinoza, *Theological-Political Treatise*, 173 (13:3).
[20] Spinoza's conviction is that 'Scripture leaves reason absolutely free and has nothing at all in common with philosophy, but that each of them stands on its own separate footing.' Spinoza, *Theological-Political Treatise*, 9 (Preface:10).

himself is capable of making this distinction, and Spinoza is quick to point out that
'Paul speaks according to his opinion . . . [and consequently] ambiguous meanings
and tentative expressions are found in many passages'; he also has no trouble
finding examples where the apostle 'corrects himself by saying that he is speaking
there in human fashion and through the weakness of the flesh.'[21] Using the epistles
to suggest that the language of the Bible is a flexible tool adapted in different ways
at different times for the purposes of effective communication could, he believed,
also lead to a more profound understanding of, amongst other things, the very
nature of God.[22]

Spinoza's conception of the deity is notoriously problematic, not least for the
difficulty in reconciling it with the God of biblical tradition. Whatever the precise
meaning Spinoza retained for the term 'God', it was to some extent synonymous with 'nature', a power without a personality, closely related to the universal,
deterministic laws of the cosmos. It therefore comes as something of a surprise to
find him claiming Paul in support of this idea.

[Paul] prefers not to speak openly. Rather, as he puts it (Romans 3.5 and 6.19), he
spoke 'in human terms', expressly admitting this when he calls God 'just'. Likewise, it is
undoubtedly due to this 'weakness in the flesh' that he attributes pity, grace, anger, etc,
to God, adapting his words to the character of the common people or (as he himself
puts it at 1 Corinthians 3.1–2) 'carnal men'. For at Romans 9.18 he absolutely teaches
that God's anger and mercy depend not upon men's works but upon God's vocation

---

[21] Spinoza offers 1 Cor. 7:6 ('But this I say by way of concession, not of command'), 7:25 ('Now
    concerning virgins I have no command of the Lord, but I give an opinion as one who by the mercy
    of the Lord is trustworthy'), and 7:40 ('But in my opinion she is happier if she remains as she is; and
    I think that I also have the Spirit of God'); and Rom. 3:5 ('But if our unrighteousness demonstrates
    the righteousness of God, what shall we say? The God who inflicts wrath is not unrighteous, is He?
    I am speaking in human terms'), 3:28 ('For we maintain that a man is justified by faith apart from
    works of the Law'), 6:19 ('I am speaking in human terms because of the weakness of your flesh For
    just as you presented your members as slaves to impurity and to lawlessness, resulting in further
    lawlessness, so now present your members as slaves to righteousness, resulting in sanctification'),
    and 8:18 ('For I consider that the sufferings of this present time are not worthy to be compared with
    the glory that is to be revealed to us'). Spinoza, *Theological-Political Treatise*, 40 (2:18), 155 (11:1), and
    159 (11:6).

[22] Paul is only one of the New Testament disciples who adapted their message as necessary. '[T]o
    avoid offending them too much with the novelty of its teaching, they [the Apostles] adapted it [the
    Gospel], so far as they could, to the minds of their contemporaries (see the First Epistle to the
    Corinthians 9.19–20), and built upon the basic principles that were most familiar and acceptable
    at the time.' Spinoza, *Theological-Political Treatise*, 162 (11:9). Supernatural imagery was one way
    of accomplishing this, and Paul was by no means the only biblical writer to engage in this kind of
    language. '[T]he prophets understood and taught almost everything in parables and allegorically,
    expressing all spiritual matters in corporeal language; for the latter are well suited to the nature of
    our imagination. Neither shall we any longer be surprised that Scripture or the prophets speak so
    inappropriately and obscurely about the spirit or mind of God, as at Numbers 11.17, 1 Kings 22.2, etc,
    or that Micah saw God seated, Daniel saw him as an old man dressed in white clothes, and Ezekiel
    as a fire, the Apostles saw him as tongues of fire, whereas Paul, when he was first converted, saw him
    as a great light. For all this is clearly well suited to the imaginings of ordinary men about God and
    spirits.' Spinoza, *Theological-Political Treatise*, 26 (1:29).

alone, i.e. upon his will. . . . We conclude therefore that God is described as a legislator or a prince, and as just, merciful etc, only because of the limited understanding of the common people and their lack of knowledge, and that in reality God acts and governs all things from the necessity of his own nature and perfection alone, and his decrees and volitions are eternal truths and always involve necessity.[23]

Although other Jewish thinkers might have drawn upon Maimonides,[24] here Paul is brought to bear in an argument that the biblical language which endows God with a personality is a necessary evil, a concession to untutored minds, which no philosopher need take seriously. Rather, God appears as something akin to the stuff of the universe, whose nature we glimpse only through the eternal laws and predetermined mechanisms of creation.

According to Spinoza, then, Paul and the biblical authors in general were prone to error, were constrained by the conventions of their times, and consciously adapted their language to their specific audiences – to such an extent that the very nature of God had been profoundly misunderstood. In all this, Spinoza implies, the Bible should be read with a willingness to recognise what is authoritative and what is not. He looks forward to the day when this critical approach would free religion from unauthoritative teachings, which he calls superstitions.[25] Ultimately he argues that, for the purposes of a just society based on solid rational foundations, only those biblical teachings that encourage right conduct are necessary.

Of course, Spinoza would have been quite capable of making the arguments out-lined above regarding the importance of reason, the universal conception of God, and his proto–biblical criticism without reference to Paul. Why is it that the apostle featured in such a positive way in the alternative vision of society described in the *Theological-Political Treatise* – especially considering that Spinoza was forced to overlook those aspects of Pauline theology with which he was at odds? The answer lies in the difficulties of articulating his political theory in the dangerous historical context in which he wrote, a context in which power remained in the hands of Christian authorities. If Spinoza had called for a 'universal religion of human reason that transcends the historical differences between the revealed faiths and that can serve as an ethical basis for a free, open and tolerant society', as has

---

[23] Spinoza, *Theological-Political Treatise*, 64–5 (4:10).

[24] Spinoza was disinclined to draw on Maimonides as a result of the twelfth-century philosopher's attempt to equate Judaism with rationalism. As Feld puts it, 'The first six chapters of the *Theologico-Political Treatise* are an extended argument with Maimonides: Spinoza many times explicitly indicates that Maimonides is the one who holds the position he is seeking to demolish. It is the Maimonidean identification of Judaism and rationalism which takes the full brunt of his criticism and his argument that prophets are not philosophers is offered to free philosophy from its religious connection.' Edward Feld, 'Spinoza the Jew', *Modern Judaism*, 9:1 (1989), 109.

[25] Spinoza believed that '[d]isputes and schisms have ceaselessly disturbed the church ever since apostolic times, and will surely never cease to trouble it, until religion is finally separated from philosophical theories and reduced to the extremely few, very simple dogmas that Christ taught to his own. . . . How happy our own age would surely be, were we to see it also free from all superstition.' Spinoza, *Theological-Political Treatise*, 161–2 (11:9).

been suggested,[26] then this would explain both his apparent anti-Judaism and his apparent high regard for Paul. On one hand, in order to undermine the authority of revealed religion in general, he had launched a polemical attack on Judaism in particular, ostensibly contrasting Christianity favourably; and yet many of his Christian contemporaries had realised that his criticisms could just as easily be applied to their own faith. On the other hand, Spinoza himself suggested that it was useful to support his arguments from scripture; and certainly, for the majority of his audience who belonged to one Christian church or another, it is clear that Paul functioned as a familiar and powerful figure of biblical authority.[27] Thus the seventeenth-century marginal Jew made a conscious effort to clothe his arguments in the apparel of the Apostle to the Gentiles.

LEV SHESTOV AND THE ANTIRATIONALIST PAUL

Although Spinoza had valued Paul for his rationality, the Russian Jewish philosopher and bitter critic of Spinoza, Lev Shestov (1866–1938), was attracted to Paul precisely because he regarded him as part of a long-term Judeo-Christian *critique* of Western rationality. Born Yehuda Leyb Schwartzman in Kiev to a wealthy Jewish family, he emigrated to France in 1921 and remained there until his death. Although the professor of Russian literature at the University of Paris produced no dedicated study, the apostle is frequently in Shestov's thought, informing his language and reinforcing his arguments throughout a wide selection of his writings.

Shestov's particular brand of existentialist philosophy is notoriously difficult to articulate, not least because language was part of the system that he wanted to critique. Fascinated by paradox and the subjective experience of the individual, he was convinced that the Western tradition of rational philosophy was bankrupt. This was because rational thought tries to describe the world in generalisations and unchanging laws that delimit what is and is not possible. Drawing upon European philosophy and literature, with which he was intimately familiar, Shestov tried to show how humanity experienced despair and loss of freedom as the result of having embraced the intellectual restrictions of the scientific worldview. The very attempt to rationalise suppressed the raw experience of lived reality and failed to

---

[26] Smith argues persuasively that Spinoza was not denigrating Judaism in order to champion Christianity but was just as concerned to undermine Christianity's claims to revelational authority. Smith, *Spinoza, Liberalism, and the Question of Jewish Identity*, 105–18, 197.

[27] For the same reason, Jesus appears frequently in the *Treatise*, where he is also presented positively as a philosopher. One particularly important example of Spinoza appealing to Paul's authority can be found in his key chapter 'On the foundations of the state, on the natural and civil right of each person, and on the authority of sovereign powers'. Here, the state of nature is distinguished from the state of religion that characterises a civil society because of the absence of religion and law, and consequently of all sin and wrongdoing: 'This is how we have conceived it, and have confirmed this by the authority of Paul'. Spinoza, *Theological-Political Treatise*, 205 (16:19).

address the most meaningful questions of individual existence.[28] What, then, was the alternative? Shestov eventually came to believe that the biblical tradition best captured the frightening yet liberating insight that everything was possible, that nothing was fixed or certain, and that, ultimately, all was beyond man's control.[29] This way of understanding life as potentiality, which he described as 'faith', was 'biblical' in the sense that its God was not the God of the philosophers, the unmoved mover, but rather the capricious God of Abraham, Isaac, and Jacob – and of the apostle Paul. Shestov's 'religious existentialism', which is most famously given expression in *In Job's Balances* (1929)[30] and his magnum opus *Athens and Jerusalem* (1938),[31] can therefore be understood as combining a radical scepticism with a profound religious sense.[32]

Shestov's interest in the Bible began relatively late, after he had left revolutionary Russia for France in the 1920s and two decades after he had first begun his crusade against reason.[33] One commentator has suggested that it was partly to make his philosophy more intelligible to a European audience that the Hebrew Bible began to feature in Shestov's work. In any case, his conception of biblical faith emerged as a positive complement to his negative evaluation of logical positivism. A nonobservant Jew who eschewed orthodox tradition, Shestov was wary of institutional

[28] '[Modern philosophy] sweeps away beauty, good, ambition, tears, laughter, and curses, like dust, like useless refuse, never guessing that it is the most precious thing in life, and that out of this material and this alone, genuine, truly philosophic questions have to be moulded. Thus the prophets questioned, thus the greatest sages of antiquity, thus even the Middle Ages. Now only rare, lonely thinkers comprehend this.' Leo Chestov, *In Job's Balances: On the Sources of the Eternal Truths*, trans. Camilla Coventry and C. A. Macartney (London: J. M. Dent and Sons, 1932), II:16.

[29] 'The business of philosophy is to teach man to live in uncertainty – man who is supremely afraid of uncertainty, and who is forever hiding himself behind this or the other dogma. More briefly, the business of philosophy is not to reassure people but to upset them.' Lev Shestov, *Apotheosis of groundlessness: An attempt in adogmatic thinking* (St. Petersberg: Obshestvennaia Pol'za, 1905), I:11, reprinted in Bernard Martin, ed., *All Things Are Possible and Penultimate Words and Other Essays* (Athens, Ohio: Ohio University Press, 1977), trans. S. S. Koteliansky.

[30] Chestov, *In Job's Balances*. Originally published in Russian (Paris: Annales contemporaines, 1929).

[31] Lev Shestov, *Athens and Jerusalem*, ed. and trans. Bernard Martin (Athens, OH: Ohio University Press, 1966). Originally published in French and German as *Athunes et Jerusalem; Essai de la philosophie religieuse* (Paris: 1938); *Athen und Jerusalem: Versucht einer religiosen Philosophie* (1938).

[32] Shestov's dismantling of all philosophical edifices has been described as 'an anguished religious quest, casting away all forms of idealism – indeed, of all moral and epistemological certainty and reassurance – in order to encounter the living God: unpredictable, irrefrangible, absurd.' Michael Weingrad, 'New Encounters with Shestov', *The Journal of Jewish Thought and Philosophy* 11:1 (2002), 49.

[33] Initially, there was nothing religious about his existentialism. From early on in his career Shestov had been convinced of the failure of philosophy to provide solace to individuals in despair, illustrating his argument by means of poetic truths penned by Shakespeare, among others. Thus the turbulent experiences of Hamlet and King Lear culminated in increased knowledge of their own inner worlds, he argued, a knowledge that shared next to nothing with the world as described by rationalists. This experience of the individual, Shestov maintained, was frequently of greater import than the abstract logic of philosophy, even though the tendency was to set it aside as inferior. For an account of the evolution of Shestov's thought, see Brian Horowitz, 'The Tension of Athens and Jerusalem in the Philosophy of Lev Shestov', *The Slavic and East European Journal*, 43:1 (Spring 1999).

religion and collective religious experience. In his Bible, which appeared to consist primarily of Genesis and some of the prophetic writings, Shestov found a powerful precedent for his idea, for the ancient texts told of various individuals' direct experience of a living God whose sovereign rule over existence appeared to them as arbitrary as it was absolute. Nor was the insight of the Hebrews limited to the Old Testament. The New Testament could, in this very important sense, be regarded as one with the Old, and this explains how Shestov came to see the Apostle to the Gentiles[34] as part of a Jewish biblical tradition that questioned worldly wisdom.[35]

As far as Shestov is concerned, Paul's message was 'true Jewish thinking'[36] and the man himself a visionary whose teachings should be read alongside those of the Hebrew prophets.[37] Indeed, Shestov regards the apostle as an astute interpreter of older biblical insights. He is particularly keen to stress how Paul confronted the philosophy of his own day, drawing heavily upon Isaiah and Jeremiah.[38] For example,

[34] Shestov appears to base his view of Paul on a very restricted reading of the New Testament. He actually cites only a few verses from the Epistles: Rom. 3:2 (twice) ('Great in every respect. First of all, that they were entrusted with the oracles of God'), 5:20 ('The Law came in so that the transgression would increase; but where sin increased, grace abounded all the more'), 10:20 ('And Isaiah is very bold and says, "I was found by those who did not seek me, I became manifest to those who did not ask for me"'), and 14:23 (twice) ('But he who doubts is condemned if he eats, because his eating is not from faith; and whatever is not from faith is sin') and 1 Cor. 1:27 ('but God has chosen the foolish things of the world to shame the wise, and God has chosen the weak things of the world to shame the things which are strong'), 1:31 ('so that, just as it is written, "Let him who boasts, boast in the Lord"'), and 13. He makes no mention of Pauline scholars, either Christian or Jewish.

[35] 'The Bible remains the book of books, the eternal book. It would be no loss to exchange the theological literature of a whole generation of later epochs against a single Epistle of St. Paul or a chapter from Isaiah.' Shestov, In Job's Balances, II:7. 'In the Letter to the Romans the apostle repeats the same thing and even more strongly: "For what does Scripture say? 'Abraham believed God, and it was reckoned to him as righteousness'" (Romans 4:3). The whole Bible – the Old and the New Testament – is supported by this kind of a justification, and most of the letters of the apostle Paul speak of this truth that is incomprehensible and goes contrary to all the habits of our thinking, a truth that revealed itself many thousands of years ago to a small, half-wild people.' Lev Shestov, Speculation and Revelation, ed. and trans. Bernard Martin (Athens, Ohio: Ohio University Press, c1982), 5.

[36] In a conversation with his disciple Benjamin Fondane (26 July 1928), Shestov mused, 'I think that Hitler really has a lot of intuition – he hates St Paul: it's true Jewish thinking.' When Fondane asked him whether 'Paul had betrayed the spirit of the Bible when he opened to the Gentiles the privileges of the chosen people? Didn't God say: "I have loved Jacob but Esau I have hated"?' Shestov answered 'Of course! And yet... in the beginning there was no such thing as Jews and non-Jews...' Benjamin Fondane, 'Entretiens avec Leon Chestov' in Nathalie Baranoff and Michel Carassou, eds., Rencontres avec Leon Chestov (Paris: Plasma, 1982). Elsewhere he described Paul ironically as 'an ignorant Jew' (Preface to Lev Shestov, Potestas Clavium, ed. and trans. Bernard Martin (Athens, OH: Ohio University Press, 1968)) and affectionately as 'an old Jew' (Shestov, In Job's Balances, II:5:33).

[37] 'The prophet Isaiah and St. Paul have warned us that human wisdom is foolishness before God and that God's wisdom is foolishness in the eyes of men.' Shestov, In Job's Balances, III:5.

[38] 'The basic motif of Paul in all of his letters is as follows: "But God chose what is foolish in the world to shame the wise" (I Corinthians, 1:27). He constantly cites the most enigmatic and mysterious sayings of the prophets, and the more audacious the prophet the more joyfully does the apostle welcome him. "Therefore, as it is written: 'Let him who boasts, boast of the Lord'" (I Corinthians, 1:31), he repeats after Jeremiah 9:24. And after Isaiah 64:4: "What no eye has seen, nor ear heard, nor the heart of man conceived, what God has prepared for those who love Him" (I Corinthians, 2:9). I

St. Paul says: Isaiah dared to say: 'I was found by those who did not seek me, I manifested myself to those who did not inquire after me' [Rom. 10:20]. How can one accept such audacious words? God, God Himself violates the supreme law of justice: He manifests Himself to those who do not inquire after Him, He is found by those who do not seek Him. Can one then exchange the God of the philosophers, the single, immaterial truth, for such a God as this?[39]

Likewise, the story of Abraham, which Shestov himself adapts as an allegory for the philosopher's journey,[40] was of tremendous significance to Paul, who referred to it repeatedly in his attempt to confound the wisdom of the Greeks with the vital reality of the life of faith.

It would be too easy to multiply quotations to prove that what St. Paul said of Abraham, who went he knew not where, would have appeared to the Greek thinkers the height of folly. And even if Abraham had arrived at the Promised Land, his act, in the judgment of the Greeks, would have been as absurd as if he had not arrived anywhere. What vitiates his act, in their eyes, is precisely what confers its immense value upon it, according to the apostle [Paul] and the Bible: Abraham does not ask reason, he refuses to admit the legitimacy of the pretensions of knowledge.... What strikes and charms the apostle [Paul] in Abraham, what he sees in him as the highest virtue, appears to Plato as a truly criminal frivolity. How indignant he and Socrates would have been if it had been given them to read what St. Paul writes in the Epistle to the Romans: "For what saith the Scripture?' Abraham believed God and this was imputed unto him for righteousness. (Rom. 4:3)[41]

The still more ancient story of the tree of knowledge was another example from the Hebrew Bible that Shestov found to be in accordance with both his own and St. Paul's teachings.[42] Fired by his all-consuming philosophical agenda, Shestov could not but see the same truth repeated a thousand times – and what difference did it make whether one read it in the story of the Fall or in an epistle from the Apostle to the Gentiles? Ultimately, knowledge, death, sin, and the Law were all terms relating to the same phenomenon. As he explained,

could write out quotations from the letters of Paul endlessly but, indeed, there is no need for this; all know them without me.' Shestov, *Speculation and Revelation*, 5.

[39] Shestov, *In Job's Balances*, III:7.

[40] 'St. Paul says that when Abraham went to the Promised Land he departed without knowing where he was going. This signifies that only he attains the Promised Land who takes no account of knowledge, who is free of knowledge and of its truths: where he arrives will be the Promised Land.' Shestov, *Athens and Jerusalem*, II:14.

[41] Shestov, *Athens and Jerusalem*, III:6.

[42] 'But "knowledge" and "works" – if one accepts the mysterious Biblical legend [of the Fall] – were precisely the source of all evil upon earth. One must redeem oneself in other wise, through "faith" as St. Paul teaches, through faith alone, i.e. through a spiritual exertion of quite peculiar nature, which we describe as "audacity". Only when we have forgotten the "laws" which bind us so fast to the limited existence, can we raise ourselves up above human truths and human good. To raise himself man must lose the ground under his feet.' Shestov, *In Job's Balances*, II:7. 'Faith, in the prophets and apostles, is the source of life; faith, in the philosophers of the Middle Ages educated by the Greeks, is the source of the knowledge that understands. How can one not recall in this connection the two trees planted by God in the Garden of Eden?' Shestov, *Athens and Jerusalem*, III:6.

The knowledge of good and evil, as well as of shame, came to [man] only after he had tasted the fruits of the forbidden tree. This is incomprehensible to us, just as we do not understand how these fruits could bring him death. And relying on the infallibility of our reason, we wish with all our powers that the mind should be dormant in the man who does not know the difference between good and evil. But the Bible does not say this. The Bible says, on the contrary, that all the misfortunes of man come from knowledge. This is also the meaning of the words of St. Paul . . . 'all that does not come of faith is sin' [Rom. 14:23]. In its very essence knowledge, according to the Bible, excludes faith and is the sin par excellence or the original sin.[43]

From this we see that, at the same time as viewing Paul as a faithful transmitter of the core teachings of the ancient Hebrews, Shestov readily acknowledged that the author of the Epistles offered him a new vocabulary with which to communicate his idea. Indeed, he believed that Paul's abrogation of the Law had become one of the classic expressions of a tradition of antirationalist thought.[44] Thus, when the apostle had exclaimed, 'The law entered that offence might abound' (Rom. 5:20), what he had meant was that the Law was 'a hammer in God's hands, that he may break man's assurance that living beings are ruled by eternal, immaterial, and sovereign principles.'[45] Shestov was also very quick to adopt Paul's language for his own purposes more generally: to speak of 'grace' as the only hope,[46] to warn against the eternal threat of rationality as 'the enemy [who] is alert, skilful, cruel and watchful',[47] and to recognise that even though one might 'understand all mysteries, and [have] all knowledge . . . [yet] knowledge, it shall vanish away.'[48] And so Shestov takes the remarkable position as a Jew and as a philosopher that Paul's

---

[43] Shestov, *In Job's Balances*, II:14.

[44] Shestov identified this tradition with a Christian antinomian one. 'There is a tradition of thought, or a question, that has run back from St. Augustine, and past St. Augustine to St. Paul, past St. Paul to what Paul found in certain passages of Isaiah, and in the Biblical story of the Fall. The same question which had confronted Luther a century earlier, presents itself to Pascal: Whence does salvation come to man? From his works, that is to say, from his submission to eternal laws; or from a mysterious force which, in the no less mysterious language of the theologians, is called the Grace of God?' Shestov, *In Job's Balances*, III:7.

[45] Shestov, *In Job's Balances*, III:8.

[46] 'Augustine, quoting St. Paul and the prophet Isaiah, spoke of grace.' Shestov, *In Job's Balances*, II:4:28.

[47] Here Shestov actually paraphrases Peter's admonition (1 Pet. 5:8), mistakenly thinking it to be Paul's: 'the last warning of an old Jew, the Apostle Paul, in whose name they were speaking. The enemy is alert, skilful, cruel and watchful. If one yields to him all is over.' Shestov, *In Job's Balances*, II:5:33.

[48] 'Arithmetic has power only in the "ideal" world subject to man, chiefly and perhaps even exclusively because this world was created by man himself and consequently obeys its author. But in the real world a different hierarchy prevails: there that which in the ideal world is smaller is "greater." The laws in general are different there; it may even be that there cannot be any question of laws there, that one wishes to know nothing about our laws there. St. Paul teaches: "Though I speak with the tongues of men and of angels, and have not charity, I am become as sounding brass, or a tinkling cymbal. And though I have the gift of prophecy, and understand all mysteries, and all knowledge; and though I have all faith, so that I could remove mountains, and have not charity, I am nothing. . . . Charity never faileth: but whether there be prophecies, they shall fail; whether there be tongues, they shall cease; whether there be knowledge, it shall vanish away" (I Cor. 13).' Shestov, *Potestas Clavium*, preface.

emphasis on faith (so often contrasted negatively with rationality or knowledge) is the correct one, and that his teachings concerning freedom from the 'law' (here understood as immaterial and eternal truths to which one subjugates oneself) could be counted amongst mankind's most important insights into the nature of existence.

Furthermore, Shestov employed Paul's own life-story to support his privileging of individual experience over abstract philosophy and to show how certain assumptions (or 'theory') could blind mankind to the deeper truths of inner knowledge (or 'facts'), which were too often discounted as unreal. History, he argued, 'agrees to admit only what is important for a large number of people'. St. Paul's revelatory experience on the road to Damascus held an honoured place in history precisely because 'St. Paul was always persuaded that he had really seen the Christ', because he had managed to persuade people to believe his account, and because he was concerned to have the memory of his vision preserved. But what of the many others down through the centuries who had been less persuasive, or who, unlike Paul, had come to doubt their own experiences? Posterity had forgotten them. Shestov believed that Paul would have agreed with him that 'the *theory* of fact hides from men the most important realm of being, and that those facts which theory does not admit are precisely the most precious and the most significant.'[49]

Insofar as the apostle added credibility to Shestov's lifelong rage against reason,[50] Paul was also useful in attacking Shestov's opponents, both ancient and modern. The Greeks would have despised the ignorance of those, like Paul, who privileged faith over reason. As Shestov put it,

The Greek wisdom could admit neither Abraham, the father of faith, nor St. Paul, nor the prophets of the Bible to whom the apostle constantly refers. The indifference, the 'proud' scorn of knowledge, would be pardoned neither in this world nor in the other.

---

[49] Shestov, *Athens and Jerusalem*, IV:4:38. Earlier he explained, 'We have no right to reject an unusual experience, even though it does not agree with our *a priori* notions. I have already shown that Nietzsche underwent a similar experience, and from it he derived the idea of his "beyond good and evil", which is simply a modernized translation of Luther's *sola fide*. And unless we are much mistaken, St. Paul's vision on the road to Damascus was another instance of the same thing. To St. Paul, who was persecuting Christ in the name of the "law", it became suddenly clear that "the law entered that the offence might abound".... Oh, how precious are these "sudden" findings, and how little does philosophy know how to make use of them, thanks to its traditional methods and its fear of the irrational "ego"! It is difficult to realize the shock that a man experiences when he makes such a "discovery", and still harder to understand how he can go on living.' Shestov, *In Job's Balances*, III:7.

[50] Camus described Shestov's writings, obsessed as they are with his one idea, as 'wonderfully monotonous'. Albert Camus, *The Myth of Sisyphus* (New York: Vintage Books, 1955), 19, originally published in France in 1942 by Librairie Gallimard. Against the charge that he misrepresented the views of ancient authorities so as to strengthen his own position, Shestov freely admitted another might criticise his choice of texts as highly selective, over-emphasising the accidental or throw-away comment. 'But the goal of these reflections', he insisted, 'consists precisely in seizing and saving from oblivion the "accidental".' Shestov, *Potestas Clavium*, preface.

St. Paul and his Abraham are only pitiful 'haters of reason,' who must be fled like the plague. [51]

Part of the reason for the hostility of their heirs towards Paul lay in the diametrically opposed views of how salvation is to be achieved. Traditionally, Paul's faith had been set in contrast to works-righteousness, but the real dichotomy is between faith and knowledge.

For the Greek philosophy . . . believed that knowledge was the only way to salvation: 'To him who has not philosophized, who has not purified himself through philosophy and who has not loved knowledge, it is not given to unite himself with the race of the gods.' If Abraham and St. Paul are not 'thinkers,' if they do not love and seek knowledge, they will never obtain salvation. The Greeks knew this well and they would never have agreed to grant anyone the right to raise and resolve the question of knowledge and the salvation of the soul: Aristotle has told us that philosophy itself resolves all questions. [52]

Thus Paul's arrogant declaration that 'All that does not come of faith is sin' (Rom. 14:23) sets him forever at enmity with the classical philosopher, who cannot accept the terrible idea that a lifetime of rational speculation was a lifetime wasted. Shestov delights in acknowledging that 'most of the ideas that [Paul] develops in his epistles and the quotations from the Old Testament with which his reflections are interspersed can awaken in educated people only feelings of irritation and revulsion.' [53] Significantly, Shestov developed his diatribe to include the attempt by theologians to reconcile faith with reason. [54] Thus the apostle could be held up as a corrective to the pursuits of the giants of modern theological rationalism, including amongst others Spinoza.

The fundamental opposition of biblical philosophy to speculative philosophy shows itself in particularly striking fashion when we set . . . Spinoza's 'to rejoice in true contemplation' opposite St. Paul's words, 'Whatsoever is not of faith is sin.' [For the] precondition of . . . Spinoza's 'true contemplation' is the willingness of the man 'who knows' to renounce God's 'blessing' [that is, God's sovereign, arbitrary control] by virtue of which the world and everything that is in the world were destined for man's use. [55]

---

[51] Shestov, *Athens and Jerusalem*, III:6.

[52] Shestov, *Athens and Jerusalem*, III:6.

[53] 'What good, then, is Plato's *catharsis*, the Stoics' struggle, the monks' *exercitia spiritualia*, and the rigorous *itineraria* of the martyrs, ascetics and mystics? Will all these tremendous, superhuman and glorious works then have served for nothing? Is it possible to "defend," through rational arguments, the God of the Bible against these accusations that are so well founded on rational thought? Obviously not.' Shestov, *Athens and Jerusalem*, II.

[54] To subject revelation to the judgement of reason is folly or, as he put it, 'even Moses himself could speak face to face with God only as long as he held to the heights of Sinai; as soon as he descended into the valley the truth that had been revealed to him was transformed into law.' Shestov, *Athens and Jerusalem*, II:10.

[55] Shestov, *In Job's Balances*, forward 2.

Strictly speaking, Paul's theology is not a necessary element in Shestov's philosophical programme. Undoubtedly, one reason he features so prominently is that Shestov, like Spinoza, recognises the moral authority of Paul within the wider Christian society and his usefulness as a common frame of reference. From this point of view, the Russian philosopher's apparent lack of compunction only supports those commentators who have questioned his Jewish authenticity.[56] And yet, Shestov's interest in the tyrannical rule of rationality down through the centuries did make the apostle important in one special sense. Because Paul (and readings of Paul by men such as Augustine and Luther) continued to shape Western civilisation, the correct reading of the epistles really mattered. If his theology had actually been more radical than was commonly understood, if he had not simply offered a critique of Judaism or of legalism but had in fact sought to bring the countercultural message of the ancient Hebrews to those living in his own day, just as Shestov himself was attempting to do in contemporary terms, then there would be profound, if not revolutionary, implications for society. After all, in contemporary terms, the message was that the very scaffold upon which Western theology and philosophy had been hung was rotten to the core. Of course, it was precisely because Shestov interpreted Paul's abrogation of the Law as a critique of the high value placed on reason that his warning cry to European civilisation was entirely the reverse of Spinoza's. The seventeenth-century philosopher had painted a political vision of a better society, a world where a rational apostle set the example and where one might collectively challenge the authority of those who would control by way of superstition. For Shestov, Paul is rather one of the enlightened few who grasps the absurdity of such a vision, and who gives the lie to the claim that there is a rational basis to faith. In terms of social activism, however, Shestov appears impotent beside Spinoza. He cannot use Paul to offer a constructive blueprint for action, other than to point the individual inwards on a quest to confront the mystery, unintelligibility, and seeming injustice of the divine will. In time, an even

---

[56] 'While the heroes and stories of the bible captivated Shestov, it is clear that the actual religion left him less enthusiastic. He did not reflect on the laws and rituals of Judaism, the institution of the rabbinate and ignored the history of the Jewish people and the problems of 'chosenness.' In short, he accepted only those aspects consistent with his teaching: the miracles of the Bible and the individual images of stubborn allegiance to God . . . By accepting both Judaism and Christianity, he maintains allegiance to the religion of his birth, yet was simultaneously free to employ Christianity's spiritual wealth.' Brian Horowitz, 'The Tension of Athens and Jerusalem in the Philosophy of Lev Shestov', 168–9. 'He cared too much for inwardness, for inner experience as an access to salvation, to rest within what was orthodox in Judaism. At the same time he was too dismayed with the Logos of the Fourth Gospel, too smitten with love for the Old Testament God, with all his arbitrary caprice, to have other than short shrift for conventional or churchly Christianity. Yet Shestov was both a Jew and a Christian; and for him the fundamental antinomies were not between the Old and New Testament, or even between religion and atheism, but rather, as the titles of his last two books clearly state, between *Speculation and Revelation*, and *Athens and Jerusalem* (1938).' Sidney Monas, 'Shestov, Lev', *Encyclopedia Judaica*, XIV, 1383–5.

more systematic negative political theology would be offered, again justified by reference to Pauline thought.

JACOB TAUBES AND PAUL'S POLITICAL THEOLOGY

The Viennese-born Jewish philosopher of religion, Jacob Taubes (1923–87), was Professor of Judaism and Hermeneutics at the Free University of Berlin. Although a trained rabbi and a self-proclaimed 'arch-Jew',[57] he was also deeply interested in marginality and limits, and described himself as living an 'uneasy Ahasueric lifestyle at the borderline between Jewish and Christian, at which things get so hot that one can only [get] burn[ed].'[58] His academic career was concerned with religio-philosophical issues such as the theological legitimation of political authority and modern conceptions of apocalyptic thought, both of which informed his treatment of the apostle Paul.[59] In Heidelberg in 1987, a few weeks before he died of cancer, he gave a series of lectures on Paul that he described as his spiritual testament.[60] The result was a carefully edited work of oral testimony that was published as *The Political Theology of Paul* in 1993.[61]

---

[57] Letter from Jacob Taubes to Carl Schmitt (18 September 1979), reproduced in appendix B of J. Taubes, *The Political Theology of Paul*, Aleida and Jan Assmann, eds. and trans. Dana Hollander (California: Stanford University Press, 2004), 110.

[58] Cited by Aleida Assmann in J. Taubes, *The Political Theology of Paul*, 143. Ahasuerus was one of the names given to the Wandering Jew of medieval legend, who mocked Christ on route to the crucifixion and, as a result, was condemned by God to exile until the Second Coming.

[59] Key influences on Taubes's thought were his teacher and the German-Jewish historian of Jewish mysticism, Gershom Scholem (1897–1982), the German-Jewish philosopher Walter Benjamin (1892–1940); and the German Catholic political theorist Carl Schmitt (1888–1985). Taubes was dependent on Scholem for his understanding of Sabbatianism and *kabbalah*; he concurred with Benjamin's pessimistic view of time as moving towards a cataclysmic ending and the call to act ethically in whatever time remains; and he agreed with Schmitt that all significant concepts of the modern theory of the state are secularised theological concepts, although he disagreed as to the precise nature and implications of this special relationship.

[60] 'Taubes did not understand his works on Paul as an academic obligation or exercise. He regarded them as an account of what lay at the centre of what unsettled him intellectually.' Preface by Aleida Assmann in J. Taubes, *The Political Theology of Paul*, xiii.

[61] The four lectures were held at the Protestant Institute for Interdisciplinary Research (FEST) in Heidelberg, 23–7 February, 1987, and originally published in German (based on the audio recordings of Aleida Assmann) as Jacob Taubes, *Die Politische Theologie des Paulus* (München: Wilhelm Fink, 1993). The English edition is Jacob Taubes, *The Political Theology of Paul*, Aleida and Jan Assmann, ed. and trans. Dana Hollander. Despite the editors' best efforts, one commentator has observed of the book: '[T]he tone – by turns confiding, anecdotal, and trenchantly judgemental – and the form – digressions, understatements, circular thought, incomplete demonstrations – are both bewildering.' Alain Gignac, 'Taubes, Badiou, Agamben: Reception of Non-Christian Philosophers Today', Society of Biblical Literature 2002, Section 2.1. The afterword in the English edition by Wolf-Daniel Hartwich, and Alieda and Jan Assman (115–42), which provides an overview and commentary on the text, has proven to be an indispensable guide for making sense of Taubes's highly idiosyncratic lectures in the presentation offered here.

Whatever his own philosophical agenda, Taubes was explicit that he wanted to approach Paul from a Jewish perspective,[62] and saw himself contributing to a liberal Jewish interpretative tradition.[63] This tradition had taken a dim view of the Apostle to the Gentiles in the past, in sharp contrast to its generally positive appreciation of his master, Jesus. As Taubes put it, a Jewish reclamation of Paul is 'a borderline that's hard to cross.'[64] He was generally suspicious of the motives of those who had written before him, and was keen to distance himself from any interest in improving Jewish–Christian understanding.[65] What appealed to Taubes was the possibility of reclaiming certain patterns of thought for Judaism that had become associated with Christianity in general and with Pauline theology in particular. But before exploring these matters, he wanted to properly categorise the apostle.[66]

For Taubes, the matter was clear: Paul had been an authentic Jew. As he explained,

[The reason that] little Jacob Taubes comes along and enters into the business of gathering the heretic [Paul] back into the fold, [is] because I regard him – this is my own personal business – as more Jewish than any Reform rabbi or any Liberal rabbi, I ever heard in Germany, England, America, Switzerland or anywhere.[67]

Taubes felt a strong sense of familiarity with Paul, 'a diaspora Jew' who reminded him of the cocky, aggressive Jewish American college students he had seen in

---

[62] 'In the course of this lecture I want to try to convey to you why Paul concerns me as a Jew....' Taubes, *The Political Theology of Paul*, 4.

[63] Taubes is dismissive of Klausner and Schoeps, complimentary about Baeck and Flusser, and interested to engage with Buber and Freud. Taubes, *The Political Theology of Paul*, 5–11, 136–8. Christian commentators cited include Harnack, Bauer, Schweitzer, Stendahl, and Barth (and Nietzsche). Schmidt suggests that Taubes's work is heavily dependent upon the reconstruction of Paul's epistle to the Romans found in Erik Peterson's *Theolgische Traktate* (Munich: Kösel, 1951), although this is unacknowledged. Christoph Schmidt, 'Review essay of Jacob Taubes' *The Political Theology of Paul*', in *Hebraic Political Studies* 2:2 (Spring 2007), 239. Taubes tended to focus on Romans but did occasionally mention other letters, including 1 Corinthians and Galatians.

[64] 'Of course I'm not speaking *ex nihilo* here [in this lecture]. This means that I still owe you a scholarly answer to the question of what tradition of Jewish religious history I stand within. Now it happens that the Jewish study of Paul is in a very sad state. There is a literary corpus about Jesus, a nice guy, about the rabbi in Galilee, and about the Sermon on the Mount; it's all in the Talmud and so on.... This apologetic literature proliferated in the nineteenth and twentieth centuries, and there is a consensus in Liberal Judaism (not in Orthodox Judaism, which hasn't moved an inch), that is, a sort of pride in this son of Israel. But when it comes to Paul, that's a borderline that's hard to cross.' Taubes, *The Political Theology of Paul*, 6.

[65] '[T]o the present day.... nothing has changed, and all of this blahblah about Jewish-Christian understanding is not worth mentioning – the world is divided into Jews and Gentiles. That there are Christians is something that has not entered [the Jewish] consciousness, so to speak. Whoever tells you anything different is an interested party. That's how it is.' Taubes, *The Political Theology of Paul*, 20.

[66] 'Names are not sound and smoke, but word and fire, and it is to names that one must be true.' Cited by Aleida Assmann in Taubes, *The Political Theology of Paul*, 143.

[67] Taubes, *The Political Theology of Paul*, 11.

Israel.[68] The apostle's Jewishness meant that Taubes believed he could understand the epistles better than non-Jews,[69] but Paul's was a special kind of Jewishness, and one with exciting potential for any philosopher interested in marginal identity. As Taubes saw it, Paul had lived and worked in a unique atmosphere, one in which the conflict between Jewish and Gentile Christians was still raging and in which the political and economic relationships within the mixed congregations was very different from the situation pertaining after the destruction of the Temple, when he believed that the spirit of the Jewish-Christians had been broken. Thus Paul had inhabited a world where what was 'Jewish' and what was 'Christian' had not yet been decided.[70]

To accomplish his reclamation, Taubes needed to undermine the Christian image of Paul. Rather than emphasise the *conversion* of Paul (from Judaism to Christianity), whereby Paul's faith is understood in terms of freedom from the Law, he stresses the *calling* of Paul (in line with other Jewish prophets). Starting with Rom. 1:1, in which Paul introduces himself as 'a servant of Jesus Christ, called to be an apostle', Taubes argued,

So what we have here is not a conversion but a calling. Whoever looks at what Galatians 1:15 says about what is commonly called the conversion, the Damascus [road] experience, knows that what is being talked about here is not conversion but a calling, and

---

[68] 'I am inclined to assume that Paul was a diaspora Jew. Whether his family originated in Palestine, whether he belongs to the tribe of Benjamin – he says he belongs. If he comes from the Galilean tradition, then it makes a lot of sense to me that he also calls himself a "zealot". Someone with zeal for the law.... If you go to Israel [today] and look ... then you will notice that there is a whole zealot group of American college boys ... who are cocky [*frech*], like any American, and, on top of that, aggressive when they want to accomplish something. Anyway, this type of zealot diaspora Jew who is to the core holier than thou, that is, who wants to outdo the normal level of piety, this is what we have before our eyes today, so to speak. You can just smell it.... That's the type he was. A diaspora Jew, but nevertheless sent by the family to Jerusalem.' Taubes, *The Political Theology of Paul*, 25–6.

[69] Taubes reports as evidence a conversation he once had with the Germanist and Greek scholar Emil Staiger: 'You know, Taubes, yesterday I was reading the Letters of the Apostle Paul. To which, he added, with great bitterness: but that isn't Greek, it's Yiddish! Upon which I said: Yes, Professor, and that's why I understand it!' Taubes, *The Political Theology of Paul*, 3–4.

[70] 'During the time of Paul ... the political balances and the economic balances were different.... [The Roman congregation] is a mixed congregation, and the conflicts within it are between Jewish Christians and Gentile Christians.... The whole question of commensality, of the common table, these are very concrete problems. Does one eat together? Does one sleep together? Is this a congregation or is this not a congregation? That wasn't as simple as it seems now. After 70 it was all smooth sailing.... With that [the destruction of the Temple, interpreted as divine punishment] the will of the Jewish Christian congregation is broken by both the Jews and the Gentile Christians. What is exciting about Paul is that we are just *before this turning point*, and the balances are totally different.... [T]he word "Christian" – this I ask you to get into your heads – doesn't yet exist for Paul. One mustn't be cleverer than the author and impute to him concepts that he doesn't have and doesn't want to have.' Taubes, *The Political Theology of Paul*, 20–21. The term 'Christian' first appears in the New Testament in Acts 11:26: 'and when he [Barnabas] had found him [Paul], he brought him to Antioch. And for an entire year they met with the church and taught considerable numbers; and the disciples were first called Christians in Antioch.' Taubes, suspicious of the historicity of much of the New Testament, ignored such references.

that this is done in the language and the style of Jeremiah [1:5: 'Before I created you in the womb, I selected you. Before you were born, I consecrated you. I appointed you a prophet concerning the nations.'].... And this is how Paul sees himself called to be an apostle – one has always to add this, otherwise one misses what is essential – from the Jews to the Gentiles.[71]

So, although Paul was undoubtedly a Jew, he was a Jew with a very special mission. What precisely had this mission entailed? Taubes read Rom. 9–11 as Paul's declaration that, like Moses, he was the founder of a new people and the representative of a new Law.[72]

For Paul, the task at hand is the *establishment and legitimation of a new people of God*. This doesn't seem very dramatic to you, after two thousand years of Christianity. But it is the most dramatic process imaginable in a Jewish soul.[73]

The Epistle to the Romans can only be understood, suggested Taubes, if it is read alongside Exod. 32, for always in Paul's mind is the story of Moses. God's anger at the rejection of his messiah had mirrored God's anger at the rejection of the Law and the worship of the Golden Calf. Moses and Paul had both been with Israel at the awful moment when relations had hung in the balance; but whereas Moses had been able to change God's mind, to convince Him to adhere to the original covenant, and had rejected the idea of founding a new people,[74] Paul had become the anti-Moses who took responsibility for the new foundation or covenant of the people of God. 'The crux of the thing', Taubes continued,

lies in the fact that Paul faced the same problem as Moses. The people has sinned. It has rejected the Messiah that has come to it. It is only from this, after all, that the calling of Paul results, as it says in Galatians.... All of what I have said appears to me to be necessary in order to understand just what Paul means when he says he wants to be accursed by Christ. These are not rhetorical flourishes, but rather the [expression of] devastation about the people of God no longer being the people of God.[75]

In offering further support for the idea that Paul had sought to create a new people, Taubes directed his attention to the Pauline reduction of Jesus' dual commandment

---

[71] Taubes, *The Political Theology of Paul*, 13–14.
[72] Taubes relates a story of how he was invited to Plettenberg in the autumn of 1979 to talk with Carl Schmitt about Romans and generated his idea of Moses who, twice, 'refused the idea that with him begins a new people and that the people of Israel should be eliminated – and of Paul who accepts the idea.' According to the story, Schmitt had said, 'Taubes, before you die, you must tell some people about this.' Taubes, *The Political Theology of Paul*, 2–3.
[73] Taubes, *The Political Theology of Paul*, 28.
[74] Taubes cites Exod. 32–4 and Num. 14–15.
[75] Taubes, *The Political Theology of Paul*, 37–8.

(which had already reduced the 613 commandments to two, love of God and love of neighbour) to the single commandment, love of neighbour.

No dual commandment but one commandment. I regard this as an absolutely revolutionary act.... [Jesus' dual commandment] belongs to the primordial core of Jesus's Christian tradition. And that Paul couldn't have missed.'[76]

Why had Paul done this? It made good sense, Taubes suggested, if Paul had been concerned not with the individual so much as with the new community he had founded and the need to integrate Jews and Gentiles within it. Nevertheless, Taubes was insistent that Paul's vision of a new people had not negated his sense of belonging to the old people and that it was this loyalty that accounted for his heartfelt pain and readiness to suffer for their sake as a scapegoat that might neutralise God's anger (just as Moses had done for Israel's salvation). For Taubes's Paul, the enmity of God for Jews (for their rejection of the messiah) had been part of an ancient love story and certainly had not implied the rejection of the Jews for the sake of the Gentiles. The election of the Gentiles had been a chapter in this story, whereby God had attempted to draw back his people to him.

The whole business about going to the Gentiles turns out in this context to be a scene of jealousy in order to make the Jews, to whom this message is directed, jealous. I didn't invent that; it says so in the text. Because he doesn't want to cast away the people, but to make them jealous.[77]

In any case, what most interested Taubes in Paul's opening up of the Covenant to the Gentiles was the authority he claimed for the consequent creation of a new community. In Paul's day, he observed, there had been only two models of human relations: the ethnic community, such as the people of Israel, and the imperial order of the Roman Empire. Paul was understood to have offered a third option, which he had defined against both. Thus the Epistle to the Romans relativises Rome's world imperialism with the messiah's claim to world dominance, and at the same time challenges Israel's self-understanding by asserting the New Israel's independence of Law (*nomos*) and peoplehood (*ethnos*). As Taubes put it elsewhere,

I read the Epistle to the Romans as a legitimation and formation of a new social union-covenant, of the developing ecclesia against the Roman Empire, on the one hand, and, on the other hand, of the ethnic unity of the Jewish people.[78]

His image of Paul was of a revolutionary thinker who, having rejecting all political and ethnic conceptions of identity, went on to disregard any authority that defined

---

[76]   Taubes, *The Political Theology of Paul*, 53.
[77]   Taubes, *The Political Theology of Paul*, 50.
[78]   This is from a course description of a lecture course 'On the Political Theology of Paul' (1986), cited in Taubes, *The Political Theology of Paul*, afterword by Wolf-Daniel Hartwich, Alieda and Jan Assman, 117.

itself in these terms. And this is the context in which he offered another corrective to Christian traditional interpretation, this time regarding the Law.

For Taubes, it was important to jettison the traditional dichotomy of Law and works-righteousness, and to acknowledge the error of regarding Pauline theology as, essentially, a critique of the Torah or Jewish religious Law. Instead, he believed that the 'nomos' or 'law' that Paul had condemned should actually be understood as referring to the 'Hellenistic theology of the sovereign'. In stark contrast with other interpretations of what Paul had meant by the Law,[79] Taubes maintained that Paul's critique of the Law represents a negation of the use of law *per se* – whether imperial or theocratic[80] – as a force of political order: for the apostle, legitimacy was denied to *all* sovereigns of the world. As Taubes put it, 'It isn't *nomos* but rather the one nailed to the cross by *nomos* who is the imperator!'[81] Taubes's Paul offered, then, a 'negative political theology' in that he offered no *political* alternative in his programme to undermine the law as a power to dominate; and this, said Taubes, had important implications for those interested in using Paul for their political theologies, for although many oppressed groups might identify with his revolutionary objectives, they could not claim the authority of Paul for the new political orders for which they called.

In offering this unusual interpretation of Paul's view of the Law, Taubes tried not only to develop a political-theological critique of the foundations of legal authority, but also to build a case for the categorisation of antinomianism as a legitimately *Jewish* enterprise. Judaism and Christianity have traditionally been stereotyped as two different approaches to religion: one is said to exemplify 'reconciliation by ritualisation' or ritualistic religiosity, whereby obedience to the Law is prized above all else; the other exemplifies 'redemption by liberation' or spiritual religiosity, whereby freedom from the Law is regarded as the key. And yet, historically, both approaches have each had proponents within both religious systems. Taubes's original contribution was to focus on 'redemption by liberation' in the *Jewish* context, for which he held up Paul as his Jewish champion. (Traditionally, of course, Paul had been regarded as the *Christian* exemplar of 'liberation' from the Law). For Taubes, Paul's critique of the Law had *not* been a Christian polemic against Judaism or the Torah, but rather one of a series of Jewish attempts to find freedom from the Law.[82] Another controversial example he gives was the seventeenth-century self-proclaimed messiah Sabbatai Zvi.

---

[79] Taubes takes exception to Bultmann's assertion that Paul shares in the same kind of universality found elsewhere in the Jewish-Hellenistic world, so that his concept of the law incorporates the Torah, the law of the universe, and natural law. Taubes, *The Political Theology of Paul*, 24.

[80] Paul goes beyond the Zealots who deny only the legitimacy of Roman Imperial law, and who hope for a new national form of rule, a theocratic law. In this context, Taubes praises Bruno Bauer, who was the first to recognise in *Christ and the Caesars* (1877) that 'Christian literature is a literature of protest against the flourishing cult of the emperor.' Taubes, *The Political Theology of Paul*, 16.

[81] Taubes, *The Political Theology of Paul*, 24.

[82] Taubes, *The Political Theology of Paul*, afterward by Wolf-Daniel Hartwich, Alieda and Jan Assman, 116–17.

The story of Sabbatai Zvi (1626–c1676) and his apostle Nathan of Gaza (1643–80) provided Taubes with the evidence he needed to justify his categorisation of Paul's antinomian theology as authentically Jewish. After all, both Nathan and Paul had been concerned to answer a profoundly Jewish question, namely, how does one rationalise the apparent failure of the messiah?[83] In comparing what he called the 'messianic logic' of the two theologians, Taubes hoped to demolish the common view of Paul's conception of faith and his attitude towards the Torah as evidence of his non-Jewish or Christian character. Basing himself heavily on his friend Gershom Sholem's work, Taubes explained that Lurianic *kabbalah* teaches that every Jew partakes of the restoration (*tikkun*) of creation by means of the 'progressive separation of good from evil' accomplished through 'performance of the commandments of the Torah'.[84] Nathan of Gaza had replaced the redeeming function of the 'works of the Law' (which had been assumed by Luria) with legitimation by means of 'pure faith' in the messiah. Just as Paul had written 'The righteous shall live by his faith',[85] so Nathan had exclaimed 'He whose soul is justified by faith shall live.'[86] Just as Paul had offered a theological rationale for the crucifixion (that is, the pure messiah must, paradoxically, become impure in order to sanctify those who are impure),[87] so too had Nathan for Sabbatai Zvi's conversion to Islam. (In Nathan's case, the idea appears to have been that evil is so thoroughly woven into the cosmos that its division from good is impossible; the good must fully identify with evil, transcending the Torah which distinguishes between good and evil, in order to transcend it.) Thus faith for Paul and Nathan is not a matter of belief in God. What both are calling for was, in fact, the impossible – for men to believe, despite the evidence to the contrary, that Jesus or Sabbatai Zvi was the messiah – and they were prepared to recognise this feat as the greatest spiritual accomplishment of all. It was clear that, to achieve this, the believer needed to discard previous assumptions along with any and all authorities upon whom they had previously depended.

---

[83] 'If there is something like a catalogue of Jewish virtues, and there is such a thing, then the word *emunah* [faith] plays a very subordinate role. That is, if you read the moral literature of the Talmud or of thirteenth-century Spain or of the fifteenth-century . . . if you read this moral literature, then [it's true that] you will also find, among the wide variety of virtues they have there, the word *emunah*. [But in contrast] In the Sabbatian literature the coverage is very dense. This is in the first place a statistical finding: Suddenly the word *emunah* appears six, seven times on each folio page. This statistical finding is incredibly instructive. The Sabbatian drama is a caricature of the Christian drama. By caricature I don't mean that it is imitated [but that both histories are those of the apparent failure of a Jewish messiah for which an explanation must be found].' Taubes, *The Political Theology of Paul*, 8.

[84] Gershom Scholem, *Sabbatai Sevi: The Mystical Messiah, 1626–1676*, trans. R. J. Zwi Werblowsky (Princeton, NJ: Princeton University Press, 1973), 42.

[85] Rom. 1:17 ('For in it the righteousness of God is revealed from faith to faith; as it is written, "But the righteous man shall live by faith"'), referring to Hab. 2:4.

[86] G. Scholem, *Sabbatai Sevi* (1973), 282, 284.

[87] Taubes cites 2 Cor. 5:21 ('He made Him who knew no sin to be sin on our behalf, so that we might become the righteousness of God in Him').

[T]he principle is clear: the inner experience of redemption is going to be *reinterpreted* in light of an external catastrophe and a slap in the face.... [T]he internal logic of events demanded a faith that is paradoxical, that is contradicted by the evidence. Paul comes and says: Here is the Messiah. People must know that he died on the cross. After all, word has gotten around.... Here is the son of David hanging on the cross!... Now try to think from the centre in a Jewish way: expelled from the community he hangs there, accursed, and has to be taken down in the evening lest the ground become impure. This is a total and monstrous inversion of the values of Roman and Jewish thought...[88]

The faith in this defamed son of David becomes an equivalent for all – now we're speaking in Pauline terms – works. This faith is more important than any works.... Here something is demanded at such a high price to the human soul that all works are nothing by comparison – to consider it for a moment from the perspective of religious psychology instead of theology.... Faith according to Paul must be understood in the emphatic sense as faith in the Messiah, who by an earthly measure cannot be the Messiah who hangs condemned on the cross.... This paradoxical faith... [this] messianic logic in the history of Jewish mysticism, is a logic that is repeated in history.[89]

Once again, then, Taubes was offering a corrective to the Christian tradition. Paul's faith had had little to do with an individual's ahistorical spiritual experience of salvation as understood in terms of a new relation with God. Nor could it be used to justify any claim to power. Rather, it had been founded on the historical experience of a catastrophe and the paradoxical realisation that salvation was to be achieved by the overturning of the previous rational universe, the abandonment of the Law and works, and the transfer of allegiance to a higher authority than that of *any* earthy rulers. Preempting any queries as to how this antiauthoritarian reading of the apostle could be reconciled with his apparently quietistic passages which called for the *status quo* and obedience to existing worldly powers,[90] Taubes reasoned,

under this time pressure, if tomorrow the whole palaver, the entire swindle were going to be over – in that case there's no point in any revolution! That's absolutely right, I would give the same advice. Demonstrate obedience to state authority, pay taxes, don't do any thing bad, don't get involved in conflicts, because otherwise it'll get confused

---

[88] Taubes, *The Political Theology of Paul*, 9–10.
[89] Taubes, *The Political Theology of Paul*, 49–50.
[90] For example, Rom. 13:1–7: 'Every person is to be in subjection to the governing authorities. For there is no authority except from God, and those which exist are established by God. Therefore whoever resists authority has opposed the ordinance of God; and they who have opposed will receive condemnation upon themselves. For rulers are not a cause of fear for good behavior, but for evil. Do you want to have no fear of authority? Do what is good and you will have praise from the same; for it is a minister of God to you for good. But if you do what is evil, be afraid; for it does not bear the sword for nothing; for it is a minister of God, an avenger who brings wrath on the one who practices evil. Therefore it is necessary to be in subjection, not only because of wrath, but also for conscience's sake. For because of this you also pay taxes, for rulers are servants of God, devoting themselves to this very thing. Render to all what is due them: tax to whom tax is due; custom to whom custom; fear to whom fear; honor to whom honor.'

with some revolutionary movement, which, of course, is how it happened. Because, after all, these people have no legitimation, as, for instance, the Jews do, as a *religio licita* [legal religion]....[91]

Thus Paul's apparent quietism actually reflected his radical apocalypticism: if one expected the imminent end of the world and believed that God has called one to found a new social order, then there was no time to waste revolting against meaningless worldly authority.[92]

With this interpretation of the apostle's theology, Taubes believed that he had returned Paul the heretic to the Jewish fold (because a messianic logic is a Jewish logic) and that, in so doing, he had also developed a more sophisticated understanding of Judaism itself – one which saw Judaism as a phenomenon that has historically, from time to time, demonstrated a tendency to seek liberation from the Law. This is, of course, a highly problematic argument. It is by no means obvious that messianism is an exclusively Jewish phenomenon, for Christianity, at least, shares this trait. It was also somewhat naïve for Taubes to have thought that his assertion that Paul and Nathan both understood the Law in terms of religio-political authority would be accepted without further debate. And the same is true for their 'messianic logic', whose antinomianism would – by definition – disqualify its Jewish categorisation as far as many in the Jewish community are concerned. Nevertheless, as we shall see, this allegedly Jewish messianic understanding of faith, as espoused by Paul, represented a powerful means by which Taubes could critique certain ideas within modern political theology.

In *Occidental Eschatology* (1947),[93] Taubes had argued that if one accepted the idea that time would one day come to an end, as he himself did, then there were profound implications for political thought. Although in 'nature' time was experienced as an eternal cycle of events, 'history' was defined as the realm of time in which men's actions altered the progression of events. A man's decision, then, really mattered. Such a philosophy demanded that individuals take responsibility for their own actions and shake off all authorities that claimed to act on their behalf.[94] This theory, which he called Apocalyptic, was deeply unnerving to many observers and went a long way towards earning him his reputation as a nonconformist, maverick

---

[91]   Taubes, *The Political Theology of Paul*, 54.
[92]   For an excellent overview of Taube's key philosophical interests, including his apocalypticism and political-theological legitimisation of authority, see Joshua Robert Gold, 'Jacob Taubes: Apocalypse from Below', *Telos* 134 (March 2006), 140–56. See also the comparative study of Taubes's political theology in Marin Terpstra and Theo de Wit, '"No Spiritual Investment in the World as It Is": Jacob Taubes's Negative Political Theology', in Ilse N. Bulhof and Laurens Ten Kate, eds., *Flight of the Gods: Philosophical Perspectives on Negative Theology* (New York: Fordham University Press, 2000), 320–53.
[93]   Jacob Taubes, *Abendländische Eschatologie* (Bern: A. Francke, 1947).
[94]   As he put it elsewhere, 'This has consequences for the economy, actually for all life. There is no eternal return, time does not enable nonchalance; rather it is distress.' Interview with Jacob Taubes (1987), cited in Joshua Robert Gold, 'Jacob Taubes: Apocalypse from Below', 145.

thinker. It certainly coloured his debate with Carl Schmitt (1888–1985), the German political theorist. In this intellectual engagement, two theoretical possibilities for relating divine and secular power had been discussed in the light of Paul's theology. In 1922, Schmitt had famously written in *Political Theology* that 'all significant concepts of the modern theory of the state are secularised theological concepts',[95] thereby stressing the structural similarities between the function of political theory in legitimating State power and the function of theology for justifying God's power. The idea that God intervenes miraculously as part of his providential role for the world correlated to the ruler's acting above the law in the interest of state order; to 'decide on the exception' was therefore the justifiable action of a sovereign.[96] Ominously, Schmitt argued elsewhere that membership of the State was defined against a common enemy who was 'existentially something different and alien'.[97] The appeal of such ideas to the Nazi regime are obvious and explain in part Schmitt's prestige and influence as a jurist during its early years. A lifetime later, in September 1979, Schmitt invited Taubes to his home in Plettenberg.[98] Taubes's own account makes it clear that the category of enemy was discussed in the context of Paul's attitude to the Jews as portrayed in Rom. 11:28, 'Enemies [of God] for your sake; but as regards election they are beloved, for the sake of their forefathers'. Whereas Schmitt focused on the earlier part of the sentence, believing that Paul's new community had been defined against and in opposition to the Jewish people who had become the enemies of God himself, Taubes emphasised the later part of the sentence, stressing the ongoing covenant with Israel.

And this is the point I challenged Schmitt on, that he doesn't see this dialectic that moves Paul, and that the Christian church after 70 has forgotten, *that he adopted not a text but a tradition, that is, the folk traditions of church antisemitism, onto which he, in 1933–6, in his uninhibited fashion, went on to graft the racist theozoology.* That is something that he, the most important state law theorist, did indeed receive as a lesson. 'That I did not know!' It is possible to read texts without noticing what their core point is.[99] [Italics added]

---

[95] Carl Schmitt, *Political Theology*, trans. George Schwab (Cambridge, MA: MIT Press, 1985), 36. The translation is of the 1934 second edition; the first edition was published as Carl Schmitt, *Politische Theologie: Vier Kapitel zur Lehre von der Souveränität* (Munich: Duncker & Humblot, 1922).

[96] Carl Schmitt, *Political Theology*, 5.

[97] Carl Schmitt, *The Concept of the Political*, trans. George Schwab (Chicago: University of Chicago Press, 1996), 27. Originally published as Carl Schmitt, 'Der Begriff des Politischen', in *Archiv fur Sozialwissenschaft und Sozialpolitik*, 58 (1927).

[98] In 1952, Schmitt had been forwarded a copy of a letter in which Taubes had described him as '*the* intellectual capacity that stands above all the intellectual scribbling' (see Appendix B in Taubes, *The Political Theology of Paul*, 107) and began sending him copies of his books; he circulated the letter, commenting, 'Letter from a Jewish intellectual who understands me better than any of my followers.' Taubes had ignored the ex-Nazi jurist, until in 1979 he wrote asking to see him. For an overview of the Schmitts–Taubes relationship, see Marin Terpstra and Theo de Wit, '"No Spiritual Investment in the World as It Is": Jacob Taubes's Negative Political Theology', 327–36.

[99] Taubes, *The Political Theology of Paul*, 51.

In general terms, Taubes agreed that political theory and theology were intimately related. But the implications, as he saw them, were very different from those suggested by Schmitt, whose theoretical conception of 'enemy' showed him to be a victim of the seductive power of the traditional, but mistaken, Christian interpretation of Pauline thought. For Taubes, the structure of theology – that is, the logic of messianic and Apocalyptic thought – did not somehow legitimate the political power, but rather pointed to the usurpation of all authority and the delegitimation of State sovereignty. And this view, which made pointless any accommodation to the prevailing political establishment, was a good thing. As Taubes tries to explain in his Heidelberg lectures, Schmitt had been interested in only one thing, namely,

that the chaos not rise to the top, that the state remain. No matter what the price. . . . I [Taubes] have no spiritual investment in this world as it is. But I understand that someone else [for example, Schmitt] is invested in this world and sees in the apocalypse, whatever its form, the adversary, and does everything to keep it subjugated and suppressed, because from there forces can be unleashed that we are in no position to control. You see now what I want from Schmitt – I want to show him that the separation of powers between worldly and spiritual is *absolutely necessary*. This boundary, if it is not drawn, we will lose our Occidental breath. This is what I wanted to impress upon him against his totalitarian concept.[100]

It would be surprising if, in making this argument to Schmitt himself in 1979, Taubes had not drawn heavily upon Paul's Jewish messianism, which he believed offered the antidote to the poisonous assumptions underlying Schmitt's political theology.[101]

As a post-Holocaust Jew, Taubes had been understandably concerned to question the foundations of political authority, and especially its theological legitimation. Partly because influential Western political theoreticians such as Schmitt appeared to have been influenced by Pauline theology, in one way or another, it seemed imperative to Taubes to offer a critique of Paul. In his reclamation of the 'Jewish Apostle to the Gentiles', Taubes suggested that the study of Paul's milieu offered an insight into a time when borders between Jewish and Christian thought had not been finalised; there was, in his view, a tantalising possibility of reaching back and reclaiming certain traditionally Christian ideas as Jewish. One such idea was the tendency to look for liberation from the law – in the sense of freedom from political authority. In other words, his focus on Paul's creation of a new people, 'a

---

[100] Taubes, *The Political Theology of Paul*, 103.

[101] Gold has demonstrated that from early on in his career, Taubes had read Paul's theology along apocalyptic lines; thus the Pauline community had been constituted of those who 'have freed themselves from all natural, organic attachments – from nature, art, cult and state – and for whom emptiness and alienation from the world . . . accordingly reached a high state.' Taubes, *Abendländische Eschatologie* (1947), cited in Joshua Robert Gold, 'Jacob Taubes: Apocalypse from Below', *Telos* 134 (March 2006), 153.

subterranean society, a little bit Jewish, a little bit Gentile,'[102] and the justification the apostle offered for doing so, allowed him to criticise both Christian and Jewish culture more generally. The Christian community had missed the political import of Paul's language of 'faith' and 'law', whereas the Jewish community had been wrong to regard antinomianism as entirely alien to Judaism and Jewish thought.

CONCLUSION

The philosophical treatments of Spinoza, Shestov, and Taubes, despite their differences, nevertheless share certain aims in common. All three oriented their work around a revolutionary vision of society, and all three regarded Paul as an influential voice in Western civilisation whose support was essential for persuading their mainly non-Jewish readerships of the failings of (Christian) authority. All three were also interested in relating Paul to rational discourse, although in different ways. Spinoza's inclination was to use the apostle in the construction of a rationalist, antisuperstitious platform from which to undermine the Church's interference in secular power. Shestov also challenged the established orders but, in his case, Paul helped destabilise what was regarded as the overly rationalist assumptions of the Judeo-Christian tradition. Taubes, like Spinoza, was particularly interested in Paul's universalism, although he was less concerned about questions regarding the universality of reason and more interested in the apostle's creation of a universal society that implied the subjection of *all* rational forms of political authority. Here, Taubes's messianic, apocalyptic logic shared a good deal with Shestov: both men were theoretically antinomian, although only Taubes tried to show that this was an authentically Jewish stance. It is also worth noting that, however much each drew upon Paul in his work, the apostle can in no wise be regarded as having shaped their ideas or their sense of identity; quite the reverse, it should be clear that it is their preexisting ideological programmes which dictated their understanding and use of him.

Having completed a brief survey of three philosophers who have drawn upon the apostle Paul in their work, it is worth noting that, although Jewish-born, all inhabited the no-man's land of Jewish marginality. Two did not adhere to religious practices whatsoever and, arguably, all three attempted to subordinate their Jewishness to the more universal worldviews of philosophy. In this regard, several of Deutscher's previously discussed observations about the non-Jewish Jew apply. All three sought to challenge, and even to subvert, a culture which was regarded as dangerously dominated by Christian norms of thought. Each one adopted a perspective that offered an alternative, historically unconventional view, whether it was rationalism (Spinoza), antirationalism (Shestov), or messianic apocalypticism (Taubes). All aimed to strike at the heart of the sources of power within society,

---

[102] Jacob Taubes, *The Political Theology of Paul*, 54.

be it the fearful sway of superstition (Spinoza), dogma and idealism (Shestov), or legal authority (Taubes). In so doing, they can be regarded as having joined the ranks of religious Jews in the modern period who have offered a critique of Christian thought by means of engaging with the apostle, with the key difference that here their focus was not upon theology *per se* but upon the legacy of Paul for understanding the place of religion in society. As we shall now see, other kinds of non-Jewish Jews have swelled these ranks.

8

∽

The Psychoanalytical Writings of Sigmund Freud
and Hanns Sachs

From its inception, psychoanalysis has had a complicated relationship with Judaism. Freud himself was anxious to prevent the association of his new science with Jews for fear that it would not be taken seriously by an anti-Semitic establishment. And yet, until Jung joined it, the psychoanalytical association was almost exclusively composed of Jews. As one contemporary, a British professor at Harvard, observed,

The famous theory of Freud is a theory of the development and working of the mind which was evolved by a Jew who has studied chiefly Jewish patients; and it seems to appeal very strongly to Jews; many, perhaps the majority of those physicians who accept it as a new gospel, a new revelation, are Jews.[1]

It is by no means only those hostile to the therapeutic system who regard it as some sort of Jewish science (as the Nazis notoriously referred to it). Anna Freud herself once described it as such,[2] and David Meghnagi has suggested that the birth of psychoanalysis should be understood as 'a cultural event within Judaism', as a sublimated answer to the problems posed by secularisation and as a rejection of an authentic integration of Jews into Christian European society. He argued that it is best appreciated when it is set alongside the rise of the sociopolitical movements of Zionism and the Bund, that is, alongside Jewish nationalism and Jewish socialism. These movements were products of the great process of secularisation of culture that had been sweeping through the Jewish world since the seventeenth century. Psychoanalysis, a German-Jewish synthesis of literature, theory, and science, was therefore one of several new worldviews that promised an alternative 'community'

---

[1] William McDougall, *Is America Safe for Democracy?* (New York: Scribner, 1921), 127.
[2] At the inaugural lecture of the Sigmund Freud Professorship at the Hebrew University in Jerusalem in 1977, Anna Freud's lecture, which was read out in her absence, noted that psychoanalysis 'has been criticized for its methods being imprecise, its findings not open to proof by experiment, for being unscientific, even for being a "Jewish science." However the other derogatory comments may be evaluated, it is, I believe, the last-mentioned connotation which, under present circumstances, can serve as a title of honor.' Anna Freud, 'Inaugural Lecture', *International Journal of Psycho-Analysis* LIX (1978), 148.

for the Jew. The psychoanalytical association promoted a new reality, one that made both the Jewish and Christian religions irrelevant.[3]

In this chapter we will see how Sigmund Freud and Hanns Sachs, two Jewish-born luminaries at the centre of this particular response to modernity, were attracted to Paul for what they regarded as his profound insight into human psychology. These secular Jews, like the philosophers of the previous chapter, drew upon the apostle's thought in their programmatic efforts to undermine common assumptions about the influence of religion upon political authority. Their writings remind us once again, if we needed to be reminded, that Jewish commentary on Paul is by no means restricted to those committed to a theological or interreligious debate.

SIGMUND FREUD, PAUL, AND THE RETURN OF THE REPRESSED

The Austrian founder of psychoanalysis, Sigmund Freud (1856–1939), wore his Jewishness lightly, even as he readily acknowledged it.[4] His controversial theories of the unconscious mind have enjoyed immense academic and popular success, constituting the foundation of a psychotherapy still practiced widely in the West and the subject of ongoing intellectual discussion. His approach to religion, for example, as provocative today as when it was first published, remains essential reading on university campuses worldwide.

---

[3] David Meghnagi, 'A Cultural Event within Judaism' in David Meghnagi, ed., *Freud and Judaism* (London: Karnac Books, 1993), 57–8, 63–4. Arguably, the same is true for race, as Gilman notes: 'As virtually all of Freud's early disciples were Jews, the lure of psychoanalysis for them may well have been its claims for a universalisation of human experience and an active exclusion of the importance of race from its theoretical framework.' Sander L. Gilman, *Freud, Race and Gender* (Princeton, NJ: Princeton University Press, 1993), 6.

[4] In *Moses and Monotheism* (1939), published shortly after he had fled Nazi Germany, Freud expresses his concern, as a Jew, in attempting to undermine Jewish tradition's claim on Moses as a Hebrew. 'To deny a people the man who it praises as the greatest of its sons is not a deed to be undertaken lightheartedly – especially by one belonging to that people.' At the same time, he could be dismissive of some aspects of Jewish thought. Knowing that his theory 'lacked objective proof', he accounts for his reluctance to publish it, thus: 'it is not attractive to be classed with the scholastics and Talmudists who are satisfied to exercise their ingenuity, unconcerned how far removed their conclusions may be from the truth.' Sigmund Freud, *Moses and Monotheism*, 11, 30. In a speech given in May 1926, looking back at his early career, Freud commented, '[F]or I myself was a Jew, and it always seemed to me to be not only shameful but downright senseless to deny it.' Sigmund Freud, 'On Being of the B'nai B'rith: An Address to the Society In Vienna', reproduced in *Commentary* (March 1946), 23. For discussions about Freud's Jewishness, see Peter Gay, 'The Question of a Jewish Science' in *A Godless Jew: Freud, Atheism, and the Making of Psychoanalysis* (New Haven: Yale University Press, 1987), 115–154, Yosef Yerushalmi, *Freud's Moses: Judaism Terminable and Interminable*, 8–14, David Meghnagi, ed., *Freud and Judaism* (London: Karnac Books, 1993), Sander L. Gilman, *Freud, Race and Gender*, Daniel Boyarin, *The Rise of Heterosexuality and the Invention of the Jewish Man* (Berkeley: University of California Press, 1997), 189–220, and Jay Geller, *On Freud's Jewish Body: Mitigating Circumcisions* (New York: Fordham University Press, 2007).

In *Totem and Taboo* (1913)[5] Freud had outlined a theory in which a psychologically traumatic experience in our distant primate past was held responsible for the emergence of religion. According to the theory, alienated male members of an ancient tribe, jealous of their polygamous leader's sexual monopoly of their mothers, had cannibalised him in a rite that had resulted in guilt-ridden reverence for, and eventually worship of, his power. Subsequently, they had transformed the previously reviled prohibitions of their murdered father figure into universal taboos and religious tradition. From this foundation[6] Freud went on to explore the nature of monotheism in the book *Moses and Monotheism* (1939),[7] in which he combined the application of psychoanalytical categories to Judaism and Christianity with a sensational, unsubstantiated account of Moses' Egyptian ancestry.[8] Arguably, the book is almost as much about the apostle Paul as about Moses, for it proposes to explain how the religion of the one logically emerged from the religion of the other.[9]

Fundamental to Freud's theory of the origins of religion was the idea that one can apply lessons learned from individual psychology to mass psychology. For example, just as a person retains childhood memories into adulthood, whether consciously or not, so too does a human collective. If animal instinct is simply a label for the phenomenon whereby animals 'carry over into their new existence the experience of their kind', Freud asked why this should not also apply to the human animal. Thus he began with the assertion that humankind 'have preserved in their minds memories of what their ancestors experienced.'[10] Again, just as an

---

[5] Originally published as Sigmund Freud, *Totem und Tabu: Einige Übereinstimmungen im Seelenleben der Wilden und der Neurotiker* (Leipzig: H. Heller, 1913).

[6] Freud maintained that since writing *Totem and Taboo* (1913), 'I have never doubted that religious phenomena are to be understood only on the model of the neurotic symptoms of the individual, which are so familiar to us, as a return of long-forgotten important happenings in the primeval history of the human family, that they owe their obsessive character to that very origin and therefore derive their effect on mankind form the historical truth they contain.' Freud, *Moses and Monotheism*, 94.

[7] Sigmund Freud, *Moses and Monotheism*. German original: Sigmund Freud, *Der Mann Moses und die monotheistische Religion* (Amsterdam: A. de Lange, 1939).

[8] In looking for historical traces for Moses, Freud alights upon the story of an Egyptian monotheist, Akhenaten. He suggests that it is this Pharaoh, whose Aton religion was a form of monotheism, who actually lies behind the Hebrew legend of Moses in the book of Exodus. Much of *Moses and Monotheism* is taken up with this investigation.

[9] Freud did not cite directly from Paul, but offered instead paraphrases of what he saw to be the essential message; for example, 'See, the Messiah has truly come. He was indeed murdered before your eyes', or 'It is because we killed God the Father that we are so unhappy', or 'We have been delivered from all guilt since one of us laid down his life to expiate our guilt'. Freud, *Moses and Monotheism*, 114, 174. He made no reference to Christian or Jewish Pauline scholarship.

[10] 'If we accept the continued existence of such memory traces in our archaic inheritance, then we have bridged the gap between individual and mass psychology and can treat peoples as we do the individual neurotic.... If the so-called instincts of animals – which from the very beginning allow them to behave in their new conditions of living as if they were old and long-established ones – if

individual neurotic experiences an event which was repressed in such a way that his subconscious generated obsessive behaviour, so the same process could be said to explain the profoundly obsessive character of religious tradition among the masses, which was not amenable to reason or logical arguments.[11]

When it came to explaining Judaism, a monotheistic tradition famously characterised by its taboos regarding incest and diet, Freud had no difficulty in identifying the Primal Father as Moses. For only if the Lawgiver had been murdered by the children of Israel would they have adhered so tenaciously to their laws down through the millennia. Consequentially, their collective guilt and veneration of the man who spoke with God had been transformed into an obsessive tradition. Not only Judaism but Christianity, too, could be understood by reference to this ancient episode. In fact, Freud believed that the comprehensive victory of Christianity over Judaism in historical terms could best be accounted for by the way in which the apostle Paul had intuitively taken advantage of the same psychological processes that he himself was now uncovering.

To Freud the amateur historian, the rise of Christianity could be partly explained in terms of timing. The period in question had been a period of widespread unease. The Jewish people had festered in unconscious guilt at the murder of Moses, and the rest of civilisation, perhaps reminded of their ancient crime against the Primal Father, also lived in a state of dread. This 'precursor of the return of the repressed' ended with the arrival of a certain Jewish 'political-religious agitator' in Palestine.[12] His followers eventually came to believe that they should disassociate themselves from Judaism. It was Paul, however, rather than Jesus, who was mainly responsible for this new religion. In recounting the history, Freud cleverly dovetailed his own theory with the theology of the apostle.

Paul, a Roman Jew from Tarsus, seized upon this feeling of guilt and correctly traced it back to the primeval source. This he called original sin; it was a crime against God

---

this instinctive life of animals permits of any explanation at all, it can only be this: that they carry over into their new existence the experience of their kind; that is to say, that they have preserved in their minds memories of what their ancestors experienced. In the human animal things should not be fundamentally different. His own archaic heritage, though different in extent and character, corresponds to the instincts of animals.' Freud, *Moses and Monotheism*, 160–61.

[11] 'A tradition based only on oral communication could not produce the obsessive character which appertains to religious phenomena. It would be listened to, weighed, and perhaps rejected, just like any other news from outside; it would never achieve the privilege of being freed from the coercion of logical thinking. It must first have suffered the fate of repression, the state of being unconscious, before it could produce such mighty effects on its return, and force the masses under its spell, such as we have observed – with astonishment and hitherto without understanding – in religious tradition.... The term "repressed" is here used not in its technical sense. Here I mean something past, vanished, and overcome in the life of a people, which I venture to treat as equivalent to a repressed material in the mental life of the individual.' Freud, *Moses and Monotheism*, 162, 208.

[12] 'The lightening of that oppression [that had seized all Mediterranean peoples as a vague discomfort, a premonition of misfortune, the reason for which no one knew] proceeded from the Jews.' Freud, *Moses and Monotheism*, 213.

that could be expiated only through death. Death had come into the world through original sin. In reality this crime, deserving of death, had been the murder of the Father who later was deified. The murderous deed itself, however, was not remembered; in its place stood the phantasy of expiation, and that is why this phantasy could be welcomed in the form of a gospel of salvation (Evangel). A Son of God, innocent himself, had sacrificed himself, and had thereby taken over the guilt of the world. It had to be a Son, for the sin had been murder of the Father.[13]

The apparent simplicity of this presentation of Christian history and theology is deceptive, however. It began by identifying the universal sense of guilt with the familiar Christian doctrine of Original Sin. For Freud, of course, the original sin was the murder of the Primal Father, who had later been deified, that is, a kind of deicide. But what did Freud believe that *Paul* had understood to be original sin? Nowhere does he describe that theological conception of original sin traditionally attributed to Paul, namely, the universal condition of sin that had followed Adam's Fall. Rather, the impression given was that Paul also thought of original sin in terms of deicide. This impression was further reinforced when Freud wrote,

It was . . . in the mind of a Jew, Saul of Tarsus, who as a Roman citizen was called Paul, that the perception dawned: 'It is because we killed God the Father than we are so unhappy.' It is quite clear to us now why he could grasp this truth in no other form but in the delusional guise of the glad tidings: 'We have been delivered from all guilt since one of us laid down his life to expiate our guilt.' In this formulation, the murder of God was, of course, not mentioned, but a crime that had to be expiated by a sacrificial death could only have been murder. . . . Original sin and salvation through sacrificial death became the basis of the new religion founded by Paul. . . . [14]

What is not clear from this is how, in Paul's mind, God the Father had been murdered. Was this synonymous with the crucifixion of Jesus? But according to the theory, Jesus had been the Son whose sacrifice was a necessary atonement for the murder of the Father. Did it refer to the killing of Moses? Although Freud claimed this in the context of Jewish history, he did not appear to claim this for Paul's theology. Nor had he suggested that the apostle's teaching had been pointing to the Primal Father. It seems that for Freud's Paul, the guilt from which mankind and the Jews awaited liberation had been the murder of God the Father, who was himself an amalgamation of several figures, including Moses and Jesus.[15] Freud himself was aware of the confusion implicit here, but argued that the story of Jesus' life and death, the details of which had soon been lost to history, had made

[13] Freud, *Moses and Monotheism*, 138–9.
[14] Freud, *Moses and Monotheism*, 213, 214.
[15] 'The awakening . . . of the memory trace [of the murder of the Primal Father] through a recent repetition of the event is of decisive importance [in activating the archaic inheritance].The murder of Moses was such a repetition, and later on the supposed judicial murder of Christ, so that these events move into the foreground as causative agents. It seems as if the genesis of monotheism would not have been possible without these events.' Freud, *Moses and Monotheism*, 162.

this confusion inevitable and was actually an essential factor for understanding Christianity's success.

It can scarcely be by chance that the violent death of another great man [that is, Jesus] should become the starting point for the creation of a new religion by Paul. This was a man whom a small number of adherents in Judea believed to be the Son of God and the promised Messiah, and who later on took over some of childhood history that had been attached to Moses [that is, father figure, lawgiver, mediator between God and the people]. In reality, however, we have hardly more definite knowledge of him than we have of Moses. We do not know if he was really the great man whom the Gospels depict or whether it was not rather the fact and the circumstances of his death that were the decisive factor in his achieving importance. Paul, who became his apostle, did not himself know him.[16]

In other words, the stature of Jesus had only increased as his memory had become fused with that of Moses. It was even possible that the messianic hope itself had had its origin in the guilt that the Hebrews had felt in killing Moses, and that Jesus should be regarded as 'the resurrected Moses'.[17] Furthermore, the way in which Christianity had gone on to resolve the similar confusion or ambivalency between the Father and the Son had proved to be one of the key innovations of the new religion.

Its main doctrine, to be sure, was the reconciliation with God the Father, the expiation of the crime committed against him; but the other side of the relationship manifested itself in the Son, who had taken the guilt on his shoulders, becoming God himself beside the Father and in truth in place of the Father. Originally a Father religion, Christianity became a Son religion. The fate of having to displace the Father it could not escape.[18]

Having 'burst the confines of Judaism', then, the followers of Paul came to equate the Son with the Father, and went on to institutionalise the identification of one with the other. Although the ceremony of Holy Communion, in which the believer partakes of the body and blood of Christ, 'repeats the content of the old totem feast', it also made a virtue out of a necessity by strengthening the conflation of Father and Son through ritual expression.[19]

---

[16] Freud, *Moses and Monotheism*, 143–4.

[17] 'It is an attractive suggestion that the guilt attached to the murder of Moses may have been the stimulus for the wish-phantasy of the Messiah, who was to return and give to his people salvation and the promised sovereignty over the world. If Moses was this first Messiah, Christ became his substitute and successor. Then Paul could with a certain right say to the peoples: "See, the Messiah has truly come. He was indeed murdered before your eyes." Then also there is some historical truth in the rebirth of Christ, for he was the resurrected Moses and the returned primeval father of the primitive horde as well – only transfigured, and as the Son in the place of the Father.' Freud, *Moses and Monotheism*, 144–5.

[18] Freud, *Moses and Monotheism*, 214–15.

[19] '[T]he Christian ceremony of Holy Communion, in which the believer incorporates the flesh and blood of the Redeemer, repeats the content of the old totem feast; it does so, it is true, only in its tender and adoring sense, not in its aggressive sense.' Freud, *Moses and Monotheism*, 141.

Freud was prepared to admit that traditions from 'Oriental and Greek mysteries' had exerted some influence in shaping this 'phantasy of salvation', but his lip service to New Testament scholarship was very much secondary to his recognition of Paul's originality. The apostle's characteristic emphasis on the Sonship of Jesus was seized upon as evidence of the psychological dynamic underlying the emergence of Christianity. Likewise, his tenet of the shadowy conception of original sin showed him to have tapped into the subconscious.[20] Paul was certainly 'a man with the gift of religion', but his power was by no means miraculous. Rather, 'Dark traces of the past lay in his soul, ready to break through into the regions of consciousness.'[21]

Paul's originality lay, first, in his doctrine of salvation, the sacrifice of a Son by which he had put to rest the ghost of ancestral guilt. Second, he had abandoned the idea of the chosen people and its visible sign (that is, circumcision), thereby ensuring the universal nature of the new faith.[22] In so doing, Freud was prepared to admit that Paul had brought about psychological liberation for a large proportion of mankind: 'Christianity marked a progress in the history of religion: that is to say, in regard to the return to the repressed.'[23] Ironically, the innovations by the 'Roman Jew from Tarsus' had achieved their success at a terrible cost for his ancestral faith; and here Freud returned to the complex relationship between the father and the son.

The ambivalency dominating the father–son relationship shows clearly, however, in the final result of the religious innovation. Meant to propitiate the Father Deity, it ends by his being dethroned and set aside. The Mosaic religion had been a Father religion; Christianity became a Son religion. The old God, the Father, took second place; Christ, the Son, stood in his stead, just as in those dark times every son had learned to do. Paul, by developing the Jewish religion further, became its destroyer. . . . From now on, the Jewish religion was, so to speak, a fossil.[24]

Of course, as Freud made clear elsewhere, religion was itself to be regarded as a fossil. Whatever its evolutionary benefits had been, he believed that this relic from our ancient past had been superseded by rational solutions in the modern age. And if religion was properly interpreted as a wish fulfilment or a neurosis, then it

---

[20] Freud, *Moses and Monotheism*, 214.

[21] Freud, *Moses and Monotheism*, 138–9.

[22] Freud, *Moses and Monotheism*, 142. Freud suggests that 'this might have been determined by Paul's revengefulness on account of the opposition which his innovation found among the Jews. . . . ' Ibid.

[23] Freud, *Moses and Monotheism*, 143. This recognition was by no means unqualified. 'In certain respects the new religion was a cultural regression as compared with the older Jewish religion. . . . The Christian religion did not keep to the lofty heights of spirituality to which the Jewish religion had soared. The former was no longer strictly monotheistic; it took over from the surrounding peoples numerous symbolical rites, re-established the great mother goddess, and found room for many deities of polytheism in an easily recognizable disguise, though in subordinate positions. Above all, it was not inaccessible, as the Aton religion and the subsequent Mosaic religion had been, to the penetration of superstitions, magical and mystical elements which proved a great hindrance to the spiritual development of the following two millennia.' Ibid., 142.

[24] Freud, *Moses and Monotheism*, 141, 143.

was surely an undesirable foundation for civilisation or culture.[25] What, then, is the place of the Apostle to the Gentiles in this famous critique of society?

Certainly, Freud's attitude towards Paul was more positive than had been many Jewish commentators before him, but a certain ambiguity remained.[26] On the one hand, Paul was an ally. He could be held up as a key figure in Western thought whose most profound teachings (properly interpreted) provided powerful evidence in support of Freudian analysis. He had instinctively understood what Freud had come to recognise, namely, the psychological power of releasing men from the gnawing societal guilt that resulted from their ancestors' murder of the Primal Father. Salvation from original sin equated to liberation from the return of the repressed. On the other hand, Paul was an arch-opponent. His invention, Christianity, was not only a religion – and therefore part of the discourse of illusion and an expression of wish-fulfilment – but it was, historically, the most influential religion that had acted upon and shaped Western civilisation.[27] To convince society that it had grown out of religion, Freud knew that he would first have to convince society of the psychological, rather than divine, origins of Pauline Christianity.

---

[25] 'Our knowledge of the historical worth of certain religious doctrines increases our respect for them, but does not invalidate our proposal that they should cease to be put forward as the reasons for the precepts of civilization. On the contrary! Those historical residues have helped us to view religious teachings, as it were, as neurotic relics, and we may now argue that the time has probably come, as it does in an analytic treatment, for replacing the effects of repression by the results of the rational operation of the intellect.' Sigmund Freud, *The Future of an Illusion*, trans. W. D. Robson-Scott (New York: H. Liveright, 1928), 72–3. German original: *Die Zukunft einer Illusion* (Leipzig: Internationaler Psychoanalytischer Verlag, 1927).

[26] James Forsyth's comparison of the Pauline and Freudian systems of thought is suggestive of the approach Freud might have adopted in a dedicated analysis of the apostle's theology. Although not actually examining Freud's writings on Paul, Forsyth points out that there are real similarities between Paul's understanding of guilt and death, and Freud's interest in discontent and the death-impulse, as fundamental to the human condition. 'Freud perceived civilisation as Paul perceived the Law – as extraneous authority which promised life but delivered death in the form of guilt.' Yet the value of both civilisation and the Law is recognised by both men, these *apparent* causes actually being understood as providing only the *occasion* for man's experience of death. James J. Forsyth, 'Freud and St Paul' in John R. May, *The Bent World: Essays on Religion and Culture* (Chico, CA: Scholars' Press, 1979), 83–93. In fact, the study of Paul by the Jewish psychoanalyst Hanns Sachs makes precisely these connections between psychoanalytical categories and Pauline terminology. Hanns Sachs, *Masks of Love and Life: The Philosophical Basis of Psychoanalysis* (Cambridge, MA: Sci-Art Publishers, 1948), 82–107.

[27] Sitting in London, a refugee from Nazi persecution, the world-famous psychoanalyst poignantly reflected on the causes of anti-Semitism. The Jews' status as a weak minority was partly to blame, in that they refused to assimilate and at the same time drew attention to themselves as contributors to civilisation. But he also believed that there was a deeper underlying motive, a motive which implicated the apostle Paul. 'Through this decision [to refuse the new doctrine of Paul] they [the Jews] are still more sharply separated from the rest of the world than they were before. They had to suffer the reproach from the new religious community – which besides Jews included Egyptians, Greeks, Syrians, Romans and lastly also Teutons – that they had murdered God. In its full form this reproach would run: "They will not admit that they killed God, whereas we do and are cleansed from the guilt of it."' Freud, *Moses and Monotheism*, 215.

HANNS SACHS, PAUL, AND LIBERATION THROUGH LOVE

A more comprehensive, and certainly more focused, psychoanalytical treatment of Paul was provided by Hanns Sachs (1881–1947). Born in Vienna in a middle class family 'which counted rabbis and merchants in its immediate ancestry', Sachs eventually gave up his law practise to become instead a practitioner of what he called 'the scientific art.' Having been deeply impressed by *The Interpretation of Dreams* (1900),[28] Sachs met Freud in 1910 and was soon drawn into the inner circle. His interests in art and literature led him to persuade his mentor to found *Imago* in 1912, a journal devoted to the psychoanalytical interpretation of cultural phenomena, which he coedited with Otto Rank for 20 years. From 1920 he trained scores if not hundreds of psychoanalysts and in 1932 he was invited to join Harvard Medical School. Perhaps his best-known publication was *The Creative Unconscious* (1942),[29] which explored the psychological processes involved in artistic creativity.[30]

Originally, Sachs had planned to write a major study of St. Paul, a thorough psychoanalysis of the life and work of the apostle. Ill health made this impossible, but in *Masks of Love and Life* (1948),[31] published posthumously, he was able to dedicate one chapter to the subject.[32] Consequentially, his approach to Paul was part of a more general project to outline a philosophical basis of psychoanalysis which treated a wide range of subjects, including leadership, appreciation of art, educational theory, sexual fantasies, pleasure, love, happiness, hate and Nazi anti-Semitism, and old age.[33]

As Sachs made clear early on, the human condition is one of anxiety and longing for inner freedom. Social conventions and prohibitions, 'some of them handed down through untold generations from our prehistoric, perhaps even from our hairy ancestors,' have come to dominate our lives. Against our wishes, we suppress and repress a wide range of behaviours,[34] and few of us have the psychological resources necessary to challenge such conventions, even quite unreasonable ones.

---

[28] Sigmund Freud, *Die Traumdeutung* (Leipzig: Franz Deuticke, 1900).

[29] Hanns Sachs, *The Creative Unconscious: Studies in the Psychoanalysis of Art* (Cambridge, MA: Sci-Art Publishers, 1942).

[30] For brief biographies of Sachs, see A. A. Roback, 'Dr Hanns Sachs (A Memoir)' in H. Sachs, *Masks of Love and Life; The Philosophical Basis of Psychoanalysis* (Cambridge, MA: Sci-Art Publishers, 1948), 11–18 and Ernest Jones, 'Hanns Sachs', *International Journal of Psycho-Analysis* 27 (1946), 168–9.

[31] Hanns Sachs, *Masks of Love and Life*. The titled was changed by the editor from *The People of a Strange Planet*, a title suggestive of Sachs's detached approach to observing the strange and often self-contradictory behaviour of humans, both individually and in wider society.

[32] Like Freud, Sachs made no references to the wider Pauline scholarship. He did, however, cite Paul's letters, including Romans, Galatians, and 1 Corinthians, and he referred once to Acts of the Apostles.

[33] In many ways, Sachs's chapter preempts the comparison of the Freudian and Pauline systems of thought found in James J. Forsyth, 'Freud and St Paul', 83–93. Although Forsyth does not actually refer to Freud's views on the apostle's thought, he does compare Freud's linking of guilt, the death-impulse, and civilisation with Paul's linking of guilt, death, and the Law.

[34] Sachs's charming list includes 'cannibalism and nose-picking, adultery and "thou shalt not put a knife into thy mouth," parricide and flatulence, commandments issued from Sinai and impositions

It is as if all of us live in fear of walking through the open doors that surround us. As his 'scientific art' informed him,

The fear of living in [the] face of an open door, the urge of thinking about it as closed – these are signs that occur in the life of every man. It is the function of civilization – and has been from the earliest stages – to see that as few as possible may escape through one of these open doors.[35]

For Sachs, psychoanalysis was the modern scientific method by which one frees oneself from the anxiety that civilisation has generated through its myriad impositions; by understanding the often arbitrary nature of social convention and by seeking out the roots for one's behaviour in one's personal history, one can achieve true inner freedom. Before Freud, however, there had also been individuals who had walked through the open doors, achieving the remarkable feat of a truly autonomous life through their own powers of intuition. Often such men had attracted followers 'due to the promise of a new road to inner freedom which they [held] out', although this promise had never been kept. History showed that these leaders, who included men of action as well as thinkers and dreamers, usually 'made their personal inhibitions become general laws; after liberating on one hand, they forged new shackles for the other.'[36] Despite their failings, Sachs suggested, such 'tortured spirits' had been especially influential when history took a sudden turning, and perhaps the most important turning in human history had been the transition from the view of the afterlife according to the ancients to the view of the afterlife according to Christianity. It was in this context that Sachs introduced Paul.[37]

According to Sachs, the apostle's originality lay in his unique approach to anxiety, which he had expressed as a duality: on the one hand there was death and, on the other, that which would lead to life, namely absolution from desire (or *Id*) and freedom from the yoke of imposed rules (or *Super-Ego*). (Here Sachs neatly mapped Paul's characteristic teachings about the flesh and the Law onto psychoanalytical categories, implying a considerable degree of overlap between the two systems.[38]) For the apostle, salvation from death meant liberation from a complex

learned in kindergarten . . . [all] grouped together without rhyme or reason.' Sachs, *Masks of Love and Life*, 55–6.
[35] Sachs, *Masks of Love and Life*, 55.
[36] Sachs, *Masks of Love and Life*, 83.
[37] 'In [Paul's] vain striving after inner freedom this spirit became the originator of a truly world-shaking event, the first and greatest missionary of newborn Christianity. Possessing, like most tortured souls, a profound, intuitive insight into the mind, he aroused forces the existence of which nobody had hitherto suspected.' Sachs, *Masks of Love and Life*, 84–5.
[38] 'He [Paul] longed for the freedom and the true life with a desire which nothing could weaken and cried out for it with a voice which is still heard over the centuries (for instance: *Romans* VIII:21). In the fire of his frenzy, the multiform aspects of the problem which confuse the ordinary observer were finally melted down to one pair of opposites. At the one end stood death. . . . In *homo sapiens* [and in contrast to other animals] the idea of death became explicit, a part of his consciousness that

set of interrelated issues. He felt tremendous guilt that his inner desires frequently conflicted with Jewish Law, leading him to sin, and he intuitively sensed that this guilt was eating away at him, killing him spiritually. As Sachs formulated Paul's insight: 'Sin, conflicting with law, fetters the inner life; death is the reward of sin, sin is death.'[39] What solution, then, did the Jewish Apostle to the Gentiles find to rid himself of this deep anxiety? The answer that he stumbled upon was a wish fulfilment or fantasy that modified the Jewish conception of the messiah, and the long-awaited hope for national emancipation, with certain features of Gentile mystery cults, namely, personal liberation from evil by means of identification with deities who died and rose again (such as Orpheus, Attis, and Osiris). As Sachs put it,

In the crucified Jesus, the two beliefs which appealed most to Paul's emotion and imagination merged and became one: the faith of the Gentiles in the divine youth whose death and resurrection promised eternal life to his believers and the Messianic hope of the Jews.[40]

Unlike Freud, Sachs suspected that this new theology had not actually been the apostle's own creation. But he thought that the apostle had become the foremost proponent of the idea of a dying and rising messiah,[41] and suggested that only an

---

was steadfastly rejected by his Unconscious. He [Paul] reacted by creating more or less satisfactory fantasies of continued existence. This anxiety, which overshadows the humans, spoiled for Paul everything in life; it became the embodiment of all frustrations ... it stood as the symbol of every defeat and inhibition, as the way leading to the impassable doors, or, in his language: by drive of desire, the law was turned into the constant threat of sin and sin was identical with death, was in fact the absolute death (*Romans* VII:7,8). Opposite death stood the absolution from sinful desire and with it the freedom from the yoke of imposed rules and inhibitions. How was it possible to make the pronounced will of God void and superfluous, to see in his Holy Law a snare and a danger, without rejecting him? To live in the tension of this dualism was more than Paul, the monotheistic Jew, could stand. The traces left on his mind by the torment remained plainly visible long afterwards. ("I am the most wretched of men. Who will release me from the body of this death?" *Romans* VII:24)'. Sachs, *Masks of Love and Life*, 85–7.

[39] 'It was not this dream of political liberation, of national victory and glory, upon which Paul fixed his hope, faith, and love. What he desired, with all the passion of his burning heart, was another and infinitely greater victory, the victory over death. He wanted to defeat destruction not only in the form of the final extinction – this was his highest, but not an isolated, aim. The same destruction as in death was hovering around him all the time, spoiling, debasing and constricting his inner life. Law and lust (*Super-Ego* and *id*-tendencies) were both active within him. "I agree with the law of Jehovah as to my inner nature, but I see another law in my members; and fights against the law of my mind and I get bound by the law of sin which is in my members." (*Romans* VII:22,23). Sin, conflicting with law, fetters the inner life; death is the reward of sin, sin is death.' Sachs, *Masks of Love and Life*, 93.

[40] Sachs, *Masks of Love and Life*, 98.

[41] 'A group of men – probably all of them, like Paul himself, Jews who had grown up in one of the Hellenistic cities outside Palestine – had tasted, directly or indirectly, of the promises of resurrection and immortality, held out by the mystery religion. In their minds, the Jewish Messiah and the crucified and resurrected God were fused into a unity. To these men the person and the teachings of the man whom the Roman authorities had executed was but of secondary interest. Paul doesn't

individual with the power of Paul's personality could have had such an impact on world civilisation.[42]

Bearing in mind that Freud had attributed Christianity's blurring of Moses' monotheism to Paul, it is interesting that there was never any question in Sachs's mind that the apostle had remained a monotheist throughout his life.[43] He explained the Hebrew roots of several terms in order to support this conviction,[44] he accepted the New Testament claims regarding the apostle's authentic Jewish background,[45] and he argued that it was Paul's Jewishness that explained the style and content of his argumentation.[46] The apostle's undiminished commitment to Israel also explained a key characteristic of his thought, namely, the tension between his loyalty to his new Gentile followers and to his fellow Jews. The evidence of this internal conflict could be seen in his frustration at his unsatisfactory attempt to redefine Israel in terms of the Church[47] and in symptomatic mistakes in his theology, such as the famous simile of grafting the wild

seem to have been the founder of this group, but its leader in the newly opened missionary field.' Sachs, *Masks of Love and Life*, 101–2.

[42] 'The discovery of Jesus as the point where the two separate rivers of religious emotion could join and flow together, the work of coordination and consolidation of elements of different origin was not done by Paul, but by other, or earlier, believers or perhaps by one of them.... But if ever a man of overpowering personality showed to the world his heart bared and divested of all petty disguises; if ever the suffering, the troubles and conflicts, the consolations, the hopes and the love of a great mind were exposed to the eyes of men, it is to be found in Paul's epistles. Originality is only a very weak term to designate this quality.' Sachs, *Masks of Love and Life*, 98.

[43] 'The word *Theos* was for Paul the exact rendering of Jehovah (*Yahveh, Elohim*) and nothing else, for Paul was, and remained a pious, zealous Jew, that is: a strict monotheist.' Regarding the idea of a dying and rising god of the mystery religions, the preconversion Paul must have 'rejected it with all the fanaticism of a monotheistic religious zealot.' Paul's eventual hope is that 'The end of everything, revealed by prophetic outlook into the future, is the return to pure and unalloyed monotheism, God being again "all in all" (*I Corinthians* XV:24–28).' Sachs, *Masks of Love and Life*, 88, 96, 100.

[44] 'The Apostle everywhere keeps up (at least in the four authentic Epistles) a sharp distinction between Jehovah, the only and almighty God, and the Messiah . . . He wanted to avoid a misunderstanding for which no possibility existed in the Old Testament. The Jehovah who rises from the dead and the crucified Messiah who rises from his grave have to be distinguished with particular care by their different names and titles, since the old monotheistic prerogative had to be kept intact and yet room made for a Messiah who had little in common with the Messiah of the Jewish tradition.' Sachs, *Masks of Love and Life*, 91–2.

[45] 'The evidence for Paul's considering himself an orthodox Jew is abundant. He calls himself proudly a "Jew descended from Jews, of the tribe of Benjamin, the seed of Abraham, circumcised in the ordained manner." At his last, ill-fated stay in Jerusalem he subjected himself to the rite of purification . . . and let it be known, at the Temple, when sacrifice could be offered for him, all this with the purpose of emphasizing that he was a pious Jew. (*Acts* XVI:26).' Sachs, *Masks of Love and Life*, 88. Information about Paul could safely be gleaned from the 'four authentic epistles' (Romans, 1 and 2 Corinthians, and Galatians) and Acts of the Apostles. Ibid., 102.

[46] According to Sachs, Paul's favourite arguments are drawn from 'the most impressive parts of the Old Testament', including the stories of Abraham, Adam, Jacob and Esau, and the rock in the desert. Later he qualifies this: 'All essential arguments are drawn either from the resurrection or from the Old Testament.' Sachs, *Masks of Love and Life*, 92, 101.

[47] 'His intense attachment to the Jews and the Jewish religion caused one of his deepest, apparently endless, conflicts. After he had become the foremost missionary to the Gentiles, defending their equal right to salvation and to the brotherhood of Christ, he tried to soothe his conscience by a curious device. The true Jews, the Jews according to the spirit, were the Christians, whatever they

olive branch (representing the Gentiles) onto the olive tree (representing Jewish Israel). As Sachs observed,

Here the conflict in the Apostle's mind manifests itself in a mistake (a symptomatic act) which is calculated to warm the cockles of an analyst's heart by bearing out Freud's theory in his *Psychopathology of Everyday Life*. . . . No gardener ever grafted a wild branch on a noble stem; it is, of course, always the other way around.[48]

As for the Gentile mystery religions, in addition to supplying Paul with the familiar mythic form of a dying and rising god, the popular cults also gave the apostle two acts of ritual, namely, baptism and communion. Both of these are, of course, of considerable interest to psychoanalysts, the first being a symbolic repetition of birth and the second being an ancient totemic act of cannibalism.[49] Having been performed within the mystery religions as ways to achieve union with the divine, 'both had probably been adopted by all the missionaries of the crucified Messiah, but certainly by none of them more ardently than by Paul.'[50] Even so, Sachs argued that such magical rituals were for Paul 'mere accessories.'[51] More effective in unifying with Christ was 'the strangest power in which the life instinct embodies itself . . . the power of love.'[52] And this had been Paul's unique achievement: for Sachs, the potency of the apostle's theology lay in his understanding of love as a unifying force – and not, as so often claimed, in his doctrine of faith.[53]

Essentially, Paul's sophisticated theology works in the following way. Anxiety, which is caused by the believer's unruly desires and subsequent failure to obey the Law, is dissolved by focusing on one desire, love. Rather than trying to suppress all desires of the Id, love is given a monopoly and thus simply eclipses them. With no

might have been before, since Jehovah had accepted the eater of unlawful food as well as the non-eater (*Romans* XLV:3) whereas the Jews, the real actual Jewish people, were only "Jews according to the flesh." Did this ingenious stratagem suffice to end his scruples? By no means. He still feels deeply afflicted. Despair breaks out in his worlds when he declares that in his supreme anguish he would wish to be accursed and separated form salvation for the sake of his brethren according to his flesh (*Romans* IX:2,3). His ultimate hope still lies with his own people.' Sachs, *Masks of Love and Life*, 88–9.

[48] Sachs, *Masks of Love and Life*, 90.

[49] 'Baptism, the coming out of the water after immersion, was the symbolic repetition of the act of birth. The psychoanalysts have learnt this equation by means of the interpretation of dreams, which contain it frequently as a typical element in the language of the Unconscious.' And likewise, 'The sacred meal is one of the oldest institutions, going back to times before the development of religion, to the truly "dark ages" of totemism. It is the most naïve, but also the most intense, way of identifying oneself with another being, by eating his flesh and drinking his blood. It means being unified with him as the child at the breast becomes one with the mother.' Sachs, *Masks of Love and Life*, 103–4.

[50] Sachs, *Masks of Love and Life*, 102.

[51] Sachs, *Masks of Love and Life*, 104.

[52] Sachs, *Masks of Love and Life*, 104–5.

[53] 'No teaching or understanding, no hope and no faith can lead to being one with Jesus: love is the only means of identification. On this point Paul is most explicit (106) and emphatic: "love is greater than faith and hope" and "even if I have the gift of prophecy and have insight into all mysteries and into all knowledge, and even if I have all the faith so that I can move mountains, but have no love, I am nothing" (*I Corinthians* XIII:2).' Sachs, *Masks of Love and Life*, 105–6.

other desires tempting the believer to sin, the Law or Super-Ego also loses its dread. The object of love is, of course, Christ, which is a perfectly natural response for someone who has understood the nature of the sacrifice made. In loving Christ, the believer seeks to become one with him, and, as he increasingly identifies with him, so he longs for the death or extinction of his Ego. Paul thus offers a remarkable theology in which love is used to reconcile us with death, with the result that, free from all anxiety, we see all the doors swing wide open before us. It is worth citing Sachs's eloquent summary of Pauline theology at length.

The reason for loving Jesus, and only him, was that his own love made the Messiah, the 'first born of the sons of God' . . . willing to die on the cross and to be buried for the salvation of mankind. This love arouses in those to whom it had been given, and who are able to accept and requite it, the longing to die, thus mediating the only way leading to the resurrection and eternal life. Here we have love made free from all anxieties and inhibitions; *before it all doors were springing open.* . . . This, to the eyes of an outside observer, is the greatest feat of about-face that has ever been performed: life and death united by love. The law, or as we call it by less forbidding names: *Super-Ego*, conscience, loses its power to forbid, to inhibit, to punish. It has no claims and no threat, since its task had become superfluous. The sinful desire which it had to keep in check: to suppress, to annihilate or, when all this had proved beyond its power, at least to repress and keep out of the Ego, this desire had ceased to exist. Relieved from the struggle and reconciled to the *Id*, the *Super-Ego* can now assume . . . and encourage the function which hitherto belonged to the *Id*, and turn, in its own particular way, from an inhibiting and deadening force to a life-giving, and even creative, one. Thus the apostle and saint is born. The Ego does not receive any longer its life-impulses from its instinctual sources in the treacherous guise of desire which the law changes into sin and death. Love, highest and purest of the life impulses alone survives; it retains its purity by giving itself up altogether to this sole aim, to be the way and the open door leading to the final consummation. Life is now no longer life, it is a constant dying in becoming one with the crucified. Death is no longer death for him who became one with the resurrected first-born of God. Paul expressed this complicated process in simple and perfectly clear words: 'For I died by means of the law so that I will live to Jehovah. I have been crucified together with the Messiah. I live no longer, but the Messiah lives in me'.[54] (Gal. 2:19)

With this highly original interpretation of Pauline theology, Sachs achieved two things. First, he provided a graceful explanation for the psychological power and longevity of Christianity as taught by the Jewish Apostle to the Gentiles. In stripping bare the psychodynamic problems facing the apostle, we come to see that Paul's theological genius is, in fact, better understood as psychological genius. Second, Sachs suggested that Paul could be held largely responsible for undermining the ancients' acceptance of the impermanence of life, and for giving Western civilisation its focus on death and the need to find salvation from it. From this perspective,

---

[54] Sachs, *Masks of Love and Life*, 105–7.

Masks of Love and Life (1948) was 'an exposé, a critique of civilization', as Sachs's editor observed.[55] The critique is accurate, for Christianity was to be regarded as the fantasy or wish fulfilment of a 'tortured soul', and however insightful that individual had been, it could only be a partial solution to the problem of anxiety. Nevertheless, the study of Paul was a highly profitable exercise, for it illustrated the potential influence of leaders (that is, those who walked through the open doors) in the historical development of the modern world. As Sachs saw it,

The most moving spectacle . . . is to see one of the loftiest and most cruelly tortured of these spirits at work, liberating and enslaving a few humble contemporaries and an indeterminable procession of later generations, the end of which is not yet in sight.[56]

CONCLUSION

There are important differences in the writings of the two psychoanalysts regarding Paul. Although Freud had understood the secret of the apostle's longevity to be his accidental discovery of the dark psychodynamics of the father–son relationship and freedom from a universal sense of guilt, Sachs had explained his power in terms of his insights into achieving personal liberation from the anxiety of death. And while both accounts necessitated a radical rereading of Paul, they did so in different ways: Freud's theory had involved a highly unorthodox interpretation of 'original sin', which related it to an ancestral murder rather than an act of disobedience in the Garden of Eden, whereas Sachs's hypothesis required a revision of the Protestant interpretation of Paul's theological priorities, downplaying his 'faith' in favour of his 'love'. Nevertheless, there were underlying similarities in their approaches, especially regarding the nature of their critiques of society. Freud's use of Paul to fire a powerful broadside against society's irrational attachment to religion was paralleled by Sachs's assertion that, despite his admiration for the way in which Paul had freed himself from the constraints of civilisation, such leaders tended to go on to generate new chains for their followers, and that only psychoanalysis offered a real solution. Perhaps most interestingly, both men had been convinced that Paul's teachings and achievements had demonstrated – even proved – important aspects of psychoanalysis and the irrational nature of the unconscious.

If we once again return to Deutscher's idea of the non-Jewish Jew, their programme of deconstruction makes perfect sense. Like the philosophers discussed in the previous chapter, both Freud and Sachs had found a perspective that offered an alternative, historically unconventional view, namely, psychoanalysis, and both sought to strike at the heart of the sources of power within society, namely, religious belief itself. Writing in 1926, Freud offered further evidence from a very personal perspective.

[55] A.A. Roback, 'Introduction' in Sachs, *Masks of Love and Life*, 26.
[56] Sachs, *Masks of Love and Life*, 84.

That which bound me to Judaism – I am obliged to admit it – was not my faith, nor was it national pride; for I was always an unbeliever, raised without religion, although not without respect for the so-called 'ethical' demands of human civilization. And I always tried to suppress nationalistic ardour, whenever I felt any inclination thereto, as something pernicious and unjust, frightened as I was by the warning example of the peoples among whom we Jews live. But there remained enough other things to make the attraction of Judaism and Jews irresistible – many dark emotional forces, all the more potent for being so hard to grasp in words, as well as the clear consciousness of an inner identity, the intimacy that comes from the same psychic structure. And to that was soon added the insight that it was my Jewish nature alone that I have to thank for two characteristics that proved indispensable to me in my life's difficult course. Because I was a Jew I found myself free from many prejudices that hampered others in their use of their intellects; and as a Jew, I was prepared to take my place on the side of the opposition and renounce being on good terms with the 'compact majority'.[57]

In addition to confirming Deutscher's views about the irrelevance of religion and nationalism for the non-Jewish Jew, and the attendant sense of isolation, Freud here boasts of his independence from the theologically derived constraints that characterise Western Christian society; even more significantly for our purposes, he *credits* his Jewishness for his orientation against the conventional worldview. This powerful sense of contrariness is suggestive for answering the question of why the Apostle to the Gentiles assumed such a significant role in the imaginations of these psychoanalysts (and, indeed, in the imagination of the philosophers). As all were quick to note, he too had been a revolutionary.

As a figure of great authority within Christianity and Christian culture who had influenced generations of theologians and leaders and who had profoundly shaped the course of Western civilisation, it made good rhetorical sense for Jewish humanist thinkers to engage with and claim the support of Paul, who was, himself, regarded as a Jew. But it is also possible to see in their attraction to the figure of Paul a reflection of their own complex issues of identity. After all, Paul's life had been one lived in the borderland between the Jewish and the Gentile communities, distanced from the Jewish people, even as he remained connected to them. And he, too, had been profoundly affected by his engagement with the wider world, having broken through the boundaries of Jewish religion and nationalism. There was surely a degree of identification with the apostle amongst these thinkers, and, perhaps, some cold comfort in finding in this misunderstood Jew an ideological ally.

---

[57] Sigmund Freud, 'On Being of the B'nai B'rith: An Address to the Society in Vienna' (May 1926), reproduced in *Commentary* (March 1946), 23–4.

Conclusion

The preceding chapters have explored some of the very different ways in which Jewish thinkers have constructed images of Paul. The range of often contradictory presentations is impressive, although arguably no more so than that offered by Christians over the same period. It seems fair to say that the one thing upon which those Jewish thinkers who have seriously engaged with the Apostle to the Gentiles can agree is that he is a vitally significant figure for the history of the Jewish people and even for Judaism, be it for good or ill. And yet such a claim sits uneasily with the fact that Paul barely registers on the popular Jewish cultural radar. If an individual's significance to a community is determined by his historical reception within that community as a whole, then one must admit that Paul's impact on the Jewish imagination has been a very minor one. It is hoped that this collected body of interpretations of the apostle will act as a corrective in bringing the historical Jewish engagement with him to the attention of a wider Jewish audience.

In Chapter one it was suggested that Jewish curiosity about Paul had its origins in the nineteenth-century emergence of historicism and the reinvention of the Jew in the modern world. Increasingly, naturalistic, rational explanations of the history of the Jewish people and their religion were privileged over supernatural, providential explanations. Inevitably, the new assumptions led to a reappraisal of Christianity, with which Judaism had struggled for so many centuries. If the Jewish comprehension of Christianity shifted at this point from an essentially traditional, providential perspective to an increasingly historicist, rationalist one, then it would make good sense that the Jewish *tête-à-tête* with Paul began at around the same time. The German biblical critics' revisionist histories of the New Testament period, which appeared to undermine the religious unity of the early Church and to emphasise the influence of pagan thought within it, generated considerable enthusiasm among many Jewish observers. Paul was associated by both Gentiles and Jews with many of the innovations that had led Christianity to break loose from its Jewish roots. He stood at the centre of this new interpretation of the past. So it was that when the apostle first captured the attention of Jewish writers, he was immediately located within an account of the parting of the ways (and Jewish history) that gave great weight to human thought and action. Insofar as its emphasis upon historicism characterises modern Jewish thought, the study of Paul represents one important area in which the transition to modernity can be observed. Without an appreciation of this phenomenon, the nineteenth-century Jewish interest in Paul seems to come out of nowhere. However, this obsession of the intelligentsia with understanding themselves from a historical perspective and negotiating a place for themselves in Western Christian society has not greatly excited the general Jewish public, few of whose members have enjoyed the opportunity to pursue social acceptance and integration to the degree that the elites did, and many of whom continued to believe that the past was explained perfectly adequately in terms of traditional conceptions of divine providence. For the masses, then, the drive to understand Christianity and, by association, Paul was a good deal less urgent. This might explain, in part, the dearth of material relating to the apostle that has characterised popular Jewish discourse. If one considers the case study of the Anglo-Jewish weekly *The Jewish Chronicle*, published continuously since 1841, the impression gained is one of sustained suspicion of Christianity and little or no interest in Paul for anything other than the purposes of religious polemic.

In Chapter two, the idea was further developed that Jewish commentary on Paul reflects specific concerns generated as a result of political and social emancipation. From this broad perspective, the basic, general strategies adopted by Jews committed to modernity (that is, holding Christian society at arm's length or embracing it) appear largely unchanged until the present day. They are useful in beginning to account in broad outline for the variety of Jewish attitudes towards Paul. Writers such as Elijah Benamozegh in Italy and Heinrich Graetz, Leo Baeck, Kaufmann Kohler, and Martin Buber in Germany, joined later by Abba Hillel Silver in the United States and Hyam Maccoby in Britain, reflected an impulse to demarcate the limits of Jewish compromise with the non-Jewish world. Although fully engaged with Christian thought, they did not want to identify with it too closely; they were suspicious of the damaging inroads of assimilation and/or concerned to protect their own conceptions of Judaism from its disorienting influence. They instinctively realised that to undermine Paul, regarded as the moral and intellectual founder of the Gentile Church, was to undermine its ubiquitous power, or at least to demonstrate that it did not have a monopoly on the truth. Consequentially, Paul's Jewish credentials were only reluctantly acknowledged; Graetz and Benamozegh attributed Paul's teachings to profound misunderstandings of Judaism, and the others pointed to the non-Jewish sources that they saw saturating the apostle's theology. By these means the apostle's credibility as the critic *par excellence* of the Jewish Law and religion was undercut, and a space for the legitimacy of the Jewish way of life carved out. Arguably, these barrier-builders are the scholars whose writings are responsible for the power and longevity of the classic negative Jewish image of Paul; their discrediting of Paul remains central to the Jewish critique of Christianity today.

The other way to locate oneself as a Jew within a wider Christian society and to maintain a legitimate space for Jewish life within it is to emphasise what is common to Jews and Christians. Bridge-builders such as Isaac Mayer Wise and Joseph Krauskopf in the United States and Claude Montefiore in Britain offered historical accounts that praised Paul's universalism, ethics, and religious sincerity, and were generally prepared to confirm his Jewish education and background (even if Wise focused somewhat eccentrically on Paul's alleged kabbalistic education). Their good will towards Paul was in part an expression of their confidence in religious progress and political emancipation. Their quickness in distancing themselves from the ostensibly traditional, negative view of Paul was a signal of their commitment to the modern non-Jewish world. In their optimism they believed that by contributing to the historical reconstruction of Paul's Jewishness, and by demonstrating their appreciation for him, they could inoculate the Gentile world against an anti-Jewish reading of the apostle. Such remain amongst the most sympathetic portrayals of Paul, although later scholars including the older Leo Baeck, but more particularly Pinchas Lapide in Israel and Mark Nanos in the United States, were committed to bridge-building within a specifically modern interfaith context. For these, Paul's attitude towards observance of the Torah could be recast to become thoroughly Jewish. Baeck interpreted Paul's view as valid from the point of view of one who believed that the messianic age had come; Lapide argued that the apostle's abrogation of the Law was relevant only to Gentile Christians, whereas the Law retained its full validity for Jews; and Nanos went so far as to argue that not only had Paul himself been a fully Torah-observant Pharisee who had expected Jewish believers to follow suit but that he had even required the Gentile Christians to keep the (Jewish) Noachide laws. Thus was an attempt made to transform the Law into an instrument of Jewish–Christian rapprochement.

Almost by definition, modern Jewish identity has been constructed in a world where the positive definition of Jewishness (in terms of a normative Judaism) can no longer be taken for granted, and the various approaches to Paul mirror this reality. It has been suggested that the three most important factors acting upon and shaping modern Jewry have been those of *anti-Semitism*, which both strengthened and weakened Jewish ties, the *Enlightenment*, which encouraged Jews to identify with a larger world beyond the boundaries of Judaism, and *Zionism*, which offered the hope of a shared national identity.[1] The remarkable figure of the apostle resonates in each of these contexts. For those who attributed Gentile hostility and Jew-hatred to Christianity itself, and who sought to protect themselves from it or to draw its sting, Paul's relevance lies in his role in the emergence and success of

---

[1] For example, these themes define the three lectures that compose Michael A. Meyer's *Jewish Identity in the Modern World* (Seattle: University of Washington Press, 1990).

the new religion. This we have already seen in the work of the barrier-builders and bridge-builders examined in the second chapter. The two other factors, the Enlightenment and Zionism, provide the essential backdrops for the intra-Jewish ideological debates discussed in Chapter three.

For those who sought to define Judaism in terms of Enlightenment values or otherwise reconcile the best thought and attitudes of their own day with the truths of Judaism, there has been a fascination with the apostle's centuries-old pursuit of synthesis with the dominant Hellenism and his radical reformulations of Jew-ish tradition. Progressive theologians of an older Anglo-North American mould, such as Emil Hirsch in the United States and Claude Montefiore in Britain, were quick to upbraid their Orthodox opponents by reference to the apostle. They argued that not only had he freed his followers from an overly rigid interpreta-tion of the Torah, a courageous act which made possible the universalisation of Judaism for the benefit of the wider, non-Jewish world, but also he could inspire the modern Jew with a theology premised upon the principle of love, in con-trast to the uninspiring, incoherent rabbinic tradition. (Others, such as Flusser, attached a negative value-judgement to such liberal attitudes to the Law.) Whether consciously intended or otherwise, the Pauline studies of later North American progressive Jewish New Testament scholars also contributed to the undermining of traditionalist conceptions of Jewish history with their casual presumptions of the apostle's Jewishness. Samuel Sandmel's reluctance to attribute to Paul the label 'Christian' was compounded by Alan Segal's unexpected claim that Paul's letters represent the best evidence extant for Jewish mysticism in the first century. Jewish feminists further illustrate the pronounced inclination of progressives to unearth evidence from their first-century studies that challenges the assumptions on which many conservative Jewish claims rest, especially with regard to attitudes towards non-Jews, marginal figures, and women. Pamela Eisenbaum in the United States stressed Paul's profoundly Jewish commitment, as she saw it, to the harmonisation (rather than the eradication) of difference within the early church; her compatriot Amy-Jill Levine likewise associated Paul's interest in Gentiles with prophetic and even Talmudic tradition; and the Israeli Tal Ilan confirmed the apostle's Pharisaic Jewish status, and his corresponding *halakhic* orientation, by attributing to it the egalitarianism of 1 Cor. 7. Perhaps the least subtle use of Paul to justify a rejection of traditionalist interpretations of Judaism was that offered by the controversial Hebrew Christians and Messianic Jews. For Paul Levertoff in Britain, Sandford Mills in the United States, and Joseph Shulman in Israel, the Jewish roots of Paul's teaching of salvation were presented precisely in order to achieve that purpose, namely, the salvation of the Jews; thus Jewish learning was used to demonstrate the folly of Jewish learning without the messiah.

For those consumed by the nationalist dream of Zionism, the third factor shaping modern Jewry, Paul could be credited with the invention of Gentile Christianity, an essentially Diaspora enterprise, which would be forever hostile to the authentic Judaism of *eretz Yisrael*. Although some liberals might have doubted this, such as Hans Joachim Schoeps in Germany, who denied vehemently that authentic Judaism could not be detached from Jewish nationalism, others could not help but interpret history through this ideological lens. For Joseph Klausner in Palestine, Paul was at once a member of the Jewish nation who had shaped world history and, as a universalist visionary, a betrayer of the Zionist soul of the Jewish people. The revisionist history offered by his compatriot, Micah Berdichevsky, who was determined to lay bare the essentially non-Jewish origins of the apostle and hence of Christianity itself, went so far as to reconstruct Paul as an idolatrous pagan priest of Damascus. Whether in the context of anti-Semitism, the Enlightenment, or Zionism, the point is that the Apostle to the Gentiles has been treated in such a way as to facilitate and reinforce a wide variety of perspectives within the modern Jewish ideological landscape.

Doubtless, the classic, negative Jewish view of Paul is alive and well, and there is no reason to believe that Paul will not continue to function as a figure of abuse in public discourse, in Jewish–Christian religious polemic, and in intra-Jewish debate for a long time to come. But at the same time others will join with those who see in the first-century apostle a pioneer in the quest to find a meaningful sense of historical continuity between the Jewish past and the Jewish future, an approach that was outlined in Chapter four. At a time when the chasm between the modern and pre-Enlightenment Jewish worlds appears so daunting and unbreachable, the figure of Paul, who himself traversed far-flung cultures and was acutely aware of the challenges facing Judaism, looks beguilingly familiar. In the eclectic writings of the eccentric Hugh Schonfield in Britain, or Richard Rubenstein, Nancy Fuchs-Kreimer, and Daniel Boyarin in the United States, one must acknowledge the role of Paul in inspiring far-reaching personal reflections, which have bound him to each as a fellow traveller on the path to religious self-understanding. Each was convinced that contemporary Jews could benefit from thinking about the questions Paul asked (if not always his answers), whether the issue be, respectively, how to commit oneself to the politics of God and to become a partner of divine activity; or how to meet the challenge of existential angst with real insight; or how to retrieve as a Jewish theological truth the idea of God's grace and to find a theological space for the non-Jew; or how to begin to counter the gender biases and ethnic bigotry of a traditional system to which one is committed without threatening its foundations. Here, none was ashamed to articulate such concerns in the language of the apostle, precisely because he was perceived as a serious partner in a perennial dialogue concerning the very nature of Judaism itself.

In addition to the contributions of Jewish theologians, religious leaders, and scholars of religion, who tend to dominate interfaith dialogue, important and distinctive Jewish perspectives on the dramatic events of the ancient 'parting of the ways' and on the controversial figure of Paul can be found elsewhere. Amongst those offering artistic, literary, philosophical or psychoanalytical interpretations of the apostle are a number who might be described as 'marginal' Jews, their idiosyncratic self-identities and the complicated nature of their backgrounds often frustrating easy categorisation. For obvious reasons they have been uncomfortable championing the Jewish community's received traditions and dialoguing with representative members of the Christian fraternity. But there are many ways to define Jewishness, and exploration of the intellectual worlds of those who regard themselves as Jewish in some sense, even if they are not committed to any kind of Judaism, is a very worthwhile endeavour. The fact that, along with so many other Jews in the modern world, they cannot easily be fitted into religious or national pigeonholes is precisely what makes them so interesting when studying their empathetic interpretations of the similarly complex character of the apostle. Their works have proved especially useful for illustrating two themes that are common to the majority of Jewish studies of Paul.

One recurrent theme has been the attempt of Jewish intellectuals to map out the relationship between Jews and Gentiles in a context where the centuries-old rules no longer seem to apply. The difficulty in achieving a coherent, satisfactory resolution for those who inhabit the cultural borderlands in particular was the subject of Chapters five and six. The common intellectual conundrum that lay beneath the three examples of German fine art, namely, Felix Mendelssohn's oratorio, Ludwig Meidner's painting, Franz Werfel's play, and the two North American novels by Sholem Asch and Samuel Sandmel was whether or not there existed a common religious essence between Judaism and Christianity. The majority agreed that there was, despite maintaining that Paul was responsible for the 'parting of the ways'. Its precise nature was described in their respective treatments of the apostle in terms of rationality, prophetic inspiration, complementary manifestations of the spirit of God, and a universal brotherhood of faith. Only Sandmel rejected the idea, even as he valued Paul as an instrument of interfaith rapprochement. As the exception that proved the rule, Sandmel's self-confidence as a religious Jew contrasted sharply with the much more complex identities and marginalised experiences of the others; one cannot help thinking that their need for Jewish–Christian integration, as mirrored in their studies of Paul, was greater than his.

Another running theme has been the gnawing tension between the need to criticise Christian thought and authority, and the desire to demonstrate one's commitment to western society. Paul's revolutionary zeal and iconic status attracted the attention of some who saw him as an ally for their own countercultural endeavours. Again, although this adoption of Paul as an ideological supporter could be said to apply to many, it was a particularly potent dimension of the work of the so-called 'non-Jewish Jews', the focus of Chapters seven and eight, including the

Dutch, Russian, and German philosophers Baruch Spinoza, Lev Shestov, and Jacob Taubes, and the German and North American psychoanalysts Sigmund Freud and Hanns Sachs. Paul was a counterpoint around which the philosophers could debate the rationality of Western civilisation's political and intellectual foundations, and he was called into service as an opponent of superstition, dogma, and politico-legal authority, respectively. For the psychoanalysts, Paul's power lay in his psychological insights into the human condition, especially with regard to guilt and fear of mortality. Sachs was effusive in his appreciation of Paul's attempt to free the individual from the unnatural constraints of civilised life, and his resolution of existential anxiety, couched as it was in the theological language of love. Freud was more cautious; although he certainly acknowledged the power of the apostle's image of the sacrifice of the Son in making restitution for the ancestral murder of the Father, he never forgot that it represented a truly formidable obstacle in his mission to rid the world of the illusion of religion.

This book set out to document the variety of meanings imputed to the iconic figure of Paul in a wide range of Jewish discourses in the modern period. It has been assumed throughout that the best kind of explanation of this variety has to do with ideology and identity politics, and there is reason to think that such an approach is especially appropriate for discussing Jewish interpretations of Paul. As has been well observed, no culture is an island unto itself and, consequently, there are no identity boundaries that are truly impermeable. For a long time now, thoughtful observers have acknowledged the symbiotic relationship between Judaism and Christianity, that is, between Jewish and Christian religious cultures. They have noted the interdependence of ritual practices, the shared vocabularies, the common fascination with 'the other', the antagonistic counterhistories, and the blurred theological boundaries. It has been suggested that it is through the process of engaging with Christian culture, of exploring the intersecting boundaries, that Jewish identity is formed (and *vice versa*), for one is repeatedly obliged to adopt a stance in response to the challenge posed by 'the other'.[2] One might agree, disagree, or compromise, but for self-reflective Jews living in a (historically) Christian society it is simply not possible to ignore the ever-present challenges. From this point of view, Saul-Paul could be thought of as an important point of overlap between Jewish and Christian cultural boundaries. Arguably, it is precisely because the apostle *is* located at an intersection between Jewish and Christian cultural boundaries that he has proved so attractive to some of the thinkers discussed and has facilitated so powerfully their exploration of questions concerning Jewish authenticity. For those Jewish inhabitants of modernity who have been both attracted to and critical of the non-Jewish world, there are powerful resonances with the state of mind of

---

[2] One of the most recent studies, which specifically focuses on the interaction between Christian and Jewish theologies in the modern period, is Marc A. Krell, *Intersecting Pathways*.

the first-century apostle who sought to be 'all things to all men' and yet who also refused to 'conform to the world'.[3] In working out their relation to Paul, there is unquestionably a sense of profound consequence in their deliberations and an awareness that their views about him are important for how they understand their own Jewishness, and for how others will perceive them.

---

[3] 'And *do not be conformed to this world*, but be transformed by the renewing of your mind, so that you may prove what the will of God is, that which is good and acceptable and perfect' (Rom. 12:2). 'For though I am free from all men, I have made myself a slave to all, so that I may win more. To the Jews I became as a Jew, so that I might win Jews; to those who are under the Law, as under the Law though not being myself under the Law, so that I might win those who are under the Law; to those who are without law, as without law, though not being without the law of God but under the law of Christ, so that I might win those who are without law. To the weak I became weak, that I might win the weak; *I have become all things to all men*, so that I may by all means save some' (1 Cor. 9:19–22).

Appendix: The Story of Abbu Gulish in *The Book of Tales*[1]

Rabbi Pinchas said, There was a story in Damascus about an idolatrous temple there. It had a priest whose name was Abba Gulish and he served before the idol many years. One time, a spirit of distress came upon him and he cried for help before the idol for many days but to no avail. After that he went outside one night and said, 'Sovereign of the Universe, hear my prayer and redeem me from my distress.' And he was cured. He stole away and came to Tiberias and converted [to Judaism] and he observed the *mitzvot* [commandments]. He was appointed administrator for the poor [but as soon as] monies were entrusted to him, the hands that had been accustomed to pilfer when they had been in the idolatrous temple, began to pilfer the dedicated money [once more]. Immediately he felt [pain] in one of his eyes and it became blind. Again, he reached out for the dedicated [funds] and felt [pain] in the other one and it became blind. And those from his [previous life and] place would come to Tiberias and see him blind and tell him, 'Abba Gulish, what were you thinking, that you scorned the idol and abandoned it so that it punished you so?' And more and more others [came and reproved him]. What did he do? He said to his wife, 'Get up! Put all other business on hold until we have been to Damascus.' And she took hold of his hand and they set off. As they arrived at the small towns within the environs of Damascus, people gathered about him and said, 'Here is Abba Gulish. The idol did right to you in that he made you blind.' He said to them, 'I have not come [for any reason] other than to seek him and to make peace with him, [and then] perhaps he will open my eyes for me!' But he was scorning them [in saying this] all the way to Damascus. Having entered [the city], the people of Damascus gathered about him, and said to him, 'Master Abba Gulish, what is the purpose of your visit?' He said to them, 'What does it look like?' They replied, '[If] you think you are scorning the idol, he is scorning you more.' And mocking them, he said, 'I have come to make peace with him, perhaps he will take pity on me. Only go and bring together all the people of the city.' They gathered crowds upon crowds on the roofs and on the ground and

[1] Story 131 in Moses Gaster, *Judith Montefiore College Ramsgate: Report for the Year 1894-5* and *Report for the Year 1895–6 . . . Together with the Ancient Collections of Agadoth, the Sefer ha-Maasiyoth* (Ramsgate: Judith Montefiore College, 1896), 90–91, reproduced in M.Y. Bin Gorion [Berdichevsky], *Shaul ve-Paul*, 13. My thanks to Noam Livne for his assistance in the production of this translation, and for his insightful comments on my analysis of Berdichevsky in general.

inside the temple to watch Abba Gulish [and what would happen] in the idolatrous temple. He told his wife to stand him on the platform that he knew was there. He went and stood on it and said to them, 'My brothers, people of Damascus, while I was a priest and serving this idol, people used to entrust me with deposits. And I was able to betray them, since the idol has no eyes to see, nor ears to hear, so as to punish me. Now I have gone to [the One] whose eyes roam the whole world and no misdeed is beyond Him to see [and punish]. And my hands wished to pilfer and take [again], as I had been accustomed, but before I even had a chance to do it, he punished me. Therefore *He* blinded my eyes.' Rabbi Pinchas ha-Cohen ben Khama said, He did not come down from the platform until the Holy One, blessed be He, restored his sight and doubled his honour and authority with the people, so that His Name was sanctified in the world. And there thousands and tens of thousands from the [Gentile] nations converted [to Judaism] and they attained [the blessing] of finding shelter under the wings of the *Shekhinah* [God's presence] though him.

Bibliography

BOOKS

Aarons, Victoria, *A Measure of Memory: Storytelling and Identity in American Jewish Fiction* (Athens, GA: University of Georgia Press, 1996).

Alter, Robert, *After the Tradition: Essays on Modern Jewish Writing* (New York: E. P. Dutton, 1969).

Altmann, Alexander, ed., *Moses Mendelssohn Gesammelte Schriften: Jubilaeumsaugabe* (Stuttgart: Friedrich Frommann Verlag, 1971).

Asch, Sholem, *Three Cities*, trans. Willa and Edwin Muir (London: 1933).

Asch, Sholem, *The Nazarene*, trans. Maurice Samuel (New York: Putnam, 1939).

Asch, Sholem, *My Personal Faith*, trans. Maurice Samuel (London: G. Routledge, 1942).

Asch, Sholem, *Mary*, trans. Leo Steinberg (New York: G. P. Putnam's Sons, 1949).

Asch, Sholem, *The Apostle*, trans. Maurice Samuel (London: Macdonald, 1949).

Baeck, Leo, *Judaism and Christianity*, trans. Walter Kaufmann (New York: Leo Baeck Institute 1958).

Baron, Salon, *A Social and Religious History of the Jews*, second ed. (New York: Columbia University Press, 1966).

Barron, Stephanie, '*Degenerate Art': The Fate of the Avant-Garde in Nazi Europe* (New York: H. N. Abrams, 1991).

Barth, Karl, *The Epistle to the Romans*, trans. Edwyn C. Hoskyns, sixth ed. (London: Oxford University Press, 1933).

Baur, F. C., *Paulus, der Apostel Jesu Christi* (Stuttgart, 1845).

Baur, F. C., *Paul: The Apostle of Jesus Christ*, trans. Eduard Zeller, 2 vols., (London: Williams & Norgate, 1873),

Baur, F. C., *Paul the Apostle of Jesus Christ*, trans. Eduard Zeller, 2 vols., second ed. (London: Williams and Norgate, 1876).

Benamozegh, Elijah, *Morale juive et morale chrétienne: Examen comparatif suivi de quelques réflexions sur les principes de l'islamisme* (Paris: Michel Lévy frères, 1867).

Benamozegh, Elijah, *Jewish and Christian Ethics with a Criticism on Mahomedism*, trans. anonymous (San Francisco: Emanuel Blochman, 1873).

Benamozegh, Emanuel, *Israël et l'humanité: Étude sur le problème de la religion universelle et sa solution* (Paris: E. Leroux, 1914).

Benamozegh, Emanuel, *Israel and Humanity*, trans. Maxwell Luria (New Jersey: Paulist Press, 1995).

Berdichevsky, Micah Yosef [Bin Gorion], *Yeshu ben Hanan*, ed. Immanuel Bin Gorion (Jerusalem: Mosad Ha-Rav Kuk, 1959).

Berdichevsky, Micah, *Miriam and Other Stories*, trans. Avner Holtzman (New Milford: The Toby Press, 2004).

Berger, David, *The Jewish–Christian Debate in the High Middle Ages: A Critical Edition of the Nizzahon Vetus* (Philadelphia: Jewish Publication Society of America, 1979).

Bin Gorion [Berdichevsky], Micah Yosef, *Shaul ve-Paul*, ed. Immanuel Bin Gorion (Tel Aviv: Moreshet Micha Yosef, 1971).

Boyarin, Daniel, *A Radical Jew: Paul and the Politics of Identity* (Berkeley: University of California Press, 1994).

Boyarin, Daniel, *The Rise of Heterosexuality and the Invention of the Jewish Man* (Berkeley: University of California Press, 1997).

Brown, Michael, *What Do Jewish People Think about Jesus? And Other Questions Christians Ask about Jewish Beliefs, Practices, and History* (Grand Rapids, MI: Chosen Books, 2007).

Buber, Martin, *Ich und Du* (Berlin: Schocken Verlag, 1923).

Buber, Martin, *Zwei Glaubenweisen* (Zurich: Manesse Verlag, 1950).

Buber, Martin, *Two Types of Faith*, trans. Norman P. Goldhawk (Routledge & Kegan Paul: London, 1951).

Bultmann, Rudolf, *The Theology of the New Testament*, trans. Kendrick Grobel (Waco, TX: Baylor University Press, 2007).

Cabezón, Jose Ignacio, and Davaney, Sheila Greeve, eds., *Identity and the Politics of Scholarship in the Study of Religion* (London: Routledge, 2004).

Camus, Albert, *The Myth of Sisyphus* (New York: Vintage Books, 1955).

Cesarani, David, *The Jewish Chronicle and Anglo-Jewry, 1841–1991* (New York: Cambridge University Press, 1994).

Chestov, Leo, *In Job's Balances: On the Sources of the Eternal Truths*, trans. Camilla Coventry and C. A. Macartney (London: J. M. Dent and Sons, 1932).

Cheyette, Bryan, *Constructions of 'the Jew' in English Literature and Society: Racial Representations, 1875–1945* (Cambridge: Cambridge University Press, 1993).

Chiesa, Bruno and Lockwood, Wilfrid, *Ya'cub al-Qirqisani on Jewish Sects and Christianity: A Translation of Kitab al-Anwar, Book I, with Two Introductory Essays* (Frankfurt am Main/New York: Verlag Peter Lang, 1984).

Citron, Marcia J., ed., *The Letters of Fanny Hensel to Felix Mendelssohn* (New York: Pendragon, 1987).

Cohen, Arthur, *The Myth of the Judeo-Christian Tradition: And Other Dissenting Essays* (New York: Schocken Books 1971).

Cohen, Bernard, *Sociocultural Changes in American Jewish Life as Reflected in Selected Jewish Literature* (Rutherford, NJ: Fairleigh Dickinson University Press, 1972).

Cohen, Lucy, *Some Recollections of Claude Goldsmid-Montefiore 1858–1938* (London: Faber & Faber, 1940).

Cohen, Shaye J. D., *The Beginnings of Jewishness: Boundaries, Varieties, Uncertainties* (Berkeley: University of California Press, 1999).

Cohn-Sherbok, Dan, *Messianic Judaism* (London: Continuum, 2001).

Danby, Herbert, *The Jew and Christianity* (London: Sheldon Press, 1927).

Davies, W. D., *Paul and Rabbinic Judaism: Some Rabbinic Elements in Pauline Theology*, second ed. (New York: SPCK, 1955).

Devrient, Eduard, *Meine Erinnerungen an Felix Mendelssohn or My Memories of Felix Mendelssohn* (Leipzig: J.J. Weber, 1872).

Dunn, James D. G., *Jesus, Paul and the Law* (Louisville, KY: Westminster/John Knox Press, 1990).

Eisenbaum, Pamela, *Paul Was Not a Christian: The Original Message of a Misunderstood Apostle* (New York: HarperOne, 2009).

Eliel, Carol S., *The Apocalyptic Landscapes of Ludwig Meidner* (Munich: Prestel, 1989).

Endelman, Todd M., ed., *Jewish Apostasy in the Modern World* (New York: Holmes & Meier, 1987).

Erikson, Erik, *Young Man Luther: A Study in Psychoanalysis and History* (New York: W. W. Norton, 1958).

Erikson, Erik, *Gandhi's Truth: On the Origins of Militant Nonviolence* (New York: W. W. Norton, 1969).

Farmer, William, ed, *Anti-Judaism and the Gospels* (Harrisburg, PA: Trinity Press International, 1999).

Flusser, David, *Judaism and the Origins of Christianity* (Jerusalem: Magnes Press, 1988).

Flusser, David, *The Sage from Galilee: Rediscovering Jesus' Genius* (Grand Rapids: Eerdmans, 2007).

Frankel, Jonathan, and Zipperstein, Steven J., eds., *Assimilation and Community: The Jews in Nineteenth-Century Europe* (Cambridge: Cambridge University Press, 1992).

Freud, Sigmund, *Die Traumdeutung* (Leipzig: Franz Deuticke, 1900).

Freud, Sigmund, *Totem und Tabu: Einige Übereinstimmungen im Seelenleben der Wilden und der Neurotiker* (Leipzig: H. Heller, 1913).

Freud, Sigmund, *Die Zukunft einer Illusion* (Leipzig: Internationaler Psychoanalytischer Verlag, 1927).

Freud, Sigmund, *The Future of an Illusion*, trans. W. D. Robson-Scott (New York: H. Liveright, 1928).

Freud, Sigmund, *Der Mann Moses und die monotheistische Religion* (Amsterdam: A. de Lange, 1939).

Freud, Sigmund, *Moses and Monotheism*, trans. Katherine Jones (London: Hogarth Press, 1939).

Gager, John G., *The Origins of Anti-Semitism* (Oxford: Oxford University Press, 1983).

Gager, John G., *Reinventing Paul* (New York: Oxford University Press, 2001).

Gaster, Moses, *Judith Montefiore College Ramsgate: Report for the Year 1894-5 and Report for the Year 1895-6 . . . Together with the Ancient Collections of Agadoth, the Sefer ha-Maasiyoth* (Ramsgate: Judith Montefiore College, 1896).

Gaster, Moses, *The Exempla of the Rabbis: Being a Collection of Exempla, Apologues and Tales Culled from Hebrew Manuscripts and Rare Books* (London/Leipzig: Asia Publishing Company, 1924).

Gaston, Lloyd, *Paul and the Torah* (Vancouver: University of British Columbia Press, 1987).

Geiger, Abraham, *Das Judenthum und seine Geschichte* (Breslau: Schletter, 1865–71).

Geller, Jay, *On Freud's Jewish Body: Mitigating Circumcisions* (New York: Fordham University Press, 2007).

Gilman, Sander, *Jewish Self-Hatred: Anti-Semitism and the Hidden Language of the Jews* (Baltimore: Johns Hopkins, 1986).

Gilman, Sander, *Freud, Race and Gender* (Princeton, NJ: Princeton University Press, 1993).

Goldstein, Morris, *Jesus in the Jewish Tradition* (New York: Macmillan, 1950).

Goodman, Paul, *The Synagogue and the Church* (New York: Routledge, 1908).

Goodman, Paul, *History of the Jews*, rev. Israel Cohen (London: J. M. Dent & Sons, 1951).

Graetz, Heinrich, *Geschichte der Juden von den ältesten Zeiten bis auf die Gegenwart* (Leipzig: Leiner, 1853–75).

Graetz, Heinrich, *History of the Jews from the Earliest Times to the Present Day*, ed. and trans. Bella Loewry (London: Jewish Chronicle, 1901).

Grochowiak, Thomas, *Ludwig Meidner* (Recklinghausen: Bongers, 1966).

Hagner, Donald, *The Jewish Reclamation of Jesus: An Analysis and Critique of the Modern Jewish Study of Jesus* (Grand Rapids, MI: Zondervan, 1984).

Harnack, Adolf, *Wesen das Christentums* (Leipzig: J.C. Hinrichs, 1901).

Harvey, Richard, *Mapping Messianic Jewish Identities* (Milton Keynes: Paternoster Publishing, 2009).

Hensel, Sebastian, *The Mendelssohn Family*, trans. Carl Klingemann, second ed. (New York: Harper, 1882).

Herford, Robert Travers, *Christianity in Talmud and Midrash* (London: Williams & Norgate, 1903).

Hilton, Michael, *The Christian Effect on Jewish Life* (London: SCM Press, 1994).

Heschel, Susannah, *Abraham Geiger and the Jewish Jesus* (Chicago: University of Chicago Press, 1998).

Hoffman, David Zvi, *Great Midrash: Exodus*, 2 vols., (Berlin: Verein MeKize Nirdamin, 1913-21).

Hoffman, Matthew, *From Rebel to Rabbi: Reclaiming Jesus and the Making of Modern Jewish Culture* (Stanford, CA: Stanford University Press, 2007).

Husik, Isaac, *A History of Medieval Jewish Philosophy* (New York: Macmillan, 1930).

Ilan, Tal, *Integrating Women into Second Temple History* (Peabody, MA: Hendrickson, 2001).

Jacob, Heinrich E., *Felix Mendelssohn and His Times*, trans. Richard and Clara Winston (Englewood Cliffs, NJ: Prentice Hall, 1963).

Kaplan, Mordecai, *Judaism as Civilisation* (New York: Macmillan, 1934).

Klausner, Joseph, *Yeshu ha-Notsri* (Jerusalem: Shtibel, 1922).

Klausner, Joseph, *Jesus of Nazareth: His Life, Times, and Teaching*, trans. Herbert Danby (London: Allen & Unwin, 1925).

Klausner, Joseph, *Mi-Yeshu ad Paulus* (Tel Aviv: Mada, 1939).

Klausner, Joseph, *From Jesus to Paul*, trans. William F. Stinespring (London: Allen & Unwin, 1943).

Klein,Charlotte, *Anti-Judaism in Christian Theology* (London: SPCK, 1978).

Kling, Simcha, *Joseph Klausner* (Cranbury, NJ: Thomas Yoseloff, 1970).

Klinghoffer, David, *Why the Jews Rejected Jesus* (New York: Doubleday, 2005).

Kobler, Franz, ed., *A Treasury of Jewish Letters: Letters from the Famous and the Humble*, II (New York: Jewish Publication Society, 1953).

Kohler, Kaufmann, *Christianity vs. Judaism: A Rejoinder to the Rev. Dr. R. Heber Newton* (New York: Stettiner, Lambert and Co., 1890).

Kohler, Kaufmann, *The Origins of the Synagogue and the Church* (New York: Macmillan, 1929).

Krauskopf, Joseph, *A Rabbi's Impressions of the Oberammergau Passion Play* (Philadelphia: Edward Stern & Co., 1908).

Krell, Marc A., *Intersecting Pathways: Modern Jewish Theologians in Conversation with Christianity* (Oxford: Oxford University Press, 2003).

Langton, Daniel R., *Claude Montefiore: His Life and Thought* (London: Valentine Mitchell, 2002).

Lapide, Pinchas, *Paulus zwischen Damaskus und Qumran* (Mohn: Gütersloh, 1993).

Lapide, Pinchas, *The Resurrection of Jesus: A Jewish Perspective* (London: SPCK, 1983).

Lapide, Pinchas and Stuhlmacher, Peter, *Paulus: Rabbi und Apostel* (Stuttgart: Calwer Verlag, 1981).

Lapide, Pinchas and Stuhlmacher, Peter, *Paul: Rabbi and Apostle*, trans. Lawrence W. Denef (Minneapolis: Augsburg Publishing House, 1984).

Lasker, Daniel J., *Jewish Philosophical Polemics against Christianity in the Middle Ages* (New York: KTAV, 1977).

Lasker, Daniel J. and Stroumsa, Sarah, *The Polemic of Nestor the Priest: Qissat Mujadalat al-Usquf and Sefer Nestor Ha-Komer*, 2 vols. (Jerusalem: Ben Zvi Institute, 1996).

Lessing, Theodore, *Der Jüdische Selbsthass* (Berlin: Jüdischer Verlag, 1930).

Levertoff, Paul, *The Confessions of St Augustine* (London: Luzac & Co., 1908).

Levertoff, Paul, *St. Paul in Jewish Thought: Three Lectures* (London: Diocesan House, 1928).

Levertov, Paul, *Ben ha-Adam: Chayey Yeshua ha-Mashiach upealeav or Son of Man: A Survey of the Life and Deeds of Jesus Christ* (London: 1904).

Levertov, Paul, *Polus ha-Shaliach o Sha'ul ish Tarsus: Chayav, po'alav u-nesi'otav or St Paul: His Life, Works and Travels* (London: 1907).

Levine, Amy-Jill, *A Feminist Companion to Paul* (London: Continuum, 2004).

Levine, Amy-Jill, *The Misunderstood Jew: The Church and the Scandal of the Jewish Jesus* (New York: Harper Collins, 2006).

Levison, Leon, *Life of St. Paul* (Edinburgh: Marshall Brothers, 1916).

Lieberman, Chaim, *The Christianity of Sholem Asch: An Appraisal from the Jewish Viewpoint* (New York: Philosophical Library, 1953).

Loewe, Herbert, *Rabbinic Anthology* (New York: Schocken Books, 1974).

Maccoby, Hyam, *Revolution in Judaea: Jesus and the Jewish Resistance* (London: Ocean Books, 1973).

Maccoby, Hyam, *The Mythmaker: Paul and the Invention of Christianity* (London: Weidenfeld and Nicolson, 1986).

Maccoby, Hyam, *Paul and Hellenism* (London: SCM, 1991).

Madison, Charles A., *Yiddish Literature: Its Scope and Major Writers* (New York: F. Ungar, 1968).

Mann, Vivian B. and Tucker, Gordon, *The Seminar on Jewish Art: January–September 1984* (New York: Jewish Theological Seminary of America and the Jewish Museum, 1985).

Martin, Bernard, ed., *All Things are Possible & Penultimate Words and Other Essays*, trans. S. S. Koteliansky (Athens, OH: Ohio University Press, 1977).

McDougall, William, *Is America Safe for Democracy?* (New York: Scribner, 1921).

Meghnagi, David, ed., *Freud and Judaism* (London: Karnac Books, 1993).

Meissner, Stefan, *Die Heimholung des Ketzers: Studien zur Jüdischen Auseinandersetzung mit Paulus* (Mohr: Tübingen, 1996).

Mendelssohn, Felix, *St. Paul* (Birmingham: 1837).

Moses Mendelssohn, *Phaedon oder über die Unsterblichkeit der Seele in drey Gesprächen* (Berlin: Stettin, 1767).

Mendelssohn, Moses, *Jerusalem oder über religiöse Macht und Judentum* (Berlin: Maurer, 1783).

Moses Mendelssohn, *Phaedon or the Death of Socrates* (London: J. Cooper, 1789).

Mendelssohn, Moses, *Jerusalem or On Religious Power and Judaism*, trans. Allan Arkush (Boston: Brandeis University Press, 1983).

Mendelssohn Bartholdy, Paul and Carl, eds., *Letters of Felix Mendelssohn Bartholdy, from 1833 to 1847*, trans. Lady Wallace (London: Longmans, 1863).

Mendelssohn-Bartholdy, Felix, *Paulus* (Bonn: N. Simrock, 1836).

Meyer, Michael A., *Jewish Identity in the Modern World* (Seattle: University of Washington Press, 1990).

Mills, Sanford C., *A Hebrew Christian Looks at Romans*, second ed. (Grand Rapids, MI: Dunham Publishing, 1969).

Montefiore, Claude G., *Judaism and St. Paul: Two Essays* (London: Macmillan, 1914).

Montefiore, Claude G., *Liberal Judaism and Hellenism and Other Essays* (London: Macmillan, 1918).

Montefiore, Claude G., *The Old Testament and After* (London: Macmillan, 1923).

Myers, David N., *Re-inventing the Jewish Past* (New York: Oxford University Press, 1995).

Nanos, Mark, *The Mystery of Romans: The Jewish Context of Paul's Letter* (Minneapolis: Fortress Press, 1996).

Nanos, Mark, *The Irony of Galatians: Paul's Letter in First-Century Context* (Minneapolis: Fortress Press, 2002).

Neusner, Jacob, *Jews and Christians: The Myth of a Common Tradition*, second ed. (London: SCM Press, 1990).

Neusner, Jacob, and Chilton, Bruce, eds., *In Quest of the Historical Pharisees* (Waco, TX: Baylor University Press, 2007).

Nemoy, Leon, *Al-Quirqisani's Account of the Jewish Sects and Christianity* (Cincinnati: Hebrew Union College, 1930).

Ortar, Ilana, *Melnikoff: The Awakening Judah* (Haifa: University of Haifa Art Gallery, 1982).

Parkes, James, *The Conflict of the Church and Synagogue: A Study in the Origins of Anti-Semitism* (London: Soncino Press, 1934).

Parkes, James, *Jesus, Paul and the Jews* (London: SCM, 1936).

Perlmann, Moshe, *Ibn Kammuna's Examination of the Three Faiths* (Los Angeles: University of California, 1971).

Peterson, Erik, *Theolgische Traktate* (München: Kösel, 1951).

Radford-Ruether, Rosemary. *Faith and Fratricide; The Theological Roots of Anti-Semitism* (London: Search Press, 1975).

Reinharz, Jehuda and Shapira, Anita, eds., *Essential Papers on Zionism* (London: Cassell, 1996).

Riches, John K., *A Century of New Testament Study* (Cambridge: The Lutterworth Press, 1993).

Rubenstein, Richard L., *After Auschwitz* (Indianapolis: Bobbs-Merrill, 1966).

Rubenstein, Richard L., *My Brother Paul* (New York: Harper & Row, 1972).

Sachs, Hanns, *The Creative Unconscious: Studies in the Psychoanalysis of Art* (Cambridge, MA: Sci-Art Publishers, 1942).

Sachs, Hanns, *Masks of Love and Life: The Philosophical Basis of Psychoanalysis* (Cambridge, MA: Sci-Art Publishers, 1948).

Sacks, Jonathan, *One People? Tradition, Modernity, and Jewish Unity* (London: Littman Library, 1993).

Salvador, Joseph, *Jésus-Christ et sa doctrine* (Paris: Guyot et Scribe, 1838).

Sanders, E.P., *Paul and Palestinian Judaism* (London: SCM Press, 1977).

Sandmel, Samuel, *A Jewish Understanding of the New Testament* (New York: Ktav Publishing House, 1956).

Sandmel, Samuel, *The Genius of Paul: A Study in History* (New York: Farrar, Straus & Cudahy, 1958).

Sandmel, Samuel, *We Jews and Jesus* (New York: Oxford University Press, 1965).

Sandmel, Samuel, *Two Living Traditions: Essays on Religion and the Bible* (Detroit: Wayne State University Press, 1972).

Sandmel, Samuel, *Anti-Semitism in the New Testament* (Philadelphia: Fortress Press, 1978).

Saperstein, Marc, *Jewish Preaching, 1200–1800: An Anthology* (New Haven, CT/London: Yale University Press, 1989).

Schmitt, Carl, *Political Theology*, trans. George Schwab (Cambridge, MA: MIT Press, 1985).

Schmitt, Carl, *The Concept of the Political*, trans. George Schwab (Chicago: University of Chicago Press, 1996).

Schoeps, Hans Joachim, *Paulus: Die Theologie des Apostels im Lichte der Jüdischen Religionsgeschichte* (Tübingen: Mohr, 1959).

Schoeps, Hans Joachim, *Paul: The Theology of the Apostle in the Light of Jewish Religious History*, trans. Harold Knight (London: Lutterworth Press, 1961).

Scholem, Gershom, *Sabbatai Sevi: The Mystical Messiah, 1626–1676*, trans. R. J. Zwi Werblowsky (Princeton, NJ: Princeton University Press, 1973).

Schonfield, Hugh, *The History of Jewish Christianity from the First to the Twentieth Century* (London: Duckworth, 1936).

Schonfield, Hugh, *The Jew of Tarsus: An Unorthodox Portrait of Paul* (London: MacDonald, 1946).

Schonfield, Hugh, *The Passover Plot* (London: Hutchinson, 1965).

Schonfield, Hugh, *The Politics of God* (London: Hutchinson, 1970).

Schonfield, Hugh, *Proclaiming the Messiah: The Life and Letters of Paul of Tarsus, Envoy to the Nations* (London: Open Gate Press, 1997).

Schumann, Robert, *On Music and Musicians*, ed. Konrad Wolf, trans. Paul Rosenfeld (New York: Pantheon, 1946).

Schweitzer, Albert, *The Mysticism of Paul the Apostle*, trans. W. Montgomery (London: ARC Black, 1931).

Segal, Alan, *Paul the Convert: The Apostate and Apostasy of Saul the Pharisee* (New Haven, CT: Yale University Press, 1990).

Shestov, Lev, *Athens and Jerusalem*, ed. and trans. Bernard Martin (Athens, OH: Ohio University Press, 1966).

Shestov, Lev, *Potestas Clavium*, ed. and trans. Bernard Martin (Athens, OH: Ohio University Press, 1968).

Shestov, Lev, *Speculation and Revelation*, ed. and trans. Bernard Martin (Athens, OH: Ohio University Press, c. 1982).

Schleiermacher, Friedrich, *The Christian Faith*, trans. H. R. Mackintosh and J. S. Stewart (Edinburgh: T&T Clark, 1928).

Schleiermacher, Friedrich, *On Religion*, trans. Richard Crouter (Cambridge: Cambridge University Press, 1988).

Shulam, Joseph, and Le Cornu, Hilary, *A Commentary on the Jewish Roots of Romans* (Baltimore: Lederer Books, 1997).

Silberstein, Laurence J., *Mapping Jewish Identities* (New York: New York University Press, 2000).

Silver, Abba Hillel, *History of Messianic Speculation in Israel from the First through the Seventeenth Centuries* (New York: Macmillan, 1927).

Silver, Abba Hillel, *The Democratic Impulse in Jewish History* (New York: Bloch, 1928).

Silver, Abba Hillel, *Religion in a Changing World* (New York: Richard R. Smith, 1931).

Silver, Abba Hillel, *Where Judaism Differed: An Inquiry into the Distinctiveness of Judaism* (New York: Macmillan, 1956).

Simon, Maurice, and Levertoff, Paul Phillip, trans., *Zohar* vol.4 (London: Soncino Press, 1933).

Skarsaune, Oskar, and Hvalvik, Reidar, eds., *Jewish Believers in Jesus: The Early Centuries* (Peabody, MA: Hendrickson Publishers, 2007).

Smith, Steven B., *Spinoza, Liberalism, and the Question of Jewish Identity* (New Haven, CT: Yale University Press, 1997).

Sperling, Harry, Simon, Maurice, and Levertoff, Paul Phillip, trans., *Zohar* vol.3 (London: Soncino Press, 1933).

Spinoza, Benedict de, *Theological-Political Treatise*, trans. Michael Silverthorne and Jonathan Israel (Cambridge: Cambridge University Press, 2007).

Sposato, Jeffrey, *The Price of Assimilation: Felix Mendelssohn and the Nineteenth-Century Anti-Semitic Tradition* (Oxford: Oxford University Press, 2006).

Stahl, Nanette, ed., *Sholem Asch Reconsidered* (New Haven, CT: Beinecke Rare Book and Manuscript Library, 2004).

Steiman, Lionel B., *Franz Werfel: The Faith of an Exile* (Ontario: Wilfrid Laurier University Press, 1985).

Stendahl, Krister, *Paul among Jews and Gentiles and Other Essays* (Philadelphia: Fortress Press, 1976).

Stroumsa, Sarah, *Dawud Ibn Marwan Al-Muqammis's Twenty Chapters (Ishrun Maqala)* (Leiden: E. J. Brill, 1989).

Taubes, Jacob, *Abendländische Eschatologie* (Bern: A. Francke, 1947).

Taubes, Jacob, *Die Politische Theologie des Paulus* (Munich: Wilhelm Fink, 1993).

Taubes, Jacob, *The Political Theology of Paul*, Aleida and Jan Assmann, eds. and trans. Dana Hollander (Stanford, CA: Stanford University Press, 2004).

Todd, Larry R., ed., *Mendelssohn and His World* (Princeton, NJ: Princeton University Press, 1991).

Todd, Larry R., *Mendelssohn: A Life in Music* (Oxford: Oxford University Press, 2003).

Troki, Isaac, *Faith Strengthened*, trans. Moses Mocatta (New York: Hermon Press, 1970), reprinted from 1850 edition.

Van Voorst, Robert E., *Jesus outside the New Testament: Introduction to the Ancient Evidence* (Grand Rapids, MI: William B. Eerdmans, 2000).

Wagner, Richard, *Judaism in Music and other Writings*, trans. W. Ashton Ellis (London: University of Nebraska Press, 1995).

Watson, Francis, *Paul, Judaism and the Gentiles: A Sociological Approach* (Cambridge: Cambridge University Press, 1986).

Welch, Claude, *Protestant Thought in the Nineteenth Century: 1799–1870* (New Haven, CT: Yale University Press, 1972).

Werfel, Franz, *Paulus unter den Juden* (Berlin: Zsolnay, 1926).

Werfel, Franz, *Juarez and Maximilian*, trans. Ruth Langner (New York: Simon and Schuster, 1926)

Werfel, Franz, *Paul among the Jews: A Tragedy*, trans. Paul Levertoff (London: A. R. Mowbray & Co., 1928).

Werfel, Franz, *Der Weg der Verheissung* (Vienna: Paul Zsolnay, 1935).

Werfel, Franz, *The Eternal Road*, trans. Ludwig Lewisohn (New York: Viking Press, 1936).

Werfel, Franz, *Das Lied von Bernadette* (Stockholm: Bermann-Fischer, 1941).

Werfel, Franz, *The Song of Bernadette*, trans. Ludwig Lewisohn (New York: Viking Press, 1942).

Werner, Eric, *Mendelssohn, A New Image of the Composer and His Age*, trans. Dika Newlin (New York: Collier-Macmillan, 1963).

Westerholm, Stephen, *Perspectives Old and New on Paul: The 'Lutheran' Paul and Hs Critics* (Grand Rapids, MI: William B. Eerdmans, 2004).

Wright, Nicholas T., *What St Paul Really Said* (Oxford: Lion, 1997).

Yerushalmi, Yosef, *Freud's Moses: Judaism Terminable and Indeterminable* (New Haven, CT: Yale University Press, 1991).

Yerushalmi, Yosef, *Zakhor: Jewish History and Jewish Memory*, third ed. (Seattle: Unversity of Washington Press, 1999).

CHAPTERS IN BOOKS

Alexander, Philip S., 'Gaster's *Exempla of the Rabbis*: A Reappraisal', in G. Sed-Rajna Rashi, ed., *1040–1990: Hommage à Ephraim E. Urbach* (Paris: CERF, 1993).

Amishai-Maisels, Ziva, 'The Artist as Refugee', in Ezra Mendelssohn and Richard I. Cohen, eds., *Art and Its Uses: The Visual Image and Modern Jewish Society*, Studies in Contemporary Jewry VI (New York: Oxford University Press, 1990).

Botstein, Leon, 'The Aesthetics of Assimilation and Affirmation: Reconstructing the Career of Felix Mendelssohn', in R. Larry Todd, ed., *Mendelssohn and His World* (Princeton, NJ: Princeton University Press, 1991).

Botstein, Leon, 'Neo-Classicism, Romantism, and Emancipation: The Origins of Felix Mendelssohn's Aesthetic Outlook', in Douglass Seaton, ed., *The Mendelssohn Companion* (London: Greenwood Press, 2001).

Deutscher, Isaac, 'The Non-Jewish Jew', in Isaac Deutscher, *The Non-Jewish Jew and Other Essays* (Oxford: Oxford University Press, 1968).

Eisenbaum, Pamela, 'Following in the Footnotes of the Apostle Paul', in Jose Ignacio Cabezón and Sheila Greeve Davaney, eds., *Identity and the Politics of Scholarship in the Study of Religion* (London: Routledge, 2004).

Endelmann, Todd M., 'Jewish Self-Hatred in Britain and Germany', in M. Brenner, ed., *Two Nations: British and German Jews in Comparative Perspective* (Tübingen: Mohr Siebeck, 1999).

Benjamin Fondane, 'Entretiens avec Leon Chestov', in Nathalie Baranoff and Michel Carassou, eds., *Rencontres avec Leon Chestov* (Paris: Plasma, 1982).

Flusser, David, ''Paul's Jewish-Christian Opponents in the Didache', in S. Shaked, D. Shulman, and G. Stroumsa, eds., *Gilgul: Essays on Transformation, Revolution and Permanence in the History of Religions* (Leiden: 1987).

Forsyth, James J., 'Freud and St Paul', in John R. May, *The Bent World: Essays on Religion and Culture* (Chico, CA: Scholars' Press, 1979).

Gay, Peter, 'The Question of a Jewish Science', in *A Godless Jew: Freud, Atheism, and the Making of Psychoanalysis* (New Haven, CT: Yale University Press, 1987).

Gutmann, Joseph, 'The "Second Commandment" and the Image in Judaism', in Joseph Gutmann, ed., *No Graven Images: Studies in Art and the Hebrew Bible* (New York: Ktav, 1971).

Hagner, Donald A., 'Paul in Modern Jewish Thought', in Donald A. Hagner and Murray J. Harris, eds., *Pauline Studies: Essays Presented to F. F. Bruce* (Exeter: Paternoster Press, 1980).

Hirsch, Emil, 'Paul, the Apostle of Heathen Judaism, or Christianity', reprinted in G. W. Foote and J. M. Wheeler, eds., *The Jewish Life of Jesus, Being the Sepher Toledoth Jeshu or Book of the Generation of Jesus*, trans. from the Hebrew (London: Progressive Publishing Company, 1885).

Ilan, Tal, 'Paul and Pharisee Women', in Jane Schaberg, Alice Bach, Ester Fuchs, eds., *On the Cutting Edge: The Study of Women in Biblical Worlds* (London: Continuum, 2003).

Krausz, Michael, 'On Being Jewish', in David Theo Goldberg and Michael Krausz, eds., *Jewish Identity* (Philadelphia: Temple University Press, 1993).

Levertoff, Olga, 'Paul Levertoff and the Jewish-Christian Problem', in Lev Gillet, ed., *Judaism and Christianity: Essays Presented to the Rev. Paul P. Levertoff* (London: J. B. Shears and Sons, 1939).

Meghnagi, David, 'A Cultural Event within Judaism', in David Meghnagi, ed., *Freud and Judaism* (London: Karnac Books, 1993).

Meyer, Michael A., 'Reflections on Jewish Modernization', in Elisheva Carlebach, John Efron, and David Myers, eds., *Jewish History and Jewish Memory* (Hanover, NH: Brandeis University Press, 1998).

Myers, D. N., 'Of Marranos and Memory', in Elisheva Carlebach, John Efron, David Myers, eds., *Jewish History and Jewish Memory* (Hanover, NH: Brandeis University Press, 1998).

Norich, Anita, 'Sholem Asch and the Christian Question', in Nanette Stahl, ed., *Sholem Asch Reconsidered* (New Haven, CT: Beinecke Rare Book and Manuscript Library, 2004).

Reffet, Michel, 'Franz Werfel and Psychoanalysis', in L. Huber, ed., *Franz Werfel: An Austrian Writer Reassessed* (Oxford: Berg, 1989).

Roback, A. A., 'Dr Hanns Sachs (A Memoir)', in Hanns Sachs, *Masks of Love and Life: The Philosophical Basis of Psychoanalysis* (Cambridge, MA: Sci-Art, 1948).

Rubenstein, B., 'A Brief Biographical Sketch', in Betty Rubenstein and Michael Berenbaum, eds., *What Kind of God? Essays in Honour of Richard L. Rubenstein* (New York: University Press of America, 1995).

Rubenstein, R., 'Reflections on Identity and Memory', in Charles Selengut, ed., *Jewish Identity in the Post-modern Age: Scholarly and Personal Reflections* (St Paul, Minnesota: Paragon House, 1999).

Schiller-Szinessy, S.M., 'St Paul from a Jewish Point of View', in *The Expositor*, ed. W. Robertson Nicoll (London: Hodder and Stoughtons, 1886), IV.

Segal, Alan, 'Paul's Religious Experience in the Eyes of Jewish Scholars', in David Capes, April D. DeConick, Helen K. Bond, and Troy A. Miller, eds., *Israel's God and Rebecca's Children: Essays in Honor of Larry W. Hurtado and Alan F. Segal* (Waco, TX: Baylor University Press, 2007).

Sanders, E. P., 'Reflection on Anti-Judaism in the New Testament and in Christianity', in William Farmer, ed., *Anti-Judaism and the Gospels* (Harrisburg, PA: Trinity Press International, 1999).

Skarsaune, Oskar, 'The Ebionites', in Oskar Skarsaune and Reidar Hvalvik, eds., *Jewish Believers in Jesus: The Early Centuries* (Peabody, MA: Hendrickson Publishers, 2007).

Stanton, Graham, 'Jewish-Christian Elements in the Pseudo-Clementine Writings', in Oskar Skarsaune and Reidar Hvalvik, eds., *Jewish Believers in Jesus: The Early Centuries* (Peabody, MA: Hendrickson Publishers, 2007).

Terpstra, Marin and de Wit, Theo, '"No Spiritual Investment in the World as It Is": Jacob Taubes's Negative Political Theology', in Ilse N. Bulhof and Laurens Ten Kate, eds., *Flight of the Gods: Philosophical Perspectives on Negative Theology* (New York: Fordham University Press, 2000).

Warren, John, 'Franz Werfel's Historical Drama: Continuity and Change', in Lothar Huber, ed., *Franz Werfel: An Austrian Writer Reassessed* (Oxford: Berg, 1989).

Wiefel, Wolfgang, 'Paulus in Jüdischer Sicht', in Marcus Barth, Josef Blank, Jochann Bloch, Frank Mussner, and R. J. Zwi Werblovski, eds., *Paulus – Apostat oder Apostel? Jüdische und Christliche Antworten* (Regensburg: Verlag Friedrich Pustet, 1977).

Wise, Isaac Mayer, 'Paul and the Mystics', in Isaac Mayer Wise, *Three Lectures on the Origin of Christianity* (Cincinnati: Bloch & Co., 1883).

Witherington, Ben, 'Contemporary Perspectives on Paul', in James D. G. Dunn, ed., *The Cambridge Companion to St Paul* (Cambridge: Cambridge University Press, 2003).

Wolin, Richard, 'Reflections on Jewish Secular Messianism', in Jonathan Frankel, ed., *Jews and Messianism in the Modern Era: Metaphor and Meaning*, Studies in Contemporary Jewry VII (Oxford: Oxford University Press, 1991).

ARTICLES AND LECTURES

Alon, Keziah, 'Christians, Jews and Others: A Study in the Literary Heritage of Scholem Ach and Avraham Aharon Kabak', *Theory and Criticism* 26 (Spring 2005). [In Hebrew]

Baeck, Leo, 'Harnack's Vorlesungen über das Wesen das Christentums' in *Monatsschrift für Geschichte und Wissenschaft des Judenthums* 45 (1901).

Baeck, Leo, 'The Faith of Paul', *Journal of Jewish Studies* 3 (1952).

Baur, Ferdinand Christian, 'Die Christuspartei in der korinthischen Gemeinde, der Gegensatz des paulinischen und petrinischen Christentums in der ältesten Kirche, der Apostel Petrus in Rom,' *Tübinger Zeitschrift für Theologie* 4 (1831).

Bentwich, Norman, 'Claude Montefiore and His Tutor in Rabbinics: Founders of Liberal and Conservative Judaism', 6th Montefiore Memorial Lecture (Southampton: University of Southamptons, 1966).

Botstein, Leon, 'Songs without Words: Thoughts on Music, Theology, and the Role of the Jewish Question in the Work of Felix Mendelssohn', *The Musical Quarterly* 77:4 (Winter 1993).

Botstein, Leon, 'Mendelssohn and the Jews', *The Musical Quarterly* 82:1 (Spring 1998).

Botstein, Leon, 'Mendelssohn, Werner, and the Jews: A Final Word', *The Musical Quarterly* 83:1 (Spring 1999).

Brumberg-Kraus, Jonathan D., 'A Jewish Ideological Perspective on the Study of Christian Scripture', *Jewish Social Studies* 4:1 (1997).

Dash-Moore, Deborah, 'Jewish GIs and the Creation of the Judeo-Christian Tradition', *Religion and American Culture* 8:1 (1998).

Eisenbaum, Pamela, 'Is Paul the Father of Misogyny and Antisemitism?', *Cross Currents* 50:4 (Winter 2000–2001).

Falk, Harvey, 'Rabbi Jacob Emden's Views on Christianity', *Journal of Ecumenical Studies* 19:1 (Winter 1982).

Feld, Edward, 'Spinoza the Jew', *Modern Judaism*, 9:1 (1989).

Flusser, David, 'A New Sensitivity to Judaism and the Christian Message', *Harvard Theological Review* 61 (1968).

Foot-Moore, George, 'Christian Writers on Judaism', *Harvard Theological Review* 14:5 (July 1921).

Freud, Anna, 'Inaugural Lecture', *International Journal of Psycho-Analysis* 59 (1978).

Freud, Sigmund, 'On Being of the B'nai B'rith: An Address to the Society in Vienna' (May 1926), reproduced in *Commentary* (March 1946).

Fuchs-Kreimer, Nancy, 'Seven Extant Letters of Rabbi Nancy Fuchs-Kreimer of Philadelphia to Rabbi Paul of Tarsus: Letter 1', The Institute for Christian-Jewish Studies, http://www.icjs.org/scholars/letters.html (accessed 29 July 2007).

Gager, John G., 'Scholarship as Moral Vision: David Flusser on Jesus, Paul, and the Birth of Christianity', *The Jewish Quarterly Review* 95:1 (Winter 2005).

Gold, Joshua Robert, 'Jacob Taubes: Apocalypse from Below', *Telos* 134 (March 2006).

Harvey, Richard, 'Passing over the Plot? The Life and Work of Hugh Schonfield (1901–1988)', *Mishkan* 37 (2002).

Hirschberg, Harris, 'Allusions to the Apostle Paul in the Talmud', *Journal of Biblical Literature* 62:2 (June 1943).

Horowitz, Brian, 'The Tension of Athens and Jerusalem in the Philosophy of Lev Shestov', *The Slavic and East European Journal* 43:1 (Spring 1999).

Hotam, Yotam, 'Berdichevsky's *Saul and Paul: A Jewish Political Theology*', *Journal of Modern Jewish Studies* 6:1 (March 2007).

Jackson, Bernard S., 'Legalism', *Journal of Jewish Studies* 30:1 (1979).

Jones, Ernest, 'Hanns Sachs', *International Journal of Psycho-Analysis* 27 (1946).

Langton, Daniel R., 'A Question of Backbone: Comparing Christian Influences upon the Origins of Reform and Liberal Judaism in England', *Melilah* 3 (2004).

Mercer-Taylor, Peter, 'Rethinking Mendelssohn's Historicism: A Lesson from St Paul', *The Journal of Musicology* 15:2 (Spring 1997).

Montefiore, Claude G., 'First Impressions of St. Paul', *Jewish Quarterly Review* 6 (1894).

Montefiore, Claude G., 'Rabbinic Judaism and the Epistles of St. Paul', *Jewish Quarterly Review* 13 (1901).

Mutius, Hans-Georg von, 'Eine jüdische Pauluskritik aus dem 16. Jahrhundert', in *Judaica* 35 (1979).

Newman, Hillel I., 'The Death of Jesus in the Toledot Yeshu', in *Journal of Theological Studies* 50:1 (April 1999).

Orwell, George, 'Stendhal', *The New English Weekly* 15 (27 July 1939).

Quiñónez, Jorge, 'Paul Phillip Levertoff: Pioneering Hebrew-Christian Scholar and Leader', *Mishkan* 37 (2002).

Rembaum, Joel E., 'Medieval Jewish Criticism of the Christian Doctrine of Original Sin', *AJS Review* 7 (1982).

Ronning, Halvor, 'Some Jewish Views of Paul as Basis of a Consideration of Jewish–Christian Relations', *Judaica* 24 (1968).

Sandmel, Samuel, 'Leo Baeck on Christianity', Leo Baeck Memorial Lecture 19 (New York: Leo Baeck Institute, 1975).

Schmidt, Christoph, 'Review Essay of Jacob Taubes' *The Political Theology of Paul*', *Hebraic Political Studies* 2:2 (Spring 2007).

Schwartz, G. David, 'Explorations and Responses: Is There a Jewish Reclamation of Jesus?', *The Journal of Ecumenical Studies* 24 (1987).

Segal, Alan, 'Paul et ses exégètes juifs contemporains', *Recherche de science religieuse* 94:3 (2006).

Silk, Mark, 'Notes of the Judeo-Christian Tradition in America', *American Quarterly* 36:1 (Spring 1984).

Sposato, Jeffrey S., 'Creative Writing: The [Self-] Identification of Mendelssohn as a Jew', *The Musical Quarterly* 82:1 (Spring 1998).

Sposato, Jeffrey S., 'Mendelssohn, "Paulus", and the Jews: A Response to Leon Botstein and Michael Steinberg', *The Musical Quarterly* 83:2 (Summer 1999).

Steinberg, Michael P., 'Mendelssohn's Music and German-Jewish Culture: An Intervention', *The Musical Quarterly* 83:1 (Spring 1999).

Stendahl, Krister, 'The Apostle Paul and the Introspective Conscience of the West', *Harvard Theological Review* 56:3 (July 1963).

Stendahl, Krister, 'Review of *A Jewish Understanding of the New Testament*', *Ecumenical Review* (July 1975).

Talmage, Frank, 'The Polemical Writings of Profiat Duran', *Immanuel* 13 (1981).

Wagner, Richard, 'Das Judenthum in der Musik' in *Neue Zeitschrift für Musik* (Leipzig: 1850).

Wecker, Menachem, 'The Challenge of Defining Jewish Art', *Forward* (18 August 2006).

Weingrad, Michael, 'New Encounters with Shestov', *The Journal of Jewish Thought and Philosophy* 11:1 (2002).

UNPUBLISHED MANUSCRIPTS

Brumberg-Kraus, Jonathan D., 'Conventions of Literary Symposia in Luke's Gospel with Special Attention to the Last Supper', Ph.D. dissertation, Vanderbilt University (1991).

Fuchs-Kreimer, Nancy, 'The Essential Heresy: Paul's View of the Law According to Jewish Writers, 1886–1986', Ph.D. dissertation, Temple University (May 1990).

Sandmel, Samuel, *The Apostle Paul: A Novel* (unpublished, undated), 472pp., in Samuel Sandmel Papers, Manuscript Collection No. 101, Series C/1/17.7 and 18.1 at the American Jewish Archives, Cincinnati, U.S.A.

Scheyer, Ernst, 'Ludwig Meidner, Artist-Poet', Manuscript, Los Angeles County Museum of Art, Rifkind Center (undated).

Setzer, Claudia, 'Understanding Paul', unpublished paper given at the twelfth *Nostra Aetate* Dialogue, Fordham University (October 2004).

VISUAL ART

Meidner, Ludwig, 'Töte das Fleisch' [Mortify Thy Flesh] (1902), ink pen, 20 × 32 cm. Private estate of Ludwig Meidner.

Meidner, Ludwig, 'Apokalyptische Landschaft' [Apocalyptic Landscape] (1912), oil painting, 94 × 109 cm. Küsters Collection, Recklinghausen.

Meidner, Ludwig, 'Pauluspredigt' [Paul's Sermon] (1919), watercolour, 68 × 49 cm. Buller Collection, Duisberg.

Meidner, Ludwig, 'Prophet' (1919), feather and brush, 111 × 73 cm. Museum of Art, Düsseldorf.

Meidner, Ludwig, 'Vision der Apostel Paulus' [Vision of the Apostle Paul] (1919), lithograph print, 25.4 × 17.62 cm. The Robert Gore Rifkind Center for German Expressionist Studies.

Meidner, Ludwig, 'Die Verzückung Pauli' [The Ecstasy of Paul] (undated), drawing? unknown dimensions. National Gallery Berlin?

REFERENCE WORKS AND ENCYCLOPAEDIA ENTRIES

Book of Common Prayer (New York: The Church Hymnal Corporation, 1979).

Dictionary of Jewish-Christian Relations, ed. Ed Kessler and Neil Wenborn (Cambridge: Cambridge University Press, 2005).

Encyclopaedia Judaica, ed. Geoffrey Widoger (Jerusalem: Keter Publishing, 1972).

Encyclopedia of Jewish Knowledge, ed. Jacob de Hass (New York: Behrman's Jewish Book House, 1934).

Jewish Encyclopaedia, ed. Isadore Singer (New York: Funk and Wagnalls Company, 1901–1916).

Routledge Encyclopedia of Philosophy, ed. E. Craig (London: Routledge, 1998).

The Standard Jewish Encyclopedia, ed. Cecil Roth (London: W. H. Allen, 1959).

The Universal Jewish Encyclopedia, ed. Isaac Landman (New York: Universal Jewish Encyclopedia Co., 1942).

Vallentine's Jewish Encyclopaedia, ed. A. M. Hyamson and A. M. Silbermann (London: Shapiro, Vallentine & Co., 1938).

Ben-Sasson, Haim Hillel, 'Hadassi, Judah', in *Encyclopedia Judaica*, VII, 1046–7.

Flusser, David, 'Paul of Tarsus,' in *Encyclopaedia Judaica*, XIII, 190–92.

Goodman, L.E. 'Jewish Philosophy', in *Routledge Encyclopedia of Philosophy*, V, 90–95.

Harvey, Warren Zev, 'Philosophy, Jewish', in *Encyclopedia Judaica*, XIII, 421–65.

Jacobs, Joseph, Kohler, Kaufmann, and Eisenstein, Judah David, 'Art, Attitude of Judaism toward', in *Jewish Encyclopedia*, I, 141–3.

Kohler, Kaufmann, 'Christianity in Its Relation to Judaism', in *Jewish Encyclopedia*, IV, 49–59.

Kohler, Kaufmann, 'Jesus of Nazareth', in *Jewish Encyclopedia*, VII, 160–78.

Kohler, Kaufmann, 'Saul of Tarsus', in *Jewish Encyclopedia*, XI, 79–87.

Lasker, Daniel J., 'Anti-Paulinism, Judaism', in *Encyclopedia of the Bible and Its Reception* (Berlin/New York: de Gruyter, 2009), columns 284–6.

Monas, Sidney, 'Shestov, Lev', in *Encyclopedia Judaica*, XIV, 1383–5.

Stern, Sacha, 'Talmud', in *Dictionary of Jewish-Christian Relations*, 416–17.

Wigoder, Geoffrey and Seckbach, Fern, 'Editor's Introduction', in *Encyclopaedia Judaica*, I, 1–16.

Scripture and Other Ancient Writings Index

OLD TESTAMENT
Genesis
  42.17, 112
Exodus
  3.1–2, 238
  32, 253
  32–34, 253
  33–34, 238
Leviticus
  12, 90
  17, 90
  18, 90
  20, 90
  24.16, 187
Numbers
  11.17, 240
  14–15, 253
1 Kings
  22.2, 240
Psalms
  2, 159
  115.3, 188
Proverbs
  21.8, 25
Ecclesiastes
  12.1, 86
Isaiah
  43.11, 190
  51, 104
  53, 72
  60.1–2, 190
  64.4, 244
Jeremiah
  1.5, 223, 253
  7.21–22, 123
  9.24, 244
  10.14–15, 188
Ezekiel
  1.26, 126
Amos
  5.21–22, 123
Jonah
  1.17, 112

Habakkuk
  2.4, 256

NEW TESTAMENT
Matthew
  23.37, 190
Luke
  1.3, 228
John
  4.22, 144
  14.1, 27
  14.8, 27
  14.11, 27
Acts
  1.1, 228
  2.21, 191
  4.24, 187
  4.26, 190
  4.29, 190
  6.11, 187
  6.14, 187
  6.39–40, 187
  7, 109
  7.47–48, 187
  7.52, 190
  7.58, 148
  8.1, 148
  9, 111
  9.1, 148
  9.1–39, 113
  9.5, 214
  9.9, 111
  9.11, 148
  9.17, 148
  9.21, 190
  11.26, 252
  11.29–30, 111
  13.2–3, 109
  13.4–15.35, 112
  13.9, 113
  13.47, 191
  14.15, 188
  15, 60, 192

15.19–21, 192
15.19–32, 90
15.36–18.22, 112
16.15, 90
16.26, 274
17, 60
17.16–34, 112
17.24, 188
18.23–20.38, 112
19.23–41, 112
20.23, 191
20.25, 191
21.24, 78
21.25, 90
21.28, 188
21.37, 148
21.40, 148
22, 111
22.1–11, 202
22.1–22, 113
22.3, 60, 61, 148
22.6, 200
22.7, 201
22.9, 201
23.6, 148, 149
23.16, 158
24.17, 112
26, 111
26.4–7, 149
26.5, 148
26.9–18, 202
26.9–24, 113
28.17, 149
Romans
  1.1, 252
  1.17, 256
  1.2, 27
  1.20, 239
  1.25, 158
  1.4, 27
  2.11, 146
  2.13, 88
  2.17–18, 158

3.1–2, 18, 129, 130
3.2, 244
3.5, 240
3.9, 238
3.20, 17, 60, 63, 119
3.28, 240
3.29, 238
3.31, 18
4.3, 244, 245
4.15, 238
4.17, 158
5, 150
5.10, 150
5.12, 73
5.12–14, 62
5.12–21, 60
5.17, 150
5.18–19, 73
5.20, 62, 244, 246
6, 61
6.1–10, 39
6.15, 60, 63
6.19, 240
7, 162
7.1–6, 60, 61, 75, 163
7.7, 18
7.7–8, 273
7.9, 15
7.12, 18
7.14, 15
7.17, 15
7.18, 15
7.20, 15
7.22, 88
7.22–23, 273
7.24, 273
8.18, 240
8.21, 272
8.22–23, 60
8.28, 146
8.29–30, 73

Romans (*cont.*)
8.35–39, 158
9.2–3, 275
9.3, 78, 149
9.3–5, 19
9.4, 144, 158
9.4–5, 129
9.5, 158
9.18, 240
9–11, 119, 253
10.4, 65, 72, 88
10.15, 191
10.18, 191
10.20, 244, 245
11, 135
11.1, 19
11.11, 78
11.25–26, 60, 62
11.26, 19
11.28, 259
11.33, 188
12, 150
12.2, 286
12.4–8, 39
12.9–21, 150
12.11, 146
13.1–7, 257
13.8, 239
13.14, 146
14.3, 275
14.23, 65, 244, 246,
    248
15.12, 147
15.33, 158
1 Corinthians
1.27, 244
1.31, 244
2.9, 244
3.1–2, 240
5.1, 25
6.12, 86
7, 132
7.3–4, 129
7.6, 240
7.12–14, 132
7.21, 133
7.25, 240
7.40, 240
9.1, 113, 202
9.19–20, 240
9.19–22, 286
10.23–26, 120
10.25, 25
11.7, 130
11.23–34, 39
12, 39

13, 244, 246
13.2, 275
14, 39
14.34–35, 136
15, 78
15.3–8, 113
15.3–9, 202
15.8, 24
15.24–28, 274
15.56, 17
2 Corinthians
3.13–16, 17
3.18, 39
5.1–10, 126
5.21, 256
6.14–7.1, 84
8.20–21, 112
10.10, 201
11.22, 149
11.32, 111
11.32–33, 78
12, 78
12.1–6, 39
12.4, 78
13–16, 18
Galatians
1.11–17, 202
1–11–12, 113
1.15, 252
1.15–16, 113
1.17, 78, 111
2, 192
2.10, 112
2.12, 129
2.20, 39
3.6–14, 127
3.10, 129
3.10–11, 17
3.19–20, 75
3.21, 19
3.25, 72
3.26–4.7, 90
3.28, 65, 129, 130, 131,
    171
4.1–6, 60, 63
4.30, 72
5.3, 88
5.6, 131
5.22, 238
6.15, 17
Ephesians
2, 87
2.8, 192
3, 87
Philippians
3.4–6, 18

3.5, 148
3.5–6, 149
Colossians
3.22, 73
1 Thessalonians
2.14–16, 18, 44
1 Timothy
1.8, 88
2 Timothy
4.17, 191
4.7–8, 191
1 John
3.1, 191
1 Peter
5.8, 246
Revelation
6.15, 190
11.15, 191
15.4, 191
15.14, 190

DEAD SEA SCROLLS
1QS
9.21–23, 151
10.17–25, 151

RABBINIC
LITERATURE

MISHNAH
Avot
1.17, 141
1.18, 147
2.8, 110
2.15, 146
3.11, 25
Tamid
7.4, 85

TOSEFTA
Avodah Zarah
8.4, 90
Demai
2, 132
2.16–17, 132,
    133
2.17, 132
Hagigah
3, 132
Shabbat
1.15, 132

BABYLONIAN
TALMUD
Baba Metzia
59b, 168

Berakhot
57b, 25
60b, 146
Derekh Eretz Rabbah
7.7, 151
Hagigah
14b, 78
Niddah
24b, 110
Sanhedrin
42b, 149
91b, 146, 147
97a, 85
98b, 62
105a, 134
107b, 25
Shabbat
30b, 25
151a, 86
151b, 61
Sotah
47a, 25

MIDRASHIM
Bereshit Rabba
12, 147
3, 133
Pesikta Rabbati
4a, 85
Ruth Rabbah
3, 25
Tanhuma Beshallah
3, 146, 147

EARLY CHRISTIAN
WRITINGS
Epiphanius, *Panarion*
    or *Against*
    Heresies
30.16.9, 24, 75
Irenaeus, *Against*
    Heresies
1.26.2, 24
Pseudo-Clement,
    Homilies
17.13.1, 24
17.19.1, 24
Pseudo-Clement,
    Recognitions
1.70ff, 24

HELLENISTIC
LITERATURE
Josephus, *Antiquities*
13.3.5, 109

General Index

Abba Gulish, 25, 108, 109, 110, 111, 112, 113, 114, 287, 288
Abba Saul, 109, 110, 111
Abraham, patriarch, 25, 72, 90, 110, 127, 131, 141, 149, 219, 221, 222, 223, 224, 225, 227, 228, 229, 243, 245, 247, 248, 274
Abrahams, Israel, 82
Acher. *See* ben Abujah, Elisha
Adam, 62, 63, 73, 141, 206, 267, 274
Adler, Felix, 101
Ahasuerus, 250
Akhenaten, 265
Akiva ben Joseph, 78, 108
al-Mukammis, David ibn Marwan, 26, 27, 33
al-Quiquisani, Yaqub. *See* Kirkisani, Jacob
Amos, prophet, 123
angels, 28, 75, 126, 157, 204, 206, 224, 246
antinomism, 144, 207, 246, 255, 258, 261
Antioch, 135, 216, 222, 223, 224, 226, 227, 252
anti-Semitism, 13, 24, 32, 34, 43, 50, 52, 74, 76, 84, 88, 92, 121, 145, 156, 180, 187, 189, 212, 270, 271, 281, 283. *See also* Jewish self-hatred
anti-Zionism, 2, 82, 98, 115–118
apocalypticism, 85, 197, 200, 258, 260
Apollos, 108, 229
apostasy, Jewish, 5, 45, 46, 101, 102, 164
Apostles' Creed, the, 157
Ariarajah, S. Wesley, 134
Aristotle, 248
Asch, Sholem, 44, 197, 211–219, 220, 230, 284
Athens, 99, 109, 112, 140, 243
atonement, 42, 53, 73, 78, 144, 194, 227, 228, 267
Atonement, Day of (*Yom Kippur*), 144, 228
Augustine of Hippo, 4, 16, 106, 141, 162, 165, 246, 249
Auschwitz, 88, 160, 161

Baeck, Leo, 14, 25, 39, 57, 63–65, 76, 77, 84–86, 92, 93, 94, 116, 121, 122, 160, 197, 251, 280, 281
baptism, 13, 136, 144, 275
Barclay, William, 143, 169

Barnabas, 109, 112, 185, 229
Barrett, Charles, 160
Barth, Karl, 15, 16, 84, 86, 115, 160, 251
Bauer, Bruno, 105, 251, 255
Baur, Ferdinand Christian, 13, 38, 74, 105, 122, 169, 175
Bellow, Saul, 210
ben Abraham, Levi, 26
ben Abujah, Elisha, 25, 77
ben Zakkai, Yochannan, 146
Benamozegh, Elijah, 13, 15, 57, 60–63, 76, 93, 115, 280
Ben-Chorin, Schalom, 92, 93, 115
Benjamin, Walter, 250
Berdichevsky, Micah Joseph, 13, 15, 25, 98, 107–114, 283, 287
biblical criticism, 4, 8, 12–19, 34, 48, 58, 68, 79, 93, 143, 150, 175, 235, 241, 252, 279
Bin Gorion, Immanuel, 109, 110
Bin Gorion, Rachel, 109
Bin Gorion, Mikha Yosef. *See* Berdichevsky, Micah Joseph
Botstein, Leon, 180, 181, 183, 188, 189, 192, 195, 196
Bousset, Wilhelm, 13, 39, 68, 82, 84, 105
Boyarin, Daniel, 8, 16, 93, 125, 128, 129, 147, 155, 169–172, 173, 283
Brown, Michael, 137
Brumberg-Kraus, Jonathan, 50, 97, 98, 121, 125
Brunner, Emil, 70
Buber, Martin, 14, 58, 67–71, 74, 76, 86, 92, 93, 94, 117, 160, 162, 251, 280
Bultmann, Rudolf, 14, 15, 16, 68, 74, 84, 105, 122, 160, 169, 255
Burkitt, Francis Crawford, 68, 156

Calvin, John, 4, 15
Camus, Albert, 247
Castelli, Elizabeth, 132
Chagall, Marc, 178, 198
Christ, 17, 18, 19, 114, 117, 155, 157, 180, 192, 194, 275

Christianity
 Catholicism, 14, 18, 39, 62, 118, 119, 134, 144, 145,
  146, 157, 199, 203, 207, 250
 Lutheranism, 191–194, 214
 mission, 17, 30, 45, 46, 47, 49, 50, 52, 53, 59, 60,
  76, 80, 98, 112, 138, 139, 140, 143, 145, 152, 188,
  215, 218, 272, 274, 275
 mysticism, 196, 199, 200
 Protestantism, 39, 62, 186, 188, 195, 196,
  237
circumcision, 27, 34, 131, 136, 142, 172, 217,
  224
Cohen, Arthur, 176
Cohen, Hermann, 94, 117
communion. See eucharist, and Paul and
  eucharist
conversion, 3, 9, 11, 24, 25, 39, 41, 45, 46, 52, 53, 58,
  59, 65, 71, 73, 90, 91, 92, 100, 101, 108, 109, 111,
  112, 113, 114, 121, 123, 124, 125, 126, 127, 136,
  142, 143, 145, 148, 151, 164, 166, 179, 180, 184,
  185, 189, 190, 193, 195, 199, 200, 201, 203, 204,
  212, 213, 214, 216, 218, 222, 223, 224, 226, 227,
  235, 252, 256, 274, 288
Corinth, 226
covenant, 17, 19, 25, 44, 66, 72, 78, 115, 120,
  127, 129, 161, 201, 226, 238, 253, 254,
  259
crucifixion, the, 106, 178, 205, 250, 256, 267

Dalman, Gustaf, 68
Damascus, 24, 25, 58, 78, 100, 111, 112, 113, 114, 126,
  134, 140, 159, 185, 192, 200, 202, 214, 225, 247,
  252, 283, 287, 288
David, King, 140
Davies, W. D., 16, 74, 122, 129, 160, 169
Day of Judgement, 61, 151, 223
Dean, Lester, 93
deicide, 35, 265, 267, 270
Deifelt, Wanda, 136
Deism, 175, 182, 188, 194, 239
Deissmann, Gustav, 84, 105
del Rossi, Azariah, 33
Delitzsch, Franz, 68, 82, 105
Deutsche Christen, 175
Deutscher, Isaac, 231, 232, 233, 261, 277, 278
dialogue, interfaith, 1, 2, 57, 86, 89, 93, 134, 135,
  165, 174, 283
Dibelius, Martin, 68, 160
Dunn, James, 16, 125, 129, 169
Duran, Profiat, 26, 28, 33

Ebionites, 24, 74, 75, 155, 156
Edersheim, Alfred, 156
Efodi. See Duran, Profiat

Eisenbaum, Pamela, 6, 7, 8, 16, 44, 93, 94, 98,
  128–131, 137, 152, 282
Eisler, Robert, 156
election, 43, 44, 53, 72, 119, 120, 161, 204, 216, 218,
  238, 254, 259
Elijah, prophet, 141, 162, 199
Elisha, prophet, 199
Emancipation, Jewish civil, 3, 30, 31, 76, 183, 231,
  280, 281
Emden, Jacob, 29
Endelmann, Todd, 50
Enlightenment, the, 2, 30, 32, 33, 34, 35, 37, 48, 51,
  76, 175, 176, 184, 189, 196, 231, 234, 235, 239,
  281, 282, 283
Ephesus, 109, 112, 185, 191
Epiphanius, 24, 74, 75
Esau, 213, 244, 274
Essenes. See Qumran
eucharist, 13, 180, 268, 275. See also Paul and
  eucharist
evil inclination, the, 140, 147
Ezekiel, prophet, 126, 158, 240

Fatum, Lone, 132
Flusser, David, 53, 93, 98, 118–121, 147, 150, 152,
  251, 282
Foot-Moore, George, 13
Frankel, Zacharias, 58
Freud, Anna, 263
Freud, Sigmund, 2, 13, 119, 160, 163, 164, 207, 231,
  232, 235, 251, 263, 264–270, 271, 272, 273, 274,
  275, 277, 278, 285
Friedlaender, Michael, 82, 93, 105
Fuchs-Kreimer, Nancy, 16, 23, 50, 94, 95, 155,
  165–169, 173, 283
Fürst, Julius, 185, 186

Gager, John, 16, 74, 88, 125, 129, 165, 169, 212
Gamaliel the Elder, 25, 61, 100, 106, 115, 140, 147,
  148, 204, 205, 206, 208, 213, 214, 217, 228
Gans, Eduard, 36
Gaster, Moses, 26, 110, 156
Gaston, Lloyd, 16, 74, 87, 129, 165, 169, 212
Geiger, Abraham, 36, 37, 38
Georgias, 63
Gilman, Sander, 50, 264
gnosticism, 39, 52, 60, 62, 66, 67, 68, 70, 74, 75, 79,
  81, 98
Goodman, Lenn, 234
grace, 120, 167, 168, 169, 246, 283
Graetz, Heinrich, 36, 37, 57, 58–60, 63, 67, 76, 93,
  94, 105, 122, 280
Greenberg, Irving, 33
Gunkel, Hermann, 13

ha-Bavli, David. *See* al-Mukammis, David ibn
    Marwan
Hadassi, Judah, 28, 33
Hagner, Donald, 37, 92, 94
Ha-Kohen, Joseph, 33
halakhah. See Law
Harnack, Adolf, 64, 251
Hasidism, 58, 67, 107, 198
Haskalah or Jewish Enlightenment, 34, 35, 107,
    179
Hatch, Edwin, 68, 99
Headlam, Arthur, 25, 147
Hebrew Christianity. *See* Judaism: Messianic
Hellenism, 13, 14, 39, 40, 65, 66, 67, 68, 69, 71, 74,
    75, 76, 84, 85, 88, 93, 99, 103, 108, 109, 114, 115,
    121, 122, 125, 134, 140, 149, 156, 157, 165, 170,
    171, 213, 215, 226, 228, 229, 245, 247, 248, 255,
    269, 273, 282. *See also* Judaism: Hellenistic
Herford, Robert Travers, 25, 105
Hertz, Joseph, 48, 143
Hillel the Elder, 66, 74, 79, 151
Hirsch, Emil, 98–102, 282
Hirsch, Samson Raphael, 58
Hirsch, Samuel, 93, 98
Hirschberg, Harris, 15, 25
History-of-Religions School, 13, 14, 16, 38, 39
Hobbes, Thomas, 63
Holocaust, the, 23, 92, 93, 95, 115, 118, 129, 161,
    260
Holtzmann, Adolf, 82

ibn Kammuna, Said ibn Mansur, 28, 33
ibn Verga, Solomon, 33
idolatry, 26, 46, 87, 111, 112, 141, 187, 188, 215, 287
Ilan, Tal, 16, 98, 131–134, 137, 152, 282
Incarnation, the, 42, 46
Inge, William, 73
Irenaeus, 24
Isaac, patriarch, 219, 222, 243
Isaiah, prophet, 72, 79, 104, 123, 140, 199, 211, 229,
    244, 245, 246
Islam, 66, 113, 256

Jacob, patriarch, 213, 215, 219, 222, 243, 244, 274
James, brother of Jesus, 24, 129, 192, 204, 205, 215,
    229
Jeremiah, prophet, 123, 199, 223, 224, 229, 244,
    253
Jerusalem, 252
Jerusalem Council, the, 60, 192, 216
Jesus, Christian views of, 14, 34, 37, 38, 42, 44, 64,
    66, 69, 72, 110, 136, 180, 193, 194, 267
Jesus, Jewish views of, 23, 24, 26, 27, 28, 29, 30, 35,
    36, 37, 38, 39, 40, 41, 42, 52, 57, 58, 61, 64, 66,

67, 68, 69, 70, 72, 74, 77, 79, 81, 83, 86, 87, 89,
    99, 101, 102, 105, 107, 108, 110, 121, 124, 139,
    150, 151, 155, 160, 192, 204, 206, 218, 242, 251,
    253, 256, 266, 268
Jew hatred. *See* anti-Semitism
Jewish art, 178–179
Jewish Chronicle, The, 23, 40, 41, 42, 43, 45, 47, 48,
    49, 50, 51, 52, 179, 280
Jewish identity, 3, 33, 36, 41, 46, 50, 89, 96, 115, 125,
    128, 152, 153, 155, 156, 160, 164, 165, 170, 172,
    174, 177, 179, 181, 189, 207, 229, 230, 231, 232,
    235, 264, 281, 285
    the problem of, 9–12, 33
Jewish philosophy, 234–235. *See also* Spinoza,
    Baruch, *and* Shestov, Lev, *and* Taubes, Jacob
Jewish Publication Society of America, 17
Jewish Reformer, The, 98
Jewish self-hatred, 45, 46, 50–51, 52, 87, 206, 235
Jewishness. *See* Jewish identity
Jonah, prophet, 112
Josephus, Flavius, 108, 109, 136, 169, 170
Jowett, Benjamin, 66, 82, 103
Judaism
    Conservative, 44, 72, 102, 105, 125, 128, 160, 169
    feminist or gendered, 2, 128–137
    Hellenistic, 15, 30, 69, 82, 98, 106, 114, 115, 116,
        122, 123, 124, 127, 128, 133, 134, 161, 164, 170,
        171, 214, 220, 224, 226, 252
    Liberal, 32, 48, 63, 82, 102, 103, 104, 105, 117, 120,
        121, 122, 124, 125, 196, 220, 251
    Messianic, 2, 10, 49, 50, 155
    mysticism, 79, 123, 125, 158, 164, 250, 257. *See
        also* kabbalah, *and* Paul and *kabbalah, and*
        Paul and mysticism
    Orthodox, 2, 72, 251
    Palestinian, 15, 16, 24, 30, 39, 60, 85, 99, 107, 114,
        115, 116, 122, 133, 134, 156, 164, 213, 214, 220
    Reconstructionist, 23, 97, 165, 168, 210
    Reform, 2, 32, 36, 37, 42, 48, 58, 60, 65, 66, 67,
        71, 72, 77, 78, 79, 81, 86, 89, 98, 100, 101, 102,
        121, 125, 128, 160, 251
Judaizers, 24, 91, 142, 227
Judeo-Christian tradition, the, 1, 2, 4, 57, 71, 73,
    81, 175–177, 196, 202, 203, 208, 209, 211, 212,
    218, 219, 229, 230, 242, 261
Jung, Carl, 263
justification by faith, 14, 16, 17, 18, 69, 192, 240, 256

kabbalah, 60, 62, 79, 256. *See also* Judaism:
    mysticism, *and* Paul and *kabbalah, and* Paul
    and mysticism
Kafka, Franz, 70
Kaplan, Mordecai, 168, 210
Käsemann, Ernst, 74, 86, 147, 160, 169

Kirkisani, Jacob, 26, 27, 33
Kittel, Gerhard, 25, 138, 143, 147
Klausner, Joseph, 14, 25, 92, 93, 94, 98, 105, 106, 107, 114, 115, 122, 138, 147, 153, 156, 160, 251, 283
Kohler, Kaufmann, 14, 50, 52, 57, 65–67, 69, 74, 76, 79, 92, 93, 94, 105, 118, 280
Krauskopf, Joseph, 13, 79–81, 281

Lake, Kirsopp, 82
Lapide, Pinchas, 17, 50, 77, 86–89, 91, 93, 168, 281
Law
    and death, 61, 62, 162, 163, 187, 271, 276
    and ethics, 48, 127, 217
    and faith, 18, 65, 69, 72, 117, 118, 127, 158, 225, 240, 252, 261
    and sense of guilt, 59, 64, 71, 102, 140, 141, 157, 166, 212, 214, 220, 221, 222, 227, 271, 273
    and sin, 17, 18, 44, 61, 62, 63, 72, 144, 205, 206, 224, 238, 244, 245, 246, 247, 273
    and the messianic age, 59, 61, 85, 86, 90, 116, 158, 163, 281
    and women, 47, 136
    as a curse, 17, 42, 71, 127, 129
    as a human construct, 235
    as allegorical, 49, 171, 221, 223, 225
    as bondage, 14, 47, 48, 51, 59, 61, 63, 100, 120, 122, 142, 215, 227, 247, 252, 255, 272
    as evil, 67, 222, 224
    as holy, 18, 28, 157, 188
    as obstacle to conversion, 53, 59, 72, 78, 101, 123, 220, 286
    as social barrier, 90, 142, 171
    Christian critique of, 13, 18, 29, 32, 37, 40, 71, 116, 124, 149, 166, 189, 214, 255
    dietary laws, 27, 28, 29, 45, 47, 72, 90, 104, 120, 132, 135, 146, 216, 217, 228, 275
    in the messianic age, 61, 67, 72, 85, 116, 158, 163, 206, 212, 217
    intra-Jewish controversies, 7, 48, 50, 72, 98, 100, 101, 102, 104, 116, 117, 118, 120, 121, 152, 153, 164, 167, 255, 282
    Sabbath, 24, 47, 48, 158, 216, 217
Le Cornu, Hilary, 147
Leeser, Isaac, 52
legalism, 14, 16, 18, 37, 40, 44, 47, 64, 69, 100, 101, 102, 119, 188, 249
Lessing, Theodore, 50
Levertoff, Olga, 139
Levertoff, Paul, 13, 24, 25, 30, 92, 98, 138–143, 147, 151, 152, 282
Levertov, Paul. See Levertoff, Paul
Levine, Amy-Jill, 16, 98, 134–137, 152, 282
Levison, Leon, 137
Loewe, Herbert, 116

Lohmeyer, Ernst, 68, 122, 160
Loisy, Alfred, 68, 82, 105
Luther, Martin, 4, 14, 15, 16, 18, 29, 44, 65, 79, 124, 143, 162, 165, 166, 169, 180, 189, 192, 246, 247, 249

Maccoby, Hyam, 16, 58, 74–76, 93, 129, 156, 280
Maimonides, Moses, 26, 35, 139, 235, 241
Marx, Adolf, 181, 185, 186
Marx, Karl, 46, 233
Mary, mother of Jesus, 144, 157, 211, 218
Meeks, Wayne, 129
Meidner, Ludwig, viii, 176, 179, 196–202, 208, 209, 284
Meissner, Stefan, 93, 94
Melnikoff, Avraham, 179
Mendelssohn, Abraham, 179, 183, 184, 185, 186, 188, 189, 190, 191, 193, 195
Mendelssohn, Fanny, 183, 184, 195
Mendelssohn, Felix, 10, 11, 12, 176, 179–196, 208, 209, 284
Mendelssohn, Joseph, 183
Mendelssohn, Moses, 35, 101, 102, 179, 181, 182, 183, 184, 189, 191, 195
messiah, 28, 39, 49, 59, 66, 72, 85, 86, 87, 90, 104, 114, 115, 116, 126, 137, 140, 144, 147, 149, 150, 151, 155, 157, 158, 159, 162, 163, 176, 204, 205, 206, 213, 215, 216, 217, 223, 225, 253, 254, 255, 256, 257, 265, 268, 273, 274, 275, 276, 282
    Jewish expectations of, 24, 59, 75, 85, 86, 107, 114, 122, 139, 140, 142, 147, 155, 156, 159, 176, 204, 213, 215, 256, 273, 274
messianic age, 61, 85, 86, 88, 90, 91, 116, 158, 163, 281
messianism, 17, 71, 85, 139, 140, 142, 143, 163, 233, 258, 260
Meyer, Michael, 31, 33, 35, 281
Mills, Sanford, 14, 98, 143–147, 151, 152, 282
Montagu, Lily, 82
Montefiore, Claude, 14, 15, 16, 38, 47, 66, 74, 77, 81–84, 91, 92, 93, 94, 98, 102–105, 115, 118, 121, 122, 124, 138, 143, 152, 160, 169, 281, 282
Moses, 17, 79, 123, 140, 199, 206, 211, 222, 224, 226, 227, 228, 237, 238, 248, 253, 254, 264, 265, 266, 267, 268. See also Paul: contrasted with Moses
mystery religions, 39, 40, 43, 67, 68, 74, 76, 85, 98, 103, 106, 273, 274, 275

Nanos, Mark, 16, 77, 89–91, 93, 125, 212, 281
Nathan of Gaza, 256
Nazism, 63, 115, 175, 180, 196, 203, 211, 259, 264, 270, 271

Neuchristen, 180, 181, 195
New Perspective on Paul, 16, 87, 90, 125, 129, 165
Nietzsche, Friedrich, 196, 199, 247, 251
Noachide laws, 90, 91, 166, 227, 281
Noah, 224
Nomos. See Law
non-Jewish Jew, the, 231–233

Occident, The, 52
Oesterley, William, 156
original sin. *See* sin: original

Pagels, Elaine, 74
Palestine, 30, 67, 105, 107, 118, 122, 142, 156, 204, 211, 213, 252, 266, 273, 283
Parkes, James, 13, 74
Paul
    and antinomism, 29, 36, 43, 45, 47, 52, 53, 59, 61, 62, 65, 71, 75, 78, 80, 88, 91, 102, 116, 121, 122, 124, 141, 163, 192, 204, 206, 207, 212, 216, 220, 246, 249, 281
    and baptism, 39, 53, 67, 109, 136, 275
    and Christ, 14, 18, 24, 27, 39, 47, 61, 65, 66, 69, 72, 73, 78, 81, 83, 85, 87, 90, 94, 126, 127, 129, 131, 135, 149, 159, 164, 166, 171, 185, 189, 192, 193, 200, 205, 212, 223, 227, 228, 236, 239, 247, 250
    and circumcision, 17, 18, 25, 28, 29, 88, 90, 129, 130, 131, 136, 143, 172, 217, 223, 224, 227, 228, 238, 269
    and death, 162, 272
    and eucharist, 39, 53, 67, 76, 275
    and faith, 69, 70
    and gnosticism, 39, 52, 60, 66, 67, 68, 70, 74, 75, 79, 81, 98
    and grace, 14, 59, 63, 73, 119, 120, 149, 150, 165, 167, 173, 192, 193, 240, 244, 246
    and idolatry, 112, 166
    and Jewish ethics, 59, 62, 67, 80, 81, 83, 281
    and Jewish mysticism, 60, 78, 79, 123, 126, 128, 282
    and *kabbalah*, 60, 62, 63, 78, 281
    and mysticism, 14, 39, 66, 67, 80, 86, 104, 126, 158
    and the Gentile Problem, 211, 213, 214, 222, 225
    and the Law, 1, 14, 17, 18, 19, 24, 25, 27, 28, 29, 39, 40, 42, 43, 44, 45, 47, 48, 49, 50, 51, 52, 53, 57, 59, 61, 63, 64, 65, 67, 69, 70, 71, 72, 75, 77, 78, 80, 85, 86, 87, 88, 90, 91, 92, 100, 101, 103, 104, 106, 116, 117, 118, 119, 120, 122, 124, 126, 127, 129, 131, 135, 136, 138, 143, 144, 146, 148, 149, 152, 153, 157, 158, 162, 163, 164, 165, 167, 170, 193, 200, 204, 205, 206, 212, 214, 216, 217,
222, 224, 225, 226, 227, 228, 229, 240, 244, 246, 247, 249, 252, 253, 255, 258, 270, 271, 272, 273, 275, 276, 280, 286
    and universalism, 29, 34, 38, 57, 72, 78, 79, 80, 81, 92, 103, 114, 115, 152, 166, 171, 172, 175, 207, 216, 225, 238, 255, 261, 269, 281, 282
    and women, 47, 170, 172
    as a prophet, 80, 92, 123, 124, 201, 209, 220, 223, 229, 230, 244, 252, 253
    as an apostate or heretic, 23, 24, 25, 27, 38, 40, 45, 46, 47, 49, 52, 77, 83, 89, 93, 94, 98, 101, 160, 164, 206, 229, 251, 258
    as anti-Semitic, 43, 50, 52, 88, 129, 229
    as Saul, 24, 41, 43, 48, 50, 51, 52, 53, 58, 59, 63, 66, 67, 100, 108, 109, 110, 111, 112, 113, 114, 116, 118, 135, 140, 153, 157, 159, 185, 186, 205, 210, 212, 213, 214, 267, 285
    contrasted with Moses, 45, 79, 140, 141, 237, 238, 253, 254, 265
    his background, 1, 24, 31, 58, 59, 67, 68, 74, 75, 76, 78, 80, 85, 99, 106, 111, 112, 115, 119, 122, 124, 125, 126, 132, 134, 138, 140, 148, 156, 157, 160, 164, 170, 213, 214, 220, 222, 226, 252, 274, 281
    in rabbinic literature, 15, 24–26
    originality of, 78, 90, 116, 143, 269, 272, 274
    personal failure to observe the Law, 59, 69, 75, 100, 104, 116, 117, 122, 140, 157, 158, 162, 164, 166, 206, 212, 214, 220, 271, 273, 275
    personal observance of the Law, 89, 91, 148, 158, 212, 216, 217
    requiring Jewish observance of Law, 88, 91, 158, 212
Paul, Jewish perspectives on
    anti-Zionist, 115–118
    artistic or literary, 179–208, 211–230
    as an intra-Jewish ideological battlefield, 97–98
    building barriers with respect to Christianity, 76–92
    building bridges with respect to Christianity, 57–76
    emergence of awareness in nineteenth century, 34–40
    gendered or feminist, 128–137
    Hebrew Christian or Messianic Jewish, 137–152, 155–160
    in Hebrew, 105, 138
    marginal or 'non-Jewish', 179–208, 211–219, 235–250, 264–270, 278
    Orthodox or traditionalist, 58–63, 67–71, 74–76, 86–89, 118–121, 169–172
    philosophical, 242–261
    popular, 23–53

Paul, Jewish perspectives on (*cont.*)
  pre–nineteenth century, 24–31
  psychoanalytical, 264–270, 277
  Reform, Liberal or progressive, 63–67, 71–74,
    77–86, 89–92, 98–105, 121–128, 160–164,
    165–169
  the question of a Jewish reclamation, 92–96
  traditional view of, 23–31, 40–51, 84, 87, 89
  Zionist, 107–114
Pauline scholarship
  authentic epistles, 17
  Christian, 12–19, 38–40, 92, 94, 105, 121, 129,
    138, 149, 156, 165, 191
  Jewish, 92–96
Paulinism, 64, 67, 69, 70, 71, 76
Peter, apostle, 24, 26, 28, 38, 109, 135, 142, 186, 204,
    226, 227, 228, 229, 246
Pfleiderer, Otto, 13, 42, 82
Pharisaism, 17, 18, 28, 30, 43, 45, 58, 61, 69, 74, 75,
    76, 78, 87, 88, 89, 92, 100, 106, 114, 115, 116, 119,
    125, 126, 127, 131, 132, 133, 134, 144, 148, 149,
    157, 158, 161, 163, 165, 166, 167, 170, 204, 206,
    207, 213, 214, 216, 223, 226, 227, 238, 281, 282
Philippi, 226
Philo of Alexandria, 122, 123, 169, 170, 234
Plato, 182, 221, 245, 248
Potok, Chaim, 210
Proudhon, Pierre-Joseph, 63
psychoanalysis, 2, 124, 160, 163, 207, 220, 263–264,
    265, 270, 271, 272, 275, 277
psychobiography, 124, 160

Qumran, 147, 151, 161

Räisänen, Heikki, 129
Rebecca, matriarch, 213
Reform Advocate, The, 98
Reitzenstein, Richard, 13, 39, 66, 74, 82, 105
Renan, Ernst, 60
resurrection
  as an eschatological event, 14, 28, 61, 135, 148,
    149, 157, 273, 276
  of Christ, 42, 71, 72, 78, 79, 89, 162, 193, 215, 228,
    268, 273, 274, 276
Rome, 42, 74, 109, 226, 228, 254
Ronning, Halvor, 94
Rosenzweig, Franz, 33, 168
Roth, Philip, 210
Rubenstein, Richard, 17, 33, 92, 93, 155, 160–165,
    169, 173, 283
Ruether, Rosemary Radford-, 167

Saadia Gaon, 26
Sachs, Hanns, 232, 264, 271–277, 285

Sacks, Jonathan, 44
Sadducees, 28, 148, 149, 161, 214
Salvador, Joseph, 37, 93
salvation, 9, 14, 43, 44, 59, 62, 65, 76, 78, 88, 94,
    101, 103, 120, 131, 135, 139, 141, 144, 149, 160,
    167, 173, 182, 184, 190, 192, 197, 212, 218, 225,
    236, 237, 246, 248, 249, 254, 257, 267, 268,
    269, 272, 274, 276, 282
Samaritans, 108, 109
Sanday, William, 25, 82, 143, 147
Sanders, Ed, 16, 74, 120, 125, 147, 156, 165, 169
Sandmel, Samuel, 14, 15, 37, 74, 92, 93, 98, 121–125,
    152, 160, 168, 169, 176, 211, 219–230, 282, 284
Sanhedrin, 75, 149
Saul. *See* Paul as Saul
Schechter, Solomon, 68, 82
Schiller-Szinessy, Solomon, 92, 107, 138
Schleiermacher, Friedrich, 180, 185, 189, 194
Schmitt, Carl, 250, 253, 259, 260
Schoeps, Hans Joachim, 14, 15, 33, 68, 74, 92, 93,
    94, 98, 115–118, 121, 122, 152, 158, 160, 163, 168,
    169, 251, 283
Scholem, Gershom, 147, 250
Schonfield, Hugh, 14, 74, 155–160, 163, 173, 283
Schubring, Julius, 180, 185, 186, 189, 192, 193
Schüssler Fiorenza, Elisabeth, 129, 132, 134, 136,
    169
Schweitzer, Albert, 14, 15, 43, 68, 69, 74, 105, 160,
    251
Segal, Alan, 6, 7, 8, 16, 93, 94, 98, 125–128, 152, 169,
    282
Shammai, 79, 148
shekhinah, 111, 146, 206, 288
Shema, the, 90, 158, 217
Shestov, Lev, 13, 232, 234, 242, 243, 244, 245, 246,
    247, 248, 249, 250, 261, 262, 285
Sholem, Gershom, 256
Shulam, Joseph, 14, 98, 143, 147–151, 152, 282
Silver, Abba Hillel, 58, 71–74, 76, 280
Simon Magus, 24, 25
sin, 15, 16, 17, 18, 39, 61, 63, 65, 72, 73, 83, 86, 101,
    103, 119, 135, 141, 144, 146, 157, 205, 206, 214,
    224, 227, 238, 242, 244, 245, 246, 248, 256,
    267, 269, 270, 273, 276, 277
  original, 28, 30, 42, 52, 53, 62, 73, 87, 88, 147,
    152, 192, 245, 246, 266, 267, 269, 270, 277
Sinai, 72, 85, 141, 216, 224, 227, 248, 271
Sloyan, Gerard, 165
Socrates, 182, 245
Son of God, 27, 39, 42, 49, 67, 77, 78, 140, 215, 218,
    236, 267, 268
Son of Man, 138, 139
Spinoza, Baruch, 2, 10, 11, 12, 29, 34, 35, 231, 232,
    233, 234, 235–242, 248, 249, 261, 262, 285

Sposato, Jeffrey, 180, 181, 183, 185, 187, 188, 189, 191, 192, 193, 194, 195
Staiger, Emil, 252
Steinberg, Michael, 180, 181
Stendahl, Krister, 16, 74, 125, 129, 147, 160, 165, 169, 251
Stephen, martyr, 140, 186, 188, 189, 193, 204, 214

Taubes, Jacob, 17, 232, 234, 250–261, 262, 285
Teresa of Avila, 199
theosophy, 81
Thoma, Clemens, 165
Thomas à Kempis, 199
Tiberias, 287
Timothy, 229
Titus, 216, 229
Todd, R. Larry, 180, 181, 193
Toledot Yeshu, 27, 28, 30, 34, 99
Torah. See Law
Tremellius, John Immanuel, 237
Trinity, the, 27, 29, 42, 46, 155
Troki, Isaac, 26, 28, 29, 33
Tübingen School, 13, 16, 24, 38, 84, 175

universalism, Jewish, 3, 71, 72, 80, 92, 99, 103, 104, 122, 152, 166, 168, 170, 177, 181, 190, 223, 232, 255, 282

van Buren, Paul, 165, 167
Vasanthakumar, Nirmla, 134

Vermes, Geza, 156
von Wartenberg-Potter, Bärbel, 134

Wagner, Richard, 180
Watson, Francis, 16, 169
Weizmann, Chaim, 105
Wellhausen, Julius, 68, 82
Werfel, Franz, 92, 138, 176, 179, 197, 202–208, 209, 220, 284
Werner, Eric, 180, 196
Wesley, John, 4
Westerholm, Stephen, 16, 129, 169
Wiefel, Wolfgang, 94
Wine, Antoinette, 132
Wise, Isaac Meyer, 13, 15, 24, 77–79, 91, 93, 281
Wissenschaft des Judenthums, 35, 36, 37, 64
works of the law, 17, 40, 61, 62, 69, 73, 104, 117, 119, 127, 129, 146, 192, 240, 245, 246, 256
works righteousness, 14, 18, 104, 141, 146, 149, 192, 224, 228, 248, 255
Wrede, Wilhelm, 13, 39
Wright, Tom, 16, 169
Wyschogrod, Michael, 93, 168

Yerushalmi, Yosef, 33, 34, 36, 231

Zechariah, prophet, 134
Zionism, 2, 32, 67, 71, 73, 105–114, 115, 153, 171, 172, 263, 281, 282–283
Zunz, Leopold, 35, 36
Zvi, Sabbatai, 29, 163, 255, 256

Lightning Source UK Ltd.
Milton Keynes UK
UKOW04f0741090815

256611UK00001B/73/P